America's 100 Best Places to Retire

Edited by Elizabeth Armstrong

VACATION
PUBLICATIONS
HOUSTON

America's 100 Best Places to Retire

Edited by: Elizabeth Armstrong

Art Direction and Cover Design: Fred W. Salzmann

Contributing Graphic Designer: W. Don DeAnda

Research Associates: Thain Allen, Kelly Boyle, Jynelle A. Gracia, Molly Robey, Lauren Tucker

Back cover photo by Jynelle A. Gracia

Published by Vacation Publications, Inc.
1502 Augusta Drive, Suite 415
Houston, TX 77057

Library of Congress Control Number: 2002111314

ISBN 0964421690

Printed in the United States of America

The Contributors

Mary Lu Abbott

Mary-Ann Bendel

Brenda Blagg

Ron Butler

Jay Clarke

Steve Cohen

Julie Cooper

Jerry Camarillo Dunn Jr.

Karen Feldman

Richard L. Fox

Dixie Franklin

Fred Gebhart

Diana C. Gleasner

Janet Groene

Mary Ann Hemphill

Linda Herbst

Bill Hibbard

Edie Hibbard

Carole Jacobs

John A. Johnson

Bern Keating

Jim Kerr

Bob Lane

Tracy Hobson Lehmann

Adele Malott

Stephen H. Morgan

Honey Naylor

Mary Lou Nolan

Stanton H. Patty

Ruth Rejnis

Carolyn Rice

William Schemmel

Marcia Schnedler

Lan Sluder

Constance Snow

Molly Arost Staub

Nina J. Stewart

Dana Tims

John Villani

Judy Wade

Claire Walter

David Wilkening

Table of Contents

Low-Cost Edens 💲   Undiscovered Havens ✳

By State

America's 100 Best Places to Retire

The Top 10

Best Art Towns
Ashland, OR
Beaufort, SC
Brevard, NC
Hot Springs, AR
Jackson Hole, WY
Ojai, CA
Palm Desert, CA
Santa Fe, NM
Sarasota, FL
Scottsdale, AZ

Best Budget Towns
Eufaula, AL
Hattiesburg, MS
Hot Springs, AR
Mountain Home, AR
Natchitoches, LA
Ocala, FL
Oxford, MS
Rio Grande Valley, TX
San Antonio, TX
Vicksburg, MS

Best Lake Towns
Clemson, SC
Coeur d'Alene, ID
Eagle River, WI
Eufaula, AL
Gainesville, GA
Lake Havasu City, AZ
Mountain Home, AR
Mount Dora, FL
Paris, TN
Petoskey, MI

Best Undiscovered Towns
Cashiers, NC
Celebration, FL
Eagle River, WI
Mountain Home, AR
Natchitoches, LA
New Bern, NC
Paris, TN
Seaside, FL
Sequim, WA
Thomasville, GA

Best Beach Towns
Cape Cod, MA
Cape May, NJ
Carlsbad, CA
Golden Isles, GA
Longboat Key, FL
Myrtle Beach, SC
Naples, FL
Ormond Beach, FL
Sanibel, FL
Whidbey Island, WA

Best Main Street Towns
Athens, GA
Dade City, FL
DeLand, FL
Georgetown, TX
Natchitoches, LA
Port Townsend, WA
San Antonio, TX
Temecula, CA
Thomasville, GA
Waynesville, NC

America's 100 Best Places to Retire

Best College Towns

Asheville, NC
Athens, GA
Chapel Hill, NC
Charlottesville, VA
Clemson, SC
Eugene, OR
Gainesville, FL
Oxford, MS
Tallahassee, FL
Williamsburg, VA

Best Small Towns

Beaufort, SC
Brevard, NC
Camden, ME
Edenton, NC
Fairhope, AL
Mount Dora, FL
Oxford, MS
Port Townsend, WA
Punta Gorda, FL
Waynesville, NC

Best Four-Season Towns

Bend, OR
Camden, ME
Charlottesville, VA
Door County, WI
Fort Collins, CO
Grand Junction, CO
Maryville, TN
Prescott, AZ
Reno, NV
Santa Fe, NM

Best Mountain Towns

Asheville, NC
Bend, OR
Brevard, NC
Cashiers, NC
Fort Collins, CO
Jackson Hole, WY
Mountain Home, AR
Prescott, AZ
Santa Fe, NM
Waynesville, NC

San Juan
Islands

Sequim

Whidbey
Island

Port
Townsend

Coeur d' Alene

Lincoln
City

Eugene

Bend

Ashland

Jackson
Hole

Reno

Fort Collins

Grand
Junction

St. George

Las Vegas

Ojai

Palm
Desert

Prescott

Santa Fe

San Juan
Capistrano

Temecula

Lake Havasu City

Fallbrook

Carlsbad

Wickenburg

Scottsdale

Tucson

Las Cruces

Green Valley

Sierra Vista

Georgetow

Kerrville

San Antonio

Rio Grande
Valley

America's
100
Best
Places
to
Retire

Camden

Eagle River

Petoskey

Door County

Cape Cod

Cape May

Charlottesville

Williamsburg

Chapel Hill

Edenton

Branson

Brevard

Mountain Home

Asheville

Pinehurst

New Bern

Waynesville

Paris

Maryville

Hendersonville

Wilmington

Cashiers

Oxford

Gainesville

Clemson

Myrtle Beach

Athens

Aiken

Hot Springs

Charleston

Beaufort

Vicksburg

Hilton Head

Natchitoches

Eufaula

Golden Isles

Hattiesburg

Thomasville

St. Augustine

The Woodlands

Pensacola

Palm Coast

Fairhope

Gainesville

Ormond Beach

Seaside

Ocala

DeLand

Tallahassee

Dade City

Mount Dora

Bradenton

Celebration

Longboat Key

Viera

Sarasota

Winter Haven

Siesta Key

Vero Beach

Venice

Jupiter

Punta Gorda

Boca Raton

Sanibel

Naples

Fort Myers

Introduction

M oving to a new town in retirement is more than just a change of scenery. It's a chance to reinvent yourself. In the past decade of interviewing retirees for *Where to Retire* magazine, we've met hundreds of people who have treated retirement as a fabulous opportunity to start their own business, go back to school, sign up for volunteer projects, resume an old hobby — or try a new one.

Like Lynn Geri and Dick Curdy, for example. They left behind busy professional lives in a Seattle suburb to open a bed-and-breakfast inn on tranquil Whidbey Island, WA. Or Jim Christiansen, age 57, who upon moving to Ojai, CA, took up surfing again, a sport that he had tried briefly after high school. And in Grand Junction, a town at the edge of the Colorado Rockies that's popular among outdoor enthusiasts, Karen and Pete Dickes are indulging their newest passion — off-road adventure in their four-wheel-drive vehicles.

Regardless of how and where they chose to spend their retirement, most of the retirees we've met share some common denominators in what they desire in a new hometown. They want comfortable climates, health-care facilities within a reasonable driving distance, and access to shopping, entertainment and cultural venues. Many also seek opportunities for continuing education and community involvement. With these criteria in mind, we set out to find appealing retirement towns across the country and profiled them in *Where to Retire* magazine.

The 100 communities compiled here represent the best of the cities and towns that have been featured in *Where to Retire*, each updated to reflect the most current data available. In the mix, you'll find "Low-Cost Edens" (💲) and "Undiscovered Havens" (❋), as well as popular vacation destinations such as Myrtle Beach, Santa Fe, Cape Cod, Tucson and Las Vegas. Check out our Top 10 lists on pages 6 and 7 to find the best college towns, beach towns, mountain towns, art towns and more.

Whatever your dreams for retirement may be, you are sure to find a place to indulge them within these pages. *– Elizabeth Armstrong*

Aiken, South Carolina

South Carolina town has charm, culture and an equestrian heritage

By William Schemmel

Aiken, situated in the gently rolling and densely wooded Sand Hill country of western South Carolina, always has proved irresistible to newcomers, although today's residents need not have fortunes or horses in order to be socially accepted. Still, at least a pastoral interest in the ponies doesn't hurt.

Almost as quick as train tracks were laid down, locomotives brought wealthy 19th-century plantation owners from steamy Charleston and the low country to the new town of Aiken. Many of them grew fond of the area's quiet beauty and temperate climate and built second homes.

Even before the Civil War, Aiken's reputation as a health resort well-suited to the genteel sports of horse racing, steeplechasing and fox hunting spread to the cities of the North. After the war, wealthy Northerners established what became known as the Winter Colony, building magnificent 50- to 100-room "cottages" with plenty of acreage to raise and run horses.

Aiken was introduced to polo in 1882, only six years after the sport crossed the Atlantic from Europe. Thoroughbreds, harness horses and steeplechasers took immediately to the balmy year-round climate. Nowadays, there's hardly a major race in America without an Aiken-reared blue blood at the starting gate.

The city's love for horses reaches a crescendo in late March and April when the Aiken Triple attracts equestrian sports lovers from all over the world to flat races, steeplechasing and harness racing on three successive weekends. From September to November and February to July, the public is invited to the Aiken Polo Club's Sunday afternoon matches. In this easy-living town, several small streets are left unpaved in deference to horses, and pedestrian "walk" buttons are placed high on poles in easy reach of riders on horseback.

Alan and Marjorie (Marge) Wood moved to Aiken in 1993. They don't ride horses, "but like everybody else in town,

we go to the racing events in the spring," says Marge.

Alan was global marketing manager for the Delaware Port Authority in Philadelphia when he retired, and Marge had a career with the U.S. Department of State, her last assignment with the economic development department of the U.S. Embassy in Malaysia. The Woods vow they'll never move again.

"We love it here," says Marge, a vivacious redhead in her mid-50s. "There's tremendous diversity among the people who live in Aiken, and there's always something to do. We have our own symphony and ballet, a good amateur theater and outdoor concerts in the summer. For a small city, we have an amazing number of good restaurants and many opportunities to get outdoors."

Several of the town's resources are legacies of the Winter Colony. Banksia, the Aiken County Historical Museum, was originally a 32-room Winter Colony mansion. Now it's the city's fascinating "municipal attic," with numerous exhibits that trace the area's colorful past.

The Thoroughbred Hall of Fame and Museum at Hopeland Gardens was a gift from Mrs. C. Oliver Iselin, a member of the Winter Colony. When she died in the late 1960s, she willed her estate to the city. Photos and trophies earned by 39 home-grown champions are proudly displayed in the hall of fame. Each has won major races like the Kentucky Derby, Preakness Stakes or Belmont Stakes.

The rest of the estate became a 14-acre public garden with canopies of magnolias, live oaks and cedars, seasonal flowers, fountains, classical statuary and a touch-and-sense trail for the visually impaired. On summer Monday evenings, Aikenites enjoy free concerts in Hopeland's amphitheater.

Also left from the Winter Colony is Hitchcock Woods, a 2,000-acre preserve originally part of the estate of Thomas Hitchcock, a wealthy New York sports-

man who brought steeplechasing to Aiken in the 1890s. Trails winding through the woods attract legions of horseback riders, walkers, joggers and bikers. Hitchcock Woods is the setting for fall and winter fox hunts and Thanksgiving Day's Blessing of the Hounds.

"Shopping is excellent," adds Marge Wood, "and when we want a change of pace or something we can't find here, we're close to Augusta and Columbia, and Atlanta is a short drive. The North Carolina, Tennessee and Georgia mountains and the beaches at Charleston and Hilton Head Island are also a short drive."

The Woods began thinking about retirement while living in India in 1980. "We wanted a place with a four-season climate," Marge says. "I'm originally from Vermont and Alan was born in England and lived in the tropics for 30 years. Neither of us is fond of severely cold weather, but we didn't want to live in Florida where it's warm all the time. We really enjoy Aiken's four seasons. And the people here are so friendly and generous."

The Woods looked at retirement sites in Louisiana, Florida and Georgia and visited Aiken several times before making their decision. They bought property in Kalmia Landing, an adult community, in 1985 and built their house in 1988. They moved permanently in January 1993.

"I wish we'd done it a lot sooner," says Alan, 72. "We like just about everything, except maybe the fire ants. The cost of living here wasn't a major factor in our decision, but housing and other things are less expensive than most of the other places we've lived."

Patio homes in Kalmia Landing offer 1,500 to 1,700 square feet of living space and sell for $119,000 to $150,000. Condos in the community start at $70,000. Clubhouse facilities include a library, dance floor, kitchen, exercise room, pool and tennis courts.

Marge feels secure at Kalmia Landing and considers proximity to medical services a big plus. "Two years ago, Alan had a stroke and I was able to get him to the Aiken Regional Medical Center in two minutes," she says. "While he was recuperating, it was great for me to be so close."

Rodney and Geneva Grandy, both in their early 60s, considered Hilton Head Island and Kiawah Island in South Carolina and Raleigh-Durham in North Carolina before relocating from New Canaan, CT, in June 1991. Geneva had lived in Aiken in the late

Aiken, SC

Population: 25,337 in Aiken, 142,552 in Aiken County.

Location: Extreme western South Carolina, 17 miles east of Augusta, GA, and 60 miles southwest of Columbia, SC. Lightly rolling country, 527 feet above sea level.

Climate:

	High	Low
January	51	35
July	90	74

Aiken has four distinct seasons, with warm summers and mild winters.

Average relative humidity: 60%

Rain: 47.5 inches.

Cost of living: 91.8, based on national average of 100.

Average housing cost: $129,000

Sales tax: 6%

Sales tax exemptions: Prescriptions, dental prosthetics and hearing aids.

State income tax: For married couples filing jointly and single filers, the rates are graduated in six tiers from 2.5% on the first $2,400 of taxable income to 7% on taxable income above $12,000.

Income tax exemptions: Social Security benefits are exempt. Retirees who are drawing income from qualified retirement plans may deduct up to $3,000 of that income.

Intangibles tax: None.

Estate tax: None, except the state's "pick-up" portion of the federal tax, applicable to taxable estates above $1 million.

Property tax: $185.30 per $1,000 of assessed value in unincorporated county; city residents pay an additional $71 per $1,000. Residential property up to five acres is assessed at 4% of actual appraised

value, over five acres assessed at 6%. With the exception noted below, the average tax on a $129,000 house on less than five acres is $586 in the county, $810 in the city. Tangible personal property, including vehicles and boats, is subject to a personal property tax that varies by county district; it is assessed at 9.75% of appraised value.

Homestead exemption: $50,000 off market value for homeowners age 65 and older after one year of residency in North Carolina.

Religion: More than 100 churches and synagogues represent some 20 denominations.

Education: The University of South Carolina-Aiken offers full four-year programs in a wide range of studies and continuing-education and evening classes. The Academy for Lifelong Learning, affiliated with USC-Aiken, has exercise classes, forum and lecture meetings, field trips, study groups and cultural programs for those 55 and older. Aiken Technical College has two-year programs in many practical areas. The main campus of the University of South Carolina is 60 miles away at Columbia. Tuition at all South Carolina public colleges is free for those 60 and older.

Transportation: No public bus system. Regularly scheduled commercial air service is available at Bush Field in Augusta, GA (35 miles), and Columbia Metropolitan Airport, SC (40 miles).

Health: Aiken Regional Medical Center is a 225-bed acute-care complex with 24-hour emergency service, neurosurgery, urology/lithotripsy, cardiac care, Carolina Cancer Center, Women's LifeCare Center, Aiken Medical Imaging Center, plastic/reconstructive surgery, nuclear medicine and orthopedics/sports medicine. About 110 physicians practice in Aiken County. Public health centers, assisted living, nursing homes and hospice programs are available.

Housing options: Housing ranges from apartment, condo and manufactured-home communities to Winter Colony mansions with extensive grounds and

stables that sell for $1 million or more. **Cedar Creek**, (800) 937-5362, is a 1,116-acre golf community. Custom brick homes on half-acre wooded homesites start in the low $170,000s. The 18-hole Golf Club at Cedar Creek, lighted tennis courts and a 25-meter competition swimming pool are among features. **Kalmia Landing**, (800) 722-7356, has about 70 1,500- to 1,700-square-foot patio homes from $119,000 to $150,000. Two- and three-bedroom condos start at $70,000. A bridge connects the adults-only community to Aiken Regional Medical Center, and all homes have special lights to direct emergency vehicles. **Woodside Plantation**, (800) 648-3052, is a golf-course community, with 300 to 400 homes priced from $189,000. Homes include club villas and attached houses. There's full-time gated and staffed security. Amenities also include a swimming pool, tennis courts and a clubhouse. **Houndslake**, (888) 346-8637, has villas, patio homes, condos and attached houses in three areas. Most are 1,050 to 3,500 square feet and sell for $125,000 to $350,000. The few available lakeside lots sell for about $59,000 to $95,000; other lots are $26,900-$65,000. Among amenities are three nine-hole golf courses, tennis, swimming pool, clubhouse and 34-room lodge. **Eden Gardens**, (803) 642-8444, is an assisted-living community with studio apartments and one- and two-room suites for individual and shared living. The single-story brick building on four wooded acres has a community dining room, library, beauty shop and activity rooms.

Visitor lodging: Holiday Inn Express, two locations, $65-$92, double occupancy, (800) 465-4329. The historic Willcox Hotel, $175-$850, double occupancy, (803) 648-1898.

Information: Greater Aiken Chamber of Commerce, 121 Richland Ave. E., Aiken, SC 29801, (800) 542-4536, (803) 641-1111 or www.aikenchamber.net.

1970s, when things were different.

"It's changed a lot, for the better, in the last 15 years," she says. "The downtown area has made a big turnaround. It wasn't very attractive when I lived here the first time, but they've landscaped the streets and there are many new businesses, restaurants and shops. I seldom go to Augusta for shopping — we have everything we need right here."

A lower cost of living was among other attractions. "Having lived in the Northeast, I knew living in the South would be a lot less expensive," Rodney says. "But cost was only one consideration. I had a successful 37-year career with Exxon, with excellent retirement benefits and good investments. So we were really looking for a place where life would be easier."

And the Grandys believe they have found that easier life. "After six years here, I have a hard time finding anything I don't like," Rodney says. "Occasionally I have to sit in traffic a whole minute or two, I don't buy as many suits as I used to, and I can't remember the last time it snowed."

For Rodney and Geneva, the easier life they found in Aiken is an active one. "It's a can-do city — people are active; they don't just sit around," says Rodney.

Three times a week, Geneva attends exercise classes at University of South Carolina-Aiken's Academy for Lifelong Learning, a program for persons 55 and older that also includes field trips, study groups, discussion groups and cultural programs. The academy also is affiliated with the Elderhostel Institute Network, which offers programs worldwide.

The Grandys are active in several civic clubs and public health and social service agencies. They play golf, climb mountains and ski in neighboring North Carolina.

The Grandys live in a lakeside home in Woodside Plantation. One of Aiken's most prestigious residential developments, Woodside has its own golf course, tennis courts and swimming pool. Homes are priced from $189,000.

Golf is a popular pastime all around Aiken. In 1997 *Golf Magazine* hailed Aiken's new Cedar Creek community as the No. 4 semiretirement golfing community in the country, which took Cedar Creek residents and management by pleasant surprise.

"It's incredible. You can't buy that kind of advertising," says Cedar Creek vice president Ray Jackson. "People here want to live their retirement in a different way than they did their working life. They're not hanging it up; they're just changing address, getting to a warmer climate where they can be active 365 days a year."

Cedar Creek is attracting newcomers whose idea of retirement is full-time action on the golf course. The community is a mix of retirees, semiretirees and families with small children and pets.

Plans call for 850 homes to be built over a 10-year development plan. Homes range in size from 1,500- to 2,000-square-foot carriage houses to custom-built houses with 2,000 to 6,000 square feet, selling from $170,000 to $550,000.

Architect Arthur Hills laid out the 7,206-yard, 18-hole golf course first. Housing sites were arranged around the course, which has gently changing elevations, creeks and streams, tree-lined Bermuda fairways and a few sand bunkers to keep the game interesting. The Cedar Creek Club House, designed like an English country manor house, has a full-service dining room, pro shop and outside porches.

Residents also enjoy lighted tennis courts, a 25-meter competition swimming pool with a 5,000-square-foot sun deck, and a 3.5-mile nature trail. Cedar Creek's 1,150 acres of pristine woods are a bird and wildlife sanctuary.

Lois and Larry Potter fell in love with Aiken when they were scouting the Carolinas four years ago. Larry was retiring as an IBM engineer in Manassas, VA, and Lois was a former teacher and director of a voluntary action center. The couple already had ruled out Florida and other states when they discovered Aiken.

"We visited Aiken four times, and each time it looked better," says Lois, 65. "We're still very happy here. By coincidence, not long after we moved here, our daughter, son-in-law and grandson moved to Columbia, SC, and my mother just moved to the Cumberland Village senior living community from Florida."

Cumberland Village, an upscale senior living community on 35 wooded acres, welcomed its first residents in 1996. Housing options include furnished studio, one- and two-bedroom apartment rentals and privately owned 1,350- to 1,600-square-foot patio homes with full services and

access to an indoor swimming pool and other amenities. The Personal Care Center is designed for residents who require assistance with daily activities.

The Potters live in Gem Lakes, an older neighborhood 10 minutes from downtown. Ranch and colonial-style homes with about 2,000 square feet sell for around $160,000. Residents range from retirees and semiretirees to young couples with children. Although Gem Lakes is not a planned community, the neighborhood has a recreation center, tennis courts, private lakes for swimming and a playground for kids.

Larry, 68, says property taxes on the couple's $160,000 house are "miniscule" compared to what they paid in Virginia. With deductions that seniors get at age 65, their annual taxes are only about $1,000. "Even without the deduction, taxes here are much lower than they were in Virginia," Larry says.

They've found plenty to keep them occupied. "We keep very busy," Lois says. "We're in the hand-bell choir at our Presbyterian church. We do volunteer work and take part in activities at the Academy for Lifelong Learning. We're also doing archaeological work with the University of South Carolina in Columbia."

For couples like the Potters, Grandys and Woods who enjoy the outdoors, recreation is abundant. Lake Thurmond, a massive U.S. Army Corps of Engineers reservoir on the nearby Savannah River, and Lake Murray, near Columbia, lure fishermen, boaters, swimmers, water-skiers and campers. Aiken State Park, 16 miles east of the city, has four lakes, nature trails and campsites.

The Blue Ridge Mountains of the Carolinas, Georgia and Tennessee are less than three hours north of the city. Due east, the same drive time will get you to such popular Atlantic Ocean resort areas as Hilton Head Island, Myrtle Beach and Kiawah Island. Big-city shopping, sports, entertainment and dining are less than an hour away in Columbia, South Carolina's capital, and two and a half hours west in Atlanta.

"The people here, our rich history, low taxes, excellent medical care, cultural and recreational activities are among the many positive things that make Aiken such a great place to retire," says Ray Jackson.●

Asheville, North Carolina

This small, vibrant city in the North Carolina mountains attracts active retirees from all over the country

By Mary Lu Abbott

While George W. Vanderbilt came to Asheville for its beautiful setting and built a 250-room chateau in the late 1800s, retirees today are finding they, too, can have the good life in the mountains of western North Carolina — and in smaller abodes.

On a high plateau surrounded by the gentle, often-misty Blue Ridge Mountains, Asheville has been a natural crossroads for centuries, creating a richly diverse community in the new millennium. Coming from such distant, and disparate, locales as New England and California, retirees today find a spirit that's simpatico with a variety of individual interests.

Settling here in 1994 from Connecticut, Jack and Sheila Ingersoll wanted a place they could truly call home after having moved many times.

"I wanted to put down roots, to know people in the town and to greet them as you walk around. I thought Asheville gave us that opportunity," says Sheila, 66. "It's somewhat a spiritual community. I thought the people had a caring spirit, and now I know they do."

Jack, 70, says, "I wanted to give back some of the good I had received over the years, and I thought there would be the opportunity here — and there has been."

An executive with IBM, Jack continued working as a consultant for several years after they moved to Asheville, then retired in 1998 and delved into a program called Leadership Asheville Seniors, which explores the history of the area, introduces participants to community leaders and matches work skills with volunteer needs.

From Marin County north of San Francisco, Louaine Elke focused on lifestyle rather than a region or particular towns for retirement. "I wanted a co-housing community, a concept started in Denmark," says Louaine, 67. While residents have their own private living unit, they also share some meals together in a community house and donate time keeping up the common grounds and tending to community business, she says.

Louaine, a college instructor with degrees in fine arts and architecture, had investigated some co-housing communities in California after her husband died in 1994 but found them all too expensive. At the invitation of a former student, she came to Asheville in 1996 to see its architecture and crafts and discovered a co-housing unit was being developed in town. "I went to a meeting (of those planning the community) and I liked the people. I felt it would go. Sometimes people sit around and talk about doing this but it never goes. In a week, I made a deposit," she says.

Beyond the lifestyle concept, "I liked Asheville — the size, the old buildings, the university campus, the arts community," she says. She returned three times to watch progress of the community, located adjacent to a creek and wooded area, and moved here in 1998.

Rick and Linda Ricordati retired here from Rhode Island in 1997, after having lived most of their lives in the Chicago area. They discovered Asheville about 20 years ago when vacationing along the Blue Ridge Parkway and Skyline Drive, a scenic route that connects the Shenandoah Mountains in the north and the Great Smoky Mountains southwest of Asheville.

"Any time we traveled, we would look at a place and say, 'Could we live here?'" says Linda, 58. "The decision about Asheville was a process of elimination. I did not want a lot of heat and humidity. That ruled out Florida and Arizona — I don't care how dry it (Arizona) is, 110 degrees is 110."

Rick adds that they checked out San Diego but felt traffic was too congested, and it was too far from their children in the Midwest. "We looked at the coasts of North and South Carolina. The winters are mild, but the summers are brutal," he says.

"There are ocean people and mountain people, and we are mountain people," says Linda.

On a master checklist of desirable qualities in a retirement destination, Asheville scores high — a small but sophisticated city with excellent health care, a reasonable cost of living and the added bonus of a university with a cutting-edge program for active seniors. Well-located, it's on Interstate 40 and the slow-paced Blue Ridge Parkway, approximately 200 miles from Atlanta, GA; 120 miles from Charlotte, NC; 110 miles from Knoxville, TN; and 60 miles from Greenville, SC.

Once they decided on the Asheville area, the Ricordatis visited several times and talked to many residents before buying property in a new development of free-standing homes. They like the diversity of Asheville. "It isn't filled with all the same types of people — all the same age or who all play golf," says Rick, 58, who retired from marketing. The cultural, educational and medical hub of a region that encompasses more than 200,000 residents, Asheville has a makeup that mixes retirees with college students, young families and professionals of all ages. Health care, manufacturing and tourism are major industries.

"We like the manageability of living here," says Linda. "It's easy to do things — to go to the grocery store or the cleaners. And if there's a little traffic, you don't mind it because the scenery is so beautiful."

"In general, the whole city is friendly and laid-back," Rick says. "It's unusual to bump into anyone who's not pleasant."

Since moving here in 1994, the Ingersolls have seen the city gain momentum. "It has gotten better. It's growing — but not too much — and downtown is really coming to life," Sheila says.

"We had dinner downtown the other night," says Jack, " and people were still walking around at 9 or 10. It's drawing a variety of ages."

Asheville entered its first boom in the early part of the 1900s, as Vanderbilt's elegant Biltmore Estate focused attention on the area. Its clean, cool mountain air soon made it a favorite resort among presidents and celebrities. Luxury accommodations opened, among them the still-grand 1913 Grove Park Inn, a massive hotel built in the style of a rustic lodge with walls of granite boulders. The downtown area blossomed with new buildings in art deco and modern designs, and farmland became housing developments with mountain views. When the Great Depression hit, Asheville and surrounding Buncombe County reeled under a massive debt and struggled for nearly five decades to pay off all its obligations rather than default on the loans. Only in the 1970s did the city really begin to recover, but there was an unexpected benefit to its long-term decline: Since the city had no extra funds for urban renewal projects popular in the '50s and '60s, its classic buildings

Asheville, NC

Population: About 69,000 residents in the city, 206,000 in Buncombe County. Asheville is the county seat and regional cultural, medical and educational hub.

Location: In the Blue Ridge Mountains of western North Carolina, about 200 miles northeast of Atlanta, GA, and 120 northwest of Charlotte, NC. It's on the Blue Ridge Parkway about 50 miles from Great Smoky Mountains National Park. Elevation varies, with the average being 2,200 feet.

Climate:

	High	Low
January	47	25
July	83	63

Average relative humidity: 58%

Rain: 48 inches.

Snow: 15 inches.

Cost of living: 100.9, based on national average of 100.

Average housing cost: $89,782 for a two-bedroom home, $132,657 for a three-bedroom home. Monthly apartment rents average $535 for one bedroom, $625 for two bedrooms.

Sales tax: 6%

Sales tax exemptions: Prescriptions and services. Motor vehicles are taxed at 3 percent.

State income tax: For married couples filing jointly, the rate is graduated from 6% of taxable income up to $21,250 to 8.25% on amounts over $200,000. For single filers, it is graduated from 6% of income up to $12,750 to 8.25% on amounts over $120,000.

Income tax exemptions: Social Security benefits are exempt. Up to $2,000 of distributions from private retirement benefits and IRAs (up to the amount reported in federal income taxes), or up to $4,000 of government pensions may be exempt. Total deductions may not exceed $4,000 per person.

Intangibles tax: None.

Estate tax: None, except the state's "pick-up" portion of the federal tax, applicable to taxable estates above $1 million.

Property tax: City residents pay a combined city-county tax rate of $1.15 per $100 of assessed value, and county residents pay a rate of $.73 per $100 of assessed value, with all homes assessed at 100 percent of market value. Annual taxes on a $132,657 home are about $1,526 in the city, $968 in the county.

Homestead exemption: Those age 65 and older can exempt $20,000 or 50% (whichever is greater) off the assessed value of permanent residence if combined income is less than $18,000 annually.

Personal property tax: Same rate as home taxes noted above apply to vehicles, boats, motor homes, mobile homes and other specified belongings.

Religion: The city has about 300 places of worship, representing Protestant, Roman Catholic, Greek Orthodox and Jewish faiths.

Education: The city has several colleges and universities, augmented by campuses in surrounding communities. The University of North Carolina at Asheville has degree programs and is home to the North Carolina Center for Creative Retirement, which has numerous programs for retirees, including the College for Seniors with four terms of noncredit classes annually.

Transportation: Asheville Regional Airport provides commuter and jet service, and the Asheville Transit Authority runs buses in the city.

Health: A regional medical center, Asheville has five hospitals and more than 500 doctors, providing a range of health care including heart and cancer centers, trauma services and emergency air transport by helicopter.

Housing options: Some retirees choose to buy older homes in city neighborhoods, while others relocate to new developments in suburban areas or adjacent communities in Buncombe County. Some developments cater to active adults but many are composed of all ages. Among choices: In the eastern part of the city, **ViewPointe** is a gated community of maintenance-free cluster homes for active adults, with a clubhouse for activities; homes are in the $160,000s-$190,000s. To the north in Weaverville, about 20 minutes to downtown Asheville, **Reems Creek Golf Club**, (828) 645-3110, attracts all ages, offering townhomes from $175,000 and homes from the $260,000s. To the south at the community of Arden, about 10 minutes from Asheville, **High Vista Falls** is a gated community for all ages with golf course, clubhouse and patio homes from the $277,000s and townhomes from the low $300,000s.

Visitor lodging: A popular vacation hub, Asheville has a wide choice of lodging, from budget to luxury and including bed-and-breakfast inns. The grand dame is Grove Park Inn, (800) 267-8413, a legendary mountainside resort with a rustic elegance; rates start at $130. Contact the Asheville Bed & Breakfast Association, (877) 262-6867, for information on most of the B&Bs.

Information: Asheville Area Chamber of Commerce, P.O. Box 1010, Asheville, NC 28802, (800) 257-1300 or www.ashevillechamber.org. North Carolina Center for Creative Retirement, (828) 251-6140 or www.unca.edu/ncccr.

didn't succumb to the wrecking ball.

Recognizing their architectural treasures from the early 20th century, residents and developers began restoring the art deco, Queen Anne, Revival and Romanesque structures and recycling them for new uses. Today more than $50 million is pledged for downtown redevelopment. Among the restorations downtown, Pack Place now houses three museums, a theater and cultural center. Galleries and shops showcase outstanding arts and crafts created in the region, augmenting the extensive collection of mountain crafts at the Folk Art Center outside town on the Blue Ridge Parkway.

Asheville's extensive cultural venues are a drawing card for many retirees who are eager to escape the hassles of living in metropolitan areas but still want some of the big-city amenities. "It's easy and inexpensive to go to performances here," says Louaine, noting that the area has community theater, university drama presentations and current productions by touring groups. It takes her as little as 10 minutes to get to performances, which usually cost less than $20 — "I figured it cost about $100 to go into San Francisco for an evening performance," she says.

Although the cost of living in Asheville runs slightly above average, it's less than metropolitan areas, and all those interviewed cited lower costs as a factor in choosing Asheville.

Each chose a different option for housing. The Ingersolls bought an older home, which they renovated. "It's 10 minutes from downtown but feels like it's in the country," says Sheila. The Ricordatis wanted a new development where they felt that making friends would be easier than in a neighborhood of longtime Asheville residents. "We pretty much built our house by phone and fax," Rick says, noting that they shuttled to and from Rhode Island during construction. They were pleased with the work, though. "The real surprise (of their move) was that we could build a house without being here, and it come out 98 percent the way we wanted," he says with a laugh.

Louaine's co-housing community has 24 units in close clusters of three or four attached homes that range from one to three stories and from one to five bedrooms. Each has a private back yard but

the front yards are common. All parking is close to the street with walkways to the houses, an architectural design intended to encourage residents to meet and greet their neighbors as they go to and from their homes.

"We have a very interesting group (of residents), ranging from a 4-month-old baby to 70s," says Louaine. "This is part of the appeal to me — I didn't want all seniors." It's a friendly group that looks after each other, she says, and takes time to chat when crossing paths outside.

"In Denmark, co-housing residents eat dinner at the community house daily. Here we do it twice a week and sometimes the men do brunch on Sunday," she says. The community house has a restaurant-size kitchen, and residents sign up for work on the cooking team. A community garden provides vegetables and herbs for the shared meals, and residents also can have their own gardens. Louaine, who is an avid gardener, has an arbor where she grows Asian pears and kiwis, among other fruits.

A guiding force for many seniors who move to the Asheville area is the North Carolina Center for Creative Retirement, established in 1988 as part of the University of North Carolina at Asheville. With "creative" an operative part of its title, the center reached out to the growing number of seniors who want to stay active in retirement and designed programs that have become national models. Its mainstay is the College for Seniors, which offers four terms annually with classes in such far-ranging topics as Understanding the Balkans, King David vs. King James, Getting Started With Computers and U.S. Leadership in Today's Global Economy. UNCA faculty, community residents and retirees who are experts in varying fields teach the noncredit classes, which draw about 1,500 seniors annually.

The Ingersolls, Ricordatis and Elke are involved in classes at the College for Seniors, which they also found to be a good way to meet people, make new friends and learn more about the community. Jack serves on the boards of the College for Seniors and Leadership for Asheville Seniors, another program of the center. Rick serves as the university's representative to United Way, and both he and his wife volunteer to assist

with the center's Creative Retirement Exploration Weekend. Held over the Memorial Day weekend, the event annually draws about 150 seniors who attend workshops to discuss the economic, social and psychological factors of relocating to this region when they retire. Participants hear firsthand experiences from seniors who have come here from all parts of the country and have time to see Asheville and surrounding communities.

With mountains at their doorsteps, Asheville residents enjoy a variety of outdoor sports, including hiking, rafting, biking and fishing. The area has a mild four-season climate with a colorful spring and fall.

The retirees interviewed consider the health care here excellent, and Louaine notes that besides traditional medicine, the city has choices of alternative medicine.

All voice a common concern about increased air pollution, which usually occurs in summer. There has been a slight upward trend in air pollution recently, with the increased population driving more motor vehicles and pollutants drifting into the area from the west, according to representatives of the Western North Carolina Air Pollution Control Agency, which monitors air quality. They say that while in the summer of '99 Asheville had some days when the ozone level rose to moderate levels, the city had only two days when air quality was rated unhealthy for sensitive groups (those susceptible to asthma and other respiratory problems) and no days rated generally unhealthy.

Rick says most people who've relocated here like it so much they sound "like a voice for the chamber of commerce — we've become that way." As for seniors considering places to retire, Rick adds, "I think Asheville should be on your list. It was right for us but it may not be for everyone." He says a golfer would find plenty of courses to play but a "water person" or boating enthusiast might not be as happy here.

Jack says that after living so many different places, "This is home — where I want to be." Sheila adds, "No matter where I lived I enjoyed it, but I never made an attachment and I wondered if I would ever find a place I could. It's happened here." ●

Ashland, Oregon

A lively town in pretty southern Oregon sets the stage for Shakespeare

By Stanton H. Patty

Sometimes it seems as if all of Ashland's 19,500 residents are hooked on Shakespeare. That includes retirees who have settled here in southern Oregon to partake of Ashland's award-winning Oregon Shakespeare Festival.

"We've seen plays all over the world, but none better than right here in Ashland," says Gerald Garland, a retired educator. But the play hasn't always been the thing in Ashland-upon-Interstate 5.

Back in 1935, Angus Bowmer, an instructor at Southern Oregon Normal School (now Southern Oregon University), dreamed of producing a Shakespeare festival on the grounds of an abandoned theater once used for events on the Chautauqua circuit. Chautauqua was the 19th-century movement that aimed to bring culture and entertainment to rural areas around the country. Celebrities such as bandmaster John Philip Sousa and orator William Jennings Bryan drew crowds here.

Ashland's city fathers agreed to give Bowmer $400 for expenses — with the provision that a boxing match be presented on the same program. The thrifty city officials reasoned that pugilism would cover the Shakespeare show's certain losses.

The fights lost money, but that first festival's two Shakespeare plays — "Twelfth Night" and "The Merchant of Venice" — turned a profit. Ever since, the annual Oregon Shakespeare Festival has been a hit.

And ever since, this pretty, little town snuggled against the Siskiyou and Cascade mountain ranges has been blending scenic beauty and the lyrics of the Bard. More than 358,000 visitors were counted here last year. The economic impact of the nine-month-long Oregon Shakespeare Festival alone was estimated at $90,203,600 last season.

Many of Ashland's retirees say they "discovered" Ashland during frequent trips here to attend the Shakespeare series. Others allow that they didn't have a burning interest in Shakespeare's works until getting involved in volunteer assignments at the festival.

John and Norma Yovich, both retired teachers, moved to Ashland 17 years ago after giving retirement a try in the U.S. Virgin Islands. The Yoviches had friends who were conducting a study of the best places to live for retirees. The friends decided on Medford, 17 miles north of Ashland by way of Interstate 5. The Yoviches traveled to Medford for a visit.

"But then we looked at Ashland and just fell in love with the town," recalls Norma. Ashland, she says, offered "just the right mix" — location, small-town living, an array of cultural assets, excellent medical care, a gentle climate for gardening, interesting neighbors and scenic mountain views.

"The (Shakespeare) festival was not the most compelling reason for moving here," says John (Jack) Yovich. "What I really liked was the idea of having a college in town." The Yoviches, both 76, are regulars at Ashland's Southern Oregon University for concerts, lectures and Elderhostel sessions.

But now they also are Shakespeare enthusiasts. "I'm hooked," says Norma Yovich, who, along with dozens of other retirees, volunteers for tasks ranging from costume repairs to ticket-taking at the festival's three theaters.

What happened in Ashland is that the Tony Award-winning Oregon Shakespeare Festival made the town a major-league destination. Along with Shakespeare came other theaters, a symphony orchestra, a range of lodging accommodations (including 62 bed-and-breakfast inns, at last count),

outstanding restaurants, art galleries and antique shops. These are all attractions sought by retirees who are determined to continue creative, vigorous lives after their working years.

For them (with apologies to the Bard of Stratford-upon-Avon), it's Ashland as they like it. An Ashland Chamber of Commerce publication states it this way: "Ashlanders don't talk much about 'quality time' because it's all quality time."

Richard and Mary Mastain didn't even consider another retirement spot before moving here from Sacramento, CA, in 1989. "I can't think of any negatives," Mary says of Ashland.

Richard, 73, was director of California's Commission on Teacher Credentialing for 16 years. Before that he was employed at Yale University, and before Yale he served in the Peace Corps in Nigeria. Mary, now 71, and their four children went along on the African adventure. Mary, a longtime reading specialist in a Sacramento-area school district, taught in a Nigerian school for a year.

It was the Oregon Shakespeare Festival that introduced Ashland to the Mastains. "We had been to Ashland two or three times for the festival and just liked the town very much," says Mary.

During one visit, the couple expressed interest in buying a 100-year-old house on Granite Street in downtown Ashland but had to wait four years before the owner was ready to sell. Their 2,800-square-foot home is across from Lithia Park, Ashland's 100-acre gem of a park where early-day locals and visitors used to imbibe a so-called healing elixir called Lithia Water.

Ashland's enterprising merchants had hopes back then that their town would become a renowned European-style spa, but interest waned. Fortunately for Ashland, Shakespeare

Ashland, OR

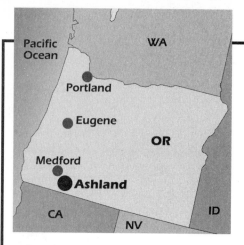

Population: 19,500 in Ashland, 184,000 in Jackson County.

Location: On Interstate 5 between San Francisco (365 miles to the south) and Portland, OR (290 miles to the north). Ashland, at an elevation of 2,000 feet, is at the southern end of the Rogue Valley, 15 miles north of Oregon's border with California.

Climate:

	High	Low
January	48	32
July	85	52

Average relative humidity: 83% in winter, 52% in summer.

Rain: 19 inches.

Cost of living: Above average (specific index not available).

Median housing cost: $289,900 in the city, $342,000 in rural areas.

Sales tax: None as such, but Ashland does have a 5% "food tax" that applies to restaurant meals, takeout foods and deli purchases within grocery stores. There is no tax on other groceries.

State income tax: For married couples filing jointly, the rate is graduated from 5% of taxable income up to $5,000 to 9% on amounts over $12,600. For single filers, graduated from 5% of taxable income up to $2,500 to 9% on amounts over $6,300.

Income tax exemptions: Social Security benefits are exempt. Federal pensions are fully exempt for those who retired before October 1991 and may be partially exempt for retirement after that date. There is a retirement income tax credit of up to 9 percent of retirement income for those age 62 and older if they meet specified income limitations.

Intangibles tax: None.

Estate tax: None, except the state's "pickup" portion of the federal tax, applicable to taxable estates above $1 million.

Property taxes: $14.95 per $1,000 of assessed value for city property owners, and ranging from $9.39 to $13.81 for rural property owners, depending on taxes assessed by school and fire districts. Homes are assessed at 85% of market value. The tax on a $289,900 home in the city would be about $3,684. The tax on a $342,000 home in a rural area would be about $2,730 to $4,015. Property tax relief is available for low-income seniors.

Homestead exemption: None.

Religion: 36 churches or religious affiliations, including synagogues and a Buddhist congregation.

Education: The Ashland School District has seven schools with enrollment estimated at 3,400. There also are several private schools. Southern Oregon University, founded in 1869, is part of the Oregon University System. Its main campus is in Ashland, with a branch campus in neighboring Medford. There are more than 6,000 undergraduate and graduate students. Rogue Community College, with its main campus in nearby Grants Pass, OR, offers a full range of community college programs.

Transportation: The regional airport is Rogue Valley International-Medford Airport, 20 miles north of Ashland. The airport is served by United Airlines and Horizon Air, a sister company of Alaska Airlines. Bus service is available from Greyhound-Trailways and, locally, from Rogue Valley Transportation District, which offers low-cost public transportation throughout Ashland. For rail service, the nearest Amtrak station is in Klamath Falls, OR, 70 miles east of Ashland.

Health: Ashland Community Hospital is an acute, primary-care facility fully accredited by the Joint Commission on Accreditation of Healthcare Organizations. The 49-bed hospital provides 24-hour emergency services, inpatient medical and surgical services, outpatient services, an intensive-care unit, an alternative family-oriented birthing center, a hospice unit and other facilities. Other medical facilities in the region include Providence Medford Medical Center (168 beds) in Medford, and Rogue Valley Medical Center (305 beds), also in Medford.

Housing options: Many Ashland-area retirees buy single-family homes, but the city also has high-quality retirement facilities. Among these is **Mountain Meadows**, (800) 337-1301, an award-winning retirement center occupying a 41.5-acre campus about one mile northeast of downtown Ashland. Resale options include single-family homes (with two or three bedrooms) priced from $390,000 to $450,000, depending on square footage, and condominiums (with one, two or three bedrooms), from $190,000 to $440,000. Mountain Meadows also has an assisted-living center with 75 apartments and 32 special-care units. Prices begin at $1,800 a month. Madeline Hill, a former administrator of the state of Oregon's Senior Services Division, founded Mountain Meadows "when I saw what was not available for my older friends." Mountain Meadows was honored by the National Council on Seniors Housing as being the best small active-adult community in America. Another Ashland retirement center with facilities for independent or assisted living is **Mountain View**, (541) 482-3292, in downtown Ashland. Mountain View has 111 apartments, including 25 apartments for assisted-living guests. Monthly rates for independent-living tenants range from $1,120 to $1,565 for a studio apartment, and starting from $2,665 for two-bedroom apartments. Assisted-living services are additional. There is a waiting list that ranges from one to three months. Mountain View is part of a chain, Holiday Retirement Corp., with 25,000 units in the United States, Canada and England. Medford also offers retirement centers, including **Rogue Valley Manor**, (800) 848-7868, with accommodations for about 750 residents.

Visitor lodging: Ashland's lodging establishments — including more than 60 bed-and-breakfast inns and country inns — offer a total of about 1,200 beds. Among motel options: Windsor Inn, $65-$159, (800) 334-2330, and Bard's Inn Best Western, $100-$150, (800) 528-1234. Among B&B options: Chanticleer Inn, $160-$195, (800) 898-1950, and Bayberry Inn, $65-$100, (800) 795-1252.

Information: Ashland Chamber of Commerce, P.O. Box 1360, Ashland, OR 97520, (541) 482-3486, or fax (541) 482-2350. Internet: www.ashlandchamber.com. Oregon Shakespeare Festival, P.O. Box 158, Ashland, OR 97520. For tickets, call (541) 482-4331. For administration offices, call (541) 482-2111. Internet: www.orshakes. org.

soon replaced the bitter bubbly from Lithia Springs as the mainstay of Ashland's economy.

Richard and Mary Mastain have a full schedule. Mary is a volunteer at the local chamber of commerce, serves on Ashland's library board and guides walks through Lithia Park. Richard plays tennis regularly with partners that he describes as "terrific people from all walks of life." A recent tennis turnout of retirees included an oral surgeon, a Navy physician, two airline pilots, a businessman and a still-performing Shakespearean actor.

The Mastains celebrated their 50th-wedding anniversary in Lithia Park. They needed a major space for the party because more than 150 guests from throughout the United States attended. "We're having a wonderful time here," says Mary Mastain.

Cherie and Gerald Garland began their retirement years in Ashland in 1990 by buying a two-story house on 45 acres of land — and adding three goats, two cats, a dog and 100 head of beef cattle. They since have traded the house and the menagerie for a condominium at Ashland's Mountain Meadows retirement community, which won the National Council on Seniors Housing award as the best small active-adult community in America.

"There comes a time," says Cherie of the switch to condo living.

Gerry, 71, was a high-school English teacher for 24 years in Oklahoma and California. Later the couple owned an educational-supplies business with stores in California and Arizona. It was the Shakespeare festival that brought them to Ashland.

"We started coming to the festival about 25 years ago," says Cherie, 67. "We'd usually see eight plays or so, then go home and jump back into the business."

But one day, while returning through stop-and-go freeway traffic to their home in Pomona, CA, there was what Gerry calls "a gray blanket of fog" hanging over the Los Angeles Basin. It was time to leave, he said.

Destination: Ashland — and the 45 acres of pasture with the big house. "We had just sort of fallen in love with the town," Gerry remembers.

Then came the day when they decided to move into Mountain Meadows. Their Ashland house sold after only five days on the market, and all the animals found good homes. The cats stayed with the property, and the dog went to live with friends. The goats moved two houses away. The cattle belonged to someone else, who had been leasing the Garlands' property for grazing. And so the Garlands settled happily into a brand-new 1,500-square-foot Mountain Meadows condominium.

"There has not been one moment of regret," says Cherie. "It was a big decision, but we were able to make it while we were of sound mind and in good health. That's the important thing."

Both sing in church choirs. Cherie also is active in the local garden club, and Gerry plays tennis several times a week. Travel also is on their schedule, and they have journeyed from Bali to Africa.

"Nothing to it," says Cherie. "We just go out the front door and lock it."

Geography — Ashland's mainline location between San Francisco and Portland, OR — was an important decision-making factor for many retired couples here. "We wanted to be in driving distance of our children in California," says Mary Mastain.

Ashland is 15 miles north of the California border — 365 miles north of San Francisco, 290 miles south of Portland. About the only drawback for Ashlanders, says Jack Yovich, is what he terms "somewhat limited air transportation." The nearest airport — Rogue Valley International-Medford Airport — is 20 miles north of Ashland. It currently is served by only two carriers, United Airlines and Horizon Air, an Alaska Airlines sister company.

"It's not a serious thing, but does makes airline travel a bit more complicated for us," Jack says.

"And yet," says Jeanne Thomas, a 22-year resident of Ashland, "things have really improved over the years here for air travel. We are getting more special fares and better service than before," says Jeanne, a receptionist at the Ashland Chamber of Commerce.

Another key factor in attracting retirees to Ashland is excellent medical care. There are first-rate hospitals both in Ashland and in neighboring Medford. And Ashland's full menu of cultural offerings is encouraging big-city physicians to move here to rear their families.

"There's so much culture here that it's sort of mind-boggling," says Mary Mastain.

And Shakespeare isn't Ashland's only attraction. Residents of all ages in this Oregon playground are outdoor-minded. They exercise along a network of walking and bicycle trails inside the city, and they golf on eight courses scattered through the Ashland-Medford region.

Close by — and, incidentally, owned by the city of Ashland — is the Mount Ashland ski area. Mount Ashland, 7,533 feet high, receives more than 300 inches of snow each Thanksgiving-through-April ski season. Cross-country skiers find more than 80 miles of trails, and downhillers have a choice of 23 runs.

Emigrant Lake, six miles to the east, is popular with water-skiers, swimmers and boaters. Crater Lake National Park (Oregon's only national park) is a drive of about two and a half hours from Ashland. And then there is Oregon's Rogue River, with world-class rafting, kayaking, jet-boating and sport fishing. Guides and outfitters are available for adventure outings.

For generous helpings of history and music, there is Jacksonville, five miles west of neighboring Medford. Jacksonville, born of a gold rush in the 1850s, is home to the Britt Festivals, a summertime musical series running the scale from jazz to the classics.

But it is the Oregon Shakespeare Festival that continues to hold the spotlight here. The 65-year-old festival is billed as the nation's oldest and largest professional regional theater company. The extravaganza begins in February and ends in October and features nearly a dozen plays.

If all the world's a stage, as the Bard said, Ashlanders will tell you that center stage is right here in southern Oregon. Verily!●

Athens, Georgia

Historic university sets the pace in Georgia city

By William Schemmel

In Athens, GA, unlike many other cities today, the action centers on downtown, where the scene is reminiscent of *Saturday Evening Post* covers.

Students and townspeople crowd the sidewalks, drifting in and out of shops that sell books, bagels, clothes, CDs, hardware and a myriad of other goods.

They settle into restaurants serving everything from tofu burgers and "California inventive" cuisine to Southern-style home cooking, barbecue, Indian, Mexican, Cajun, Chinese, Japanese and German dishes.

The lively downtown "looks like the downtowns many people remember when they were younger," says Joan Zitzelman, spokeswoman for the Athens Convention and Visitors Bureau.

A major contributor to the action is the University of Georgia, temporary home to about 30,000 students. From downtown, the landmark Arch serves as a commemorative gateway to the historic campus.

UGA is the nation's oldest chartered state university, founded in 1785, but buildings and classes didn't come until 1801, with the birth of the town of Athens. City fathers named the community for the Greek capital, seeking to establish it as another "classic city" known as a center of culture and learning.

Indeed, the new Athens did become a major educational center, with UGA fostering great pride and a fervent following among Georgia residents and its graduates.

Today UGA's abundance of cultural, educational and recreational activities draws not only young students but also seniors seeking an active retirement lifestyle. Here they find theater, lectures, films, the Georgia Museum of Art, the State Botanical Garden, a continuing-education center with extensive enrichment classes and the popular Georgia Bulldogs athletic programs.

Many graduates come back to Athens when they retire.

Helen Rode, 63, grew up in Athens and attended the university. She and her husband, Ed, 66, lived in the Chicago area for most of his 40-year ministry with the United Methodist Church.

When he retired, they considered a few other areas, "but we wanted the cultural activities and other amenities of a university town, and I remembered what a wonderful place Athens was," she says. "We were delighted to find that it still has a wonderful small-town feeling, even though it's much larger than it was then."

The city now has a population of about 100,000, including students. Large oak and elm trees shade historic homes and churches, including many antebellum mansions with tall white columns. At the university, the Greek Revival-style chapel, the president's residence and several other buildings on the original campus date back to the early or mid-1800s.

Ed says another factor in choosing Athens was its below-average cost of living, which he calls "much lower than in Illinois."

"We have a modest income and we needed an affordable home. Plus, we wanted to get out of the cold Chicago winters. It stays hotter here than it does in Illinois, but it rarely snows, and the falls are beautiful," Ed says.

They purchased a 30-year-old home in a subdivision of medium-sized houses. "It's a lovely home that was really well cared for," he says. "I've always had a dream of having a home in a community I enjoyed being in. It's very satisfying."

Helen adds, "It's such a beautiful town, with so much going on all the time. It's hard to be bored. But we can get to Atlanta in about an hour or so, and we're also within a short drive of the Georgia mountains and a few hours from the Georgia and South Carolina beaches."

Okel and Gennis Dawson moved to the Athens area after their home of 32 years in Homestead, FL, was destroyed by Hurricane Andrew in 1992.

"We'd been thinking about moving away from South Florida for a good while," says Gennis, 70. "When the hurricane took everything, we didn't see any reason to stay.

"Our son had become the dean of environmental design at the University of Georgia, and he encouraged us to move to the Athens area. We're very happy with the decision.

"Everything, especially property taxes, is much cheaper here, and property values are much better," she says.

The Dawsons live in the Great Oaks subdivision in Oconee County, a rapidly growing bedroom community about 10 minutes south of downtown Athens. Houses in Great Oaks are valued at $120,000 to $175,000.

"We have a two-story house on two-and-a-half acres of land. That enables us to have a garden," says Gennis, adding that it helps cut down on their grocery bills.

The Dawsons found a warm welcome in their new home.

"I didn't know my next-door neighbor in Homestead," Gennis says, "but when we went to a church of 150 members here, 120 shook our hands. People are so friendly."

The Dawsons often go into Athens for dining, football games and other activities. They say they feel safer from crime here than they did in South Florida.

"We're happy where we are," says Okel, 76, a machinist who retired from International Paper Co.

Other residents are equally enthusiastic about the area's assets.

"First-class health care is abundant," says Buddy Allen, president of

Heyward Allen Motor Co. Athens is a medical center for northeast Georgia, offering two acute-care facilities, Athens Regional Medical Center and St. Mary's Hospital. Both have advanced surgical technology and treatment programs.

Jack Wilson, who moved from Atlanta a year ago, finds the city a comfortable place for singles.

"There are plenty of inexpensive apartments and rental houses," he says. "You can get a decent place for much less than you'd pay in Atlanta or other big cities. There's always something to do here. You can eat very well and very inexpensively. Athens has crime problems like every other place, but I generally feel safe here."

The average housing cost in Athens is $142,000. Property taxes are reasonable, aided by a $10,000 homestead exemption.

The city takes up most of Clarke County, which is the state's smallest county in land area and one of its most densely populated. Although much of the available land in Clarke County has been developed, a few new subdivisions are still being built.

Athens, GA

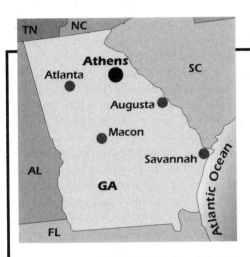

Population: 100,266, including 30,000 University of Georgia students.

Location: In Georgia's southern Piedmont Plateau region, 65 miles northeast of Atlanta.

Climate:

	High	Low
January	48	31
July	92	69

Average relative humidity: 60%

Rain: 52 inches.

At an elevation of 750 feet, Athens has a moderate four-season climate with cool winters, colorful falls and hot, humid summers. Snow is infrequent and light when it occurs.

Cost of living: Below average (specific index not available).

Average housing cost: $142,000

Sales tax: 6%; 7% on food and perishables.

Sales tax exemptions: Prescriptions, hearing aids, eyeglasses.

State income tax: For married couples filing jointly, graduated from 1% of taxable income up to $1,000 to $340 plus 6% on amounts over $10,000. For single filers, graduated from 1% of income up to $750 to $230 plus 6% on amounts over $7,000.

Income tax exemptions: Social Security benefits are exempt. Up to $14,000 in retirement income is exempt for each

taxpayer age 62 and older. Up to $4,000 of earned income can be included in the $14,000 exemption.

Intangibles tax: None.

Estate tax: None, except the state's "pick-up" portion of the federal tax, applicable to taxable estates above $1 million.

Property tax: $32.70 per $1,000 of assessed value, with homes assessed at 40% of fair market value. With homestead exemption listed below, yearly tax on a $142,000 house is $1,530.

Homestead exemption: $10,000 off assessed value for full-time residents.

Religion: More than 200 churches and synagogues serve all denominations.

Education: The main campus of the University of Georgia offers undergraduate and graduate programs, day and evening classes, community classes without credit and a wide range of continuing-education courses in languages, cultural studies and other subjects. College classes are free for all Georgia residents age 62 and older; continuing-education classes have fees. The Athens Area Technical Institute offers day and evening vocational and technical courses.

Transportation: Athens Transit System provides bus service throughout the area, and the university operates a bus system for use by students, faculty and staff. There are daily commuter flights to Charlotte, NC, a hub for air connections nationwide; regularly scheduled limousine service goes to the Atlanta airport.

Health: Athens is a regional health care center. St. Mary's Hospital (private) and Athens Regional Medical Center (public) together have about 500 beds and offer 24-hour emergency care and all other major services. More than 170 physicians practice in all medical specialties. The Navy Corps Supply School has medical

and dental facilities available to military retirees.

Housing options: Five Points is a quiet neighborhood near downtown and the university, with frame and brick homes built in the '30s-'50s; prices range from about $150,000 to $350,000 and up for older homes. In Clarke County, the **Village at Jennings Mill** has large contemporary homes from $135,000 on an 18-hole private golf course. **Kingston Greens**, a golfing community in Madison County, about 20 minutes north of downtown Athens, has three-bedroom homes on large wooded lots from the $130,000s. South of Athens in Oconee County, **Stonebridge** has three- and four-bedroom homes for $230,000-$350,000, and **Laurel Shoals** homes start in the $240,000s. For more information call Mike Geyer with Coldwell Banker Upchurch Realty, (706) 202-1660. The Athens area has numerous rental apartments, condos and houses.

Visitor lodging: Holiday Inn, adjacent to downtown and UGA campus, doubles $79-$107, (706) 549-4433; Courtyard by Marriott, near downtown and campus, $79 double, (706) 369-7000; Holiday Inn Express, near campus and downtown, $79 double, (706) 546-8122. Rivendell Bed and Breakfast, between Athens and Watkinsville, contemporary country home in a quiet wooded setting about 15 minutes from downtown, $70-$90, (706) 769-4522. Rates at most Athens area lodgings are higher on football weekends.

Information: Athens Convention and Visitors Bureau, 300 N. Thomas St., Athens, GA 30601, (800) 653-0603 or www.visitathensga.com. Athens Area Chamber of Commerce, 220 College Ave., Athens, GA 30601, (706) 549-6800 or www.aacoc.org.

Large wooded lots in Hampton Park start at $23,900, and three-bedroom homes with tennis and pool privileges start at $127,000.

Those who enjoy in-town living in an older neighborhood prefer the Five Points area. Close to downtown and the university campus, most of the frame and brick homes were developed between the 1930s and early 1950s. The neighborhood shopping area has grocery stores, a deli, antique shops, bookstores and a good mix of locally owned restaurants and shops. Smaller homes that need work sell for about $80,000, while brick homes in good condition are in the low $150,000s. Some newer homes are selling for $200,000 or more.

Much of the area's new growth is taking place in once-rural counties like Oconee to the south and Madison to the north. Homes in developments such as Harrowford Estates, Skipstone, Laurel Shoals, Great Oaks and Twelve Oaks in Oconee County and Kingston Greens in Madison County are priced from $130,000 and up. Some large custom-built homes are valued at $1 million-plus.

In addition to its thriving downtown and neighborhood shopping areas, Athens has numerous other shopping districts and one major regional mall. Georgia Square has four anchor department stores — Macy's, Penney's, Sears and Belk — as well as specialty shops, services and cinemas.

Residents offer little criticism of the city, though newcomers must adjust to the huge influx of football fans, who help fill the 82,000-seat stadium.

Ed Rode notes that traffic can be heavy and "there are plenty of 'Chicago drivers' down here," referring to the aggressive nature of some on the road.

The Rodes can think of only one thing they miss from their previous home. "You can't get Illinois corn in Georgia. Fresh corn out of the field just can't be replaced, but then you can't get good Georgia peaches, watermelons and peanuts in Illinois," he says.

The city hosted some segments of the Summer Olympic Games in 1996, furthering its bond with ancient Greece. The university's football stadium was the setting for the semifinals and finals of women's and men's soccer, and its 10,000-seat basketball coliseum was the scene of Olympic volleyball competition.

In the months before the games began, the city was the training site for national Olympic teams from several different countries, including Australia and Sweden.

"We know we have a wonderful community, and we enjoyed showing it off to people from so many states and foreign countries," says Zitzelman of the Athens Convention and Visitors Bureau.●

Beaufort, South Carolina

Newcomers settle into island life in coastal South Carolina

By Lan Sluder

An irresistible combination of dependably warm weather, laid-back island living, historical charm and welcoming attitude to newcomers has turned the once-sleepy community of Beaufort into one of the fastest-growing retirement areas in South Carolina.

The town of Beaufort, about midway between Charleston and Savannah, is the seat of Beaufort County, which in recent years has led the state in population growth. The county has doubled in population since 1980. The Greater Beaufort area has 12,950 residents.

Beaufort is in the heart of what's called the Lowcountry. The Lowcountry is more a state of mind than a specific geographic locale, but roughly it runs along the coast from around Georgetown, SC, to somewhere south of Savannah, GA. It includes the South Carolina Sea Islands of which Beaufort is a part.

Even if you've never been within miles of Beaufort, you've probably seen the town. Beaufort (pronounced as in "beautiful," say local boosters) was Forrest Gump's hometown in the blockbuster film of the same name. Beaufort and its collection of atmospheric Southern mansions have been featured in many other movies, including "The Prince of Tides" with Barbra Streisand and Nick Nolte and "The Big Chill" starring William Hurt and Glenn Close.

Because Beaufort was a Union headquarters and hospital zone in the Civil War, it was spared the destruction of many other Southern towns. Beaufort's 304-acre historic district has 150 antebellum and pre-Revolutionary homes. The oldest, the Thomas Hepworth House, dates to 1717.

While suburban areas around Beaufort have their share of franchise sprawl, Beaufort's historic district is an almost picture-perfect Southern coastal town. The graceful old homes on Bay Street, one of the town's main thoroughfares, have views of the Beaufort Bay (a part of the Beaufort River) framed by ancient live oaks and palmetto palms.

But it's not history or Hollywood that draws most retirees to Beaufort. It's that magic five-letter word — water, says Ron Kay, 57, who moved here with wife Carrol from Miami in 1989 to open a bed-and-breakfast inn, TwoSuns Inn B&B.

"People don't necessarily want to live on the water, just be near it," says Ron, who notes that almost one-half of the guests at his six-room inn are considering Beaufort for retirement or relocation.

Peggy Masterson, 62, who with husband Greg, 70, moved to the Beaufort area in 1991 from Barrington, IL, agrees. "Our interest was very much being in a community at the ocean. We are both beach people, and I swim daily in the ocean," she says. Peggy and Greg live at Fripp Island, a gated community on the water about 17 miles east of downtown Beaufort.

The city of Beaufort itself is on an island, Port Royal Island, and most of the surrounding communities are on the scores of islands that together make up the South Carolina Sea Islands. However, these are not islands edged with sandy beaches, but barrier islands whose shores are mostly salt marsh. The nearest ocean beach is at Hunting Island, about 16 miles from downtown Beaufort.

As you drive east from Beaufort on Highway 21 toward the Atlantic, you are struck by the beauty of the marshes, which are washed twice a day by tides with a tidal variation (the difference between low and high tides) of up to 11 feet. Vistas of the dominant cordgrass, which grows to five or six feet in the marsh, may remind you of enormous fields of wheat.

Here, east and south of the town of Beaufort on a cluster of islands, some so close together that you may not realize that only short bridges separate one from another, are a growing number of planned communities. Prized waterfront building lots with deep-water access go for $200,000 or more.

Beaufort's coastal setting, however, is a curse as well as an attraction. Hurricanes are a fact of life, although most recent transplants have never experienced a killer storm. In 1893, a fearsome hurricane — by all accounts the strongest storm to hit the region in recorded memory — killed more than 2,000 people as a tidal wave rushed over low-lying areas. Another hurricane in 1940 did serious damage. Beaufortonians note with irony that a scale developed to measure the force of wind is called the Beaufort scale after the early 19th-century British admiral who invented it.

Twice in 1996 area residents faced mandatory evacuations because of hurricane threats. These storms, however, veered off and didn't do much damage. Still, the sea and usually fine weather are the main reasons people move to Beaufort, says Jean Lebro, former executive vice president of the Greater Beaufort Chamber of Commerce.

That holds true both for those moving to escape cold Northern or Midwestern winters and for those from Florida and other hot-weather areas who like the fact that Beaufort has a four-season climate. While summers can be hot and humid — and in Beaufort summers begin in March and end around Christmas Eve, some say — sea breezes exert a moderating influence. Homes in Beaufort traditionally all faced south to catch the prevailing breezes.

Maybe it's the weather or something in the water, but the Beaufort lifestyle is definitely laid-back. "There's a peace and serenity here that you don't find in some other towns," says Peggy Masterson.

Another couple, Norm and Suzanne Green, who moved to Dataw Island from Chester Township, NJ, in 1994, also like the Beaufort style. "We liked the gentle lifestyle — it has a nice rural feel to it," says Norm, 69. Dataw is a gated planned community of about 500 homes on an 870-acre island developed by ALCOA about six miles east of Beaufort. Villas and homes sell for $250,000 to $500,000.

"It offers the type of atmosphere we were used to," says Nancy Hicks, 70, who with husband Scott, 71, moved from Peterborough, NH, to Dataw in 1996. This area has "the feel of a small town, yet it's close enough to Charleston for big-city amenities," she says.

Residents note that Hilton Head is only about 35 miles from Beaufort, but the pace of life is entirely different. Hilton Head has a population of about 34,000, of whom about one-third are retirees, but the island gets more than 2.5 million visitors a year. Tourists come to play its

Beaufort, SC

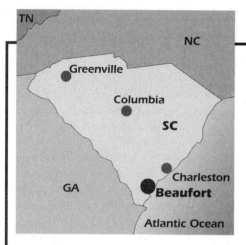

Population: 12,950 in Beaufort, 120,937 in Beaufort County.

Location: The city of Beaufort is in northern Beaufort County on the southeastern coast of South Carolina. By car it is about one hour north of Savannah, GA, and one and a half hours south of Charleston, SC. Hilton Head is about 45 minutes away.

Climate:

	High	Low
January	59	38
July	89	71

Beaufort has a mild, four-season climate, although summers are very warm. Hurricane season is June-November. Average water temperature in the Atlantic Ocean is 52 in January and 84 in July.

Average relative humidity: 53%

Rain: 49 inches on average, with the most rain May through August. Light snow occurs very rarely.

Cost of living: About average (specific index not available).

Average housing cost: $146,000

Sales tax: 5%

Sales tax exemptions: Prescriptions, dental prosthetics and hearing aids. There is a maximum of $300 sales tax on motor vehicles. Those 85 and older are exempt from 1% of sales tax.

State income tax: For married couples filing jointly and single filers, the rates are graduated in six tiers from 2.5% on the first $2,400 of taxable income to 7% on taxable income above $12,000.

Income tax exemptions: Social Security benefits are exempt. Retirees who are drawing income from qualified retirement plans may deduct up to $3,000 of that income.

Intangibles tax: None.

Estate tax: None, except the state's pickup portion of the federal tax, applicable to taxable estates above $1 million.

Property tax: In the city of Beaufort, $244.80 per $1,000 of assessed value, with homes assessed at 4% of appraised value. Annual tax on a $146,000 home in the city would be about $1,430. Tax rates in districts outside Beaufort range from $192.10 to $261.40. Tangible personal property, including vehicles and boats, is subject to a personal property tax that varies by county district; it is assessed at 10.5% of appraised value.

Homestead exemption: $50,000 off fair market value for residents age 65 or older.

Religion: More than 25 churches and synagogues.

Education: The University of South Carolina has a campus in Beaufort offering four-year and continuing-education programs. Members of the USC-Beaufort's Creative Retirement Center — now totaling about 800 — can take an unlimited number of special CRC courses for a flat fee of $150. Webster University and Park College, based elsewhere, offer degree programs locally. Technical College of the Lowcountry offers courses in computers and other subjects.

Transportation: Major airlines serve the airports in Savannah (45 miles) and Charleston (70 miles).

Health: Beaufort Memorial Hospital is a fully accredited 182-bed hospital with more than 100 board-certified doctors on staff. Larger hospitals and more specialists are available in Charleston and Savannah.

Housing options: The Beaufort area offers a wide choice of housing options, from antebellum homes in the historic district (a large renovated antebellum home may be $600,000 or more) to waterfront or golf-course living in a planned community. Among the planned communities in the area are **Callawassie Island**, (800) 221-8431, with homesites from $45,000 to $350,000 and homes from $275,000 to $600,000; **Dataw Island**, (800) 848-3838, with homesites from $50,000 and homes ranging from $250,000 to $500,000; and **Fripp Island**, (843) 838-2411, with homesites from around $30,000 to $250,000, and villas and homes from $165,000 to $1.6 million. The houses at **Newpoint**, (843) 986-2300, are inspired by the traditional coastal architecture of historic homes in Savannah and Charleston and feature old-fashioned porches and picket fences. The neighborhood is on Lady's Island, across the river from Beaufort. Home prices range from the low $200,000s to more than $1.5 million. West of Beaufort on the Broad River, **Habersham**, (843) 846-1000, offers interior lots from the $40,000s and marsh-front lots from the $400,000s, and homes from the mid-$200,000s to more than $1 million. Homes in other neighborhoods around Beaufort County start at under $100,000. Two-bedroom rental apartments range from around $400 to $800 a month.

Visitor lodging: Beaufort has 17 inns and several chain motels. Beaufort Inn has 21 luxurious rooms, $145-$300, and an award-winning restaurant, (843) 521-9000. The more casual five-room Two-Suns Inn occupies a 1917 building overlooking Beaufort Bay, $105-$168, (800) 532-4244. Best Western Sea Island Inn is an attractive motel in downtown Beaufort, $109-$125, (843) 522-2090. Hunting Island State Park has rental cabins for $78-$125 and a 200-site campground near the beach, (843) 838-2011.

Information: Greater Beaufort Chamber of Commerce, 1106 Carteret St., P.O. Box 910, Beaufort, SC 29901, (800) 638-3525 or (843) 524-3163 or www.beaufort sc.org.

30 golf courses and more than 300 tennis courts and to shop its many factory outlet stores.

It's nice to be able to go to Hilton Head for outlet shopping, says Peggy Masterson, or to Savannah (less than an hour away) or Charleston (about an hour and a half by car) for major purchases and entertainment. Still, she notes, it's good to come back to the quieter atmosphere of Fripp Island and Beaufort.

But transportation is a concern for some residents. The nearest interstate, I-95, is about 25 miles away. Both Savannah and Charleston have airports, but flying from them often requires a change of planes in Atlanta or Charlotte.

For those who look for it, however, there's plenty to do in the area. There are thriving little theater groups and music societies. Beaufort's art galleries, many specializing in Lowcountry art, are known throughout the region.

Good food is important to Beaufortonians, and while Beaufort doesn't have the selection of ethnic eateries to be found in larger cities, the best of Beaufort restaurants rival those in Charleston or Savannah. Locals gather at Plums or Bananas, two popular downtown lunch spots, dine expansively at Beaufort Inn or get together for a Lowcountry boil. Lowcountry boil, also known as Frogmore stew after the Frogmore section of Beaufort County, is a combination of shrimp, sausage, corn on the cob, red potatoes, onions, seafood seasonings and sometimes crabs, all boiled together in a large pot.

The Beaufort area offers almost unlimited outdoor recreational opportunities. In addition to nearby Hilton Head's golf options, there are 11 public and private courses around Beaufort, including nationally noted ones at Fripp, Dataw, Callawassie, Spring and Cat islands, among others.

Boating is big in Beaufort, and many planned communities have their own marinas. Hunting Island, near Fripp, is one of South Carolina's most popular state parks. The 5,000-acre park has four miles of beach, a lighthouse and a subtropical maritime forest of great beauty. The ACE Basin, a large coastal wilderness area defined by the Ashepoo, Combahee and Edisto rivers, is just north of Beaufort.

Alligators thrive at Hunting Island and elsewhere around the Sea Islands. As dangerous as gators can be — they occasionally devour dogs and can outrun humans for short distances — the peskiest creatures on the islands also are among the smallest. No-see-ums, biting gnats so tiny they can get through screen doors and windows, are bugaboos of many retirees. Mosquitos can be fierce in remote marsh areas and at Hunting Island State Park but are not much of a problem in areas where there is regular mosquito control sprayings, residents say. Cockroaches (locals call them palmetto bugs) are big and not at all rare.

Many Beaufort residents point to the Creative Retirement Center at the University of South Carolina at Beaufort as an important source of local activities and educational opportunities. Through the campus in Beaufort, and at satellite locations serving Hilton Head and the Del Webb Sun City development near Bluffton, the CRC offers more than 50 courses for members in everything from gardening to Greek history. CRC members can take as many courses as they wish for a flat fee of $150, says Peggy Masterson, who edits the CRC newsletter, Second Wind.

The Beaufort area also occupies a special place in African-American history. Penn Normal School on St. Helena Island east of Beaufort was established by Quaker missionaries as the first school for freed slaves. In the early 1960s, Dr. Martin Luther King Jr. used Penn Center, as it is now known, as a training and meeting facility for civil rights workers. Today its mission is to preserve Gullah heritage, the culture developed by former slaves on the Sea Islands. Sea Island Creole, also called Gullah, combines elements of English and West African languages and still is spoken by some people in the area.

Critics say that Beaufort's special lifestyle could eventually be threatened by the area's growing popularity.

The chamber of commerce's Jean Lebro says her office gets about 40,000 requests for information a year, many from people considering relocation to Beaufort. But she admits that there is some local resistance to more growth. Those who moved to Beaufort some time ago note that traffic congestion has increased, especially on some of the two-lane roads.

If water, weather and lifestyle are Beaufort's big selling points, it is an intangible quality that clinches the sale for many transplants. Put simply, Beaufort is one of the most welcoming and friendliest places anywhere.

Old towns, especially old port towns in the South, often have a veneer of hospitality, but scratch that and you find that newcomers — those whose roots go back less than three or four generations — are never quite fully welcomed into the heart and soul of the community.

But for a variety of historical and cultural reasons, Beaufort isn't like that. The Civil War broke the back of an aristocratic plantation economy that once made Beaufort one of the richest areas of America, famed for its Sea Island cotton and rice. Many of Beaufort's old guard moved away, replaced by contingents of Northerners who stayed on after the war ended or moved here later. This infusion of new blood has continued, off and on to the present day, because of Beaufort's growing lure for retirees and other transplants.

In 1891, a U.S. Navy station was established on Parris Island (it's now a Marine Corps boot camp and training base). Along with Parris Island, a naval hospital and Marine air station have pumped millions of dollars into the local economy, but they also have added a cosmopolitan layer to the area. Today the Beaufort area is home to a sizable group of retired military, including a number of senior officers such as Gen. Norman Schwarzkopf, the Gulf War commander, who has a place here.

All of these factors mean that Beaufort, while its roots run deep, is neither provincial nor closed to outsiders. Says innkeeper Ron Kay, "Beaufort is one of the most hospitable small towns on the entire East Coast. Period."

"It was so easy to make friends here," says Suzanne Green. "Everyone is in the same boat, looking for new friendships."

Jean Lebro, former head of the Greater Beaufort Chamber of Commerce, is a relative newcomer. A self-proclaimed "damn Yankee from Boston," Jean moved to Beaufort four years ago. "Beaufort really welcomed me," she says.

Still, there's a limit to Beaufort's hospitality. "Never say, 'this is how we did it up North,'" Jean advises potential newcomers.●

Bend, Oregon

Pine forests and rugged mountains make Central Oregon hard to resist

By Fred Gebhart

Most days, Mirror Pond in downtown Bend looks like the perfect picture postcard. Its waters reflect the snowcapped Cascade Range along with towering ponderosa pines, blazing yellow roses and a sapphire sky. River otters blithely scamper across bike paths, and bald eagles cruise nearby rivers looking for a meal. On winter days, you wonder how rainbows happen over one shoulder while falling snow obscures the silhouette of the Cascades on the other side.

Bend sits on the sunny eastern side of the Cascade Range in Central Oregon, and it's easy to see why early explorers like Kit Carson escaped harsh mountain winters and blistering desert summers by lingering along the Deschutes River as it rushed through the high desert near Bend.

For financial planner Max Jacobs and his wife Sandra, these attributes were exactly what they were seeking in retirement. One of Max's five business partners in Laguna Beach, CA, had grown up in Bend and suggested that the couple give the small Oregon town (population 52,029) a look when it came time to retire. And as it turned out, the area's jumble of jagged lava flows, waterfalls, buttes, acres of forests, alpine lakes and crystal-clear rivers suited Max and Sandra perfectly.

"We checked into the River House, a hotel that straddles the Deschutes River, in 1992, and walked outside to Drake Park," Max remembers. "We were just enchanted when we saw Mirror Pond. We knew we wanted to leave the Los Angeles area when I retired in 1994, and this looked like the place."

Californians Dick and Joan Gilles had the same reaction. Both liked the San Francisco area where they were living but wanted a smaller home with what Dick called "a little bit of land" around it when he retired from his longtime job as product engineering director for an aerospace company.

"The trail that led us to Bend was a long one," Dick explains. "We started looking up and down the West in 1990. One of Joan's friends had a sister in Bend who suggested we look here for the golf and the fishing. Once we saw Bend in 1994, we kept coming back three or four times a year until we found the right property."

Bend offers everything from manufactured housing in long-established parks to custom-built mansions overlooking forests that will never be developed. Dick, now 67, and Joan, 66, looked at, and passed over, traditional subdivisions, gated communities and one of the most successful resort developments in the Pacific Northwest, Sunriver.

The basic equation, Dick explains, was a combination of housing budget, space and facilities, especially golf. The plan was to sell their 2,400-square-foot house in San Ramon, CA, and pay cash for something smaller. It had to be far enough from the neighbors that they didn't hear toilets flushing and TVs blaring. And Dick wanted to store their 32-foot trailer on site.

"There are a lot of communities that are terrific," he found, "but many restrict you to parking your RV in a parking area instead of on the property. I want our trailer where I can work on it at my leisure, not theirs."

They had considered Florida for retirement, but heat and humidity sent them back to the West. They also looked in coastal Oregon, Palm Springs and Las Vegas before Joan's friend brought Bend's charms to their attention.

"We had plenty of choices from Sunriver to Redmond," Dick says. "There are a lot of opportunities for less money than we ended up paying. But when you talk value for the money, we're still convinced it was a bargain."

The bargain was $220,000 for a 9-year-old, 1,800-square-foot house on 2.7 acres in Boones Borough, a rural development eight miles north of Bend. The one-square-mile subdivision has 225 lots surrounded on three sides by untamed juniper forests controlled by the Bureau of Land Management. The nearby Deschutes and Crooked rivers and Tumalo Creek lure fly-fishers from around the world eager to test their catch-and-release skills against wily trout and salmon. And there are more than two dozen golf courses within a 30-minute drive.

That's not to say that Bend is a garden of Eden. Gardening, in fact, can be a challenge because of the short growing season. Although the sun shines close to 280 days most years, the gardening season is barely three months long. Central Oregon was settled by cattle ranchers, not farmers, and while there's no shortage of water for home gardens, frost can come to the high desert anytime from Labor Day to Memorial Day.

"I've lost two crops of tomatoes this year," Dick sighs. "I planted too early. I'm probably not going to get any tomatoes at all, but the peppers survived."

Max, 64, and Sandra, 61, don't mind the short growing season, but they aren't avid gardeners. They came to Bend for the natural beauty, the small-town feel and the outdoor activities.

"It never gets really hot in summer, although it can get cold for a few days in winter," says Max. "That's hard for somebody from Southern California, but compared to Idaho or Montana, Bend is a piece of cake. And if you're a golfer, which we aren't, this is paradise. The courses are all affordable and most of them are open to the public."

The Jacobses bought their property

as an investment, sight unseen. They fell in love with the area and saw growth potential in Boones Borough.

Back in Southern California, they instructed a real estate agent to buy a lot in their $24,000 price range.

When they finally saw their property nine months later, 2.5 acres bordering BLM forest with more than 80

Bend, OR

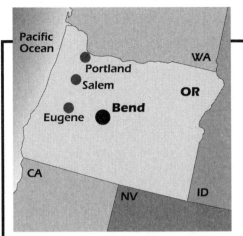

Population: 52,029 in Bend, 115,367 in Deschutes County, with 13.1 percent of city residents age 65 or older.

Location: In the high desert of Central Oregon, just east of the Cascade Mountains, Bend is the economic and recreational hub of the eastern two-thirds of the state. Bend sits astride Highway 97, 180 miles north of Medford, 162 miles south of Portland and 121 miles east of Eugene. Elevation is 3,628 feet.

Climate:

	High	Low
January	39	18
July	85	46

Average relative humidity: 45%

Rain: 12 inches. **Snow:** 34 inches. Bend averages 280 days of sun annually.

Cost of living: 113.2, based on national average of 100.

Median housing cost: $173,000 in Bend, $213,000 for a single-family home on rural acreage. The value of rural property is determined largely by the availability of water.

Sales tax: None.

State income tax: For married couples filing jointly, the rate is graduated from 5% of taxable income up to $5,000 to 9% on amounts over $12,600. For single filers, graduated from 5% of taxable income up to $2,500 to 9% on amounts over $6,300.

Income tax exemptions: Social Security benefits are exempt. Federal pensions are fully exempt for those who retired before October 1991 and may be partially exempt for retirement after that date. There is a retirement income tax credit of up to 9 percent of retirement income for those age 62 and older if they meet specified income

limitations.

Intangibles tax: None.

Estate tax: None, except the state's pickup portion of the federal tax on taxable estates in excess of $1 million.

Property tax: The tax rate in Bend is $14.67 per $1,000 of assessed valuation. Tax rates in Deschutes County range from $8.77 (desert areas) to $17.72 (Redmond) per $1,000 of assessed valuation. Since the passing of Measure 50 in 1997, homes are assessed at 90% of the 1995 market value; for subsequent years, the growth in assessed value is limited to 3% a year. The yearly tax on a home currently assessed at $173,000 in Bend is approximately $2,538.

Homestead exemption: None.

Religion: There are more than 100 places of worship in Bend, nearly all Christian and conservative.

Education: Central Oregon Community College, which has 1,600 students, offers noncredit classes and workshops at centers in Bend, Sunriver, Redmond and other nearby towns. Seniors age 62 and older receive discounted tuition for some classes.

Transportation: The nearest air access is Redmond Municipal Airport, 16 miles north, served by Horizon Airlines and United Express with service to Portland and Seattle. Avis, Budget, Hertz and National have car-rental outlets at the airport. Bend Municipal Airport (5.5 miles northeast) and Sunriver Resort Airport (17 miles south) have general aviation services, charters and car rentals. Amtrak provides passenger service via Chemult, 60 miles south of Bend.

Health: St. Charles Medical Center has a trauma center with its own air ambulance service, Air Life. The 181-bed facility offers the latest in medical technology with more than 200 local physicians on staff. Specialties include radiation oncology, neurology, neurosurgery, open-heart surgery, radiology, urology, pathology, emergency medicine, rehabilitative medicine, family practice, cardiology, dermatology, orthopedics, psychiatry and men's and women's health services.

Housing options: Many retirees buy homes in existing neighborhoods in Bend,

with average home prices around $170,000. Prices are somewhat less in nearby Redmond, and higher in **Sunriver**, (541) 593-1000, a 3,300-acre mountain resort 15 miles south of Bend. A quarter of the resort's 3,200 homes and 600 condominiums are occupied full time, primarily by retirees drawn to 54 holes of golf, 35 miles of paved bike paths, a 5,500-foot private airstrip and nearly two dozen restaurants. Prices range from the high $180,000s for a studio to well over $1 million for a 10,000-square-foot mansion; the average price is $340,000. At **Broken Top**, (800) 382-7690, homes start at $395,000, or residents can custom-build homes on lots starting at $89,900. The gated community is on the west side of Bend and offers a 27,000-square-foot clubhouse and 18-hole golf course. **The Falls at Eagle Crest**, (888) 70-FALLS, opened in 1998, 15 miles north of Bend in Redmond. The 208-home neighborhood for those 55 and older offers homes from the low 200,000s to the high $300,000s. **Bend Villa Court**, (541) 389-0046, has 123 apartment units for independent or assisted living. Monthly fees range from $1,700 for a studio to $2,150 for two bedrooms. All units are unfurnished, but fees include three daily meals (plus a fully equipped kitchenette), housekeeping and laundry, local transportation and utilities. **The Summit Assisted Living**, (541) 317-3544, has 65 units, studios to two-bedrooms, ranging from $2,497 to $3,793 per month with all meals, light-duty nursing, housekeeping and activities included.

Visitor lodging: There are more than 2,400 hotel and motel rooms in Bend, with another 2,000 rooms in nearby towns and recreational areas, including Best Western Inn and Suites, $69-$109, (541) 382-1515; Hampton Inn, $69-$89, (541) 388-4114; and The Riverhouse, $69-$155, (541) 389-3111.

Information: Bend Area Chamber of Commerce/Visitor and Convention Bureau, 63085 N. Highway 97, Bend, OR 97701, (541) 382-3221 or www.bendchamber.org.

full-grown junipers of their own, it was a gem. Max retired on schedule in 1994 and the couple moved to a rented house in Redmond, about 20 minutes north of Bend. The interim move got them out of crowded Southern California and gave them the time to look for the perfect house in Bend.

Eventually, though, they decided to build on the lovely lot they had bought as an investment. "We just couldn't find an existing home that really met our needs," says Max, who with Sandra decided on plans for a two-story, 2,400-square-foot country farmhouse with porches on all four sides and passive solar heating. The solar design tempers both the occasional 90-plus summer days and winter nights that drop into the teens.

Snow rarely stays on the ground more than a few days, Max says, though he warns prospective buyers to check weather with potential neighbors. The area is a checkerboard of microclimates that change dramatically with elevation, exposure and rivers.

Sunriver, for example, 15 miles south of Bend, turns its three golf courses and 30-plus miles of bike trails to cross-country skiing every winter. Mount Bachelor, another 15 miles south, is one of the top downhill ski destinations in the West.

Sunriver is an important part of the Bend community. Several of the area's finest restaurants are in Sunriver, supported by the nearly 3 million tourists who visit Bend every year. The Sunriver Music Festival brings some of the biggest names in classical and jazz to Central Oregon every August.

The music festival meshes with Bend's own Cascade Festival of Music as well as the free Munch & Music series that fills Drake Park with up-and-coming pop, blues and world beat groups on midsummer Thursday evenings. Two theater groups provide live entertainment year-round, and a new county performing arts center in Redmond offers space for touring theater and performance companies.

There is, of course, a downside to Bend. The nearest international airport is Portland, a 3.5-hour drive or an expensive commuter flight from Redmond. "There just isn't enough business to push the airlines to drop their prices," Max gripes, "although that's changing as the population grows."

Traffic is another complaint. Highway 97, the main north-south artery, has regular traffic jams in Bend. But a bypass built in 2000 has helped ease the congestion. And while downtown Bend is alive with boutiques and art galleries, the closest upscale department stores are in Portland. Local shopping malls tend toward Kmart, Home Depot and Sears.

Jobs are another sore point. Bend is traditionally a ranching and lumber region, with little skilled and professional employment. Population growth and the resulting housing boom is creating construction jobs, but retirees should count on living on their retirement income or make plans to create their own jobs. Sandra Jacobs found part-time work in a local accountant's office, but such opportunities are rare.

Taxes are on the high side — what taxes there are, that is. There's no state sales tax, for instance. "We get hit pretty hard on property taxes and personal income taxes," Max says. "But I just saved 8 percent on a Ford Ranger over what I would have paid in California. That kind of savings goes a long way toward easing the pain of income taxes."

Indeed, Bend's charms far outnumber its few drawbacks, Max says. "It's a vibrant place, a gorgeous place — art galleries, festivals, restaurants, scenery, hiking, out-of-this-world photography," says Max. "We love it." ●

Boca Raton, Florida

Arts and culture and cool sophistication characterize this Florida resort community

By Jay Clarke

Retirement is a time to slow down and take it easy, right? Florida would seem to be just the spot, but Boca Raton may not be the place to rest on your laurels. There's an industrious quality to life in retirement here.

"I am tremendously busy," says Aaron Lintz, 68, who moved to Boca Raton in 1990 from Washington, DC. "I play golf six days a week, and I'm a volunteer with the Service Corps of Retired Executives and with RSVP (Retired Senior Volunteer Program)."

Aaron, a salesman during his working years, also keeps a finger on the pulse of his telemarketing business. His wife, Elaine, plays golf three times a week, enjoys bridge and does volunteer work.

Bruce Benefield reports a similar experience. "For the first two years after I retired, I was busy adding on to this house," says Bruce, 69, who also moved from the Washington, DC, area to Boca Raton. "Then I got involved in the homeowner association and became president."

Still at it, Bruce, a retired Air Force colonel and vice president of TRW, is on the alumni board of directors of his alma mater, the University of Miami, and does some volunteer tax counseling. His wife, Barbara, 66, is active in the local garden club and tends the beautiful garden that surrounds their waterfront home. She's also into aerobics and started a local chapter of her sorority, Kappa Kappa Gamma.

"I have to be busy," says Stan Perlstein, 71, who moved to Boca Raton from the Philadelphia area just a year ago. An interior designer, Stan says that for the first two weeks of his retirement, he "stood at the refrigerator all the time" and gained unwanted weight. So now he's working in design again. "I have to get out of the house."

So does his wife, Gladys, 56, who taught kindergarten and once worked at Bloomingdale's. "Maybe I'll go work in a department store again," she muses.

For all three couples, retirement is not an abdication of life but an opportunity to grow in different ways.

"What this (retirement) has done for me is that it's given me the opportunity to do things other people did, and I love it," says Aaron, whose career in sales kept him out of town and away from home for long periods. "I never played golf before we moved here.

"In some ways, we're living life like we did up North," he says of the lifestyle he and his wife have chosen. "We lead separate lives during the day, but we go out to eat a lot and we spend weekends together."

"It took us a while to get acclimated to retirement," Elaine admits, but neither now misses their former home. The first time they went back to Washington, DC, after moving to Boca Raton, Elaine says, "We stayed a month. Next time it was three weeks, then two weeks. Then it was 10 days, and now my husband says that's too long."

"We broke away from the North completely," confirms Aaron. "This is our home; this is the way we want to live."

The Benefields, too, have settled comfortably into their home in a residential neighborhood where there's a mix of ages. "When we moved in, there were no children on our block," says Barbara. "Now there are seven. We like that."

Barbara even has adjusted to the climate. "What I like about Florida is that it rarely rains all day," she says, noting that downpours occur but soon end. In Washington, she says, daylong drizzles are more common.

Bruce also had little trouble adapting to Florida. "I even bought a convertible — always wanted one," he says. And, like a lot of other Floridi-

ans, the Benefields have a boat. Since they live on a canal, their 23-footer is docked just a few steps from their back door — providing a quick escape to the water if the mood strikes.

Stan and Gladys Perlstein, who live near the Benefields, also have a boat. Stan bought the 42-footer when he lived in a Philadelphia suburb before he retired, but he didn't get to use it as often as he would have liked. Now he believes he'll be able to put it to more frequent use.

But Stan actually is somewhat surprised to find himself living here. "I really hated Florida," he admits. "Dad lived on Collins Avenue (in Miami Beach), and when I came to visit, all I saw were old people. There were nurses in the lobby. I didn't want to live like that when I retired."

Stan thought about moving to Mexico but now is glad he settled on Boca Raton. One reason may be that Boca is unlike most other communities that attract retirees. It does not make any special pitch for retirees, doesn't have subdivisions just for retirees and, frankly, doesn't want to become known primarily as a retirement haven.

Says Mike Arts, president of the Boca Raton Chamber of Commerce, "Our median age has been going down — from 44 to about 41 — since I came here 14 years ago."

Particularly noticeable, he says, is the increasing number of second homes. "Boca's population increases 12 percent in the winter season."

Though they may not live in communities especially designed for them, retirees find that Boca Raton has much to offer. "You won't find much ticky-tack here," the editor of the *Boca Raton News* said in a 1992 profile of the city. "We don't have an underclass. We don't have smokestacks or even industry that's unsightly. It's what we don't have that makes this place what it is," said Wayne Ezell, the editor in 1992.

That still holds true. Boca always has attracted clean industries. Giant IBM built personal computers here and had a massive presence for years. It has since moved most of its PC manufacturing out of state, but newer companies keep moving in.

Culture plays an important role in Boca Raton, whose location in south Palm Beach County puts its residents within easy reach of the arts in Fort Lauderdale and West Palm Beach.

Boca Raton has its own cultural scene, as well. Partly because it is an upscale community, Boca is home to many art galleries. It also boasts an art museum, pops orchestra, theater and concerts at Florida Atlantic University and many other venues for music and drama.

Boca, too, has an undeniable panache. Comedians like Jay Leno and Billy Crystal work "Boca" into their gags, usually coupled with "money." The city's upscale reputation is so

widespread that the often-heard phrase, "It's so Boca," is instantly understood even outside Florida. Being Boca means being upscale in an unmistakable but not flashy way.

Nowadays what's so Boca in Boca is Mizner Park. It's Florida upscale, a palm-lined mall of more than 50 specialty shops, cafes and art galleries.

It was Mizner who created Boca Raton 71 years ago. The man who haddesigned many of the grand mansions and clubs of Palm Beach wanted

Boca Raton, FL

Population: 74,764 within city limits, 195,000 in the metropolitan area.

Location: On the Atlantic Coast of Florida between Fort Lauderdale and West Palm Beach.

Climate:	High	Low
January	76	63
July	90	78

Average relative humidity: 75%

Rain: 60 inches.
May-October is the rainy season, October-April the dry season.

Cost of living: Above average (specific index not available).

Average housing cost: Single-family homes average $215,000. Average condo co-op cost is $154,131.

Sales tax: 6%

Sales tax exemptions: Groceries, medicines, professional services.

State income tax: None.

Intangibles tax: Assessed on stocks, bonds and other assets. Tax rate is $1 per $1,000 in assets. The first $20,000 in assets is exempt for individuals. For couples filing jointly, the first $40,000 is exempt. Those who owe less than $60 need not pay.

Estate tax: None, except the state's "pick-up" portion of the federal tax, applicable to taxable estates of more than $1 million.

Property tax: $21 per $1,000 of assessed value, with homes assessed at 100% of market value. Annual taxes on a $215,000 home are about $3,990, with the homestead exemption noted below.

Homestead exemption: $25,000 off assessed value of permanent, primary residence.

Religion: There are more than 50 houses of worship in Boca Raton.

Education: There are five institutions of higher learning in Boca Raton, including a state community college, Palm Beach Community College, and a state university, Florida Atlantic.

Transportation: Boca Raton is conveniently located about halfway between Palm Beach International Airport (25 miles north) and Fort Lauderdale International Airport (20 miles south). Miami International Airport (47 miles south), with direct flights to many foreign destinations, is about an hour away. Boca Raton Airport is home to about 286 corporate and individually owned aircraft and has a station on the Tri-Rail commuter train line, which runs between West Palm Beach and Miami. Ten to 15 trains run in either direction daily. Amtrak's two northbound and two southbound trains daily stop at nearby Delray Beach and Deerfield Beach. Palm Beach County bus service is provided by PalmTran; fare is $1.25 for adults with discounts for seniors and disabled passengers. Door-to-door service is available to seniors and disabled adults under a Dial-a-Ride program.

Health: The not-for-profit Boca Raton Community Hospital, with 394 beds and 24-hour emergency service, is the largest in south Palm Beach County. West Boca Medical Center, a private facility, has 185 beds and 24-hour emergency care. Several other hospitals are in the area, including Delray Community Hospital in Delray Beach, North Broward Medical Center in Pompano Beach and North Ridge Medical Center in Fort Lauderdale. A number of specialized health-care centers also are found in Boca Raton, including the Mae Volen Senior Center.

Housing options: The older coastal communities tend to be more expensive, with condominium units starting at $500,000, while new developments in unincorporated areas west of the city offer many amenities in lower price ranges, with condos and estate homes starting at $200,000.

Visitor lodging: Rates are seasonal — lowest in summer, highest in winter. The Boca Raton Resort and Club, built by Addison Mizner, is the most prestigious hotel in the region, charging about $180 in summer, $270 in winter, (561) 395-3000. Among chain hotel choices are Best Western University Inn, about $59 low season, $145 high season, (561) 395-5225; Holiday Inn West Boca, about $75 low season, $145 high season, (561) 482-7070; and a few miles north of Boca Raton, Delray Beach Marriott, about $139 low season, $289 high season, (561) 274-3200.

Information: Greater Boca Raton Chamber of Commerce, 1800 N. Dixie Highway, Boca Raton, FL 33432-1892, (561) 395-4433 or www.bocaratonchamber.com.

to create a town all his own 22 miles south of that bejeweled resort. It was his grandest vision.

Mizner sketched out polo fields, grand plazas, playhouses, a golden-domed city hall and lavish homes for the wealthy. He planned to build a castle on an island in a lake for himself and a cathedral for his mother. He even designed modest bungalows for workers.

"All of the charms of the Riviera, Biarritz, Menton, Nice, Sorrento, the Lido and Egypt are to be found in Boca Raton," a Mizner brochure boasted immodestly.

Alas, only part of his plan became reality. Mizner did build the hotel, now known as the Boca Raton Resort and Club. One of the top hotels in Florida, the landmark pink hostelry counts among its assets a half mile of private beach, two 18-hole golf courses and 48 clay tennis courts.

Mizner also built a grand avenue, El Camino Real, that was 20 car lanes wide and had a canal in its median. The road still exists, although the canal was filled in long ago. He built 29 modest homes for workers and an administration building, all in the Spanish Mediterranean style he created for Palm Beach, and they, too, still are in use.

But Florida's real estate bubble burst in the 1920s and the rest of Mizner's dream never was realized. The hotel, though, provided an image that set the stage for Boca Raton's resurgence after World War II.

Living costs in upscale communities can be a problem, but the Lintzes say their overall costs in Florida are less than they were in the Washington, DC, area. Dining out costs less, Aaron reports, and there's no state income tax. Clothing also costs less — and is far more casual. Aaron hasn't bought a suit since moving to Boca Raton.

The Benefields and the Perlsteins also agree that lifestyles are more informal in Florida than in their preretirement communities. Suits and other dressy outfits stay mostly in the closet, they say. But some costs creep higher. Entertainment options in Boca Raton are good but on the expensive side, says Aaron Lintz. "We pay $65 for the theater."

Home insurance, too, has been on the rise since Hurricane Andrew caused billions of dollars in damage to South Florida in 1992. In fact, the Benefields find quite a few costs to be higher in Boca Raton than in Washington. They say their real estate taxes have doubled. "And homeowner's insurance is also at least twice as high," says Bruce. "Fuel is higher here, too," Stan Perlstein notes.

So with many choices available to today's retirees, what made this trio decide to move to Boca Raton? All cite location and easy access to airports, cultural facilities, shopping and climate.

"Boca Raton is not as densely populated," says Aaron. "People here are pretty friendly," Bruce observes. And, adds Stan, "Everyone knows Boca."

Indeed, everyone knows Boca. After all, Boca Raton still reflects much of the spirit and ambiance Mizner planned for it. Even though newer homes and buildings no longer mimic Mizner's designs, his grand style still overlays the city — one of the reasons it has become such a stylish retirement haven. ●

Bradenton, Florida

Newcomers find it easy to get involved in this town on Florida's west coast

By Karen Feldman

Spanish conquistador Hernando DeSoto, who landed in Bradenton in 1539, searched the region in vain for gold. But modern-day visitors can mine all manner of riches with just a bit of digging.

At first, the casual observer might see little happening in this laid-back city of 49,504. But on closer inspection, they'd discover a community on the move, endowed with sprawling beaches along the Gulf of Mexico and a multitude of golf courses, plus easy access to Sarasota to the south and sprawling Tampa-St. Petersburg to the north.

"Sometimes newcomers can't fully appreciate the city initially," says Marie Deitrich, vice president of the Manatee County Chamber of Commerce. "But we have everything here: We still care about each other as neighbors.... We've got beautiful beaches and still have a community feel. You go to a baseball game and see people you know. People here are more savvy than some give them credit for."

Marie, who has lived in the area for 30 years, thinks Bradenton "has come into its own. Everything is happening at the same time: There's downtown waterfront development, a new city center, and Lakewood Ranch has been a humongous boon to the area."

The city is connected to the rest of the world by Sarasota-Bradenton International Airport, from which 10 carriers transport 1.6 million travelers a year. And less than an hour away lies the even larger Tampa International Airport, from which two dozen airline companies serve 11.5 million passengers annually.

It was this mix of accessibility and sense of community that prompted Paul and Janet Trudeau to leave Burlington, CT, their home of 34 years, in October 1996. They'd considered and ruled out other locales, including southern California as well as the Carolinas, where winters would still be too chilly for their taste.

"I like to go in the water any time of year," says Paul, a retired insurance company executive. "We both love the ocean."

While staying at a relative's home in nearby New Port Richey, he says they "drove around Florida until we found Bradenton. We wanted proximity to the Gulf. We wanted a community with arts and theater, a college town."

Bradenton already has those things and continues to grow in scope and population, drawing most of its residents from the northeastern and midwestern states. More than 50 percent of the population is 45 and older. As a result, there are many recreational, medical and housing options that cater to this older population.

With all the cultural opportunities of Sarasota within easy reach, the Trudeaus found an apartment close to the Gulf at a price that suited them. And it didn't take long for them to find friends. "We joined a church right away. We met people in the apartment complex. And we attended dances," says Paul, 60.

They also volunteered their services to a variety of organizations and met still more people that way. Paul joined the Elks. They linked up with Volunteer Service of Manatee, through which they got involved with the chamber of commerce, a landscaping project at a school, helping out at Bradenton Ballet performances and serving as museum tour guides. "There aren't too many days when we are at home just sitting around," says Janet, 59.

Retired elementary school teachers Ben and Georgette Thomas had a similar experience. After living in South Windsor, CT, for 28 years, the couple moved to Bradenton in June 1991.

They'd considered Asheville, NC, and Florida's Gulf coast from St. Petersburg south.

They wanted warm weather — which eliminated Asheville from consideration — as well as a place where they'd have access to culture and be able to be a part of it, too. "Within a reasonable distance, we wanted a symphony orchestra, a theater large enough to bring in the Broadway touring companies, an opera guild, community theater. It began to narrow the scope," says Georgette, 67, who refers to Bradenton as "a big small town."

"Prior to our teaching (Georgette is a graduate of the Juilliard School of Music), we both performed opera and musical comedy," says Ben, 72, "and we were looking for a place where we could perform. We found that Bradenton is probably the best place in Florida. Within three-quarters of an hour, I'm in Sarasota or Tampa. There are any number of theaters in the area."

It didn't take the Thomases long to get involved in their new community. They joined RSVP — Retired Senior Volunteer Program — and helped create Seniors Offsetting Schools (SOS), through which retirees work with schoolchildren. Both perform in community theater. Not long ago, Georgette played Miss Daisy in a community theater production of "Driving Miss Daisy."

A diabetic, Georgette knows regular exercise is vital, so she walks daily — along the beach when she can. Ben likes to take his boat out to fish in the tranquil bays of the region.

They purchased a 1,650-square-foot home in Highland Lakes, a development with 126 homes, a small clubhouse and a pool, about seven miles from the beach. Over the time they've had it, the house has appreciated about 40 percent, according to Georgette. "We live here instead of Sarasota because our home would have cost $10,000 more than here," Ben says.

Those looking for property will find a wide range of housing options and price ranges, says Lynn Parker, the relocation director and branch manager for Wagner Realty in Bradenton. Four golf communities — all with easy access to Interstate 75 — offer maintenance-free villas, patio homes and single-family homes, with prices starting at $140,000 for a villa, $170,000 for a patio home and from $200,000 for a single-family home.

Along the bays and on the county's two barrier islands, Anna Maria Island and Longboat Key (half of which lies in Sarasota County to the south), the choices are condos or single-family homes, she says. A modest home on the Gulf might be had for about $150,000. More affordable for many people are neighborhoods where homeowners can dock their boats in

Bradenton, FL

Population: 49,504 in Bradenton, 264,002 in Manatee County.

Location: On the west coast of Florida just north of Sarasota, 45 miles south of the Tampa-St. Petersburg area. Easily accessible via Interstate 75 and Interstate 275 as well as Sarasota/Bradenton International Airport and Tampa International Airport.

Climate:

	High	Low
January	72	50
July	91	72

Average relative humidity: 52%

Rain: About 52 inches annually

Cost of living: 102.1, based on national average of 100.

Median housing cost: $142,600 for a new single-family home ($117,500 for condominiums).

Sales tax: 6%

Sales tax exemptions: Food, some services and medicine.

State income tax: None.

Intangibles tax: Assessed on stocks, bonds and other assets. Tax rate is $1 per $1,000 assets. The first $20,000 in assets is exempt for individuals. For couples filing jointly, the first $40,000 is exempt. Those who owe less than $60 need not pay.

Estate tax: None, except the state's "pickup" portion of the federal tax, applicable to taxable estates above $1 million.

Property tax: $20.74 per $1,000 in Bradenton, with homes assessed at 100% of market value. The annual tax on a $142,600 home, with exemption noted below, is $2,439.

Homestead exemption: $25,000 off the assessed value of a permanent, primary residence.

Religion: There are 165 Protestant and seven Catholic churches, four synagogues and 62 other houses of worship in Manatee County.

Education: Manatee Community College operates a branch in Bradenton. In Sarasota, there are several colleges, including the University of South Florida, Eckerd College, the Ringling School of Art and Design, New College and the University of Sarasota. In Tampa, there are campuses of the University of South Florida, Eckerd College, Tampa College, the University of Tampa and the University of Sarasota. These colleges offer a variety of degrees ranging from associates to doctorates. Noncredit courses for adults also are available.

Transportation: Sarasota-Bradenton International Airport provides service to many U.S. cities with a combination of major air carriers and commuter carriers. Tampa International Airport, 45 minutes north, offers hundreds of flights daily to destinations throughout the world. Amtrak provides train service to much of the United States from Tampa. Manatee Area Transit provides local bus service.

Health: There are two primary healthcare hospitals: Manatee Memorial with 512 beds and Columbia Blake Medical Center with 383 beds. Charter Hospital of Bradenton is a psychiatric hospital. There are 36 licensed nursing and congregate-care facilities. The county has 534 physicians and 130 dentists.

Housing options: There are many options available in the Bradenton area, including single-family and condominium complexes. **Lakewood Ranch,** (800) 30-RANCH, a 5,500-acre community, offers two 18-hole golf courses, a private country club and housing by several builders, ranging from modest condos from the $100,000s to estate homes over $3 million. Other golf communities include **Rosedale,** (800) 881-9080, **Palm-Aire,** (877) 779-2473, **University Park,** (800) 394-6325, and **The Preserve at Tara,** (941) 751-9000, offering maintenance-free villas and patio homes starting at about $140,000 and single-family residences from $200,000. Along the Gulf of Mexico, modest dwellings can be had for about $150,000. Boating communities, with access to the Intracoastal Waterway and Tampa Bay, offer condos in the $90,000-to-$100,000 range and single-family residences ranging from $175,000 to $500,000. In inland neighborhoods that aren't on the water, a two-bedroom home with a pool averages $125,000, while a condominium can be had for $75,000 to $80,000.

Visitor lodging: Hotels and motor inns abound in this popular tourist destination. A sampling includes the Comfort Inn-Bradenton, $53-$99, (941) 747-7500; Holiday Inn-Riverfront, $99-$149, (941) 747-3727; and the Park Inn Club and Breakfast, $84-$114, (941) 795-4633. For those seeking a waterfront spot, there's Tradewinds Resort, $89-$289, (941) 779-0010 on Bradenton Beach. There are beach-front accommodations on Longboat Key at The Colony Beach & Tennis Resort, $195-$1,395, (941) 383-6464; the Longboat Key Hilton Beach Resort, $99-$239, (941) 383-2451; and the Resort at Longboat Key Club, $170-$1,120, (941) 383-8821. Rates are per night, double occupancy.

Information: Manatee County Chamber of Commerce, 222 10th St. W., P.O. Box 321, Bradenton, FL 34206, (941) 748-3411 or www.manateechamber.com.

canals behind their homes and still have access to the Intracoastal Waterway and the Gulf of Mexico.

Among the newest and most popular developments in the area is the 4,000-acre Lakewood Ranch. "It still is an active ranch and farm," Lynn Parker says, "but they've broken off part and created a new community that has homes geared to young upscale families and active retirees." Builders offer a range of housing, from small condos to regal estate homes.

It was precisely because of the myriad choices that the Trudeaus opted to rent for a while so they could thoroughly investigate various neighborhoods before deciding where to buy a place. Their experience as renters has been a positive one in a 200-apartment complex about four miles from the Gulf of Mexico. They find their neighbors and other city residents to be "warm-hearted, friendly people," Paul says.

"People whom we have just met briefly have invited us into their homes," he says. "One day a lady on a bicycle — she must have been 85 years old — led us to a friend's home just to show us something of the neighborhood."

Though both couples have wide circles of friends, there are a few parts of their Northern lives they miss, such as family and old friends. "And Connecticut in the fall. I really miss that season," Georgette says.

On the other hand, Ben says, "I was happy to get rid of the snow blower, lawn mower, the responsibilities of a larger home. My life has changed so much. I can't consider going back. I'd be bored to death in Connecticut."

Boredom isn't something from which either the Trudeaus or the Thomases suffer. "If you are bored in retirement, it's because you are boring," Georgette says.

The city offers a wealth of volunteer opportunities, fraternal groups and more than 230 houses of worship. Keep Manatee Beautiful, a group that encompasses volunteers, businesses and government agencies, provides year-round opportunities to help beautify beaches, roads and public places. The Art League of Manatee County displays the works of local artists, offers classes, demonstrations and workshops, and teams up with other groups to sponsor cultural events. The league works with the Goodtime Jazz Club, for example, to sponsor Jazz on the Riverfront, a weekend of live jazz during the winter tourist season.

While its larger neighbors to the north and south get most of the publicity, Bradenton boasts much of interest, especially of a historical nature, a rarity in a state where development often paves over the past.

The city proudly claims its connection to DeSoto, who began his four-year, 4,000-mile trek through the southeastern portion of the country in his futile search for El Dorado, the lost city of gold. Modern-day visitors can get a taste of DeSoto's 16th-century world at the DeSoto National Memorial along the Manatee River where, from December through March, park employees dress in period costumes and portray the way the early settlers lived, including cooking and musket-firing demonstrations. Each spring, the city hosts a month-long Florida Heritage Festival to commemorate DeSoto's landing.

The Manatee Village Historical Park focuses on the region's 19th-century life, with a collection of historical buildings, including a Cracker farmhouse, one-room schoolhouse, church and smokehouse. Staff members here also wear period dress.

Downtown at the South Florida Museum lives the city's mascot, Snooty the manatee, in a 60,000-gallon aquarium. At age 46-plus, the 750-pound vegetarian is the oldest living manatee in captivity, having taken up residence at the museum at the age of 10 months. He and his companion Mo afford a rare close-up view of these gentle sea mammals that seek out Florida's warm waters during the winter months. The museum also displays various aspects of the region's history, maintains an old-time medical wing and runs star and laser shows at the Bishop Planetarium.

During the winter, the Royal Lipizzaner Stallions of Austria take up residence at Colonel Hermann's Ranch in Manatee County. And come March, residents and visitors alike flock to McKechnie Field to watch the Pittsburgh Pirates play spring-training games.

For culture, Sarasota has few equals of its size. It is home to the Asolo Theatre Company, The Players, Sarasota Opera, Sarasota Ballet of Florida, the Florida West Coast Symphony and a number of vocal and chamber ensembles. It draws big-name entertainment to the Florida State University Center for the Performing Arts and Van Wezel Hall.

There are still more cultural opportunities in Tampa and St. Petersburg. A sampling includes the Salvador Dali Museum, The Florida Aquarium, the Florida International Museum, the Museum of Fine Arts, the Tampa Bay Performing Arts Center and Busch Gardens. Tampa's Ybor City has a rich Cuban heritage and has become a popular nightspot. In St. Petersburg, the Pier is a multilevel complex filled with restaurants, shops and clubs.

Many retirees are drawn to Florida by the weather and the opportunity to be outdoors. In Bradenton, options include golfing at any of 30 courses, tennis and racquetball, fishing and, of course, the beaches on Anna Maria Island and Longboat Key.

The mix works well for many, as the Trudeaus and Thomases can attest. Neither couple has plans to move out of the area anytime soon. For others considering relocation, Georgette Thomas suggests, "Make an itemized list of what you need to keep yourself mentally and physically healthy in your retirement, and certainly explore Bradenton, because there is such a variety of things to do." ●

Branson, Missouri

Missouri Ozarks are alive with the sound of music

By Mary Lou Nolan

Puffs of mist cling to Table Rock Lake, holding up the start of the Tri-Lakes Triathlon. So 50 swimmers wait, waist-deep in water, shivering under their orange rubber caps.

Nearby are dozens of volunteers, many of them retirees, in orange vests, orange caps or orange buttons, just as alert as the athletes, but smiling, not shivering. It's a crisp September morning, a bright sun is burning off the last of the mist, and an event they have worked on for months is about to begin. Swimming, biking and running courses are laid out, checkpoints are staffed, stop watches are set.

As a whistle splits the air, the athletes — and the volunteers — plunge into action. You can't tell who will enjoy it more.

Volunteers are integral to the quality of life in Branson, MO, a country-music-mad boom town in the Ozark Mountains. They staff the Branson/Lakes Area Visitor Center, stamp books at Taneyhills Community Library and raise money for the expanding Skaggs Memorial Hospital. New businesses struggling for a foothold in the self-proclaimed "America's Live Entertainment Capital" get help from SCORE, the Service Corps of Retired Executives.

"I think this town would collapse without volunteers," says Norma Root, the library's only paid employee.

Retirees underpin the volunteer community here, mixing good works with golf and fishing, bridge matches, dinner clubs and church socials. Their lives are full — too full for some of their spouses — and the strains of country music only add to their enjoyment.

"I'm about ready to leave him and get a man who stays home," jokes Effie Evans, who retired here with her husband Ken.

But the music boom also has strained local resources. Lower-income housing is in short supply, and some residents worry about trees being cut and lake water being dirtied as a result of the expansion. On the other hand, traffic, once a legendary nightmare, has undergone tremendous improvement.

The boom also has brought a new sense of urgency to some volunteer pursuits. A spinoff group of 19 local churches, for example, assists people with little money who come to Branson in search of jobs. The Christian Action Ministry, with about 70 volunteers, helps with food, rent and utility payments. It operates a pantry and is considering opening a shelter, with community support, says Charles G. Mitchener, a retiree who spearheads the program.

The ministry is just one of the volunteer activities that Mitchener threw himself into when he and Ellie, his wife, moved to Branson from Carmel, IN, near Indianapolis, nine years ago. The couple considered spots in North Carolina and the Cumberland Plateau area in Tennessee before buying a four-acre lot north of Branson and building a home. Then Mitchener, who retired as chief financial officer for a Midwestern farm cooperative, got busy.

"I decided when I retired that I would like to put some of those skills back into a community," says Mitchener, 67.

He's also active with the Red Cross, SCORE and Lives Under Construction, a ranch for troubled teenage boys southwest of Branson. And Mitchener was on hand at Table Rock State Park that crisp Saturday morning in September, working as a volunteer. He and Ellie checked in athletes as they crossed under the balloon-festooned goal posts that marked the finish line.

Retirees in orange Tri-Lakes Triathlon Volunteer buttons chatted like golf buddies before the race got under way. Bob Glenn, a retired state patrolman, and his wife, Jerrie, moved here from Ames, IA, 10 years ago. Glenn started working on the triathlon in January. His condo neighbor, Bill Silva, a retired Speed Queen employee from Ripon, WI, helped get members of the Amateur Radio Club in Kimberling City involved as volunteers.

Much of what appeals to retirees about the Branson area was apparent at Table Rock State Park that day.

The land itself is a big draw. Steep wooded hills of the Ozark Mountains fall away to sprawling Table Rock Lake, one of three that define the Branson/Lakes Area in western Taney and southern Stone counties. Table Rock, with 750 miles of shoreline, is known for water sports and bass fishing; Taneycomo, which winds northeast like a river channel for 22 miles, is known for trout; Bull Shoals, east of Branson, flows through the least populated, least developed land.

The climate is mild, especially compared to the Upper Midwest, from where many residents have moved. But the four seasons are distinct, usually with some snow in the winter and hot, humid days in the summer.

Climate and green, open spaces were a big draw for the Glenns. "I like the four seasons," Jerrie Glenn says, adding that the foot of snow blanketing the hills in February "is beautiful — I love this."

There also is a neighborliness nurtured by Branson's small-town atmosphere. Its relatively low cost of living and crime rate, low taxes and conservative values have attracted many retirees over the years. Perhaps that's why complaints about growth, and especially traffic and the lengthening tourism season, are so common.

"You lose all patience when you have to deal with it every day," Ellie Mitchener says.

"I've learned to be quite a wild driver now, with all the tourists," she says, smiling. "You learn to take the back roads, and to go out in front of the tourists, who are wondering which way to go."

Branson has only 6,050 residents, while the Lakes Area has about 34,000. But more than 5.7 million people visited in 1999 as more big-name entertainers opened music shows here.

Branson is home to nearly 50 indoor entertainment centers, with a total seating capacity in excess of 60,000. Branson's main strip, 76 Country Boulevard, also is home to some 7,000 motel rooms, more than 140 restaurants and huge amounts of neon.

Some of the long-time music shows, with locally known entertainers and hillbilly humor, have suffered as bigger, fancier shows have opened. But the big-name entertainers now draw fans to Branson from across the country. Among country musicians performing here are Mel Tillis, Willie Nelson, Jim Stafford, Cristy Lane, Ray Stevens and Charlie Pride. Andy Williams broadened the scene a bit when he opened the $8 million Moon River Theater in '92, and Wayne Newton has his own theater.

Tourism, long the area's leading industry, got a significant — some say overwhelming — boost in December '91, when "Sixty Minutes" aired a segment on Branson's boom. The chamber of commerce tripled the number of phone lines, added staff and began moving toward a year-round season.

"'Sixty Minutes' launched us, in giving us an identity internationally," says Dawn Erickson, the chamber's communications director. "We have not had what you would call a quiet time since then."

"I'm a country-western music lover from way back," Jerrie Glenn says, although the effect of the intense publicity concerns the Glenns. Both worry that the influx of tourists will lessen the quality of life in Branson, but the Glenns still feel at home here. A recent three-week trip to the Southwest only confirmed that.

"We talked to our friends and saw some nice places, but they didn't sway us," Bob Glenn says. "We like it every

Branson, MO

Population: 6,050 in town, 34,000 in area.

Location: Busy commercial, entertainment center in Ozarks of southwestern Missouri. Hilly, wooded terrain in two counties with three major lakes.

Climate:[1]

	High	Low
January	41	22
July	93	68

Average relative humidity: 58%

Rain: 41 inches.

Snow: 15 inches.

Has four distinct, though not harsh, seasons. Snowfall normally light. Spring and fall are mild, summers warm and humid.

Cost of living: Below average (specific index not available).

Median housing cost: $107,276 for single-family house in Taney County; prices higher in many areas popular with retirees. A lake-front house runs from $125,000 to $3,400,000.

Sales tax: 7.225%.

Sales tax exemptions: Food, prescription drugs, some medical supplies, professional services.

State income tax: For married couples filing jointly and single filers, graduated from 2% of taxable income up to $200 to $315 plus 6% on amounts over $9,000.

Income tax exemptions: Social Security benefits subject to federal tax are taxable. There are exemptions in private pensions of up to $5,000 for each taxpayer and in federal, state and local pensions of up to $6,000 per taxpayer, all subject to specified income limitations. The total pension exemption claimed cannot exceed $6,000.

Intangibles tax: None.

Estate tax: None, except the state's "pickup" portion of the federal tax, applicable to taxable estates above $1 million.

Property tax: Rate is $41.76 per $1,000 of assessed value in Branson, including schools, fire, ambulance, health and city taxes. Homes are assessed at 19% of market value. Property tax on a $107,276 home is about $851.

Homestead exemption: There is a property tax credit for homeowners age 65 and older filing jointly with a household income of $27,000 or less.

Religion: 36 Christian churches in Branson.

Education: Classes available at The College of the Ozarks, a private, four-year liberal arts college.

Transportation: None. Car necessary. Springfield Regional Airport is 45 miles north.

Health: Skaggs Community Health Center, a non-profit care center with 107 beds and a staff of more than 400 has completed a $4.5 million renovation to expand adult cardiac surgical services.

Housing options: Most retirees live in single-family homes outside the city. Besides resale homes, there are new homes in the $85,000-$500,000 range available within a five-mile radius. Custom-built homes on the south side of Table Rock Lake are popular with retirees. The **Branson North** development has $100,000-plus homes on spacious lots in a quiet, wooded area. Kimberling City, also on Table Rock Lake, attracts upper-income retirees; Forsyth and Hollister attract moderate-income retirees. Condominiums are available, both in Branson and on the lakes, and **Branson Manor**, (417) 334-3800, offers subsidized housing for the elderly in Branson.

Visitor lodging: More than 20,000 motel/resort rooms available, with rates of $20 to $250-plus a night. Super 8 Motel, (417) 334-8880, by Branson's main strip, $48-$70. Deer Run Motel near Silver Dollar City, (417) 338-2223, $45-$89. Big Cedar Lodge, (417) 335-2777, a 72-year-old resort overlooking Table Rock Lake, $119 and up.

Information: Branson/Lakes Area Chamber of Commerce, P.O. Box 1897, Branson, MO 65615, (800) 214-3661 or www.bransonchamber.com.

[1]Climate data based on information for nearby Springfield.

bit as much here as any place we've seen."

"Sixty Minutes" also lured people looking for work, some of whom just packed up and moved to Branson, says Al Moon, a real estate agent and retired banker. Jobs were available, but they often were seasonal with wages of $5 and $6 an hour. And lower-income rental housing is in very short supply in Branson, where land values have climbed.

Efforts are under way to add rental housing and to build the labor force. One potential answer is to recruit retiring military people who are looking for income to supplement pensions, Moon says.

Major traffic relief is in the works. Branson voters approved $10 million in taxes in 1991 for city road improvements, and a $100-million-plus project that will build an Ozark Mountain Highroad around Branson is in progress.

The music boom also may be affecting the type of retirees drawn here. For years they tended to be well-to-do people who vacationed in the Lakes Area because of its natural beauty, Moon says. A couple bought land, often with a lake view, built a spacious home and took in an occasional music show.

As the music industry grows, and more visitors and bus tours pass through, Moon thinks more retirees will be moderate-income music fans.

Retirees now looking in the area are typically from the Midwest and are searching for homes in the $65,000-$100,000 bracket, Moon says. Older homes in Branson run $60,000-$65,000; moderate-priced housing typifies the nearby communities of Forsyth, Hollister and Rockaway Beach. Kimberling City, with homes in the $100,000-plus range, is at the high end.

The area seems especially popular with Californians, some of whom are Midwestern natives who want to put the West Coast lifestyle behind them.

"This is just a better place to live, a better life for them," Moon says.

That's what Ladd Chase found here. Over a bridge hand at the Branson Com-munity Center, Chase describes how he left the furniture business behind in Long Beach, CA, when he moved into a Branson condo six years ago.

"I like the lakes, I like the fishing, I like the country music shows. I wouldn't live anywhere else," says Chase, 75. "Traffic doesn't bother me — I know the back roads."

Not everyone agrees. Just ask people at the next bridge table.

Ethelmae Henss and her husband helped develop Branson North, an older suburban development of spacious homes on wooded lots. But after more than 30 years in the area, she's concerned about the rapid pace of growth. "It happened too fast," she says, echoing many older residents.

As the Branson area grows, residential development is pushing outward, says Rex L. Asselin, a real estate broker and a chamber of commerce director. He speaks from experience.

In 1992 Asselin sold the 4,400-square-foot home he and his wife built in 1968 to the company that built Wayne Newton's new theater. The house was bulldozed, and a 3,000-seat theater, restaurant and two motels were built on the 32-acre plot in a once-rural area on Branson's outskirts.

Asselin himself moved 12 miles north of Branson, where he built a 5,500-square-foot house with indoor pool on a large tract of land.

"Branson's not a quiet place," he says. "But you can live within a 15-minute drive of Branson and have a quiet country living."

That describes Dean and Peg Courtney, who recently added a deck to their three-bedroom mobile home on a secluded lot south of Hollister. The couple vacationed in the area for about 10 years, then moved down after Dean Courtney retired as postmaster in Caney, KS.

Courtney, who is a member of the Lions Club, says his church "adopted" the couple after their first visit. "We haven't sat still since we got here," he says.

He also works at Silver Dollar City, a theme park where turn-of-the-century crafts and amusement rides are featured. During the busy season last year, he worked in cash control in the office.

"It's just like a bank," Courtney says. "It's office work without the responsibility of the postmaster."

Courtney says his wages help pay for "extras," and he enjoys the fellowship. During winter months the couple often travels to a warmer location, like the Texas coast.

"I feel like a person who retires and then goes back to work looks at it differently," says Courtney, 59. "If you are using it as supplemental income, you have a different attitude. You don't have to do it."

Ken and Effie Evans were drawn here more than 20 years ago from Oak Park, IL, when Ken was about to retire from Swift & Co. in Chicago. He was a native of northern Missouri and the couple had traveled in the area. Then their daughter took a teaching job south of Kansas City, about four hours away.

"'I know when Daddy retires he's going to come back to Missouri,'" Evans recalls his daughter saying. "Well, I don't remember telling her that, but she could feel how much we enjoyed it."

The Evanses bought a lot in the Branson North subdivision in 1970, built a spacious one-story home and moved in 1974.

"Coming from Missouri, loving the hills and the Ozarks, this was it," Evans says.

The growing traffic and congestion is irritating. And Ken has never liked the humid summer days. But the Evanses keep a busy schedule. As sight chairman for the Lions Club, Ken helps arrange glasses and surgery for needy people. And both are active in the Presbyterian church.

Still happy here?

"Wouldn't be anywhere else," Ken says.

"Yes, I've been very happy here," Effie agrees. "You have your church, and we have a dinner club we belong to. And we have lots of friends here."

But Effie advises potential visitors to find out the best routes for traffic in advance.

"Anyone who wants to come should send for a map," she says.●

Brevard, North Carolina

Small-town friendliness adds to beauty of North Carolina town

By Diana C. Gleasner

With a main street worthy of a Norman Rockwell painting, Brevard sits tucked neatly in a valley surrounded by the heavily forested mountains in western North Carolina.

People gather for summer concerts in the park, and going to the bank is as much a time to visit with neighbors as to do business.

The 2,230-foot altitude contributes to a moderate four-season climate with mild winters and cool summers, and crime is not a serious concern.

Yet for many residents, these attractions aren't the main appeal of Brevard.

"It's the friendliness of the people and the pace of life we like best," says Bob Reaume, 63, who moved with his wife, Joyce, 61, from Connecticut four years ago.

Joyce adds, "At the slightest problem, neighbors come to help."

George and Eva Stephenson, 63 and 51 respectively, moved from Florida and like the small-town atmosphere and feeling of safety in Brevard, which has only about 6,700 residents.

"It's a dry county (no liquor sales) and that has a tranquil effect on adults and children alike, since the children don't have to suffer through the hangovers of their parents," says Eva. She thinks the area's lower drug usage helps keep crime down, too.

Jack and Barbara Cronin, formerly of Princeton, MA, didn't want to retire to an adult-only community. They appreciate the mix of ages in Brevard, and the laid-back attitude and relaxed lifestyle, says Jack, 64. Barbara, 61, likes the opportunity to take an active role in a "real community."

Making friends in Brevard was easy, says Jack. "We went to church and before we got home people were waiting at our door to welcome us."

All three couples assimilated quickly by taking a course at Brevard College called "Inside Transylvania," which introduces newcomers to the facilities of the community and Transylvania County.

"We met the local politicians, medical professionals and academics," says Joyce Reaume. Other speakers acquainted new residents with the Brevard Music Center, police department, volunteer agencies and the nearby Pisgah National Forest.

Brevard College, a two-year liberal arts school, offers a range of courses. Joyce, who currently is taking macrobiotic cooking and landscaping, sometimes teaches a course in sign language. One of the Reaumes' five children is hearing-impaired, and Joyce had been a full-time teacher of the deaf before coming to Brevard.

Bob Reaume took beginning piano and cartooning, and both he and Joyce enjoyed a course called "Great Decisions," an analysis of the U.S. role in international affairs. The Cronins, who are in a swimming program at the college, took conversational French and a course in Chinese cooking.

The three couples have further woven themselves into the community by contributing their time and talents. Jack Cronin teaches adult students as part of the Transylvania Literacy Council and serves as the council's chairman and president. Barbara also works with literacy students, is a full-time church organist and takes calls on the 911 mental health hot line.

The Reaumes tutor in the School of Forestry, in the public schools and in the literacy program. George Stephenson is active in Kiwanis and both he and his wife plan to get involved in the literacy program or in the public schools.

The town's rich cultural scene centers on Brevard College, the Blue Ridge Community College campus in Brevard and the Brevard Music Center. During its annual six-week Summer Music Festival, the center sponsors more than 50 events including Broadway musicals, operas, chamber music, symphony and pops concerts featuring internationally renowned guest artists. The center has a nationally recognized summer music camp for promising young artists.

Aficionados of authentic mountain music may drop in at Silvermont Mansion any Thursday evening for a live performance. These inspired (and free) concerts set the toes tapping as the dulcimer, fiddle, banjo, bass fiddle, guitar and harmonica celebrate the musical heritage of the region's original Scotch-Irish settlers.

Brevard Little Theater presents popular plays, while the Arts Council sponsors a weeklong annual Festival of the Arts in mid-July. It features musicians, tours, food, special events and the arts and crafts of local artists.

Retirees enjoy the natural beauty of the Blue Ridge Mountains. The county's 200 waterfalls have given it a nickname, Land of Waterfalls. At 411 feet, Whitewater Falls is the highest cascade east of the Rockies, while beautiful Looking Glass Falls is probably the best known. Sliding Rock, a 150-foot natural water slide, is a popular local attraction. Shining Rock Wilderness area and more than 200 miles of clear streams and rivers add to this idyllic scene. The area has more summer camps than any county in the country.

Pisgah National Forest just north of Brevard covers more than a third of Transylvania County. It has 470 miles of hiking trails plus opportunities for rock climbing, cross-country skiing and tubing. At Cradle of Forestry, where scientific forestry was first taught in America almost 100 years ago, the U.S. Forest Service operates an interactive hands-on museum. The forest shelters a black bear sanctuary and has one of the largest trout hatcheries in the East. Visitors to the fish hatchery can see the origins of the trout that later stock local streams.

Golf enthusiasts find year-round challenges on public and private courses in the area. Sapphire Lakes, a private 18-hole championship course, has been listed among the top 50 of *Golfweek* magazine's "Best of the Best." Etowah Valley Championship Club in Henderson County is open to the public. Glen Cannon, although private, allows guests from out of the area. Among other private courses are Sherwood Forest, Lake Toxaway Country Club's Holley Forest, Horsepasture Club and Connestee Falls.

Other area recreational opportunities include tennis, swimming, fishing, hunting, square dancing, camping, canoeing, kayaking and horseback riding.

Nearby attractions lure visitors who come to experience the Blue Ridge Parkway, considered one of America's most scenic drives, and Great Smoky Mountains National Park. Asheville, a 40-minute drive north, offers additional shopping and amenities. At Asheville, the 250-room Biltmore Estate, largest private residence ever built in the New World, has guided tours through the home and gardens. Thomas Wolfe's boarding house, the setting for his novel "Look Homeward, Angel," has been restored

Brevard, NC

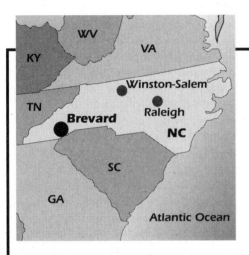

Population: 6,789 in town, 29,334 in Transylvania County.

Location: In the scenic Blue Ridge Mountains of southwestern North Carolina, 30 miles south of Asheville. Brevard, the county seat, is adjacent to Pisgah National Forest. The French Broad River flows through the area, creating mountain streams and waterfalls. Elevation is 2,230 feet.

Climate:

	High	Low
January	50	25
July	85	61

Average relative humidity: 55%
Rain: 66 inches.
Snow: 6.2 inches.
Moderate four-season climate with mild winters and cool summers. Average number of days with snow coverage is five.

Cost of living: Below average (specific index not available).

Average housing cost: $167,281
Sales tax: 6.5%

Sales tax exemptions: Prescription drugs, eyeglasses, some medical supplies.

State income tax: For married couples filing jointly, the rate is graduated from 6% of taxable income up to $21,250 to 8.25% on amounts over $200,000. For single filers, it is graduated from 6% of income up to $12,750 to 8.25% on amounts over $120,000.

Income tax exemptions: Social Security benefits are exempt. Up to $2,000 of distributions from private retirement benefits and IRAs (up to the amount reported in federal income taxes), or up to $4,000 of government pensions may be exempt. Total deductions may not exceed $4,000 per person.

Intangibles tax: None.

Estate tax: None, except the state's "pick-up" portion of the federal tax, applicable to taxable estates above $1 million.

Property tax: City tax rate is $5.20 per $1,000 valuation and county rate is $6.41 per $1,000 valuation, with homes assessed at 100 percent of appraised value. City residents pay both city and county taxes. Tax on a $167,281 home within the city is about $1,942 yearly. Tax on a $167,281 home in the county is about $1,072.

Homestead exemption: Homeowners age 65 and older, or disabled, living in the home and earning $18,000 or less per year qualify for an exemption of $20,000 or 50% of the value of the home, whichever is greater.

Religion: More than a dozen denominations are represented.

Education: Brevard College, a two-year liberal arts college, offers an extensive continuing-education program, and Blue Ridge Community College's Brevard campus offers a wide variety of courses. Transylvania County Library's 65,000 volumes include large-print books. Bookmobile covers rural area.

Transportation: No public transportation. Car necessary. Asheville Regional Airport is 25 miles away.

Health: Transylvania Community Hospital has 94 beds and provides in-patient medical, surgical, obstetrical, coronary and intensive care, outpatient services, in-home services, drug and alcoholism treatment. Emergency services are staffed 24 hours. Highland Hospital Resource Center offers psychiatric services. Three-level care at Brian Center, a 140-bed facility, includes skilled, intermediate and nursing home care.

Housing options: Glen Cannon Properties, (828) 966-4242, has wooded residential homesites from $25,000 and condos starting at $160,000; Glen Cannon Country Club, to which residents may belong, has a golf course, tennis courts, pool and clubhouse. **College Walk**, (800) 280-9600, is a retirement community with independent and assisted living. It is adjacent to Brevard College.

Visitor lodging: Inn at Brevard, $99-$225, (828) 884-2105, has 12 guest rooms in a historic bed-and-breakfast setting. Womble Inn, $65-$85, (828) 884-4770, a B&B, has seven guest rooms furnished in antiques, all with private bath. Located 17 miles west of Brevard, Greystone Inn, (828) 966-4700 or, outside the state, (800) 824-5766, offers resort accommodations in a historic mansion on Lake Toxaway; prices are $265-$595 per couple, including meals.

Information: Brevard Chamber of Commerce, P.O. Box 589, 35 W. Main St., Brevard, NC 28712, (828) 883-3700, (800) 648-4523 or www.brevardncchamber.org.

to its 1906 image.

The gentle mountains have become a haven for retirees who enjoy a four-season climate without lengthy cold winters or long hot summers. Besides attracting retirees from the Northeast, the area draws people from Florida seeking to escape its steamy summers.

Eva Stephenson, a native Floridian, fell in love with the mountains on a vacation. When she and her husband moved here, she was thrilled with the first big snow. She says she doesn't miss Florida's hot weather — "it zaps your energy."

Jack Cronin is quick to say he doesn't miss what he calls the "Taxachusetts" government he left behind in Massachusetts, and his wife adds that she doesn't miss the heating bills from their New England house.

A favorable economic climate in Brevard, while not the primary motivation for most retirees to relocate here, is a definite attraction. According to the North Carolina Department of Budget and Management, Brevard's cost of living is below the national average.

In looking ahead to retirement, Bob Reaume, a former engineer, developed a detailed financial plan and for years focused on building a nest egg to meet their goals. Each month Bob calculates the couple's net worth and makes appropriate adjustments. So far the Reaumes are on target with money to meet their needs.

"If we want something, we buy it," he says. "Joyce is a frugal shopper and I don't have great needs. Every once in a while I buy a new tool for my wood shop."

The Reaumes find the cost of living, especially housing and taxes, lower than in Connecticut, although the difference is not dramatic.

The Stephensons are delighted that insurance is much less expensive than where they lived in Haines City, FL, but they now have to pay a state income tax, which Florida did not have.

The Cronins find small-town living much more economical than life in a big city. While Jack jokes that retirement is a time when "my wife is blessed with twice as much husband and half as much money," these parents of five admit they have more discretionary income than ever before. "Not that it's that much, but we have fewer people helping us spend it," Jack says.

Medical services are especially important, as Jack puts it, "to those of us who are getting less young." Transylvania Community Hospital provides medical, surgical, coronary and intensive care, diversified in-home care and 24-hour emergency services. He describes the local hospital as "terrific, reflective of this caring community."

Bob Reaume, whose cardiac problems began in his 40s, checked area medical resources thoroughly before retiring to Brevard. The Reaumes' peace of mind is helped by having a hospital "right up the road" and emergency helicopter service that transports patients to an Asheville cardiology group in just 11 minutes. A recent trip to the Mayo Clinic for a second opinion confirmed Bob's conviction that he is getting excellent local care.

Joyce Reaume says they looked into continuing-care facilities before making a decision to move to Brevard.

"We didn't want to burden our children, and we also didn't want to have to pick up and move to a whole new area of the country," she says.

Brian Center, a 140-bed facility, offers various levels of care as do local communities with assisted-living units.

If Brevard has flaws, retirees have to think long and hard to come up with them. Bob Reaume is surprised at the amount of rain, lightning and thunder. Jack Cronin notes that the laid-back style of living does not apply to mountain drivers, and he misses the fresh fish and seafood he and his wife enjoyed in New England.

While the Cronins take great pleasure in the nationally acclaimed Brevard Music Festival, Barbara mentions the increase in summer traffic and congestion generated by the festival's popularity. George Stephenson misses Florida's warm winter weather.

All three couples suggest that prospective retirees spend time in the area before making a decision to move here. When the Reaumes arrived in Brevard, they thought they would just love living way up on a mountain, but renting such a home for a year brought them back down to earth.

"With 24 curves you couldn't see around, we wore out brakes and tires like you wouldn't believe," says Bob.

The Reaumes now are settled in a self-designed home two miles from downtown in a woodsy area called Deerlake Village. They describe it as a community within a community, with a current population of 80 families that includes seniors as well as young couples with new babies.

Eva Stephenson, however, yearns for a house higher on the slopes, declaring, "All that's missing from my paradise is a wide-open view of the mountains." Husband George concurs, adding, "We found beautiful views with a lousy house, and beautiful houses without views, so we had to compromise on the view somewhat."

Jack Cronin says, "I only regret we didn't find Brevard earlier."●

Camden, Maine

Despite high cost, Maine coastal town's natural beauty makes it perfect for some retirees

By John A. Johnson

When Al and Ina Doban decided to retire several years ago, they had the financial means to move anywhere in the country.

They chose Camden, a small town on the coast of Maine.

It was a move that startled their friends and neighbors in Hagerstown, MD. After all, Maine is not generally recognized as a premier retirement area.

"Our friends were surprised we chose Camden, but they had never been here," says Ina, 59. "Al and I vacationed here in 1987 and it was the first vacation I had ever been on that I didn't want to go home."

Al, 64, agrees: "Our one-week vacation in Maine turned into a four-week stay. When it was time to retire, Camden seemed the perfect place for us to go."

Nestled at the base of the Camden Hills, which rise almost 1,400 feet above one of the state's most picturesque harbors, Camden is considered special not only by retirees and vacationers but also by Maine natives.

Camden was settled in 1769 by James Richards, his wife, Betsy, and their cook. The family came to cut timber and fell in love with the natural beauty of the mountains and the sea.

That beauty attracted other families, and Camden was incorporated in 1791 as the 72nd town in Maine. There were 331 residents at the time.

Over the years the town became a center for boat building, gristmills and tourism. A summer colony soon sprang up and today the population of 5,254 swells to almost 15,000 during June, July and August.

Generally, people who retire to Camden are financially comfortable. The cost of living is higher than in many parts of the country, especially when it comes to buying a house and paying real estate taxes.

"The same house you pay $400,000 for in Camden probably would cost $150,000 back in Maryland," Al says.

"But that didn't deter us. Ina and I sat down to look over potential retirement spots in Florida, North Carolina, Arizona and California and we compared everything to Camden."

Ina explains it simply: "We asked ourselves if we wanted to save $1,000 a year and live in North Carolina or a few thousand a year living in Florida. The answer was always no. We wanted to live in Camden. It's worth the extra costs."

The Dobans aren't alone in their feelings. Many Camden residents are retirees. In fact, more than 35 percent are age 55 or older. They have come from all across the United States, but primarily from the Northeast — Massachusetts, New York and New Jersey. Most have spent vacations in the Camden area or have lived in Maine at one time or another.

Sandy and Mary Lou MacKimm, for example, lived in Waterville, ME, for five years during the early 1960s. "We moved all around the country for Sandy's work, but we loved Maine the most," says Mary Lou, 63. "We have a summer camp in another part of the state, so it was natural for us to consider Maine for our retirement home."

The only other spot the MacKimms considered was in North Carolina. "We have five children and two grandchildren. We knew they would visit us in Maine, but we weren't sure about (their coming to) North Carolina," Sandy, 64, says.

The MacKimms retired here from Barrington, IL, choosing Camden in part because they felt it would be easy to make friends.

"Sandy was an executive with a chemical company, and there are many retirees here with similar educations and company responsibilities," Mary Lou says. "We felt comfortable right from the start."

Town manager Roger A. Moody says, "Our retirees seem to like the fact that Camden is a real town, that it wasn't created just for those of retirement age. We have all age groups and occupations here, and there's a vitality to the town that retirees seem to enjoy. In addition, our neighborhoods are mixed and the retirees don't feel isolated."

The town has three subsidized housing developments for older people but no other retirement communities.

A popular yachting center, Camden is home to many of the passenger schooners offering weekly summer trips along the Maine coast. It's also a popular stop for private yachters as they tour Penobscot Bay.

Many of Camden's activities center on its harbor, home port for several yacht races throughout the summer, including the annual race from Camden to Castine. During these events, as the boats head home toward the Camden Yacht Club, they raise their spinnakers and create an exciting parade of color that tourists and residents alike eagerly flock to each year.

Along Camden's typical New England Main Street, fine clothing boutiques, gift and book stores, handcraft shops and galleries keep visitors browsing for hours. A variety of restaurants can be found throughout the town, and accommodations range from fine inns to cozy bed-and-breakfasts.

In addition to the waterfront, activity in Camden centers on the public library, located at the top of Main Street. Next door is the Camden Amphitheatre, which is the town green and the arena for summer and fall arts and craft shows and various entertainment.

Across from the green is the town park, bounded by a beautiful waterfall and one of the oldest boatbuilding shops in the United States. With its grand view of the harbor, the park is a lovely spot for boat watching and picnicking.

Prominently placed in the town park

is a is a Robert Willis sculpture of Edna St. Vincent Millay, the Pulitzer Prize-winning poet and Camden's most famous native.

Mementos of Millay still abound in Camden — from the stately Cushing-Hathaway Mansion that she owned on Chestnut Street to the plaque on Mount Battie commemorating her most famous work, "Renascence."

Just north of the town along coastal U.S. 1, Camden Hills State Park spreads across 5,000 acres at the foot of Mount Battie. A paved road ascends from the campground to Mount Battie's 900-foot summit, which offers a wonderful panorama of Penobscot Bay, nearby towns and the rolling inland countryside.

Camden claims to be the only town on the East Coast where you can ski from the top of a mountain (at the Camden Bowl) and see the Atlantic Ocean as you descend. The area has golf courses and health clubs.

Outdoor activities are important, the town manager says, because retirees who move to Camden tend to be younger and more active.

Vaughan and Vera Lee, 64 and 63 respectively, retired to Camden from Stratford, CT. They enjoy hiking, swimming, boating, golfing, canoeing and cross-country skiing, all of which are found in the Camden area.

"Camden affords us almost a total lifestyle," Vera says. "Because of our proximity to the lake and the town, which is only five to seven minutes away, we feel we have the best of all worlds."

Sandy MacKimm says Camden offers plenty of opportunities to stay busy. Retirees spend a lot of time doing volunteer work with such groups as Habitat for Humanity, the Rotary Club, the garden club, the book club, the yacht club, or just visiting sick townspeople. The Longstreet Society, engaged in historic preservation, is a favorite organization for many retiree volunteers.

"I've had to learn to say 'no' to some requests," says Vera. "When you come to Camden, you aren't allowed not to become involved."

Full medical care is available at the Penobscot Bay Medical Center. Recently when Sandy was ill, he found care came from more than the doctors and nurses there.

"I found an outpouring of love that was just great," he says. "Our friends and neighbors cooked for us, stopped by to see me in the hospital and were willing to do anything we needed. There are some very caring people in this area."

Camden, ME

Population: 5,254

Location: Midcoast Maine, about one hour north of Portland and one hour south of Bar Harbor. Surrounded by Camden Hills and Penobscot Bay.

Climate:

	High	Low
January	32	14
July	75	55

Average relative humidity:[1] 59%

Rain: 46 inches.

Snow: 35-40 inches.

Coastal conditions are tempered by the Atlantic Ocean, resulting in cooler summers and warmer winters than in other regions of the state.

Cost of living: Above average (specific index not available).

Average housing cost: $213,500

Sales tax: 5% sales, 7% prepared food and lodging.

State income tax: For married couples filing jointly, the rate is graduated from 2% of taxable income up to $8,250 to 8.5% on amounts over $33,000. For single filers, graduated from 2% of taxable income up to $4,150 to 8.5% on amounts over $16,500

Income tax exemptions: Social Security benefits are exempt. There is an exemption for pension income of up to $6,000 per person of the amount included in federal adjusted gross income. This exemption must be reduced by the amount of any Social Security benefits received.

Intangibles tax: None.

Estate tax: None, except the state's "pick-up" portion of the federal tax, applicable to taxable estates of more than $1 million.

Property tax: Rate is 17.85 per $1,000 of assessed value, with homes assessed at 100% of full market value. Tax on a $213,500 home is about $3,686, with $7,000 exemption noted below.

Homestead exemption: $7,000 off the assessed value of the home. There also are property tax/rent refunds for low-income and elderly residents.

Religion: 18 churches, one synagogue in Camden-Rockport area.

Education: Husson College, a four-year accredited business school, offers courses at the local high school. A branch of the University of Maine-Augusta is located 12 miles south of Camden in Thomaston.

Transportation: None; car needed. Nearest commercial airport is in Bangor, about one hour away.

Health: Penobscot Bay Medical Center has 109 beds, 80 physicians and is a full-service regional hospital.

Housing options: Most housing is neighborhood single-family homes. The **Lily Pond Drive** and **Chestnut Street** areas are popular with retirees; housing prices are $175,000-$650,000. **Quarry Hill**, (207) 230-6116, offers independent and assisted living. There are three subsidized elderly housing projects: **Highland Park**, (270) 236-2736, with 44 units; **Megunticook House**, (207) 236-6168, with 34 units; and **Mary Gardens Estates**, (207) 230-0618.

Visitor lodging: The Lord Camden Inn, (207) 236-4325, a historic property on Main Street, starting at $90-$140 off-season, $160-$220 in season. The Lodge at Camden Hills, (800) 832-7058 or (207) 236-8478, rooms and suites (some with fireplaces, kitchens and Jacuzzis) in a wooded setting, starting at $79-$199 off-season, $125-$225 in season.

Information: Rockport-Camden-Lincolnville Chamber of Commerce, P.O. Box 919, Camden, ME 04843, (207) 236-4404 or www.camdenme.org.

[1]Relative humidity based on readings for Portland.

Although residents accept Camden's cold weather and higher costs as prices to pay for living here, these factors are unattractive to some retirees. While winters are milder on the coast than elsewhere in Maine, they're still cold — January highs hover at the freezing mark and the lows dip into the teens. Snowfall averages 35-40 inches a winter, but the warming effect of the water prevents heavy accumulation.

Most retirees live year-round in Camden because they enjoy activities in all seasons. Spring — or lack of it in Maine — is the exception.

"We like to go away each spring to Europe, especially Portugal," says Mary Lou. "It's the only time that Maine is not beautiful. There is no real spring."

But that doesn't dampen her enthusiasm for Camden.

"I would recommend Camden to anyone willing to live in a colder climate and able to put up with a few inconveniences, such as the lack of a big department store," Mary Lou says.

Retirees say the only major drawbacks to living in Camden are the traffic in the summer and the lack of parking in town.

Unless retirees have friends here, getting to know people can take some reaching out, the couples note.

"We had an advantage because Vaughan's family had been vacationing here each summer for several years," Vera says. "We fit right into the social scene."

Both the MacKimms and the Dobans met people through organizations they joined and through volunteer work.

For those interested in retiring to Maine, the cost of living is a factor. While some costs are kept down because of the mix of retirees and a working class, most consider Camden to be expensive.

"I don't dare think about what it's costing me to live here," says Al. "But we planned well for our retirement (the Dobans both worked at Mack Truck). We worked with a financial planner and had a 30-year plan."

The MacKimms and Lees also planned for retirement for many years and were well prepared. Still, with interest rates falling and costs rising, they have had to be more aware of finances than they thought would be necessary.

None of the couples has changed their lifestyles, however, although traveling has become more of a luxury.

"We used to do a trip a year," says Vaughan. "We've cut that out. Of course, I've bought a boat and that has something to do with it."

While each has different reasons, they all love Camden, agreeing that the pros outweigh the cons.

Vera Lee sums it up best: "Vaughan and I have traveled worldwide, and there's no place else that has the ambiance that Camden has for us."●

Cape Cod, Massachusetts

When summer crowds depart, residents settle in for the quiet life

By Stephen H. Morgan

Summer is high season on Cape Cod, southern New England's favorite beach vacation spot. Traffic picks up on the bridges over the Cape Cod Canal from Friday afternoon through Monday morning, clogging the Cape's main arteries and making it tough to get around — unless you know the back roads. Beaches are crowded, their parking lots full. And tee times, restaurant tables, ferry tickets — well, everybody seems to want the same things at the same time.

All that changes after Labor Day, when the summer people head home to work and school. "It's quieter, less traffic, less hassle, and you can make left turns easily," says Edward Kleban, 64, a retired certified public accountant from White Plains, NY.

What's left are weekending couples, late-season vacationers whose children are too young for school and, of course, the small-town community life of Barnstable County's 222,230 year-round residents, about 23 percent of whom are age 65 or older.

"The Cape is swarming with retirees," says Carol Kleban, 61, a retired marketing-research executive who is current president of the Nauset Newcomers Club. The club keeps its nearly 800 members hopping from Labor Day to Memorial Day but shuts down in summer because everybody is too busy. "We struggle with an inundation of guests in season," Carol explains.

At the September monthly meeting, members sign up for interest groups, which include everything from canoeing, bicycling and horseback riding to bridge, dine-around groups (both at restaurants and in members' homes), square dancing and needlework. People get a chance to make friends through common interests and to connect with local organizations that need volunteers.

"When we moved here in May '94, we literally knew no one," says Carol, despite having vacationed here on and off for 15 years. Neighbors told them about the club, and they've since gotten involved in local cultural and civic groups. "Now it's unbelievable."

Most retirees settle in the Upper Cape — the part closest to the canal — or the Middle Cape, says Michael J. Frucci, former executive director of the Cape Cod Chamber of Commerce in Hyannis. Some are snowbirds who head south in winter, and about 85 percent come from Massachusetts, Connecticut, New Jersey and New York.

"Most everybody comes first as a visitor," says Frucci. "Then they buy a vacation home, which becomes a permanent home."

One couple who bucked that trend is Peter and Carolyn McDermott of Glendale, CA. "On the Cape, they call you a 'wash ashore' if you weren't born here," says Carolyn, 54, a Los Angeles native who never saw snow until she was 21. "I was a 'drag ashore.' . . . I never thought I would ever move to a cold climate."

The McDermotts had scouted other retirement locations before buying a home in Harwich, a small Outer Cape town of beaches and cranberry bogs. Sun City, AZ, was "too organized a retirement place," says Peter, 64. "We wanted to be involved in a community and see children . . . and mix with all kinds of people." They also spurned the gated community they visited in Las Vegas and the heat of Phoenix and Palm Springs.

A hospital administrator for Los Angeles County who had grown up in the New York-New Jersey area, Peter often traveled back East for hospital seminars. Carolyn, who worked for the county health services department, came along on one trip in 1992, and they tacked on a Cape visit with Peter's cousin in Orleans.

On a lark, they asked a real estate agent to show them around. They ended up offering a "ridiculously low"

$200,000 for a cedar-shingled Williamsburg colonial — with an asking price 50 percent higher — that had been sitting vacant on an acre of land in a tiny development near Round Cove Pond. The real estate market was sliding, and to their surprise the offer was accepted. "We didn't believe we could buy this much house," Peter said.

Two years later Peter moved into the Harwich home to oversee renovations, and two years after that they sold their $400,000 Glendale home and Carolyn retired. Now they're involved in a dizzying array of activities.

Through the Nauset Newcomers Club, they go saltwater canoeing in Pleasant Bay, Carolyn is learning how to garden the Cape's sandy soil and Peter is learning how to get on the Internet. Together they are uniformed volunteers with the Coast Guard Auxiliary, advising boaters on marine safety and courtesy, and Carolyn is the volunteer coordinator for the Harwich Cranberry Festival, the town's biggest annual event.

Peter loves the seasonal Cape climate, something he missed in California. For Carolyn, after a rainy first summer, "the jury's out" regarding weather, but not on her West Coast worries about "snobbish" New Englanders. "Here I know my neighbors," she says, "which I never did in L.A."

Cape Cod's climate is cool compared to the Sunbelt, but it is probably the mildest climate in New England because of the moderating waters surrounding it.

The climate was the main attraction for Doris Childs, a social-studies teacher from Manlius in upstate New York's snow belt. She retired two years ago, not long after her husband, William, died. "I wanted to live somewhere the climate was mild and where it was close to the ocean," she says.

She considered coastal Maine, where she has friends, and the New Jersey shore, where she had once lived. But she liked the Cape's ambiance better and settled on a $200,000 three-bedroom contemporary home with a cathedral ceiling in Brewster. "It's like living in the country without being in the country," she says.

Doris is only two blocks from the beach on Cape Cod Bay, whose waters are warmer and tides more dramatic than the Atlantic Ocean or Nantucket Sound beaches. "The tide goes out a mile and you can walk way out," she says. "Then the water comes in and you can swim."

The 65-mile-long Cape, a peninsula that varies from one to 20 miles wide, basically is a sandbar left by the last glaciers. It was made into an island by the completion of the Cape Cod Canal in 1914.

Wind, tide and overuse take their toll annually on the Cape's natural resources. In the 1960s, a 27,000-acre swath

Cape Cod, MA

Population: 222,230 in Barnstable County; 23% are 65 and older. Town of Barnstable (which includes Hyannis) 47,821, Falmouth 32,660, Yarmouth 24,807, Sandwich 20,136, Bourne 18,721, Dennis 15,973, Harwich 12,386, Brewster 10,094, Mashpee 12,946, Chatham 6,625, Orleans 6,341, Eastham 5,453, Provincetown 3,431, Wellfleet 2,749, Truro 2,087.

Location: In southeastern Massachusetts, Cape Cod is an arm-shaped peninsula separated from the mainland by a canal and extending into the Atlantic Ocean.

Climate:

	High	Low
January	40	25
July	78	63

Average relative humidity: High.

Rain: 45 inches at Chatham.

Snow: Usually minimal, occasionally heavy.

Cost of living: Higher than average (specific index not available).

Median housing cost: In most towns $215,000-$260,000 for a single-family home. Higher in Provincetown ($342,687), Orleans ($378,431), Chatham-Truro ($330,468). Lower in Mashpee ($176,285) and Yarmouth ($161,622).

Sales tax: 5%

Sales tax exemptions: Groceries, clothing priced less than $175, prescription drugs, some medical supplies.

State income tax: 5.3% on earned income and dividends earned from a Massachusetts bank (12% on capital gains and interest not earned from a Massachusetts bank).

Income tax exemptions: $700 per person age 65 or older in addition to a personal exemption. Social Security benefits and federal and state contributory pensions are exempt.

Intangibles tax: None.

Estate tax: None, except the state's "pick-up" portion of the federal tax, applicable to taxable estates above $1 million.

Property tax: Per $1,000 of valuation, with property assessed at 100% of market value: Barnstable $11.87, Bourne $12.87, Brewster $10.69, Chatham $6.94, Dennis $6.23, Eastham $9.20, Falmouth $8.24, Harwich $8.90, Mashpee $9.25, Orleans $5.36, Provincetown $6.30, Sandwich $12.86, Truro $7.96, Wellfleet $6.93, Yarmouth $11.10. Rates do not include land bank fees (a 3% surcharge on real estate property tax bills).

Homestead exemption: $500 off the property tax for persons over age 70 under certain conditions. There is a "circuit breaker credit" for taxpayers 65 and older who meet specific income limits.

Religion: Well over 100 churches throughout the Cape cover a variety of denominations; Hyannis has a synagogue.

Education: Adult education classes are available at Cape Cod Community College in Barnstable, at high schools and regional vocational technical schools and, through Elderhostel, at institutions such as the Marine Biological Laboratory in Woods Hole and the Cape Cod Museum of Natural History in Brewster.

Transportation: Cape Cod Regional Transit Authority provides bus service along eight routes on the Upper and Middle Cape, plus Hyannis-Provincetown.

Its B-Bus minibuses make door-to-door trips throughout the Cape with pickups by reservation one day ahead. Plymouth & Brockton Street Railway buses go to downtown Boston and Logan Airport. There's air service and (summers only) Amtrak service from Hyannis to Boston and New York. Ferries to Nantucket and Martha's Vineyard depart from Woods Hole and Hyannis.

Health: Cape Cod Hospital, a 218-bed acute-care hospital in Hyannis, and 83-bed Falmouth Hospital have merged; they are affiliated with more than 20 medical-service providers around the Cape. The 60-bed Rehabilitation Hospital of the Cape and Islands is in East Sandwich.

Housing options: Single-family homes, condos (starting about $75,000), rental homes and apartments. Retirement communities include **Thirwood Place**, (508) 398-8006, $3,000 to $5,000 per month; **Heatherwood at Kings Way**, (508) 362-4400, $130,000-$275,000; **Mayflower Place**, (508) 790-0200, all in Yarmouth. **Wise Properties**, (508) 945-5291 in Chatham and Harwich, $155,000-$250,000. **New Seabury**, (508) 477-8300, is a second-home community in Mashpee with prices of $209,000-$6 million. Golf communities include **Ballymeade** in Falmouth, **Willowbend** in Mashpee and **The Ridge Club** in Sandwich with average new-home prices of $470,000-$1 million.

Visitor lodging: Hotels, motels, housekeeping units, bed-and-breakfast inns and weekly rentals of cottages and condos are among options. Call the chamber of commerce for listings.

Information: Cape Cod Chamber of Commerce, P.O. Box 790, Hyannis, MA 02601, (888) 332-2732 or www.capecod chamber.org. The Cape Cod Canal Region and most towns also have their own chambers of commerce.

from Orleans to Provincetown — including wetlands, forest and some 30 miles of beaches — was set aside as the Cape Cod National Seashore. Other protected areas include the Audubon Society's Wellfleet Bay Wildlife Sanctuary, the Ashumet Holly Reservation and Wildlife Sanctuary in Mashpee and the Monomoy National Wildlife Refuge in Chatham.

All these areas are accessible for hiking, bird-watching and other outdoor activities. There's also Nickerson State Park in Brewster and miles of paved bicycle paths of the Falmouth Shining Sea Bikeway and the South Dennis-to-Eastham Cape Cod Rail Trail, about 80 beaches, more than 20 golf courses (public and private), and no end of places to go fishing or put a boat in the water.

Many retirees cite the Cape's cultural attractions as favorites, such as the summertime Monomoy Theatre in Chatham and Cape Cod Melody Tent in Hyannis, as well as the year-round Cape Cod Symphony Orchestra, the Academy Playhouse in Orleans, museums in Provincetown, Brewster, Sandwich and other places, and an endless variety of adult-education classes and library events.

Some like to visit Boston, one and a half to two hours away by car, with its art and science museums, theater and musical events, sightseeing, restaurants and night life. Providence, RI, also is a cultural mecca. There are major shopping malls in Falmouth, Hyannis, Mashpee and South Dennis.

Maude and Raymond Dugan were Cape Cod regulars by the time they moved to Chatham year-round in June 1984. With their five children, they had vacationed in Brewster, an easy drive from their home in Ramsey, NJ. They bought a large lot in South Chatham in 1973 and built a three-bedroom Cape ranch house as a year-round home rather than an uninsulated cottage, even though it originally was used as a vacation home.

"We always knew we wanted to retire to Cape Cod, but not necessarily to this house," says Maude, 72, who worked as a registered nurse in northern New Jersey high schools, then in hospices.

When Ray, now 75, retired from New Jersey Bell's management in 1983, they hired a local builder to enclose the side porch and convert it to a dining and reading room with beautiful built-in bookcases while they took the "trip of a lifetime" through the South Pacific.

The cozy cedar-shingled home — on a private way where few cars pass — is only a 10-minute walk from Ridgevale Beach, one of the small so-called private beaches that serve local renters and year-rounders while tourists head to Harding's, the town beach nearby. The neighborhood association maintains two footbridges that give access to the beach, arching the tidal streams that ebb and swell in grassy wetlands where geese and herons feed.

For Maude, Chatham offers a great library ("I read a lot") and convenience to community theaters, chamber music and Cape Cod Symphony concerts, plus opportunities to volunteer at hospices, join the choral group and take community college classes. Ray golfs in spring and fall ("it's too crowded in summer"), and in winter drives north to Vermont, New Hampshire and Maine to ski with old friends from New Jersey.

The Dugans find Cape prices comparable to New Jersey, where they still visit friends and family — but their property taxes are about $5,000 lower. And they don't feel put off by Chatham's wealthy image. "It's quiet money," explains Maude. "The guy you see at the hardware store with no toes on his sneakers is probably the one who is president of some large corporation."

Residents say each of the 15 Cape Cod towns has its own character. Chatham, surrounded by water on three sides at the Cape's "elbow," is notable for its shop-lined, walkable center; Harwich has several centers. Brewster is a bedroom town; Orleans a commercial hub. Outer Cape towns have a quiet, beachy feel until you reach busy, urban Provincetown at the tip.

Back toward the canal, parts of Dennis are quietly suburban, while Yarmouth has a bit of highway honky-tonk. Hyannis is an urban center and one of seven villages that comprise sprawling Barnstable. Falmouth is a leafy retreat, despite its big ferry terminal and famous oceanographic institute at Woods Hole.

The Cape's biggest town, Barnstable, has less than 50,000 people. Most towns are governed by a board of selectmen, and some hold the traditional New England town meeting each year.

Sunbelt-style retirement communities aren't yet a big part of the Cape's senior scene, but they are growing in popularity, particularly as a second move.

Among options is The Melrose in Harwichport, which Betty Budell, 78, describes as "like living in a fine resort hotel" because of the 29-unit development's attractive common rooms, 24-hour concierge service and good security. She and her husband, Bill, 84, call it "an ideal setup."

Prices at The Melrose start at $225,000, with long-term lease options starting at $2,250 per month. At Heatherwood they start at $130,000, plus hefty monthly fees for meals and use of facilities. New Seabury resort in Mashpee, while defining itself as a second-home community rather than a retirement community, is another attractive option, with condos starting at $209,000 and single-family waterfront homes with prices into the stratosphere.

In comparison, a modest home on the Upper or Middle Cape might go for $112,000 to $140,000, says chamber of commerce director Frucci. That's for a two-bedroom house with living room, dining room and kitchen, a full basement and one-car garage, on a 1,500- to 2,000-square-foot lot.

Few retirees complain about prices, except that gasoline costs more in the summer tourist season. Most say their property taxes went down dramatically, even when making an even trade in terms of housing prices. Peter McDermott found haircuts half the price of cuts in California, but the Klebans say food and dry-cleaning costs are higher than in New York state.

None expresses concerns about personal safety. "We still have our California attitude," says Peter McDermott, who locks his car and put a security system in their house. "But crime is no big deal here. You get the occasional theft, but it's nothing like in a metropolitan area."

Doris Childs says her neighbors check the furnace when she's away and look out for each other in other ways. "I feel very safe here," she says.

It's a quiet lifestyle that tends to draw you in with the beauty and comfort of the surroundings.

"You tend to fall in love with the Cape," says Doris.●

Cape May, New Jersey

History and nature combine in a unique Jersey shore town

By Carolyn Rice

When Jane and Jim Bonner retired to Cape May in 1993 from Philadelphia, they weren't sure what they were going to do with their time

"Between raising eight children and our careers, we hadn't developed any hobbies," says Jane, 66. "Still, we had no intention of taking on new jobs." But that changed in a hurry in Cape May, where a spirit of loyalty and volunteerism is infectious.

Cape May could be called the "big toe" of New Jersey. The peninsula sits at the state's southeastern point where the Delaware Bay meets the Atlantic Ocean. Like most shore towns, Cape May boasts beaches, ocean breezes, great seafood restaurants and a bulging summer population.

Cape May, however, adds a lot more to the usual coastal mix. It has the largest concentration of 19th-century houses in the United States and a year-round schedule of events and activities.

It was Cape May's spirit and vision that kept it from becoming just another shore town. When a huge spring storm destroyed the town's boardwalk and much of its beach in 1962, the town used federal disaster funds to restore and preserve its historic buildings — instead of tearing them down for modern motels, as many developers wanted to do. When the wrecker's ball loomed again in 1970 over the Emlen Physick Estate, a masterpiece of Victorian architecture, the townspeople rallied once more, founding the Mid-Atlantic Center for the Arts (MAC).

MAC volunteers raised $90,000 to buy the decaying property, patched the roof, installed windows and mowed the lawn. Since then, the entire downtown district of Cape May has been declared a national landmark, the Physick Estate has become a fascinating museum of Victorian-era culture, and volunteers and part-time employees conduct a year-round series of walking and trolley tours

for thousands of annual visitors, using the proceeds to finance MAC operations.

When senior staff at MAC learned that Jane Bonner had been the executive director of the senior volunteer program in Delaware County, PA, they offered her a part-time job as volunteer coordinator. Jim, 72, a former sales agent for an air freight company, was recruited to be the part-time manager of the city's recycling program.

Beyond their part-time jobs, the Bonners have converted part of their sprawling 1912 "cottage by the sea" into a guest house and host a local cable TV program called "Gray Matters." On the show, they give information about activities and services available to seniors and interview politicians and area senior citizens who have unusual hobbies or skills.

"Cape May turns out to be a great place for retirees who want to volunteer or work part-time. MAC prefers to hire retirees to be guides because they provide continuity and enthusiasm," notes Jane.

Retirees with an interest in history find it easy to become involved in MAC, which pays volunteers and prospective employees to take its extensive training program. This includes a complete history of Cape May and the Physick Estate, a grounding in the day-to-day life of Victorians, and lectures on architecture and art of the 19th century. Anyone who takes a paid position must pass a comprehensive test.

Volunteers (some 200 of them) may do anything from gardening, driving a trolley, or opening up their homes to various tours. "The inside of Cape May's Victorian homes can be just as fascinating as the outside. We're so lucky that so many people volunteer to show their homes to strangers," says Jane.

Opening one's home to the world can only be done in a place that feels safe, and Cape May does. Chief Robert Boyd

of the Cape May Police Department says burglary and other property crimes are rare. "Our most common crime is bicycle theft," he says, adding that the police force doubles in size during the summers to add the security necessary to control seasonal crowds.

One thing that draws visitors to the Cape is its extensive collection of historic accommodations. The community has more than 50 bed-and-breakfast inns, many of them owned and managed by people who have retired from other careers.

When Terry and Lorraine Schmidt sought to retire from their banking and administrative careers in Trenton, they knew they wanted to live near the ocean. "But we didn't want to live in a town that closes the day after Labor Day," says Lorraine.

Still in their 40s when they left their jobs in the state's gritty capital for small-town Cape May in 1987, the Schmidts wanted to go into business for themselves. As a former executive with the New Jersey Casino Control Commission, Terry understood something about taking a gamble, but he also knew to develop a business plan.

"Our decision to open an inn in Cape May was more a business one than an emotional one, but we're very happy we made it," notes Terry.

The Schmidts' retirement business is the Humphrey Hughes House, a home originally built for a Philadelphia physician in 1903. "Once we chose Cape May, we contacted a Realtor to find out what was available. We bought the Humphrey Hughes House for $700,000. It's worth at least twice as much today," explains Terry.

The inn has been successful enough to now have a full-time manager. The Schmidts have purchased a private residence a few blocks away, giving them some much-needed privacy. While the inn is open year-round, during the winter it only accommodates guests on weekends. "As we get older, we intend to work less and less," Lorraine says.

She is enthusiastic about Cape May as a retirement hometown for anyone who loves history or just wants to live in a friendly, walk-everywhere kind of place. "I don't see any negatives," she says, noting that property values are increasing.

Peg Roth, a real estate agent and a former vice president of the Chamber of Commerce of Greater Cape May, echoes that sentiment. "We see a steady stream of retirees coming into Cape May. Most come from Maryland, Philadelphia and northern New Jersey," she says.

A popular area for retirees is Village Green near the Coast Guard base. A two-bedroom quad unit costs as little as $170,000. Single-family homes in the heart of town start around $350,000 and can cost much more if the home has historic significance or coveted ocean views. (There are very few ocean-front properties.) "Many people purchase second homes in Cape May and eventually retire to them," says Peg Roth.

That's the approach Edward and Jane Zane took. Having fallen in love with Cape May in the 1950s (even though other shore resorts were much more fashionable at the time), the Zanes bought a duplex in 1976 for weekend use. They lived in Turnersville, NJ, near Philadelphia. Edward, 69, was a line installer for New Jersey Bell and Jane, now 75, worked for a bank in Philadelphia.

"Where else is there a seaside resort town with tree-lined streets for walking?" asks Jane. "We don't like the gated, more wealthy communities where every house has a huge fence or gigantic hedge to block the views of passers-by. In Cape May, people are proud of their houses and gardens and want them to be seen." The Zanes' garden is a case in point, having won the Cape May Garden Club's monthly award.

Knowing that they would move to Cape May when Edward retired from his job at age 65, the Zanes bought an older single-family house near the beach

Cape May, NJ

Population: 4,034 in the city, 102,326 in Cape May County.

Location: In southeastern New Jersey. Cape May is a thumb-shaped peninsula separated from the mainland by a canal. It divides Delaware Bay and the Atlantic Ocean.

Climate:

	High	Low
January	40	24
July	85	68

Average relative humidity: 73%

Rain: 46 inches. **Snow:** 16 inches (snow cover rarely lasts more than a day).

Cost of living: Above average (specific index not available).

Median housing cost: Mid-year market summary for 2002 showed a median price of $279,900. Housing costs are higher in town than in the surrounding area. Average monthly rent is $700.

Sales tax: 6%

Sales tax exemptions: Groceries, clothing, and prescription and nonprescription drugs.

State income tax: For married couples filing jointly, the rate is graduated from 1.4% of taxable income up to $20,000 to 6.37% on amounts over $150,000. For single filers, graduated from 1.4% of taxable income up to $20,000 to 6.37% on amounts over $1 million.

Income tax exemptions: Social Security benefits are exempt. Federal, state, local and private pensions are taxable. Up to $15,000 of taxable pension is exempt for married couples age 62 and older, up to $11,250 for single filers age 62 and older.

Intangibles tax: None.

Estate tax: None, except the state's "pick-up" portion of the federal tax, applicable to taxable estates above $1 million.

Property tax: $1.78 per $100 of assessed value, with homes assessed at 100% of market value. Annual tax on a $279,900 home is about $4,982.

Homestead tax exemption: There is a homestead rebate that ranges from $100 to $775, depending on income, filing status and the amount of property tax paid.

Religion: There are 11 churches in Cape May City, and the nearest synagogue is in Wildwood. Cape May County has 116 houses of worship.

Education: Adult education classes are available at Atlantic Community College, Cape May Institute, Rutgers University Extension programs and Cape May County Technical School.

Transportation: New Jersey Transit provides bus service to Atlantic City, Philadelphia and New York City. The nearest airports are Atlantic City International and Philadelphia International. The County Department of Aging provides free transportation for seniors to medical facilities (including Veteran's Hospital in Wilmington, DE) and essential shopping.

Health: Burdette Tomlin Memorial Hospital, 10 miles north, has 242 beds. Major medical facilities are available in Philadelphia and Wilmington, both a 90-minute drive.

Housing options: Village Green, a 10-year-old area with ranch-style homes, has quad units for $170,000-$200,000. Houses in the historic district start at $200,000 and go into the millions if they have been renovated as inns.

Visitor lodging: The Virginia Hotel is a full-service, luxury hotel in the historic district, $80-$365 depending on season, including continental breakfast, (609) 884-5700. The Humphrey Hughes House is an elegant B&B inn, $105-$270 depending on season and type of room, (609) 884-4428.

Information: Chamber of Commerce of Greater Cape May, P.O. Box 556, Cape May, NJ 08204, (609) 884-5508 or www.capemaychamber.com. Cape May County Chamber of Commerce, P.O. Box 74, Cape May Court House, NJ 08210, (609) 465-7181 or www.cmccofc.com.

in 1991, tore it down and rebuilt it before moving in. They also sold their first duplex and purchased another one, which they rent to year-round residents.

"There's always something to do here," says Edward, who served as treasurer for the local historical society and as a volunteer for Cold Spring Village, a re-creation of a 19th-century farming village just a few miles from town.

While history buffs and antique collectors find Cape May almost divine, they aren't the only folks who enjoy the good life in New Jersey's far south. Nature lovers and anyone who likes being active outdoors will take to Cape May.

For starters, the climate generally is welcoming. The ocean takes the edge off both winter and summer, and temperatures drop below freezing only 15 days a year. Snow melts before it becomes a nuisance. While some may find 46 inches of annual rainfall and an average humidity of 73 percent a little too wet, the gardens love it.

The Cape also is a good place to view wildlife. It is rated as one of the 10 best bird-watching destinations in the world by the Audubon Society. In prehistory, migrating birds selected the narrow peninsula as their resting and feeding ground on annual flights between the Arctic and South America. Butterflies, too, make the Cape a way station — as do several species of whales and dolphins.

"Cape May is ideal for many migrating species because it is halfway between their northern and southern habitats," explains Dr. Paul Kerlinger, director of the Cape May Bird Observatory. Commonly observed species include red-throated loons, snowy egrets, ospreys, peregrine falcons and many types of sandpipers and terns. Many retirees get caught up in birding once they settle on the Cape and take part in the observatory's annual census.

Biking and walking also are popular. People who might not have enjoyed bicycling back home find that the area's lightly traveled roads and flat terrain make it quite pleasurable. Walkers have their choice of venues, and the walker-friendly historic district is particularly popular with retirees.

The shopping district is a pedestrian mall, and sidewalks are in good repair on block after block of brightly painted, garishly trimmed Victorian houses. After the infamous 1962 storm that blew away the boardwalk, it was replaced with a concrete promenade. "It's easier to walk on than a boardwalk," says Jane Zane.

Boardwalk aficionados will find miles of it in Cape May Point State Park, bridging marshes and meandering through mangroves to various birding lookouts. When the grandchildren come to visit, retirees take them to the Wildwood boardwalk eight miles north of Cape May. This is where they'll find beach amusements and the widest expanse of white sand in the state. While Cape May's beach has been slowly eroding, Wildwood's beach is growing.

Although Cape May residents may not have a huge beach to brag about (it's a more-than-adequate strip of sand), most are glad to be living on solid ground. Unlike most shore towns in New Jersey, Cape May is not on a barrier island.

With the convergence of two large bodies of water, fishing and boating enthusiasts will find plenty of opportunities to pursue their interests. Cape May has the second-largest commercial fishing port on the East Coast — a tribute to the wealth of these waters.

Golf, too, is a popular sport with about 10 courses in the surrounding area, including the 18-hole Cape May National Golf Club. Tennis courts are abundant; seniors particularly like the town courts next to the Emlen Physick Estate.

Like most shore towns, Cape May has its share of eateries featuring fried fish, hot dogs, saltwater taffy and hamburgers. The town also boasts top-rated restaurants, most of which are open all year, but a few close January through March.

There's also a three-season roster of cultural, educational and just plain fun events and festivals. Spring kicks off with tulip, kite and music festivals. The Cape May Music Festival features a six-week schedule of classical, jazz and blues artists. In the summer, there are antique shows, a seafood festival, a wine-and-food festival, and theater — including the Cape May State Equity Theater and the Cape May Kids Playhouse.

Activities peak during a 10-day period in October known as Victorian Week, which features historic house tours, Victorian fashion shows and sing-alongs. The Christmas season also is jammed with activities. Things get quiet during the winter, and many retirees choose that time to vacation in warmer climates.

The Cape May Institute offers a year-round roster of Elderhostel programs. It also conducts photography, writing and preservation workshops at various times of year, and a summer series of philosophy lectures.

For more extensive entertainment opportunities, Cape May residents like the area's proximity to Philadelphia (80 miles) and Atlantic City (49 miles). Public transportation is available to both at reduced rates for senior citizens.

Convenient location, mild climate, lots to do, and a friendly atmosphere all make Cape May rate highly as a retirement locale. As Jane Zane puts it, "A day doesn't go by when we don't say how blessed we are to live here." ●

Carlsbad, California

Sea breezes and Mediterranean charm sweeten life in this Southern California coastal town

By Richard L. Fox

It's springtime in this coastal Southern California village, and massive fields of ranunculuses and other hard-to-pronounce flowers erupt in blazing colors of red, orange, pink and yellow, drawing thousands of visitors from across the Southwest. It's summertime, and hordes of youngsters and their parents and grandparents stream into one of the world's largest family-oriented theme parks. It's autumn, and golfers, fishermen, sunbathers and festival-goers flock to this sun-splashed oceanside resort seeking refuge, recreation and relaxation.

Into this magical potpourri of sun, sand, surf and surprises, New Jersey retirees Jack and Gwen Nelson came seeking the perfect place to spend their retirement years. "We were looking for a community with sidewalks, a nearby college and a good library," says Jack. "We found that and a whole lot more in Carlsbad."

Carlsbad evokes images of a charming Mediterranean town, with balmy sea breezes, sun-splashed sidewalk cafes and delightful antique shops and boutiques. Its attributes also include a predictably temperate climate, scenic vistas, excellent shopping and diverse residential neighborhoods, and San Diego is within easy range for more shopping options, cultural and sporting events, dining and entertainment.

For centuries the area was the home of Luiseno Indians, who camped by and fished in coastal lagoons that dot the landscape. In the mid-18th century, Spanish explorers staked claim to this remote territory for their king. In 1798, Franciscan missionaries established the largest of 21 missions in California, Mission San Luis Rey, a few miles north.

With the discovery in the 1880s of mineral waters believed to have healing properties, Carlsbad borrowed its name from the popular Karlsbad Spa in Bohemia and began establishing a reputation as a tourist destination. A giant step was taken in the opening of these coastal lands between Los Angeles and San Diego when the Arizona Eastern Railway built the Carlsbad Depot (now the Tourist Information Center) in 1887.

The introduction of irrigation waters in 1914 brought an economic boom to the area through increased cultivation of vegetables, fruits and flowers. Now more than 200,000 people visit Carlsbad's famous Flower Fields, a mile-long garden of multicolored blossoms that has attracted spring visitors for more than 60 years. The area's newest attraction, Legoland, opened last March to enthusiastic crowds and was expected to bring 1.8 million youngsters and chaperones to the Danish toy manufacturer's only U.S. theme park in its first year of operation.

For many retirees, California's reputation for expensive real estate and high costs of living has precluded relocation. But some, including the Nelsons, have done comparison shopping and found the state more affordable than they thought.

"We had decided to write off California for retirement because of everything we read about high costs of housing, taxes and general living expenses," says Jack. "Then we read an article that caused us to compare property, sales and income taxes in New Jersey and California. We found that New Jersey was much higher than California."

Pleasantly surprised, the Nelsons looked at 10 towns in Southern California, from Santa Rosa to San Diego, and also considered Boulder, Fort Collins and Colorado Springs, CO; Las Cruces and Albuquerque, NM; Seattle, WA; and Philadelphia, PA. Just as the Nelsons thoroughly researched places to retire, they looked hard at available housing before selecting their retirement home.

"We looked at 80 houses, and this was the best built," says Jack, a 66-year-old former Rutgers University professor. "The contractor built it for his mother."

They bought a 2,300-square-foot ranch-style home with stucco and wood siding in May 1998 for about $300,000 "in old Carlsbad, less than a mile from downtown and 1.5 miles from the ocean," says Jack. It's an ideal location for two favorite hobbies, walking on the beach every morning and sampling new restaurants. "We test a lot of restaurants," Gwen adds.

Carlsbad's wide array of housing styles complements the diverse lifestyle choices of its residents. Oceanside condominiums and expansive estates are available for those who enjoy a close relationship with surf and sand. Victorian cottages and beautifully restored historic homes in walking distance of downtown are favored by those seeking convenient access to small-town living. New, upscale suburban developments, notably Aviara and La Costa east of Interstate 5, offer a choice of golf course, lagoon and ocean views from high-end homes running $300,000 to $1,000,000-plus. Carlsbad by the Sea, a luxurious, oceanfront continuing-care retirement community in California mission-style architecture, provides on-site health care, a diverse recreational program, transportation and an innovative program of services fostering good health and well-being.

Manley and Linda Sarnowsky chose a home in the upscale planned community of Aviara, just off Interstate 5 and only minutes from the ocean and downtown, when they moved from St. Louis, MO, in April 1998. Manley, a 58-year-old retired Ralston-Purina executive, and Linda, 57, had visited potential retirement sites in North Carolina, New Mexico and other areas of California before settling on Carlsbad. "We stayed here three full weeks and bought on our first visit," Linda recalls. "We knew we wanted to be near the coast, and we wanted new housing. Once we found the right house we knew this was the place. Carlsbad Village is so attractive, and we just fell in love with the area."

"We had always thought about (retiring in) California, but we thought it would be too expensive," says Manley. "We set a limit on what we would pay for a house, and it turned out to be what we paid almost to the dollar."

"The cost of living is higher than St. Louis," Linda adds, "but that's the only negative here. There are trade-offs. You may have to pass up some things you would like in order to live in a beautiful place."

Asked how they made new friends after moving to Carlsbad, Manley says, "It was easy for me. We joined El Camino Country Club, and I went to the golf course. I play just about every day." Manley says he misses the golf courses back in St. Louis, but they were more crowded. "I have three courses (here) I can get on quite easily," he says.

Linda doesn't golf, but she does "a lot of walking and reading." She joined the Newcomers Club, Ameri-

can Association of University Women, Aviara Women's Club and an investment club. "We've also been inundated with houseguests since we moved out here. I sometimes feel like I'm running a B&B — but I love it," she adds.

Another transplanted couple, Morris and Gladys Hayes, were pleased to find their living expenses in California less than what they were in their preretirement days in Altoona, WI. Morris and Gladys had lived in Altoona for 30 years when they decided their annual one-week stay in a time-share unit at Carlsbad Inn was just not enough.

"We liked coming here so much that we decided to think about retir-

Carlsbad, CA

Population: 78,247
Location: On the California coast, 31 miles north of San Diego.
Climate:

	High	Low
January	65	47
July	78	68

Average relative humidity: 69%
Rain: 7.15 inches.
Cost of living: Above average (specific index not available).
Average housing cost: $336,000
Sales tax: 7.75%
Sales tax exemptions: Food products, prescription medicines and services.
State income tax: For married couples filing jointly, graduated from 1% of taxable income up to $11,496 to 9.3% on amounts over $75,450. For single filers, graduated from 1% of taxable income up to $5,748 to 9.3% on amounts over $37,725.
Income tax exemptions: Social Security benefits and railroad pensions are exempt.

Estate tax: None, except the state's "pick-up" portion of the federal tax, applicable to taxable estates above $1 million.
Property tax: $10.24 per $1,000 of market value or purchase price plus 2% per year, whichever is lower. With the exemption noted below, the annual tax on a home valued at $336,000 would be $3,369.
Homestead exemption: $7,000 on owner-occupied property.
Religion: There are about 30 churches and synagogues.
Education: California State University at San Marcos, 10 miles east, offers undergraduate and graduate degree programs. Two nearby community colleges, MiraCosta in Oceanside and Palomar in San Marcos, offer vocational and general education courses.
Transportation: Coaster is a commuter rail service to San Diego. San Diego International Airport is 30 miles south.
Health: Tri-City Medical Center, just north in Oceanside, is a 450-bed general and acute-care facility. Just south of Carlsbad, Scripps Memorial Hospital-Encinitas has 139 beds. There are 48 physicians and surgeons in Carlsbad, and more than 400 in the area.
Housing options: Homes on or near the ocean, within walking distance of downtown, in historic neighborhoods and in new, upscale suburban developments are available in escalating price ranges. Plan to

spend $125-$200 per square foot for new housing. Older homes can be purchased for around $100 per square foot. **Carlsbad by the Sea** is an award-winning continuing-care retirement community housed in an attractive California mission-style complex near the Pacific Ocean. Programs focus on health and well-being, and amenities include a fitness center, lap pool, hydro-therapy pool and spa services such as facials, massages and herbal wraps. Floor plans range from 800 to 1,800 square feet. Entrance fees are $164,000 to $484,000 and monthly service fees are $2,050 to $3,675. For information, call (800) 255-556 or visit www.carlsbadbythesea.com.
Visitor lodging: Twenty hotels, motels and bed-and-breakfast inns in the community offer a wide range of accommodations and prices. Carlsbad Inn Beach Resort, $178-$250, (800) 235-3939. Pelican Cove Inn, a bed-and-breakfast inn, $90-$180, (888) 735-2683. La Costa Resort and Spa, $345-$570 and up, (800) 854-5000. Four Seasons Resort, Aviara, starting at $395, (800) 332-3442. Rates are per night, double occupancy.
Information: Carlsbad Chamber of Commerce, 5620 Paseo del Norte, Suite 128, Carlsbad, CA 92008, (760) 931-8400 or www.carlsbad.org. Carlsbad Convention and Visitors Bureau), 400 Carlsbad Village Drive, P.O. Box 1246, Carlsbad, CA 92018, (800) 227-5722 or www.carlsbadca.org.

ing here," says Gladys, 78, a former high school music teacher. "We wintered here in 1996-97 and started looking at real estate. We looked at five properties and bought within 24 hours — four blocks from the ocean."

They found that their property taxes were half what they paid back in Altoona, "and utility bills are about a seventh of what we paid in Wisconsin," Morris says. He estimates their home in a 70-unit condominium development has appreciated modestly since they purchased it in February 1997 — "about $3,000," he says.

Morris, 80, a former music professor at the University of Wisconsin-Eau Claire, says they were captivated by the "quaintness" of Carlsbad Village.

"They built the shopping area about four miles from the village," he says, "and the city fathers have made a point, religiously, to keep fast-food chains and things like that out of the village. Crime is low, and the transportation system is excellent."

Carlsbad is getting its share of relocating in-state retirees as well. Bill and Pat Northridge had lived in La Crescenta, north of Los Angeles, more than 40 years when they decided to seek relief from the increasingly frenetic pace of their hometown. "It took awhile to shake the L.A. County hurries," Pat says, "but the laid-back attitude of the people here in San Diego County has finally rubbed off.

"When our real estate agent found this area in Aviara we did not hesitate to buy," she adds. "One mile to the ocean, which is always in view, yet we're in a forest of protected vegetation and trees all through the hills running up from the Pacific."

Bill and Pat enjoy Aviara's scenic trails, which boast ocean views and wind through exotic vegetation and past a cool, clear lagoon. Bill attends San Diego Padres baseball games, and they both engage in "a bit of competition (among neighbors) to have a beautiful community and keep it that way," says Pat.

Carlsbad's population has grown from about 300 at the turn of the 19th century to about 75,000. There are nine retail shopping centers in the area, including Carlsbad Company Stores, an eclectic mix of upscale retailers, designers, manufacturers' outlets, art galleries, restaurants and financial institutions. With the opening of Legoland, and a large luxury resort, golf course and upscale shopping facilities on the drawing board, some residents worry that the small-town, resident-friendly atmosphere of Carlsbad is being threatened.

But at this point, there's only one thing Linda Sarnowsky doesn't like about Carlsbad: "It's a little far from downtown San Diego," she says. "It takes 30 to 40 minutes to get downtown."

Those who want to avoid busy Interstate 5 to San Diego can take a more leisurely scenic drive down coastal Highway 101. Better yet, residents can board the popular Coaster at one of two Carlsbad stations and enjoy a comfortable commuter train ride downtown.

Normally quiet and uncrowded, Carlsbad draws a crowd of 90,000 shoppers during the Carlsbad Village Faire, the largest one-day street fair in California, in May and November, and a popular farmers market fills downtown streets with eager buyers during the peak growing season. Among major sporting events attracting large numbers of visitors to Carlsbad annually are the San Diego Marathon, with more than 5,000 competitors; the Carlsbad 5000, a premier racing spectacular with more than 10,000 runners participating; and the Mercedes PGA golf championship and Toshiba Tennis Classic held on the grounds of La Costa Resort and Spa.

Seniors can take courses at MiraCosta College, next door in Oceanside, and Palomar College, 15 minutes away in San Marcos. Both are community colleges. The Cal State University campus in San Marcos provides a range of undergraduate and graduate courses.

Jack and Gwen Nelson are glad they made the move from New Jersey. When they aren't walking on the beach or "testing restaurants," Jack is busy revising his latest college textbook and Gwen is either reading, knitting or cooking.

"We may eventually move out of Carlsbad, but not for a long time," Jack says. "We may need an assisted-living home some day, but it will be in this area."

If you're planning a move to Carlsbad, "you better hurry up," advises Linda Sarnowsky. "It's not getting any cheaper. Try to get in on the front end of a new development." ●

Cashiers, North Carolina

This western North Carolina village has the ambiance of a mountain resort

By Mary Lu Abbott

In search of "downtown" Cashiers, I pulled into the corner gas station/food mart at U.S. Highway 64 and State Highway 107 and interrupted a conversation of local patrons to ask, "Where's the main part of town?"

They looked at each other, chuckled and nodded to the young clerk to provide an answer. "Well, I guess this is it, ma'am," she said.

Indeed, city folks sometimes have a hard time recognizing Cashiers. In the blink of an eye you've passed through town and again are deep in the mountains and forests of western North Carolina.

Called the "crossroads" by residents, the intersection of highways 64 and 107 forms the heart of Cashiers, an unincorporated community that attracts many retirees. To one side of the intersection the small Village Green acts as a gathering spot and playground, and beyond it is a cluster of enticing shops and businesses with a mountain resort ambiance. Down from the Village Green on Highway 107 north, a few gift stores and crafts galleries, antique shops, professional offices and a hardware store and mercantile occupy small wood and stone buildings nearly hidden among tall fir trees.

Gloria Joseph, a former resident of West Bloomfield, MI, a Detroit suburb, is happy that Cashiers is small. "I don't want it to be built up. The purpose in coming here is to get away from all development," she says, although she acknowledges that at first she was reluctant to settle in this mountain community about 65 miles southwest of Asheville.

"Friends told us about Cashiers, and when we went to Florida for a wedding, we stopped here on the way back. My husband fell in love with it and bought a lot then," says Gloria, 58, who worked for a steel company before she retired. "I didn't want to leave Michigan. We had built our home there and had a lot of blood, sweat and tears in it."

Gloria changed her mind over the next five years, though, as she and Jeff, 64, a Chrysler employee, came back to vacation in the area. They built a home in the Sapphire Valley Resort area east of Cashiers and moved permanently in 1990.

Situated at 3,486 feet, the town is surrounded by mountains 4,000 to 5,000 feet high. Narrow two-lane roads twist and turn through canyons, climb through forests and skirt the edge of ridges with precipitous drop-offs. On some mountain curves, the narrow road makes it difficult for one large vehicle to pass another, and the speed limit in many stretches is only 20 to 30 mph. Those who know the area navigate the snaking roads faster than newcomers and visitors. Road signs suggest that slower drivers pull over to let others pass.

"At first, I was terrified by the roads with no guardrails, but now I drive with one hand — the other's on the armrest — and people have to pull off for me," Gloria says with a laugh.

For hundreds of years people have found their way over these mountains and into Cashiers Valley, first American Indians coming to hunt, then permanent settlers in the early 1800s. By the mid-1800s, it was gaining a reputation as a summer resort where well-to-do Southern families came to escape the heat and humidity of coastal areas. Mountain lodges and second homes sprang up, and an active social scene developed among the "summer people." The early activities of hunting, fishing and horseback riding soon expanded to include golfing, hiking, swimming and tennis.

Now Cashiers is more popular than ever as a resort, its permanent population of about 1,678 residents mush-rooming to 8,000 or more with the summer people, many of whom have second homes they've built or bought in developments around Cashiers. While Cashiers draws vacationers from a variety of areas, the migration of Southerners has remained strong. Residents of metropolitan Atlanta frequently escape here for the weekends, but perhaps the largest contingent comes from Florida. Residents of South Florida in particular pack up and head to the cool mountains for the entire summer to escape their sultry season.

Lester and Mary Freeman of Miami, FL, built a vacation home outside Cashiers in 1988 and moved permanently in 1991. Like the Josephs and many others who summer here, when it came time to retire, the Freemans decided there was no better place than Cashiers.

"We didn't have to think about it," says Mary, 67. "We loved the atmosphere when we visited here during the summer months. We liked the scenic beauty, and we had friends with summer homes here."

When John and Rosalyn Perdue prepared to retire and leave Mobile, AL, their home of 36 years, they knew they wanted to relocate to these mountains but weren't sure exactly where to settle.

"We looked all over western North Carolina. We wanted a cooler climate with a change of seasons. When we saw Cashiers, we knew this was the place," says John, 74.

Like other retirees, the Perdues were drawn by the scenic beauty of the area, with its gentle, often misty mountains, many waterfalls and clear streams.

"It's centrally located between a lot of larger towns for shopping, cultural and entertainment needs," John adds. The hub of the region is Asheville, about an hour away. Greenville, SC, is about 70 miles to the southeast, and Charlotte, NC, and Atlanta each are about two hours away.

Retirees are settling in several towns in the area, in particular Highlands, 10 miles southwest on Highway 64, and Franklin, about 30 miles farther west on Highway 64. Highlands sits highest, at an altitude of about 4,100 feet, while Cashiers is lower by about 600 feet, and Franklin, the largest town, spreads over the foothills at about 2,100 feet.

"Franklin gets hot in the summer," says Rosalyn, 71. "We wanted someplace cooler. We looked at Highlands but were discouraged by the (high) prices. We were on our way back to Greenville (where their daughter lives) and decided to go through Cashiers. We were impressed at how it had cleaned

Cashiers, NC

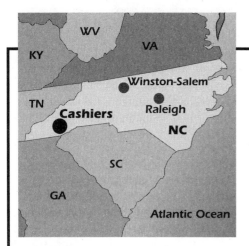

Population: About 1,678 year-round residents in Cashiers, about 8,000 in summer. Jackson County has about 33,121 residents.

Location: In the Blue Ridge Mountains of western North Carolina, about 65 miles southwest of Asheville. Elevation is 3,486 feet.

Climate:

	High	Low
January	46	26
July	82	59

Average relative humidity: 56%

Rain: 91 inches.

Snow: 12 inches.

Cost of living: Below average in Jackson County (specific index not available), but homes tend to be higher-priced in the Cashiers area.

Average housing cost: About $150,000, though many homes are in the $200,000 range and some go above $1 million.

Sales tax: 6.5%

Sales tax exemptions: Prescriptions, services and automobiles.

State income tax: For married couples filing jointly, the rate is graduated from 6% of taxable income up to $21,250 to 8.25% on amounts over $200,000. For single filers, it is graduated from 6% of income up to $12,750 to 8.25% on amounts over $120,000.

Income tax exemptions: Social Security benefits are exempt. Up to $2,000 of distributions from private retirement ben-efits and IRAs (up to the amount reported in federal income taxes), or up to $4,000 of government pensions may be exempt. Total deductions may not exceed $4,000 per person.

Intangibles tax: None.

Estate tax: None, except the state's "pick-up" portion of the federal tax, applicable to taxable estates above $1 million.

Property tax: Residents of Cashiers pay the Jackson County tax rate of $4.80 per $1,000 of assessed value. Homes are assessed at 100 percent of market value, and appraisals are done every four years. Taxes currently are based on 2000 appraisals. Annual taxes on a $150,000 home are $720.

Homestead exemption: Homeowners age 65 and older, or disabled, living in the home and earning $18,000 or less per year qualify for an exemption of $20,000 or 50% of the value of the home, whichever is greater.

Personal property tax: Same rate as real property (homes) on the depreciated value of boats, mobile homes, motor homes and campers and other specified belongings.

Religion: The community has several Protestant, Roman Catholic and nondenominational places of worship, but no synagogue.

Education: Southwestern Community College in Sylva and a branch in Franklin offer classes. The University of North Carolina at Asheville, about 65 miles away, has an extensive program and activities for seniors.

Transportation: There's no local bus service. Nearest airports are at Asheville and Atlanta, about two hours away.

Health: The community has a medical clinic affiliated with the Highlands-Cashiers Hospital, about six miles from Cashiers on U.S. Highway 64. The 24-bed hospital offers extensive services, including cardiac care, and is linked with re-gional medical facilities to provide specialized care locally. For advanced surgical procedures, residents go to Asheville or Atlanta.

Housing options: There are many residential communities in the Cashiers-Glenville-Sapphire area, offering lots and new and resale homes, townhouses and villas in the mountains and on lakes and golf courses. Most construction is wood and stone. Among popular options for retirees are **Holly Forest**, with homes priced from $160,000-$450,000, and **Emerald Cove**, $175,000-$225,000 (contact Fairfield-Sapphire Valley Resort, (828) 743-3441, for information on these two communities); the new **Trillium Links and Village**, (828) 743-9951 or (888) 464-3800, custom homes $350,000-$695,000, homesites $60,000-$600,000; **Country Club of Sapphire Valley**, $175,000-$950,000; and **Cullowhee Forest**, $250,000-$650,000. The chamber of commerce provides a directory listing several real estate agencies in the area.

Visitor lodging: Options range from log cabins to elegant homes, bed-and-breakfast inns, resorts and lodges. Oakmont Lodge, (828) 743-2298, offers log cabins with fireplaces starting at $59 November to June and $128 the rest of the year. Cottage Inn, (828) 743-3033, has accommodations for $80-$140, depending on season. The Millstone Inn Bed & Breakfast, (888) 645-5786, open March through December, has 11 rooms starting at $150. Sapphire Valley Resort, (800) 533-8268, about three miles outside Cashiers, has golf, tennis, hiking, fishing, canoeing and a variety of accommodations from hotel rooms to four-bedroom homes; hotel rates are $90-$350 a night.

Information: Cashiers Area Chamber of Commerce, P.O. Box 238, Cashiers, NC 28717, (828) 743-5941 or www.cashiersnc.com.

up. It used to have a lot of junkyards and old cars along the highway.

"We stopped to see a realtor and five months later bought a lot. We wanted to buy something to renovate. We said we would never build another house (after building one in Mobile) but we couldn't find anything we wanted, so we did build," says Rosalyn.

When they moved in 1991, theirs was the third house in an area a couple of miles from Cashiers on Highway 64 toward Highlands. "We were the first full-timers in the area and we thought we were going to be alone out here for a while. Now there are 18 homes and four of us are full-timers," Rosalyn says. She retired from a position as a school library media specialist, and John concluded a career as a structural engineer.

Cashiers residents say their community and Highlands are more resort-oriented than Franklin. Gloria thinks Cashiers has more pizazz because of its specialty shops, which purvey fine art, mountain crafts, gourmet foods, decorative arts, gardening gifts and antiques.

"We're similar to Highlands, but they're more commercialized, more developed. They're incorporated and we're not. There are advantages and disadvantages to incorporation," says Jeff. Without a local governing authority, development can be helter-skelter, but "a few wealthy families bought a lot of the land around here and make sure that what goes in is desirable," says Jeff. "There are a lot of very active people who are guiding growth control. It's in good shape."

Cashiers relies on Jackson County and local volunteers to provide needed services. Emergencies are handled by a volunteer fire department, a rescue squad with a full-time ambulance crew supplemented by volunteers, and the Jackson County Sheriff's Department. Cashiers residents take pride in their new branch of the Jackson County Public Library, which also has a meeting room for concerts and other programs. A community center hosts activities for seniors. The local Cashiers Medical Center is affiliated with the Highlands-Cashiers Hospi-

tal, located between the two communities.

"The hospital was a deciding factor in our move," says Rosalyn. "We're five miles and about eight minutes from the hospital. It took longer than that to get to a hospital in Mobile. This is a good hospital — it's hooked up (for electronic consultations) with other medical facilities in the region, and some staff from Emory University Hospital (in Atlanta) come for visits or are on call. Some Emory doctors have homes up here."

For all three couples, a major factor in relocating here was its lower cost of living. "We can live here 40 to 50 percent cheaper than we can in Miami," says Lester, 70, who owned a telecommunications company. "Taxes and insurance are much less. We used to do a lot of dining out — on-the-town sort of thing. We have far fewer opportunities to spend money." And that includes "even the places to buy clothes — there's no Bloomingdale's," adds his wife, Mary.

For Jeff and Gloria, the savings were dramatic. "Michigan taxes were $10,000-$12,000 annually. Here they are $1,000-$1,200," Jeff says. "Transportation expense is far less. When we were in the city we spent about 25 percent of our lives in a car. We went from two cars to one when we moved here. We live right across the street from the golf course and I have a golf cart."

High among the attractions cited by residents are the outdoor activities, including hiking, walking, golfing, fishing and rafting. The area is "good for your health because it's hard not to be involved in physical activities," says Jeff.

The beauty of the changing seasons also beckons people outdoors. Red maples and pink azaleas herald spring, followed by the rosy hues of rhododendrons, white and pink mountain laurels and fragrant magnolia blossoms covering the mountains into the summer. Fall paints the peaks and knolls a myriad range of reds, oranges and golds.

Winter brings chilly days and several snowfalls, but extreme cold and heavy snow are rare. Retirees have

mixed reactions to the winters, depending on where they have lived previously. Those who came from the North, such as the Josephs, consider the winters quite mild. Some people from the South love the opportunity to see snow, and others consider January and February good times to flee like "snowbirds."

"We love the snow," says Rosalyn, who rarely encountered it in Mobile. "We don't mind being snowed in with a fireplace. We have four-wheel-drive vehicles. You really need them up here," she says, while noting that highways are plowed for snow and remain open in winter.

The Freemans don't like the "rainy, dismal days" that sometimes come in winter, so they escape back to Miami frequently. "When you live in South Florida, the sun shines every day. I am very much affected by gloomy weather," says Mary. Lester adds that they experience "horizon deprivation" when they are surrounded too long by mountains rather than skies. The Freemans suggest that anyone considering retiring to Cashiers full-time rent for a year and try it out through a winter.

The Josephs advise retirees resettling here to compare the price of buying furniture in North Carolina to the cost of moving furnishings. Since so much furniture is manufactured in the state, it's often less expensive here.

The retirees find more to praise than to fault in Cashiers. Those who moved from metropolitan areas like its low crime and the lack of congestion. Being a resort area has fostered the growth of good cafes, delis and gourmet restaurants, though some close for a while during winter. The couples say it's easy to meet people and step into the active social scene through churches and community volunteer programs.

For Rosalyn and John Perdue, living in Cashiers is like one long vacation. "Our friends wondered how we found the place and how we could drive on the (narrow, twisting) roads without being bothered, but we're not," says Rosalyn. "We have exactly what we want," adds John.●

Celebration, Florida

Retirement dreams come true in this Florida town created by Disney

By David Wilkening

The idea of retiring to Walt Disney World may seem like a childhood fantasy, but when Disney founded a town adjacent to its Orlando theme park in 1994, it was a dream that became reality. The first residents moved into their homes in Celebration four years ago, and while the development is not age-restricted, many of its residents are young-at-heart retirees. In accordance with general Disney philosophy, residents here are supposed to live happily ever after. For many, that's not a difficult assignment.

New residents Rod Owens and his wife, Peg, found that it really is a small world after all, as the Disney ditty goes. They had planned a retirement relocation, and their search for a new community took them about 17,000 miles in a small motor home. But eventually they found their new home only 30 miles from the old one.

"After my husband retired, we started traveling. But we were always looking for someplace else to live," recalls Peg Owens. The couple had what seemed an almost perfect retirement location on a lake in Central Florida near the garden-rich tourist attraction of Cypress Gardens. But while living on a lake sounds like a fine lifestyle, "it was quiet but boring," says Peg.

The couple wanted to live in the South in a community with good sidewalks. "My husband jogs every day, and we knew we wanted somewhere with the mobility of being able to walk on sidewalks," she says. They were considering various places they visited, but their search came to an end on the day they read about a new community planned by Walt Disney World in Florida.

Celebration, less than an hour from their home, was so popular before it even opened that a drawing was held to determine the buyers of the first 500 homesites available. There were 5,000 entries, and Rod, a retired dentist, and Peg were among the lucky ones.

Their good fortune allowed them to become two of Celebration's first residents when they moved into their home in the summer of 1996. What they found when they arrived was a small-town atmosphere and a downtown that featured retail shops, restaurants, a town hall, a post office, grocery store, offices and cinema. Not only did they have sidewalks on which to jog, they also had access to a lake ringed with a wide promenade that is a focal point of the town.

One of Disney's theme parks, EP-COT (Experimental Prototype Community of Tomorrow) originally was to have been a place where people lived and worked. Walt Disney died long before that ever took place, but he probably would have approved of the magic of Celebration, a community with Southeastern ambiance and pre-1940s-style architecture. When complete, it will have 12,000 to 15,000 residents in homes overlooking plenty of green space. The 4,900-acre site just south of busy U.S. Highway 192 near Interstate 4 is surrounded by a 4,700-acre protected greenbelt.

Disney wanted its community to be perfect, just like its theme park, and it is said that the creators of Celebration spent a decade studying successful towns of the past and present to create a close-knit community — but one that also is technologically advanced to meet the needs of the 21st century. Famous architects of Disney's new town included Robert Stern, Aldo Rossi, Michael Graves and Philip Johnson.

The technology is evident in various ways, such as Florida Hospital Celebration Health, a 60 bed healthcare facility offering comprehensive care and a 60,000-square-foot fitness and wellness center. Another example is the community's own Intranet, which links homes, schools, healthcare facilities, office and retail areas, providing such online services as e-mail, chat rooms and bulletin board announcements.

But there are homey small-town touches such as homes with front porches designed to promote social interaction. Even the par-72 Celebration Golf Club has been designed to have the feel of a city park. Popular with retirees such as the Owenses are the many miles of nature trails and bicycle paths.

Also popular among retirees is an over-50 group of volunteers. But what the Owenses and others find particularly enticing about Celebration is its wide mix of age groups that all seem to share a sense of community.

"You get a great feeling of community here that I don't think you find at mobile home parks or retirement areas," says Peg Owens. Virtually everyone she knows at Celebration is involved in some type of charity or civic organization. Her husband, Rod, 57, helps out with Give Kids the World. Peg, 51, started a garden club when Celebration first opened and has watched it grow from 15 to almost 60 members.

If there is a negative side to Celebration, the Owenses feel it is nearby busy U.S. Highway 192. "We do hate the traffic there," Peg says. As best they can, the Owenses and other residents avoid getting out at rush hour and other peak traffic times.

The Owenses praise the wide choice of housing available, ranging from apartments to garden, village, cottage and estate homes. Prices start in the $230,000s for a garden home and reach $750,000 to $1 million at the estate level. The Owenses chose a 2,400-square-foot home that has a small lot but provides them with plenty of privacy because of the layout.

Houses are designed in six styles: Classical, Victorian, Colonial Revival, Coastal, Mediterranean and French. There are six home types: estate, village, cottage, garden, townhouse and bungalow. These types allow for a variety of lifestyles that range from a traditional large home on a golf course that might be 90 feet wide by 130 feet deep to compact cottage homes like those found in the downtown areas of some of Florida's cities and towns. Bungalow homes, the smallest at 39 feet wide by 79 feet long, are reminiscent of Coral Gables, FL, or Pasadena, CA, in the early 1900s. Thirty-seven of 47 bungalow sites were snapped up the first day they became available in September 1999.

The community is not gated, but the Owenses say that's no detriment. Perhaps partly because there always are people out participating in various activities in the community, there is little concern about crime.

"All ages are here. We love seeing and hearing the children. There are wide sidewalks everywhere. Children are skating by. Families are walking by. You feel perfectly safe," says another resident, Melie Sue Ablang. She and her husband, Ernie, a physician, also were among the lucky lottery winners who first moved here. Like the Owenses, the Ablangs read about Celebration in a magazine.

At the time, they were living in Chesapeake City, MD. "Ernie had always loved Disney, so we flew down and took a look," Melie Sue says. They made up their minds almost immediately. Sight unseen, evaluating it from a picture, they bought a village home with a garage apartment.

"Back home in Chesapeake City, we told our kids we were packing up and retiring to Disney World. Their mouths were open. Their eyes were wide. They said, 'You're doing what?' But they quickly got over the shock," recalls Melie Sue.

The Ablangs helped start the Celebrators, an over-50 retirement club that now has about 60 members and meets monthly to hear guest speakers. Melie Sue is active in the garden club and does work with the Celebration Foundation, an independent, nonprofit organization established to promote and conduct activities in the town's community buildings. She and Ernie also are active in the local Presbyterian church.

Like the Owenses, Melie Sue and Ernie don't want to live in a community peopled entirely by retirees. They

Celebration, FL

Population: 2,736, eventually reaching 12,000 to 15,000 when the development is completed.

Location: In the northwest corner of Osceola County, 10 miles southwest of downtown Orlando and just south of Walt Disney World, about 20 minutes from Orlando International Airport.

Climate:

	High	Low
January	72	49
July	92	73

Average relative humidity: 55%

Rain: 48 inches annually.

Cost of living: 98.4 in Orlando, based on national average of 100. Housing costs in Celebration are above average.

Average housing cost: The average home in Celebration costs $377,000, according to a local real estate company.

Sales tax: 7%

Sales tax exemptions: Food, some services and medicine.

State income tax: None.

Intangibles tax: Assessed on stocks, bonds and other assets. Tax rate is $1 per $1,000 in assets. The first $20,000 in assets is exempt for individuals. For couples filing jointly, the first $40,000 is exempt. Those who owe less than $60 need not pay.

Estate tax: None, though there's a "pickup" portion of the federal tax, applicable to taxable estates above $1 million.

Property tax: $16.32 per $1,000 of assessed value. Real property is assessed at 100% of value. The annual tax on a $377,000 home, with exemption noted below, is about $5,745.

Homestead exemption: $25,000 off the assessed value of a permanent, primary residence.

Religion: All major religions are represented in Osceola County. Community Presbyterian Church is located in Celebration.

Education: Four-year colleges in the area include the University of Central Florida and Rollins College. There also are several junior colleges, including Seminole Community College, Valencia Community College and others. Noncredit classes for adults are available at various outlets, including The Knowledge Shop.

Transportation: Orlando International Airport is a major airport providing direct service both nationally and internationally. But the area's major bus transportation system, Lynx, does not serve Celebration.

Health: Florida Hospital Celebration Health, a 60-bed facility that offers acute care, is located in Celebration. There are several other major hospitals in the Orlando area.

Housing options: New residents can choose from apartments to estates. Prices start in the $230,000s for garden homes, $250,000 for townhomes and cottages, $350,000 for village homes and $750,000 for estates. Monthly apartment rentals can be had for $700-$2,000.

Visitor lodging: The 115-room Celebration Hotel is built in 1920s-style wood-frame design, with rooms from $165 to $380, (888) 499-3800 or (407) 566-6000. Near the theme parks are other options in all price ranges.

Information: Celebration Realty, 910 Beak St., Celebration, FL 34747, (877) 696-8696, (407) 566-HOME or www.celebrationfl.com.

relish the variety of age groups they encounter daily. And, "there's always something going on," says Melie Sue.

Community-sponsored events range from St. Patrick's Day treasure hunts, periodic car shows, pumpkin-carving events at Halloween, founders day weekends, basketball tournaments and even artificial snow at Christmas.

Along with the Ablangs and the Owenses, Pat and Joe Storey also were among the first settlers here. And the Storeys have equal praise for Celebration, though they are moving — very reluctantly and by necessity, says Joe, a retired Navy pilot. He had already retired and they were living in another part of Orlando when Celebration first came to their attention.

"Our next-door neighbor was an architect and construction project manager for Celebration," recalls Joe. "He kept us advised what was going on down here.

"We figured that if someone who was on the inside of this project was enthusiastic enough to plan to move here, we would just follow along and see what was going on."

The Storeys visited the preview center and watched a presentation. "We liked what we saw," but that early in development, "it was a leap of faith," says Joe. However, Pat thought so highly of the plans for Celebration that she told her husband, "We should move there even if we have to live in a closet."

Needless to say, they didn't have to live in a closet, and they relied on Disney's longstanding reputation for high quality in making their decision to buy. "We knew about their track record, and judging by that, we thought it would be a beautiful place. And it is. It's a great, great place," Joe says.

Then why are they moving? "We're moving to a CCRC (continuing-care retirement community) because of our health. To get to places you have to visit, such as getting your car repaired, you have to drive down a very busy highway (U.S. Highway 192) for at least five minutes. My wife hates it. As long as you don't leave Celebration, that's no problem. But outside the gates, access gets less convenient as you get older," Joe says.

The Storeys particularly liked the sense of community in Celebration, and they found it easy to make friends. They say they will miss those friends when they move, but they had no trouble selling their home. "Homes only last about two weeks on the market," Pat says. And some homes have appreciated $100,000 or more since Celebration opened just a few short years ago, she adds.

That level of appreciation is lamented by friends of the Owenses who considered Celebration but instead retired in Tampa. Now the Owenses say their frequently visiting friends wish they had moved to Celebration. But it's too late — they can no longer afford the prices.

The Ablangs also are thinking of moving again, although they say they love their home. But they'll be staying in Celebration, perhaps moving to a larger home so Ernie can have more space for his hobby, woodworking. Both Ernie and Melie Sue do miss their children, "but they visit a lot because business conferences bring them to the Orlando area. We get to see them often," Melie Sue says.

And that brings up one of the best things about Celebration — its proximity to Walt Disney World. With the theme park just a short drive away, residents who have children and grandchildren say they've never been more popular. "We even have a back road that takes us straight to Disney World without getting on the busy highways," says Melie Sue Ablang.●

Chapel Hill, North Carolina

This small, historic city in North Carolina
grew up around the nation's first state university

By Jim Kerr

___

If people are retiring twice to the same place, you know it's got to be good. And that's what Charles and Janet Paddock did — both times for the same reasons. As a career U.S. Navy pilot, Charles was stationed in every far-flung corner of the globe, from Iceland to North Africa, Australia to Europe, the Mediterranean to Hawaii. But when it came time to hang up his wings and touch down to a quieter life, the former Navy captain and aircraft carrier pilot and his wife chose Chapel Hill.

It was the perfect compromise climate from the extremes they had experienced, including Charles' last assignment in Oahu, HI. Chapel Hill, a beautifully preserved 209-year-old city in the rolling hills of central North Carolina, met all their other criteria as well, including a location with superb educational and health facilities. Twenty years later, after Charles' second career in tax consultation with H&R Block, the Paddocks moved less than 10 minutes away from their former home in Chapel Hill to Carol Woods, a continuing-care retirement community.

"We were tired of mostly hot climates where we'd been stationed, but since we had both grown up in Indiana, we also wanted a change of seasons without the severe winters," says Charles, 73.

Chapel Hill, with a population of 48,715, retains a small-town ambiance in a highly cosmopolitan environment. The town is anchored by the University of North Carolina in a region renowned for higher learning. With Duke University just minutes north in Durham, North Carolina State University 30 miles east in the state capital of Raleigh, and an array of high-tech companies in the area, the Research Triangle formed by the three cities boasts more doctorates per capita than anywhere in the country — and perhaps the world.

When the University of North Carolina was chartered in 1789, making it the oldest state university in the United States, the local terrain and atmosphere contributed heavily to the decision. It is said that a search committee had a pleasant picnic under a shady poplar tree at a crossroads near the New Hope Chapel. Today the same canopy of deciduous trees, including oaks, maples and hickories, shelters many well-heeled neighborhoods of Colonial, Georgian and Victorian homes.

Visitors can get a feel for Chapel Hill's history by stopping at the Horace Williams House, headquarters of the local preservation society, and picking up a map for a self-guided walking tour of downtown. The map highlights homes that date from the early 1800s to the early 1900s, most of them built for UNC professors.

Joan Vanderweert, 67, a former teacher, and husband Garrett, 67, a Toys-R-Us executive, feel energized by the youthful faces and attitudes they encounter here every day.

"That sort of feeling doesn't exist in most places, even New York," says Joan, who still maintains a second home in Wyckoff, NJ. "I've been teaching all my life, and intellectual pursuits interest me. They have shortened courses at Duke and UNC at the masters level for people like us, and it's fun being around students and young people."

She calls their townhouse life at a community called Southern Village "a different kind of retirement" where the Vanderweerts come and go as they like and where most of the residents are students rather than retirees. The Vanderweerts bought their two-story, two-bedroom townhouse more than two years ago in an area that was recently incorporated into Chapel Hill's southern boundaries. Other similar communities are springing up nearby.

The UNC campus, a square mile of red-brick, Georgian-style buildings amidst a wooded and grassy landscape, is a beehive of activity where 24,000 college students study, socialize and generally dominate the scene during the academic year. Nearby, busy Franklin Street is an assortment of bookstores, casual clothing outlets and restaurants, from pizza parlors and sandwich shops to moderate and upscale dining. Traffic is heavy, even on quiet days. And following any big Tar Heels football or basketball victory, Franklin Street is not the place to be unless your tastes run toward wild celebrations.

The university offers a vast smorgasbord of opportunities in education and the arts, including campus theater, symphony concerts and other musical events, as well as museums such as the Ackland Art Museum and the Morehead Planetarium. The UNC medical complex includes a top-ranked medical school and hospitals for children, women, neurologic and psychiatric patients, and general adult patient care. Providing some of the most advanced medical care in the Southeast, UNC hospitals are leaders in organ transplants, burn care, cancer treatment, diabetes, gastrointestinal diseases, obstetrics and pediatrics.

Duke University, with its renowned medical facilities and programs for retirees and the aging, is minutes away by car or bus, and Raleigh, an easy drive down Interstate 40, offers symphony concerts, off-Broadway plays, ballet, museums, arts and craft shows and, in late October, the popular state fair.

Like most top-rated places to live, Chapel Hill and its environs are rapidly expanding with familiar growing pains. Carrboro, a railroad depot and mill town that attracted blue-collar workers beginning in the 1890s, has grown up adjacent to Chapel Hill with a population of 16,782. Houses, apartments, condos and shopping malls are rapidly filling in farmland and replacing the closed-down flour and cotton mills, and the population is expected to expand dramatically in the next few years.

Meanwhile, the tiny historic towns of Hillsborough and Pittsboro (both with ties to the Revolutionary War and Civil War) are located 15 miles north and south of Chapel Hill respectively. Both are known today for their antique shops

Chapel Hill, NC

Population: 48,715 permanent residents, plus 24,000 students during the regular University of North Carolina session, 16,782 in adjacent Carrboro and 118,227 in Orange County.

Location: Rolling, wooded hills in central North Carolina, three hours from the Atlantic coast and three hours from the Blue Ridge Mountains, on the western point of the Research Triangle formed by Chapel Hill, Raleigh (30 miles to the southeast) and Durham (to the immediate northeast).

Climate:

	High	Low
January	51	27
July	89	66

Average relative humidity: 54%
Rain: 41.43 inches.
Cost of living: Above average (specific index not available).
Average housing cost: $237,355
Sales tax: 6.5%
Sales tax exemptions: Prescription drugs, eyeglasses, some medical supplies and most services.
State income tax: For married couples filing jointly, the rate is graduated from 6% of taxable income up to $21,250 to 8.25% on amounts over $200,000. For single filers, it is graduated from 6% of income up to $12,750 to 8.25% on amounts over $120,000.
Income tax exemptions: Social Security benefits are exempt. Up to $2,000 of distributions from private retirement benefits and IRAs (up to the amount reported in federal income taxes), or up to $4,000 of government pensions may be exempt. Total deductions may not exceed $4,000 per person.

Estate tax: North Carolina's inheritance tax was repealed in 1999, but the state takes a portion of the federal tax, applicable to taxable estates above $1 million.
Property tax: The rate is $17.31 per $1,000 assessed market value in Chapel Hill and $16.64 per $1,000 in Carrboro. The tax on a $237,355 home in Chapel Hill would be approximately $4,109.
Homestead exemption: Homeowners age 65 and older, or disabled, living in the home and earning $18,000 or less per year qualify for an exemption of $20,000 or 50% of the value of the home, whichever is greater.
Religion: Churches represent a dozen denominations, with an emphasis on humanitarian issues and community focus.
Education: There are more doctorates per capita in Chapel Hill than any other town in the country. The University of North Carolina was the first state university in the United States and was chartered in 1789. Duke University is located in nearby Durham, and North Carolina State University is located in Raleigh, the state capital.
Transportation: Chapel Hill Transit provides regular daily bus service throughout Chapel Hill from 6 a.m. to 11 p.m. weekdays during the school year, with somewhat less-frequent service on weekends and during the summer. The fare is 75 cents, and both annual and semiannual passes are available. A shared-ride service also is offered, as well as Triangle Transit Authority service between Chapel Hill, UNC Durham and Duke University for $1. I-40 connects Chapel Hill with Raleigh and RDU International Airport, located between the two cities.
Health: UNC Hospitals has more than 750 attending physicians and 500 interns with specialized care for patients with complex medical problems, as well as a complete range of routine services geared for all ages. Outpatient surgery programs also are offered, eliminating costly hospital stays. Nearby Duke University Medical Center in Durham also

contributes to an area physician-to-patient ratio that is five times the national average.
Housing options: Many options for single-family houses, apartments, condos and continuing-care retirement communities (CCRCs) are available in Carrboro, Hillsborough and Pittsboro as well as Chapel Hill. A few minutes south of Chapel Hill, **The Preserve at Jordan Lake**, (800) 252-5263, is a new master-planned community on 600 wooded acres nestled against a 14,000-acre lake. **Carol Woods**, (800) 518-9333, a CCRC on the outskirts of Chapel Hill, has both single-family cottages and townhouses in three-unit buildings. **Carolina Meadows**, (919) 942-4014, is another CCRC with 391 apartments and villas on 170 acres. New courtyard and patio homes at **Fearrington Village**, (919) 542-4000 or (800) 277-0130, start at $242,000, single-family homes at $248,000. Resale single-family homes range from $140,000 to $400,000. A guide to a wide range of housing alternatives, from independent-living and assisted-living CCRCs in Orange County, is available by calling Orange County's information line, (919) 968-2087 or www.co.orange.nc.us.
Visitor lodging: There are numerous hotels, inns and bed-and-breakfast facilities, ranging in price from $69 at the Days Inn, (919) 929-3090, to $220 and up at the Fearrington House Inn, (919) 542-2121. Other options include Windy Oaks Inn in Chapel Hill, starting at $135, (919) 942-1001; UNC's Carolina Inn, (919) 933-2001, and the Siena, (919) 929-4000, both priced $150 and up; Hampton Inn, $59-$94, (919) 968-3000; and Best Western University Inn, $50-$100, (919) 932-3000.
Information: Chapel Hill-Carrboro Chamber of Commerce, 104 S. Estes Drive, Chapel Hill, NC 27514, (919) 967-7075 or www.chapelhillcarrboro.org. Chapel Hill-Orange County Visitors Bureau, 501 W. Franklin St., Suite 104, Chapel Hill, NC 27516, (919) 968-2060 or www.chocvb.org.

and crafts and have garnered their own share of relocated retirees.

Nearby Jordan Lake is a heavily used recreational area for hiking, picnicking, swimming, camping, boating and fishing. Dr. John Shillito, 78, a retired neurosurgeon who practiced at Childrens Hospital of Boston, keeps a small Boston whaler in a slip at the 14,000-acre lake but laments that he doesn't always have much time to use it these days. Six years ago, he and his wife, Bunny, 69, a paramedical professional, retired to Fearrington Village, eight miles south of Chapel Hill. Today they seem to be always on the go.

"Most people here are like us — active socially and academically," John says. "Bunny volunteers for anything."

Both work out three times a week at a spa in Chapel Hill and belong to several of the 70 or so clubs available at Fearrington. John's skill with, and passion for, photography has led him to teach courses at two area community colleges and Duke University, while Bunny is involved with several community services, including Meals on Wheels and the Habitat for Humanity Store in Pittsboro. Both get involved in courses at Duke University's Institute for Learning in Retirement, where John is currently studying the U.S. Constitution.

"Such a collection of students you've never seen," he says of the current 800 enrollees. "All you have to be is retired."

Fearrington Village now has about 1,800 residents, about 80 percent of them retirees. The development is quiet, pastoral and distinctly upscale, with townhouses and single-family homes spread over 1,100 acres and anchored by a 33-room, five-star inn and restaurant. To preserve both the Scottish heritage and the rural atmosphere, owner-developer R.B. Fitch took an unusual but eye-catching approach when he imported a few rare belted Galloway cows in the 1980s. They have since flourished to 50 head. "We don't eat them, of course," affirms Fitch. "They're just mascots, chosen because they're different." Most locals refer to the black cows with white bands around the middle as "Oreo cows."

Meanwhile, Carol Woods, where the Paddocks live, also lives up to its name as a pine-forested community in north Chapel Hill. Flowering trees and shrubs like dogwood and azaleas blend with the big blue and white hydrangeas that Janet Paddock tends in her back yard. Spring and fall linger on the 500-foot plateau, with warm summer days reaching into the upper 80s and generally mild winters where cold temperatures and snow are aberrations.

"Everyone laughed when they saw we had brought our blue snow shovel," says Lew Woodham, who, with his wife, Ann, moved to Carol Woods in June 1999 from New York state.

Neighbors weren't laughing, however, when they borrowed the shovel following a freak storm the year the Woodhams moved in, but the occasion was an isolated one. The Woodhams' neat and comfortable cottage is one of 292 townhouses and cottages on 120 wooded acres at Carol Woods.

Comfortable weather aside, Lew and Ann had a long checklist when they left Schenectady, NY, in search of a retirement location. Lew, 67, had been a social worker and youth program coordinator, and Ann, 66, had been a homemaker and community volunteer. Their list of requisites, like that of most retirees drawn to Chapel Hill, had included a culturally active community, first-class medical facilities and both local and far-reaching modes of transportation. At least one son still had "itchy feet," and Raleigh-Durham International Airport connected him with his parents when he was off in Thailand, India and Kosovo.

When Carol Woods became the site of a day camp for 8- to 13-year-olds last summer, Lew jumped in as coordinator. It might have been farmland 20 years ago, but today the area has plenty of facilities for kids to swim, fish, make art objects and listen to storytelling by foster grandparents who, like Lew, thrive on independent thinking in an active community.

"Here, we have 400 activity directors," he says.

Like most Chapel Hill retirees, Charles Paddock is very much involved in the Retired Senior Volunteer Program, and for the past 15 years has helped low- and middle-income families prepare their taxes through the IRS Volunteer Income Tax Assistance Program.

It's hard to imagine that Chapel Hill was once just a remote crossroads with a church and rest stop for the occasional stagecoach. Today it is a lively university town that has attracted retirees from all walks of life. Says John Shillito: "The cross-section of residents here is amazing — top Army brass, big corporate CEOs, doctors, professors, scientists, administrators. And they don't hit you over the head with it. It takes a while to find out what someone did before retirement."

Chapel Hill appeals to the active, intellectually curious retiree, says Lew Woodham. "There are more programs and activities for seniors. Come to Chapel Hill if you're not looking to retire."

"I can't imagine anyone not liking it," says Janet Paddock.●

Charleston, South Carolina

America's 'most mannerly city' offers Southern hospitality and gracious living

By Lan Sluder

In historic Charleston, SC, founded in 1670, even the trees are old. The Angel Oak, a gnarled live oak tree on nearby Johns Island, is believed to be at least 1,400 years old, making it one of the most ancient living things in America.

Charleston lays claim as the home to America's first museum, first horse race, first golf course, first steam locomotive passenger train service, first theater building and first prescription drug store. The city was the site of the first major American victory in the Revolutionary War and the first shots of the Civil War.

It has America's oldest public gardens, oldest membership-based preservation society and oldest plantation home open to the public, along with the world's oldest Reform Judaism synagogue and the oldest Baptist church in the South.

History is around nearly every cobblestone-paved corner, but that's only a small part of the city's appeal to visitors and, increasingly, to retirees. For one thing, etiquette expert Marjabelle Young Stewart has given it the title of America's "most mannerly city" for seven years in a row.

Charleston's seafood and Southern restaurants are legendary, and the city is home to one of the country's top culinary institutions, Johnson and Wales University. Its cultural life — highlighted in late spring by the Spoleto Festival, which this year celebrated its 27th anniversary — is vibrant, with a nationally recognized symphony orchestra, dance and theater troupes and art galleries.

With more than 20 area golf courses (including the Ocean Course at Kiawah Island, which has hosted the Ryder Cup), Charleston offers excellent year-round recreation. There also are many tennis facilities and myriad boating and fishing opportunities. Its beaches attract sun lovers from all over — from semifunky, colorful Folly Beach (where George Gershwin wrote the score to "Porgy & Bess") to the Isle of Palms with its six miles of wide beaches, to tony, beautiful Kiawah Island.

Population: 549,033 in the Charleston metropolitan area (Charleston, Berkeley and Dorchester counties), 309,969 in Charleston County, and 96,650 in the city of Charleston.

Location: Charleston is on the Atlantic coast of South Carolina, midway between Myrtle Beach and Savannah. By car it is two hours to either Myrtle Beach or Savannah, and two and a half hours to Columbia, South Carolina's capital.

Climate:

	High	Low
January	59	38
July	89	71

Semitropical but with four distinct seasons. The climate is affected by proximity to the coast. Coastal areas are generally cooler in summer and warmer in winter than inland areas.

Average relative humidity: 86%

Rain: 52 inches annually. Snow is rare.

Cost of living: 103, based on national average of 100.

Median housing cost: $153,800 for existing single-family homes, according to first-quarter 2002 data from the National Association of Realtors. Homes in desirable areas such as the historic district or in gated island communities are much higher.

Sales tax: 5% state plus 1% local tax in Charleston, for a total of 6%

Sales tax exemptions: Prescription drugs, prescription prosthetics and hearing aids are exempt.

State income tax: For married couples filing jointly and single filers, the rates are graduated in six tiers from 2.5% on the first $2,400 of taxable income to 7% on taxable income above $12,000.

Income tax exemptions: Social Security benefits are exempt. Retirees who are drawing income from qualified retirement plans may deduct up to $3,000 of that income.

Intangibles tax: None.

Estate tax: None, except the state's "pick-up" portion of the federal tax applicable to taxable estates above $1 million.

Inheritance tax: None.

Property tax: Property tax varies by community, but averages about 1.3% of actual value in the metro Charleston area. A $153,800 home would be taxed at $1,999, based on the average. A personal property tax is assessed on vehicles and boats.

Homestead exemption: South Carolina residents 65 and older and those totally disabled or blind get an exemption on the first $50,000 of fair market value.

Religion: Due to a long history of religious tolerance, Charleston traditionally attracted people of many different religions, and today nearly every religious group is represented. Charleston is often called "The Holy City" or "City of Steeples." There are more than 180 churches in the city of Charleston alone.

Education: Charleston is home to four colleges and universities — The Citadel, College of Charleston, Charleston Southern University and Limestone College. There are two community colleges, Trident Technical College and Miller-Motte Technical College. Most offer nondegree adult programs at moderate cost. In addition, Johnson and Wales University trains culinary students, and the Medical University of South Carolina is the largest medical school in South Carolina.

"I love it, and I tell everybody we love it," says Bob McCloskey, 62, a retired senior executive with Eaton Corp., who with wife Betsy, 60, lives part of the year on Kiawah Island and the rest of the year in Cleveland. The McCloskeys began visiting the Charleston area on vacation in the late 1970s.

With several other couples, they bought two vacation cottages on Kiawah and later bought a lot and built a home on the island. In 1997 they bought another lot and built their present place, a 5,300-square-foot, five-bedroom home on a lagoon. Bob, who has a 15 handicap, says he loves the golf and is a member of the Kiawah Island Club.

Three counties constitute the metro area: Charleston County with around 310,000 people, Berkeley with around 143,000, and Dorchester with about 96,000. The three counties make up what is called the Trident.

Within this sprawling, 3,163-square-mile tri-county area are dozens of individual towns and communities.

While Charleston has affordable middle-class subdivisions and neighborhoods that would not look out of place anywhere in the Southeast, two residential choices are Charleston's claim to real distinction. One is its famed historic district downtown. The other is the collection of barrier islands around Charleston, where the Atlantic Ocean, salt marshes and sand dunes paint a heady picture of breezy seaside living.

The downtown historic district, which is made up of a number of different neighborhoods, is framed by the confluence of the Ashley and Cooper rivers. The most sought-after area is called Below Broad, south of Broad Street at the tip of the peninsula. Homes here, mostly dating from the mid-18th to mid-19th centuries, usually go for $600,000 or more, with many selling for more than $1 million.

Other historic district neighborhoods include the French Quarter, named for the French Huguenots who once lived here, and Ansonborough, both slightly less pricey than Below Broad. Mazyck-Wraggborough, Har-leston Village and Radcliffeborough are less expensive.

Neighborhoods east of the Cooper River, which include Mount Pleasant, Sullivan's Island and the Isle of Palms, are among the fastest-growing locales in the region. Mount Pleasant, an area with a population of around 48,000, and one of the fastest-growing municipalities in the state, is a bedroom community with a variety of homes, old and new, starting at under $200,000.

Sullivan's Island is a laid-back beach community, once the place where African slaves arrived to be sold in Charleston's slave market. The Isle of Palms is a rambling residential beach area, and at its tip is Wild Dunes, a large resort and vacation home development. Other upscale developments include Dewees Island, a private island accessible only by boat, and Daniel Island, an ambi-

Charleston, SC

Transportation: Interstate 26 terminates in Charleston and connects about 60 miles northwest of Charleston with I-95. U.S. Highway 17 is a major north-south route. Charleston International Airport, off I-26 about one-half hour from downtown, is served by Continental, Delta, Midway, Northwest, TWA, US Airways and United Express, with a total of more than 50 daily departures. Amtrak provides daily service to Charleston. By water, the Intracoastal Waterway crosses Charleston Harbor.

Health: The Charleston area has 10 hospitals with a total of more than 2,100 beds and more than 17,000 health-care workers. The 596-bed Medical University of South Carolina Medical Center is a nationally recognized teaching hospital. Roper Hospital, part of CareAppliance Health Services, and Charleston Memorial Hospital are two other large medical centers. There also are a number of medical clinics around the area, including Kiawah-Seabrook Medical Care on Johns Island.

Housing options: William Means Real Estate/Christie's (Helen Geer), (843) 577-6651 or www.charlestonrealestate.com, specializes in historic district properties. **John M. Settle II, ReMax Realty,** (843) 556-4505 or www.johnsettle.com, handles residential properties around the area. Developments on the barrier islands around Charleston include: **Daniel Island,** (800) 958-5635 or (843) 971-7100, www.danielisland.com; **Dewees Island,** (800) 444-7352 or www.deweesisland.com; **Kiawah Island Real Estate,** (800) 277-7008 or (843) 768-3400, www.kiawahisland.com; **Seabrook Island Realty,** (800) 358-6556 or (843) 768-2560, www.seabrookrealty.com; and **Wild Dunes Real Estate,** (800) 562-9453 or (843) 886-2500, www.wilddunesrealestate.com. Located 20 miles from downtown Charleston, **Southern Palms** is a Jensen's Residential Community for those age 55 and older, featuring manufactured homes with a clubhouse, swimming pool and organized activities. Homes start in the $70,000s; for information, call (843) 875-6441 or visit www.jensencommunities.com.

Visitor lodging: Charleston is famous for its intimate inns and B&Bs, of which there are dozens in the historic district. The nine-room Two Meeting Street Inn, $165-$310 (no credit cards), is one of the most charming, (843) 723-7322 or www.twomeeting street.com. Hampton Inn Historic District, $99-$249, offers attractive accommodations in a historic setting, (800) 426-7866 or (843) 723-4000, www.hamptoninn. com. Visitor accommodations also are available at Kiawah, (800) 576-1570 or www.kiawahresort.com; Seabrook, (800) 845-2233 or www.seabrook.com; and Wild Dunes, (888) 845-8926 or www.wild dunes.com.

Information: The Charleston Metro Chamber, P.O. Box 975, Charleston, SC 29402, (843) 577-2510 or www.charlestonchamber.net, offers a free relocation package.

tious development that is still in its early stages. The latter ultimately may have as many as 7,000 homes and 15,000 people, with a planned "island town" where residents will live and work.

West of the Ashley River is a group of islands that are diverse in size and population: James, Johns, Folly, Kiawah and Seabrook. James Island, closest to downtown Charleston, has a mix of lower-middle and middle-class areas, along with upscale sections such as the Country Club of Charleston area, where homes on the Intracoastal Waterway can go for the low seven figures. Some houses on Johns Island are old and shabby. Folly, sometimes compared to Tybee Island near Savannah and even to Key West, is getting new attention from developers and buyers. Beach erosion here continues to be a serious problem, despite expensive beach reclamation and renourishment projects.

Kiawah Island consists of 10,000 acres with 10 miles of beautiful beach and five golf courses, designed by Gary Player, Pete Dye, Tom Fazio, Jack Nicklaus and Clyde Johnston. It's one of the 250 wealthiest communities in America, and the wealthiest in South Carolina; the average home sale in 2001 was more than $1.3 million. Slightly less up-market is nearby Seabrook Island, with lots from around $60,000 to more than $2 million, condos from around $135,000 to $600,000, and homes mostly from $400,000 to around $2.5 million.

Despite some pricey real estate in the historic district and on the islands, the median sales price for existing single-family homes in metropolitan Charleston is a more down-to-earth $153,800, according to the latest statistics from the National Association of Realtors. Modestly priced property is available in suburban areas. North Charleston, a commercial and industrial area, has some of the least-expensive housing in the region, with the average home selling for about $60,000. Some upscale developments are in the works here. Intersected by I-26, this area was once home to the North Charleston Navy Center, which closed in the mid-1990s.

Tom and JoAnn Nipper chose the historic district as their pied à terre for retirement. As a senior executive at Belk department store — he retired as chairman of the central division, with responsibility for 59 Belk stores — Tom moved to Charleston after postings in Wilmington and Charlotte, NC. It took a while, Tom says, to find just the right place, but they found it: a renovated mid-19th-century "single" house. A single house is a unique Charleston architectural style. It has a single room on the street with additional rooms behind it. Usually there is at least one porch — or piazza, as Charlestonians call it — on the side.

A single house may be just one or several stories high. The house Tom, 61, and JoAnn, 59, bought has three levels, with three bedrooms and three and half baths. It has dens on both the second and third levels. The floor-level windows fold up so that for a party the windows become open doors. The interior is mostly natural cypress and mahogany with heart pine floors. In the back is an architecturally designed garden, and there's off-street parking, rare in Charleston.

Tom and JoAnn immediately felt at home in their new community. "I don't know that there's a more friendly city than Charleston — people took us in right away," he says. Active in civic affairs, Tom is on the board of the Spoleto Festival and headed up this year's United Way campaign. JoAnn is active in volunteer work and at the Charleston Stage Company at the Dock Theater, the oldest theater building in America. The couple enjoys being able to walk to restaurants and other activities downtown.

While the Nippers wanted a historic house, many who retire to Charleston are looking for a place on or near the water. Dick Murdock, 60, a retired corporate pilot who traveled the world flying with General Electric, looked at several island locales around Charleston, including Wild Dunes and Seabrook, but eventually chose Kiawah Island.

"It's one of the most beautiful places I've seen in the world," Dick says. He and wife Jan, 54, now live in a three-bedroom, 3,000-square-foot home at Kiawah. Dick says he enjoys the year-round outdoor activities such as boating and tennis. Jan is a bicyclist and enjoys riding on miles of firm, packed beach sand at Kiawah.

Henry and Gayle Fellers moved to Seabrook Island in 1997 from Knoxville, where Henry, 56, was an environmental engineer and Gayle, 52, was a psychologist. Henry is retired but does some consulting work in Charleston. Gayle no longer has a private psychology practice but runs a learning center for children on neighboring Johns Island. The center has more than 100 volunteers, mostly from Seabrook and Kiawah islands, who tutor kids from lower socioeconomic groups. Gayle also teaches as an adjunct professor at The Citadel in Charleston, one of nine institutions of higher learning in the Charleston area.

The Fellerses rented for a year while their home, a typical Lowcountry traditional-style house, was being built. Building in this area can be a long process, often taking up to 18 to 24 months, Gayle says. "We call it the Slow Country," she says, noting that the booming local economy means that it's difficult to get subcontractors in a timely fashion. The final quality is high, she says, but it can take a long time to finish the job.

The former Tennesseans live on the marsh about a half-mile from the ocean. "You can hear the ocean at night," Gayle says. "Friends from New York thought it was traffic."

Deer, raccoons, otter, bobcats and all kinds of wildlife run through their yard, which has live oaks and magnolias, Gayle says. The natural beauty is special, Gayle says, but the downside is that the no-see-ums and mosquitoes "can be terrible" when the sea breezes die down.

It's been very easy to make friends, Gayle says. "We're all transplants here," she says, and most are from the Northeast. She does not know many other couples from the South at Seabrook, she says.

A drawback is the drive to Charleston, which on the two-lane roads takes about 45 minutes. The fact that the state chose to repair both of the old-fashioned drawbridges to Charleston at the same time doesn't help, she says. There's a Piggly-Wiggly supermarket about seven miles away, but residents drive into Charleston for other shopping needs. "You learn to combine errands and make a day of it," Gayle says.

The long drive and the lack of a large

hospital nearby (there is a medical clinic on Johns Island) are reasons why some residents of Seabrook and Kiawah might eventually move away as they get older, she says. But there's wonderful theater, a great art community and orchestra in Charleston, Gayle notes.

The metropolitan area's population tops half a million, and with so many bottlenecking bridges over rivers and inlets, narrow one-way streets and meandering roads, at times the traffic seems to be worse than in a city of twice that population. Plus, there's the impact of four million tourists a year, most of whom arrive by car. Only one interstate highway, I-26, leads to Charleston.

Ocean breezes moderate the heat in seaside areas, but inland a few miles the thermometer on some days tops 100 degrees, with humidity over 80 percent. In antebellum times, wealthy Lowcountry planters spent summers in the mountains of North Carolina, and to-day not a few retirees arrange to travel in the summer or return to cooler climes of former homes in New England or elsewhere.

Many newcomers pay high premiums for homeowners and flood insurance if they live in a flood plain near the coast. The combined cost of the Fellerses' home insurance is about $6,000 a year, Gayle says.

Memories of Hurricane Hugo in 1989 still linger. While the damage from Hugo has long since been repaired, some wary retirees keep the Weather Channel on around the clock when hurricane season arrives.

Seabrook Island residents Peter and Annie Van Every installed hurricane shutters on their waterfront house as a precaution. The couple lived in San Francisco, North Carolina, London and Switzerland before moving to Seabrook in 1999. They had visited the area on a number of occasions, beginning in 1982.

Annie, 52, is an artist and potter. When they built their 5,000-square-foot house with a dock on a creek, marsh and lagoon at Seabrook, they included a pottery studio for Annie. "The biggest room in the house is my studio," she says. She sells her one-of-a-kind pottery pieces, which she describes as "funky, with a Southwestern or African look," in galleries in Charleston. Annie also works several days a week at a crafts co-op downtown.

Husband Peter, 58, formerly general counsel for a large international corporation, is a "triathlete," says Annie. That means he plays golf and tennis and fishes, she says, all of which are excellent at Seabrook.

Though Annie says she loves the Southwest and admits she was interested in living there after retirement, she's enjoying the Charleston area. "People here are really friendly," Annie says.●

Charlottesville, Virginia

Retirees follow Jefferson's lead to Virginia

By Bob Lane

There's nothing like the presence of 20,000 college kids to help keep you young, and Charlottesville, home to the University of Virginia, is a college town with a growing appeal to retirees fleeing the congested, high-priced suburbs of northern Virginia and the Northeast. Escapees from Washington, Philadelphia, New York and other big cities seem delighted to find this central Virginia combination of livability, affordability and sophistication.

"I'm amazed at the people from all over the U.S. and the world who are moving here," says Harold Schrock, 67, who with wife Theodora, 59, came from northern Virginia. "We couldn't be happier," says Harold, a retired homebuilder. Indeed, two of his sisters have followed him to the area.

Those moving to "Thomas Jefferson's Virginia" needn't leave behind the worldly pleasures they've learned to love, either. Supermarkets in Charlottesville sell fresh sushi and organic produce. Restaurants serve Brazilian, Thai, Vietnam-ese, Indo-Pakistani, Japanese, Szechuan, German and Greek food (not to mention Southern-style fried chicken and cheeseburgers). There are lattes to sip at Starbucks and a dozen other coffee houses. Jazz and Shakespeare weekends are as common as crabgrass. Sports buffs can follow polo, steeplechase racing, lacrosse and mainstream NCAA football and basketball. Nearby are mountains to climb, ski slopes to explore, golf courses to conquer and lakes to fish.

All around Charlottesville are the liv-

Population: 45,049 in Charlottesville, 79,236 in Albemarle County.

Location: Charlottesville is in the Piedmont Plateau of Central Virginia. It is 110 miles southwest of Washington, DC, and 70 miles northwest of Richmond. Beginning just west of Charlottesville are the Blue Ridge Mountains. Shenandoah National Park, the Skyline Drive and the Blue Ridge Parkway all are within a short drive of Charlottesville.

Climate:

	High	Low
January	44	26
July	86	65

Average relative humidity: 52%

Rain: 47 inches.

Snow: 24 inches.

Cost of living: The overall cost of living in Charlottesville is estimated to be 5 percent higher than the national average.

Housing costs: The median residential sale in Albemarle County was $219,000 in 2001. However, real estate prices vary greatly, ranging from under $100,000 for a small condo to more than $1 million for a large home in an exclusive development. In mid-2000, residential listings with the Charlottesville Area Board of Realtors ranged from $40,000 for a mobile home on 2.5 acres to $7,750,000 for 10-bedroom, eight-bath, 8,600-square-foot home and farm. Local real estate agents say retirees mov-ing to the area are likely to spend $200,000 to $350,000 or more for a newer home in a desirable neighborhood. One-bedroom apartments in desirable areas typically rent for $500 to $750 a month, and two-bedroom apartments for $700 to $950. Student demand for apartments is high.

Sales tax: 4.5% (3.5% state and 1% local)

Sales tax exemptions: Medicines are exempt. The state is phasing in a reduction of sales tax on food for human consumption, and some food items are exempt.

State income tax: For married couples filing jointly and single filers, the rate is graduated from 2% of taxable income up to $3,000 to 5.75% on amounts over $17,000.

Income tax exemptions: Social Security benefits are exempt. There is an $800 personal exemption for residents age 65 or older. There is a $6,000 deduction per person from adjusted gross income for residents age 62-64, and a $12,000 deduction per person for residents 65 and older.

Intangibles tax: None.

Estate tax: None, except the state's pick-up portion of the federal tax, applicable to taxable estates above $1 million.

Property tax: Albemarle County prop-erty taxes are $7.60 per $1,000 of assessed value. Charlottesville residents pay $11.10 per $1,000 of assessed value. Homes are assessed at 100% of market value. Annual tax on a $200,000 home in Charlottesville would be about $2,220. Personal property taxes are assessed on automobiles and other vehicles; the rate in Charlottesville is $42.80 per $1,000 of valuation.

Homestead exemption: Low-income persons 65 and older may qualify for reductions in property tax rates.

Religion: The metropolitan area is home to more than 200 churches and synagogues representing most religions and denominations, including Buddhist, Greek Orthodox and Mennonite.

Education: Retirees can take courses at the University of Virginia or at Piedmont Virginia Community College. Virginia's Citizen Scholar Program allows residents age 60 and older who have lived in Virginia at least one year to audit credit courses or enroll in noncredit courses on a space available basis, at no charge. Participants may attend any of Virginia's state institutions of higher learning, including Piedmont Virginia Community College and the University of Virginia through its Division of Continuing Education. Credit classes also are free for those with taxable incomes of $10,000 or less; for others, tuition for credit coursing echoes of history, from the homes of presidents Jefferson, Monroe and Madison to the bedroom of John-Boy Walton. For vinophiles there's another plus: Central Virginia is one of the East Coast's principal wine grape growing regions, with more than 50 vineyards in operation. Thomas Jefferson is considered the father of American wine, as he made his own wines, encouraged Americans to drink wine and selected the first wines to be stocked at the White House.

Most retirees who relocate to Charlottesville say the presence of the University of Virginia was what first attracted them to the area. "I've always been drawn to a university town," says Jeanne Chamales, 58, who first visited Charlottesville on the college tour circuit with her daughter. "The university brings so much to the area, including speakers from around the world," adds Jeanne, who moved to Charlottesville with husband John, 59, from Washington, DC, in 1993.

Bruce Copeland, 75, who with his wife, Carol, also 75, moved to Charlottesville from West Virginia in 1996, agrees. "The university has been a plus, even more so than we expected," he says.

UVa, as it is known, was founded in 1819 by Thomas Jefferson as his last great act of public service. Jefferson spearheaded the legislative initiative to charter the university, chose its location, planned its curriculum, designed its first buildings and served as its first rector. The Rotunda, which Jefferson modeled on the Pantheon in Rome, was designed, with the adjoining two-story Pavilions housing faculty and one-story rooms housing students, to be the heart of Jefferson's "academical village" or community of scholars. Having survived a fire and several redesigns, the neoclassical Rotunda and companion buildings along what Virginians call "the Lawn" remain to this day the focal point of the university. During the United States Bicentennial in 1976, the American Institute of Architects recognized Jefferson's academical village design as the most significant achievement of American architecture in the past 200 years.

Today, the University of Virginia has more than 13,000 undergraduate and 8,000 graduate students, about 30 percent of them from outside Virginia. UVa competes with other top state universi-

Charlottesville, VA

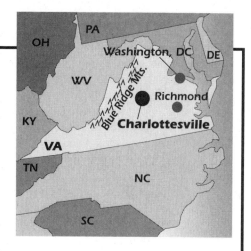

es at UVa is $211 per credit hour, but may very by class.

Transportation: Charlottesville-Albemarle Airport is a small, modern airport with service to Philadelphia, Pittsburgh, Cincinnati, Charlotte, New York and elsewhere on regional commuter carriers Comair/Delta Connection, United Express, US Airways Express and Continental Express. Many Charlottesville residents drive to Washington or Richmond for jet service. Interstate 64 runs east-west through Charlottesville, connecting with I-95 in Richmond, I-81 in Staunton and I-85 in Petersburg. AMTRAK provides passenger rail service with a station in Charlottesville.

Health: The University of Virginia Medical Center, a 591-bed regional acute-care research and teaching hospital, has been rated among the top hospitals in the country. Martha Jefferson is a private 180-bed acute-care hospital.

Housing options: The Charlottesville area offers a wide choice of housing choices. Among them: **Forest Lakes** is a planned development in northern Albemarle County off Highway 29, with townhomes and single-family homes from $125,000 to $150,000, (800) 455-7222. **Glenmore**, a gated country club community in eastern Albemarle County, has homes from $390,000 to more than $1 million, (800) 776-5111, and

Fontana, near Route 20 and Route 200 East near Charlottesville, offers homes from $230,000 to $350,000, (877) 984-6310. Contact local agents for information about **Ednam Forest** in western Albemarle County, with homes from $440,000 to $800,000, and **Lake Monticello**, a recreation residential area in adjoining Fluvanna County, with lots from around $10,000 and homes from $95,000 to $500,000 and higher. **Branchlands** is a moderately priced retirement village with apartment suites offering housekeeping and meal service, (434) 973-9044. **Real Estate III**, the largest real estate firm in the area, offers a package of information for those relocating to Charlottesville; contact Linda Oliver, relocation director, at (877) 979-7464. Other real estate professionals who can provide information for prospective residents include Karen Kehoe, **Re/Max Excellence**, (800) 818-7629, and Stephen T. McLean, president of **McLean Faulconer Realtors**, (434) 295-1131.

Visitor lodging: Charlottesville has more than 20 motels and hotels and nearly as many bed-and-breakfast inns, with about 3,000 rooms altogether. Within walking distance of UVa and the Medical Center are several pleasant chain properties, including Hampton Inn, $80-$130 for doubles, (800) 426-7866, and Red Roof Inn, $69-$110, (800) 843-7663. A new Courtyard by Marriott recently opened, (800) 321-2211. Silver Thatch Inn, (434) 978-4686, is Charlottesville's oldest country inn, dating from around 1780. The inn has seven rooms, several with fireplaces and canopy beds, with doubles from $125 to $170. Boar's Head Inn, (800) 476-1988, on 53 acres at the University of Virginia, is a resort with Colonial-era furnishings, a restored gristmill, tennis courts, golf, spa, hot air ballooning and an excellent restaurant. The inn's recently renovated 171 rooms go for $188 to $500.

Information: Charlottesville Regional Chamber of Commerce, P.O. Box 1564, Charlottesville, VA 22902, (434) 295-3141 or www.cvillechamber.org. It offers a newcomer package for $13.50, including shipping and handling.

ties and even with Ivy League colleges for student talent. The university's architecture, law and medical post-graduate programs are nationally ranked as among the best in the country.

Retirees say the cultural activities, bookstores, sports and youthful sense of intellectual curiosity that accompany campus life are, for them, the most important aspects of a university town. For example, Charlottesville has more than two dozen bookstores, and the University of Virginia has 14 libraries with more than 4.4 million volumes. UVa has an active drama department, and there are several community theater groups in the area.

For baby boomers who recall their college days in the era of long-haired hippies, flower power and the Rolling Stones, the appearance of University of Virginia students "on Grounds" — UVa-speak for on campus — may be a surprise. While a few sport pierced orifices and tattoos, most seem fresh-scrubbed and refreshingly clean-cut. On a warm spring day, students lounge in small groups on the Lawn or participate in a race for charity. At "The Corner" on Main Street, inexpensive eateries attract hungry young undergrads and older townies alike.

UVa is not the only college in the area. Piedmont Virginia Community College, on a hill across from Monticello, has about 7,000 students. PVCC, in partnership with Mary Baldwin College, also offers a four-year adult degree program.

The availability of superb medical care is another reason for Charlottesville's appeal to retirees. The University of Virginia Health System includes nationally known schools of medicine and nursing, along with the UVa Medical Center, a 591-bed regional acute-care hospital with nearly 600 board-certified or board-eligible physicians on staff. The Medical Center has been rated one of the top 100 hospitals in the United States by HCIA-Sachs, a health-care information research firm, and the Health Network, a health-oriented cable television network. It has specialty treatment centers for heart disease, cancer, digestive and neurological disorders and other health problems. Also in Charlottesville is Martha Jefferson Hospital, a well-regarded, 180-bed private hospital.

Bob and Pat Zimmer decided to move to Charlottesville from Mobile, AL, in 1997 in part because of a need for specialized medical care. Bob, 76, has rheumatoid arthritis and needed a knee replacement. "The medical school here keeps a lot of spare knees on hand," Bob jokes. But even retirees who are in good health say that knowing that such good medical care is close at hand is a comfort to them.

Having moved to a college town, many retirees find they develop a new interest in college sports, especially less-well-known sports. Football and men's basketball are the big-time sports at UVa, and the Cavaliers — or Wahoos or just 'Hoos, as they're locally known — have had nationally ranked teams. But the university fields teams in many sports, including swimming, golf, volleyball and crew. Tickets for these events are far cheaper and easier to obtain than for the major events.

Retirees who want to stay active find a lot to do at the Senior Center, a nonprofit community organization open to anyone age 50 or over. The Senior Center, in its own modern building, has some 60 groups and activities such as investment clubs, lecture series, arts and crafts groups, fitness classes and computer classes, according to executive director Peter Thompson. A travel program through the center offers day trips to Washington, DC, for $30 a person, as well as other travel opportunities.

Shopping options in the Charlottesville area are varied. The area has one enclosed mall, Fashion Square, anchored by JC Penney and Belk department stores. Retirees say they would like to see other national department stores in Charlottesville, but they note that for major shopping expeditions they can go to Richmond or Washington. Charlottesville's Historic Downtown Mall is a gentrified pedestrian-only shopping center with brick streets, flowers and a good selection of restaurants and shops. U.S. Highway 29, a major thoroughfare, sports the usual collection of strip centers and suburban chains. While traffic and congestion don't compare with the situation in northern Virginia and other population centers, suburban sprawl, especially along the Highway 29 corridor, is a growing concern for many residents.

No state in the Union takes a back seat to Virginia in its important role in American history, so exploring the past is a favorite pastime of Charlottesville residents and visitors. The most famous site, of course, is Monticello, Thomas Jefferson's incomparable plantation home on a hill about two miles southeast of modern-day Charlottesville. "All my wishes end, where I hope my days will end, at Monticello," said Jefferson, and indeed he did die there, on July 4, 1826, precisely on the 50th anniversary of the adoption of the Declaration of Independence. Monticello is open to the public year-round, and local residents get a discount on admission.

Also in the Charlottesville area are the homes of presidents James Madison and James Monroe, both open to visitors. Several museums in the area focus on the history of Virginia, and the Civil War battlefields of Chancellorsville and Fredericksburg are within easy driving distance. One more contemporary attraction is Walton's Mountain Museum, on Route 617 in Schuyler about 20 miles southwest of Charlottesville. Earl Hamner Jr., author of the books that were the basis of the popular TV series, "The Waltons," grew up in Schuyler.

Virginia's long history and Charlottesville's collection of notable FFVs, or First Families of Virginia, have led some prospective retirees to fear that local residents would be snobbish and stand-offish, but retirees to Charlottesville generally say that has not been the case. Brian Mandeville, a former senior executive with a medical devices company in Minneapolis who moved here with wife Jean in 1996, says, "The people are wonderful, grand, friendly, good-mannered — trust and a handshake just come with this community."

Agrees Jeanne Chamales, "The people are so friendly and hospitable. There is that Southern hospitality thing that is the real thing — holding the door for you, not cutting you off in traffic."

Not everyone is totally in love with Charlottesville, however. Bob and Pat Zimmer, who moved here in search of good medical care and to be closer to family in Washington, say that while their neighbors at Brookmill condominiums are very nice, they find Charlottesville "kind of boring," according to Pat. They say that compared to other areas where they lived after Bob retired as a plant manager for Anchor Hocking, including Hendersonville, NC, and Mobile, AL, the arts community in Charlottesville seems surprisingly small, especially for a university town, and there's not as much as they'd like in the way of shopping and cultural activities. They also say they feel the University of Virginia doesn't reach out to retirees the way some other colleges do.

But there seldom are complaints about the weather. The moderate four-season climate in Charlottesville appeals to many retirees. In one survey of weather professionals, the American Association of State Climatologists, Charlottesville rated behind only Asheville, NC, as having the "most desirable climate in the Eastern United States." New residents such as Brian and Jean Mandeville, who moved to Charlottesville from Minneapolis, say the four-season climate is one of the things they like best about the area. Both are runners and golfers.

Charlottesville is not for those seeking a consistently warm climate, however. The area gets an average of about two feet of snow a year, and snow skiing is a winter sport at Wintergreen and other ski areas in the mountains just to the west of Charlottesville. The winter of 1995-96 dropped about 55 inches of snow on Charlottesville, making it the snowiest winter in a century, but on average, about one in 10 winters sees no snow at all.

Spring is usually pleasantly mild in Charlottesville, inviting outdoor activities, and fall brings invigorating weather and colorful autumn foliage, especially in the nearby Blue Ridge Mountains. Summers can be hot, with temperatures hitting the 90s. To beat the heat, "we play tennis at 7:30 in the morning," says Bruce Copeland. Humidity, while much higher than in dry Western states, is lower in the Shenandoah Valley area than in most of the rest of the East Coast except parts of New England. The growing season extends to 200 days or more, making it an ideal climate for gardening. In late spring and summer, violent thunderstorms and, on rare occasions, even tornadoes may occur.

Although Charlottesville itself is in Virginia's Piedmont Plateau at an elevation of just 480 feet, it is within shouting distance of some of the East's most beautiful mountain scenery in the Shenan-

doah Valley and Blue Ridge Mountains. The Chamaleses are typical of retirees who were attracted by the scenery. "We were drawn by the mountains. The landscape here is so beautiful. The mountains are friendly, not so high that they are overpowering," says Jeanne, who previously lived briefly in Washington, DC, and for 13 years in New Jersey.

Richard Worch, 65, a retired civil engineer with the Federal Aviation Administration, who now lives with wife Betty, 64, on a hill overlooking the Blue Ridge Mountains, can't say enough about the natural beauty of the area. "We love the area, the scenery, watching the change of seasons from our house," he says. Richard and Betty moved to Charlottesville from Washington, DC, in 1996.

Those relocating to Charlottesville have a variety of options for housing, from moderately priced downtown condos catering to retirees to gated golf communities to horse farms going for a million dollars and up.

"Some move to golf communities like Farmington Country Club or Glenmore, or subdivision neighborhoods like Ednam Forest, but there are plenty of people who retire to farms out in the county," says Stephen T. McLean, president of McLean Faulconer Realtors.

Says Karen Kehoe, an agent with Re/Max Excellence Realty in Charlottesville, "Many retirees like Branchlands. It is near the Senior Center. They can have dining with other seniors if they desire. Another area retirees like is Brookmill, which is located just adjacent to Senior Center, although this neighborhood has a mix of all ages."

Harold and Theodora Schrock, who moved from northern Virginia, live in a house they built on four acres near the town of Ivy, west of Charlottesville. It's a 4,000-square-foot contemporary designed by a West Coast architect. An unusual feature is the octagon-shaped sunroom, 20 feet across with a 24-foot-high ceiling and two rock walls to absorb heat in winter. The octagonal shape is a nod to the famous architecture of Jefferson's Monticello. The Schrocks' house also has extensive decking — some 2,000 square feet — with mountain views.

Brian and Jean Mandeville say their biggest decision when they moved to

Charlottesville in early 1996 was "whether we wanted to buy a lot of acreage and live on an old horse farm in the country, or in a new neighborhood." They decided on Glenmore, a gated golf community with homes from $390,000 to $1 million-plus, because they felt it would be easier to meet people and to get involved. They built a 6,000-square-foot, two-story, Virginia-style brick home with American traditional features. "We can look out our back window and see Monticello," says Brian.

One drawback, or advantage, depending on your point of view, about Albemarle County is that a significant part of the land is tied up in large family owned farms and estates, some of several thousand acres. This keeps the area looking rural in the Jeffersonian gentleman farmer tradition, but it means that land is expensive. Buildable lots can cost $80,000 to $200,000 or more. The Jefferson Highway area, for example, has been called the area's Millionaire's Row. This is fox hunt country, and working horse farms and estates line the road.

But the Charlottesville area has many middle-class communities as well. For example, Forest Lakes is a planned community of townhomes and single-family homes north of town, with prices starting at around $125,000. Land and housing generally are cheaper in surrounding counties, including Fluvanna to the southeast and Greene to the north. Parts of both counties are less than a half-hour commute from Charlottesville. Says Kehoe, the real estate agent, "Retirees from out of state are looking strongly also at Lake Monticello, a 20-minute ride from Charlottesville. It's a 300-acre lake with boating, golf, dining, swimming, sandy beaches, etc. It's a planned community with something for everyone. Prices start in the $90,000s and go to $500,000. What a mix, eh?"

Housing costs, of course, are relative, and opinions of retirees depend on where they have lived in the past. Bruce Copeland, for instance, says that his home about two miles from Charlottesville is a bargain compared to Evanston, IL, another college town (home to Northwestern University), where he and his wife previously lived. "We have a nicer home here, at one-third of the cost of the house in Evanston, and taxes are a quarter of taxes there," he says.●

Clemson, South Carolina

College spirit enriches this lakeside town in the rolling South Carolina hills

By Mary Lu Abbott

Two centuries ago, as calendars turned into the 1800s, Americans were discovering a verdant corner of South Carolina, building second homes there and retiring to enjoy the scenery and climate. As the new century unfolds, the scenario plays anew for modern-day retirees in the foothills of the mountains that bond the Carolinas and Georgia.

Known as the "upcountry," or upstate, the region about halfway between the metropolitan areas of Atlanta and Charlotte retains its natural beauty, the rolling hills and towering trees enhanced by a string of lakes. Glimpses of the distant Blue Ridge Mountains provide visible evidence for their name. Historically agricultural, the region also is attracting light industry and high-tech companies, some of their buildings set along country roads where signs still alert drivers to the possibility of deer darting from the woods.

Nestled in the hills of historic Pickens, Oconee and Anderson counties are a number of small towns, the most notable being Clemson about 11 miles from the traffic on Interstate 85. On the shores of Lake Hartwell and partially hidden among canopies of trees, Clemson exudes a serene aura, blending history and tradition with the energy and vibrancy of the renowned university for which it's named.

David and Julia Wise had plane tickets to Arizona to check out retirement sites there when a friend suggested they consider the Clemson area. "We came and liked it so much we bought a house in two days," says Julia. "We like the weather and the four seasons — spring and fall are glorious. We're close to the mountains, and it's a half-day drive to the ocean."

David was a veterinarian with the Air Force, so the Wises moved frequently, and they sampled a couple of other retirement sites before settling here. After spending a summer in Beaufort, SC, on the coast, they decided it was "too hot and buggy," and after a year in Cascade, CO, they thought it was too isolated. When they came to this region, they first bought in Seneca, about five miles from Clemson, and for several years David served the university as veterinarian. In 1994, they moved to the Clemson Downs retirement community, where they have a spacious apartment and enjoy community activities that include classical concerts in a new entertainment facility.

Chuck and Betty Cruickshank, who lived in upstate New York outside Rochester, discovered Clemson when they came through the area to visit their sons at the University of Georgia at Athens. "The Finger Lakes area (of New York) looks like this. It reminded us of home — without the snow," says Betty, 68. They also considered retiring to nearby Asheville, NC, and to Florida.

Though the town's population is only about 12,000, that represents a major growth since 1960 when residents numbered about 1,500. Each fall, the population more than doubles as about 17,000 undergraduate and graduate students start classes at the university.

Beyond simply sharing names, the town and university are closely intertwined and form an integral part of South Carolina history that's dear to the hearts of thousands of Southerners. Clemson was home to the eminent orator and statesman John C. Calhoun, 1782-1850, who was in national politics for 40 years, serving about 20 years in Congress (most of them as a senator), as secretary of war for James Monroe, as vice president for John Quincy Adams and Andrew Jackson and as secretary of state for John Tyler. Many may recall from U.S. history classes that Calhoun, Daniel Webster and Henry Clay were eloquent, powerful speakers of their time and that Calhoun became a staunch states' rights advocate.

Born at Abbeville to the south, Calhoun bought a small two-story cottage here in 1825 when he was vice president and expanded it for his family, establishing a plantation known as Fort Hill. The community became known as Calhoun and was part of the Pendleton District, which was attracting wealthy, well-educated plantation owners and other well-to-do families who wanted to escape the sultry summers in the "lowcountry," as the swampy coastal area is called. They came "upcountry" to build homes in the mountains where summers were more moderate and there were cool streams and abundant waterfalls.

Calhoun's daughter, Anna Maria, married Thomas Green Clemson, an advocate of science education and its application in agriculture. Clemson bought the plantation from Calhoun, and like other Southerners after the Civil War pondered the economic future of the region. Upon his death in 1888 without any heirs, he bequeathed the plantation and the rest of his estate to South Carolina to start an agricultural and mechanical college. Thus Clemson was founded in 1889, graduated its first class in 1893 and over the years diversified its curriculum and became a major university. A national historic landmark open to visitors, the Calhoun home sits on a tree-covered hilltop surrounded by college buildings. Most of the campus and some of the town that grew around it, now named Clemson, were part of the plantation.

"The combination of small town and university gives it a unique quality," says Walter Cook of the attributes that he and his wife, Grace, like about Clemson. "Students bring a vitality and energy to the community."

In their 60s, the Cooks were pleasantly surprised at the numerous events in which they could participate and the educational stimulation from the university. They moved here in 1991 from western Pennsylvania after he retired from Quaker State Corp., and for three years he worked in corporate development for the university.

The Wises, who are in their early 70s, like the Clemson area for its "large number of people with the same cultural and educational level and social interests as ours," says David. Julia enjoys the diversity of the town, from its many university offerings to its proximity to Atlanta.

The Cruickshanks also take advantage of the cultural programs, entertainment and sports provided by the university. "The new Brooks Center for the Performing Arts is a beautiful theater with perfect acoustics, and there's

Clemson, SC

Population: About 11,939 residents in town, about 17,000 enrolled in Clemson University.

Location: In the foothills of the Blue Ridge Mountains in the northwestern corner of the state, about 30 miles southwest of the booming Greenville area and about 125 miles from Atlanta to the southwest and Charlotte to the northeast. Altitude is 850 feet.

Climate:

	High	Low
January	50	30
July	88	68

Average relative humidity: 54%

Rain: 51 inches.

Snow: 6 inches.

Cost of living: Average (specific index not available).

Average housing cost: $125,000 in the Clemson-Pendleton area, including some lake property.

Sales tax: 7%

Sales tax exemptions: Prescription drugs.

State income tax: For married couples filing jointly and single filers, the rates are graduated in six tiers from 2.5% on the first $2,400 of taxable income to 7% on taxable income above $12,000.

Income tax exemptions: Social Security benefits are exempt. Retirees who are drawing income from qualified retirement plans may deduct up to $3,000 of that income.

Intangibles tax: None.

Estate tax: None, except the state's portion of the federal tax, applicable to taxable estates above $1 million.

Property tax: Clemson homeowners pay a tax rate of $292 ($88 city, $204 county) per $1,000 in valuation, with homes assessed at 4% of market value. Owners receive sales tax credits from the city (currently .001543 of the market value) and county (currently .001496 of market value) and property tax relief from the state for up to $399.20 for homes valued above $100,000. Gross yearly tax on a $125,000 home would be about $1,460 without credits or exemptions. A personal property tax is assessed on vehicles and boats.

Homestead exemption: In addition to the credits noted above, at age 65 owners receive an exemption of $20,000 off the market value of their homes and further credits based on the homestead exemption.

Personal property tax: Same city and county tax rates and sales tax credits apply to vehicles and boats, which are assessed at 10.5% of market value.

Religion: There are about two dozen places of worship in the immediate area. Jewish synagogues are located in nearby Anderson and Greenville.

Education: Seniors can audit classes free at Clemson, which also offers some noncredit, continuing-education programs.

Transportation: Clemson Area Transit runs free bus service around the campus and town. There's Amtrak service, and Greenville-Spartanburg Airport has commercial jet flights.

Health: The 160-bed Oconee Memorial Hospital, located in neighboring Seneca, has 110 doctors and provides emergency services, including cardiac care. More extensive medical services are available in Anderson, about 20 miles away, and in Greenville, the regional hub, about 30 miles away.

Housing options: There are older neighborhoods and newer subdivisions in Clemson and adjacent Pendleton, and there are gated communities, some with golf courses, around the adjacent lakes, particularly Keowee. Among options popular with retirees: **Heritage Oaks**, a landscaped subdivision with green spaces in Pendleton, is about 3 years old and has homes from the $99,000s to the $140,000s. **Magnolia Point** in Pendleton includes lawn maintenance for its single-family homes, which run $98,000-$102,000. In Clemson, **Country Walk** is a master-planned community with a pool, clubhouse and putting green among amenities; homes start at $200,000. **Clemson Downs**, (864) 654-1155, is a retirement community with private homes and apartments, assisted-living apartments and a nursing care center. Around the lakes, **Keowee Key**, (800) 537-5253, is one of the region's premier resort communities with a golf course, country club and water sports; condominiums and townhomes start around $65,000 and homes from about $125,000. Among the real estate agencies that can help locate homes is Carolina Real Estate, (864) 654-6202.

Visitor lodging: The Clemson-Pendleton area has B&B lodging, motels and rental properties on the lakes. Among choices are the Hampton Inn, (800) HAMPTON, which has double rooms from $69.

Information: Clemson Area Chamber of Commerce, P.O. Box 1622, Clemson, SC 29633, (800) 542-0746, www.clemsonchamber.org.

a Clemson Little Theater," says Betty. Besides numerous university productions and performances, there are concerts and programs by emerging and established artists from elsewhere. Betty says ticket prices usually are lower here than in larger cities nearby.

Come fall, Clemson's colors show not only in beautiful foliage but also in university sports as the orange carpet is rolled out for the football team to come thundering into Clemson Memorial Stadium to the roar of 80,000-plus fans. The site is more commonly known as Death Valley Stadium, so named back in the 1940s by an opposing coach whose team suffered frequently at the hands of the Clemson Tigers. The nickname was enhanced in the 1960s when an alumnus placed a rock from Death Valley, CA, on the players' route into the stadium. Facing a tough foe, the Clemson coach suggested the players rub the Death Valley rock for good luck as they passed it. After the win that day, the ceremonial touching of the rock by each player has become an opening tradition for every game.

With many championships to their credit and repeated trips to bowl games, the Tigers draw large crowds to their stadium, which officially seats about 80,000. Rising 177 feet on one side and 159 feet on the other side, the stadium exerts a commanding presence in this small community where trees are taller than nearly all the buildings. The stadium also hosts major concerts.

With years of experience, the town seems to know how to handle an influx of 80,000 or more fans for games and other events. Several highways provide access, and main routes become one-way into town before major events and one-way out afterward. Those in the know come early or stay late and enjoy tailgate parties. The town also has many restaurants and

more accommodations than many other towns its size.

Betty says the football fans, many of them repeat visitors and alumni, generally know where they're going and where to park, but traffic problems sometimes arise when first-time visitors come for concerts in the stadium. School spirit and support run high throughout the community. Orange tiger paw prints color streets, and merchants in the downtown shops adjacent to the campus offer Clemson memorabilia and items in the school's dominant colors, orange and white.

A part of the Calhoun plantation, the South Carolina Botanical Garden by the campus showcases the area's colorful and fragrant seasons, from camellias in winter to azaleas and daffodils in spring, with wildflowers, rhododendron and honeysuckle leading into summer's annuals and perennials and chrysanthemums and bright foliage in fall.

The Cruickshanks volunteer at the botanical gardens and established a namesake garden of hostas, which they tend regularly. They play golf and hike in the mountains. The Wises enjoy gardening, walking and bird-watching and have assisted in rehabilitation of injured wild animals. Julia helped found the "Keep Oconee Beautiful" Association, which now numbers more than 500 members and assists in keeping the county clean.

The Cooks both do several types of volunteer work at the university, particularly at the Brooks Center for the Performing Arts, and they play golf and tennis. The university has a golf course, and several others are located in the surrounding counties.

Some retirees relocate here for the lake recreation and outdoor sports. Sailing, windsurfing, water-skiing, fishing, canoeing and boating are popular on Lake Hartwell, which borders the town, and adjacent lakes

Keowee and Jocassee, both taking names from the Cherokee Indian heritage of the area. Many gated communities are built along the lake shores; the best-known development is Keowee Key with its country club, golf course, marina, hiking trails and condominiums, townhomes and homes for sale and rent. For those who want action, the nearby Chattooga River rushes through the mountains, offering white-water trips through rugged back country.

All three couples say it's easy to make friends in the community, which is accustomed to welcoming new students each year. "I know someone's life history after standing with them for five minutes in the checkout line," says Julia, who was born in England and adjusted to making new friends often as the Wises moved in the Air Force.

The couples find little to fault in the area, though Grace dislikes the summer humidity, which can be high at times. She and her husband were surprised by a personal property tax on cars and found their state income tax higher here than in Pennsylvania. The Wises were surprised to see abandoned vehicles and appliances outside some homes in the country, a reminder of rural poverty.

For those who might consider the area for retirement, David says, "I would encourage them, but they need to understand that this is not a big city."

"Come well ahead of time and look it over; talk to people who live here. Be curious and satisfy yourselves that it's a fit," says Walter.

Chuck, who's 71, suggests not moving too far out from town. "The action is here in Clemson. We could have bought a place at Keowee Key but we wanted to be close-in to take advantage of what the university offers," he says. ●

Coeur d'Alene, Idaho

The Idaho Panhandle offers a playground of rivers, mountains and lakes

By Richard L. Fox

Lewis and Clark put it on the map. French-speaking explorers and fur traders named it. Now tourism, retirees and refugees from urban concerns are shaping Coeur d'Alene, the hub of Idaho's panhandle.

In the course of their expedition to find a Northwest Passage in the early 1800s, Meriwether Lewis and William Clark were met by the Nez Perce Indians 100 miles south of present-day Coeur d'Alene. Dispatches to President Thomas Jefferson recounted their explorations and brought new details about this great Western territory to map makers, opening the region for exploration and eventual settlement.

The name Coeur d'Alene, roughly translated as "heart like an awl," refers to the keenly sharp negotiating skills of the Schee-Chu-Umsh Indians, whose village occupied the area when French traders arrived several decades after Lewis and Clark.

Today, the Coeur d'Alene Indians are based about 30 miles to the south, where they have achieved economic success with a popular bingo and gaming casino. The rugged wilderness and mystique of which Lewis and Clark wrote still permeate this region.

"When I first came here, the town reminded me of my hometown of Newport Beach, CA, when I was a child," says Shirlee Wandrocke. "The town, the lake, the mountains just overwhelmed me (along with) the warm, congenial, lovely people. I just have a spiritual feeling living here."

Shirlee, 59, made what might be termed a reconnaissance move to the area in 1983, leaving husband Dick, 63, in Newport Beach to manage the family business. She commuted back and forth until 1990, when Dick turned the business over to their son and joined Shirlee in Coeur d'Alene. Their first home sat on a hillside over-

looking the Spokane River where it joins Lake Coeur d'Alene, but they recently moved to a new home that sits on one acre of land right in town.

The Wandrockes looked at potential retirement sites in Washington, Oregon and Jackson Hole, WY, before deciding on Coeur d'Alene. "It measured up to all of our requirements. We had to live within an hour's drive of a large city (Spokane) for concerts and symphonies. We also wanted to be near an airport because of our children living in Southern California. We had to be in sight of water . . . and it had to have a decent hospital, because I was bringing my mother with me," Shirlee says.

The desire to live "in sight of water" is shared by natives and newcomers to the area. Rustic cabins, lake villas, condominiums and 10-acre estates all share spectacular views of the lake and surrounding mountains.

With a population greater than 34,000, Coeur d'Alene is the seat of Kootenai County in the northwest Idaho Panhandle. It sits on the north shore of Lake Coeur d'Alene near forests and mountains that beckon climbers, hikers, bikers, skiers and snowmobilers. Some might expect this town to be merely a launch pad for recreational opportunities in the hinterlands.

"Not so," says Dick Compton, 63, who spent 33 years traveling around the country and the world for IBM before retiring to Coeur d'Alene in 1993 with his wife, Janette, a native of the town.

Janette, 64, likes the small-town atmosphere. "It doesn't matter who you are or where you've been — you are accepted," she says.

"Cultural opportunities are good, health-care facilities are good — and getting better — and crime is a minimum issue. There are no gangs and (there is) good law enforcement," says

Dick, who finds that civic leaders are more accessible in Coeur d'Alene. "You can know the people who are prominent and influential in the city and become involved much easier than in a large city like Seattle. It's the right size," he says.

Shortly after retiring here, Dick became involved in local politics and was elected chairman of the Kootenai County Board of Commissioners. He also serves on the board of Jobs Plus, which recruits small businesses to the area.

Coeur d'Alene has experienced a growth spurt in the last few years, creating mixed feelings among residents. "Whether you like it depends on whether you are buying or selling," says Dick. "Prices of real estate have gone up considerably. We're having a tough time absorbing the growth that's going on — the social and economic changes."

He feels that the local economy is good. "When we grew up around here there wasn't a lot of employment... there's more now — more opportunities for young people to go to work in meaningful jobs," he says.

Jim and Margie Porter moved to the area from Diamond Bar, CA, in 1990. "Our home has probably tripled in value since we bought it," says Jim. "Five acres used to run $20,000. Now it runs from $60,000 to $80,000."

The influx of new residents has increased local traffic, as Dick Wandrocke notes. "When Shirlee moved here (in 1983) there were two stoplights. When I moved here (in 1990) I could go anywhere in town from my home in five minutes. Now it takes 20 to 25 minutes. I still haven't adjusted to that, and I'm frequently late for meetings," he says.

Shirlee takes it in stride. "You could not drag me back to California — just too many people," she says. The traffic is horrendous. I go insane when I drive down there."

With more than 300 businesses, shops and restaurants, downtown Coeur d'Alene is clean, open and tourist-oriented. The trendy, fashionable shops of Coeur d'Alene Resort Plaza spill into the downtown shopping district. Other shopping venues include Silver Lake Mall and, in neighboring Post Falls, a factory outlet mall with 60 stores.

Small, picturesque communities that range in size from 225 to 10,000 residents cozy up to the borders of Coeur d'Alene. Jim and Margie Porter chose Hayden Lake (population about 7,000), eight miles to the north.

"We found a perfect place in Hayden Lake," says Jim, 67. "A great house... five acres of timber. It's just heaven."

"We built a barn and bought a horse for Jim and a pony for our grandchildren," adds Margie, 63. "We have an acre of grass. When you're out on the patio you feel like you're in the national forest."

Jim's 10 bypasses and a pacemaker were not enough to move the couple from their home in Hayden Lake, though Jim did travel to famed Scripps Institute in California for his most critical surgical needs. He still splits his own firewood, storing up enough for winter. "When I can't chop wood, take care of that acre of lawn (and) my horse, and put the hay up for the winter, we'll probably have to move," he says.

"But we won't move out of the area," Margie declares.

Lake Coeur d'Alene is the nucleus that binds together the town, a large resort and many recreational areas.

Just one of some 60 lakes in a 60-mile radius, this 26-square-mile, huckleberry-hued playground is an outdoor paradise.

Homesites and boat docks line the lake's forested 135-mile shoreline. Standing out on the horizon is the Coeur d'Alene Resort, an expansive complex with a multistoried hotel, marina, boat rentals, private beach, cross-country and downhill skiing and more. The fairways of the resort's championship golf course frame the water's edge, and cruise boats ferry sightseers for a close-up view of the nearly five-million-pound, one-of-a-kind floating green on the 14th hole.

The steamboats that moved mining and lumbering supplies in the early 1900s are gone. Now boats take off with parasailers in tow, and sailboats and cabin cruisers barely leave a wake as

Coeur d'Alene, ID

Population: 34,514 in Coeur d'Alene, 108,865 in Kootenai County.

Location: At the edge of scenic Lake Coeur d'Alene in northern Idaho's panhandle. Elevation is 2,187 feet.

Climate:

	High	Low
January	35	22
July	86	52

Average relative humidity: 46%
Rain: 27 inches. **Snow:** 80 inches.
Cost of living: Slightly above average (specific index not available).
Median housing cost: $122,672, according to the Coeur d'Alene Chamber of Commerce.
Sales tax: 5%
Sales tax exemptions: Prescription drugs and most services are exempt.
State income tax: For married couples filing jointly, the rate is graduated from

1.6% of taxable income up to $2,173 to 7.8% on amounts over $43,460. For single filers, graduated from 1.6% of taxable income up to $1,087 to 7.8% on amounts over $21,730.

Income tax exemptions: Social Security benefits and railroad pensions are exempt. There is an exemption at age 65 or older for federal and some state and local pensions of up to $18,432 for single filers and $27,648 for married couples filing jointly. The deductions must be reduced by the amount of Social Security benefits received.

Estate tax: None, except the state's "pickup" portion of the federal tax, applicable to taxable estates above $1 million.

Property tax: At the average rate of $14 per $1,000, the annual tax on a $122,672 home would be about $1,017, with $50,000 homestead exemption noted below.

Homestead exemption: State law exempts 50% or $50,000 (whichever is less) of assessed value of the primary residence, exclusive of land value.

Personal property tax: None
Religion: 26 Catholic and Protestant denominations are represented.
Education: Lewis-Clark State College's Coeur d'Alene Center offers the final two years of a baccalaureate degree program

in a number of disciplines. The University of Idaho Coeur d'Alene Center allows students to complete undergraduate and graduate degrees.

Transportation: Spokane International Airport, 35 miles west, is served by seven major carriers.

Health: Kootenai Medical Center has 187 beds and 24-hour emergency care. The North Idaho Immediate Care Center and North Idaho Cancer Center, both in Coeur d'Alene, offer additional healthcare facilities. Six major medical centers and hospitals are less than an hour away in Spokane, offering advanced medical and surgical procedures.

Housing options: Arrow Point Resort offers two-bedroom, two-bath condos on the lake starting at $180,000. **Coeur d'Alene Place**, with parks and a trail system, has new homes priced from $100,000 to the low $200,000s. Lakeview homesites are expensive, starting at $160,000 in one area minutes from town.

Visitor lodging: The Coeur d'Alene Resort, $99-$199 in winter, $179-$449 in summer, (800) 688-5253. There are more than 50 hotels and motels in the area.

Information: Coeur d'Alene Area Chamber of Commerce, P.O. Box 850, Coeur d'Alene, Idaho 83816, (208) 664-3194 or www.coeurdalene.org.

they lazily ply the calm waters. Heron and osprey circle high above the vessels in summertime, and in January and February avid bird-watchers scan the skies for bald eagles, which fish the lake for kokanee salmon as they migrate to warmer climes.

The Coeur d'Alene, Spokane and St. Joe rivers, flowing in and out of the lake, abound with salmon, trout and bass. In some places, white-water rapids provide a thrill a minute for rafters, canoeists and kayakers.

Mountain peaks are visible to the north, south and east of Coeur d'Alene. National forests and state parks make up more than 50 percent of the Idaho Panhandle.

"Camping is absolutely wonderful up here," says Shirlee Wandrocke.

"You can go anywhere and find campgrounds — primitive or with all of the facilities."

There also are opportunities for biking, hiking and climbing, and it's not uncommon to spot a moose, elk, deer or mountain lion in the higher elevations during summer months.

When temperatures dip (the average January low is 22 degrees), boats are put in dry docks, and snowmobiles, skis, snowshoes and ice skates are brought out of storage. Those who enjoy ice fishing break out their ice picks and cold-weather gear to try their luck on area lakes.

Four alpine ski resorts at elevations of 6,000 to 7,000 feet offer trails for downhill skiers, while literally hundreds of miles of cross-country and snowmobile trails crisscross the mountains.

Jim and Margie Foster love the cold and snow. "We don't go south like the snowbirds," Margie says. "We stay here with our two snowmobiles and play." But she cautions those thinking about moving here to consider the weather. "Everyone can't handle the winters. Some friends tried it for four years, gave up and moved to Arizona," says Margie.

"The good news is there's four seasons. The bad news is there's four seasons," jokes Dick Compton. "We get some snow and we get some winter. If you're concerned about being able to cope with that, you may want to look south." ●

Dade City, Florida

Picturesque small town evokes memories of a slower-paced time

By Jay Clarke

A common thread runs through Dade City's retirees — a love of country living. The small-town ambiance is an attribute that all of the retirees here cite, although there are many other attractions. Some relocated retirees even find that Dade City reminds them of their former homes while offering the pleasing retirement lifestyle they were seeking when they moved.

"We had been coming to Florida for a number of years," says Tom Brennan, 72, former chief justice of the Michigan Supreme Court and later a law school professor. "Years ago we sent our middle daughter to St. Leo College (near Dade City) and we had a condo in Innisbrook. As we began spending more time in Florida, we wanted to build, but we weren't crazy about Innisbrook," says Tom, explaining that he and his wife, Polly, decided it had become too crowded for their tastes.

Then, while revisiting the area, they came upon the Lake Jovita Golf and Country Club development, which opened in August 1999 and has homes from $170,000 to more than $1 million. "We fell in love with the place. It had rolling terrain reminiscent of home in Michigan. But what turned out to be the most pleasant surprise was Dade City," Tom says.

"I brought down all these boxes of files and Polly didn't want them in the house, so I rented an office downtown," he says. "That began a love affair with Dade City. I go into the office almost every day, have coffee at the local bakery, take lunch at a table in back with judges and old-timers. I've found the city to be very delightful, a friendly place. A walk around downtown gives you a real high."

Another aspect that pleases the Brennans is meeting home folks. "Where we were in Innisbrook, everybody was from somewhere else. Here we meet people from Dade City," Tom says. So, even though Tom had been active in the public life of Michigan, moving from Lansing to Dade City wasn't a difficult choice. Polly, also 72, loves the town as well, Tom says, and both have had no trouble developing a busy social life.

The downtown that Tom loves is dominated by a white-domed courthouse, a regal structure that dates to 1909. But activity revolves around the 30-odd antique shops that line the streets, spawning a tourism industry. "Bus tours from St. Petersburg, Clearwater and Tampa come here on day trips," says Phyllis Smith, executive director of the Dade City Chamber of Commerce. The occupants alight to shop.

Another visitor destination is the Pioneer Museum, a grouping of historic buildings brought here from all over the region, as well as a collection of artifacts from the early 20th century. Such structures as a train depot, school, church and country store — even a moonshine still — are spread over several acres.

And just outside of town is Dade Battlefield, where Major Francis Dade was ambushed and killed by Seminole Indians while leading troops from Fort Brooke (Tampa) to Fort King (Ocala) in the 1830s. The incident started the Second Seminole War and immortalized Dade. This city is named after him, as is Miami-Dade County to the south, the most populous in Florida.

The site of the ambush is now a state park whose picnic grounds are busy every weekend the year around. A small museum tells Dade's story, and next to it the park has rebuilt a log redoubt similar to what Dade troops hastily constructed while under attack.

Within a few miles of Dade City are several small towns that are part of the city's outreach. One of them is the village of St. Leo, home of Florida's only abbey, a lovely complex on a lake that was founded by German monks in the 1890s. It's also the site of St. Leo University, a Catholic liberal arts school no longer run by the Benedictine monks, and a public golf course owned by the abbey. San Antonio, a bedroom community that conducts a popular yearly rattlesnake festival, stands next to St. Leo, and a few miles south of Dade City is Zephyrhills, a city of about 9,000 known internationally for its bottled water and skydiving center.

Like any other small town, Dade City is immensely proud when one of its hometown boys makes good. That's why a large sign at the city limits announces that Dade City is the boyhood home of tennis star Jim Courier. Though he still visits, Courier has moved away, but the Bellamy Brothers, well-known country singers, still return to their farm home here when not traveling the world on tour.

On Dade City's annual calendar are a variety of events from bluegrass festivals and antique shows to Indian pow-wows and bicycle races. Biggest is the Kumquat Festival in January, centered on the small citrus fruit that is often used to make jellies or decorate dishes. Dade City claims to be the kumquat capital of the world, and this year's fete drew more than 30,000 visitors. San Antonio's Rattlesnake Festival, held every October, is another major hoopla. In the past it has attracted television coverage from as far away as Japan.

And this past March, Dade City inaugurated a new event, the Little Everglades Steeplechase. It's the only steeplechase in the state as well as one of only 21 in the nation — and it was constructed as a labor of love by a new Dade City retiree, Bob Blanchard.

Bob and his wife, Sharon, maintained two homes for many years, one in Cashiers, NC, and another in Tampa. Retiring from a holding company, he sold his home in Tampa and has just built another — his prime residence now — on a 1,775-acre ranch just outside Dade City.

"Both of us like the country. We have Hanoverian horses and 300 cattle, and we have room. The closest neighbor is a mile away," Bob says. The semi-isolation also is changing their lives in other ways. "We used to be much involved in (community) activities in Tampa, but that's dropping off sharply," Bob says.

Though retired, Bob admits he likes to keep busy. "I have to have projects," he says. The steeplechase track — a not-for-profit operation — is one of them. "It's a world-class track, with jockey quarters, judging towers and ancillary facilities," he says. The facility will be used only once a year, when it opens the nation's steeplechase season in March. Last March, in its first race season at the new track, Little Everglades attracted 3,500 spectators.

The country-town atmosphere of Dade City also is part of what attracted Robert "Smoky" Stoever and his wife, Wilma, to move from their home in Southbridge, MA, after they retired in 1993. "Our kids were shocked when we moved here," Smoky says. "But my best friend lived nearby, and we liked the weather and the country living."

Smoky and Wilma were among the first to move into the then-new Southfork Mobile Home Community here. They have a spacious double-wide home with three bedrooms, dining room, living room with fireplace and a porch on a tree-lined street, and four grapefruit and orange trees in the back yard.

"Senior park living is great," says Smoky, 70. "Nobody (who lives here) is working, so we're able to do things together. We have a lot of dances, potluck suppers, pancake breakfasts. We take bus trips to the dinner theater, to Clearwater or Cape Canaveral."

Before moving to Florida, Smoky also had looked in Kentucky, home of his wife's family, and in southern Illinois. But Dade City won out, and life here seems to agree with him. "I do what I want to do," he says. He's into flowers and gardening, and his wife, Wilma, calls him the "shuffleboard king of the park."

Wilma, 69, who worked in home-care nursing in Massachusetts before her retirement, still keeps a hand in nursing, working as a volunteer at local hospices. She also is quite active in Southfork community organizations.

And what about their children, who were so surprised about their parents' move to Florida? Six of the eight still live in Massachusetts, but they've mel-

Dade City, FL

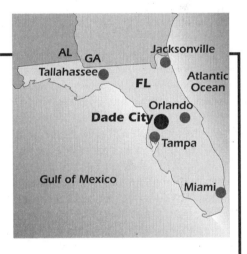

Population: 6,258 in Dade City, about 40,000 in the region.

Location: About 45 miles north of Tampa.

Climate:

	High	Low
January	72	49
July	92	71

Average relative humidity: 60%

Annual rainfall: 49 inches.

Cost of living: Below average (specific index not available).

Average housing costs: $120,000 for a single-family home.

Sales tax: 6%

Sales tax exemptions: Groceries, medicine and professional services.

State income tax: None.

Intangibles tax: Assessed on stocks, bonds and other assets. Tax rate is $1 per $1,000 in assets. The first $20,000 in assets is exempt for individuals. For couples filing jointly, the first $40,000 is exempt. Those who owe less than $60 need not pay.

Estate tax: None, except the state's "pickup" portion of the federal tax, applicable to taxable estates of more than $1 million.

Inheritance tax: None.

Property tax: $26.50 per $1,000 valuation in Dade City, $21 per $1,000 in Pasco County, with homes assessed at 100% of market value. The tax on a $120,000 home would be about $2,518 in the city and $1,995 in the county, with homestead exemption noted below.

Homestead exemption: $25,000 off assessed value of primary, permanent residence.

Religion: 64 churches.

Education: Nearby are St. Leo University, (352) 588-8242, offering four-year liberal arts degrees, and Pasco Hernando Community College, (352) 567-6701, whose two-year degrees are transferable to the state university system. Three four-year colleges are within 40 miles: Florida Southern College in Lakeland and the University of South Florida and University of Tampa in Tampa.

Transportation: Nearest major airport is Tampa International, about 47 miles. Dade City is Amtrak's only stop in Pasco County.

Health: Two hospitals are within 10 miles. Pasco Regional Medical Center has 120 beds, and East Pasco Medical Center has 139 beds. Both have 24-hour emergency services. Several nursing homes and home health care services are available in the area.

Housing options: Lake Jovita Golf and Country Club, (800) 267-2768, (352) 567-7000 or www.lakejovita.com, opened in August 1999 on 1,054 acres. It offers single-family homes from $170,000 to more than $1 million and has a clubhouse, swimming pool and 18-hole golf course. Another 18-hole course is under construction. **Southfork Mobile Home Community**, (352) 523-0022, with attractive manufactured homes on tree-lined streets, has a pool, clubhouse and shuffleboard courts. **Edwinola**, (352) 567-6500, a large congregate living facility, has about 185 units in a renovated landmark structure in town. **Tampa Bay Golf and Country Club**, (800) 588-2108, has a pool and golf course.

Visitor lodging: The 52-room Best Western of Zephyrhills is seven miles from Dade City, $53-$89, (813) 782-5527.

Information: Greater Dade City Chamber of Commerce, 14112 Eighth St., Dade City, FL 33525, (352) 567-3769 or www.dadecitychamber.org.

lowed. When winter blows in, they aren't a bit sorry that their parents have a place in Florida they can visit.

Smoky Stoever is one of many retirees who have gravitated to this city from distant states. Some have moved from no farther away than Tampa, 45 miles south. Dennis and Gloria Huffman, for example, moved to Dade City a year ago after many years in Tampa. That may not sound like much of move, but the Huffmans, both 59, say that despite their proximity, the two cities are vastly different.

"Tampa is flat and palm trees, like most of Florida," Gloria says. "Out here there are hills and live oaks. It looks like North Carolina. We moved here because of that."

Actually, they had lived in quite a few places before settling in Tampa in the 1980s, including Jackson, MS; Hartford, CT; and Jacksonville, FL. So when they began thinking of retirement, they had a pretty good idea of what they wanted. Still, says Gloria, "We looked at the 'best' retirement places — Naples, Sarasota, even the mountains of North and South Carolina. We spent 10 days in a cabin in the mountains, but that was too isolated for me."

In 1999 they visited Lake Jovita Golf and Country Club, liked what they saw, bought a lot and constructed a house there. "We like golf," Gloria says. "In Tampa we lived in a nice place with nice golf and tennis. But there were not enough retirees there. Here you can always find someone to play with."

Another plus, Gloria says, is the plethora of activities available to Lake Jovita residents. She ticks off some of them: "They have a fitness center; we go there two or three times a week. Some ladies have a knitting class. Every Tuesday we meet for lunch and play cards. Wednesday night is family night, with a big dinner buffet. Thursday night is poker night. The Couples Club plays golf every first and third Sunday."

Dade City suits them well, too. "There's not a lot of traffic here, no parking meters. Everybody's real friendly, very laid back. It's easy to make friends and there are no cliques. It's like a little country town," Gloria says.

Bob and Sally Davis also moved from a nearby Florida town, Lutz, a suburb of Tampa that got too big for them. But as Bob had been an executive in the Postal Service, they had lived previously in many other places — Alabama, Mississippi and Tennessee, among them. "We moved every three years," Sally sighs. "We looked around for five years, but we knew we liked the Tampa area. My husband is a big golfer, and he can play golf the year around here."

Like other retirees, the Davises like Dade City's country-town atmosphere. "Everybody's friendly, comfortable. It reminds me of the town I grew up in — Jasper, AL," Sally says. "There's always something going on. Groups meet for suppers, for walking, for sewing. We go to concerts. Anything we want to do, we do," she says.

"And there are younger couples here, too," she says. Though retired, both are still relatively young: Sally is just 60, and Bob is 63.

Retirees say that few who experience Dade City ever express longing to return to urban life, although they do enjoy the big-city amenities in nearby Tampa. "Any kind of entertainment I want is just 25 minutes away," says Sally, echoing the feeling of most others.

The cost of living is another attraction. "It seems a little less in Florida — there's no income tax," says Tom Brennan. "Insurance, taxes, utilities — they're all less," says Sally Davis. "Taxes are less, utilities cheaper," agrees Gloria Huffman. "But food costs about the same."

Smoky Stoever, however, finds his costs considerably less, in part because of the type of home he has. "The insurance is less, the energy costs less, the eating out is cheaper," says Smoky, who worked in security positions both as a career soldier and as a civilian. And because he leases the land his mobile home stands on, and because it is technically a vehicle, he only has to buy a license tag every year. He pays no real estate taxes. "Taxes were high in New England," he notes.

Whatever the cost, though, Dade City's retirees seem to think life in Florida is worth it. As Tom Brennan says, "If I had to choose between Michigan in January and Florida in August, I'd choose Florida."

He did, and thousands of others have done the same. ●

DeLand, Florida

University scene enriches life in central Florida town

By Janet Groene

Bypassed by interstates and eclipsed by its more famous neighbors, Walt Disney World and Daytona Beach, little DeLand seldom gets attention amid all the attractions of central Florida. But seniors are discovering that this quiet community of 21,000 residents has many makings of a nice retirement town.

From its stately domed courthouse to oak-lined streets and elegant Greek Revival, Victorian and Tudor university buildings, DeLand evokes a sense of permanence. Its mixture of architecture is more reminiscent of classic Small Town U.S.A. than nouveau Florida, where concrete-block construction dominates.

In DeLand and the surrounding area, retirees find a blend of cultural and recreational opportunities. As the home of Stetson University, a private school with 2,500 students, it offers a wide range of cultural pursuits for a town its size. And, it's a recreation crossroads, ideally located near Ocala National Forest, 45 minutes west of the Atlantic beaches and in the middle of central Florida's pleasantly hilly lake district.

Retirees from urban areas of the North have found this small town has more of what they're looking for in retirement than many other places.

Vic Laumark, 63, and his wife, Muriel, 54, considered New Hampshire, the western Carolinas and northern Florida for retirement after living in a New York City suburb and overseas while he was with Exxon.

But after three visits to DeLand in a three-month period, they chose the town for its good fishing, hunting and social opportunities, they say.

Norman and Kay Laws, in their mid-60s, looked for five years at spots in Hawaii, California, Arizona, Texas and central Florida before retiring to DeLand when he left Chicago State University, where he was a professor.

Al Reeves, 63, and his wife, Jean, 60, also considered other Florida sites and Chapel Hill, NC, before moving to DeLand from Rochester, NY, where he was with Kodak.

"We've found a real home here. We're really happy," says Jean as she and Al exchange greetings and banter with neighbors in Whisperwood. On a sunny Sunday, the manufactured-home community crackles with activities and conversations among residents.

The couples say the small, college-town atmosphere and the music, drama and lecture programs of Stetson University, one of the South's oldest and best liberal arts schools, were a major draw.

While DeLand's cultural offerings aren't as extensive as in the metropolitan areas where they formerly lived, retirees say there are trade-offs. They have to drive only a few miles to attend world-class speeches, symphonies, operas or touring theater productions under university auspices. Plus, parking is hardly a problem at these events.

Recent appearances have been made here by such luminaries as Archbishop Desmond Tutu, ex-President Jimmy Carter, author Derek Humphrey, Russian poet Yevgeny Yevtushenko, and jazz great Taj Mahal. An even wider choice of events, including national sports, is within a 30-minute or one-hour drive to Daytona or Orlando.

Beyond its cultural events, Stetson plays an integral part in the community. Its students mingle with senior citizens in funky coffeehouses and avant-garde theaters, giving the community an eclectic blend that is lacking in some Florida cities.

The town was founded in 1876 by Henry A. DeLand, a manufacturer from New York, who planted oak trees 50 feet apart to border the streets. Development started along the St. Johns River, a major waterway that brought settlers to the state long before roads were built, but the town grew away from the river when U.S. 17, now a quiet byway, became a major route between Miami and New York.

DeLand persuaded John B. Stetson, the hat-maker, to establish a school in the town. Founded as DeLand Academy in 1883, it later became Stetson University and is the home of the oldest higher education school building in the state. The original Henry DeLand home now is restored as a museum, open to the public.

The towering oaks that once lined the stately streets and earned the town the nickname "Athens of Florida" have been decimated by storms and street projects, but new live oak trees have been planted along Woodland Boulevard, locally known as "The Boulevard."

Outdoors enthusiasts enjoy such nearby attractions as a wildlife refuge with a smorgasbord of bird life; DeLeon Springs State Park, thought to be the original Fountain of Youth; and Blue Springs State Park, one of the state's most fabled manatee refuges.

The area's sprawling St. Johns River system is a fishing and boating bonanza, yielding lunker bass on its lakes and drawing swimmers and divers to its sweetwater springs and wildlife enthusiasts to jungle-lined shores.

Aboard rental houseboats, awed visitors from all over the world roam the river, looking at colorful birds, curious raccoons, sunning turtles, manatees munching fragrant water hyacinth, alligators, and even a colony of wild monkeys along the banks.

One of the nation's biggest, freshest and folksiest farmer's markets is held each Wednesday at the county fairgrounds west of downtown. And the historic downtown area itself is becoming a magnet for antique shoppers and nostalgia buffs.

Lower costs of living, better climate, less pollution and lighter traffic are factors that attract retirees to this area.

"The cost of living, including no state income tax, was a large influence," says Vic Laumark of the move to DeLand. "We figure we can live here for $3,500 less annually than in New Jersey."

The three couples interviewed waltzed happily into local life through the Newcomers Club, church and the many volunteer opportunities they found. New residents must leave the newcomers group after three years, so all three couples have "graduated" — with regrets — but are busier than ever.

The Reeveses enjoy chess, bicycling, crafts and bowling. Both are involved as volunteers in a Florida state program for first-time juvenile offenders in which they hear juvenile cases and recommend courses of action to the judge.

Muriel Laumark's enthusiasm as a newcomer led her to a new career, welcoming other new arrivals for the Florida Greeting Service.

The Lawses, who live on a canal just 10 minutes by water from the St. Johns River, are active in the yacht club and other water-oriented activities as well as church, garden club and service clubs.

In sharing tips for other retirees planning a relocation move, both the Laumarks and the Reeveses point to things they would do differently.

When moving, number your boxes and keep an inventory of everything you pack, the Laumarks caution. They also advise insuring your goods for replacement value. In their move, some of their boxes were lost, and they

DeLand, FL

Population: 20,904 in DeLand, 43,343 in Volusia County.

Location: In central Florida's hilly lake district, about 20 miles from Daytona and about 40 miles from Orlando.

Climate:[1]

	High	Low
January	72	49
July	92	73

Average relative humidity: 55%

Rain: 48 inches.

Winters are warm and dry; summers are hot and muggy.

Cost of living: Below average (specific index not available).

Median housing cost: $85,500. Prices for new three-bedroom, two-bath homes start at $105,000.

Sales tax: 6.5%.

Sales tax exemptions: Medical services, prescription drugs, most groceries.

State income tax: None.

Intangibles tax: Assessed on stocks, bonds and other assets. Tax rate is $1 per $1,000 in assets. The first $20,000 in assets is exempt for individuals. For couples filing jointly, the first $40,000 is ex-

empt. Those who owe less than $60 need not pay.

Estate tax: None, except the state's "pickup" portion of the federal tax, applicable to taxable estates above $1 million.

Property tax: Within the city limits, $24.15 per $1,000 of assessed value. Outside the city limits in Volusia County, $21.90 per $1,000. Homes are assessed at 80% of market value. Including the exemption below, tax on an $85,500 home in the city is $1,048, and $950 outside the city.

Homestead exemption: $25,000 off assessed value for primary, permanent residence.

Religion: 56 Protestant churches, one Catholic church and one synagogue.

Education: Stetson University, a private liberal arts college in DeLand, offers non-degree classes and Elderhostel programs geared to those age 55 and older. DeLand also has a branch of Daytona Beach Community College.

Transportation: There's no local air service. Votran provides bus service for Volusia County. DeLand is served by Greyhound, Amtrak and several taxi and van services to the Daytona Beach and Orlando airports, 20 and 40 miles respectively.

Health: The 156-bed Florida Hospital Deland is the area's major health facility. The 97-bed Fish Memorial Hospital is south of town in Orange City. Many local patients go to Orlando or Daytona Beach for specialized services. There are 150 medical doctors.

Housing options: There's a wide range of single-family homes, condos and man-

ufactured-home communities, some catering to adults only. **Trails West** and **Brandywine** are planned urban developments of single-family homes and townhomes; **Bent Oaks** and **Longleaf Plantation** have upscale homes, and **Whisperwood** offers manufactured homes starting at $39,000 on rented lots. **Victoria Park**, (866) 842-7275, is a multigenerational, master-planned community with parkland, championship golf course and recreation center. It is comprised of several neighborhoods, including **Victoria Gardens**, which is designated for active adults. Independent living in continuing-care communities is available at the **Alliance Community**, (386) 734-3481; **Florida Lutheran Retirement Center**, (386) 736-5800; and **John Knox Village**, (800) 344-4504. Retirement apartment complexes include **Hugh Ash Manor**, (386) 736-2500; **College Arms Towers**, (386) 734-2299; and **Woodland Towers**, (386) 738-2700.

Visitor lodging: DeLand has many small, private motels, campgrounds and fish camps. Other options include the DeLand Country Inn, $49-$79, (386) 736-4244; Holiday Inn, $85, (386) 738-5200; and Howard Johnson Express, $49-$69, (386) 736-3440. Book early; rooms fill quickly during special events at Stetson or at the Daytona International Speedway.

Information: DeLand Area Chamber of Commerce, 336 N. Woodland Blvd., DeLand, FL 32720, (386) 734-4331 or www.delandchamber.org.

[1]Climate data for nearby Orlando, from National Climatic Data Center.

couldn't prove the boxes even existed, let alone the value of the contents.

Jean Reeves' chief regret was that they got rid of too many items from their home in Rochester.

"We had a big house sale and sold almost everything we owned, so we had to purchase many of the items here at higher prices," she says.

The Lawses credit "a lot of planning" with their smooth transition.

DeLand's wide choice of local housing is reflected by the three lifestyles chosen by the couples: manufactured-home subdivision, waterfront property and acreage in the country.

The Reeveses didn't want the expense and upkeep of a standard house so they looked for a manufactured home in an adult community — one that also would accept their 80-pound dog. After a search, they found what they wanted in a development in which manufactured homes start at $38,900 and sites rent for $169 monthly. The monthly fee covers lawn mowing, recreation facilities and other amenities. By contract, their rental fee cannot rise more than 6 percent a year.

The two other couples have homes built on site, one on three country acres and the other on a canal leading to the St. Johns River.

Like many others in the area, all three couples consider themselves DeLandites but actually live in neighborhoods outside the city limits, which cover only a small area. Because of the large number of county government and university buildings in DeLand, 34 percent of the city's property is tax-exempt. As a result, the town has one of the highest property tax rates in the county. Adjoining and nearby neighborhoods zealously guard against annexation, although thousands of their residents come into DeLand for shopping, church, medical treatment, meetings, entertainment and recreation.

While Florida does not have a state income tax, it does have a tax on intangible assets, which applies to stocks, mutual funds and some bonds, though there are some exclusions. The tax is a bookkeeping nuisance since taxpayers must compute the value of all applicable holdings as of Jan. 1 each year. Taxes are based on the asset's value that date, regardless of the value when the tax is paid, which can be as late as the following June 30.

Although one couple interviewed reports that this tax costs them $1,400-$1,500 yearly, they say that's much lower than the taxes they paid where they previously lived. With its exemptions, the Florida intangibles tax has little effect on many taxpayers. It falls heaviest on those who have large stock portfolios.

The Laumarks and the Reeveses express concern about crime. Burglaries in the Reeveses' neighborhood prompted their community to organize a neighborhood watch program.

The Lawses note that power outages are frequent in their area, and say they must reset clocks three or four times a month.

Al and Jean Reeves miss having a major shopping center nearby.

The medical care is not as extensive as found in metropolitan areas, the Lawses add, but they find it adequate. For more specialized care, residents usually go to Daytona Beach or Orlando, both nearby.

Would any of them move away? No — but Al and Jean Reeves would like to have a summer home in North Carolina. Florida's summer weather is more humid than they expected.●

Door County, Wisconsin

This wooded Wisconsin peninsula is rich in arts, culture, scenery and recreation

By Bill and Edie Hibbard

Door County, Wisconsin's limestone "thumb" that juts north eastward into Lake Michigan, often is compared to Cape Cod, but with an Upper Midwest flavor. A variety of scenic villages are nestled at water's edge, with fascinating islands to explore and recreational and cultural activities galore. And like Cape Cod, Door County counts legions of vacationers, more than 2 million each year.

The same things that appeal to vacationers also convince an increasing number of people to retire here. The continuously changing scenery of the 80-mile-long peninsula, the abundance of recreational activities and the flowering of the arts make it a prime place to live. To these advantages, add a vitality in the air, friendly locals, excellent medical services and good roads.

For retirement, Door County is particularly attractive to couples who want to interact with their neighbors, stay active in community affairs and desire four well-defined seasons, including — yes — snow and ice in winter. But winter here is milder than in many other areas at this latitude. The Door peninsula is only six to 20 miles wide, and the water on each side moderates both the cold in winter and the heat in summer. When snow comes, roads are plowed quickly and residents get around easily,

"Winter is my favorite season," says Ted Kubicz, who with wife Agnes has lived in Baileys Harbor in Door County for 16 years. "You can sleep longer, you get fewer visitors and it's quiet. I like to read, so it's the perfect time to finish a good book."

And life doesn't end when the tourists go home. "Even in winter, there's plenty to be doing," says Agnes, who is involved in a multitude of activities.

George and Barbara Larsen, who have lived near Sister Bay for 14 years, concur. "We just love winter here — it's beautiful and quiet," says George, who adds that winter gives him more time

for genealogical research on his computer. "In summer, you're often busy with guests," says Barbara. "In winter, there's lots more activity with your Door County friends."

Harvey and Alice Kroboth, who recently completed their second Door County retirement home near Carlsville, take a different tack. They also own a home in Arizona and spend five months or so there in winter to be near a daughter and grandchildren. But, as their grandchildren grow older, the Kroboths expect to be spending winters in Door County and have no qualms about it.

Harvey, 75, and Alice, 71, retired to Door County from the Milwaukee area, where Harvey, whose career started in art and advertising, had been assistant manager of the Milwaukee Journal promotions department. After 30 years at the newspaper, he took early retirement and joined Kohls Department Stores, setting up photo and production sections of the company's advertising department.

After about four years with Kohls, he retired permanently to Door County, where he and Alice had built a cottage in 1974 near Juddville on a bluff overlooking Green Bay. They had visited other parts of the state, but "this area appealed to us more than the others. It is so different from the rest of the state. It has some truly unique features — the shoreline, the little villages, the small-town atmosphere," he says. The art community and the artistic opportunities in Door County also played a part in their decision, adds Alice.

"We came here by chance in 1962 and loved it," says Harvey. "In addition, it was the right distance from Milwaukee," about three hours by car. After retirement in 1984, they built a larger year-round home on the property and used the cottage as a guest house. A few years ago, they decided that they didn't want the upkeep of two houses, so they

bought another bluff-top lot overlooking the bay about 10 miles to the south and had a sleek contemporary home built there.

They bought at the right time. "We bought the lot for $79,000, and now they're going for $138,000," Harvey says.

In 16 years in Door County, Harvey has melded in smoothly, serving on the county's board of adjustment, Scandia Retirement Center's board of directors, Miller Fine Arts Center committees, Peninsula Music Festival's publicity committee and St. Peter's Lutheran Church's planning committee. He also found time to teach basic drawing at the Peninsula Art School in Fish Creek and The Clearing in Ellison Bay, a 65-year-old school that teaches arts, crafts, humanities and other courses in the Danish Folk School tradition. He's a member of the Door County Art League, the Nor-Door Bird Carving Club, which sprang from a seminar at The Clearing, and the Peninsula Golf Association, which operates the 18-hole course in Peninsula State Park. He works two or three days a week as a starter at the course. "The pay is minimal, but I can play free on my days off," says Harvey.

One of his most memorable experiences was helping to prepare for publication a biography of Door County's dean of watercolorists, Gerhard Miller. Miller acknowledged Harvey's help in the book and presented an original watercolor to him in appreciation.

Alice Kroboth is an accomplished quilter and has continued this avocation in retirement. She has taught classes in quilting at The Clearing and produced quilts to harmonize with and be displayed with pottery at the prestigious Hardy Gallery. One of her quilts gleaned $2,000 for a church fund-raiser.

Harvey believes that the cost of living is slightly higher in Door County than in Milwaukee because of high real estate valuations and consequent taxes, but he finds groceries, gasoline and restaurant meal prices about the same as elsewhere. He also notes that younger retirees seem to be buying lots and building along their road, "people who are able to do it at 50 or 55."

When the inevitable vacationing houseguests arrive at the homes of Door County retirees, active options include sailing, powerboating, water-skiing, wind surfing and fishing for king salmon, steelhead, brown and lake trout, bass and walleye in the waters of Lake Michigan to the east and its Green Bay arm to the west. Each waterfront village in Door County boasts its own marina.

Snorkeling and diving abound, too. Door County took its name from Death's Door Strait at the northern tip of the peninsula, a graveyard — along with the rest of peninsula's 250 miles of rugged shoreline — for sailing ships and other vessels. Divers visit some of the wrecks when the water is clear.

Visitors also haunt gift shops and art galleries that carry an amazing array of paintings, sculpture, carvings and pottery. Seminars on photography, music, nature and other topics are conducted at Lawrence University's Bjorklunden (a 425-acre estate that offers weeklong seminars), The Clearing, Birch Creek Music Center and the Peninsula Art Center. Concerts are held at Birch Creek Music Center and the Door Community Auditorium, with an annual Peninsula Music Festival each August offering appearances by such performers as Willie Nelson, Joan Baez and Debbie Reynolds.

Museums dot the peninsula, including a few stately lighthouses and the new Door County Maritime Museum at Sturgeon Bay. Peninsula Players Theater is the oldest professional resident summer theater in the nation. In addition, theater-goers can chose from options at the Door Community Center,

Door County, WI

Population: 27,961 in Door County; 9,437 in Sturgeon Bay, the county's only city.

Location: Door County sits on a peninsula jutting into Lake Michigan in the eastern part of Wisconsin. Sturgeon Bay is about 40 miles northeast of the city of Green Bay and about 140 miles north of Milwaukee.

Climate:

	High	Low
January	23	9
July	81	63

Average relative humidity: 73%

Rain: 27 inches.

Snow: 40 inches.

Cost of living: About average (specific index not available).

Average housing cost: $153,900

Sales tax: 5.5% (5% state, 0.5% county)

Sales tax exemptions: Most food for home preparation, heating fuel for residential use (electrical and natural gas only, November through April), newspapers and magazine subscriptions, most prescription medications and equipment,

caskets and burial vaults.

State income tax: For married couples filing jointly, graduated from 4.6% of taxable income up to $10,750 to 6.75% on amounts over $155,100. For single filers, graduated from 4.6% of taxable income up to $8,060 to 6.75% on amounts over $116,330.

Income tax exemptions: No more than 50% of Social Security benefits are included in Wisconsin taxable income. There is a credit of $25 for those 65 and older.

Intangibles tax: None.

Estate tax: None, except the state's "pick-up" portion of the federal tax, applicable to taxable estates of more than $1 million.

Inheritance tax: None.

Property tax: Varies by municipality. The rate in Sturgeon Bay is $26.31 per $1,000 in valuation. The annual tax on a home valued at $153,900 would be about $4,049.

Homestead exemption: For homeowners with a gross income of up to $24,500, the state allows a homestead credit of up to $1,160.

Religion: 50 churches are maintained by 18 denominations, including Baptist, Catholic, Episcopal, Lutheran, Methodist and Moravian. Nearest Jewish synagogue is in the city of Green Bay.

Transportation: Cherryland Airport at Sturgeon Bay offers charter service, and there are small airports at Ephraim and Washington Island. The regional airline hub is Green Bay, with limousine service

available. Senior transportation assistance is available in Door County.

Health: Door County Memorial Hospital in Sturgeon Bay has 89 beds. Additional specialists are available in Green Bay, an hour by car or ambulance. There also are seven clinics in the county.

Housing options: Single-family homes, townhouses, condominium units and apartments are available as year-round or part-time residences. Assisted-living facilities are available in Sturgeon Bay and Sister Bay.

Visitor lodging: The county has 4,200 rooms for visitors, according to the Door County Chamber of Commerce. They range from cabins to bed-and-breakfast inns, condominium resorts and hotels to campgrounds. Some are timeshares. Check www.doorcountyvacations.com for rate ranges, information and online inspections or call (800) 52-RELAX for a free vacation guide. At New Yardley Inn in Baileys Harbor, a bed-and-breakfast inn, rates are $130-$175 in peak season and $105-$155 off-season, (888) 4-YARDLEY. At Inn at Baileys Harbor, rates are $72-$135 in peak season and $59-$75 off-season, (920) 839-2345. At Cherry Hills Lodge, a small resort in Sturgeon Bay, rates are $115-$155 in peak season and $89-$129 off-season, (800) 545-2307.

Information: Door County Chamber of Commerce and Visitor Information Center, 1015 Green Bay Road, Box 406, Sturgeon Bay, WI 54235, (920) 743-4456 or www.doorcountyvacations.com.

American Folklore Theater in Peninsula State Park, Door Off Broadway and Door Shakespeare at Bjorklunden.

Hiking and biking are popular in the five state parks in the county, including Peninsula State Park, the state's largest. Birding and ecological walks are held in the parks and at The Ridges, a privately held wildflower sanctuary in Baileys Harbor. Golfers can tee off at nine full-size courses, and cross-country skiing, snowmobiling and ice fishing are popular in winter.

George and Barbara Larsen had rented vacation places in Door County since 1957, and they knew they would retire to Door County. "We were among six couples that came here each summer," says Barbara, 73. "All six built homes here and three of us have retired here."

"When we moved here, we were so familiar with things that it was like moving from one end of town to the other," says George, 76. "I hadn't been here a week and I felt I was at home."

"There's a small-town feel," says Barbara. "Tradespeople get to know you; they help you out when needed. People here really care about one another."

When the Larsens were retiring from their jobs as faculty members in the Sheboygan, WI, school system — George as a high school choral music teacher, Barbara as an elementary school librarian — they found a piece of land they liked inland. Before they ended negotiations, however, the owner suggested they also look at a lot her brother owned nearby on a bluff overlooking Green Bay.

"The sun was setting as we came up on it," George recalls, "and we agreed this was it." They had their seven-room ranch house built there in 1986 and have enjoyed the often-spectacular sunsets ever since.

The Larsens' activities since retiring equal whole new careers. Barbara has written and published four books of poetry and teaches poetry writing and appreciation and life-history writing at The Clearing. She is regional vice president of the Wisconsin Fellowship of Poets, a 400-member organization. She takes regular dance-fitness classes, and when they are not scheduled, she does yoga on her own.

Besides acting as hosts at open houses

at Bjorklunden, Barbara and George regularly take one to four of the seminars scheduled there each summer. They live at Bjorklunden's lodge for one of the seminars "as a vacation," Barbara says. They also are active in fundraising for Scandia Retirement Village in Sister Bay and are avid supporters of the Peninsula Music Festival.

When the Door Community Auditorium was being built, George served as liaison between the board and the architect. He also directed the Peninsula Chamber Singers, a 100-voice choir, for 10 years. Now he's assembling historical archives for Bjorklunden. Many that existed for the program that dates back to 1980 were lost in a fire that destroyed the old lodge in 1993.

Both Alice Kroboth and George Larsen have had positive experiences with local medical facilities. Alice says, "I had to have rotator-cuff surgery at Door County Memorial Hospital in Sturgeon Bay (the county's largest community, about 20 miles from her home) and I was impressed with the quality of the doctors and the treatment. It was a good job and I'm back to normal. All reports we've had from others who've gone there have been good, too."

George, who uses a wheelchair as a result of polio he contracted in 1956, also praises Door County Memorial Hospital and local paramedics who, he says, have been quick to respond when needed.

Another local couple, Ted and Agnes Kubicz of northern Illinois, discovered Door County separately, Ted with his first wife and Agnes as a guest of her employer. Once they'd discovered it, each continued to visit year after year. After they married 24 years ago, they spent all their summer vacations here. Each took early retirement — Ted, now 81, from the advertising department of a GTE (now Verizon) subsidiary, and Agnes, 72, as secretary to the senior vice president for government affairs of United Airlines.

During their visits they often walked along Lake Shore Drive in Baileys Harbor, stopping occasionally to admire their "dream house." One day in 1977 they found a sign in front of it and realized it was for sale. They made an appointment, liked what they saw on a quick tour, and made an earnest-money

payment then and there for the 50-year-old, natural limestone home.

"When we moved in we found we had a septic system and a crawl space," says Ted. "We had no idea about some of the basics. But we lucked out and we've never regretted the way we did it." They retired to Door County seven years after purchasing the home.

Although Agnes says you can be as busy or as lazy as you like in Door County, the Kubiczs choose to be busy. They have volunteered at Bjorklunden, which lies just south of their home, and at The Ridges wildflower sanctuary, and they take classes at The Clearing. Season ticket holders for the Peninsula Music Festival, they also are members of its sustaining committee, picking up artists in Green Bay, sometimes providing housing for them, preparing lunch on rehearsal days and distributing posters and brochures. They also find time to attend performances by the Peninsula Players, the Birch Creek musicians and the American Folklore Theater.

Agnes is president of Immanuel Lutheran Church's women's group and sings in the choir. She also sings with the Peninsula Chamber Singers, which has performed in Germany and Austria recently and plans a concert in New York City's Carnegie Hall next spring.

In what has become a morning ritual, the Kubiczs meet friends for breakfast on the western side of the peninsula, then drive through Peninsula Park. "We like to see the cross-peninsula scenery and how it changes," explains Ted. "We often see our favorite kingfisher at Kangaroo Lake, and we've seen blue herons along the road and sandhill cranes in the fields." As their property backs up against a wooded bluff, they often host deer, foxes, wild turkeys and groundhogs in the yard.

They enjoy watching a trio of mute swans that paddle by just offshore in summer and trumpeter swans that stop for a rest in March on their migration. "There may be more beautiful areas of the world, but I'm not sure they have as much activity," Agnes says.

"Each year we have to make a list of things we haven't done, so we can do them the next year," Ted adds. "We think it's a great place to retire," Agnes concludes.●

Eagle River, Wisconsin

Wisconsin lake area sparkles with fresh air, clear water

By Dixie Franklin

The north-central Wisconsin town of Eagle River is a life-size diorama, with low storefronts bordered by flowers in summer and roofs silhouetted against winter snow by strings of tiny holiday lights. In this dioramic setting moves a parade of tourists and local residents — including a growing number of retirees.

The natural beauty of four seasons, a clean environment and a perfect combination of woods and waters help attract retirees to the town of 1,443 people. A laid-back lifestyle and the spontaneous friendliness of its people add to its charm. Folks like to boast that the air here is fresher, the lakes clearer, forests greener and snows whiter than anyplace else.

"I came from a place where you could see the air," says Bob Johnson, a retiree who didn't stay retired long. Formerly a merchant and clothing manufacturers' representative, he now is executive director of the Eagle River Information Bureau.

After retiring to Arizona and living in a community where he had to purchase bottled drinking water, he and wife Carol returned to northern Wisconsin. "The other day while fishing, I could see my lure in 17 feet of water," he marvels.

Summers bring idyllic 85-degree temperatures, and autumns mean glorious displays of reds, oranges and bronzes painted across the forests. Winter snow comes in mid-November and lingers until March, with mid-January temperatures in the high teens and 20s. Most year-round retirees are defensive about their winters and are reluctant to admit to "cabin fever."

"From a calendar standpoint, our winters are long, but I have an unbelievable number of personal projects that keep me busy," says Adrian Willis, a retired marketing manager who lived in Battle Creek, MI, before moving to Eagle River. "And there is a side benefit to our winters. Once it gets cold, it stays cold, as opposed to ups and downs in temperature."

Johnson agrees. "In winter, it's cold, but it's white, clean and crisp. There is no isolation. Our infrastructure is good, and roads are plowed immediately after a snow."

The town and its surrounding lakes and forests make it a popular year-round tourism destination. The town of Eagle River sits in a bend of the river of the same name. The river links 28 navigable freshwater lakes known as the Eagle River Chain of Lakes, one of the world's largest such inland chains. Summer population increases to about 6,500 in the immediate area. For residents living along the chain of lakes, the easiest way to town may be by water. There's a marina just a block from the heart of town.

Many storefronts along the seven-block business district are reminiscent of the 1920s and 1930s, with a railroad depot converted to an information center, a corner bank-turned-gift shop, an old-fashioned soda fountain and a cinema that shows first-run movies through the summer months.

There are souvenir and craft shops, boutiques, galleries, antiques, a candy store, markets and restaurants. At the Colonial House Restaurant, visitors still can drop coins in the nickelodeon while waiting for their sodas. B.J.'s Butcher Shop makes its own sausages, and Bonson's Fine Foods bakes the famous Wisconsin Kringles, fruit-filled pastries with just enough dough to hold the filling together.

First as summer tourists, then as year-round residents, retirees are discovering the pleasures of an area that they boast is "above the tension zone," free of city hassles. The area is especially attractive to outdoor enthusiasts who are as happy here in winter as summer because of the snow sports. And artists wax creative in a North Woods setting where it is not unusual to see whitetail deer, otter, beaver and occasionally a bear during an afternoon drive.

Eagles still nest in the forests of tall, craggy pines along the Eagle River, which flows from Watersmeet Lake on the Wisconsin River to connect the Eagle Chain. Before 1870, the only Europeans to pass this way were occasional fur traders.

In the 1870s, lumberjacks came to harvest virgin white pine. They built a large sawmill in the river's bend, and the town grew around it. Lumbering and the forests still fill a vital role in the economy, both in the harvest of timber and creation of a natural environment of forests and lakes for tourism. The Nicolet National Forest to the east and Northern Highlands State Forest to the west guarantee many outdoor opportunities.

Vilas County, of which Eagle River is the county seat of government, boasts 549 named lakes and 773 smaller unnamed lakes among its rolling, forested hills. Seventy-three rivers and streams carve their way through forests predominantly of pine, maple and birch. Lakes and rivers are enjoyed by fishermen, boaters, waterfowl hunters — and just plain romantics who relish a sunrise or sunset across a placid lake.

Fish catches include the legendary fighting muskies, walleye, northern pike, bass, trout and many species of pan fish. Most any summer weekend will find lakes teeming with fishing boats, sailboats, pontoons, canoes, kayaks and jet skis.

Retiree Herman Smith, formerly a recreation and resource agent for the University of Wisconsin Extension Service, says he saves his fishing for midweek when waters are less crowded, leaving weekends for the tourists.

With such a wealth of recreational opportunities, it's no surprise that real estate on the water is most popular, especially along the Eagle River Chain of Lakes. Residential properties range from summer cabins to impressive year-round homes worth $275,000 and more.

Bruce Bryer of Tri-County Realty, a local agency, says the average cost of homes near Eagle River has increased as much as 20 percent in the last two years. Newcomers should plan to spend up to $225,000 for a 1,200-square-foot cottage on the water, Bryer says.

A municipal water and sewer system serves the city and adjacent area, although some homeowners depend on private wells and septic systems. There are three banks, a public library, pharmacies, insurance agencies and a fire department staffed by more than 20 volunteers. A county newspaper is published weekly.

Homes in town offer many advantages, but shoreline property is the first choice of many retirees. Adrian Willis lives on the river, which provides entertainment year-round — even in winter, when the current prevents it from freezing over entirely.

Adrian and his wife, Gen, moved to Eagle River when their two sons purchased a marina on the Chain of Lakes. They spend pleasant spring days watching minks build dens in the banks of the river. Later in the season the minks parade their young across the lawn.

James Slagle first came to Eagle River as a tag-along on his father's fishing trips. The retired school principal lived in Minnesota and elsewhere in Wisconsin before moving to Eagle River.

"From childhood on, I've always enjoyed the woods," he remembers. Four years ago, James and his wife, Sandra, purchased an "insulated shell of a house on Lower Nine Mile Lake east of Eagle River, and I did much of the remodeling myself." Summer evenings often find the Slagles paddling their canoe on the lake.

Herman and Betty Smith are not newcomers; they have lived in the same big house on the edge of town for the last 40 years. Herman says it is time to move to a smaller house, but they're not moving far. They're look-

Eagle River, WI

Population: 1,443 in Eagle River, 21,033 in Vilas County.

Location: Eagle River is in the lake country of north-central Wisconsin, 140 miles northwest of Green Bay. Elevation is 1,642 feet.

Climate:

	High	Low
January	25	10
July	85	60

Average relative humidity: 50%

Rain: 28 inches.

Snow: 60 inches.

Idyllic summers, long winters (from late November to May).

Cost of living: Average (specific index not available).

Average housing cost: $90,000 for a 1,200-square-foot house away from the water, $200,000-$225,000 on the water.

Sales tax: 5.5%

Sales tax exemptions: Groceries, prescription drugs, professional services, hearing aids, eyeglasses, prosthetic devices.

State income tax: For married couples filing jointly, graduated from 4.6% of taxable income up to $10,750 to 6.75% on amounts over $155,100. For single filers, graduated from 4.6% of taxable income up to $8,060 to 6.75% on amounts over $116,330.

Income tax exemptions: No more than 50% of Social Security benefits are included in Wisconsin taxable income. There is a credit of $25 for those 65 and older.

Intangibles tax: None.

Estate tax: None, except the state's "pick-up" portion of the federal tax, applicable to taxable estates above $1 million.

Property tax: About $17.11 per $1,000 of assessed value, which is set at 107.49% of market value. Yearly taxes on a $150,000 home would be about $2,759.

Homestead exemption: For homeowners with a gross income up to $24,500, the state allows a homestead credit up to $1,160.

Religion: 12 Protestant churches, one Catholic church.

Education: Nicolet College and Technical Institute at Rhinelander, a two-year school, offers classes at Eagle River. Courses are offered through the Institute for Learning in Retirement, with unlimited classes for $30 annually, (715) 365-4512.

Transportation: There's no public transportation, but the Kalmar Senior Center arranges some city transportation. Regional transportation is available via commercial commuter service at Eagle River Regional Airport and by commercial commuter service at Rhinelander-Oneida County Airport, 25 miles south.

Health: The 25-bed Eagle River Memorial Hospital handles general health care. The town has 12 dentists, and doctors from Rhinelander and Woodruff offer satellite services.

Housing options: Homeowners choose among lakeside and river properties, forested acreages and city-size lots. Many homes are summer cottages that have been winterized; others represent new construction. Some lake areas have property and homeowner associations.

Visitor lodging: Rustic cabins and modern resorts are located throughout the area. In addition: American Days Inn-Eagle River, $50-$70, (715) 479-5151; Chanticleer Inn, $79-$330, depending on cottage, (715) 479-4486.

Information: Eagle River Chamber of Commerce, P.O. Box 1917, Eagle River, WI 54521, (800) 359-6315 or www.eagleriver.org. Vilas County Chamber of Commerce, 330 Court St., Eagle River, WI 54521, (715) 479-3649 or www.vilas.org.

ing at a house down the street.

There are no planned housing facilities for retirees, and as the area has become more popular for year-round living, housing availability has become more limited. Some retirees are solving the problem by building new homes or purchasing older summer cottages and remodeling them for year-round use.

Even though he has faced a heart attack and bypass surgery, Herman Smith doesn't worry about the availability of medical service. The 25-bed Eagle River Memorial Hospital maintains an active medical staff of 14, with specialists in surgery, urology, cardiology, internal medicine, orthopedics and occupational therapy. It maintains 24-hour ambulance service, with trained emergency medical technicians. An air ambulance also is available to transport patients to other regional hospitals or to medical facilities in Milwaukee.

The hospital is affiliated with the 75-bed Howard Young Medical Center at Woodruff, 25 miles west, which has a staff of more than 45 physicians plus consultants. The medical center was named for a New York art dealer who owned a summer home in nearby Minocqua. Upon his death, he bequeathed $20 million to the hospital.

The Eagle River Hospital can arrange for Meals on Wheels for homebound residents who require special diets prescribed by a physician. Other senior meals are served at the local Kalmar Senior Center.

There's no public transportation in Eagle River, but Kalmar Senior Center schedules free senior van service for medical appointments and shopping. For other chores, residents say there often seems to be a neighbor going in the right direction.

"There is so much to do, I don't feel like I'm retired yet," says James Slagle, who is among the many who add vitality to the community by volunteering through the hospital, churches, clubs and Senior Eagle River Volunteer Enterprise (SERVE).

Through church activities, the Slagles have made many new friends. They also participate in the Youth Futures Committee, a group of students and mature citizens who are developing ideas and activities as an alternative to alcohol and drugs for area youth. James also serves on the hospital board.

Some retirees take advantage of continuing-education programs offered through Nicolet College and Technical Institute at Rhinelander. The college brings classes to Eagle River, and the Institute for Learning in Retirement also offers classes to seniors.

For entertainment, retirees tend to look first to outdoor recreation. Eagle River has one 18-hole golf course and one nine-hole course (there are 16 golf courses within a 20-mile radius) as well as tennis courts, parks, beaches and picnic areas. After summers spent fishing (the license is $17 for persons age 65 and older), boating and hiking, residents look forward to winter ice fishing, snowmobiling and cross-country skiing over miles of forest trails.

Shows at a community theater liven up the winters. At Hazelhurst, 30 miles southwest, the Northern Lights Playhouse presents professional theater throughout the year. There also are numerous festivals, including the October Cranberry Fest.

For dining out, opportunities range from fast foods to nice supper clubs. A number of restaurants offer access from land and water.

Herman Smith sums it up for many retirees who live in Eagle River. "For us, there is no other place," he says.●

Edenton, North Carolina

Lovely bay-front town takes pride in its Colonial past

By Jim Kerr

On the Fourth of July, the folks of Edenton, a 300-year-old town that knows something about American history, gather in the park fronting Edenton Bay to celebrate with games, food and fireworks. Brick buildings from the 19th and 20th centuries line Broad Street, the main downtown thoroughfare, as kids and adults amble southwest toward the park. And as they approach the waterfront, the buildings grow more historic until they reach the oldest, a Jacobean-style structure known as Cupola House, built in 1725.

Crape myrtle trees, brimming with bright purple and white flowers, decorate the town, and well-groomed magnolias and oaks shade carefully restored Federal, Georgian, Greek revival and Victorian homes. A breeze off the bay tempers the warm July afternoon as hundreds of Edenton's 5,500 residents gather in a scene Norman Rockwell might have conceived.

But while broad strokes of Americana characterize the event and give it a New England flavor, Edenton is a bona fide Southern town, laid out in 1712 along the north bank of Albemarle Sound at the mouth of the Chowan River in the northeastern corner of the state. It is North Carolina's second-oldest town and its first Colonial capital, and Cupola House was its first customs house. For several decades leading up to the American Revolution, goods were cleared here and distributed from perhaps 100 ships anchored in the same bay that now overlooks the annual Independence Day picnic.

Winds of change have swept over Edenton, but through good times and bad, the little town has persevered as a functioning community. English settlers ventured south from Virginia beginning in the 1650s, and while the town still is closely linked with immigrants from the former Northern colonies, most today come as tourists and retirees attracted by the town's historic ambiance, sense of community and progressive, if laid-back, pace.

"We wanted our kids to grow up in a small town where we could also retire," Mary Jo Sellers says. "It's a move we have never regretted."

Their children, now 14 and 18, were just youngsters when Mary Jo and Larry Sellers moved to Edenton in 1992 from the Washington, DC, area where Larry and his partners owned a string of Ben Franklin stores. The couple had seen an ad in the Washington Post for waterfront property outside town, but they were captivated by Edenton's historic character, and instead bought a large 1920s-era house in town. A year later they sold it and bought their double-porched, Georgian-style house on Blount Street. Located two blocks north from the Cupola House, it was built in 1772 and had been Edenton's second customs house.

Being on the daily historic walking tours, the pilgrimage tour in April and Edenton's Christmas candlelight tours every December doesn't bother the Sellerses in the least. "People make you feel so good about your home and where you live," Mary Jo says, "and we like to talk to people from our front porch. We feel we have bragging rights."

Each morning Larry and Mary Jo stroll under the oaks and crape myrtles to the Lovin' Oven downtown for coffee and socializing with friends. Later in the day, the local hardware store clerk doesn't mind spending a few minutes with Larry to find a 15-cent item. Everyone in Edenton seems to have time to be helpful and neighborly.

Community spirit doesn't arise only on the Fourth of July, either. It has been bred here beginning with the actions of men and women who were in the forefront of American history, including a signer of the Declaration of Independence and a signer of the U.S. Constitution. The newly restored Chowan County Courthouse on East King Street, a national historic landmark, dates to 1767, making it the oldest continually operated government building in the state.

And the degree of cooperation between elected officials and volunteer organizations today has led many newcomers to believe Edenton embodies the best qualities to be found in small town America. Located in a convenient, yet out-of-the-mainstream corridor of the state along U.S. Highway 17, the town is 75 miles southwest of Norfolk, VA, 140 miles southeast of Richmond and 135 miles east of Raleigh. "People like to say it's an hour and a half from everything," Mary Jo says. "And that includes the beach at the Outer Banks, an easy and pleasant drive."

Edenton is the county seat of Chowan County, the smallest county in the state with 181 square miles and a population of 15,000. Lumber, cotton and peanuts are the long-time staples of the area's agribusiness, and while Edenton is no longer a commercial port, pleasure boating is a substantial "industry," with three marinas and two recreational boat manufacturers. There are waterfront condominiums along one marina, and many residents are boating and fishing enthusiasts. Larry and Mary Jo keep a jet ski at the ready behind a friend's house.

Carolina boaters enjoy wide-open sailing on Albemarle Sound and have long known about historic and boater-friendly Edenton, where visiting craft are offered two free nights at the town-operated, nine-slip marina. But anyone driving along U.S. Highway 17 en route between Hampton Roads and Raleigh could easily miss the town, whether by accident or on purpose. Such was the case with Steve and DeAnn O'Neil, a couple researching retirement locations a few years ago from their home in Chantilly, VA, just west of Washington, DC.

"Every two years we went to real estate expos in DC looking around," remembers Steve, who retired three years ago as a full colonel after 29 years of service in the Army. "We planned a schedule of visits no farther south than North Carolina, and to places close enough to our daughter in Maryland.

Edenton, NC

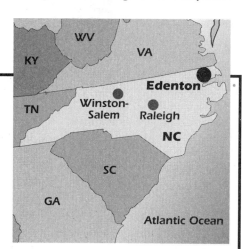

Population: 5,000 in Edenton, 15,000 in Chowan County.

Location: In Chowan County along Edenton Bay on the north shore of Albemarle Sound, approximately 135 miles northeast of Raleigh, NC, 90 miles southwest of Norfolk, VA, 140 miles south of Richmond, VA, and 60 miles from the Atlantic Coast and Outer Banks.

Climate:

	High	Low
January	52	31
July	85	72

Average relative humidity: 76%

Rain: 47.9 inches.

Snow: 4.6 inches.

Cost of living: Below average (specific index not available).

Average housing cost: $80,000 for older homes in town but outside the historic district and not on the water, to $450,000 for historic, waterfront homes in town, and $250,000 to $350,000 in new waterfront or country club developments.

Sales tax: 6.5%

Sales tax exemptions: Prescription drugs, eyeglasses, some medical supplies and most services.

State income tax: For married couples filing jointly, the rate is graduated from 6% of taxable income up to $21,250 to 8.25% on amounts over $200,000. For single filers, it is graduated from 6% of income up to $12,750 to 8.25% on amounts over $120,000.

Income tax exemptions: Social Security benefits are exempt. Up to $2,000 of private retirement benefits and distributions from IRAs and up to $4,000 of government pensions may be exempt. Total deductions may not exceed $4,000 per person.

Estate tax: None, except the state's "pickup" portion of the federal tax, applicable to taxable estates of more than $1 million.

Property tax: $1.085 per $100 of assessed value in the city, $0.73 per $100 in the county. Homes are assessed at 85% of market value. Tax on a $100,000 home would be about $922 in the city, and $621 in the county.

Homestead exemption: North Carolina residents 65 and older, with combined incomes of $18,000 or less, are exempt from the first $20,000 or 50% of assessed value, whichever is greater.

Religion: 35 Protestant churches of various denominations, but primarily Baptist, and one Catholic church, St. Anne's.

Education: College of the Albemarle is a public, two-year community college serving the seven-county Albemarle region with locations in Chowan County, Dare County and Elizabeth City, home of Elizabeth City State University, 30 miles from Edenton. East Carolina University in Greenville, NC, is 65 miles away.

Transportation: Four-lane U.S. Highway 64 and Highway 17 connect Edenton with Raleigh-Durham-Chapel Hill. State Highway 32 runs north to Virginia's Hampton Roads area and Norfolk. Closest international airports are Norfolk, VA, and Raleigh-Durham, NC, located 70 and 140 miles from Edenton, respectively.

Health: Chowan Hospital, a recent addition to University Health Systems of East North Carolina, provides state-of-the-art services by an academic medical center with 111 beds. Albemarle Hospital, a 182-bed regional medical center, has more than 100 resident physicians representing various medical specialties. Emergency helicopter service is available through Nightingale for specialized treatment in the Hampton Roads area. Eastcare Emergency Helicopter is also available from Pitt County Memorial Hospital. Edenton-Chowan County operates three strategically located rescue squad units. There is one nursing home with 160 beds.

Housing options: Homes in Edenton's historic district are frequently for sale and range from $250,000 to $800,000, but there is rarely waterfront property available in town. Waterfront lots are being sold at Phase II of nearby **Edenton Bay**, where new houses cost from $300,000. Waterfront homes outside town on the Chowan River, Albemarle Sound and other waterways, as well as those near Edenton Country Club, start around $250,000. Homesites a few minutes from downtown but not on the water start at $25,000, and resales in the area are $100,000 and up. A few small, restorable houses are still available at the Preservation North Carolina-controlled **Cotton Mill Village** in Edenton for around $45,000, (252) 482-7455. At **Swain Apartments**, (252) 482-5211, a restored school building in town that shares space with the Arts Council, there are 30 comfortable apartments for seniors. Houses can be rented in town for $1,000 to $1,300 a month. **Britthaven** is Edenton's only long-term care facility, (252) 482-7481. At **Albemarle Plantation**, (800) 523-5958, a large, waterfront golf course and marina real estate development on Albemarle Sound 17 miles from Edenton off U.S. Highway 17, approximately 250 homes have been built with 650 homesites available, ranging from $48,000 to $450,000.

Visitor lodging: There are half a dozen area motels and hotels, including Hampton Inn, (252) 482-3500, and Travel Host Inn, (252) 482-2017, both located at Exit 227 off Highway 17, with rooms ranging from $65 to $85, depending on season. More conveniently located in the heart of the historic district are half-a-dozen bed-and-breakfast inns, all in restored houses, including the elegant Lords Proprietors' Inn, $170 per night, (252) 482-3641; Granville Queen, $95-$105, (252) 482-5296; Captain's Quarters, $85, (252) 482-8945; and The Albemarle House, $95, (252) 482-8204.

Information: Edenton-Chowan Chamber of Commerce, 116 E. King St., Edenton, NC 27932, (252) 482-3400, (800) 775-0111 or www.co.chowan.nc.us/commerce.htm. Also see www.edenton.com.

We looked first in Maryland and Virginia, then mapped out routes for two separate trips to North Carolina."

The first was to the Asheville-Hendersonville area in the western mountains. The second was to the Triangle area of Raleigh-Durham-Chapel Hill in the central Piedmont, which also included a swing east to the historic town of New Bern, which succeeded Edenton as the state's Colonial capital. But while Edenton was on their list of stops as they headed home, the long trip began to weigh on them, and when they reached the U.S. Highway 17 bypass around the little town, DeAnn suggested they skip it. "I said, 'If we do, we'll never know,'" Steve recalls.

That was seven years ago. It was February and snowing. The real estate agent they talked to apologized for the coldest day of the year, but the O'Neils were undaunted.

"We drove down Broad Street and saw St. Anne's Catholic Church right in town," Steve says. "We wanted something near the water, something historic. We saw all the beautiful homes. I was impressed."

While they liked the idea of living in a historic town, the O'Neils did not want an older home. Steve had grown up in an old 900-square-foot house, and he wanted something with space and a view. They selected a large lot at the Edenton Bay development, a large finger of land on the sound connected to the town by a single-lane wooden bridge. The residential property is part of a huge family-owned peanut and cotton plantation considered the oldest continually operating plantation in the state.

The O'Neils rented a house in town for 10 months in 1996 while their Cape Cod-style house was being built. While approximately 600 homesites are being considered on the plantation, only a few dozen have been built thus far in three or four areas of Phase I along the Albemarle Sound. Many face southwest, where the expansive waterway extends to the low-country horizon, affording remarkable views.

"There's not a night that goes by when the sunsets aren't more spectacular than in Hawaii, where we lived for five and a half years," Steve says. "The sky turns the most gorgeous of colors, and no two are ever the same."

In Steve's long military career, the O'Neils had moved 28 times. Now it was time to settle in, but they had no intention of becoming disconnected recluses. They joined the 250-member St. Anne's Church as well as Edenton's active Arts Council. The town was getting artsy with the influx of new talent. There were art lessons, sewing and cooking classes. Steve, who served two years as the homeowners association president in his neighborhood, also unlimbered his clubs at the nearby Edenton Golf Club, a pastime interspersed "with that other old standby, yard work."

Soon after their arrival there was an influx of new entrepreneurs in town, opening shops and restaurants, and the choices increased from one barbecue place to half a dozen eateries specializing in various cuisines. Together the O'Neils began making lots of new friends. "One thing I learned about living in a small town," DeAnn says. "It's always social time. A 15-minute trip to town takes an hour or more, stopping to talk to people."

Just a mile or so down the road, Dave and Peggy Blomquist enjoy the same sunsets from the living room or veranda of the home they built at Edenton Bay in 1995. Dave often travels to Atlanta and the Midwest as a freelance writer and industrial consultant, and he finds easy access from both the Norfolk and Raleigh airports. The couple had lived outside Frederick, MD, but an article dubbing Edenton as the "prettiest small town in America" drew them down U.S. Highway 17 in 1994.

"It was charming," Dave says. "It's a real, working town with a functioning and thriving downtown. At 13 feet above sea level, we're the highest point in our neighborhood of Hardy's Hill." He calls their 2,900-square-foot East Hampton Cape Cod-style house "our boat on the water."

Despite the convenience of living in town, many retirees find prices lower and life just as enjoyable on the outskirts of town and in rural settings. When Arch and Jane Edwards first moved here in 1980 from a rural area outside Richmond, they found similar country living in an 1800-era house five miles outside Edenton. Today they own the 18-room Lords Proprietors' Inn, one of seven bed-and-breakfast hostelries in town.

"I was 44 years old when we came here," Arch says, "and I've seen no change in the nature of the population. I was charmed when I first saw it. I had never seen a town as lovely and well-maintained and as prosperous. Attracting and keeping civic-minded people has been a key to Edenton's success."

Instead of tearing them down, Edenton restores and uses older structures. Part of an old brick school was converted into an auditorium for theater performances, while another portion was made into 30 apartments for senior citizens. The Edenton Cotton Mill, founded by locals as a regional marketplace in 1898, formed the nucleus of a village that operated until 1995 when it was donated to Preservation North Carolina, a statewide nonprofit organization that promotes the preservation of heritage sites.

Fifty-seven homes and several empty lots have been sold at low prices to residents or newcomers willing to invest in restoration or construction. A tranquil courthouse green, laid out on the waterfront in 1712, is anchored at the north end by the Chowan County Courthouse, built in 1767 and considered the finest Georgian courthouse in the state. It was recently restored by the Department of the Interior as a national historic landmark.

Life here is almost like being suspended in another time, but with instant access to a modern outside world. Although major shopping malls are miles away, and there are times when a trip is necessary, most products that can't be purchased in town can be ordered by mail or found on the Internet. Larry Blomquist, who telecommutes from his waterfront home, says, "Living is easy here. Even though we do drive a lot to DC to visit our son, I've done entire projects from home without ever leaving."

When Larry Sellers needed a new vehicle, he knew what he wanted. But instead of roaming big city dealers, he bought the exact model and color he was looking for on e-Bay and had the car trucked to Edenton from a dealer in Kansas. Edenton may not be a major port of the Americas as it once was in the 1700s, but as Larry's experience proves, goods get here a lot faster.●

Eufaula, Alabama

Enjoy life on a lake in this historic, affordable Alabama town

By Jay Clarke

Ask retirees how they selected the town of their dreams and you'll get a variety of reasons. Bill Fleming's answer, however, is one of the best. "There's one Sunday and six Saturdays every week when you live in Eufaula," he says.

Bill and his wife, Abie, moved to Eufaula in 1998 after scouting several other locales. Eufaula, which lies on the high bluffs of the Chattahoochee River, is known for its wealth of antebellum homes and the recreational opportunities offered by dam-created Lake Eufaula.

"We started thinking about a retirement place about five years before I retired in 1996. It had to be on the water, had to be in the South, had to be a small town. We had enough of big towns," says Bill, 62, who moved to Eufaula from Germantown, TN, in 1998. President of a managed health-care administration, he and Abie had lived in Germantown for 15 years.

Before deciding on Eufaula, they looked at Destin, FL, and Hot Springs Village and Hebrew Springs, AR. Eufaula seemed to fit the bill best. It was on water (Lake Eufaula and the Chattahoochee River), it was a small town in the South, and the cost of living was reasonable. "An added value was its antebellum heritage and strong feelings about ancestry. This town really feels very strongly about where they came from," Bill says.

So they bought a lot on the lake. Bill drew the house plans and acted as his own general contractor in its construction. They moved into the house in 1998, but Bill says he's still working on the property. "I built a dock, but I'm working on a boat, a 23-foot classic mahogany runabout," he says. His next project will be a biplane. "We love to do aerobatics and water sports," explains Abie.

Eufaula's small-town ambiance also impressed retirees Hank and Joy Bryan, who had lived in many cities during his career in upper management of General Electric. Another attraction was the low cost of living. "You get twice as much here for half the price," says Hank, 77. He estimates that living costs in Eufaula are 30 to 40 percent less than in Atlanta, where he spent some of his last active years at GE before retirement.

Like the Flemings, the Bryans looked at several prospective retirement sites, among them San Antonio, TX; Hot Springs, AR; and Naples, FL. "We both wanted to live on the water," Hank says of Naples, "but my wife didn't want to be on the Gulf." In Eufaula, they found a house under construction on the lake. "It was 90 percent completed, so we bought it and finished it off," he says.

That was back in 1984. In the years since, the Bryans have taken integral roles in the town. "We founded the Humane Society here, and I built the animal shelter. I'm on the board of the church and county chairman of the Republican Committee of Barbour County. My wife was the first and only woman ever to serve on the city council. She's now on the city's parks and recreation board, the vestry of the church and is a director of the Humane Society."

The Bryans lived on the lake for 12 years, moved to a smaller house closer to town and then back into a larger house on the country club golf course "because we found we couldn't accommodate all our children and grandchildren when they came to visit," Hank says. Joy, 65, is an excellent golfer and tests her skills on the course behind their house. Hank, meanwhile, breeds show dogs as a sideline.

Hank admits that moving to Eufaula has taken some adjustment. The town doesn't have the dining and medical facilities of the larger cities where the couple had lived, he says, nor the cultural resources. "And I wish we had a movie house," he adds. "But there's so much else in our sense of values that compensates for that."

High among these is Eufaula's remarkable cache of 19th-century structures, many of which were built before the Civil War. While many buildings in the South were razed by Union troops, notably during Gen. William T. Sherman's notorious "march to the sea," Eufaula escaped destruction when the war ended just as the Union troops under Gen. Benjamin H. Grierson were advancing on the town.

Today more than 700 structures in Eufaula are listed on the National Register of Historic Places. Most renowned is the 17-columned Shorter Mansion, built in 1884 and an outstanding example of Neoclassical Revival architecture. Since 1965 it has been the headquarters of the Eufaula Heritage Association, which sponsors the town's biggest event, the annual Eufaula Pilgrimage and Antique Show. Alabama's oldest tour of homes, it takes place in April when the azaleas and dogwood trees are in full bloom, providing a colorful backdrop for the stately homes on view.

Another notable Greek Revival home is the 1854 Couric-Smith house, the homestead of Charles M. Couric, great-grandfather of NBC Today Show anchor Katie Couric. The home and the city received national attention in 1999 when Couric traced her family's roots to Eufaula.

Fendall Hall, an 1860s-era Italianate home, contains three rooms with fine Victorian-era murals painted by a French artist. Owned by the Alabama Historical Commission, it is open to the public the year around. Also built in Italianate style in the same era is Kendall Manor, whose interior has Waterford chandeliers, hand-stenciled walls and a carved walnut staircase. It is now an elegant bed-and-breakfast inn.

The 1850 Dean-Page Hall is topped with a belvedere, built so a servant could keep a lookout for river steamboats. Eufaula's oldest frame building is the 1836 Tavern, which served as an inn and a Confederate hospital before becoming a private residence.

This plethora of historic structures is what attracted Dr. Calvin Wingo and his wife, Pat, to Eufaula when they retired from their university teaching positions in northern Alabama. "We have an interest in old houses and have done some renovations," says Pat, 60. "So we bought an old house and are constantly working on it — a labor of love." The Italianate-style home they purchased here was started in the late 1850s, but the Civil War interrupted its construction and it was not completed until after hostilities ceased.

But old homes are not the only reason the Wingos came to Eufaula. "The people are so delightful, so warm and receptive," Pat says. "It's just a grand place to live." The Wingos also participate in community groups like Eufaula Pride, whose members pick up litter and clean abandoned lots, and are active in their church and the home preservation movement.

Eufaula fulfills their desires in another way as well. It's a small town close to larger cities that have better facilities for medical care, shopping and travel. Columbus, GA, and Dothan, AL, each are less than an hour away, and the Gulf beaches are only

three hours by car, Pat notes.

"We have a hospital in town that is certainly adequate, and we have some fine doctors," she says. "But we would go to Birmingham for major medical needs."

And though big cities have much wider choices in dining, Pat says Eufaula has some interesting restaurants that are not part of chains, like Cajun Corner and Old Mexico, "and we have caterers who do fancy meals. Those of us who live here all the time enjoy the local restaurants." Eufaula has 35 restaurants, about half of which are fast-food outlets.

Her husband, Calvin, 61, likes to fish,

Eufaula, AL

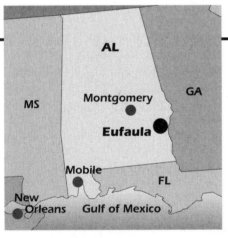

Population: 13,908. Some 2,262 of the city's residents are age 62 or older.

Location: Eufaula lies in southeastern Alabama on the banks of the Chattahoochee River, which forms the border of Alabama and Georgia. It is 50 miles equally from Dothan, AL, and Columbus, GA, 88 miles from Montgomery, AL, and 168 miles from Atlanta, GA.

Climate:

	High	Low
January	58	37
July	91	71

Average relative humidity: 72%

Annual rainfall: 68 inches.

Cost of living: Below average. The nearest indexed city is Dothan, AL, at 89.80. The national average is 100.

Average housing cost: Approximate cost of a new 1,800-square-foot home is $135,000. A 5- to 10-year-old, 1,800-square-foot home costs about $100,000.

Sales tax: 8%

Sales tax exemptions: Prescription drugs.

State income tax: For married couples filing jointly, graduated from 2% of taxable income up to $1,000 to 5% on amounts over $6,000. For single filers, graduated from 2% of taxable income up to $500 to 5% on amounts over $3,000.

Income tax exemptions: Social Security benefits and most private and government retirement pensions are exempt.

Estate tax: Like most states, Alabama has no estate tax except the state's "pickup" portion of the federal tax on estates valued at more than $1 million.

Inheritance tax: None.

Property tax: Eufaula has an ad valorem tax rate of 44 mills, or .044, with homes assessed at 10 percent of market value. The tax on a $135,000 house, without the homestead exemption, is $594.

Homestead exemptions: Up to $4,000 for the state exemption, plus up to $2,000 for the county exemption.

Religion: More than 50 churches serve Eufaula residents, the majority of them Baptist.

Education: Vocational subjects are taught at Wallace Community College, (334) 687-3543 or www.sstc.cc.al.us.

Transportation: Nearest commercial airports are in Dothan, AL, and Columbus, GA, each 50 miles from Eufaula. Dannelly Field in Montgomery, AL, is 88 miles away. Hartsfield International

in Atlanta is 164 miles.

Health: Lakeview Community Hospital has 74 beds and a 24-hour emergency department. It also offers home health and senior circle programs.

Housing options: There are no planned developments for seniors. The home sites most popular among retirees are along the lake and in historic homes. Assisted-living residences include **River Oaks East**, (334) 687-3089; **River Oaks West**, (334) 687-6089; and the **Gardens of Eufaula**, (334) 687-0430.

Visitor lodging: The Eufaula area has 11 hotels and motels, including such chains as Best Western, Comfort Suites, Days Inn, Econo Lodge and Ramada, as well as 101 rooms and 29 cabins in Lakepoint Resort State Park. Sample minimum rates (plus taxes but less such discounts as those offered through AAA and AARP) are: Ramada, $49.50, (334) 687-2021; Best Western Eufaula Inn, $39-$49, (334) 687-3900; Jameson Inn $57, (334) 687-7747; and Lakepoint Resort State Park, $59 for rooms or $79-$188 for cabins, (800) 544-5253.

Information: Eufaula/Barbour County Chamber of Commerce and Tourism Council, 102 N. Orange Ave., P.O. Box 697, Eufaula, AL 36072, (800) 524-7529, (334) 687-6664 or www.eufaula-barbourchamber.com. For more information on retiring to Alabama, contact Alabama Advantage, (800)235-4757 or www.alabamaadvantage.com.

and Lake Eufaula is one of the best places in the South, if not the country, to dip a line. Considered by many to be the "bass capital of the world," Lake Eufaula is a year-around fishery. In the past two years, the 85-mile-long lake has experienced an explosion in the number of bass, according to Tom Mann, one of America's most renowned fishermen and the owner of Mann's Fish World here. "It's the best fishing in 10 years," he says.

Mann, also famed for the fishing lures he has designed, displays freshwater fish native to the area in a 38,000-gallon tank and in 10 smaller ones at his attraction. He also has built what is possibly the only memorial anywhere to a fish. It's a $4,000 marble monument that commemorates Leroy Brown, a legendary bass that Mann trained to jump through a hoop and whose funeral was attended by 700 people.

Lake Eufaula also was the lure for Johnny Tweddle, 66, a pilot for a major airline who retired here in 1995. "I had old military friends who had a place on the lake," he says. "So I had bought a home on the lake in 1982 and leased it out."

In 1992 he regained the home and started commuting back and forth to his main residence in Fairfax, VA. When retirement neared, he and his wife, Carolyn, considered moving to Florida. "But we like rolling hills and the four seasons. And I like living on the lake," he says. So they settled in Eufaula.

Like many other retirees here, the Tweddles like being busy. Johnny sings in a choral group that gives benefit concerts at Christmas and in spring to help finance scholarships for music majors. Carolyn, 65, belongs to a garden club and sings in the church choir. "We stay busy all the time," he says.

Especially attractive to retirees here is the Eufaula Community Center, which has a swimming pool, sauna, two racquetball courts, a fitness room, three meeting rooms, a community room with a two-level walking and running track, an activity room, concession area and child-care playroom. Annual membership is $150 for a single senior, $200 for senior couples. The daily charge for nonmembers is $3, and a 15-visit coupon book can be had for $25.

The region also is popular with bird-watchers and nature lovers who converge on the Eufaula National Wildlife Refuge on the eastern edge of the Mississippi Flyway. Covering 11,184 acres on both sides of the Chattahoochee River, the refuge is a habitat for such endangered species as the bald eagle, wood stork and peregrine falcon.

Johnny and Carolyn do miss some of the options available to them in their former Virginia home. "There's a definite limitation here. We miss the Kennedy Center (in Washington), the plays, the concerts," he says. "We do try to do the bulk of our shopping here, but occasionally we go to Columbus (GA) or Dothan (AL)."

Aside from taxes and real estate, which he says run considerably less, Johnny says the cost of living in Eufaula is "pretty much on a par" with Fairfax. In comparison with other parts of the country, Eufaula boasts lower living costs overall.

"People aren't afraid to speak out, as they are in some other towns," Johnny Tweddle says. "It's a nice small town, very friendly." ●

Eugene, Oregon

From hiking and biking to volunteering and taking classes
— this Oregon city keeps retirees on the go

By Stanton H. Patty

While it's not true that all of Eugene's citizens — including retirees — can be found gasping on running trails or pedaling to exhaustion on bicycle paths, it sometimes seems that way to visitors. If contented retirees here had a theme song, the lyrics would emphasize that you're never too old to fashion an active lifestyle, and the attraction has much to do with "location, location, location" in scenic Oregon.

Robert and Mary Bergfeld, both 60, strap on backpacks and go hiking in the Cascade Range. Dee Valenti, 71, teaches safe driving to fellow seniors and volunteers at the local tourist bureau. Francis and Lorraine Evenhuis, both in their mid-80s, moved 15 times before settling in Eugene and volunteering at Eugene's Sacred Heart Medical Center. Their schedule is filled with concert dates through the music-minded University of Oregon.

Sam and Helen Romm, also in their 80s, are taking classes in current events and taxation at the University of Oregon. George and Mary Jeffrey, both in their late 60s, are busy with classes offered through Oasis, a national educational program for people age 50 or older. Subjects range from yoga to computers. "The idea is to keep people thinking," George says.

Other local retirees agree. Francis (Frank) Evenhuis puts it this way: "We are not retired mentally." Says Sam Romm with a chuckle, "We get around."

Retirees cite the gentle climate, dazzling scenery, first-class medical care and a rich menu of cultural activities as reasons for moving to the Eugene area. But geography, they say, is a key attraction. Eugene is on the Interstate 5 corridor in western Oregon, 110 miles south of Portland and 193 miles north of the California border. The North Pacific Ocean — and Oregon's acclaimed coastal highway — is only an hour or so to the west. The Cascade Mountains — with hiking trails, fishing streams and ski slopes — are about the same distance to the east.

"Couldn't be better," says Bob Bergfeld. "And I'm a gardener," he adds. "You can grow things here that we could only dream about when we lived in

Population: 137,893 in Eugene, 52,864 in Springfield, 322,959 in Lane County.

Location: On Interstate 5 at the southern end of the Willamette Valley in western Oregon's Lane County. Portland, OR, is 110 miles to the north. Eugene is at an elevation of 422 feet.

Climate:

	High	Low
January	45	33
July	80	50

Average relative humidity: 80% in January, 38% in July.

Rain: 42 inches.

Cost of living: Above average (specific index not available).

Median housing cost: $148,801

Sales tax: None.

State income tax: For married couples filing jointly, the rate is graduated from 5% of taxable income up to $5,000 to 9% on amounts over $12,600. For single filers, graduated from 5% of taxable income up to $2,500 to 9% on amounts over $6,300.

Income tax exemptions: Social Security benefits are exempt. Federal pensions are fully exempt for those who retired before October 1991 and may be partially exempt for retirement after that date. There is a retirement income tax credit of up to 9 percent of retirement income for those age 62 and older if they meet specified income limitations.

Intangibles tax: None.

Estate tax: None, except the "pick-up" portion of the federal tax, applicable to taxable estates of more than $1 million.

Property taxes: Because of levies for schools, fire districts, libraries and other agencies, there is a wide range of tax rates across Lane County. In Eugene, the 2001 rate was $18 per $1,000 of assessed value. In Springfield, the rate for 2001 was $15.8017. Property-tax relief is available for low-income seniors.

Homestead exemption: None.

Religion: There are 192 churches in Eugene/Springfield. Affiliations include Adventist, Assemblies of God, Baptist, Buddhist, Catholic, Christian, Church of Christ, Church of God, Christian Science, Disciples of Christ, Episcopal, Evangelical, Foursquare Gospel, Friends, Full Gospel, Islamic, Jehovah's Witnesses, Jewish, Lutheran, Mennonite, Methodist, Mormon, Nazarene, Orthodox, Pentecostal, Presbyterian, Unitarian, United, Unity and Universal.

Education: University of Oregon, in Eugene, has about 17,400 full-time students, www.uoregon.edu. Other options in Eugene are Lane Community College, www.lanecc.edu, and Northwest Christian College, www.nwcc.edu.

Transportation: The Eugene Airport, www.eugeneairport.com, is served by Horizon Air, America West, United Air Lines and United Express. Greyhound Bus Lines provides mainline transportation, and Porter Stage Lines connects Eugene with Florence on the Oregon Coast. Amtrak has northbound service from Eugene to Portland, Seattle and Vancouver, BC, and southbound service to points in California. Lane Transit District buses provide dependable service throughout Eugene/Springfield and Lane County. All buses are equipped with wheelchair lifts and bicycle racks.

Health: In Eugene, Sacred Heart Medical Center has 438 beds. Specialties include cardiology, orthopedics and trauma care, www.peacehealth.org. In Springfield, McKenzie-Willamette Hospital has 114 beds. Specialties include trauma care, intensive care and diagnostics, www.mckweb.com.

New Jersey."

But isn't New Jersey known as the Garden State? "I'm not knocking New Jersey, but they could call Oregon the Garden State, too," Bob says diplomatically.

Eugene has company in this ideal location. Its neighbor, Springfield, is just across I-5 to the east, and locals describe their hometowns together as Eugene/Springfield. With a combined population of 190,757, the two communities form the second-largest metropolitan area in Oregon after Portland.

Residents — and that includes many retirees — have a passion for the vigorous life. They even have kind things to say about running in the rain for which the Northwest is famous. "River rafting and jet boating are fun, too," says Dee Valenti. "It's good to be adventurous. Age doesn't matter all that much."

Folks here also have a high-voltage interest in culture. The Hult Center for the Performing Arts in downtown Eugene, one of the region's best, is the

centerpiece. With affection, audiences have nicknamed the building the "Incredible Hult."

The cultural catalog includes symphony, opera, ballet, chamber music, choral groups, live theater and more. The highlight of the season is the annual Oregon Bach Festival, a 17-day, 50-event marathon of concerts, educational programs and social occasions. The 34-year-old Bach Festival is held in June and July. "It's amazing that a community this size can have something so wonderful," says Mary Bergfeld.

The Bergfelds arrived in Eugene after Mary wrote a computer program so she and Bob could sift through communities they were considering for their retirement years. Among the essentials: Mary wanted a university community with excellent health facilities and definite seasons. She hoped to find "financial advantages" such as relatively low taxes, and Oregon has no sales tax. And she wanted to be near the Pacific Crest Trail, a popular West Coast hiking route,

in an area with moderate weather for gardening.

"The computer flashed Eugene, OR, and Bellingham, WA. Eugene won," recalls Mary, who with Bob had hiked the Oregon and Washington Cascades and Washington's Olympic Mountains on vacations several years ago.

The couple spent most of their working years in the Midwest and on the East Coast before moving from New Jersey to Eugene in December 1999. Bob was general manager of a chemical-manufacturing company when he retired. Mary had been a systems analyst for an electronics manufacturer, and the Bergfelds found themselves able to retire early. "The economy has been very good," Mary says. "We were fortunate."

The Bergfelds bought a 10-year-old hillside home about five miles from downtown Eugene. They were impressed that Eugene was a very tolerant community, says Mary. "People with very different views are able to live

Eugene, OR

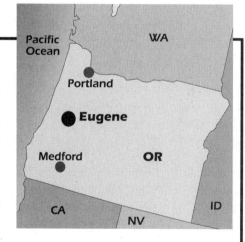

Housing options: Many Eugene/Springfield retirees buy single-family homes or condominiums. The area also has high-quality retirement facilities. Among these is **Cascade Manor,** (541) 342-5901, with 77 apartments equipped with kitchenettes for independent tenants. Cascade Manor offers continuing care with facilities that include a nursing wing. The 35-year-old building in Eugene's South Hills district is situated on five acres, with gardens and walking paths. Transportation is provided for medical appointments. Cascade Manor also schedules day trips to the Oregon coast and other attractions, plus an overnight trip to the Oregon Shakespeare Festival in Ashland. One-time entrance fees range from $39,000 for a studio unit to $115,000 for a two-bedroom apartment. Monthly fees are $1,139-$2,319 for single occupants, $1,656-$2,836 for two occupants, covering meals, utilities, housekeeping and other services. Home to other active seniors is the historic **Eugene Hotel,** (541) 343-8574, a 90-unit apartment house in downtown Eugene. The 77-year-old building is within walking distance of shops, restaurants, banks and other facili-

ties. Rentals are open to independent tenants age 58 or older. Monthly charges range from $1,000 for a studio unit to $2,500 for a two-bedroom apartment. The monthly fee includes dinners each evening, Sunday brunches, housekeeping, utilities, cable TV, shuttle transportation and parking for residents and guests. Also popular with seniors is **SongBrook,** (541) 461-4000, a 140-unit manufactured-home park for tenants age 55 or older. SongBrook is in the western section of Eugene, about six miles from downtown. Residents own their homes and lease sites. Facilities include an 8,000-square-foot community center with an indoor swimming pool, exercise room, card room and meeting space. Leases are $373-$445 per month, depending on lot size and location. SongBrook opened in 1994.

Visitor lodging: The Eugene/Springfield area has 3,100 guest rooms in hotels, motels and bed-and-breakfast inns. Courtesy Inn, in downtown Eugene, has double-occupancy rates beginning at $44.99, (541) 345-3391. Other options: Downtown Motel, also in Eugene, $40, (541) 345-8739; Best Western New Oregon

Motel, near the University of Oregon campus, $69.50 for AAA members, $77.50 for non-AAA members, (541) 683-3669; and Shilo Inn in Springfield, just off Interstate 5, beginning at $59.95, (541) 747-0332.

Information: Convention and Visitors Association of Lane County, 115 W. Eighth Ave., Suite 190, Eugene, OR 97401, (800) 547-5445, (541) 484-5307 or www.visitlanecounty.org. Eugene Area Chamber of Commerce, P.O. Box 1107, Eugene, OR 97440, (541) 484-1314 or www.eugene-chamber.com. Springfield Chamber of Commerce, P.O. Box 155, Springfield, OR 97477, (541) 746-1651 or www.springfield-chamber.org.

together pleasantly. And people here are willing to settle for less materially and more spiritually."

Bob enjoys the absence of lengthy commutes. "A traffic jam here, if it happens at all, is only five or 10 minutes long," he says. "And if they are going to do any major street work, you read about it in the paper the night before."

Sam Romm, another local retiree, also was impressed by the ease in which retirees can get around. The retired elementary school principal from New York City is particularly happy with the Lane Transit District, the area's award-winning public transit system. All of the buses are wheelchair accessible and fitted with bicycle racks. "It's marvelous," Sam says. "Schedules are exact and it gets you everywhere you need to go."

Sam and his wife, Helen, a retired school secretary, moved into a downtown Eugene apartment about 10 months ago. Their son, Dr. Richard Romm, a Eugene cardiologist, coaxed them out of New York after 50 years. "It's a new life for us," says Helen, "and it's good. We were here only a few days and had five calls from local people. That made me feel right away like we belonged."

Sam, accustomed to sometimes-brash New Yorkers, appreciates the courteous ways of local residents. "People here actually say 'thank you' and mean it," he says. "It's an amazing thing." Sam is adjusting to the easygoing tempo of western Oregon, but he says there is one thing he won't change: "I still read my New York Times every day."

George Jeffrey, 69, and his wife, Mary, 67, also appreciate amenities they find in friendly Eugene. George and Mary were on the move for decades before retiring to Eugene in 1998. George's career was in the insurance business, and that rooted the couple in Portland, Eugene, Los Angeles, Seattle, San Francisco and Chicago.

"This is just beautiful country," says Mary. "It's big enough to have many of the big-city amenities and small enough not to be overwhelming. We made the right decision."

Both George and Mary volunteer at Oasis, the educational program for the 50-and-over set. Offerings range from computer classes to concerts, and most classes are held in Eugene's Meier & Frank department store. Oasis also arranges tours, and recent trips have included outings to Ashland (181 miles to the south), for the noted Oregon Shakespeare Festival, and to the Oregon coast. "Oasis is a terrific program, and there's no cost to join," says George.

Are there any negatives about living in Eugene/Springfield? "Well, sometimes there's lots of rain," Mary says. "But that's what keeps things green."

For Frank and Lorraine Evenhuis, retiring to Eugene was a matter of returning to a state they had come to love earlier in their careers. Frank was an English professor at several universities, retiring finally from Eastern Michigan University. Lorraine retired from the Michigan Bell telephone company.

Their cross-country careers included stints in Oregon's Monmouth area, not far from Eugene, and in the college city of Bellingham in the northwestern region of Washington state. "We fell in love with the Pacific Northwest," says Lorraine. "We left part of our hearts here when we moved on. Oregon is not outdone by any state in the union for beauty."

Is this their final move? "Absolutely," says Frank. "It is too lovely to leave." The couple is enchanted with the area's sea-to-mountains setting. But just as important, they say, are the cultural advantages available to the entire community through the University of Oregon. "There is wonderful music," says Lorraine. "And tickets cost less than they would be in big cities."

The Evenhuises bought a two-bed-

room, hillside condominium in the southern part of Eugene that has what Lorraine describes as a "view of our mountains." Those would be the nearby foothills of the Cascade Range. "Just gorgeous," she says.

Another area retiree, Dee Valenti, chose Springfield's Chalet Village, a mobile-home park reserved for tenants age 55 or older. "I've always wanted to live in a mobile home, and now that I'm alone I can," says the single mother of five grown daughters. "It's great."

In fact, Dee is president of the homeowners association at the 120-unit park, where she purchased a two-bedroom mobile home and converted the second bedroom to a computer room. In addition to her duties at Chalet Village, Dee volunteers at the senior center in Springfield, works part time at the Convention and Visitors Association of Lane County and teaches a "55 Alive" driving course for seniors. The motoring class, with two four-hour sessions, is designed by AARP.

Dee spent most of her life in Wisconsin, then moved to the Eugene area four years ago from Virginia. The busy retiree has time for hobbies, too, attending concerts and exploring the Northwest by van with a tour company called Day-Breaks in Oregon Inc. Recent destinations have included Jacksonville, an early day gold-rush town in southern Oregon, and the Oregon Coast Aquarium in Newport, OR. Coming up is a visit to a Native American-owned casino in Lincoln City, OR. "I'll surely make that trip. It's a great way to travel," Dee says. "You sign up for trips that cost maybe $20 or so for the day and then enjoy the people you're traveling with."

Dee's sentiments are echoed time and again by contented retirees. "This is a great place to live," she says. "Everyone is so nice. There are so many things to see and places to go that you're always running out of time. I feel like a kid out of school."●

Fairhope, Alabama

Retirees find friendly neighbors and affordable living in this bayfront Alabama town

By William Schemmel

Stan Grubin doesn't really need anybody to tell him how fortunate he is to be retired in Fairhope. But he loves to hear it, all the same.

"My brother-in-law is a judge who lives in one of the nicest areas of Denver," Stan says. "When he and my sister come down to visit us, he always says, 'You people are getting away with something. This place is too nice.' He can't believe how clean and pretty our town is and how friendly people are."

Stan, 71, and his companion, Joyce, 61, relocated to the Mobile Bay city of 12,480 from Mission Viejo, CA, in 1997.

"Joyce was born in Pascagoula (MS) and grew up in Pensacola (FL), so we'd been coming to the Alabama Gulf coast for several years," Stan says. "Every time we came, we'd look for a place to retire. We finally hit Fairhope, and it was so pretty. There were flowers everywhere, nice shops and restaurants, and beautiful, well-kept residential neighborhoods. And the people were so friendly and welcoming. It reminded us of Monterey and Carmel in California."

It's no coincidence that Fairhope seems like utopia to Stan Grubin and other retirees. In 1894, Midwestern followers of economist George Henry's single-tax theory chose the site on Mobile Bay for an experimental colony. They named it Fairhope, in the "fair hope" it would succeed — and it did.

Under the single-tax theory, land was owned by a corporation and leased to individuals for the good of the community. Those who used the land paid rent to the corporation, which enabled the corporation to combine property taxes, city taxes and sales taxes into a single tax on the land. Lasting legacies of the colony include the bayfront municipal pier and park, which was donated to the town in the 1930s. The municipality was established in 1908.

The city's progressive climate has attracted many writers, craftspeople and artists who lend their talents to the annual Fairhope Arts and Crafts Festival and other cultural activities. Alabama native Fannie Flagg wrote her best-selling novel, "Fried Green Tomatoes at the Whistle Stop Cafe," while living in Fairhope.

One of the first Alabama communities with a horticulturalist on the municipal payroll, Fairhope has an attractive downtown with wide streets and brick-edged sidewalks lined with art galleries, boutiques and good restaurants. Flower baskets adorn streetlights and utility poles, and every year more than 200 new trees are planted on city streets and in parks.

Large single-family homes, many with cedar shake roofs and lovely gardens, patios and swimming pools, fill residential neighborhoods. Spacious lots, many with waterfront views, are beautified by live oak trees, Spanish moss and lush stands of azaleas, camellias and other flowering plants. Planned communities such as Rock Creek, Quail Creek and Fairfield Place have a variety of housing styles with easy access to golf, tennis and social activities. Rental apartments and condos also are available. Homestead Village and the Hamlet at Carroll Place have independent and assisted-living apartments and cottages.

Retirees like Stan Grubin were attracted by the low cost of living in Fairhope. "Our home is a 2,000-square-foot patio house, called a villa, in Quail Creek," Stan says. "It's on the 18th fairway of the municipal golf course. We've done a lot of improvements, including a screened back porch, which Joyce just loves. We can sit out there and it's like looking at a movie set. Compared to where we lived in California, where we could hear the hum of a freeway day and night, it's so quiet that we can hear the crickets."

Stan and Joyce are enthusiastically involved in their adopted hometown.

Stan, who worked in management for churches in California before his retirement, plays golf two or three times a week. He volunteers for the Mayor's Christmas Parade, coordinates a weekly seniors golf tournament and helps his neighbors set up computers. Joyce is part of a tai chi aerobics group, volunteers at a hospital wellness center and spends much of her free time in her garden.

True to its Midwestern roots, Fairhope continues to attract many retirees from Iowa, Michigan, Wisconsin, Indiana and other Midwestern states. Almost 25 percent of the population is 65 or older. Gary and Jean Wilson made the move from Wisconsin in January 1999.

"If you can't find something to do in Fairhope, you simply aren't looking," says Jean, who left a law partnership in Baraboo, WI, to move to Fairhope. "The James P. Nix Center has something going on all the time."

A club for seniors, the Nix Center's weekly calendar includes video exercises, billiards and table tennis, board games, golf and tennis tournaments, tai chi exercises, health screenings, nutritional lectures, arts and crafts, line dancing, financial advice, grief support, travel talks and many other programs.

Retirees are invited to volunteer at the Nix Center, local hospitals and annual festivals like the Mayor's Christmas Parade as well as a huge arts and crafts festival in spring. Volunteers staff the Eastern Shore Art Center, a 12,000-square-foot privately supported gallery that displays works by local, regional and national artists and sponsors concert, film and lecture series and art education classes.

In whatever free time remains, Fairhope residents can enjoy the single-tax colony's best-loved legacy, the beautiful bay-front park with a municipal pier extended by a quarter mile into Mobile Bay. Around the pier are duck ponds and seasonal plantings by the town's accomplished gardeners. Fairhope's 2.5 miles of beach are the stage for boating and fishing tournaments and the yearly Jubilee. One of Fairhope's most eagerly anticipated happenings, Jubilee is a natural late summer phenomenon when bottom-dwelling fish, shrimp, crabs and other sea creatures, delirious from a sudden lack of oxygen in the water, rush en masse to shore. Waiting are hundreds of seafood lovers, armed with every bucket, scoop, net and cooking pot they can get their hands on.

Fairhope protects its beauty and en-

Fairhope, AL

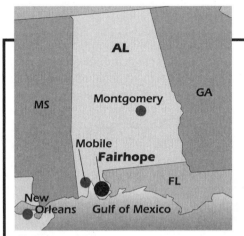

Population: 12,480 in Fairhope, 16,581 in Daphne, 5,423 in Spanish Fort, 1,876 in Point Clear, 140,415 in Baldwin County.

Location: On the eastern shore of Alabama's Mobile Bay, a half-hour by car from Mobile, 45 minutes from the Gulf of Mexico beaches and Pensacola, FL.

Climate:

	High	Low
January	62	42
July	91	72

Average relative humidity: 73%
Rain: 67 inches.
Subtropical climate with mild winters, balmy springs and delightful autumns. Summers are long, hot and muggy with frequent thunderstorms. Occasional hurricane threats in September and October.

Average housing cost: $193,079 for Fairhope/Point Clear, $157,799 for Spanish Fort, and $190,710 for Daphne/Montrose.

Cost of living: Below average (specific index not available).

Sales tax: 6% (2% county, 4% state)

Sales tax exemptions: Prescription drugs.

State income tax: For married couples filing jointly, graduated from 2% of taxable income up to $1,000 to 5% on amounts over $6,000. For single filers, graduated from 2% of taxable income up to $500 to 5% on amounts over $3,000.

Income tax exemptions: Social Security benefits and most private and government retirement pensions are exempt.

Intangibles tax: None.

Inheritance tax: None.

Estate tax: None, except the state's "pickup" portion of the federal tax, applicable to taxable estates of more than $1 million.

Property taxes: $42.50 per $1,000 of assessed value, with homes assessed at 10 percent of market value. Taxes on a $190,000 home are $808 a year, not including the homestead exemption.

Homestead exemption: Homeowners under age 65 are entitled to a maximum $4,000 homestead exemption. Homeowners 65 and older who have an annual adjusted gross income of less than $12,000, and those homeowners retired due to disability, are entitled to an exemption up to $5,000 of assessed value.

Religion: More than 100 churches and synagogues represent all major faiths.

Health: Thomas Hospital in Fairhope is a 150-bed facility that offers acute care, with a 24-hour emergency department, surgery and nuclear medical expertise. Mercy Medical, a Sisters of Mercy facility in Daphne, has a rehabilitation center, subacute care, long-term and Alzheimer's care, hospice and home health services. Baldwin County Mental Health provides a 24-hour crisis line, rape crisis center, family and group counseling, and alcohol and drug abuse treatment. There are five nursing homes and seven assisted-living facilities in the area. Helicopters can transfer patients to hospitals in Mobile and Pensacola.

Transportation: There is no regularly scheduled public transportation system. The Baldwin County Rural Area Transport System (BRATS) transports the handicapped and indigent to doctors, shopping centers and other areas. The state-operated Mobile Bay Car Ferry connects Dauphin Island and Gulf Shores. Mobile and Pensacola airports are an hour away.

Education: Continuing-education courses in business, education and liberal arts are offered at the University of South Alabama at Baldwin County, an accredited branch of the main campus in Mobile.

Most courses meet once a week at the Fairhope campus downtown. The Eastern Shore Art Center and Bay Rivers Art Guild offer continuing-education courses in painting, pottery, photography and other media.

Housing options: Quail Creek and **Rock Creek,** planned communities in Fairhope, have 1,800- to 2,000-square-foot patio homes starting at $175,000. Larger homes of 2,400 to 3,000 square feet start at $250,000. Built around the 18-hole Fairhope Municipal Golf Course, Quail Creek has its own tennis courts, pool and clubhouse. Rock Creek, (251) 928-2223, has a semiprivate 18-hole course, tennis, pool and clubhouse. **Fairfield Place,** (251) 928-6200, is a new subdivision five minutes from downtown with homes from the $170,000s to high $300,000s. **Arbor Gates,** (251) 928-2002, is an upscale one- to three-bedroom apartment development with monthly rental from $545 to $820. **The Hamlet at Carroll Place,** (251) 928-5413, and **Homestead Village,** (251) 929-0250, have independent and assisted-living cottages and apartments.

Visitor lodging: Fairhope Inn and Restaurant, a bed-and-breakfast inn in the center of town, has three guest rooms and a carriage house with private baths, $120-$175 including full breakfast, (251) 928-6226. Marriott's Grand Hotel, a resort on Mobile Bay, has seasonal rates of $139-$450, (800) 544-9933. Gulf State Park, on the beach at Gulf Shores, has seasonal rates of $50-$214 for hotel rooms, $55-$111 for furnished cabins and $12-$25 for camping; call (800) 544-4853 for hotel reservations or (251) 948-7275 for cabins and camping information.

Information: Eastern Shore Chamber of Commerce, 327 Fairhope Ave., Fairhope, AL 36532, (251) 621-8222 or www.eschamber.com. City of Fairhope, (251) 928-2136 or www.cofairhope.com.

viable character with some of Alabama's most stringent zoning laws. And it has won national recognition for its dedication to preserving trees in its parks and along streets, both in commercial and residential areas, every year since the National Arbor Day Foundation created its Tree City USA award in 1983.

Alabama and Florida Gulf coast beaches are about 40 minutes by car from Fairhope. Gulf Shores and Orange Beach, on the Alabama Gulf, are vacation destinations with hotels, condos, seafood restaurants and championship-caliber golf courses. Urban attractions also are within easy reach. Mobile, Alabama's second-largest city, is about a half-hour across Mobile Bay. Pensacola and Florida's Gulf coast are about 45 minutes away.

Baldwin County, which includes Fairhope, is Alabama's largest in area and the fastest-growing in population. The South Alabama Regional Planning Commission projects that the county's current population of 140,415 will increase by 20 to 30 percent during the next 10 years.

Other Baldwin County communities include Point Clear, a resort and residential community of 1,876 residents on Mobile Bay. An attraction there is Marriott's Grand Hotel, a resort with golf, tennis and boating facilities. Nearby communities also include the 19th-century resort town of Daphne, population 16,581; Bay Minette, the county seat with about 7,820 residents; and Spanish Fort, population 5,423.

The Gulf coast was Jean and Gary Wilson's introduction to Fairhope. "It wasn't a major decision for us," Jean recalls. "We had a condo at Gulf Shores and had been coming down here for several years. My husband is originally from Birmingham, and when he retired from Rayovac in Madison (WI), we decided to move down here full time."

The Wilsons purchased a 2,400-square-foot home in Quail Creek. "I'm in my 40s and my husband is in his 50s, so we say we're only partly retired," Jean says. "I was appointed by the mayor to the zoning and planning committee and the Fairhope First Civic Association, which plans various events. We play a lot of golf and my husband works part time at the golf pro shop."

The Wilsons say the cost of living is one of Fairhope's many tangible pluses. "You can really stretch your money here," Jean says. "Home prices may be a little high by Alabama standards, but you can get a lot more house for the money here than in Wisconsin. And taxes and utilities are much lower. I'd recommend it to retirees or anyone else looking for a less-stressful place to live. Other than the summer heat and humidity, I can't think of any real drawbacks to living here."

Helen and Bob Rudy, who moved from Michigan in 1997, second that endorsement. "We didn't look at any other areas. When we saw Fairhope, it was a gut feeling. I guess you could call it love at first sight," Helen says. "It's such a beautiful area, and the people are so friendly."

The Rudys, both in their 70s, moved into a custom-built, 1,800-square-foot villa in the Quail Creek community, where they found a social network ready to make them feel at home. "My husband plays golf several times a week. He belongs to Kiwanis and volunteers for local events," Helen says. "We get together with friends for lunch and dinner, we play bridge and tennis and enjoy the pool and the art galleries and activities in town. If you can't find enough to do, it's your own fault.

"Taxes and utilities are definitely less expensive," she adds. "Here we get one utility bill. In Michigan we'd get three or four."

Barbara Lawson began visiting the Alabama Gulf coast in the 1950s, but when she retired from teaching in Columbia, TN, 11 years ago, she looked all over south Florida before coming back to the Alabama coast and settling in Fairhope.

"I love golf and the Gulf, and they drew me back here," Barbara says. "I can't say that I've really retired. If you're able-bodied, they won't let you do that. They want to put your expertise to work. I've worked for the chamber of commerce for a while, then the mayor got me involved with all kinds of activities."

Barbara now is a senior specialist for ERA Brazeal & Harris Real Estate. "The city is growing, but we're not losing the small-town charm and quality of life that makes this such a wonderful place to live," she says. "I can help people find what they're looking for — and be as happy here as I am."●

Fallbrook, California

This pastoral community is surrounded by horse ranches and avocado groves

By Mary-Ann Bendel

Fallbrook is an undiscovered jewel in the retirement landscape, tucked away from the fray of Southern California gridlock. "You don't drive through Fallbrook on your way to someplace else," says Bob Leonard, director of the Fallbrook Chamber of Commerce. And therein lies its charm.

Nestled among the coastal foothills of north San Diego County, it has been compared visually and in terms of climate to Monte Carlo. To the east there is Palomar Mountain, and on the west is Camp Pendleton, the U.S. Marine base. A half-hour inland from the ocean, Fallbrook lies an hour from San Diego and two hours from Los Angeles.

The town is a visual delight, with its flower fields, vineyards and fruit groves. At an elevation of 1,000 feet, the native flora is live oak, coastal oak, sycamore and eucalyptus. Early in the morning, it just smells good here.

Main Street has a dusty Old West feeling, with some buildings dating to the late 1800s. You are likely to see more pickups than luxury cars on the roads. And in little restaurants like the homely Wayside Cafe, regulars have their own coffee mugs hanging from the beams. Much of Fallbrook's business is done here. Fallbrook is so low-key that most of the stores on Main Street are closed on Monday.

However, don't be fooled. Fallbrook is a place with a deep sense of community. This unincorporated village has 160 volunteer organizations. It depends on service and volunteer groups to take care of the community. The town welcomes retirees to help keep the town a safe and pleasant place to live.

During a devastating brush fire in February 2002, the community pulled together and showed the state of California what individuals can do if they support one another. Retirees Joe and Carlotta Littell lost their home in the fire. "Within a couple of hours, we had

nine offers for a house to live in as long as we needed it. Plumbers, electricians and restaurants have refused to give us a bill," says Joe, 77.

Other retirees are just as enthusiastic. Jan Reed-Massman, 52, and her husband, Dr. Jim Massman, 68, have been married 27 years and spent 25 of them in Augusta, GA. Jim was a physician at the Medical College in Augusta when he retired. They moved to Fallbrook two years ago and love it.

They left a home with property and now have a condo in an area called Village Creek. "We found Fallbrook by word of mouth," Jan says. "There is no traffic here and there are lots of good things about the community, with a sense of isolation." She still works as a clinical social worker, and Jim keeps busy volunteering with the sheriff's patrol. He also loves the local Vintage Car Club. "He is fantastically happy here," Jan says.

While the Massmans downsized into a condo, two other relocated couples bought homes with some property. Phyllis Audiss, 63, and her husband, John Ortis, 61, moved to Fallbrook two years ago from Pleasanton, CA, in the northern part of the state. They both worked for Pacific Bell. Phyllis was in the computer section and John was project manager in database administration. They bought a single-story house on two acres and now have their first real yard. They have a beautiful view of a racetrack and the horses grazing there.

"We found Fallbrook on a fluke," says Phyllis, who has joined the newcomer and garden clubs while her husband hikes and works on the Internet. "I like the whole quiet atmosphere — seeing the stars at night," she says.

Ruth and Jack Ratterree, both 65, also moved to Fallbrook two years ago. He was the principal clarinet player in the Phoenix Symphony, and she was a trust administrator for the Northern Trust

Bank in Phoenix.

"We love Fallbrook — the quiet is very nice after a hectic city life," Ruth says, noting that they have an acre of property. Jack is very happy in Fallbrook, playing golf daily. Ruth does miss longtime friends back in Arizona, though, and in some ways, moving from a large city to a rural area has not been easy. But she feels she can make the adjustment.

Fallbrook offers retirees a myriad of housing options. Some people choose to buy a couple of acres a few miles out of town to grow avocados and raise horses. Others choose a place like Poets Square right downtown. "We have well designed large homes on little lots. Two models have lower-level master bedrooms," says Karen Schlonsky, broker for the Poets Square housing development. The homes there range from $200,000 to $300,000 and are 2,200 to 2,600 square feet in size.

There are modest homes here, but it takes time to find them. Some people look for a home here for five to 10 years before they retire and then buy. Marines at Camp Pendleton may buy a home during a posting here and rent it out until they retire. Bob Tilley and his wife, Rene, both 64, bought a home during his last military posting and stayed after retirement. "Fallbrook is a magical place," says Joe, who volunteers full time for four months of the year with the Marine Corps Scholarship Fund.

Many hold out for a good buy on high-end properties. "Prices here range from $300,000 to $2 million for a vineyard or horse property," says Joann Rapaszky, a real estate agent with Coldwell Banker Landmark Group in Fallbrook. "There are people sort of hidden in the hills who are writers, painters and sculptors," she adds.

Less-expensive options include mobile home parks. Valley Oaks Mobile Ranch is located seven miles out of town and is surrounded by oak trees. "Double-wides 20 by 60 feet range from $50,000 to $100,000," says assistant manager John James. "About 30 percent of the people here are retirees."

There also is an option, Silvergate Retirement Residence, for retirees who need assisted living. Living accommodations range from studio apartments to one-bedroom suites. "We are here for people who can't manage a house anymore," says administrator Dorothy Pratt, noting that Silvergate soon will add 36 new units. Another 32 new units are planned to serve the needs of Alzheimer patients.

In terms of day-care facilities for Alzheimer patients, Fallbrook is in the forefront. "The key to caring for Alzheimer patients is to treat them like adults," says Joy Glenner, president of the George G. Glenner Alzheimer Family Centers. Her late husband, for whom the family centers are named, established the first Alzheimer day-care program in the United States 20 years ago.

The local center is on the grounds of the Fallbrook Health Care Center, which has helped 15,000 families to cope with the disease. Volunteers from the community help with music therapy, crafts and vegetable gardens. Marines from Camp Pendleton come in their dress blues to visit the patients. Staff members wear street clothes, lending an ambiance that is less institutional.

Some retirees are active in the huge local avocado industry, which is celebrated each April in an annual avocado festival that includes a 20-mile bike ride and packinghouse tours, along with avocados sold by the pound or the tree. (Next year's festival will be April 13.) Most growers have between one and five acres, but some are as large as 20 acres. Typical are Jeff and Jill Cole, who had a 2.5-acre avocado ranch for 25 years. They sold it and moved to a new home in Sycamore Ranch, a development on a golf course. Jill, a fourth-grade teacher at Live Oaks Elementary School, plans to retire next year. "We are used to property, so we have about an acre and a half now," Jill says.

Active environmental groups like the Fallbrook Land Conservancy have many volunteer retirees working to preserve and enhance the rural lifestyle and natural beauty of the area. This nonprofit, tax-exempt organization manages more than 800 acres of open space. The conservancy has 1,000 members, and the majority are retirees. "Our main goal is to preserve our rural open space," says Sue Thorne, administrative assistant. She sends a newsletter to members twice a year.

Another facet of this organization is caring for the Santa Margarita Trail. This riding and hiking trail along the Santa Margarita River on 1,500 acres of Fallbrook Utility land is a delight for nature lovers. Horses are popular in Fallbrook, which boasts a number of equestrian ranches that raise quarter

Fallbrook, CA

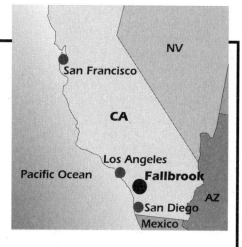

Population: 37,334
Location: The rural community of Fallbrook is located in the northernmost corner of San Diego County, 15 miles from the Pacific Ocean. Bordered on the west by Camp Pendleton Marine Base, Fallbrook is bisected by Interstate 15, which provides access to Los Angeles, San Diego and Orange and Riverside counties.
Climate:

	High	Low
January	63	42
July	90	76

Average relative humidity: 30%
Rain: 11 inches.
Cost of living: Above average (specific index not available).
Average housing cost: $350,000
Sales tax: 7.25%
Sales tax exemption: Food for home consumption and prescription drugs.
State income tax: For married couples filing jointly, graduated from 1% of taxable income up to $11,496 to 9.3% on amounts over $75,450. For single filers, graduated from 1% of taxable income up to $5,748 to 9.3% on amounts over $37,725.
Income tax exemptions: Social Security benefits and railroad pensions are exempt.

Estate tax: None, except the state's "pick-up" portion of the federal tax, applicable to taxable estates of more than $1 million.
Inheritance tax: None
Property tax: Tax is 1% of appraised value. The annual tax on a home valued at $350,000 would be about $3,500.
Homeowner's exemption: If you own and occupy your home as your principal place of residence, you may apply for an exemption of $7,000 off assessed value for an annual savings of about $70 on property taxes. New property owners will automatically receive an exemption application. For information, call the Assessor's Office, County of San Diego, (619) 531-5772, or visit www.sdarcc.com.
Religion: Most denominations are represented locally.
Education: Palomar College is 15 miles from Fallbrook in San Marcos. Courses from accounting to zoology are $11 per unit. Palomar offers free classes to seniors at the Fallbrook High School from 4:30 to 8:30 p.m. when the high school is not in session. Among courses are four levels of math, English, art history, physical education, yoga, step aerobics, weight training, speech, Spanish and political science.

Transportation: Taxi and limousine service is available locally, but there is no public transportation. However, shuttles are available to take Alzheimer patients to day-care programs.
Health: Fallbrook Hospital is a superb hospital for its size. It has 47 beds and a 24-hour emergency room and offers general acute care.
Visitor lodging: Best Western Franciscan Inn, $63-$81, (760) 728-6174. Fallbrook Country Bed and Breakfast Inn, $95-$101, (760) 728-1114.
Information: Fallbrook Chamber of Commerce, 233 E. Mission Road, Suite A, Fallbrook, CA 92028-2555, (760) 728-5845 or www.fallbrookca.org.

horses, plantation walkers and Arabians.

For retirees interested in birds, the 46-acre Los Jilgueros Preserve just south of the downtown area has more than 50 species. Jilguero is the Spanish name for linnet, or house finch. Another local passion centers on trees. At one time the area was a huge oak forest. The avocado growers cut it down, and now residents want to reforest the oaks, sycamores and alders.

"We have planted 4,000 trees in eight years," says Jackie Heyeman, a volunteer with Save Our Forests. With help from a grant from the National Tree Trust, SOF has established a nursery to provide a supply of trees for public beautification projects. Volunteers now are replanting hills burned in the fire of February 2002.

Much of Fallbrook's social life revolves around such clubs as the Rotary, Lions, Kiwanis and VFW Post 1924. As in many communities, local churches also play a central role. "This is a very spiritual community," says Rev. Don Kroger, rector of St. John's Episcopal Church. "All the churches are growing and there is no rivalry between them — there's lots of fellowship here."

Fallbrook is a very active and intellectual retirement spot. There are more than 100 area artists. Frank Hopkins is a graphic designer who works all over the country. He moved here from Orange County in 1972. "I like the rural atmosphere here," he says. "The downtown has a nostalgia of the past about it."

For senior art lovers, there are galleries, outdoor murals and bronze sculptures. Local residents donate sculptures to enhance the downtown area. The Fallbrook Art Works houses a working bronze foundry and a ceramic facility. The Art Institute has art classes and workshops, a ceramics studio and hot glass studio. Many classes are accredited with Palomar Community College in nearby San Marcos.

The Art and Cultural Center is a self-supporting, nonprofit facility. Exhibits throughout the year may include such topics as wildlife, sculpture, glass, aviation, metal, watercolor and even 16th-century bobbin copper lace. The center places an emphasis on art education for children. Every third Thursday there is an art walk downtown.

There are many creative volunteer opportunities. The 1940s era Mission Theatre on Main Street has been transformed into its former Art Deco glory. The production "Scrooge" has become a local Christmas tradition for many residents.

The Bob Burton Center for the Performing Arts at the Fallbrook High School opened in November 2001 with a black tie affair featuring local resident Rita Coolidge. The center is a joint project of the community and schools. The Fallbrook Music Society volunteers help bring classical music performers to junior high students. Their annual outdoor Concert on the Green each summer draws hundreds of people.

The sense of history runs deep in Fallbrook. The first Girl Scout troop west of the Mississippi started here 135 years ago, and it is still here. The Fallbrook Women's Club is 95 years old and helps support 14 different organizations. Most members have lived in Fallbrook a long time but welcome new members willing to help with everything from college scholarships to getting blue bears for the Fire Department to give to sick children.

History buffs can enjoy the Fallbrook Historical Society. The Fallbrook Gem and Mineral Society looks at the geology of the area and in spring, the local Pala Tourmaline Mine welcomes visitors. For flower lovers, the Green Thumbs of the Fallbrook Garden Club maintain a wildflower and butterfly garden at Live Oak Park.

A major activity here is golf. Fallbrook has six top golf courses within five miles, and there are 60 scattered throughout north San Diego County. Many golfers come to play these courses and return to retire here. Seniors play well into their 80s in this climate, which many retirees feel is the best in the world.

"Fallbrook is the ultimate place to live," says world traveler Joe Littell.●

Fort Collins, Colorado

Colorado city intent on preserving beauty, quality of life as it grows

By Claire Walter

Massachusetts-born John and Camille Trolla lived in Southern California for more than 40 years. When it came time to retire, they moved within sight of the Rocky Mountains.

The Trollas picked Fort Collins, CO, because, as John, a former school teacher puts it, "You see blue sky with clouds, smell clean air, watch the leaves changing."

John, 68, retired two years before their California house sold. As soon as it did, Milly, 66, left Disneyland after 24 years in personnel and purchasing, and in two weeks they had relocated to a new life in Fort Collins.

Jack O'Neill of Huntington, NY, spent four days in Fort Collins while visiting a brother in Denver.

"I was impressed by the cleanliness and beauty," the former high school guidance counselor recalls. "I was also impressed by the young people. Then I saw a house I liked." He phoned his wife, Ellen, and said, "I'm going to make a bid on a house, OK?" She agreed.

That deal didn't fly, but Jack told the real estate agent he wanted something in that neighborhood. The O'Neills bought a home sight unseen, didn't even attend the closing, and the agent found tenants for the house until the O'Neills were able to move.

"Everything was handled by mail," Ellen marvels. "In New York, you don't do anything without lawyers."

The couple, now both 60, say people are amazed that they would buy a home without seeing it first. They recall one woman's reaction when they related the story while asking her for directions to their new home when they first arrived.

"You let him buy a house you had never seen!" the woman exclaimed to Ellen.

"I never saw it either," Jack piped up. But the house turned out to suit them perfectly, even fulfilling a longtime dream. "I always wanted to live on a cul-de-sac," says Jack — and now he does.

Set where the prairie crumples into rolling foothills, Fort Collins offers a palpable sense of space and freedom, yet has such urban amenities as good shopping, a lively cultural scene, fine health care and decent public transportation. Founded as a military post on the Cache La Poudre River, Fort Collins made the transition to a civilian settlement in the 1870s, when Colorado A&M (now Colorado State University) was founded. CSU, Colorado's second-largest college, has more than 20,000 students, who bring to the city a youthful energy that appeals to retirees.

The downtown area, known as Old Town, is a national historic district and remains the vibrant heart of the city, with a classic main street. Although Fort Collins has two major indoor malls and many neighborhood shopping areas, Old Town draws residents and visitors alike to its interesting shops, cafes, restaurants and street festivals.

The city's major thoroughfares are spaced a mile apart, forming a neatly planned grid. Most retail and commercial development is clustered around big intersections and along the boulevards. Neighborhoods often are complemented by parks providing green space.

The community has made a concerted effort to preserve and enhance the beautiful setting. Height limitations on buildings assure that the foothills, not skyscrapers, will dominate the view. Utility lines are buried, and there's been an aggressive tree-planting program.

Broad, tree-lined boulevards are easy to drive, but Fort Collins is not totally car-dependent. Nearly 60 miles of bike routes and a 14-mile protected path for cycling, jogging and walking get heavy year-round use, and a downtown river walk is in the works. Additionally, the city's Transfort bus system is gaining riders at 30 percent a year.

Despite being close to the Rockies,

the weather is relatively mild. Hot summer days are moderated by cool nights, and cold winter nights usually turn into warm, sunny days. With low humidity, even extreme temperatures rarely are uncomfortable. At Fort Collins' 4,979-foot elevation, snow melts quickly and is usually off streets and sidewalks in hours. (Even the indoor climate is good: Restaurants with 30 or more seats must have a no-smoking section, and many are totally smoke-free.)

This booming city of 118,652 — up an average of about 2.5 percent annually since the mid-'80s — is working to balance a healthy economy with planned growth, rather than the kind of mindless development that has driven people from other places.

Ward Luthi is a land-use and transportation planner by profession and founder of Walking the World, a hiking program for people age 50 and older. His Citizen Planners is a grass-roots group studying environmental and development issues.

"We're seeing an exodus from California, and one place they're coming is Colorado," Luthi says. "It tells you there's something here that people want, and there's something out there they don't want anymore. Remember, those people went to California not too long ago because California had what we have now."

Fort Collins' healthy climate, both physically and fiscally, has fueled robust growth, but natives and newcomers alike are concerned with retaining quality of life. Few want to squelch growth, but most residents want to manage it.

"I left Hawaii because we ruined paradise," says 72-year-old John Peacock, retired president of a commuter airline there. He got involved with Challenge Fort Collins, a citizens' group studying and planning Fort Collins' future.

Like other cities in the state, Fort Collins is seeking ways to get residents out of their cars and into some form of public transportation. Peacock envisions the Front Range Railroad, a high-speed train linking Fort Collins with Denver International Airport and other Front Range cities along the eastern edge of the Rockies. He foresees managed growth along the rail corridor rather than at random.

A consensus is growing that, in order to preserve the prized sense of community in the area, there should be buffer zones, or green areas, established between towns. Such zones would keep towns from growing into each other and becoming a congested megalopolis. Residents are still discussing what constitutes buffer zones, though, with one camp wanting them to remain as farmland and another finding golf courses, parks or individual houses on 35-acre tracts acceptable.

While big skies and open spaces provide an expansive umbrella for the whole city, its lifestyle and weather continue to captivate residents. Norman and Eleanor Christiansen, both 71, lived all over the country while he was a newspaper publisher. In the early '70s, they spent five years in Boulder, another Colorado university town.

"We chose Colorado because of its climate and beauty," Eleanor says. "We

Fort Collins, CO

Population: 118,652 in city, 251,494 in Larimer County.

Location: In northeastern Colorado, 60 miles from Denver. The city, at an altitude of 4,979 feet, perches on rolling plains against the backdrop of the Rocky Mountains.

Climate:

	High	Low
January	40	13
July	86	56

Average relative humidity: 37%
Rain: 15 inches.
Snow: 51 inches.
The city has a sunny, four-season climate, averaging 296 days of sunshine a year, 116 of them clear and 180 partly sunny. There's measurable snowfall (1/10 inch or more) on an average of 25 days a year, with 3 inches or more falling on five of those days.
Cost of living: 107.3, based on national average of 100.
Average housing cost: $205,000
Sales tax: 6.5%
Sales tax exemptions: Professional services, prescription drugs, some medical supplies.
State income tax: For married couples filing jointly and single filers, taxable income is taxed at 4.63%.
Income tax exemptions: There is an

exemption from taxable pension and Social Security benefits of up to $20,000 for each person ages 55-64 and up to $24,000 for each person age 65 and older.
Intangibles tax: None.
Estate tax: None, except the state's "pick-up" portion of the federal tax, applicable to taxable estates above $1 million.
Property taxes: The property tax rate in Fort Collins is $87.29 per $1,000 of assessed value, with homes assessed at 9.15% of market value. The tax on a $205,000 home is about $1,637 a year.
Homestead exemption: The homestead exemption for senior citizens provides an actual-value reduction to a maximum of $100,000. This applies only to a primary residence for citizens over the age of 65. Also, this exemption is applicable only to a primary residence that has been owner-occupied for the 10 years immediately preceding the subject tax year.
Religion: The city has 73 churches and two synagogues.
Education: Colorado State University has continuing-education non-credit classes days and evenings; tuition is half-price for students age 60 and older. Front Range Community College's Larimer campus offers more than 90 low-cost adult-education classes through its continuing-education program. Fort Collins Parks and Recreation also has classes, and Poudre Valley Hospital's Aspen Club for people age 50 and above offers many free services and classes on health, wellness and other issues.
Transportation: Transfort, the city bus system, operates daily except Sunday on about 17 routes; the fare for those age 60 and older is 50 cents, and transfers

are free. SAINT/Care-A-Van provides free on-request or regularly scheduled door-to-door rides for registered clients age 60 and older and for citizens with disabilities. There's frequent bus service to Denver and Cheyenne, WY, and Airport Express operates hourly buses to the new Denver International Airport (about an hour-and-a-half drive from Fort Collins). There are commuter flights between Denver and Fort Collins-Loveland Airport.
Health: Poudre Valley Hospital, with 250 beds, has in- and outpatient services, including regional heart and neurosciences centers. Specialty and teaching hospitals are located in Denver. There are assisted-living facilities and nursing homes in Fort Collins. In addition, Meals on Wheels provides hot meals to the homebound, Elderhaus offers day care for the elderly and Senior Chuckwagon delivers lunches for those 60 and older.
Housing options: More than 65 percent of the homes in Fort Collins have been built since 1970, many in new subdivisions. Most are single-family homes, but patio homes, condominiums and a few full-service, high-rise apartment buildings also are available. Among the new subdivisions, Among subdivisions, homes start at $225,000 in **Paragon Estates**, **Indian Hills**, **Nelson Farm** and **South Ridge**, and slightly higher at $250,000 in **Stone Ridge**.
Visitor lodging: The city has 20 hotels and motels, including the Fort Collins Marriott, (970) 226-5200, $89-$169 for a double room, and Plaza Inn, (970) 493-7800, $50-$100.
Information: Fort Collins Area Chamber of Commerce, 225 S. Meldrum St., Fort Collins, CO 80521, (970) 482-3746 or www.fcchamber.org.

love the mountains, the outdoors, nature. Fort Collins has everything — cleanliness, beauty, bike paths, culture. And it's the right size — between a big city and a tiny town."

Norman says their moves have allowed them to analyze many different places to live. He adds, "There are no negatives here. It's nice to go to the theater one evening and the next day put on your fishing clothes and go fishing."

Carl and Grace Hittle have lived all over the world, but they settled in Fort Collins. Carl, an eastern Colorado native, received his doctorate in agronomy from what is now CSU, where he met Grace, daughter of a professor. His career took them to Central America, Sri Lanka, Nepal and India. The couple, both 72, selected Fort Collins because it is a college town with good medical care and access to the mountains.

Carl is part of a group that hikes once a week in summer and snowshoes in winter, usually in Rocky Mountain National Park, the Indian Peaks Wilderness or Roosevelt National Forest for the day.

The Trollas also hike, but they've discovered greater joy in paleontology. They prospect a ridge above a local cement plant (they've befriended the company's geologist), and sometimes they head for Wyoming's rich fossil beds. They identify and clean the specimens and mount them on wooden plaques that John shapes and Milly finishes.

The Christiansens prefer sightseeing, with a lunch stop in a picturesque town. "We take trips all around the mountains," Norman says. "In the East and Midwest, people are so confined in winter. In Florida where we once lived, people don't go out in summer."

The Fort Collins climate, with lots of sunny days, fosters year-round outdoor activities. While winter brings snow and cold temperatures, heavy snowfall and long stretches of freezing temperatures are uncommon.

For the O'Neills, who retain a distinct Eastern, urban outlook (Ellen grew up in Boston, Jack in New York), having the Rockies as a visual backdrop and occasional destination suffices. When their daughter, a New York City police officer who patrols Times Square, visited, she said the neighborhood was so quiet that she couldn't sleep. "Is everyone dead around here?" she asked the first morning.

Fort Collins may seem too quiet to an NYPD Blue, but retirees find lots to do. The Christiansens participate in Bible study, and Norman swims at a local pool. The Hittles found the Newcomers Club an excellent way to make new friends. Their "Retired Couples Out to Lunch" group grew so large that it had to be split into two eating parties.

Carl also joined Poudre Golden K, a Kiwanis group for men age 55 and older. "I never had time for that before," he says.

RSVP — the Retired Seniors Volunteer Program — provides another avenue to be involved in the community and meet people.

Ellen O'Neill, a former nurse, took a temporary job one Christmas as a cooking demonstrator at a local store and found it "so much fun" that she stayed on three days a week. With a low 3.5 percent unemployment rate, Fort Collins has part-time jobs for retirees who want them. Jack is an officer (and self-appointed social director) of his community homeowners' association and was accepted in the Fort Collins Civilian Police Academy. His interest in police procedure stems from his youngest daughter's career.

Most housing subdivisions in Fort Collins have no clubhouse, outdoor pool or golf course, but these facilities are available in the community. Of the eight golf courses, four are public, three are country clubs and one is semiprivate. EPIC — the Edora Pool and Ice Center — opened in 1987 and has a year-round ice rink and swimming facilities. A 40,000-square-foot senior center recently opened with a swimming pool, fitness center, library, wood and metal shops, and other facilities.

Boyd Lake, Carter Lake and Horsetooth Reservoir offer beaches and boating, and both cross-country and downhill skiing are nearby. Sports fans attend CSU varsity games or go to Denver for Broncos, Nuggets and Rockies games. Free summer concerts, a fine local symphony and shows at Lincoln Center, an exceptional performing-arts facility with two stages, provide Fort Collins' cultural underpinnings.

Single-family homes still dominate the housing scene, but patio homes are increasing in favor, especially among retirees. Paragon Point, South Ridge and Stone Ridge are three new subdivisions in the southeastern part of town. Stone Ridge has only single-family detached homes to retain the look of a traditional neighborhood.

"Many retirees like a semblance of what they left," says Linda Hopkins, of The Group, Inc., Fort Collins' largest real-estate agency. She says most area retirees prefer homes where no one lives above or below them.

"They want enough maintenance provided so they can travel and know the chores are covered but without a burdensome homeowners' organization running everything. The developer puts in the front yard and mows and maintains it, but residents have a courtyard to do with as they wish. A lot of people are willing to give up mowing, but they still like a petunia and a tomato plant. They give up the chores and keep the fun," Hopkins says.

Among other housing options, Park Lane Towers, a high-rise near Old Town, offers security and full building services. "When a unit comes on the market, it's snapped up right away," says Helen Gray, relocation director at The Group. The Preserve, a large apartment complex near the university, is popular with seniors. Collinwood is a new, exceptionally attractive assisted-living facility. Many of the 80 units are suites, and all are furnished with residents' own possessions. Meals, housekeeping, laundry and 24-hour nursing service are provided.

"People retire here because of the climate and the size of the community," says Gray, "The university is also a big drawing card, not necessarily for educational purposes but for the diversity and activities it brings to town. Every college town has a vitality. People often say, 'Fort Collins reminds me of such-and-such,' and the place they name is usually a college town.

"When people come to Fort Collins, it feels like a nice place to be. It's comfortable and safe," says Gray.●

Fort Myers, Florida

This Southwest Florida city has a flourishing cultural scene and affordable housing

By Karen Feldman

If the fact that Thomas Edison obtained close to 1,000 patents in his lifetime isn't proof enough of his ingenuity, his choice of Fort Myers as his winter home is a clear sign of his visionary gift. In 1886 the inventor and his bride, Mina, arrived by steamer for their honeymoon. Thus began their lifelong love affair with Fort Myers, where they built a winter home along with a laboratory and botanical garden on the banks of the Caloosahatchee River.

Edison's good friend, Henry Ford, created his own estate next door. Together they entertained such luminaries as Harvey Firestone and Charles Lindbergh at a time when Fort Myers had fewer than 900 residents and lacked both air conditioning and mosquito control.

Today, their estates have become the most popular attractions in a city that boasts 48,208 full-time residents, a number that almost doubles during the balmy winters when so-called snowbirds flock south. Like their famous predecessors, many winter visitors come for a brief respite from the cold but wind up putting down roots in this thriving city on Florida's southwest coast.

"Many people are drawn to the area for the first time on vacation," says Marietta Mudgett, executive director of the Greater Fort Myers Chamber of Commerce. "They go to the Edison Home and the beaches and they keep it in their memory banks when they think of retiring."

Fort Myers has been dubbed the City of Palms after the mile of towering royal palms planted along both sides of McGregor Boulevard, which runs from downtown past the Edison and Ford estates and on toward the county's barrier islands. It is the seat of county, state and federal government offices and a cultural center in Lee County.

Although the city itself has no beaches, it is situated just miles from the Gulf of Mexico and the beaches on Sanibel and Captiva islands and Fort Myers Beach. A mild climate, an abundance of golf courses and other natural attractions make it a popular choice among retirees, Marietta Mudgett says.

Yet another draw is the range and affordability of real estate. "The market is good. Property is appreciating slowly. The county as a whole is appreciating by about 4 or 5 percent a year, but some areas are as high as 10 or 12 percent,"

Population: 48,208

Location: On the Southwest Florida coast, about 120 miles south of Tampa and 130 miles northeast of Miami.

Climate:

	High	Low
January	74	53
July	91	74

Average relative humidity: 54%

Rain: 53 inches.

Cost of living: Slightly below average (specific index not available).

Median housing cost: $124,700

Sales tax: 6%

Sales tax exemptions: Food, some services and medicine.

State income tax: None.

Intangibles tax: Assessed on stocks, bonds and other assets. Tax rate is $1 per $1,000 in assets. The first $20,000 in assets is exempt for individuals. For couples filing jointly, the first $40,000 is exempt. Those who owe less than $60 need not pay.

Estate tax: None, except the state's "pick-up" portion of the federal tax, applicable to taxable estates of more than $1 million.

Inheritance tax: None.

Property tax: Fort Myers residents pay $23.695-$25.695 per $1,000 of assessed value, with homes assessed at 100% of market value. Yearly tax on a $124,700 home with homestead exemption below is about $2,362-$2,562, depending on location.

Homestead exemption: $25,000 off the assessed value of a permanent, primary residence.

Religion: Fort Myers has churches representing all major religions as well as some less common ones, including Reform, Conservative and Orthodox synagogues. Additional houses of worship operate in nearby Cape Coral, North Fort Myers and Sanibel Island.

Education: A variety of adult education classes are taught at high schools in and around Fort Myers. Edison Community College offers continuing-education programs and several two-year degree programs and soon will offer four-year degrees in several disciplines via the Internet. Florida Gulf Coast University is a four-year state institution offering 26 graduate and undergraduate programs as well as seminars and special programs.

Transportation: Southwest Florida International Airport offers a variety of domestic and international flights, adding more each year. Public bus transportation is provided by Lee County Transit with year-round routes and trolley shuttles. Greyhound buses also operate from Fort Myers, connecting to its nationwide system. Interstate 75 connects Fort Myers to Tampa and points north, and U.S. Highway 41 is the main thoroughfare through the area.

Health: Because of the large number of retirees in the area, Fort Myers abounds with medical options. Lee Memorial Health System is a not-for-profit, full-service, acute-care hospital system that includes two Fort Myers hospitals, the 220-bed HealthPark Medical Center and the 427-bed Lee Memorial Hospital Cleveland Avenue campus, a number of medical practices and other services, such as the Diabetic Treatment Center and the Neuroscience and Stroke Center. The for-profit Columbia Healthcare Corp. also

says Denny Sharma, a broker associate with Arvida Realty Services in Fort Myers.

Among that latter group are homes along canals and the Caloosahatchee River, which snakes along the edge of downtown and on toward the Gulf and barrier islands. Single-family homes and condos in the Fort Myers area fall in the $130,000-to-$200,000 range, from a basic three-bedroom home at the low end to 3,000 square feet with modern amenities at the high end.

Few homes in Fort Myers date much before the early 1920s, Sharma says, with smaller houses in the older, centrally located Edison Park and Dean Park running $150,000-$250,000 and larger homes costing about $350,000. Some homes priced at the lower end may need renovations. Condos start at about $100,000, and golf-course communities offer a mix of condos and single-family homes starting at about $130,000.

Anyone wanting to build a home can choose from a wealth of builders and lots that run $30,000-$80,000 and more, utilities included. Downtown apartments and condos provide another option of late, the result of efforts by entrepreneurs who are renovating old buildings and turning them into living space.

The downtown area, largely abandoned a decade ago as malls lured consumers away, is undergoing a renaissance as an arts-and-entertainment district, with boutique shopping, bars and restaurants and a resident theater company in a historic theater. All combine to encourage people to live and play as well as work downtown. The whole region has undergone a cultural awakening in the past two decades, with the opening of new theaters, art galleries, restaurants, shops and movie theaters as the county more than doubled in size from 205,266 residents in 1980 to 440,888 today.

The Barbara B. Mann Performing Arts Hall is the home of the Southwest Florida Symphony Orchestra and Chorus and the venue for concerts and shows like "Miss Saigon" and "Phantom of the Opera." The Broadway Palm Dinner Theater presents musicals and other productions year around.

For sports fans, there's spring training with the Boston Red Sox at the City of Palms Park downtown and the Minnesota Twins at the Lee County Sports Complex. From April through August, the Twins' farm club, the Miracle, plays ball at the complex. There's hockey with the Florida Everblades and basketball with the Sea Dragons at nearby Estero's TECO Arena, which also offers ice and in-line skating to the public at designated times.

Tee and Gene Lawrence have lived in Fort Myers long enough to remember the way things used to be and to appreciate how far the city has come. The couple moved to Fort Myers from Piqua, OH, in 1976. "We were in our 50s," remembers Tee, now 74. "We didn't really have enough money to retire, but we were bored where we were."

Although they had long spent vacations in Fort Lauderdale, "by the time we wanted to move, Fort Lauderdale

Fort Myers, FL

has two Fort Myers hospitals. The 400-bed Southwest Florida Regional Medical Center is a full-service hospital that includes the Heart Institute, a chest pain unit and a kidney transplant program. The 120-bed Gulf Coast Hospital is an osteopathic facility that offers a full range of services. Family Health Centers of Southwest Florida provide basic medical care to clients with limited incomes, including the Senior Outreach Center designed to offer lower-cost medical care to older clients. The Senior Friendship Centers are staffed entirely by retired medical professionals who volunteer their time. Seniors receive basic medical care for little or no money, depending upon ability to pay.

Housing options: A full range of housing options is available in Fort Myers, both within the city limits and in the surrounding unincorporated areas. Condominiums start at $100,000, depending on amenities. At a golf community, two-bedroom condos run $130,000-$180,000, and on the river they can run $250,000 or more. For single-family homes, prices range from about $80,000 for a smaller, older home in a residential neighborhood up to $180,000-$600,000 for a three-bedroom home in a golf community and $250,000-$2.5 million on the river. The following master-planned communities offer amenities such as golf, tennis, a clubhouse, social clubs and planned activities: **Heritage Palms**, (941) 417-2500; **Sun City Fort Myers** and **Gateway Golf and Country Club**, (800) WCI-2290; **Lexington Country Club**, (800) 875-0153; and **Herons Glen** in North Fort Myers, (800) 521-9557. **Shell Point Village**, (239) 466-1111, is a continuing-care community with independent living in apartments ranging from studios to three-bedroom suites and on-site assisted living and skilled nursing care.

Visitor lodging: The Li-Inn Sleeps B&B is within walking distance of the Edison-Ford Winter Estates as well as the downtown arts and entertainment district, $55-$125, double occupancy, (941) 332-2651. The Holiday Inn SunSpree Resort sits on the edge of the Caloosahatchee River and has a restaurant, boat docks and pool minutes from downtown and the city's historic neighborhoods, $89-$139, (800) 664-7775 or (941) 334-3434. Coral Bridge Suites at the southern end of town offers suites with full kitchen, $89-$119 for a one-bedroom suite, (800) 527-1133 or (941) 454-6363. **Information:** Greater Fort Myers Chamber of Commerce, 2310 Edwards Drive, Fort Myers, FL 33901, (941) 332-3624 or www.fortmyers.org. Lee County Visitor and Convention Bureau, 2180 W. First St., Fort Myers, FL 33901, (941) 338-3500 or www.Lee IslandCoast.com.

wasn't the place I wanted to be," she says. "It was entirely too hectic." Then they visited retired friends in Fort Myers. They liked it so much that they bought a little stone cottage.

"We knew we were going to retire in Florida somewhere," says Gene, 79. "We liked the casual atmosphere of Fort Myers. It was an easygoing place where I could throw away my ties."

They returned to Ohio, but as the temperature plummeted, so did their attitude about the place in which they'd raised their children. So they sold Gene's credit business and headed south. Once they settled into their new home, Gene began dabbling in real estate, while Tee took a job in property management. But it wasn't long before she discovered a major problem with her adopted hometown.

"My interests were in arts and theater, and this was a wasteland," she says. She joined a group of like-minded residents to found the Lee County Alliance of the Arts. Today the alliance is an umbrella organization for a wealth of local arts groups, occupying the 12,000-square-foot William R. Frizzell Cultural Center, which houses three art galleries, an outdoor theater and a 150-seat indoor theater. The Theatre Conspiracy performs innovative shows there, as does the Edison Community College drama department.

She also took part in preserving and restoring the historic Arcade Theater, built in 1908 as a vaudeville playhouse in downtown Fort Myers. After a rousing fund-raising campaign that included a local performance by Mikhail Baryshnikov and his dance troupe, it was painstakingly refurbished in 1991 and today houses a professional theater group, the Florida Repertory Theater.

In 1978, the Lawrences moved to their current three-bedroom, three-bath house. Built in the mid-1950s, it's in a quiet residential area just two miles from the Edison-Ford Winter Estates. They paid $40,000 for the 1,800-square-foot home, which has more than doubled in value since then, Tee says. While the prospect of moving into a more modern house appeals to them, they like their neighborhood and its central location, so they plan to stay put.

Gene continues to buy and sell homes, offering mortgages to people who might

otherwise be unable to get them from conventional banks. Tee, who finally retired in 1995, keeps busy with the arts alliance and has begun taking tap-dance lessons. They attend exercise classes twice a week through the Senior Friends program at Southwest Florida Regional Medical Center. Both find the city a good choice for retirement.

"Fort Myers has more oldsters than many cities, so it has more facilities for us," Gene says. "There are a lot of good doctors here, the restaurants give you a discount, and there are programs like Senior Friends," which offers health seminars, exercise and computer classes, among other things.

Bill and Mary Barbour, who lived in northern New Jersey for most of their married life, never considered retiring anywhere else. Bill, 78, retired as chairman of Fleming H. Revell, a publisher of inspirational and religious books, after a 39-year career. Mary, 76, worked as an executive secretary at Vick Chemical Co. for several years and spent many more as "a professional unpaid volunteer," as she describes it.

They'd been vacationing for about five years in their condo on Sanibel Island, but when they decided to retire, there was only one choice: Shell Point Village, in southern Fort Myers not far from the Sanibel causeway.

Owned by the Christian and Missionary Alliance, the not-for-profit life-care community on the shores of the Caloosahatchee River offers homes and apartments as well as assisted living, skilled nursing and rehabilitative care and a full range of activities and services. Upon moving in, residents pay an entrance fee of $65,000-$375,000, depending upon the housing unit selected, then a monthly fee of $900-$3,200, which covers utilities, basic housekeeping, nursing and assisted-living care as needed.

Bill Barbour's parents had retired to a similar type of community on the state's East Coast years before. "We knew the concept and it was a fabulous place where we wanted to be," he says.

The Barbours had made friends by attending church at Shell Point when they were vacationing on Sanibel, so their social life started up quickly. Now they add to their list of friends as new people move into their 105-unit build-

ing — "Bill makes a loaf of bread for each new person," Mary says — and as newcomers join their church or get active in community events.

Companionship without the yard work but with plenty of golf was what drew John and Doris Lynch to their current home, a condominium at Heritage Palms, a new U.S. Home development in Fort Myers. Like the Barbours, John and Doris had vacationed on Sanibel since the 1970s when they bought a time-share unit there.

John drove a tractor-trailer for a Newark, NJ, plastics company, and Doris worked in personnel at AT&T until they retired in 1992 and moved from their home of 40 years in Old Bridge, NJ, to a mobile home in south Fort Myers. "We knew where we were going," says John, 73. "We knew the area, liked the climate and the convenience of everything, like stores and doctors."

They thought the mobile home would be their permanent residence, but they started having second thoughts after they were twice ordered to evacuate as hurricanes threatened the area. Besides that, "staying there all year was too lonesome," says Doris, 68. "Everyone went home each spring."

So they found Heritage Palms, which was centrally located and has 36 holes of golf. They bought a two-bedroom, two-bath condo that overlooks a large lake and clubhouse and moved in January 1999. The change suits them both.

"There's a lot more room, the clubhouse is open all year and we're not lonesome," says Doris, who with her husband likes to play golf, visit the beach on Sanibel, shop and entertain. "Everybody here is very friendly," says Doris. "Everybody's anxious to make friends. We're all in the same boat because it's a new community."

Ask any of these retirees what they like least about the area and they all have the same answer. It's the heavy traffic of the winter tourist season. But they also say the weather and lifestyle make the traffic worth enduring.

For those considering retirement in Fort Myers, Doris Lynch advises: "Do it, because it opens up another world. It opens up a more outdoor type of life." Adds her husband, John: "If we were up in New Jersey, we'd be in the house most of the time. Down here, we're out all the time. The weather is beautiful." ●

Gainesville, Florida

Renowned medical facilities and Florida's largest university attract retirees

By David Wilkening

Some people move to Gainesville for the climate, the culture and the easygoing Florida lifestyle. But there are a lot of other reasons — including a top-rated university and excellent medical care — that help account for the fact that almost one in every 10 residents of the city is 65 or older.

Joe Werner moved to Gainesville because he got tired of traveling to town by ambulance. Joe retired in 1991 after a career as an attorney in St. Petersburg and, seeking a peaceful country life, he bought a five-acre farm in rural Dixie County, home to only 14,000 residents. But when a touchy pancreas required emergency care, Joe was rushed three times to the renowned Shands Hospital 50 miles away in Gainesville.

"After about the third trip of 50 miles, when the ambulance was bumping over rutted back roads and the medics were trying six or seven times to get an IV into my arm, I said to myself, 'I'm going to move'," recalls Joe.

Joe sold his farm and found another home for the 75-pound stray dog who had moved in with him there. Then he bought a condominium in Gainesville near the million-square-foot Oaks Mall and paid just under $50,000 for it.

The area's geographic location is midway between Atlanta and Miami and about 120 miles north of its better-known cousin, tourist-famous Orlando. A city of 100,000 people in the heart of north-central Florida, Gainesville basks in Gulf breezes that make summer days generally warm, with dry and mild winters. The most prominent city in Alachua County (population about 218,000), Gainesville has an average year-round temperature of 69 degrees.

The mild climate was an important consideration for Lucille Schlichting, who moved to Gainesville in 1989 from Long Island, NY, five years after her late husband, Bill, had a stroke that paralyzed his right side.

"We decided that we were tired of the cold weather and the rising tax rates," recalls Lucille, who recently celebrated her 70th birthday. The Schlichtings followed their daughter and son-in-law, who had moved to Gainesville from Long Island to start an auto upholstery business. The younger couple had determined they could better afford a start-up business in Florida over higher-taxed and generally more expensive New York.

A talented commercial artist before his stroke, Bill Schlichting died in 1992. "But he was comfortable in his last years here because the climate was easier on him and he had a chance to watch his grandchild grow into a beautiful and talented artist herself," says Lucille.

Just as Orlando is heavily influenced by tourism, the face of Gainesville is shaped largely by Florida's oldest and largest university, the University of Florida. Walter Gardner, 80, says that the university was one of the three major reasons he and his wife, Jacky, moved here after first leaving their native Minneapolis, MN, to retire in Virginia.

"Gainesville has the finest medical facility in the Southeast. And there are no snowbirds," smiles Walter, who along with Jacky, 75, is active in various university-related clubs and associations.

The Gardners first came to Gainesville to visit friends. They said their initial reaction was that it was a friendly town with a good climate that is influenced culturally by the presence of the university.

The sprawling school of almost 47,000 students serves as a major focal point. The college's sports teams are nationally known, particularly the NCAA champion football team. The university's cultural facilities include an impressive 1,800-seat Center for the Performing Arts, a venue for everything from popular music to opera, jazz and country music concerts. The university also lures a variety of speakers and a host of cultural events throughout the year.

Even in the summer, when school attendance dwindles, there is no shortage of cultural activities. There's the small but distinguished Hippodrome State Theater, where plays are acted out on a round stage in a former U.S. Post Office building constructed in 1909. Plays also are produced by the Gainesville Community Playhouse, the Santa Fe Players, Across-Town Repertory Theater and Florida Players Theater.

Other performing arts groups also have flourished, including the Gainesville Civic Chorus, Gainesville Ballet Theater, Danscompany, Dance Alive!, Gainesville Symphony Orchestra and Gainesville Friends of Jazz. Art lovers often find their way to the Samuel P. Harn Museum of Art, which houses five permanent exhibits.

It's not unusual for retirees to continue their education by enrolling in the University of Florida. Santa Fe Community College also offers a variety of noncredit courses.

Gainesville's strong lure for nature lovers is as obvious as the presence of the university. Almost two-thirds of Alachua County's 969 square miles is a wilderness of forests, punctuated with scenic lakes and wetlands.

The 62-acre Kanapaha Botanical Gardens has paved pathways for wheelchairs that lead to a herb- and plant-strewn rock garden. The largest bluff oak tree in Florida is found here. For the more adventurous, the Devil's Millhopper is a giant sinkhole with a half-mile nature trail and a 232-step wooden stairway to take visitors to the bottom.

Parks abound in the area. There are 40 nature parks within 50 miles of Gainesville for picnicking, hiking, swimming, camping, boating and fishing. The Gainesville Parks and Recreation Department maintains 30 parks and plans a year-round schedule of recreational activities and competitive sports for all ages. Area anglers have easy access to six freshwater lakes, all with boat ramps, and two provide accommodations and campsites with covered boat slips.

Golfers can choose among seven courses, five of which are public or semiprivate. Lighted golf at night is as inexpensive as $12 a round between March and November at the Villages of West End Golf Club, a predominantly par-three course. For those who want to make their way around on bicycles, Gainesville has 60 miles of roadways with on-street bicycle lanes that have won the city a ranking among the top 10 in the United States by Bicycling Magazine.

The median housing price is an affordable $85,000, according to the Gainesville Chamber of Commerce. A new 1,800-square-foot single-family home on an 8,000-square-foot lot starts at about $150,000. Such a home typically would have three bedrooms, two full baths, a living and dining area, a family room with a fireplace, and a two-car attached garage. There also are many luxury apartment complexes, condominiums and retirement communities.

One popular retirement area is Bailey Village, a residential assisted-living community where a monthly fee covers three meals a day, daily housekeeping, weekly linen and laundry service, supervised medication and an extensive

Gainesville, FL

Population: About 95,447 in Gainesville, 217,955 in Alachua County.

Location: In north-central Florida midway between Atlanta and Miami, about 120 miles north of Orlando. Jacksonville is 78 miles northeast.

Climate:

	High	Low
January	66	43
July	91	71

Rain: 52 inches.
Alachua County has a 255-day growing season and an average temperature of 69 degrees.

Cost of living: Below average (specific index not available).

Median housing cost: $85,000

Sales tax: 7%a

Sales tax exemptions: Groceries, prescription medicines and professional services.

State income tax: None.

Intangibles tax: Assessed on stocks, bonds and other assets. Tax rate is $1 per $1,000 in assets. The first $20,000 in assets is exempt for individuals. For couples filing jointly, the first $40,000 is exempt. Those who owe less than $60 need not pay.

Estate tax: None, except the state's "pickup" portion of the federal tax, applicable to taxable estates above $1 million.

Property tax: In Gainesville, $28.52 per $1,000, with homes assessed at 100% of appraised value. The tax on an $85,000 home would be about $1,711 a year, with the homestead exemption.

Homestead exemption: $25,000 off assessed value for permanent, primary residences.

Religion: There are approximately 300 places of worship for all faiths in the Alachua County area.

Education: Gainesville is home of Florida's oldest and largest university, the University of Florida. Santa Fe Community College offers a variety of noncredit enrichment courses. The area's Community Education Program offers classes in subjects as diverse as arts, computers, natural history and sports. Alachua County Library District has 10 locations and bookmobile service, and books can be mailed to homebound patrons. The library also sponsors dozens of free programs throughout the year.

Transportation: The Regional Transit System provides local bus service as well as minibus transportation for the handicapped. The Gainesville Regional Airport offers 32 nonstop flights each day, linking the area with hub cities such as Atlanta, Charlotte, Miami and Orlando via five major carriers. Amtrak provides rail passenger service. Interstate bus transportation is offered by Greyhound-Trailways. There is good highway access; Interstate 75 skirts Gainesville on the west, making it the main link with major metropolitan centers such as Atlanta and the Tampa-St. Petersburg area. U.S. Highway 301, U.S. Highway 441 and State Highway 26 join Gainesville with other communities in Alachua County and northern Florida.

Health: Shands Hospital and the University of Florida Health Systems (UFHS) is the area's best-known medical complex, encompassing four acute-care hospitals with a total of 800 beds, two specialty hospitals and two licensed home-health agencies. North Florida Regional Medical Center is a 278-bed acute-care facility. Gainesville Veterans Affairs Medical Center is a 480-bed medical, surgical and psychiatric facility.

Housing options: Haile Plantation, (800) 226-8802, is a master-planned community composed of walking and bicycle trails, tennis courts, playgrounds, swimming pools and an 18-hole golf course. Homes are priced from the mid-$100,000s. For high-rise living, the 12-story **Lakeshore Towers**, (352) 376-4456, near the university and Shands is an adult-oriented rental community offering both furnished and unfurnished apartments with balconies and a view. Security includes a door attendant on duty after hours. Air conditioning and heating are included in rental fees, which start at $500 a month for an efficiency unit of 400 square feet. The standard lease agreement is for one year, but the rental community works with newcomers who are unsure of their housing plans.

Visitor lodging: Days Inn, $50-$125, is near the University of Florida and Shands Hospital, and shuttle service is available, (352) 376-2222.

Information: Gainesville Area Chamber of Commerce, P.O. Box 1187, Gainesville, FL 32601, (352) 334-7100 or www.gainesvillechamber.com.

activity program. Programs are tailored to the needs of residents, either on a long- or short-term care schedule.

Lucille Schlichting has lived in the Cedarwood Apartments complex since she came to Gainesville seven years ago. Her unit is in a heavily treed complex with tennis courts and a swimming pool that she enjoys virtually every day. Her large two-bedroom apartment often serves as a temporary hotel for the many guests and relatives who pass through town.

Because Shands Hospital is a leading referral center for the state and the entire Southeast, people from all over — some with rare, diagnostically baffling diseases — are drawn to Gainesville. Because so many guests at the nearby Radisson Hotel are hospital visitors, the hotel boasts in brochures that it "treats patients, too" and offers free hospital transportation. Shands Hospital's 576-bed tertiary-care facility on the campus of the university includes cardiovascular medicine, neurological services, cancer services and transportation.

Shands at Alachua General Hospital, also in Gainesville, is a full-service center with 423 beds and 200 physicians on staff. The facility offers cardiac care, cancer care, neuroscience, neonatology, women's health and emergency care. Of particular note to seniors, the hospital sponsors Senior Advantage, a health-benefits program for people age 55 and older.

Other area hospitals include North Florida Regional, a facility with a maternity unit rated one of the top 10 in the country by Child Magazine. Veterans Affairs Hospital is a 480-bed federally funded medical center that provides medical, surgical and psychiatric patients with primary, secondary and tertiary care. And the Gainesville area supports six nursing homes offering a variety of care and a dozen retirement communities providing independent and assisted living.

Special services for retirees are offered by the Center for Aging Resources, a unit of the Mid-Florida Area Agency on Aging, (800) 262-2243. It was set up in 1986 to help seniors and their families negotiate the maze of programs and benefits that serve the elderly. Resource specialists at the agency use a computerized network to access a wealth of practical information about local, state and national resources — everything from local transportation services to pharmaceutical resources.

In part because of the hospitals, there are an unusual number of local opportunities for volunteers to perform various types of social work. Under the umbrella of the Retired Senior Volunteer Program, several hundred retirees work in museums, libraries, hospitals and nursing homes.

Among the volunteers are Joan and George Nehiley. George, 77, regularly visits local hospitals to help patients confined to wheelchairs. Joan, 73, spends part of each Thursday helping to distribute meals at a local food bank.

Before they retired, George was a guidance counselor for Dade County schools, and Joan was a secretary-treasurer. After they found themselves victims of crime several times in Miami, they moved to Gainesville about 12 years ago. They already were familiar with the area, where George attended the university before embarking on his own educational career.

The Nehileys like the warm climate and felt welcome in their new community. "There are a lot of active senior programs, and it's just a very friendly town," says Joan.

In common with much of Florida, Gainesville's growth as a city came only after the turn of the 19th century. As early as 1529, Spanish explorers trekked through what now is Alachua County. Later they built missions and used the area's fertile land for the production of food and cattle to feed themselves and the Seminole Indian popu-

lation.

The British occupied Florida from 1763 to 1783, when Spain regained control. In 1817, the Spanish king granted nearly 300,000 acres of northern Florida land to a powerful Cuban merchant. The land grant was voided two years later when Florida became a U.S. territory.

Alachua, believed to have been named after a Seminole word for a large sinkhole in a wetlands area, became the territory's ninth county. Gainesville, which was established in 1854 at the end of the Second Seminole War, was named in honor of a military hero, Gen. Edmund Gaines. The new city grew from a core of only 250 original settlers, and until the late 1800s, Alachua County was little more than a citrus capital. However, a series of freezes in the late part of the century pushed that industry farther south.

Today, visitors to the area often come to see Florida's second-oldest town, Micanopy, founded in 1821. The small city just 13 miles from Gainesville is popular for its antiques, art and curio shops.

Gainesville itself has a distinct personality in that it is home both to retirees who have their careers behind them and young college students who have yet to decide what to do with their lives. This is not always an easy truce, as Joe Werner points out.

"This town is not exactly built around retirees," Joe says when pushed to find fault with the area. He is reminded of that fact when driving too slow to suit young motorists behind him or when he pauses a little too long at a traffic signal. Students sometimes are quick to lean on the horn, he says.

Still, that seems to most retirees a small price to pay for living here. The Nehileys, who live in a subdivision that offers a mix of younger residents and retirees, put it in perspective. "Young people help keep you young," suggests Joan.●

Gainesville, Georgia

Georgia setting wins a gold medal from retirees

By William Schemmel

The secret was safe for a while, but many residents of Gainesville say the word spread during the summer of 1996: This small north Georgia city is a nice place to live.

That's when the summer Olympic Games were held in Atlanta, and communities on Lake Sidney Lanier had front-row seats. A section of the lake three miles north of downtown Gainesville was selected as the venue for canoeing and rowing competitions.

City officials say that some Olympic visitors have returnd permanently since they experienced the beauty of the lake and the mountains surrounding Gainesville.

Lake Lanier — a 38,000-acre U.S. Army Corps of Engineers reservoir with a 607-mile wooded shoreline — is one of the most popular inland waterways in the nation, and it is a major reason retirees are moving to Gainesville.

With a population of 25,578, Gainesville is the largest city on the lake. Almost 22,000 acres of this mammoth inland sea, created by a dam on the Chattahoochee River, are in Hall County, which has nearly 140,000 residents.

Gainesville also is the gateway to northeast Georgia's Appalachian Mountain vacation lands. National forests, mountains as high as 4,800 feet, waterfalls, lakes, scenic rivers, craft towns and tourist centers are a short drive north of the city.

For visitors who elect to stay here permanently, Gainesville boasts an attractive selection of residential communities, moderate property taxes, excellent medical care and plenty of indoor and outdoor recreation. Proximity to metropolitan Atlanta — only 52 miles south on an interstate highway — is another major plus.

Pat and Bud Schick visited Gainesville and Hall County many times over a five-year period before making their move from LaCrosse, WI.

"When I retired (from the Wisconsin Highway Department) at age 55, we got a trailer and spent 10 to 12 weeks at a time on the road," says Bud, 62. "We seriously considered the Asheville, NC, area and several Tennessee Valley Authority lakes. But we kept coming back here.

"We decided on it for several different reasons," he says. "It's sheltered from storms by the Appalachians and has a pleasant four-season climate. We get some cold weather and even a little snow — but nothing like we had in Wisconsin. And the fall foliage in the mountains is as beautiful as you'll find anywhere.

"We like being close to the mountains and, of course, to Lake Lanier. We enjoy fishing, swimming, boating, golf, tennis — all of which the lake has plenty of."

Pat adds: "It's the people that really decided us. They're so friendly — I was surprised at being so readily accepted. We can enjoy the advantages of a small town, and we're only an hour from the shopping, dining, entertainment and other advantages of Atlanta."

The Schicks enjoy the best of Gainesville's two worlds. They're only a few minutes from town, but their three-story brick home in the Cherokee Forest subdivision is only a few yards from the lake.

Developed originally in 1988, Cherokee Forest is typical of the area's many lake-front residential communities. About a third of the homes, on large, wooded, gently rolling lots, are owned by retirees or preretirees who enjoy the lake, a pool and tennis courts on the property.

Lake-front lots sell for $100,000 and up. Away from the lake, lots with mountain views are about $30,000 and up. Homes in Cherokee Forest are valued at $350,000-$600,000.

Another option is Chestatee North, a patio-home community on Lake Lanier. About half of its residents are retirees, and the available homes here average about $350,000. Amenities include pools and tennis courts.

Royal Lakes is another subdivision popular with retirees. The 500-acre community is not on Lake Lanier, but it has two small lakes on the property and a golf course. Lots sell for $60,000-$95,000, with homes from $270,000-$1 million.

Bob and Gloria Molloy moved to the Chattahoochee Country Club area of Gainesville from Lufkin, TX. They lived in an apartment while their home was under construction.

The Molloys' home is 500 feet off the road and backs up to Lake Lanier. "The good Lord willing, we'll die in that house," Gloria laughs.

"I miss my wonderful friends in Texas, but I have made some wonderful friends here, so I would not go back," Gloria says. "It's a great town if you want to pitch in and take part in the life of the community. Organizations and clubs welcome your participation, but you have to reach out."

Both Gloria and Bob are involved in church activities, and Gloria also donates time to the Newcomers Club and does some bell-ringing for the Salvation Army.

One of the few drawbacks to the area, she says, is a lack of good restaurants, although they are readily available in Atlanta. The Molloys like to travel, so they also appreciate the proximity to Hartsfield International Airport in Atlanta.

"The people here are very friendly," says Gloria, 66. "But it's more than that. The two colleges (Brenau University and Gainesville College) and the military academy (Riverside Academy) give the town a special mix of people."

Brenau University, a small, private college, and Gainesville College, a two-year unit of the state university system, both offer day and evening continuing-education courses. BUL-LI (Brenau University Learning and Leisure Institute) is extremely popular with retirees.

Many retirees also appreciate the cultural opportunities available through the colleges. "The colleges offer a lot of entertainment and music," says Janet Hutts, 68, who moved to Gainesville from Rhode Island with husband Wilsie, 71.

"I like living close to the water and the mountains, " says Wilsie. "And I like Gainesville because it's still small — you can go anywhere in town in 20 minutes."

They originally considered several other retirement areas in Georgia, South Carolina and Texas, but Gainesville's climate, medical services and proximity to Atlanta and their children and grandchildren won them over.

An industrious city with many well-kept residential neighborhoods, the center of Gainesville is the downtown courthouse square. Most of the art deco-style government buildings were constructed after a disastrous tornado in April 1936. Some of the city's most important cultural activi-

Gainesville, GA

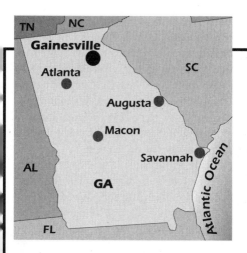

Population: 25,578 in Gainesville, 139,277 in Hall County.
Location: In the foothills of northeast Georgia's Appalachian Mountains, 52 miles north of Atlanta.

Climate:

	High	Low
January	50	31
July	87	67

Average relative humidity: 60%
Rain: 53 inches.
Snow: 3 inches.
Elevation of 1,279 feet fosters a moderate four-season climate. Hot summer days cool off in the evening. Severe cold spells, with some light snow, are brief. Fall foliage is spectacular.
Cost of living: Below average (specific index not available).
Average housing cost: $138,000
Sales tax: 7%
Sales tax exemptions: Prescription drugs, hearing aids, eyeglasses.
State income tax: For married couples filing jointly, graduated from 1% of taxable income up to $1,000 to $340 plus 6% on amounts over $10,000. For single filers, graduated from 1% of income up to $750 to $230 plus 6% on amounts over $7,000.
Income tax exemptions: Social Security benefits are exempt. Up to $14,000 in

retirement income is exempt for each taxpayer age 62 and older. Up to $4,000 of earned income can be included in the $14,000 exemption.
Intangibles tax: None.
Estate tax: None, except the state's "pick-up" portion of the federal tax, applicable to taxable estates above $1 million.
Property tax: In Gainesville, $9.64 per $1,000 of assessed value, based on 100% of fair market value plus $7.30 per $1,000 based on 40% of market value. With $2,000 homestead exemption noted below, annual taxes on a $138,000 home are $1,708. In unincorporated Hall County, the rate is $24.76 per $1,000 assessed valuation, based on 40% of fair market value. With homestead exemption, taxes on a $138,000 home are about $1,347.
Homestead exemption: $2,000 off assessed value for full-time residents. Taxpayers who are 62 or older and have an income of less than $10,000 can claim a $4,000 exemption and request a school tax exemption.
Religion: About 100 Protestant churches, one Catholic church. Nearest Jewish congregations are in Atlanta and Athens (30 miles).
Education: Brenau University, a small, private school, offers evening and weekend programs. Gainesville College, a two-year unit of the University System of Georgia, offers day and evening continuing-education courses. Lanier Technical Institute also offers continuing-education courses in many practical fields. The main campus of the University of Georgia is 30 miles away at Athens.
Transportation: Hall Area Transit public bus system. Atlanta's international airport is 60 minutes south.

Health: Northeast Georgia Medical Center, a 703-bed facility, serves a 20-county area of northeast Georgia, offering emergency care and extensive specialized and critical-care services. The "Senior Partners" program offers a package of health-related services for those age 50 and above, available for free. About 200 medical doctors and 70 dentists practice in Gainesville and Hall County. The county has seven nursing homes with about 600 beds.
Housing options: Subdivision communities on Lake Lanier are the most popular retirement locations. Cherokee Forest, Brittany Pointe, Chestatee North, Royal Lakes and other developments offer large, wooded lots on gently rolling terrain. Some have lake frontage ($100,000 and up); some interior lots have mountain views (high $20,000s and up). Some older resale homes are available in Gainesville, which also has a limited number of rental apartments and condos. Two-bedroom units rent for $500-$900 a month.
Visitor lodging: The Dunlap House Bed & Breakfast, a 1910 home in the Green Street Historic District downtown, $105-$155 including breakfast, (770) 536-0200. Holiday Inn, in downtown Gainesville with pool, restaurant and lounge, $59-$75, (770) 536-4451. Emerald Pointe Resort, with pool, tennis, restaurant, lounge, water sports and golf, $119-$350, (770) 945-8787. Campsites at Lake Lanier Islands, with water and electricity hookups, hot showers and picnic areas, are $20-$30 a night, (770) 932-7270.
Information: Greater Hall Chamber of Commerce, P.O. Box 374, Gainesville, GA 30503, (770) 532-6206, www.ghcc.com or www.gainesville.org.

ties take place on Green Street, a tree-shaded avenue of stately Victorian homes a few blocks from the square.

The Georgia Mountains Museum is a repository of information about the culture and history of the mountains. Permanent exhibits include books, arts and handicrafts by North Georgians. The Mark Trail Memorabilia Exhibit honors north Georgia native Ed Dodd, who created the nationally syndicated comic strip character.

The neighboring Quinlan Art Center has a year-round schedule of art exhibits, films, lectures, classes, workshops and music performances. The city's arts umbrella includes the Gainesville Symphony Orchestra, Gainesville Chorale, Gainesville Music Club, Pro Musica, Children's Theater, the Northeast Georgia Writer's Club and Gainesville Ballet. The Gainesville Theatre Alliance, a joint program of Brenau University and Gainesville College, offers half a dozen yearly stage productions.

Excellent and readily available medical service is cited by numerous retirees. The Northeast Georgia Medical Center is a 703-bed complex that serves a 20-county area of northeast Georgia. Services include cardiac catheterization, intensive care and coronary care units, an outpatient surgery center, cancer care, dialysis, endoscopy, enterostomal therapy, nutritional counseling, cardiology lab and a gynecologic and urologic care unit.

The city and county parks departments operate more than two dozen recreation areas, with tennis courts, swimming pools, softball fields, boat ramps, picnic pavilions and other amenities. Eight golf courses are open to the public.

Two 18-hole courses are in the Lake Lanier Islands recreation area. Operated by a state recreational authority, it was developed on the hilltops that bobbed above the waters of the lake when it was formed in 1958. In addition to the two championship golf courses,

Lanier Islands' numerous recreational amenities include two resort hotels (Renaissance Pine Isle Resort and the Emerald Pointe Resort), a sand swimming beach with boat rentals and water slides, festivals and summer concerts, camping and cottages, and some of the finest fishing in North America.

Many Gainesville retirees dock their boats at Lanier's spacious marinas. The U.S. Army Corps of Engineers has developed several multipurpose recreation areas around the lake.

Gainesville claims to be the "broiler chicken capital of the world," and many retirees originally came here as executives in the poultry industry. Other Gainesville retirees have backgrounds in diversified manufacturing and service industries. Some pre-retirees commute to jobs in metropolitan Atlanta.

"It has the values we were brought up with, and the culture of a small Southern town," says Gloria Molloy. "I hope we will never have to move." ●

Georgetown, Texas

This award-winning Texas Hill Country town carefully preserves its history

By Nina J. Stewart

Given its modern sophistication, it's sometimes hard to believe that the fastest-growing city in the fastest-growing county in Texas once was a rough-and-tumble staging town for vast cattle drives up the old Chisholm Trail. Located on the banks of the San Gabriel River on the edge of the Central Texas Hill Country, Georgetown is a progressive town of 28,339 with a rich pioneer history.

Georgetown residents came together in 1998 to celebrate their town history with a sesquicentennial blowout, which featured gala parties, parades, a mock longhorn cattle drive and other historical remembrances. Founded as an agricultural community in 1848, early Georgetown settlers — mostly Czechs, Germans, Mexicans and Swedes — realized prosperity after the railroad arrived 30 years later.

Residents then forsook their simple log or frame houses for more elaborate and stylish Victorian homes and shops. This surge of building and planning can be seen in the beautiful old town district, which was awarded a Great American Main Street Award in 1997 for its charming renovation and preservation of 180 historic buildings and houses.

Georgetown is so proud of its old town and Victorian structures that its Heritage Society keeps a trained staff of docents available to give tours and lectures designed to bring the town's pioneer history to life. The olden-days flavor is enhanced by antique street lamps that grace brick walks and tree-shaded streets.

No county seat in Texas is complete without a town square, and Georgetown does not disappoint. Bed-and-breakfast inns, city administration offices, quaint restaurants and lovely shops all grace the town square, which is crowned at its center by Williamson County's domed courthouse, erected in 1910. Visitors are reminded of Texas' participation in the Civil War by a statue on the courthouse lawn that pays tribute to its Confederate forces.

History buffs and budding anthropologists can find plenty more in the area to intrigue them. "Leann," one of the earliest-known immigrants to Texas and estimated to have lived between 8,000 to 7,000 B.C., was discovered by archaeologists in a burial ground near Georgetown. The area once was home to roving bands of Tonkawa Indian tribes in centuries past, and the discovery of pottery and arrowheads is not uncommon.

One tourist draw is the Inner Space Caverns, only a half-mile from downtown. Discovered in the late 1960s, the living caverns were formed nearly 80,000 years ago, and its depths are reached by cable car. Visitors take in the stunning stalactites and stalagmites as well as remains of prehistoric mastodons, wolves and other Ice Age animals captured for eternity in the caverns.

Housing in Georgetown is plentiful and varied, with a median housing cost of $125,000. One housing development designed in a "neotraditional" manner is Georgetown Village, an ungated community. An attractive feature of the development is the notion that housing should reflect the more appealing look of a traditional village, with smaller streets, a town center and pleasant living and work spaces. Housing prices start at $140,000 and run to $300,000.

But certainly one of the most powerful reasons retirees flock to the area is Del Webb's beautiful Sun City Georgetown. Harold and Jean Steadman bought a lot in the desirable community in 1995 and built their dream home the following year. "We would not have moved to Georgetown without Sun City, although we have come to enjoy the town," says Harold, 74.

The former Houston-area Southwestern Bell sales manager and his wife, a retired teacher, lived in Buchanan Dam, TX, for 10 years before moving to Sun City. Jean, 72, says she found making friends easy even though she and Harold didn't have friends or relatives already living in the area. "There are so many activities at Sun City, you can't help but meet people," she says.

Both find satisfaction in community involvement. Harold is president of the drama club at Sun City and is a director of the convention and visitor's bureau and the Palace Theatre. Jean volunteers with Friends Who Care, an organization that provides mentoring for schoolchildren. She also tapes books for the blind in Austin at the Texas State Library, and both are active in their church. "We started a new Methodist church with 15 initial members in March of 1997," says Harold. "Now we have about 225 members."

But not everyone prefers planned retirement communities. Ann McVey, 79, found Georgetown another way — through "trial and error." Just before her husband died, he urged her to move from Odessa in search of a retirement lifestyle that suited her. So, in 1993, with a pioneering spirit that would have made her ancestors proud, she left her home of 47 years and moved to Georgetown.

"I stayed at the Ramada Inn and looked at property in Georgetown's Berry Creek Country Club. I immediately fell in love with it and picked out a lot," says the former State Farm insurance employee. She built a 2,200-square-foot home to her liking in the prestigious development, choosing a screened porch, tile roof and stucco exterior. "My children liked it so much that they wanted to move with me," Ann says.

Making friends was made easy with the help of her neighbor, a friend of 30 years who also happened to be her State Farm underwriter. While Ann misses her friends in Odessa, she doesn't miss the West Texas sandstorms and hail in the spring. She keeps busy by volunteering with the Georgetown hospital auxiliary and works in the public affairs office.

Another local retiree, Bob Jones, 51 and a retired major in the U.S. Marine Corps, already knew of Georgetown's charm, since he had spent his boyhood school days here and had visited friends and family periodically during his military career. Georgetown's excellent school system was another draw when he and his wife, Jerri, a lieutenant colonel in the Marine Corps, considered retirement locales. They have two sons still in school.

While still on active duty and living in Okinawa, Japan, the Joneses selected a building site six miles from Georgetown in 1995 and built a one-

Georgetown, TX

Population: 28,339 in Georgetown, more than 249,967 in Williamson County. Georgetown is the county seat of Williamson County.

Location: On the eastern edge of Central Texas' Hill Country, 26 miles north of Austin off Interstate 35, 40 miles south of Temple, and equidistant from Houston and Dallas-Fort Worth. Altitude in Williamson County ranges from 454 to 1,265 feet.

Climate:

	High	Low
January	59	39
July	95	74

Average relative humidity: 56%
Annual rainfall: 34.2 inches.
Snow: Trace.
Cost of living: Below average (specific index not available).
Median housing cost: $125,000
Sales tax: 7.75%
Sales tax exemptions: Food and produce, pharmaceuticals, some agricultural services.
State income tax: None.
Intangibles tax: None.
Estate tax: None, except the state's "pickup" portion of the federal tax, applicable to taxable estates of more than $1 million.
Property tax: $2.39 per $100 valuation, with homes assessed at 100% of market value, less homestead and age

exemptions. Georgetown Independent School District levies $1.68 per $100, Williamson County levies $.395 per $100, and the city levies $.31 per $100. The tax on a $125,000 home is about $2,557, with the $18,000 homestead exemption noted below.
Homestead exemptions: $18,000 off the assessed value of permanent, primary residences. Taxpayers over age 65 get an additional $10,000 off the assessed value.
Religion: More than 40 churches serve 16 denominations.
Education: Southwestern University, a four-year liberal arts college in Georgetown, has 1,320 students. In nearby Austin, opportunities include the University of Texas (48,000 students), St. Edward's University (3,200 students) and Austin Community College (25,000 students), among other options.
Transportation: North/south Interstate 35 runs west of downtown Georgetown. Austin's international airport, Bergstrom, is about a 45-minute drive. Georgetown has a municipal general utility airport for business and executive jet activity.
Health: Georgetown Hospital is a 98-bed general, acute-care facility with surgical, diagnostic and emergency services. Scott and White Clinic at Sun City Georgetown has internists and family practitioners. Georgetown also is home to a range of therapy and rehabilitation clinics as well as a cardiovascular center. Residents can select from 134 doctors and 21 dentists.
Housing options: Options range from single-family residences and apartments to manufactured homes, estates on acreage, farms and planned

communities. Many retirees choose to buy property and build a home in developments or subdivisions near town. **Sun City Georgetown**, (888) 932-2266, a Del Webb retirement community, offers housing ranging from cottages to luxury homes from $120,000 to more than $500,000. Ask about a Vacation Getaway program that allows visitors to sample lifestyles at the development for a small fee. **Berry Creek Country Club**, (512) 930-9995, offers five neighborhoods and existing housing with a median price of $175,000, from garden homes to estates as well as acreage home sites. The country club has two championship 18-hole golf courses, swimming, tennis and racquetball courts. **Georgetown Village**, (512) 930-2322, is an ungated community with homes starting at around $140,000 in "neotraditional" style.
Visitor lodging: Visitors can choose between five motels (Comfort, La Quinta, Days Inn, Holiday Inn Express and San Gabriel Motel) or six bed-and-breakfast inns. Average motel room costs are $79 per night, double occupancy. A historic Victorian landmark, Inn on the Square, is a bed-and-breakfast inn featuring antiques and stained glass. Rooms range from $85 to $125 per night, (888) 718-2221 or (512) 868-2203. There also are four RV parks.
Information: Georgetown Chamber of Commerce, P.O. Box 346, 100 Stadium Drive, Georgetown, TX 78627-0346, (512) 930-3535 or www.georgetownchamber.org. Georgetown Convention and Visitors Bureau, P.O. Box 409, Georgetown, TX 78627, (512) 930-3545 or www.georgetown.org.

story, four-bedroom, 3,100-square-foot brick home on two acres. The development is not a planned community, but homesites are restricted to a minimum of one-acre lots on paved streets.

The Georgetown area's semirural setting has become a popular draw in Central Texas, especially among retirees who ache to spread out on their own land. "There were only about 30 homes in our neighborhood when we built. Now there are over 100 homes," Bob says.

Jerri, 46, is a dedicated golfer and president of the Women's Golf Association. Bob's hobbies are closer to home, where he gardens and enjoys coin collecting. Both volunteer with the chamber of commerce, their church and the school system. Jerri recommends that retirees moving to Georgetown "get involved early on within the community in order to meet people."

Jerri likes the fact that Fort Hood, with its commissary and medical services, is only 40 miles north in Killeen, making Georgetown even more attractive to military retirees like the Joneses. Also popular with local retirees is the opportunity to participate in college courses. Options are many in nearby Austin, home of the University of Texas, first in the nation in National Merit scholars. But one of the jewels in Georgetown's crown is Southwestern University, Texas' oldest educational institution.

Formed in 1873 when the Texas Conference of Methodist Churches decided to consolidate schools, Southwestern has a reputation for being one of the most prestigious private universities in the South, bringing cultural and economic benefits to the city. It also has a pretty campus with lovely limestone architecture welcoming all who enter. Plus, retirees in Sun City can take advantage of the Senior University in the development, where visiting college professors in the area provide lectures on a wide range of topics.

And there's outdoor recreation as varied as the imagination. Lake lovers enjoy the five miles of Lake Georgetown, only a few minutes by car from town. The park and lake offer residents and visitors alike wilderness hiking trails, fishing, swimming, boating, camping and picnicking. The U.S. Army Corps of Engineers maintains the lake and ensures its health and beauty.

In addition to the lake, the city offers two country clubs, three swimming pools, five golf courses, 38 tennis courts, a racquet club and 14 parks totalling 200 acres. Ann McVey no longer golfs, but that doesn't stop her from walking the golfing paths of Berry Creek Country Club every day.

Sports fans also have plenty to cheer about. Austin's Ice Bats, a minor league hockey team, and sports teams at the University of Texas provide the excitement. And local baseball fans soon will realize a dream: Hall-of-famer Nolan Ryan won approval to bring a minor league team to nearby Round Rock, and voters recently approved the construction of a new stadium.

Situated between rich, black farmland and rolling Central Texas hillsides, the Georgetown area also is considered desirable for its beauty and its temperate climate. The hills are rich with limestone cliffs, granite outcrops, wildlife, springs and gorgeous wildflowers. Winter freezes are few and far between, and summers are hot but not uncomfortably humid. Rapidly changing weather can include the threat of tornadoes, but the twisters normally are less powerful than those farther northwest in the Texas-Oklahoma "tornado alley" corridor.

The city's allure and natural beauty have attracted many new residents and businesses, making Georgetown part of the second-fastest-growing metro area in the United States. Georgetown's Convention and Visitors Bureau is proud of the city's rapid growth, but not everyone is completely pleased. Jerri Jones feels road construction has not kept up with the influx of residents, which causes traffic complaints.

Others simply like the charm of Georgetown and don't want it to change. "Some people would like to put a fence around Georgetown and keep everybody out, but that's not the way the world works," says Harold Steadman. "Besides," says Jean Steadman, "we are beginning to get some nice restaurants here because of the population growth, and I'm not opposed to that."

And despite the growth, Georgetown seems to be winning the battle to maintain its quaint atmosphere. Bob Jones marvels that Georgetown "still has that small-town feel, yet the closeness to metropolitan amenities." And that, he says, is reason enough to make him glad he moved to Georgetown.●

Golden Isles, Georgia

Georgia's coast has history, nature and a slower pace

By William Schemmel

On the Golden Isles, a string of barrier islands on Georgia's Atlantic Coast, there's a sense of history and security that's hard to find in today's world. For many retirees who move here, the islands offer a convenient escape to a different time and place.

"There's a wonderful magic about this part of the world. It has recaptured the feeling, the ambiance, the security of the 1950s," says Kate Minnock, who has found retirement contentment on Georgia's St. Simons Island. It's the most populous of the Golden Isles, which include Jekyll Island and Sea Island.

While some retirees are attracted by the less-developed nature of the islands, others prefer being closer to mainland amenities, choosing homes in nearby Brunswick and elsewhere in Glynn County. The area is midway along the coast between Savannah, GA, and Jacksonville, FL.

About the size of Manhattan, 14,000-acre St. Simons is connected to Brunswick, the county seat, by a toll causeway (35 cents per car). Resort hotels, condos and private homes are thinly spread along the hard-packed sand beaches. The 17,000 islanders, and thousands of yearly visitors, can play golf and tennis, shop in major supermarkets, art galleries and gift shops and dine and enjoy nighttime entertainment in a variety of restaurants and clubs.

However, most of the island remains an undeveloped realm of forests and salt marshes teeming with birds and wildlife. At the island's southern end, St. Simons Lighthouse has been a landmark since 1872.

Like all the Golden Isles, St. Simons is rich in history. In the late 1730s, the English who founded the Georgia colony built Fort Frederica at the island's northern end as a defense against Spanish invasion from Florida. The fort — whose ruins are now a national monument — never was tested, but when the

Spaniards did invade in 1742, their defeat at the Battle of Bloody Marsh left England firmly in control of the Georgia coast.

Bloody Marsh is the back yard to Kate and Tom Minnock's five-bedroom, two-story Cape Cod house in the central part of the island. They moved to St. Simons after first retiring to Hawaii from California, where he was an educator and she was a marketing executive.

If they had it to do over, "I would skip Hawaii and come straight to St. Simons Island," says Tom, 60. "When we first thought about retirement, Hawaii was our first choice. We spent the first few months doing nothing, got bored and went back to work."

After five years in Hawaii the Minnocks decided to move back to the mainland. "We looked at places all along the Georgia and South Carolina coasts, but we always kept coming back to St. Simons," he says.

Boredom is not a problem on St. Simons. Both Minnocks find plenty of ways to stay busy. Tom was coordinator for cultural, arts and athletic activities in conjunction with the 1996 Summer Olympic Games in Atlanta and nearby Savannah. Kate, 51, is administrator at a shelter for abused children in Brunswick. The Minnocks enjoy walking the island's beaches, fishing, crabbing, biking and golfing.

"The Newcomers Club is very active with new retirees," says Tom. "We also take trips with Friendship Force International, which is a people-to-people organization that enables you to stay in the homes of people in places like Russia, Ireland and Australia. There are also civic clubs, historical and arts groups."

Weather, security and cost of living were other attractions for the Minnocks.

"I like the weather," says Tom. "It's a little cooler here than Hawaii and Florida, and hurricanes are rare. I think the

last one that did any damage was about 30 years ago."

The Minnocks feel safe on St. Simons. "Especially when we're here on the island, we don't think about it (personal security)," Kate says. "When I'm in Brunswick I might lock my car doors.

The cost of living was another factor in the Minnocks' move.

"Most everything, including real estate, taxes and food, is much more reasonable here than in California or Hawaii," says Tom.

Gail Kellis, former president of the Brunswick/Golden Isles Board of Realtors and an agent with Golden Isles Realty, says that St. Simons' relaxed atmosphere, mild climate, stately live oak trees draped with Spanish moss and other assets attract increasing numbers of retirees.

The island offers them a wide range of housing options, from country club communities around golf courses to single-family homes on the beach and one- and two-level condos. But the days of inexpensive beach houses are gone, she says.

"It's getting to the point that you really have to look hard to find anything on St. Simons for under $100,000," she says.

Although St. Simons is undergoing rapid changes, the Minnocks say they're not concerned about overdevelopment. "Every once in awhile, a genius will come in who wants to change this into a mecca when it already is one," says Kate.

"When you're at ground level, it seems like we're being overdeveloped, but when you go up in a plane, as we did recently, you can see that maybe only 10 percent is being developed," she says. "The Sea Island Co., which owns The Cloister resort, owns so much of St. Simons. They allow only a small part to be developed at a time, and it's always very carefully planned."

A small bridge divides St. Simons

from Sea Island. Owned by the Sea Island Co., the tiny island is home of The Cloister, one of the most distinguished resort hotels in the country. Spanish-style villas and other huge estates along the Sea Island beach are valued in the millions of dollars.

Neighboring Jekyll Island, reached by its own causeway from Brunswick ($3 per car toll), also has an illustrious history. From 1885 to 1942, the island was the private retreat of many of Ameri-

Golden Isles, GA

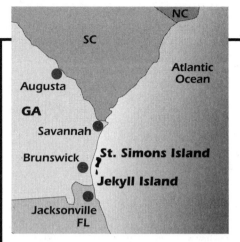

Population: 67,953 in Glynn County, 15,600 in Brunswick, 17,000 on St. Simons Island, 1,000 on Jekyll Island, 700 on Sea Island.

Location: Georgia's Atlantic Coast, 75 miles south of Savannah, GA, and 65 miles north of Jacksonville, FL. St. Simons, Sea Island and Jekyll Island are connected to the mainland by toll causeways from Brunswick.

Climate:

	High	Low
January	61	42
July	90	74

Average relative humidity: 60%
Rain: 55 inches.

A subtropical climate boasts short, mild winters and hot, humid summers with frequent thunderstorms. The last hurricane causing serious damage was Hurricane Dora in 1964. Elevation: Brunswick, 10 feet; the islands, 0-30 feet.

Cost of living: Below average (specific index not available). Housing costs on the islands are higher than average.

Median housing cost: $100,000 in mainland Glynn County and Brunswick; $237,500 on the islands.

Sales tax: 6%

Sales tax exemptions: Prescription drugs, hearing aids, eyeglasses.

State income tax: For married couples filing jointly, graduated from 1% of taxable income up to $1,000 to $340 plus 6% on amounts over $10,000. For single filers, graduated from 1% of income up to $750 to $230 plus 6% on amounts over $7,000.

Income tax exemptions: Social Security benefits are exempt. Up to $14,000 in retirement income is exempt for each taxpayer age 62 and older. Up to $4,000 of earned income can be included in the $14,000 exemption.

Intangibles tax: None.

Estate tax: None, except the state's "pick-up" portion of the federal tax, applicable to taxable estates of more than $1 million.

Property tax: In Brunswick, $35.46 per $1,000 valuation, with property assessed at 40% of market value. Tax on a $100,000 home, with $10,000 homestead exemption noted below, is $1,064. In the islands and other unincorporated areas, $26.74 per $1,000 valuation with property assessed at 40% of market value. Tax on a $237,500 home, with homestead exemption, is $2,273.

Homestead exemption: $6,000 off assessed value for full-time residents. Other age- and income-related exemptions available.

Religion: More than 100 churches and synagogues represent a wide spectrum of denominations.

Education: Coastal Georgia Community College, a two-year unit of the state university system, offers day and evening classes in the arts and sciences, languages and vocational/technical fields.

Transportation: No public bus system; a car is necessary. There's frequent commuter air service to Atlanta from Brunswick; nearest major airports are at Savannah, GA, and Jacksonville, FL.

Health: Southeast Georgia Regional Medical Center in Brunswick is a comprehensive 345-bed complex with complete diagnostic facilities and a 24-hour emergency department, coronary intensive care, mental health unit, breast imaging center and radiation oncology center. The county has 134 physicians and four nursing homes.

Housing options: On St. Simons Island, choices include country club communities such as **The Island Club** and **Sea Palms Resort,** with single-family homes on the golf course for $225,000-$1.5 million and above. Condos in the **Village** area, near the lighthouse and marina, are $150,000-$250,000. There are inland condos available on St. Simons Island from $90,000 and up. Ranch and stucco homes in **East Beach** start at about $400,000. On Jekyll Island, development is restricted and no new homes are planned. The island has 586 residences, most of them ranch-style dwellings built in the '50s-'70s. Prices range upward from $200,000, with three-bedroom ocean-front homes starting at about $450,000. On Sea Island, homes start at over $1 million; virtually all homes on Sea Island are custom-built. In Brunswick and mainland Glynn County, options range from secured-gate country club developments such as **Oak Grove** ($260,000-$1 million) to new subdivisions **Shadow Lake** ($130,000-$140,000) and **Serenoa Cove** ($310,000-$345,000), and older developments **Marshes of Mackay** ($118,000-$345,000) and **Deerfield** ($90,000-$94,000).

Visitor lodgings: Jekyll Island Club Hotel, a restored Victorian-style hotel in the historic district, has standard doubles for $139-$349, (912) 635-2600. Villas-by-the-Sea, a hotel condominium on the Jekyll Island beach, has studios to three-bedroom suites with kitchens for $89-$254, (800) 342-6872 in Georgia and (800) 841-6262 elsewhere. The King & Prince Hotel, a deluxe resort on the St. Simons beach, has a variety of rooms and villas for $125 and up, depending on season, (800) 342-0212. Days Inns of America, away from the beach on St. Simons' main commercial thoroughfare, is $71-$98, (800) 325-2525. To rent a house ($400-$2,200 per week), call Parker-Kaufman Realty, (912) 635-2512 on Jekyll Island or (912) 638-3368 on St. Simons.

Information: Brunswick & Golden Isles Visitors Bureau, 4 Glynn Ave., Brunswick, GA 31520, (912) 265-0620 or www.bgivb.com, or Brunswick and Glynn County Development Authority, P.O. Box 1079, Brunswick, GA 31521, (912) 265-6629 or www.brunswick-georgia.com.

ca's wealthiest families. Vanderbilts, Rockefellers, Morgans, Pulitzers, Goodyears, Cranes and Astors built elegant "cottages" where they spent their winters socializing and making big deals.

In 1947, the state of Georgia purchased the island, including the plutocrats' cottages, for the modest sum of $650,000. It's now a state park administered by the Jekyll Island Authority.

Ten miles of sand beaches are uncrowded even on the busiest holidays. Jekyll Island homeowners and visitors also enjoy 63 holes of golf, miniature golf, a driving range, picnic shelters, a fitness center, an outdoor summer theater festival, nature trails, indoor and outdoor tennis, marinas, water slides, an indoor Olympic-size swimming pool and other amusements.

The millionaires' cottages are a main attraction. Several are restored and open to the public in the attractively landscaped Jekyll Island Club Historic District. The Jekyll Island Club, the turreted Victorian landmark where the aristocrats dined and socialized, now is a full-service resort managed by Radisson Hotels.

The 1,000 full-time residents on Jekyll Island live in 586 mostly ranch-style homes built from the mid-1950s to the mid-1970s. Since state law stipulates that no more than 35 percent of the island's high ground can be developed, no new residential areas are foreseen.

Residents have full ownership of their homes and may make any changes they desire. However, the state retains ownership of the land, which is leased to homeowners under long-term agreements.

Jack and Pat Overholt purchased their three-bedroom ranch-style home near the ocean in 1977. After renting out the house for 10 years, they moved into it in 1987.

"When we bought it, it was a typical Jekyll Island rancher, with about 2,000 square feet," says Jack, 66, a former executive with Sara Lee Bakeries in Chicago. "We've since put on a significant addition. Before you can make addi-

tions, you have to submit your plans to the Jekyll Island Authority for approval. They're fairly flexible and are mainly concerned that you don't infringe on your neighbors."

The Overholts' home now is valued at about $200,000 on land leased until 2049. Frank Cerrato, a broker with Parker-Kaufman Realty, says large homes that front the ocean sell for $280,000 to $395,000, while some homes away from the beach can be found for about $140,000.

Potential retirees who might want to test the island's waters, literally and figuratively, can rent a place for $400 to $2,200 a week. They may find the cost of living and the island's subtropical climate attractive inducements to move here. Both were major points in the Overholts' decision.

"After living in the Chicago area, you look for a milder climate," says Pat, 61, a former elementary school teacher. "We had looked in Florida, but we preferred a little more change of seasons. Very rarely does it get so cold here that you can't go out and be active, even in the middle of winter."

Jack enjoys having a variety of activities. "I think the thing I like best is the lack of restrictions on our lifestyle," he says. "We're outdoor people, and neither of us wanted to retire and go into limbo."

Pat works with the Elderhostel program, which offers educational programs to senior citizens about the history, culture and environment of the Golden Isles. Jack is involved with Jekyll Island Museum Associates, which provides volunteers as workers and docents in the historic area.

The Overholts like to fish and play golf and tennis, activities available in abundance. "But we wouldn't want to be stuck here all the time," says Jack. "Jekyll gets pretty quiet when the summer vacationers go home. We travel a lot, visiting relatives and seeing other parts of the country and places overseas."

Among the things she misses, Pat says,

is "the accessibility to a large city. But I don't miss the congestion and hard winters."

Jekyll's shopping, dining and nightlife are limited. A strip shopping center has a small grocery store, drugstore, bank and a few other shops that cater mainly to the island's visitors. Most dining and entertainment are in the 10 hotels.

The Overholts gladly endure the minor inconveniences for the peace and security of Jekyll Island.

For serious shopping and a choice of restaurants, the Overholts must make the half-hour trip into Brunswick, where malls have chain supermarkets and other major stores. Convenience to shopping and medical services prompts many retirees to buy homes in Brunswick.

"About 20 percent of the people in Brunswick are retirees," says Winifred Capps with Capps-Century 21 Realty. "Many of them have come from Florida and the Northern states. Housing in Brunswick is less expensive than the islands, and many of the older houses are brick, which many people prefer to frame or stucco."

Oak Grove, one of the most exclusive communities, has 24-hour gated security and an 18-hole golf course. Homes sell for $260,000-$2 million. Homes in older developments facing the picturesque tidal marshes start at $118,000. Restored Victorian houses in the Old Town District near downtown Brunswick sell for about $150,000, while fixer-ups cost $70,000 or less.

The area's major medical center and only commercial airport are in Brunswick. Only commuter air service to Atlanta is available; many residents drive 65 to 75 miles to larger airports in Savannah and Jacksonville.

While the Minnocks and the Overholts like to travel, they also like to come home to Georgia's Golden Isles.

"There is a great deal of love, understanding and trust among the people who live here," says Tom Minnock. "I have never met a more gracious, warm, loving group of people."●

Grand Junction, Colorado

Hiking, fishing and biking make this Colorado town a hit with outdoors enthusiasts

By Steve Cohen

You can't ask much more of a community that makes relocating retirees feel like they are getting younger rather than older. And that's what retirees say about Grand Junction, perhaps known best for the nearby natural wonders of the Colorado National Monument. The town of 42,000 on the western slope of the Rocky Mountains is becoming home to retirees seeking an energetic outdoor lifestyle.

Grand Junction is cradled in the fertile Grand Valley, which lies between three natural barriers. The Little Bookcliffs cut across the northeastern skyline. The world's largest flat-topped mountain, Grand Mesa, covers the southeast. And the incredible monolithic rocks and plunging canyons of the Colorado National Monument create a western wall.

"The thing I like best about this town is the beautiful valley," says Dick Gerhardt, 57, a retired traffic manager from Philadelphia who moved to Grand Junction in 1997 with his wife, Aylene, 60, a retired schoolteacher. "We're a day trip from the Grand Canyon, Albuquerque or Yellowstone National Park. We have mountains all around us where we can hike, ski or snowmobile. The town next to us is known for its fruit, so we have lots of fresh fruit," he says.

The Gerhardts seriously considered other retirement sites but also liked Grand Junction's friendly residents and moderate weather. "We used to go down to Pine Isle, GA, about 80 miles northwest of Atlanta, but discounted it because of high humidity. My wife's first choice was Maui, HI. We used to go there every summer for a couple of weeks," he says.

Colorado was Dick's preference. "We used to come out to Colorado every Christmas to ski, beginning in 1986," Dick says. When he suggested Colorado, Aylene was receptive but didn't want to live in an area where winters were long and hard. "That's when we started looking around the state and discovered this area that's known as the banana belt," Dick says.

Eight local vineyards and abundant cherry, peach and apple orchards around Grand Junction attest to the moderate climate. With above-freezing low temperatures averaging 35 degrees in January, and with only 25 inches of snow a year, winter in Grand Junction is not exactly the roughest in the Rockies.

The Grand Valley was carved from rugged geography by the Colorado and Gunnison rivers and was one of the last settled regions in the lower 48 states. Grand Junction takes its name from its location at the confluence of the two great rivers. And it's not far from some of the West's most fabulous sites.

Another couple, Bill and Jane Stewart, both 78, discovered Grand Junction the second time around during their retirement. Originally from Topeka, KS, where Bill sold insurance and Jane was a homemaker, they spent their first 16 years of retirement in Vero Beach, FL, and had a second home in Vail, CO. Now they spend much of their winters at a second home in the Phoenix area. "But we still come back to Grand Junction," Jane says.

The winters here are colder than Jane would like, and she's not much of a fan of the occasional snow, but Bill likes to be in or near the mountains. "The winters are quite mild," he says. "I like to do a lot of hiking. I come back in the winter from Phoenix to ski."

Their son lived in Grand Junction, and they had visited three or four times over a period of about a year before deciding to move here. They knew at the time that their son would be leaving, but they moved anyway. Their home backs up to the public golf course at the Seasons at Tiara Rado, a master-planned community that has more than 100 homes completed of 240 projected.

"The primary reason we left Florida was allergies I picked up while living there," Bill says. "And we sure don't miss the humidity and the bugs," adds Jane. Solid health care provided by two regional hospitals, as well as a growing list of seniors-oriented services in the Grand Valley, add to the reasons people like the Stewarts feel comfortable here.

"We find people of all ages, including a growing number of retirees, moving here from all over to enjoy and participate in the outdoor Western lifestyle Grand Junction offers," says Karin Mast, promotions coordinator for the Grand Junction Visitor and Convention Bureau. "While we don't have retirement communities that are exclusively for retirees, we do have several beautiful master-planned communities," she says.

"What people tell us is that the biggest reason for choosing to relocate to Grand Junction is because there's just so much to do around here," she says. "The Grand Valley is home to eight wineries. The Colorado National Monument, which is practically right next door, contains 20,000 acres of incredible rocks and canyons. You can hike the canyons, visit Indian ruins, spot bald eagles and deer. And we have access to seven raftable rivers, from mild float trips to exciting whitewater."

The Grand Valley also is located within the famed "Dinosaur Diamond" of western Colorado and eastern Utah. The area is internationally known for its wealth of dinosaur excavation sites, exhibits, fossil trails and hands-on paleontological activities. There are several historic and scientific museums, a symphony orchestra and live theater at venues that include Mesa State College.

"We're getting bigger and better all the time, culturally," says Karin Mast. "And how many places are there where you can ride on 1,000 miles of mountain bike trails ranging from paved roads to challenging single tracks, or glimpse a herd of 100 wild horses in the Little Bookcliffs Wild Horse Area, a 30,000-acre recreation area north of Grand

Junction? You can rock climb or hike in the monument in the morning, play golf on the Grand Mesa in the afternoon, and sip a terrific Merlot or Chardonnay from the valley at night."

Attractions like these are why Grand Junction was really the only place that Pete Dickes, 57, and his wife, Karen, 53, considered for retirement. Pete, a banker, and Karen, a data processor, moved from Aurora, IL, 40 miles outside Chicago. Beginning in 1984, they

Grand Junction, CO

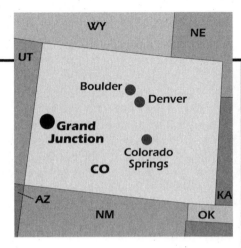

Population: 41,986 in Grand Junction, 116,255 in Mesa County.

Location: On Interstate 70, 258 miles west of Denver. Grand Junction lies in a fertile high desert mountain valley at an elevation of 4,586 feet.

Climate:

	High	Low
January	36	15
July	94	64

The weather is very dry and relatively warm for Colorado's western slope.

Average relative humidity: 8%-18%

Rain: 8.64 inches.

Snow: 25.4 inches.

Cost of living: 99.1, based on national average of 100.

Average housing cost: Countywide, residential property averages $146,948. Condos and townhouses average $83,356.

Sales tax: 7.65%

Sales tax exemptions: Prescriptions, groceries and residential energy.

State income tax: For married couples filing jointly and single filers, taxable income is taxed at 4.63%.

Income tax exemptions: There is an exemption from taxable pension and Social Security benefits of up to $20,000 for each person age 55-64 and up to $24,000 for each person age 65 and older.

Intangibles tax: None.

Estate tax: None, except the state's "pick-up" portion of the federal tax, applicable to taxable estates of more than $1 million.

Property tax: The average mill levy is 87 mills. The assessment rate on residential properties is estimated at 9.155% of actual value. A $146,948 home with an assessed value of $13,445.74 ($146,948 multiplied by .0915) would have a tax due of approximately $1,170 ($13,445.74 multiplied by .087).

Homestead exemption: The homestead exemption for senior citizens provides an actual-value reduction to a maximum of $100,000. This applies only to a primary residence for citizens over the age of 65. Also, this exemption is applicable only to a primary residence that has been owner-occupied for the 10 years immediately preceding the subject tax year.

Religion: There are more than 100 churches of varying denominations, as well as two synagogues.

Education: Mesa State College offers programs for adults.

Transportation: I-70, U.S. Highway 6 and U.S. Highway 50 pass through the area. Walker Field is an airport served by United Express, America West and Sky West-Delta, as well as charter services. Bus and train service is available from Greyhound and Amtrak, respectively. Rental cars are provided by Avis, Budget, Enterprise, National, Sears and Thrifty. Shuttle and taxi services are available from several local firms.

Health: There are three hospitals in Grand Junction with a total of 395 beds. An assisted-care facility, Grand Villa Assisted Living Community, (970) 241-9706, offers one-bedroom, 430-square-foot apartments for $2,606 monthly, and one-bedroom, 470-square-foot apartments for $2,668 monthly. Another assisted-care facility, offering 72 one-bedroom apartments in three buildings, is located in Fruita, five miles west of Grand Junction. There are 14 nursing homes in the Grand Junction area, with a total of 1,000 beds.

Housing options: Retirees are snapping up properties becoming available in two custom golf course communities being built in the shadow of the Colorado National Monument. **The Seasons at Tiara Rado** has completed the sixth phase of seven proposed neighborhoods that will comprise a total of 240 home sites. Current prices for home sites range from about $90,000 to $270,000. For information, call (970) 242-9482 or visit www.theseasonsgj.com. **Redlands Mesa** golf course community is newer, combining golf and outdoor recreation in a 500-acre development featuring a world-class golf course designed by Jim Engh, with more than a third of the community dedicated to natural open space, and approximately 400 home sites priced from $99,500 to $400,000. For information, call (877) 501-6372 or visit www.redlandsmesa.com.

Visitor lodging: Grand Junction Visitor and Convention Bureau recommends about 30 motels and hotels. About half of those are national chains. The largest motel is a 292-room Holiday Inn, with indoor and outdoor pools, a hot tub, restaurant and lounge, $74-$89, double occupancy, (888) 489-9796. The Grand Vista Hotel carries a AAA three-diamond rating. It features an indoor pool and hot tub open 24 hours, restaurant and lounge, $69-$109, some including breakfast, (800) 800-7796.

Information: Grand Junction Chamber of Commerce, 360 Grand Ave., Grand Junction, CO 81501, (970) 242-3214 or www.gjchamber.org. Grand Junction Visitor and Convention Bureau, 740 Horizon Drive, Grand Junction, CO 81506, (800) 962-2547 or www.visitgrandjunction.com.

visited every year, in different seasons, and always found it to their liking. They bought a lot in 1997, built a home and moved in on the last day of 1999.

"The town is extremely friendly," Karen says. Pete recalls a helpful store clerk who impressed him soon after he moved to Grand Junction. "I went to the Sears store to purchase a Skil saw," Pete says. "We weren't able to find one, and I purchased another item on my Visa card and left. The next day I had a phone call from the clerk, who had located the saw I was looking for, had gone to the office to get my name from the Visa transaction, looked up my telephone number, and left a message that she had the Skil saw if I still wanted it. That wouldn't happen in Chicago."

They're happy here, according to Pete. They're also happy with their home in the Seasons at Tiara Rado. A small drawback is that the development doesn't have a clubhouse, but they belong to the Bookcliffs Country Club nearby, where they play a lot of golf.

"I'm sitting here at home looking at the Colorado National Monument," Karen says. "It's absolutely beautiful." She also appreciates the area's four seasons and moderate climate. "The weather out here is just very, very good," she says. "It has very low humidity, around 15 percent," Pete adds. "It's perfect for golf."

"Every time we go away to Aurora, I miss being here," Karen says. "When I get about 50 miles outside of Denver I feel like I'm coming home. And that's amazing, considering I left a place I've lived all my life. It felt like home here immediately."

Part of the attraction is the opportunity for recreation. "Within two hours we can be in the mountains, we can be in a snow resort, we can be in a desert. It's amazing the variety of places we can get to from this central location," Karen says. "Active seniors would enjoy living in this town. People are always out walking or hiking or biking. It's the most active area I've ever seen. People get out and go.

"You would think we're going back in age instead of aging," Karen says.

In part because of their active lifestyle, the Dickes have found that their tastes in autos have changed from a Pontiac Grand Prix and Mazda RX-7 to a four-wheel-drive Honda Sierra and a Jeep Wrangler. "Pete and I have gotten into off-roading," Karen says.

For Bill and Jane Stewart, the activity of choice is golf. The Stewarts eat dinner at their country club every day, then play nine holes of golf. They like it here so much that they are building a bigger house just a block and a half away in the Seasons at Tiara Rado.

"We're moving from the 14th tee to the 17th tee," Bill says. "We love the Seasons and we decided we need a larger home. It's a wonderful place for almost anyone who has grown up in a small town or for those looking for a little slower lifestyle."

Bill does note that it's an overnight trip to a large city — Denver or Salt Lake City — for cultural activities. Jane acknowledges a challenging fact of life far from Florida's malls. "I'm here, I'm adjusted to this life," sighs Jane, "but I can't spend all the money I want!"

Dick Gerhardt doesn't particularly care for summer heat that averages 93 degrees in July. It's a dry heat, but in summer he's learned to do his outdoor chores early, getting them done before midmorning. Otherwise he waits until late in the evening.

And there were a few surprises. "We paid $24 to register a car in Pennsylvania, old or new," he says. "Here, it cost me $650 to register a new car. A friend bought a new motor home, and the tax was $5,000."

Overall, though, he finds the cost of living lower. Dick had several requirements on his relocation wish list, "a lower cost of living, and decent year-round weather being the most important." He and his wife researched books and traveled quite a bit in the year before they retired, and yet the place they chose was not found in any of the books they read.

"We came out here first in 1996 to ski. After skiing, we drove to this area, looked around, liked what we saw, went home and put our house up for sale," he says. "When we had a firm buyer, we flew out, spent a week and a half, picked out a house and bought it," says Dick, who selected a home in a new subdivision that was under construction. "The next time we came we were following a moving van."

For those who enjoy hiking, downhill skiing, snow-shoeing, or target and trap shooting, Dick feels the Grand Valley is really special. "You don't need a target range here — you just go out into the desert," Dick says, noting that 65 percent of the 3,400-acre county is federally owned forest or desert and also prime recreation space. There also are six area golf courses.

"Anyone who likes fishing, hunting, snow-skiing, hiking, mountain biking — any kind of outdoor activity — would enjoy living here," he says. ●

Green Valley, Arizona

Retiree-friendly community is an oasis in the southern Arizona desert

By Judy Wade

The 5,000 acres that comprise Green Valley lend a sense of history and tradition to a community only three decades old. The land was part of the original San Ignacio de las Canoa land grant conveyed to members of the Spanish monarchy more than 400 years ago. Today the names Canoa and San Ignacio figure prominently in the names of Green Valley streets and developments.

This unincorporated town 25 miles south of Tucson is a community of age-restricted retirement developments mixed with a few family subdivisions. Located in the Santa Cruz River Valley at an elevation of 2,900 feet, Green Valley is consistently seven degrees cooler than Tucson and 10 degrees cooler than Phoenix, two and a half hours to the north.

Green Valley is long and narrow, radiating out from both sides of Interstate 19, with main thoroughfares fed by quiet residential streets. To the east, the Santa Rita Mountains provide magnificent views as well as pine-forested venues for picnicking and hiking. On the horizon to the west is the Duval Copper Mine, a working mine that appears as a distant berm kept watered and treed so as not to create dust or become an eyesore.

The Santa Cruz River, mostly dry but subject to occasional flooding, parallels the freeway. The general impression is of a neat and tidy community that fits comfortably into the desert's austere beauty.

The weather was a deciding factor when Dave and Jan Evans moved from Rockford, IL, six years ago. Winters were cooler than they expected. "I have an orange and a grapefruit tree, and I have to cover them about a dozen times in the winter," says Dave, 68.

Green Valley's first small houses were built in the 1960s by a company that expected retirees to buy them as second homes. By 1973, Fairfield Homes, a large developer, had become the dominant builder and was offering two-bedroom villas at first intended as winter homes. But it didn't take long for residents to realize that Green Valley was delightful all year, and arriving newcomers wanted larger, full-time homes.

Helen and Gene Honderich, both 77, chose a Fairfield home when they moved from Grosse Pointe, MI, in 1989. Their townhouse overlooks the 16th fairway of the San Ignacio Golf Course, with a 270-degree view of the Santa Rita Mountains beyond. They say the view more than makes up for leaving a home on the Detroit River with access to Lake Erie.

"We discovered Green Valley while visiting Tucson and were impressed with its newness, good traffic flow and absence of slums," says Gene. They also were pleased to find property taxes considerably less than in Michigan.

Monterey Homes, a builder of neighborhoods in California, Texas and Arizona since 1985, is developing three active-adult communities in Green Valley. Canoa Ranch is a gated community offering 10 floor plans priced from the mid-$100,000s. The Legends, also gated, has six home styles available with prices from the $120,000s. At Las Campanas, homebuyers can choose from 10 floor plans with starting prices in the low $130,000s.

Green Valley also has a variety of resale housing options. Red tile roofs create a Mediterranean atmosphere in some areas, and flat-roof territorial styles establish a Southwest feel in others. Most have desert landscaping, with few traditional grass lawns.

This diversity is one of the town's big attractions, says Joe Steinmetz, associate broker with Long Realty. "We have a lot of older little townhomes and villas in the $30,000-to-

$40,000 price range that are especially popular with retirees, as well as $400,000 homes," he says.

Pueblo Estates, a manufactured home community that is age-restricted, has resales from about $53,500 to $95,000, including the lot, according to Steinmetz. La Posada, a continuing-care retirement community, is set in a shady mature pecan grove. It offers garden homes, apartments and assisted living and always has a waiting list.

When the Evanses moved from Illinois, they purchased one of the town's oldest homes, built in 1964. An add-on room provides art studio space for Jan, 67, where she works in mixed-media acrylic. Although their home is air-conditioned, they say they rarely use it, preferring an evaporative cooler that works efficiently in the dry climate. The large yard backs up to a wash, where the Evanses occasionally see coyotes. Finches, doves, flickers, cactus wrens and Gila woodpeckers are frequent visitors to the desert plantings in their yard.

Nature plays a large part in Green Valley's personality. On either side of a main street called Camino del Sol, lush fairways connect velvety golf course greens. Three of the town's seven courses are private, with the remaining four open to public play.

Green Valley sits on a productive aquifer, a subterranean zone that stores accessible water and keeps these desert greens grassy. It is projected to meet the town's water needs for decades to come, relieving dependency on ground sources and allowing Green Valley to live up to its name.

Green Valley Recreation Inc., a nonprofit organization, is the equivalent of a municipal department of parks and recreation. It operates six major recreational complexes and six neighborhood centers with swimming pools, meeting rooms, a theater and auditorium, and other sports, recreation and leisure facilities. Membership is based on the deed restrictions of each residential property. The Evanses, avid tennis players, note that their court fees went from more than $150 per month to zero when they moved to Green Valley.

Everyone in Green Valley is careful to emphasize that it is a town rather than a city. "A city and all its ills is something that many of our residents are trying to escape," says Inez Peters. "This is a small town with neighborhoods and a feeling of community."

Green Valley's small-town personality appealed to Dave and Dee Haynes, 64 and 62 respectively. They left Cupertino, CA, because of its traffic, crowds and high cost of living. "We bought our first place here in 1980 and vacationed here until I retired, then moved permanently," says Dave. In 1988 they purchased a single-family home in an area of Green Valley that is not age restricted.

With a median age in Green Valley of 72.2 years, and 90 percent of the population over the age of 55, it's no surprise that senior sensibilities run high. Fairfield builds only age-restricted communities, with one buyer in a couple required to be at least 45 to 55, depending on the community. A few local builders offer family subdivisions, but it is the retirement market that prevails.

Four shopping centers have major supermarkets and department stores as well as large discount stores and major drug chains. Small boutique apparel shops and specialty stores are part of the retail mix. Residents say they do as much shopping as possible in Green Valley to take advantage of the town's 5.6 percent sales tax. In nearby Tucson, the sales tax is 7 percent.

But residents seek health care in Tucson because Green Valley is not yet large enough to support its own hospital. Gene Honderich appreciates the fact that area doctors and hospitals are accustomed to treating a large geriatric population.

Fine dining and cultural opportunities also are best sought in Tucson, where a renowned symphony orches-

Green Valley, AZ

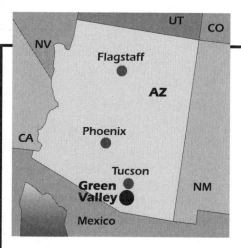

Population: 17,283 in Green Valley, 843,746 in Pima County.
Location: In the Santa Cruz River Valley midway between Tucson, AZ, and Nogales, Mexico. Elevation 2,900 feet.
Climate:

	High	Low
January	65	37
July	98	71

Average relative humidity: 25%
Rain: 16 inches.
Snow: Rare.
Clean desert air and low humidity are big drawing cards. From July through September, humid air from Mexico rushes north to cause afternoon thunderstorms with lightning displays, helping to keep the area cool.
Cost of living: About average (specific index not available).
Average housing cost: $140,000
Sales tax: 5.6%
Sales tax exemptions: Prescription drugs, groceries.

State income tax: For married couples filing jointly, graduated from 2.87% of taxable income up to $20,000 to 5.04% minus $2,276 on amounts over $300,000. For single filers, graduated from 2.87% of taxable income up to $10,000 to 5.04% minus $1,138 on amounts over $150,000.
Income tax exemptions: Social Security benefits and up to $2,500 on federal, state and local government pensions are exempt.
Intangibles tax: None.
Estate tax: None, except the state's "pick-up" portion of the federal tax, applicable to taxable estates above $675,000.
Property tax: $11.20 per $100 of assessed value, with homes assessed at 10% of market value. Taxes on a $140,000 home are approximately $1,568 a year.
Homestead exemption: None.
Religion: 21 churches represent more than a dozen denominations.
Education: College courses are offered at local off-campus facilities by the University of Arizona and Pima Community College. In Tucson, the University of Arizona offers a wide range of degree courses, some of which are available to seniors at no cost on a space-available basis.
Transportation: There's no town transportation. Citizen's Auto Stage provides

bus service between Nogales, Tucson and Phoenix, stopping in Green Valley. Tucson International Airport is 23 miles north, with shuttle service to and from Green Valley.
Health: Green Valley has four medical clinics, six dental offices, two nursing homes and four ambulances with trained emergency medical technicians. Full-service hospital care is available in Tucson.
Housing options: There's a wide selection of new and resale homes ranging from $29,000 to $700,000. Sandstone Ridge Apartments has one-bedroom rentals from $610 per month on an annual basis, $1,850 per month for a furnished unit during the peak winter season. New active-adult communities in Green Valley from Monterey Homes include **Canoa Ranch**, priced from the mid-$100,000s, (800) 528-4930; **Las Campanas**, from the low $130,000s, (877) 658-5444; and **The Legends**, from the $120,000s, (888) 829-0984.
Visitor lodging: Best Western, $59-$100, double occupancy, (800) 344-1441. Tubac Golf Resort (20 miles south of Green Valley), $80-$150 summer, $140-$235 winter, (520) 398-2211.
Information: Green Valley Chamber of Commerce, P.O. Box 566, Green Valley, AZ 85622, (800) 858-5872, (520) 625-7575 or www.greenvalleyazchamber.com. Also see www.arizonaguide.com.

tra, ballet season and theatrical events are part of an active cultural scene. Green Valley has the usual fast-food chains as well as a couple of cowboy steakhouses and good Mexican restaurants, and there's a bowling alley and a branch of the Tucson Public Library. There's one movie theater in the area. A local arts council regularly schedules exhibits and sponsors musical and dance performances.

Fifteen miles south of Green Valley, the little city of Tubac is a hub of artistic activity with more than 80 galleries and studios, shops and restaurants. It offers a series of exhibitions and performing arts presentations September through May.

The variety of churches appealed to the Honderichs, who were attracted to Valley Presbyterian because of its aesthetics. "It is architecturally designed with a beautiful view of the mountains, and it has an excellent musical program. We both belong to the choir," says Gene, who also is active in barbershop quartet singing.

A landmark just a few miles north of town is the stunning mission San Xavier del Bac. It appears on the horizon to the west of Interstate 19 as a magnificent monument to the tenacity of early Catholic fathers. "The White Dove of the Desert" is considered one of the finest examples of Spanish mission architecture in the country. It is open for tours and daily mass.

Other things to do in the area include exploring the cool, shadowy depths of Madera Canyon, about 15 miles east of Green Valley. Just 40 miles south, the Mexican border city of Nogales offers unique shopping opportunities. An hour's drive south, Patagonia Lake has recently opened for fishing and boating.

One of the most-visited attractions is the Arizona-Sonora Desert Museum, a 45-minute drive from Green Valley. Native plants and animals in their natural habitat give visitors an opportunity to get close to desert bighorn sheep, coyotes, javelinas and more.

The Pima County Sheriff's Department is the primary law enforcement agency for the area, keeping the crime rate far below the national average. Many residents belong to Friends in Deed, the largest and oldest of several service organizations. It provides no-cost blood pressure checks and assistance with Medicare, and its members visit the homebound and arrange for wheelchairs, crutches and walkers.

Most residents move to Green Valley from other areas of Arizona, but a large wall map in the chamber of commerce office shows that other states are well-represented — 889 from California, 890 from Illinois, 658 from Colorado, 675 from Minnesota and 446 from New York.

If there is a drawback to life in Green Valley, Dave Haynes attributes it to snowbirds who come only for the winter, doubling the population. Traffic is a little heavier and grocery lines are a little longer, at least temporarily.

But Dave acknowledges that there's another way to look at it: In the winter, there's double the number of friendly neighbors in Green Valley.●

Hattiesburg, Mississippi

Newcomers quickly feel at home in Mississippi university town

By Richard L. Fox

In the early 1990s, Tom and Jane Moseley were looking for a town where they could spend their retirement years — "just a nice place where we could be integrated into the community," Tom recalls.

They left their home near Atlanta in 1992 and settled into Hattiesburg, a city of about 45,000 residents in southern Mississippi. Now Tom, 60, a retired IBM engineer, and his wife, Jane, 58, a homemaker, are so well integrated into their new community that Tom is the featured commentator on a retiree-attraction videotape produced by the Hattiesburg Area Development Partnership.

"The first and foremost attraction for us was its friendly people," says Tom. "This is a thriving town . . . the leaders have a great 'can-do' attitude."

This also is a town that rolls out the red carpet for retirees. In January 1995 the Mississippi Department of Economic and Community Development named Hattiesburg the first "certified retirement city" of its Hometown Mississippi Retirement program. The statewide mission promotes Mississippi as a retirement haven and helps city leaders market their communities to relocating retirees. Cities must meet a long list of criteria in order to be certified, including good health-care facilities, available housing, educational and cultural opportunities and a retiree-attraction committee.

An integral part of Hattiesburg's retiree-attraction effort is the Retirement Connection. A division of the Area Development Partnership, this organization is staffed by senior volunteers — called "connectors" — who contact prospective new residents and share information about Hattiesburg as well as their own experiences.

Charles and Helen Short received a phone call from a Hattiesburg connector shortly after visiting the town. "The information and assistance we received from that group was vital in our decision to move to Hattiesburg," says Helen, 67. The Shorts moved in June 1995 after 35 years in Rochester, NY.

"When we moved down here, we were the 100th retired couple," recalls Charles, 69. "So we got a little publicity from that." They also got a reception, a key to the city from the mayor and a basket of goodies.

"A few months later we sat down and wrote a letter saying, 'Thank you, Hattiesburg,' for all of the things Hattiesburg had done to make us feel so warmly received. We got quite a bit of press from that and made even more new friends as a result. We had about 20 calls from people saying, 'We're so glad you're here,'" says Charles.

Bill and Nancy Litwiller, 68 and 65, moved to Hattiesburg from Hampstead, NC, where they had lived for 10 years after a long career in overseas government service. They found the Retirement Connection to be a tremendous help to their relocation. "We had friends we didn't even know — before we arrived here," says Nancy, who along with her husband now is active in the group herself.

Recently Hattiesburg has been cited in a number of national publications for its "livability," low cost of living and retiree-oriented programs. The U.S. Conference of Mayors awarded the city the Livability Award for communities of less than 100,000 residents.

If there's one thing upon which everyone in Hattiesburg agrees, it is that 12,000-student University of Southern Mississippi and 2,200-student William Carey College are largely responsible for the town's growing reputation as a great place to live.

Prominently situated on a pretty, oak-shaded campus just west of downtown, USM is credited for bringing a youthful exuberance and vitality to Hattiesburg, along with social, cultural and educational opportunities generally found in much larger cities. William Carey College is a private, Baptist-affiliated, four-year liberal arts college.

For many retirees, the university's Institute for Learning in Retirement (ILR) is the ultimate example of the community's outreach to its retired population. Established under the auspices of the university and Mississippi Hometown Retirement, the organization is run by retirees for retirees and offers dozens of courses year-round, with retirees often serving as instructors.

Seminars and a luncheon lecture series bring large numbers of people to its off-campus location. Members attend ILR classes for about $15 each and, if 65 and older, can obtain a $30 "listener's license" to audit regular university classes on a noncredit basis. Other perquisites include discounts on all continuing-education courses at USM and honorary University Club membership.

The Litwillers have taught and taken courses at the institute and number it high among their reasons for retiring to Hattiesburg. Helen Short, who was a microbiologist at the University of Rochester in New York, lectures at ILR, and she and Charles, a former marketing executive, regularly attend classes there.

Helen credits what she calls the "centrality" of Hattiesburg for its special qualities. "It has a small-town environment and yet all of the amenities," she says. "At Christmastime, people come from 100 miles away to do their shopping and participate in festivities."

Heavily traveled Hardy Street is Hattiesburg's primary east-west artery. It is named for founder Capt. William H. Hardy, who first recognized the area's potential when surveying a new railroad route; the city itself is named for his wife, Hattie. Hardy Street connects a busy, attractive downtown to the university, hospitals, restaurants and shopping malls that extend to the west.

Hattiesburg boasts a number of restored late 19th- and early 20th-century homes, churches and commercial buildings listed on the National Register of Historic Places. A 1985 historic conservation ordinance encourages the restoration of homes and buildings in six separate historic districts. The largest is 23-block Hattiesburg Historic Neighborhood District, which features Victorian, Queen Anne and Greek Revival-style homes. During a Victorian Christmas celebration each December, the district becomes a holiday wonderland.

A striking 53,000-square-foot public library near downtown features a circular 167-foot mural in its atrium. Painted on sandblasted stainless steel by local artist William Baggett, the mural depicts life in Mississippi before a 16th-century visit by explorer Hernando de Soto, and scenes extend all the way to contemporary times. Other library highlights include a 100,000-volume collection, computer lab, books by mail and a growing collection of large-print books. At Lunch With Books sessions held at the library, university profes-

sors and writers host lunchtime discussions on such topics as rare book collecting and famous authors.

Hattiesburg was settled just south of the confluence of the Bouie and Leaf rivers, and the gently undulating terrain is marked by lakes, great oaks and towering pines. An exploration of recreational resources reveals an exceptional array of golf courses, public tennis courts, miles of landscaped walking and jogging trails, and water parks for swimming, fishing, boating, camping and hiking. South of town off U.S. High-

Hattiesburg, MS

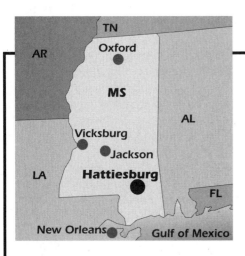

Population: 44,779 in Hattiesburg (not including 19,000 college and university students).

Location: In southeastern Mississippi, 115 miles northeast of New Orleans.

Climate:	High	Low
January	59	39
July	91	70

Average relative humidity: 74%

Rain: 60 inches.

Cost of living: 92.9, based on national average of 100.

Average housing cost: $106,700

Sales tax: 7%

Sales tax exemptions: Prescription drugs.

State income tax: For married couples filing jointly and single filers, the rate is graduated from 3% of taxable income up to $5,000 to 5% on amounts over $10,000.

Income tax exemptions: Social Security benefits, public and private pensions, IRAs and annuities are exempt. There is an additional $1,500 personal exemption for residents age 65 and older.

Intangibles tax: None.

Estate tax: None, except the state's

"pick-up" portion of the federal tax, applicable to taxable estates of more than $1 million.

Property tax: In Hattiesburg, $165.28 per $1,000 of assessed value, with homes assessed at 10% of appraised value. The rate in unincorporated areas of the county is $118.99 per $1,000. With exemptions noted below, annual property tax on a home in Hattiesburg appraised at $106,700 is about $1,763 for homeowners under age 65 and about $524 for homeowners age 65 or older.

Homestead exemption: There is a $300 tax credit for all homeowners. For those age 65 and older, the first $75,000 of appraised value is exempt from taxation.

Personal property tax: For automobiles, there is a tax of $165.28 per $1,000 based on 30% of the depreciated value, less a tax credit of 5.5% of the assessed value.

Religion: There are more than 150 places of worship, including churches and synagogues.

Education: The University of Southern Mississippi offers undergraduate and graduate degree programs. William Carey College is a four-year private liberal arts school. USM's Institute for Learning in Retirement is a self-run, self-directed association of retirees offering a variety of courses.

Transportation: Amtrak offers direct service from Hattiesburg east as far as Atlanta and west as far as Los Angeles. Hattiesburg-Laurel Regional Airport has connecting flights to Memphis. Jackson International Airport is 90 miles away, and

New Orleans International is 105 miles away.

Health: Forrest General Hospital is a 537-bed, full-service regional medical center serving 17 counties. Wesley Medical Center has 211 beds. More than 300 medical professionals in Hattiesburg practice 32 specialties.

Housing options: Prices for condominiums and townhomes in older developments start around $85,000. Currently, a limited number of condominiums and townhouses are available, but more are planned. **Timber Ridge** has three-quarter-acre lots from $10,500 and homes with underground utilities from $120,000. There are several manufactured-home parks in the city and rural areas with new homes for $50,000-$75,000. Homes in historic districts go on the market for about $120,000-$300,000. Master-planned developments include **Canebrake**, (601) 264-0403, a lakeside golf-course community with homes for $160,000-$1 million; **Timberton**, a popular golf community just minutes from downtown with homes for $180,000-$350,000; and **Lake Serene**, which has homes on large, wooded lakeside lots with resale prices of $180,000-$550,000.

Visitor lodging: Comfort Suites, $88-$160, double occupancy, (601) 261-5555. Hampton Inn, $58-$68, (601) 264-8080.

Information: Area Development Partnership, P.O. Box 751, Hattiesburg, MS 39403-0751, (800) 238-4288 or www.hattiesburg-adp.org.

way 49, Paul B. Johnson State Park has a 300-acre lake, cabins, nature trail, canoe and boat rentals, and fishing and picnic areas.

Hattiesburg's convenient hub location at the intersection of several highways means easy access to Jackson, New Orleans and popular Gulf Coast beaches, all within a two-hour drive.

Hattiesburg serves as southeast Mississippi's regional medical center and has won notice for the quality of its health care. Forrest General Hospital and Wesley Medical Center have a total of 748 beds and 300 medical professionals. Hattiesburg Clinic has 170 physicians and health care professionals, making it the largest multispecialty group practice in the state. Both hospitals have programs that provide seniors with 100 percent of Medicare-approved hospital costs, plus health education, paperwork assistance and various cafeteria and gift-shop discounts.

A stellar array of museums, art galleries, parks and gardens promote interest in the visual arts, and performing-arts forums present plays and musical performances to enthusiastic audiences. The 1,000-seat Saenger Theatre hosts a variety of events; the restored art deco movie palace is a local landmark on the National Register of Historic Places. At noon on Thursdays during May and October, the Hattiesburg Arts Council sponsors brown-bag concerts in Fountain Park.

As expected in a college town, the university is a source of diverse cultural happenings. The music school features concerts by bands, choirs, a symphony orchestra and vocal artists, while the theater and dance departments perform each spring and fall. The C.W. Woods Art Gallery hosts major traveling shows as well as solo and group exhibitions. For sports fans, USM has an NCAA Division I athletic program.

Affordability figures prominently in Hattiesburg's increasing popularity with retirees. Retirement income such as Social Security benefits, pensions and IRAs are exempt from state income tax, and a generous $75,000 homestead exemption for homeowners age 65 and older helps ease property tax burdens.

When Tom Moseley compared taxes and household expenses such as insurance and utilities between his former home in Dunwoody, GA, and Hattiesburg, he found that living costs were reduced by more than $9,000 a year in Hattiesburg. Charles and Helen Short also noticed a substantial decrease in their cost of living. "Our property tax went from $5,000 to $1,000, and we went from 1,700 square feet in Rochester to 2,700 square feet here," says Helen.

Bob James, chairman of the Retirement Connection and a Coldwell Banker real-estate agent, says newcomers can find a variety of housing at very reasonable prices.

"Thirty- to 40-year-old, well-maintained subdivisions in town have condominiums and townhouses in the $60,000s and single-family homes in the $50,000s to $90,000s," he says. "There are several manufactured-home parks in the area with new homes selling for $50,000 to $75,000. Historic districts have a half-dozen homes on the market at any time, most priced from $120,000 to $250,000."

Lake Serene, a master-planned development outside the city, has homes on large wooded lots situated around several lakes for $180,000 to $550,000. Timberton, south of town with an 18-hole golf course and clubhouse, offers new homes for $180,000 to $350,000.

The Moseleys live in Canebrake, an upscale lakeside community located six miles from town. Amenities here include security guards, walking trails, tennis courts and a golf course under construction. "About 20 retired couples live here," says Tom Moseley. "It's a nicer house, with tremendous amenities, in a nicer neighborhood than Dunwoody, and we paid one-third less for our house here.

"It also has 92 doctors living there," Tom continues. "I tell people (that) if I don't feel well, I stand out in my front yard and just yell out my symptoms and get advice from a dozen specialists."

The Litwillers also bought a house in Canebrake. Bill describes it as a two-story Arcadian-style home, similar to a Cape Cod with deep porches at the front and back. When they aren't playing golf, their favorite pastime, the Litwillers enjoy reading, computers, gardening and traveling.

Charles and Helen Short bought a 1-year-old house in Bent Creek, a subdivision eight miles from town that currently has 173 homes. "It's a young community. We are the old geezers, surrounded by young people. You can count the number of retirees on one hand," says Charles, who enjoys living among younger residents.

Hattiesburg was the recipient of 10 additional police officers via a federal grant under President Clinton's community-oriented policing initiative. Neighborhood enhancement teams patrol higher-crime areas by foot and bicycle, getting to know residents on a first-name basis and leading to a greater degree of cooperation and willingness to report criminal activity.

All three couples — the Moseleys, Litwillers and Shorts — were hardpressed to come up with drawbacks to living in Hattiesburg. "If you get down to brass tacks," Charles Short says, "there's really not a thing we don't like."

For some, the heat may take some adjustments, though. "The first summer we were here it just about wiped us out," says Helen Short, "but now that we're accustomed to it we have no problem with it."

"We were attracted by a small city that literally has everything," says Nancy Litwiller. "The university is an integral part of the city. The Institute for Learning in Retirement is just wonderful. Medical facilities are outstanding. I think, bottom line, (it's) the people... so kind and so generous and so caring."

"Get connected!" advises Bill Litwiller. "Listen to what the connector has to say. He's a volunteer. He's not selling anything. He'll tell you what's here."●

Hendersonville, North Carolina

This North Carolina town shines in its scenic setting of mountains, rivers and forests

By Richard L. Fox

Not long ago, Hendersonville was considered an undiscovered haven by many retirees. But with a 35 percent increase in population in the last 10 years, it can no longer claim to be undiscovered, although the descriptive word "haven" still applies to this scenic retreat nestled on a Blue Ridge mountain plateau in the southern highlands.

"The growth rate is a plus," says Bill Johnson, a retired bank president who moved here in 1997 from Rockville, MD. "Hendersonville is a nice small town that is growing very rapidly but has a long way to grow before becoming a large metropolitan-type place."

Bill, 61, and his wife, Barbara, 59, feel the town's growth — much of it generated by relocating retirees — provides an opportunity to help shape the direction in which it moves. "We enjoy being involved in that growth," says Bill. He is not shy about explaining his philosophy of how a town should work. "If you want to become involved in politics you can," he says. "But you don't have to have government-run agencies to get things done. People all over this town are volunteering their services to make it a better place. That's why our taxes are so low."

The Johnsons didn't know anyone when they moved to Hendersonville, but Bill says that, too, is a plus. "That's one of the common bonds everyone has," he says. "You really strike up new acquaintanceships quite easily." In fact, he warns, residents quickly can become socially overextended. "We don't have any spare time anymore," he says. "It's not a popularity thing — people here are just so amenable to meeting new people."

"It's nice to move into a community where everyone is open to meeting new people," Barbara adds. "It's a great place to grow old because it's not a real glitzy place."

The town's founding is attributed to William Mills, a Revolutionary War soldier, in the 1780s. Chartered in 1847, the struggling backwoods town got a shot in the arm with completion of a railroad line from Charleston, SC, in 1879. Sweltering Carolina lowlanders and Floridians flocked to this easily accessible, cool mountain retreat for relief from summertime heat and humidity.

For years summer tourism kept merchants busy and smiling. But downtown traffic dwindled after World War II when new suburban shopping malls began springing up in small towns across the country. Hendersonville took steps to ensure the survival of its downtown and in 1986 became a federally designated Main Street city. Today, the fruits of that decision can be seen in the restored historic buildings, wide sidewalks, colorful planters, comfortable benches and free parking along tree-lined Main Street. Antique shops, galleries, boutiques and trendy restaurants now occupy once-empty storefronts, enticing tourists and residents back to the town center.

Only on a late summer weekend in early September, when some 250,000 people descend on downtown Hendersonville for the annual North Carolina Apple Festival, does the town take on the semblance of a major metropolitan area. Then its broad main street fills with apple-munching shoppers, browsers and sightseers in a carnival atmosphere.

"We came, saw it and said, 'this is it,'" recalls Jim Finch about the move he and wife Joan made in 1990. After living 32 years in the hectic northern Virginia suburbs of Washington, DC, the Finches were ready for the slower pace promised by this small highlands community. As they experienced the scenic beauty of the surrounding Blue Ridge and Great Smoky mountains, discovered the recreational possibilities of the nearby French Broad and Nantahala rivers, and found a new —

and affordable — condominium under construction in a master-planned community, the decision was sealed.

Jim, a two-career Navy commander and former principal of Annandale High School in Fairfax County, VA, and Joan, a home economist, say they loved living in northern Virginia, "but Hendersonville is the place to retire," says Jim. "The first year you are here, you are the Club Med," he says. "Everyone wants to come down for a visit and see the beautiful mountains. We have six granddaughters and they love this place. I take them whitewater rafting, kayaking, canoeing and hiking."

The Oaks, a 198-unit condominium complex within minutes of downtown, provides everything the Finches were looking for in housing, and at an affordable price. "We bought down," Jim says happily. "We spent less for a new house here — with more square footage — than we got for our old house in Virginia."

He now serves on the homeowners' board at The Oaks and has responsibility for building maintenance and upkeep of common grounds. "We had a condo at Cocoa Beach and sold it," Jim says. "If you want to be part of a community, you can't live half a year here and half a year there."

Another couple at The Oaks, Robert and Amy Foster, discovered Hendersonville 10 years ago while visiting her brother, who had retired to Lake Lure, a small resort community 20 miles east. Amy noticed there was little commercial activity around Lake Lure and asked her brother where he shopped, bought groceries and went to the library. When the answer kept coming up Hendersonville, she told her husband that they should take a look at the town.

They did and liked what they saw. "The Oaks was new, and we found a very spacious condominium — over 2,000 square feet — at a very good price," Amy remembers. "With annual property taxes of

"$1,700 versus $5,000 in Syracuse," Robert adds.

"We were sick of the snow. I didn't want to shovel anymore," Amy says of Syracuse. "We liked the mountains and scenic beauty of the area — the small town, the four seasons," she says of Hendersonville.

The Fosters immediately became active, joining a church, the Welcome Wagon and Opportunity House, a nonprofit arts, crafts and cultural center with more than 1,400 members. Robert, a former television executive for an ABC affiliate in

Syracuse, had district oversight responsibility for 41 Rotary clubs in upstate New York and quickly assumed fund-raising and leadership activities for the local club. Amy, who taught high school Spanish, volunteers her language skills and participates in Habitat for Humanity projects.

The Fosters, Finches and Johnsons all were surprised by the array of cultural organizations supported by the small populations of Hendersonville and Flat Rock, a tiny, historic village four miles south. The Henderson County Arts Council and

Art League of Henderson County promote visual art programs throughout the year, including monthly art shows and an annual Sidewalk Art Show in which 110 artists from 16 states display and sell their works.

For music lovers, the 30-voice Carolina Chamber Singers, 100-voice Hendersonville Chorale, 70-piece Symphony Orchestra and swing band perform for enthusiastic audiences in all seasons. The renowned Brevard Music Center is a scenic 20-minute drive southwest of town.

Hendersonville, NC

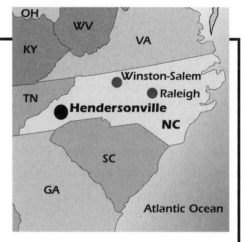

Population: 10,420 in the city, 89,173 in Henderson County.

Location: On a plateau 2,200 to 3,000 feet above sea level, between the Blue Ridge and Great Smoky mountains, 25 miles south of Asheville and 15 miles north of the South Carolina border.

Climate:

	High	Low
January	47	25
July	84	62

Average relative humidity: 60%

Rain: 52 inches annually.

Cost of living: Average (specific index not available).

Average housing cost: $163,239

Sales tax: 6.5%

Sales tax exemptions: Prescription medicine, eyeglasses, some medical supplies, gasoline, motor vehicles and most services.

State income tax: For married couples filing jointly, the rate is graduated from 6% of taxable income up to $21,250 to 8.25% on amounts over $200,000. For single filers, it is graduated from 6% of income up to $12,750 to 8.25% on amounts over $120,000.

Income tax exemptions: Social Security benefits are exempt. Up to $2,000 of distributions from private retirement benefits and IRAs (up to the amount reported in federal income taxes), or up to $4,000 of government pensions may be exempt. Total deductions may not exceed $4,000 per person.

Intangibles tax: None.

Estate tax: None, except the state's "pickup" portion of the federal tax, applicable to taxable estates above $1 million. North Carolina's inheritance tax was repealed in 1999.

Property tax: In Hendersonville the rate is $9.50 per $1,000 of assessed (market) value. The rate increases for downtown and Seventh Avenue homes by $2.50 and $1 per $1,000, respectively. In unincorporated Henderson County the rate is $5 per $1,000. The annual tax on a $163,239 home is $1,551 in Hendersonville, $816 outside the city.

Homestead exemption: The first $20,000 or 50% in appraised value (whichever is greater) is exempt for North Carolina residents age 65 and older with incomes of $18,000 or less.

Religion: More than 135 churches and a Jewish synagogue.

Education: Blue Ridge Community College enrolls more than 1,500 students. Its Center for Lifelong Learning is member-directed and offers popular workshops, seminars and lectures for over-50 members.

Transportation: There is no local public bus system. Interstates 26 and 40, U.S. highways 25, 64 and 176, and the Blue Ridge Parkway serve the area. Asheville Regional Airport, 10 miles north of the city, provides air service to national and international destinations.

Health: Margaret Pardee Memorial Hospital is a 262-bed full-service facility with 204 physicians on staff. Park Ridge Hospital has 103 beds and 150 physicians on staff.

Housing options: Carriage Park is a gated community on 399 acres offering such amenities as tennis courts, walking trails and a heated indoor pool. Homesites are priced from the $60,000s, homes from the mid-$200,000s, (800) 639-8721. **Riverwind,** an adult manufactured-home

community, offers deeded lots, clubhouse and pool. Home and land are priced from $79,900, (800) 452-3058. **Highland Lake,** a 100-acre resort with hiking trails and golf course, has single-family homes from the $140,000s to $300,000s, (877) 257-5223 or (828) 692-1359. **Lake Pointe Landing,** a retirement community, has villas, rental apartments, assisted-living services and a life-care center with skilled nursing, (800) 693-7801 or (828) 693-7800.

Visitor lodging: The area boasts 17 motels and a dozen lodges and inns, including Hampton Inn, $44-$96, (800) 531-0202; Holiday Inn Express, $88-$98, (828) 698-8899; Woodfield Inn, $79-$189, (800) 533-6016; Waverly Inn, $119-$195, (800) 537-8195; and Highland Lake Inn, $89-$393, (800) 762-1376 or (828) 693-6812.

Information: Contact the Hendersonville Chamber of Commerce, 330 N. King St., Hendersonville, NC 28792, (828)692-1413 or www.hendersonvillechamber.org. Henderson County Travel and Tourism Center, (800) 828-4244 or www.historichendersonville.org. Hendersonville Board of Realtors, (828) 693-9642.

Flat Rock Playhouse, designated the state theater of North Carolina in 1961, has been open since 1940, with a brief hiatus during World War II. The Playhouse stages 10 professional sellout productions between May and October, performed by local and summer stock actors and actresses from across the nation. Three smaller acting companies, including the all-volunteer Little Theater group, founded in 1966, entertain audiences with performances by local artists.

Carl Sandburg, America's poet laureate, historian, author and lecturer, lived in Flat Rock at his home, Connemara, for 22 years. Built in 1838, the home houses his 10,000-piece collection of books and papers and hosts thousands of visitors annually. Other popular tourism sites include St. John's in the Wilderness Episcopal Church (1836), historic Woodfield Inn, the 1879 Hendersonville Train Depot, the Singleton Centre Art Studios, the 19th-century Johnson Farm, and Bonclarken, the Associate Reformed Presbyterian Church camp that features the 1886 Heidelberg House and Gardens.

With an elevation of 2,200 to 2,800 feet above sea level, Hendersonville avoids the extreme summer temperatures of piedmont cities and towns only a few miles south and east. Cooler temperatures and an average annual 52-inch rainfall foster the growth of hemlock, spruce, rhododendron and towering Carolina white pines reminiscent of the giant redwoods of California. Winter temperatures sometimes dipping into the 20s and low 30s bring occasional light snow to the area.

Spring, summer and colorful fall beckon residents to lush green golfing fairways, white-water rivers, dark blue mountain lakes, verdant forests and inviting mountain trails that punctuate the landscape within a 10-mile radius of Hendersonville. Popular outdoor retreats include Great Smoky Mountains National Park and the Pisgah, Nantahala and Cherokee national forests west and northwest of the city; the 320-acre Foothills Equestrian Nature Center in Tryon, a few miles southeast; and the 426-acre gardens of the North Carolina Arboretum near Asheville. Breathtaking scenic vistas, natural habitats for wildlife viewing, and miles of hiking, biking and equestrian trails surround Hendersonville.

The Mills and French Broad rivers just north of town are popular venues for fishing, boating, kayaking and canoeing. Farther west, the white-waters of the Nantahala offer excitement and adventure for more daring outdoorsmen.

One statistic that illustrates the impact of retiree migration to Henderson County is the dramatic increase in Social Security payments to county residents. In 1980, Social Security benefits totaled about $47.5 million. By 1990 that figure had grown to $117 million, and in 1998 to almost $200 million, according to Hendersonville Magazine, which estimates that $16.5 million in Social Security benefits is distributed monthly to county residents.

A growing population and greater disposable income have attracted new shopping facilities, including numerous shops and department stores in the Blue Ridge Mall, the World of Clothing, and other discount and factory outlets. "Some people go to Greenville (SC) or Asheville for more upscale shopping," Bill Johnson says. "We're getting a new Super Wal-Mart. That's the big news around here."

The Fosters and Finches have used local medical facilities and rate them "very good" for a small community. Two hospitals, Margaret Pardee Memorial and Park Ridge, provide 24-hour emergency services, advanced diagnostic equipment, a certified cancer care center and excellent medical, surgical and intensive care services. Asheville, 25 miles away by interstate highway, is a regional medical center with five hospitals and more than 500 doctors. It provides big-city health care facilities, including heart and cancer centers, trauma services and emergency air transport.

The fast growth of Henderson County's population has put pressure on the home-building industry to keep up with demand, and new housing developments are popping up all over the county. Riverwind and White Oak Park are attractive manufactured-home communities favored by retirees on a budget. Heritage Hills and Heritage Lodge have single-family homes with housekeeping, maintenance, transportation, some meals and personal care options. Lake Pointe Landing and Carolina Village both offer independent-living quarters, assisted-living apartments and long-term care.

Kenmure, Carriage Park, Wildwood Heights, Champion Hills, Cummings Cove, Highland Lake and Etowah's Reach are some of the neighborhoods attracting retirees with a variety of amenities, including great mountain views, clubhouses, pools, golf courses and hiking trails. Demand for resales in The Oaks is strong, according to the Fosters, with "word of mouth" selling most properties before "for sale" signs can be erected.

Danny and Donna (Oz) Ogletree migrated to the area in 1998 after highly successful careers in environmental-process systems and real estate sales and marketing, respectively, in the piedmont area of the state. Oz's family has lived in the tiny community of Centre Friends (also known as Pole Cat Creek), birthplace of two famous Carolinians, O. Henry and Edward R. Murrow, since 1750, so the move from the familiar rolling foothills of midstate to the mountainous southern highlands was a major relocation decision. History, art and music aficionados, they were lured by the opportunity to pursue these interests, and they bought a home in Flat Rock, the historical-cultural center of the area.

Now working as a real estate sales team in the Hendersonville office of Beverly-Hanks and Associates — "Maybe she and I will retire in the year 3000," Danny says — they have helped hundreds of retirees find their dream homes in one or another of the 154 subdivisions in the area. Continuing-care retirement communities, including Carolina Village, Givens Estate, Tryon Estates and Deerfield, usually are fully occupied, Danny says.

"There are at least nine assisted-living facilities in the area," Oz adds, but she believes the area needs "more and better transitional homes for seniors between home ownership and assisted living."

The Johnsons found just what they were looking for, but Barbara suggests potential newcomers "vacation here to check out the area." Her husband, Bill, believes visitors who like small-town ambiance will find that there's no better place.

"You can go to Hilton Head and live in a strictly resort environment, but one of the great aspects of this place is that it has resort features, beautiful developments and homes all around the mountain," he says. "You can live in remote scenic areas, but you can get into town in a matter of minutes. It is very convenient, and you feel more connected to the town because you live so close in." ●

Hilton Head, South Carolina

This South Carolina barrier island blends a pristine natural environment with the amenities of a small city

By Jim Kerr

There are many surprises hidden in the woods as you motor along U.S. Highway 278 on Hilton Head Island, SC. The road is a four-lane divide, fringed on both sides by a thin forest of pines and palmettos. Birds and animals native to the semitropical lowcountry — blue herons, dwarf deer, alligators — lurk beyond the road, and wide beaches hosting seagulls and sandpipers stretch along the coast of this 12-mile-long barrier island.

But the biggest surprise on this island refuge of birds and animals is the evergrowing presence of man and all his trappings. Only on close examination, behind the veil of woods, does Hilton Head reveal the attributes of a city — shopping malls, restaurants, theaters, offices and a dozen burgeoning resort and residential complexes.

To a large degree, the primordial wetlands and ancient ecosystem that has sustained the flora and fauna on Hilton Head for thousands of years is still here, co-existing with a human urban environment of 34,000 permanent residents who interact and co-habit the island with 2.4 million annual vacationers. Yet no neon signs disturb the night. Only subtle signage reveals the whereabouts of all these people.

"The first time we saw the island, we knew it was the place for us," says Bob Houlihan, who, with his wife, Pat, retired here permanently in January 2001. "We wanted walks on the beach, golf and wildlife. But Pat grew up in Manhattan and we were both used to cities, and we didn't want a retirement community."

Atop a wooden bridge railing, which crosses a tidal lagoon behind the Houlihans' townhouse, sits a great blue heron. He comes here every day at the same time, perching above fishing grounds in this section of an 11-mile lagoon network that meanders through the community. Extending about a mile from the Atlantic beach to just past

Highway 278, the residential complex is called Palmetto Dunes. It's one of 11 so-called "plantations" on Hilton Head — gated communities with golf courses, a variety of housing choices and a large slice of nature's salt-marsh environment.

"The birds alone are beyond beautiful," Bob says. "Our blue heron comes twice a day to feed and stalk the lagoon. There are 50 turtles and a 6-foot resident alligator we call Charlie who suns himself on the bank."

Like many who retire to Hilton Head, the Houlihans traveled along a figurative line of connecting real estate dots. For the first 26 years of his career, Bob, now 66, was a New York City police officer, working his way up to inspector. From a security post at New York's Chemical Bank, he went on to the credit-card division and a job with MasterCard before retiring as a consultant for foreign banks.

The couple first came to Hilton Head in 1984 as vacationers on the recommendation of Bob's boss at Chemical Bank. They bought two time-share units in the Shipyard Plantation adjacent to Palmetto Dunes, then found their townhouse in 1995, renting it out for two years while Bob continued to work in New York. But when a debilitating stroke forced him into permanent retirement in 1997, they sold their New York house and began dividing their time between a rented townhouse there and Hilton Head.

"It became clearer and clearer with each trip that this was where we wanted to retire for good," says Bob, now almost fully recovered from the stroke. "We never seriously considered anywhere else."

The growing attachment to the island felt by the Houlihans, and the progression from vacation to retirement, was exactly what the founders of Hilton Head's now formidable resort and real estate empire had in mind. It was in

1956 that Charles E. Fraser bought out his father's interest in the Hilton Head Co. and began developing Sea Pines, the island's largest and most prestigious plantation.

That same year a two-lane swing bridge was opened, connecting Hilton Head Island, the largest barrier island on the East Coast, with the mainland. Some 48,000 cars traveled across it that first year, but by the time a new four-lane bridge replaced it in 1982, the number of annual visitors had increased to half a million, with a full-time island population of 12,500.

Except for a brief period in the 1970s, when real estate and development slumped, modern-day Hilton Head Island has never looked back. Although ancient Indians hunted prehistoric mammals here 10,000 years ago and the Spanish discovered it in 1521, it was an English sea captain named William Hilton who established the English presence here and gave the island its name in 1663.

Charleston, located 90 miles north, was established a few years later, and Savannah, GA, 45 miles south, came into being in 1733. The closest city, historic Beaufort, founded in 1711, is only 30 miles away. The Civil War and its aftermath altered Hilton Head and isolated it for almost 100 years before it found its present-day niche as a resort and burgeoning island community.

"It's perfectly located midway between New York and Miami," notes David Warren, director of marketing for Sea Pines Co. "Someone's first contact here may be in a group setting — a corporate meeting, business seminar or golf tournament. Then they vacation here with the family. After five visits they buy a condo to rent out or a time-share to use or trade. Then they retire, find the condo too small and buy a house."

The "guest for life" concept envisioned by Charles Fraser sometimes begins with the game of golf. There are 23 golf courses on Hilton Head Island, most of them public, with an overflow of another dozen or so that have spawned in the immediate vicinity of Bluffton, a small but rapidly expanding town across the Intracoastal Waterway. Most of these golf course communities are mirror images of Hilton Head's gated plantations, with links designed by noted architects like Arthur Hills, Robert Trent Jones II, Jack Nicklaus, George Fazio and others. Real estate on the Bluffton side, however, is considerably less expensive than on the island, and Bluffton's once modest population has swelled over the past 10 years.

Like Pinehurst and Myrtle Beach, golf is king on Hilton Head Island.

"It takes a lot of our time," says Bill Bury, 64, a retired American Airlines pilot who plays four or five days a week. He and his wife, Susan, 59, live in Leamington, a single-family neighborhood within Palmetto Dunes. Their golf and social associates at the club are a diverse and interesting lot — retired couples from South Africa, London, Spain and "every walk of life." Susan is a professional photographer who has converted a studio business in Bethel, CT, into a beach operation at Hilton Head.

"The beach is a mile away and I ride my bike there everyday," she says. "I'm not working as much as I used to, but through word of mouth I've developed a visiting family portrait business in a kind of beach party atmosphere."

Bill, a certified public accountant before he was a commercial pilot, worried about being disconnected from a thriving freelance tax consulting business. His 28-year career with American produced a lot of pilot and flight attendant clients, and while he lost a few in the move, he employs electronic communication technology to do the job today, spending long hours during tax time and a couple of hours a day the rest of the year poring over returns and providing retirement planning.

While Hilton Head's median age is 46, 24 percent of residents are 65 or older. Most retirees, like Bill and Susan Bury, spend a tranquil life tucked away in the forest and manicured marshland of well-maintained plantation neighborhoods where the architecture and earth tones of residences blend with the natural setting. But even though gated privacy ensures a slow pace inside, the community is an active one.

"We met a lot of people right away," Bill says. "They were more interested in volunteer work than keeping up with the Joneses. Many teach English, sell things for charity, do student mentoring. There's something for every interest."

The town of Hilton Head Island, incorporated as a municipality in 1983, offers up cultural and commercial amenities similar to any big city. There are more than 250 restaurants on the island, many providing the kind of fine dining made possible by the patronage of 2.4 million tourists a year. The arts are also alive, with exhibits, galleries, a Coastal Discovery Museum, live theater and a symphony orchestra.

"We were active theater-goers when we lived in New York," says Bob Houlihan, "and the Self Family Arts Center located just outside Palmetto Dunes does some very creditable productions. Savannah is 40 minutes away with a symphony and similarly good productions, and Charleston isn't that far, either."

Pat, 64, a homemaker, likes to read on the beach, take yoga classes, work at the church thrift store and play golf three times a week. She spent a year helping her husband, who had been an English major at Long Island University, learn to read, write and speak again after his stroke. Now he's doing something he

---

Population: Hilton Head Island has approximately 34,000 permanent residents with 2.4 million annual visitors. Nearby Bluffton Township, which includes the town and Daufuskie Island, has 21,000 residents. Beaufort County, the fastest-growing county in the state, has a total population of 121,000.

Location: A foot-shaped barrier island off the Atlantic coast of South Carolina, Hilton Head is about 45 miles north of Savannah, GA, 90 miles south of Charleston, SC, and 30 miles south of historic Beaufort, SC. The island is 12 miles long and three to five miles wide.

Climate:

	High	Low
January	58	48
July	88	75

Average relative humidity: 79%

Rain: 47 inches.

Cost of living: 104.4, based on national average of 100.

Average housing cost: A wide range of real estate prices from $80,000 for a condo to $5 million for a waterfront home gives Hilton Head Island an average close to $400,000.

Sales tax: 5%. Persons 85 and older pay a reduced sales tax of 4%. A maximum $300 tax is imposed on the purchase of vehicles and boats.

State income tax: For married couples filing jointly and single filers, the rates are graduated in six tiers from 2.5% on the first $2,400 of taxable income to 7% on taxable income above $12,000.

Income tax exemptions: Social Security benefits are exempt. Retirees who are drawing income from qualified retirement plans may deduct up to $3,000 of that income.

Intangibles tax: None.

Estate tax: None, except the state's "pickup" portion of the federal tax, applicable to taxable estates of more than $1 million.

Property tax: 4% of appraised value for residents and 6% for nonresident property owners is multiplied by various millage rates of Hilton Head's six districts. For most residents of Hilton Head, the property tax rate is .204. There is a $100,000 exemption off market value for a portion of the school operations levy after the homestead deduction has been taken, which effectively lowers the property tax rate to .1283 for the first $100,000 of the home's market value. The state imposes a personal property tax of 10.5% on the assessed value of automobiles, boats, recreational vehicles and airplanes, based on their purchase price.

Homestead exemptions: The first $50,000 of the fair market value of a home is exempt from property taxes for citizens age 65 or older.

Education: The University of South Carolina has a campus in nearby Beaufort with about 2,000 students, and a smaller branch in Hilton Head, where it shares facilities with the Technical College of the Low Country at the Hilton Head College Center.

Transportation: Hilton Head Island regional airport has daily service from Char-

always wished he could do: teach adult literacy.

Stew and Judy Brown of Chagrin Falls, OH, outside Cleveland, also began connecting the dots to a new life here beginning in the 1990s. They first came to play golf in 1992 on the recommendation of a friend and wound up buying a time-share unit from Marriott. In 1998 they found their dream home in the Long Cove Plantation.

The fabulous tidal marsh view from the living room window was the clincher. Stew, 61, a former regional vice president for Dow Chemical, occasionally shoos away the island deer nibbling in his back yard, but more often than not they're left on their own while he's working in Beaufort as a volunteer in the Senior Corps of Retired Executives (SCORE) program. Judy, 57, volunteers her time with the Junior League and the orchestra.

While golf on Long Cove's private Pete Dye-designed course was a big plus for the Browns, it was secondary to the is-

land's water and salt-marsh environment. The couple keeps a 23-foot boat nearby on Broad Creek, which they use for recreation and sojourns to Savannah and Beaufort.

Water travel to Savannah is shorter and less congested than by road, and if there is one major drawback to Hilton Head Island, many residents agree, it's the traffic. When the six-mile, $81 million Cross Island Parkway opened in January 1998, slicing across the north end of the sneaker-shaped island, it considerably reduced the load on Highway 278.

But traffic on this major thoroughfare, which connects most of the larger plantations, is always heavy, especially during spring when school break periods run into the April golf tournament. The wide public beaches offer solace, however, as does the 4,000-acre Pinckney Island National Wildlife Refuge in Port Royal Sound, with its miles of bike paths and hiking trails, thousands of birds and no human inhabitants.

Hilton Head Island includes an eclectic mix of nationalities, with residents at various income levels. Descendants of Civil War-era slaves, who developed a folk culture and language known as Gullah, live and work on the island where annual festivals highlight Gullah crafts and folklore. The island also has the largest population of Hispanics, about 4,000, of any municipality in the state.

The likelihood of visits from family and friends was a consideration for many retirees to Hilton Head Island. But the island's family-friendly atmosphere and accessibility has proven to be a magnet. The Burys' grandchildren visit every summer, delighting in golf cart rides to the beach. And last year, the Browns spent 24 weekends entertaining out-of-town guests.

"The permanent residents attract a lot of out-of-towners," Judy Brown says. "We share the beaches and roads, but the infrastructure handles it all quite well." ●

Hilton Head, SC

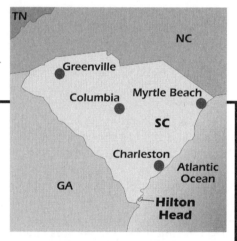

lotte, NC, and Atlanta. Savannah International, 45 minutes away, offers many additional flights. Taxis and private vehicles are the only way around the island.
Health: Hilton Head Medical Center and Clinics, a privately owned acute-care hospital, has 54 acute beds and 15 non-acute beds with more than 100 board-certified or board-eligible physicians in more than 30 specialties. The hospital is fully certified for Medicare, Medicaid, Blue Cross/Blue Shield and Tricare. The Bluffton-Okatie Outpatient Center also provides outpatient services and procedures. A primary care center and physicians offices are located at the facility. Savannah and Charleston hospitals and medical centers provide more extensive care and treatment facilities.
Housing options: Real estate values have rocketed on Hilton Head Island. Today, waterfront homes can range from $1 million to $5 million. Residential property at **Sea Pines**, (800) 846-7829, ranges from $250,000 for condos to

$300,000-$1 million for single-family homes to $3.5-$8 million for oceanfront homes. Prices are not much lower in other plantations, although there is an occasional condo under $200,000. Homes at **Tide Pointe**, an assisted-living complex of villas and homes, start at $210,000. Off the island, single-family homes in several Bluffton-area communities start at $120,000, including Del Webb's **Sun City Hilton Head**, (800) 978-9781, a 5,100-acre development nine miles west of Hilton Head Island. **The Crescent**, (800) 572-0708, a Centex Homes Community in Bluffton, has homesites from the $70,000s and fairway-view homes from the low $200,000s.

Visitor lodging: An array of accommodations ranging from luxury beachfront villas with private swimming pools to motels and bed-and-breakfast inns are available. More than 7,000 villas and time-shares are geared to families with about 3,000 hotel and motel rooms, plus two RV resorts and one off-island camp-

ground. The Marriott Hilton Head, (843) 686-8400, located at Palmetto Dunes, has been recently renovated, including all 500-plus rooms, which start at around $100 a night during the off-season. The nearby Hilton Oceanfront Resort, (800) 845-8001, with 323 rooms, starts at $120 off season. Both resorts are on the beach. Rooms at the Main Street Inn, located on the north end of the island, (843) 681-3001, range from $120 to $200 per night depending on the season.
Information: Hilton Head Island Chamber of Commerce, P.O. Box 5647, Hilton Head Island, SC 29938, (800) 523-3373, (843) 785-3673 or www.hiltonheadisland.org.

Hot Springs, Arkansas

In the Arkansas mountains, retirees find cosmopolitan living without the congestion

By Marcia Schnedler

Native American paths led from all directions to the sacred Valley of Peace, where 47 hot, healing springs bubbled from the rolling Ouachita (Wash-i-taw) Mountains. This was neutral ground, even in times of war, where strangers from faraway places met, made friends and traded ideas as well as useful and exotic items.

So from time immemorial, Hot Springs has been a place of relaxation, rejuvenation and hospitality. This storied Spa City has attracted everyone from American presidents to Al Capone and his gangster pals.

In 1832, Hot Springs became America's first national reserve. Today, its row of opulent early 20th-century bathhouses is part of Hot Springs National Park, which also encompasses forested mountain ridges and valleys surrounding the town.

But this Garland County seat, with a population of 35,750, is much more than a collection of thermal baths. The historic area and manicured parks around Bathhouse Row serve as the centerpiece of a growing district of fine arts, family attractions, shopping and dining spots. The town's calendar is packed with festivals and events, from the Arkansas Senior Olympics to Oktoberfest, documentary film and music festivals and an extravaganza of Christmas lights.

Hot Springs is surrounded by streams and five sparkling lakes — including Arkansas' largest man-made body of water — and is perched at the edge of a national forest that leads west into Oklahoma. Boaters, anglers, hunters, hikers, canoeists, bird-watchers, golfers and others who love the outdoors flock to the region.

Garland County has a lower-than-average cost of living, mild winters and a housing market varied enough in price, location and amenities to fit divergent wants, needs and budgets. It's no surprise, then, that Hot Springs attracts not only vacationers, but active retirees.

When Glenn and Dolores Quade retired from jobs in northern Illinois and

Wisconsin, they bought a new car and headed west on an 8,500-mile journey. Looping back, they stopped at Dolores' father's winter home in Hot Springs.

"We pulled in here in mid-February and it was 72 degrees," says Glenn, 71. "We were impressed by the town and its quaint charm, and by the people themselves. If you were looking at a map, people would ask if they could help you find something. If a shop didn't have what you needed, they'd call their competitors to find where you could get it."

So they promptly bought a 3,000-square-foot home on the shore of Lake Hamilton on the south end of Hot Springs. They planned to use it during the winter.

"My mom and dad had always had two homes for the seasons, and I thought I was just going to do the same thing," says Dolores, 64. "But on the way home, Glenn asked why we wanted two homes, particularly since the weather is nice in Hot Springs all year around. I do like seasonal change, and springs and falls here are especially gorgeous, while winter is a soft season."

Another transplanted couple, Fred Sims, 68, and his wife, Betty, 64, had traveled the United States and the world thanks to his job as an oil refinery technologist. Betty had worked in the retail business whenever possible. When they retired in 1991, they lived in Baton Rouge, LA.

"I was 62 the first time I visited Hot Springs," Fred recalls. "I fell in love with the terrain — the hills, the mountains, the lakes. I really enjoy fishing, boating and small-game hunting. But the really great thing is just getting out in those woods."

In addition to milder weather and outdoor recreation, they found the cost of living lower in Hot Springs in everything from groceries and gasoline to utilities. And, as an added bonus, their daughter and her family live in Hot Springs, too.

The Simses decided on a Spanish-style home in a Hot Springs neighborhood. "We like being close to grocery stores, hospitals, organizations and our grandchildren, who often stop by on their way home from high school," Fred says. "And we fell in love with the First Baptist Church near us."

The average housing price in Hot Springs is $112,000. "In the older sections of the city, homes sell for $30,000 to $40,000. And you can find a nice, well-maintained, three-bedroom, two-bath home with a two-car garage in the $80,000 range," says Carol Caldwell, who operates Century 21 Caldwell Realty. "In new areas near Lake Hamilton, you'll pay around $140,000 for a 2,300-square-foot home, a very good value. You can find homes in the $175,00 to-$1 million range in one fast-growing area, but they don't appeal much to retirees," she adds.

"You'll also find some very nice mobile home parks with manufactured homes on permanent foundations, and clubhouses," she says. "You can buy a house and lot there for around $60,000. Although the average rental price is around $450, the type of place in which a retiree would like to live, with two bedrooms, is in the $600-to-$650 range."

The Hot Springs area offers hundreds of activities, and both the Quades and the Simses leave themselves little time to relax. Betty Sims works 16 hours a week to receive medical benefits, Fred says, while he works at the Oaklawn thoroughbred racetrack — the only one in Arkansas — during its January-through-April season.

"It's a lot of fun meeting people, and it lets us travel during late spring through fall," Fred says. He also enjoys hunting and fishing trips with his son-in-law.

The Simses have volunteered at a new medical clinic for low-income families run by a group of Hot Springs churches. And Fred is active in the Masons as a member of a Shrine clown unit.

"We do a lot for children, help in fund raising for diabetes research, and go all over Arkansas in parades and meeting kids," Fred says. Betty volunteers through her church and such other groups as the Women's Welcome Club. She plays cards four times a month, and enjoys working with handicrafts, such as making toy bears for one of the local hospitals.

Glenn Quade has helped organize the state Senior Olympics held at Hot Springs each year, and both he and Dolores volunteer at the Mid-America and Hot Springs museums. Glenn, who enjoys woodworking, even made some of the Hot Springs Museum's display cases. Dolores also volunteers at a local hospital.

The couple takes advantage of the adult-education program at Garland County Community College. "Glenn is

Hot Springs, AR

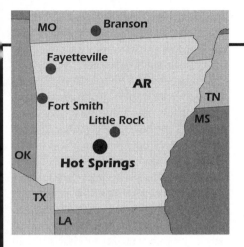

Population: 35,750 in Hot Springs, 8,397 in Hot Springs Village, 88,068 in Garland County.

Location: Hot Springs is in central Arkansas about 50 miles southwest of Little Rock. It lies in a valley of the rolling Ouachita Mountains and is surrounded by lakes and national forests. Hot Springs claims the only national park within a city thanks to the thermal waters that gave the town its name.

Climate:

	High	Low
January	43	31
July	82	67

Average relative humidity: 55%

Rain: Average annual rainfall is 54.3 inches, fairly evenly distributed but slightly higher January through May.

Snow: Averages about four inches annually and usually does not remain on the ground beyond 24 to 48 hours.

Cost of living: 92.9, based on national average of 100.

Average housing cost: $112,000 in Hot Springs. In Hot Springs Village, resale homes range from $60,000 to $800,000, and townhomes from $50,000 to $320,000.

Sales tax: 7.65% on most items, plus an additional 3% tourism tax is collected from hotels, motels and restaurants.

Sales tax exemptions: Prescription drugs and medical services.

State income tax: For married couples filing jointly and single filers, graduated from 1% of taxable income up to $3,199 to 7% on amounts over $26,700.

Income tax exemptions: Social Security benefits and up to $6,000 on most public and private pensions is exempt.

Intangibles tax: None.

Estate tax: None, except the state's "pick-up" portion of the federal tax, applicable to taxable estates above $1 million.

Inheritance tax: None.

Property tax: Property is assessed at 20% of the market value. The effective rate is determined by the school district in which the property is located. In Hot Springs school district No. 6, the rate is $41.60 per $1,000 of assessed value. In Lake Hamilton No. 5, it is $37.40. In Hot Springs Village, it is $34.60-$36.10, depending on location. The annual tax on a home in district No. 6 valued at $112,000 would be approximately $932. Personal property, such as cars, boats and RVs, is subject to tax at the same rate.

Homestead exemption: A tax refund of up to $300 is available to homeowners. In addition, homeowners age 65 or older may have the value of their home frozen.

Religion: Hot Springs has more than 90 churches representing 32 denominations. Hot Springs Village has more than 16 churches with new congregations under formation.

Education: Garland County Community College, with an enrollment of 2,300, offers continuing-education programs. Hot Springs also has two vocational-technical schools with adult education, plus continuing education at three senior and community centers. Henderson State University and Ouachita Baptist University are in Arkadelphia, 36 miles south, and the University of Arkansas is in Little Rock, 50 miles away.

Transportation: Hot Springs has an intracity transit system, one bus line, a municipal airport served by one commercial airline, and a shuttle service to Little Rock National Airport.

Health: Hot Springs and the Garland County area are served by three major hospitals with a total of 572 beds, 128 practicing physicians, 28 clinics and seven nursing homes. Among their specialties are acute care, arthritis and other rehabilitation programs, home health care, cardiology, cancer and radiation therapy centers. In Hot Springs Village are a medical and diagnostic clinic, cardiac rehabilitation unit, an urgent-care center, and a long-term care facility with independent-living apartments.

Housing options: Quite varied, from the gated **Hot Springs Village** with wooded, golf-front and lake-side lots with townhouses to custom-built homes, to in-town homes and apartments in Hot Springs, waterfront homes and condos on nearby lakes, and upscale mobile home parks. For information about Hot Springs Village, call Cooper Communities, (800) 266-7373. **Meyers Realty/Better Homes and Gardens**, (501) 624-5622 or (800) 467-0622, frequently works with relocating retirees and offers a relocation packet. The company's Web site is www.meyersrealty.com.

Visitor lodging: Arlington Resort Hotel and Spa, $78-$172, (501) 623-7771. Lake Hamilton Resort, $74-$155, (501) 767-8576. Econo Lodge, $59, (501) 525-1660. In Hot Springs Village, Village Villas Vacation Rentals, $69-$210, (800) 411-8070.

Information: Ask for a free relocation packet from the Greater Hot Springs Chamber of Commerce, P.O. Box 6090, Hot Springs, AR 71902, (800) 467-INFO or www.hotsprings.dina.org. For a statewide retirement and relocation guide, call (800) NATURAL.

a gourmet cook and has taken classes there," Dolores says. He's also just finished remodeling their kitchen to incorporate commercial-quality appliances and counter tops. Dolores is a master gardener and has taken classes in flower arranging.

As jazz fans, they belong to the local society and look forward to Hot Springs' annual jazz and blues festival. They own two boats and go fishing occasionally, and Dolores is an avid swimmer — even plunging in on her Oct. 11 birthday.

Hot Springs Village, a gated Cooper Community about 12 miles north of Hot Springs itself, offers an equally active lifestyle that suited Larry and Beverly Severson. When they retired, they were living in northern Illinois. They and their children had been downhill skiers, owning a condominium in Steamboat Springs, CO. But that didn't appeal to the Seversons as a year-round retirement location, and they gave the condo to their sons. Marco Island, FL, which they had visited with friends, didn't attract them, either.

"People were too old there," Larry says. Then they looked over Hot Springs Village on the way north from a visit to Dallas. They immediately were enchanted by the beautiful terrain — and the golf. Beverly, 71, is an avid golfer, and they built a 2,200-square-foot home on a lot overlooking a course.

"Being from Door County, WI, I missed the water," Larry says. So they sold their first home and built a 3,300-square-foot place, including a boat dock for their party barge, on the shore of Lake Balboa, the largest of the community's six spring-fed lakes.

Beverly golfs three or four times a week on one of Hot Springs Village's seven 18-hole courses, where green fees are $5. Several of the courses have restaurants and driving ranges. There also is a country club, which the Seversons joined as social members.

The Seversons are active church members, and Beverly has served as president of several local organizations.

Hot Springs Village, with a population of about 8,397, boasts 13 lighted, pro-surfaced tennis courts, a fitness center with an indoor pool, whirlpool, sauna and massage, and a family-oriented games area with outdoor pools, basketball courts, miniature golf course and fenced-in playground. Its $2.5 million performing arts center offers concerts, plays and other cultural activities, while the community center is the site of meetings of more than 100 social and civic clubs. All of these amenities are owned by the property owners association and are funded by a monthly assessment fee of $26.

While 80 percent of Hot Springs Village residents are retired, about 45 percent are under age 65. Some 480 school-age children also live there.

The price of home sites at Hot Springs Village varies. The average lot size is 90 by 160 feet, about a third of an acre. An interior lot runs $6,000 to $10,000, while one close to golf or a lake will cost $8,000 to $25,000. A golf-front lot averages $30,000, and a lake-front lot $120,000. Resale homes range from approximately $60,000 to $800,000, with townhomes running from about $50,000 to $320,000.

Hot Springs Village has medical offices, banks, restaurants, grocery stores, service stations, a florist, video store, beauty salons, clothing stores, stockbrokers, attorneys, hardware store, travel agency, bakery and even a watch repair shop.

Hot Springs itself offers an even greater variety of shopping opportunities, including such department stores as Dillard's, J.C. Penney and Sears, as well as furniture and antiques shops and clothing and accessories boutiques.

And there are the bathhouses. "Betty loves the baths and the pedicures and manicures and massages," Fred Sims says.

"Glenn gives me the whole works on my birthday," Dolores Quade says.

They and other retirees, as well as younger residents and visitors, especially love the old downtown that has made a remarkable comeback in recent years.

Its crown jewel is the Fordyce Bathhouse, the most opulent of the eight remaining spas along Bathhouse Row. Outfitted in fine wood, marble, stained glass, period furnishings and old-time exercise and therapeutic equipment, it serves as the national park's visitor center and museum. The Buckstaff is the only 1920s bathhouse still in operation, but newer ones can be found at the venerable Arlington and Majestic hotels as well as the more modern Hilton.

Up and down Central Avenue, across from Bathhouse Row, are more than 20 fine arts, crafts and antiques galleries that sponsor a monthly Friday-night Gallery Walk. Just down the street is Hot Springs' newest museum, Window to the World, opened in a restored department store and brothel that had been empty since 1958. Sue Koenig, who retired after 31 years of teaching in Denver and Saudi Arabia, had collected thousands of exquisite handmade handicrafts, costumes and other items from dozens of trips around the world. She visited friends in Hot Springs Village, liked the area, then found and remodeled the old building to display some 23,000 pounds of art.

In the same tradition as Sue Koenig's museum, Hot Springs offers a variety of ethnic as well as American restaurants. "There are restaurants galore, from German, Chinese and Japanese to Thai, Italian and Greek," Glenn says.

Fred enjoys two excellent steakhouses, Hamilton House and Coy's, and as a former Louisianan approves of the cooking at Cajun Boilers. Or they can dig into the down-home barbecue at McClard's, one of Bill Clinton's favorite hangouts when he was growing up in Hot Springs.

Most of all, these relocated retirees enjoy the friendly, active environment. "We have a lot of friends who visit us here, and the first thing they have to do is the baths," Fred says. "Some friends like art, and there is some very, very good local talent here. We enjoy walking down, getting a sandwich, hearing a concert. And Sunday afternoon, after church, it's the Arlington Hotel brunch with big-band music."

Like many newcomers to Hot Springs, the Simses quickly felt at home in their new town.

"I found a lot in common with the people here," says Fred Sims. "It doesn't take you long to fit in."●

Jackson Hole, Wyoming

A chic Old West town anchors this alpine valley in northwest Wyoming

By Mary Lu Abbott

In the summer, Joe and Gainor Bennett walk outside their home and cast for cutthroat trout in the Snake River, and in the winter they slip on skis to explore white meadows, all beneath one of nature's most spectacular canvases, the majestic Teton Range in Wyoming.

"I go cross-country skiing along the river with our dogs," says Gainor. "We always see deer. Sometimes we see moose — they're big critters. They bring you to attention."

Close encounters with moose aren't uncommon in any season in the beautiful alpine valley known as Jackson Hole. Rather ungainly looking with flattened antlers, moose munch their way along the banks of streams and rivers, enjoying willow and cottonwood trees in particular. Buffalo, elk, eagle, osprey, great blue heron, trumpeter swan, otter, beaver and bear also call this region home. So do many retirees such as the Bennetts, both 65, who moved here in 1990 from Salt Lake City, UT, where he was in the mining business.

"We like the outdoors — we ski, bicycle, fish — and we wanted a country setting. We're not golfers and didn't want a Southern golfing community," Gainor says, adding that they were familiar with Jackson Hole from vacationing and visiting relatives in the area.

Many visitors succumb to the magnetism of this mountain-ringed valley, which stretches about 60 miles from the town of Jackson on the south to the entrance of Yellowstone National Park on the north. Presiding over the broad sage-covered flats bisected by the Snake River are the high glacier-carved peaks of Grand Teton National Park, perhaps the most dramatic alpine scenery in the country.

From the valley floor of about 6,500 feet elevation, the Tetons jut abruptly upward more than a mile, with seven peaks topping 12,000 feet and the Grand Teton crowning the range at 13,770 feet. With glaciers and canyons in clear view, the peaks run most of the length of the valley, possessing an in-your-face closeness that is unusual to find without hiking to higher elevations. Against a deep blue sky and reflected in lakes beneath them, the towering Tetons at times seem like a painted backdrop.

Jack and Carole Nunn, who both attended the University of Wyoming at Laramie, had honeymooned and vacationed in the area before moving here from Boulder, CO, in 1995.

"We loved it and said if the opportunity ever presented itself to live there, let's move," says Jack, 52, who was a bank president in Boulder and is a native of Casper, WY. When their kids were grown, Jack and Carole, 50, decided they wanted something new, so they traded the Colorado Rockies for the Tetons. "We like the mountains, the open space and the fewer people here."

A pathologist from El Paso, TX, Dr. Richard Juel, 56, first saw Jackson Hole about 10 years ago when he spoke at a professional conference. "I came in September and the aspens turned (colors) over the four days I was here," he says. "I went home and told Susan (his wife), 'This is it.' I fell in love with Jackson."

Richard sold his clinical lab in 1991, and he and Susan took a road trip through Colorado to the Tetons to look at possible places to retire. There was no question where they wanted to settle when Susan saw Jackson Hole for the first time. The next year they bought a home southwest of Jackson, outside the community of Wilson, and split time between here and El Paso, where Susan, 48, still had a computer consulting business. In 1994, they decided to forsake the desert permanently for Jackson Hole, where their home sits on 14 acres with two streams and views of both the Tetons and the Gros Ventre Range to the east.

The Bennetts, the Nunns and the Juels are part of a boom that has hit Jackson Hole in the last decade, pumping the population of the county from about 11,000 in 1990 to 18,251 today. Long a popular gateway to the Grand Tetons and Yellowstone in the summer and a highly regarded ski resort, Jackson Hole has caught the fancy of many urbanites seeking a return to nature and a quieter lifestyle. Some newcomers exited the fast lanes suffering from burnout in high-pressure jobs, while others have taken early retirement, sometimes still dabbling in their businesses. A few movie stars, including Harrison Ford, hang their hats here.

Where the Marlboro Man meets Ralph Lauren and Martha Stewart, Jackson Hole succeeds in being both the real and the trendy Old West. Working cattle spreads sit beside guest ranches, and real wranglers down beers with city slickers at saloons. Everyone dresses casual, wood stoves still provide heat in some places, and old log cabins have become cozy restaurants.

Despite the area growth, Jackson remains a small town of about 8,650 residents. Elk antlers form arches around the town square, and wooden sidewalks pass chic Western storefronts such as Eddie Bauer, the Nature Company and, yes, a Ralph Lauren outlet.

"I haven't had a tie on that I recall since moving here," says Jack.

Don't mistake this jeans-and-boots, outdoorsy environment for a back-woods place, though. It's sophisticated, chic country with good restaurants and cultural opportunities to satisfy the many former urban dwellers who have moved here. The top card is the Grand Teton Music Festival, entering its 37th year of classical concerts that have gained international attention.

Each summer, a resident company of 200 musicians gathered from major symphonies around the country performs orchestra and chamber music in a concert hall at the foot of the ski resort at Teton Village, 11 miles northwest of Jackson. The July-August series enjoys enthusiastic support among Jackson Hole residents. In the winter, individual artists and ensembles are brought in for performances at the National Museum of Wildlife Art Cook Auditorium on the north edge of Jackson.

Given Jackson Hole's isolation

and small population, Jack says many people are surprised at the high quality of the festival and other cultural attractions here. A major arts center, Jackson Hole has an estimated 40 galleries and museums, a summer dance festival, a live theater, arts and crafts festivals and special events. The National Museum of Wildlife Art houses 2,000 paintings, sculptures and photographs in a low-profile stone building overlooking the National Elk Refuge. Besides its exhibits, the museum sponsors discussions on art, the environment and music. Gainor says many residents also take advantage of educational programs at the Snake River Institute and the Teton Science School.

Mountain men in the early 1800s christened the area, using the word "hole" for a high valley amid mountains and naming it for fur trapper Davey Jackson. French-Canadian trappers called the highest peaks Les Trois Tetons, or "the three breasts," now known as the Grand, the Middle and the South Teton. With the creation of Yellowstone to the north as the nation's first national park in 1872, fur trapping gave way to big-game hunters, tourists and settlers who established cattle ranching as the major business in the valley.

In 1929, the Teton Range became a national park. The late John D. Rockefeller Jr. fell in love with the area and began buying valley land fronting the mountains to keep it from being overdeveloped. In 1950, he donated 33,000 acres to expand the park, which now includes most of the valley starting on the north edge of Jackson and extending to the tip of Jackson Lake about six miles from the south entrance to Yellowstone. Between the town and the park lies the elk refuge, a long flat meadow where up to 10,000 elk migrate to spend the winter.

The preservation of the land as parks, forests and wilderness has contributed to Jackson Hole being part of the largest undeveloped natural ecosystem in the temperate zones today. And, it has left only 3 percent of Teton County privately owned and available for development, thus making land—and homes—extremely prized, particularly if there's a mountain view.

With the boom of interest in the area in

Jackson Hole, WY

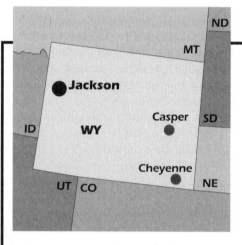

Population: About 8,650 in Jackson, the county seat, and 18,251 in Teton County.
Location: In northwest Wyoming, with the "hole," as fur trappers called a high alpine valley, running about 60 miles from the town of Jackson on the south to the entrance of Yellowstone National Park on the north and encompassing Grand Teton National Park. The valley is about 20 miles wide, rising in elevation from 6,200 feet in Jackson to 6,800 toward the north end; mountains ringing the valley top 13,000 feet.
Climate:

	High	Low
January	28	2
July	79	41

Average relative humidity: 50%
Rain: 15.27 inches.
Snow: 87 inches.
Cost of living: Above average (specific index not available).
Average housing cost: The average price of single-family homes sold in 2001 was $477,000 in the town of Jackson.

The average price of condos was $279,590 in Jackson.
Sales tax: 6%
Sales tax exemptions: Professional services, prescription drugs.
State income tax: None.
Intangibles tax: None.
Estate tax: None, except the state's "pick-up" portion of the federal tax, applicable to taxable estates of more than $1 million.
Property tax: In Jackson, $59.02 per $1,000 in assessed value. In the county, $59.72 per $1,000. Homes are assessed at 9.5% of market value. Annual property tax on a $477,000 home in Jackson is about $2,706. In some areas, separate water and sewer fees may apply.
Homestead exemption: None.
Religion: About two dozen places of worship are located in the area, including the beautiful, small Chapel of Transfiguration in Grand Teton National Park.
Education: Continuing-education classes are offered in Jackson through the University of Wyoming at Laramie and Central Wyoming Community College in Riverton.
Transportation: There's local bus service within town, to the airport and to Teton Village at the Jackson Hole Mountain Resort. The airport has daily jet service.
Health: St. John's Hospital, a full-service facility with 40 beds, 50 doctors on staff and a nursing home with 60 beds, provides most types of health care, though residents go elsewhere for more critical problems, such as heart bypasses. Salt Lake City, UT, 265 miles away, is a regional medical center.
Housing options: With national parks and forests covering 97 percent of county land, there's limited space for development of homes. While Jackson has old and new homes and condos, many newcomers prefer to buy or build outside town to get views of the Tetons, but be prepared for prices as high as the mountains. **Bar B Bar Meadows**, north of town, has lots from $575,000. To the west of town, **Teton Pines** and **Spring Creek Resort** are popular, but you'll pay $600,000 or more for a condo and from $800,000 for lots. South of town, **Rafter J** has homes in the $350,000 range, though not all have Teton views. **Jackson Hole Realty**, (888) 733-9009, can provide information on subdivisions and developments throughout the area.
Visitor lodging: Jackson Lake Lodge, in Grand Teton National Park, open from mid-May through early October, from $124, (800) 628-9988. Snake River Lodge at Jackson Hole, open all year, from $300 to $1,400, (800) 445-4655. Lodging in town, at Teton Village and in the park includes numerous small motels, guest ranches and cabins.
Information: Jackson Hole Chamber of Commerce, P.O. Box 550, Jackson, WY 83001, (307) 733-3316 or www.jacksonholechamber.com.

the last decade, housing costs have sky-rocketed. According to the Jackson Hole Report, which provides statistical analyses of local real estate sales, the average price of single-family homes sold in 2001 was $1,000,988 in the Jackson Hole valley and $477,000 in the town of Jackson. The average sales price of condominiums was $498,000 in the valley and $279,590 in Jackson. The least expensive condo listing during that period was a one-bedroom, 620-square-foot unit in Jackson for $148,000. The least expensive single-family home was a two-bedroom, 975-square-foot house for $270,000, also in the town of Jackson. For more information, see www.jacksonholereport.com.

"I've seen a doubling of property value in our area in the last five years," says Richard.

While property values are up, Jack thinks housing costs aren't as unrealistically high now as they were a few years ago. The Nunns recently bought a new home that they had considered when they first arrived in 1995. They had been put off by its high price tag and instead chose an older home and remodeled it. When the new home didn't sell, the Nunns looked at it again, got a better deal and moved into it in 1997.

"Houses are still expensive here," Jack cautions. "There are very few single-family homes under $200,000."

"Be prepared to pay more than you think to get what you want (in a house)," says Gainor, who adds that many who are thinking of building a log home are shocked to learn such construction may run $200 a square foot.

While housing is costly to buy, homeowners get a break with comparatively low property taxes, in part because homes are assessed at 9.5 percent of market value. Overall, Jackson Hole is tax-friendly; there's no state income tax, though there is a sales tax of 6 percent.

Gainor says food prices also help boost the cost of living above average. "We can get anything — even fresh fish every day — but prices are dear because of transportation. We seem to be at the end of the food chain," she says. It's 265 miles to Salt Lake City, the nearest metropolitan area.

Though Jackson has numerous stores, the scope of shopping is somewhat limited. Most of the apparel stores stock casual, outdoors-oriented wear. "We have the high end and the low end — for instance, Scandia Downs and Kmart," says Gainor. "We

support the local shops, but I keep my catalogs for some middle-of-the-road and traditional things like suits."

The couples say crime in the area is minimal. Jack adds, "We were used to locking our car all the time. The joke up here is that if (residents) took the keys out of the ignition, they wouldn't be able to find them."

"By and large, it's a trusting, open community. If you're going to be gone only a short while, many people normally don't lock their houses. The UPS and FedEx men just open the door and throw things in," says Gainor.

St. John's Hospital in Jackson serves the valley, providing all types of care except such procedures as heart surgery. "We have the best equipment and best care for a community this size that I've ever seen," says Richard, the pathologist.

Newcomers seem to have little trouble making friends. "We've met wonderful people. It's been easy to establish the type of friendships you had where you had been 25 years. The people here are active and talented," says Jack.

The music festival and social events connected with it foster friendships. All three couples are active supporters of the festival. Gainor is chairwoman of the festival auxiliary, and Carole is among its members. Gainor's husband, Joe, is a vice president of the board, and Susan serves as a trustee. Joe and Jack also are involved in other community organizations.

While Jackson Hole has many amenities, it is small. "Sometimes you get 'valley fever' — you want to get out. Sometimes you need a city fix," Gainor says.

All of the couples do sound a warning about the weather: The winters are long, cold and hard. The average high temperatures for December (26 degrees) and January (28 degrees) are below freezing, and for November, February and March are only in the high 30s. Nighttime temperatures below zero are common in midwinter.

"We have snow six months of the year. November starts getting seriously cold, and by early December we have a foot of snow," says Gainor. "If you don't really enjoy a good long winter, it's not the place to move to."

Jack says, "You have to enjoy outdoor sports in the winter to live here on a full-time basis. If you get out and enjoy the winter, it's livable." While Jackson Hole has low humidity and sunny days that

ameliorate the cold, Jack thinks the area has more overcast days than winters in Colorado.

Winter brings cross-country skiing, and downhill skiing at Jackson Hole Mountain Resort, Snow King Ski Area in Jackson and Grand Targhee Ski Resort on the back side of the Tetons, plus snowshoeing, dog-sledding, snowmobiling, ice skating and other activities.

Many residents escape during the transition months as fall turns to winter and as winter gives way to spring. "In November, you can't hike, bike or ski and the fishing season is over. Late April and May are the mud season (when snow is melting). These are great times at other places in the country, though, so many people go away then," Gainor says.

Gainor cautions gardeners about the area's short growing period, with only about 45 days that are considered frost-free. She says some things such as tomatoes and squash can't be grown because the nights are too cold. For nine months, the low temperature averages 32 degrees or colder; June and August have an average low temperature of 37 degrees and July climbs to 41 degrees, all still quite nippy.

While winter may take some adjustment, late spring, summer and fall are glorious. Snow usually has melted in the valley by May, though the mountains still are cloaked in white, glistening against deep blue skies. Over the summer, snow melts off the lower part of the Tetons but remains at high elevations. Starting in June, wildflowers begin to carpet the valley, each having its own season to paint the flats, meadows and canyons blue, lavender, yellow, red, orange, white and pink.

Newborn elk, buffalo, moose and deer play in the protective sight of their mothers. While most of the elk and buffalo migrate northward, many moose stay in the valley, often wandering onto the highway to create traffic jams of tourists who can't quite believe they're seeing the real thing. Bear sometimes are spotted in the mountains and valley.

Come September, snow falls on the peaks, frost coats the area and aspens turn Jackson Hole a brilliant gold. The valley is filled with the sound of male elks bugling as they gather their harems and move southward to the refuge. Residents put up their fly-fishing rods and kayaks and bring out the skis and snowshoes. It's all in the nature of living here.●

Jupiter, Florida

Retirees give high marks to this Florida Gold Coast town

By Molly Arost Staub

In some respects, Jupiter is typical of Florida's lure for retirees — it enjoys warm weather and sunshine, it boasts lower costs of living than many other areas of the country, and it has the opportunities and facilities for year-round golfing, tennis and boating. But Jupiter has its own special charm that makes it one of the last outposts of rural ambiance and unhurried lifestyles before you hit the hustle and bustle of South Florida's larger cities.

Ideally situated for aficionados of water sports, Jupiter basks on the Intracoastal Waterway south of the federally designated "wild and scenic" Loxahatchee River. Parks provide ramps for waterway access, and boats and skis can be rented at a variety of marinas. And for some retirees, Jupiter's superior health-care facilities provide icing for the cake.

Typical are Bob and Annamarie Broeder, who were lured by the winter climate and good weather for golf. Before moving here in 1993, they began visiting Annamarie's brother in Jupiter in 1985, then rented a condo before buying their current unit in Indian Creek, a development boasting an 18-hole golf course and clubhouse.

Previously they had lived in Grass Valley, CA, for 17 years. "We visited Phoenix but found it too hot," says Bob, 72, machine shop supervisor at Stanford University before he retired. Besides playing golf, he walks two miles daily and has become active in the Elks Club. He also helps provide transportation for seniors who need rides to their medical appointments.

Annamarie, 67, likes the social scene in Jupiter. "It's really easy making friends here in a condominium development," she says. "We meet people at the pool and in golf club events."

Avid travelers, they like to cruise from Miami — easily accessible to South Floridians — aboard Carnival, Royal Caribbean and Holland America vessels. They also travel on Jupiter Parks and Recreation Department-sponsored trips to Walt Disney World, Cypress Gardens, Universal Studios and Branson, MO. "There are nice activities and trips for seniors," Annamarie says.

She and Bob love the winter climate, and they return to California in the summer when South Florida gets hot and muggy. Bob suggests that anyone considering retiring to Florida's Atlantic coast "rent for three months during the summer to see if you can handle the heat." As for expenses, he says, "utilities and taxes are less here, and real estate is much less expensive."

Both are impressed with the area's medical facilities, which Bob says are "better equipped to handle seniors" than most hospitals. "We live a 10-minute trip to the hospital. What I miss least about where we formerly lived was the one-hour drive to the hospital," he says.

Besides the lack of snow skiing, which was nearby when they lived in California, about the only thing the Broeders miss is not having a garage and garden in their condo lifestyle. "We like to putter in the lawn and can't do that here," says Annamarie.

Another activity Bob loves is fishing, and opportunities are plentiful along the Gold Coast and its Atlantic beaches. Although fishing licenses are required for fresh- and saltwater fishing, he appreciates that they are free to residents over 65. Year-round boating lures many here, and numerous marinas cater to their needs.

Fishermen, nature lovers and beach aficionados enjoy the nearby John D. MacArthur Beach State Park, a sea turtle nesting area from May through August, where ocean swimming and

diving are available, and Jonathan Dickinson State Park featuring campgrounds, canoe rentals and boat ramps.

The fishing and good weather are products of the Gulf Stream, which runs close to shore in this area. A long maritime association is illustrated by the signature red-brick Jupiter Lighthouse, built in 1860, which boasts a museum of lighthouse memorabilia and local artifacts.

Another couple pleased with the myriad activities here is Tom and Mary Kirby. "You almost never find us home because we're always so busy," says Tom, 75.

When he and Mary, 73, aren't doing volunteer work at the parks and recreation department in Jupiter — such as working in the art gallery or helping organize five-kilometer runs and an annual beach cleanup — they're liable to be at the new Roger Dean Stadium watching spring training games of the Montreal Expos and St. Louis Cardinals or farm teams in the summer. They've made many friends through their volunteer work, "and my wife is an excellent cook," Tom says of Mary, who also enjoys painting.

Those interested in the arts find many opportunities in nearby West Palm Beach at the Norton Gallery of Art and Palm Beach's galleries — not to mention the legendary shopping along tony Worth Avenue. Broadway shows and concerts are held regularly at the Kravis Center for the Performing Arts, and more theater is available at Palm Beach's Royal Poinciana Playhouse.

The couple's choice of Jupiter also was influenced by family concerns. After living 25 years in Farmingdale, NY, they moved to Jupiter in 1985, primarily because their daughter lived here. Tom had worked as a bookbinder at McGraw-Hill for 19 years, then in construction and at the Cedar Creek Water Treatment Plant on Long Island. Mary was an assistant manager at Chemical Bank.

"I would never move back," Mary says. "And we have two grandchildren here."

Nearby attractions to lure the grandchildren (whether they're residents or visitors) beyond the ocean and pool include the expanding Dreher Park Zoo and Lion Country Safari. The Burt Reynolds Ranch and Film Studios includes a museum exhibiting movie memorabilia from the native son's films, plus a small petting farm for little ones.

Two county parks, Burt Reynolds East and Burt Reynolds West (reflecting the actor's many contributions to the area and the pride Jupiter has in him), offer boat ramps, picnic areas and the Florida History Center and Museum, spotlighting prehistoric, Seminole Indian and Spanish colonial influences.

The Kirbys previously considered Ocala, FL, and bought property there, but the section where it was located was never developed. They visited the Jupiter area many times over an eight-year period but unfortunately found themselves victims of crime soon after they moved. "Someone broke into our car before the plates were off the car," Tom says.

Jupiter, FL

Population: 39,328
Location: On the east coast of Palm Beach County north of West Palm Beach.
Climate:

	High	Low
January	74	54
July	90	73

Average relative humidity: 76%
Rain: 58.5 inches.
Cost of living: About average (specific index not available).
Average housing cost: $157,000
Sales tax: State tax is 6%, and there's a 4% Palm Beach County tourist development tax required of any person who rents or leases accommodations for a period of six months or less.
Sales tax exemptions: Food, some services and medicine.
State income tax: None.
Intangibles tax: Assessed on stocks, bonds and other assets. Tax rate is $1 per $1,000 in assets. The first $20,000 in assets is exempt for individuals. For couples filing jointly, the first $40,000 is exempt. Those who owe less than $60 need not pay.
Estate tax: None, except the state's "pick-up" portion of the federal tax,

applicable to taxable estates of more than $1 million.
Inheritance tax: None.
Property tax: $21.67 per $1,000 of assessed value, with property assessed at 100 percent of market value. The annual tax for a home assessed at $157,000 would be about $2,860, with the homestead exemption noted below.
Homestead exemption: $25,000 off the assessed value of a permanent, primary residence.
Religion: There are 29 churches and one synagogue in Jupiter.
Education: Florida Atlantic University offers courses at its convenient Northern Palm Beach Campus in Palm Beach Gardens. Palm Beach Community College's Edward M. Eissey campus in Palm Beach Gardens offers academic courses and continuing education for retirees at its Etta Ress Institute of New Dimensions.
Transportation: Palm Beach International Airport is a major airport 20 minutes from Jupiter. North County Airport in West Palm Beach opened in 1994. Amtrak serves major U.S. destinations from West Palm Beach, and Tri-Rail is a commuter rail service running between West Palm Beach and Miami, with special trains added for major events. Palm Tran is a countywide bus system.
Health: The 156-bed Jupiter Medical Center is totally comprised of private rooms. Its highly regarded departments include the Comprehensive Cancer Care Center, Women's Diagnostics, Diabetes Educa-

tion, Health and Rehabilitation, Sleep Disorders Center and Pain Management Clinic.
Housing options: The following are mixed-dwelling communities, including condominiums, villas (semidetached homes) and single-family homes. **Indian Creek** is a community with resales ranging from $150,000 to $195,000 for single-family homes, $95,000-$150,000 for condominiums. For information, contact Diane Turton Realtors, (561) 746-4466. **Jonathan's Landing** offers 24 subdivisions with homes ranging from $500,000 to $2 million. All are resales. Monthly maintenance fees average $350. **Admiral's Cove**, (561) 744-8800, is an upscale community with most homes located on the Intracoastal Waterway. They range from $300,000 to $6 million with an average monthly maintenance fee of $500.
Visitor lodging: The only oceanfront property, the Jupiter Beach Resort, has been heading toward full time-share ownership but still functions as a luxury hotel with rates of $140-$500, (800) 228-8810. Numerous motels and campgrounds include the Best Western Intracoastal Inn, $65-$99 and higher in peak season, (561) 575-2936, and Wellesley Inn at Jupiter, $79-$149, including continental breakfast, (561) 575-7201.
Information: Jupiter-Tequesta-Juno Beach Chamber of Commerce, 800 N. U.S. Highway 1, Jupiter, FL 33477, (800) 616-7402 or www.jupiter fl.org.

"Then we built the house of our dreams in Jupiter Farms, but I got sick and panicked, so we bought a condominium in the Indian Creek development nine years ago," says Tom. "It has an 18-hole golf course, a clubhouse and tennis courts. We feel safe here."

Health care is another powerful draw for the Kirbys. "I rave about the medical facilities, which are great, especially for the elderly," says Tom. "I've been in the emergency room about 15 times at the hospital at the Jupiter Medical Center. And the Comprehensive Cancer Care Center is wonderful."

He admits he misses the change of seasons "and visiting places with nice trees and hills. But at my age, I wouldn't like the cold." The summer season also can be a drawback, "muggy and buggy," he says. The thing he misses least, though, is New York traffic. "People don't know what a traffic jam is until they've been in one in New York City," he says.

And he also doesn't miss the higher cost of living in New York. "There's no comparison between the cost of living here and up north, and housing costs 40 percent less here," says Tom, noting that heating expenses and real estate taxes also are lower.

Their condo has appreciated in value since they bought it, he says.

But another couple, Sophie and Charlie Dineen, found the cost of living in Jupiter higher than they experienced in their preretirement communities in Alabama and New York. Charlie, 70, a former regional president for Manufacturers Hanover Trust, lived in Olean, NY, about 80 miles south of Buffalo, and Sophie, 60, moved to Jupiter from Tuscaloosa, AL.

Charlie considers South Florida an expensive place to live, although he notes that lower real estate taxes and the lack of a state income tax reduce costs. But he says it costs more to dine at restaurants than in upstate New York, and "dry-cleaning costs are unbelievable here."

Still, they're happy they chose Jupiter. "I had a seasonal place at PGA (in Palm Beach Gardens) and had always planned to move to Florida," says Charlie, who retired and moved to Jupiter in 1987. "I didn't consider any other place. I didn't want any part of the winter weather any longer. I love to play golf, and there's only a 10- to 12-week window when you can golf in western New York. Now I play golf five days a week."

After his wife died, he met and married Sophie 10 years ago. But she owned a horse and wanted to live in an area where her equine companion could be boarded nearby. "Jupiter had places to board a horse — there's a big community of horses in Jupiter Farms," she says, explaining their decision to buy in the Ranch Colony development of The Links. "Jupiter was a small town 10 years ago," Sophie says, "and it's still kind of rural."

What Charlie misses most are his four children and seven grandchildren, who all live in New York. He also misses having a basement, and he has had difficulty finding reliable workmen for chores around the house. "I think we were taken the first few years," he says.

"Another mistake I made, based on the seasonal community I lived in, was that I envisioned that everything had to be in pastel colors," he adds. "I gave away some beautiful wood furniture and antiques to my kids. Now I'm sorry I didn't keep it."

But he rates Jupiter's hospitals and medical care very highly. "I'm very pleased with the excellent care by the doctors and nurses and the Jupiter Medical Center, where I've been three times," he says. It's a refrain echoed by many seniors in these parts.●

Kerrville, Texas

Friendly folks welcome newcomers to the heart of the Texas Hill Country

By Tracy Hobson Lehmann

From any direction, the drive into Kerrville is downhill. This peaceful community nestles comfortably in the Guadalupe River valley. Travelers arriving from the northwest cross vast ranchlands on the Edwards Plateau, where sheep, goats and cattle outnumber people, before the road begins to twist and turn, climb and descend into the town that is the major population center of the Texas Hill Country.

From the west, the road follows the crooks and bends of the Guadalupe (the locals say GWAH-da-LOOP). Along this route, limestone cliffs loom like magnificent monuments above green water, and trees form a canopy of green over the roadways. Herds of exotic game animals populate pastures west of Kerrville, introducing a safari element to the drive.

From the southeast, verdant limestone hills rise up along Interstate 10. Live oaks and wildflowers color the scene in spring and summer. In fall, gold and red leaves of red oaks and other trees daub autumn hues on hillsides that fade from green to blue to purple in the distance as they stack against the horizon.

It's the welcoming embrace of the Texas Hill Country landscape that lures tourists and retirees to Kerrville, and it's the warmth of the community that makes them stay in the town of 20,425 located an hour northwest of San Antonio and two hours west of Austin.

On their first visit to Kerrville, Butch and Carol White were expecting the same pancake-flat metropolitan scenery they had found when visiting their son in Dallas. The hills that rose in the distance caught them by surprise. "We came up Interstate 10 from San Antonio," Carol recalls. "The view was spectacular."

If it wasn't love at first sight in Kerrville, the get-acquainted date sold the Whites. Turns out more than the view was spectacular.

Climate was a top priority for Butch, 65, and Carol, 63, when they chose a retirement community in 1994. As he wrapped up a 32-year career as a junior high school teacher and she retired from teaching kindergarten and first grade, they considered retiring in Tennessee or North Carolina. On visits there, they found both the weather and the people cool.

Next on their list was Arizona. Because Butch has Parkinson's disease, they wanted to live where the weather was mild year-round so he could remain active to stave off the effects of the degenerative illness. Before they moved from Alton, IL, outside St. Louis, MO, their son in Dallas convinced them to visit the Texas Hill Country.

During their January visit, the Whites marveled at 73-degree temperatures. "I said, 'No question, this is it,'" Butch recalls. The decision was cemented when they flew home to Illinois and had to chip ice off their car doors.

The climate and healthy environment long have been a draw to the Kerrville area. The picturesque community became renowned for its healthy climate during the nation's tuberculosis epidemic in the 1920s. Patients from all over the country converged on the town — formerly known for producing cattle, sheep and cypress shingles — to breathe the clean air. In 1921, the U.S. Department of Health deemed Kerr County the healthiest place in the nation. The hamlet, perched 1,645 feet above sea level, boasts pleasant temperatures, low humidity and moderate rainfall year-round. The city remains clean with nonpolluting industry such as health care, jewelry manufacturing, aircraft production, tourism, ranching and summer youth camps.

In November 1994, the Whites moved into Windmill Ridge, an adult community of manufactured homes west of Kerrville. When they settled into their triple-wide mobile home, they were among the first residents in the restricted neighborhood. As the Whites became acquainted with Kerrville and as more neighbors moved in, they discovered the people were as warm as the climate. "Down here, everybody talks to you like they've known you all your life," Butch says.

Neighbors helped each other lay sod in the new development, and friendships began to grow with the budding landscapes. "It's the warmest group of people I've ever been associated with," Carol says. "We're from all walks of life and from all different parts of the country, but we've become friends."

Last year at Thanksgiving, the Whites opened their home to any Windmill Ridge resident without holiday plans. Carol set a formal lunch table with china and silver, and 25 people gathered for a potluck feast. They spent the afternoon watching football on television and talking on the back deck that overlooks a greenbelt. That night, the crowd reconvened for leftovers. "It's like an extended family," Carol says of her neighborhood. "Nobody bugs you, but they are there when you need them."

Neighbors offer transportation for shopping, medical appointments or trips to San Antonio. They also volunteer to watch houses, water plants and gather mail for people who are away. Groups of Windmill Ridge residents sometimes load up RVs for out-of-state treks with their neighbors or for daylong shopping excursions to San Antonio or a major outlet mall in nearby San Marcos.

With good friends and good weather, the Whites stay active. On the days he doesn't play golf, Butch hits golf balls at the driving range in Windmill Ridge. The member-owned Riverhill Country Club offers an 18-hole course with bentgrass greens and a 16-acre lake, and the Comanche Trace master-planned community features a Tom Kite-designed championship course and a 15-acre practice facility. The refurbished municipal golf course in town and the links in nearby Fredericksburg and Comfort offer additional options for golfers.

Golf isn't Butch's only game. The former physical education teacher earned a silver medal in the basketball free-throw competition at the Senior Games, an annual rite of spring that draws about 1,000 participants to Kerrville. The event is a qualifying site for the Texas Senior Games State Championships.

Kerrville, TX

Population: 20,425 residents in the city and 43,653 in Kerr County. About one-third of the residents are retirees.

Location: Set on the Guadalupe River in the Texas Hill Country, Kerrville is about 60 miles northwest of San Antonio and 105 miles west of Austin, the state capital.

Climate:

	High	Low
January	60	32
July	94	68

The area averages 275 days of sunshine each year, and the altitude is 1,645 feet.

Average relative humidity: 55%

Rainfall: 31.5 inches.

Cost of living: Below average (specific index not available).

Average housing cost: $130,504 for the first half of 2002, according to the Kerrville Board of Realtors.

Sales tax: 8.25%

Sales tax exemptions: Food and produce, pharmaceuticals and some agricultural services.

State income tax: None.

Intangibles tax: None.

Estate tax: None, except the state's "pick-up" portion of the federal tax, applicable to taxable estates above $1 million.

Inheritance tax: None.

Property tax: Paid to the city, county, school districts and other special taxing entities. Taxes are assessed at 100% of valuation. Rates in the city of Kerrville are $2.62 per $100 valuation. The tax on a $130,000 home in the city is about $3,406, without exemptions.

Homestead exemption: Each taxing entity offers different homestead exemptions. Kerr County reduces the appraised value of a qualifying homestead by $3,000, and school districts offer a $15,000 homestead exemption in accordance with state-mandated minimums. Residents over 65 who qualify for homestead exemption receive an additional $10,000 reduction from the school district and another $3,000 from the city of Kerrville. Additionally, the Kerr County Appraisal District freezes property taxes for residents over 65.

Religion: Some 90 churches represent 20 denominations. The nearest Jewish synagogues are in San Antonio.

Education: Schreiner College, a four-year private liberal arts college with an enrollment of about 800, offers classes for area residents. San Antonio College has online classes (www.accd.edu/sac/distance/distance.htm), and Kerrville Independent School District provides adult education classes. Art and drama classes are available through the Hill Country Arts Foundation. The Dietert Senior Center, (830) 792-6020, has volunteer-led classes on topics ranging from computers to dance.

Transportation: There is no local transportation system. The Dietert Senior Center, (830) 792-4044, offers wheelchair-accessible van service in town weekdays and shuttle service to San Antonio weekly. Charter flight service is available from San Antonio to Louis Schreiner Field, the city-county airport. Commercial airline service is available in San Antonio, a one-hour drive from Kerrville. Limousine service is available to and from San Antonio International Airport.

Health: Kerrville's three major hospitals are a 148-bed regional referral center, a 221-bed Veterans Administration hospital, and a 210-bed state psychiatric hospital. A local radiation therapy center offers care for cancer patients, and residents have access to a 15-station dialysis center. Emergency helicopter and ambulance services are available from San Antonio.

Housing options: Single-family houses, condominiums, townhouses, duplexes and apartments all are options. **Vicksburg Village**, (830) 896-5316 (Take-It-Easy Realty), an over-55 community that currently has 115 homes and room for about 150, offers prices of $120,000-$185,000. The community has a clubhouse with heated pool and landscape maintenance for front yards. **Windmill Ridge**, (830) 895-3003, is a manufactured-home community west of Kerrville. The land-lease community, which is restricted to adults, features a clubhouse, golf driving range, walking trails, RV storage and homes priced at $50,000-$100,000. South of town, **Riverhill Country Club**, (830) 257-1400, offers garden homes, townhouses and single-family homes priced at $180,000-$3 million. Country club members have access to tennis, golf, swimming and dining, but residency does not require club membership. **The Meridian**, (830) 257-7561, is a gated 55-plus community with houses starting at $160,000. The 43-acre development has 147 homesites, a walking trail, heated pool and spa. **Comanche Trace**, (877) 467-6282, is a new, upscale golf course community with homes from $187,500 and homesites from $70,000. Retirement communities, assisted living and nursing homes also are available.

Visitor lodging: A popular tourist spot, Kerrville has a variety of lodging options, from more than 1,000 hotel and motel rooms to bed-and-breakfast inns to cabins and RV parks. Hotels include Inn of the Hills River Resort, $78-$130, (800) 292-5690; Y.O. Ranch Resort Hotel, $109, (877) 967-3767; and Best Western Sunday House Inn, $69, (800) 677-9477. Riverhill Country Club, (830) 896-1400, offers nightly rental cottages and casitas.

Information: Kerrville Area Chamber of Commerce, 1700 Sidney Baker, Suite 100, Kerrville, TX 78028, (830) 896-1155 or www.kerrvilletx.com. Kerrville Convention and Visitors Bureau, 2108 Sidney Baker, Kerrville, TX 78028, (800) 221-7958 or www.ktc.net/kerrcvb/.

Carol gets exercise on the walking trails that meander over the rocky hills in the community's country setting. The mild climate also allows the couple to watch wildlife from their deck. Deer cross the greenbelt regularly, as do wild turkeys and rabbits. A roadrunner makes a daily pilgrimage across their front yard, and wilder species such as a fox, coyote and cougar also have been spotted.

They also like to take in the scenery in surrounding areas. "When you go out in any direction, you see something different," including cliffs, waterfalls and pastoral settings, says Carol. Butch is captivated by the clean streams, the waterways that drew settlers to the area in the 1840s. "We're used to the muddy Mississippi," he says. "Every stream here, you can see to the bottom."

Outdoor activity and community involvement also keep retirement hopping for Harvey and Marsha Fritter, who spend time most days on the golf course at Riverhill Country Club. "Our friends said we would go crazy when we retired because we would have nothing to do," says Harvey, 82. "Truth is, we find more to do."

Marsha, 77, is president of the board at the member-owned country club. They golf and play bridge and enjoy the company of friends in dinner clubs. Harvey is active in a Bible study group, served as president of the library auxiliary and has taken art classes through the Hill Country Arts Foundation.

"One of the reasons our retirement has been great is because it has been very active with an active circle of friends," Harvey says.

The Fritters moved to Kerrville from Maryland in 1987 and immediately felt comfortable. "It took about two hours to feel at home," Harvey says, noting that many people move from out of state without knowing anyone in the community. "The people are interesting and are also interested in meeting people and getting acquainted," Marsha adds.

Like the Whites, the Fritters explored the Texas Hill Country on the advice of a family member. Marsha, a West Texas native who grew up in the flatlands, had never visited the south-central part of the state. Her brother suggested the area, and they planned to spend a month exploring Kerrville and surrounding towns.

They rented a house at Riverhill Country Club, and their Kerrville stay stretched to three months. "It's just a beautiful little town. It had everything," Marsha says. After their three-month familiarization visit, the Fritters decided to call Kerrville home. That was in 1987, and they haven't had a twinge of homesickness for Maryland.

Though Marsha had lived in the Baltimore-Washington, DC, area for more than 40 years, where she first worked for the FBI during World War II and retired as a branch manager for a bank, she was ready to come home. "I was glad to get back to Texas," she says.

"When you marry a Texas girl, part of the vows are, 'I promise to take you home again,'" adds Harvey, who retired from a petroleum servicing business started by his father. Harvey and Marsha built a house at the country club on the south end of town, where they enjoy the proximity to golf, tennis, swimming and a restaurant at the clubhouse. "We knew when we got older we wouldn't want to drive so much," Harvey says. "Here we can take the golf cart and be at the clubhouse in five minutes. We can eat there, or they will bring meals to us."

When their children and grandchildren visit from Maryland, they revel in outdoor activities in Kerrville and the surrounding area. Whether hiking at nearby Lost Maples State Natural Area, hiking at the Kerrville-Schreiner State Park, swimming in the Guadalupe River or climbing the granite dome of Enchanted Rock in Fredericksburg, outdoor enthusiasts have plenty of options for soaking up the fresh air.

The Fritters appreciate the arts offerings of the small town. Though they held season tickets to the Majestic Theater in San Antonio for many years, they find the local roster satisfying. The Smith-Ritch Point Theatre in Ingram offers outdoor performances on the banks of the Guadalupe River in spring and summer and indoor performances in winter. The Kerrville Performing Arts Society sponsors symphony performances in winter. The Fritters look forward to the annual Harvest Moon dance, which turns the pedestrian-oriented Main Street into an outdoor ballroom for one autumn evening.

It is that type of small-town living that appeals to Ruth and Randall Nyman,

who settled into the adult community of Vicksburg Village three years ago. "I love the way everybody waves at everyone here," says Ruth, 81. "We moved here and didn't know a soul. Everybody we would meet would say 'howdy,' 'good morning' or 'how are you.' They didn't know us from Adam, but they were friendly."

Kerrville is the second retirement home for the Nymans, who relocated to Kerrville from Sarasota, FL. "We moved from Fort Worth to Florida like you're supposed to," says Randall, 82. "We had a boat and a swimming pool." Then a doctor admonished the retired pediatrician and his wife to get out of the sun.

They had visited Kerrville with Ruth's sewing club and liked the proximity to their daughters in Dallas, Denver and Los Angeles. With one call to the chamber of commerce, Randall was flooded with informational brochures. In investigating the community, they liked the location on Interstate 10 and found the medical facilities outstanding.

"At this stage in life, you need lots of doctors," Randall says. "Sid Peterson (Memorial Hospital) is one of the top hospitals in the state." The Fritters and the Whites echo his praise of the city's medical care, and all three couples report low utility bills and a strong sense of security.

After renting an apartment, the Nymans found a lot in Vicksburg Village, a community geared to over-55 residents. Its clubhouse includes an indoor pool and a meeting place for the residents' weekly coffee klatch. A monthly fee to the homeowner association covers maintenance of front yards, freeing residents who don't want the hassles of yard work or who want to leave town for extended periods.

While the Nymans enjoy the friendly community, they are less enthusiastic about increasing congestion in the area, which reports annual growth of about 3 percent. They also would like to see a grocery store on the north side of town, near where they live. But the inconvenience of going to the nearest store is minor, Ruth admits, since it's only seven minutes from their house. It's a small complaint about the town they call home.

"We had a choice," Randall says. "We could have gone anywhere we wanted, and we chose Kerrville."●

Lake Havasu City, Arizona

Water, mountains and desert meld in popular Arizona oasis

By Judy Wade

In 1963 when chain-saw magnate Robert P. McCulloch began constructing Lake Havasu City, the place looked dismal.

The lake, formed when Parker Dam 21 miles to the south impounded the Colorado River, was surrounded by dirt terraces, bare of trees and vegetation. A single Spartan motel didn't do much to entice visitors.

McCulloch was a visionary, however. He promised a job with his company to anyone willing to relocate. Early guests were flown in to a rough, graded airstrip and then taken to see lakeview lots selling for $5,000.

Still, the place languished. Phoenix newspaper articles joked about the "big mudhole," smugly pointing out that summer temperatures there topped even Phoenix's legendary heat. For almost two decades Lake Havasu City's progress was unremarkable.

Then in the mid-'80s, the town began to boom, thanks in part to an anomaly in the Arizona desert, the London Bridge. Brought to Havasu by McCulloch and reconstructed in 1971, the bridge became a major tourist attraction, helping visitors discover the developing recreation area.

Today Lake Havasu City is a sparkling oasis with about 47,000 residents. The once-harsh landscape is green with golf courses and gardens. Imaginative resorts cluster at lakeside, and good restaurants offer eclectic dining. Beyond city borders, the Sonoran Desert melts into the foothills of the Mohave Mountains on one side and the Chemehuevi on the other.

The population is growing at a rate of 5 percent per year. Almost one-third of residents are seniors. Winter visitors continue to swell the numbers between Christmas and Easter, but the city is becoming much more of a year-round community. Fewer and fewer snowbirds migrate home, note local residents.

By 2010 the city is expected to max out at around 60,000 residents. Because it is surrounded by state land there is no space to expand unless the city is able to acquire publicly held property.

The appeal of water and weather lured John and Oweita Augsburger to Havasu.

"We lived on a lake in northern Indiana, and I was raised on the Gulf of Mexico, so we both like water," says Oweita, 51. "Here you have everything — mountains, water, sun and the convenience of Las Vegas, Phoenix and Los Angeles." The cities are within three to five or so hours by car, and there are commuter flights to Phoenix and Los Angeles.

The Augsburgers had vacationed at Lake Havasu City for 20 years but did look elsewhere in Arizona and in the Caribbean before deciding on the site for retirement. They built a mountainside adobe-style home with a lake view.

While climate is a big drawing card, it also may be the city's most apparent flaw. Beautiful warm winter days with temperatures in the mid-70s give way to July and August scorchers that can top 110 degrees. John, 59, suggests retreating to the 7,000-foot Hualapai Mountains, an hour away, where temperatures can be 30 degrees cooler. Some residents leave the city for several weeks during the late summer.

Retirees Jean and Bob Ramsdell aren't fond of the heat either, but say the trade-off is worth it.

"You might have two bad months, but I still like the other 10," says Bob, 76. "We have air-conditioned homes, cars and stores. If I have to run around, I do it early in the morning."

The Ramsdells moved to Havasu from Massachusetts, finding that their chronic sinus conditions were greatly alleviated in the dry desert climate.

Many Havasu residents rely on the 45-mile-long lake to help stay cool. Its waters are in the pleasant 80s from about mid-April into early fall, chilling to the mid-50s during winter months. On its shores, the natural sand beach of Rotary Community Park has shaded picnic tables and volleyball and softball areas.

Streets curve up and away from the lake, providing many homesites with views. Although architectural styles vary, Spanish-Mediterranean home designs prevail. Traditionally, lots have been sold individually or in small groups. Young families, retirees and winter-only residents share neighborhoods. While Lake Havasu City's first large planned subdivision is on the way, there still are no planned retirement communities.

Lot prices have skyrocketed — a lot that sold for $17,000 in 1976 is now on the market for $65,000. Golf-course lots can go for as much as $158,000. While $100,000 homes are the norm, custom homes can cost $600,000. Less pricey options are manufactured homes; three areas are zoned for them, two of which offer deeded lots for sale.

The London Bridge remains a focal point in the community. In the 1960s, when it was still British, the stone landmark was indeed, as the nursery rhyme declared, falling down, sinking into the Thames under the burden of increased traffic. Entrepreneurial Londoners put it on the market and McCulloch submitted the winning $2.46 million bid. The bridge was dismantled, its pieces numbered and transported to Lake Havasu. Today excursion boats and pleasure craft pass under its arches, passengers craning to see numbers still visible on many blocks.

The bridge seems appropriate in the Arizona desert in a Disneyesque sort of way, especially since Lake

Havasu City was planned by C. V. Wood, who also designed Disneyland. London Bridge is not just a quirky anachronism, though. It provides access to parks, a hotel and other businesses on a sliver of land called The Island. It also shelters the shops of English Village at its mainland end.

The city's two premier golf courses offer sweeping views of the bridge and lake. Hitting the links in 100-plus temperatures may sound like a bid for heatstroke, but courses open at daylight. Residents can get in 18 holes and be home by late morning, before temperatures peak. Late afternoon usually is the hottest time of the day. London Bridge Golf Club, where the Ramsdells belong, has two championship courses, where weekday greens fees are $50 and $35, including cart; lower rates apply after 1 p.m. Havasu Island and Queens Bay golf courses are other options.

Well-priced eateries, from the fun and funky to truly elegant, encourage dining out. At the unexpectedly European Cafe Mocha Tree, linen tablecloths and crystal chandeliers set the scene for French-style cuisine served by waiters in tuxedo shirts and cummerbunds. Bridgewater Cafe in the London Bridge Resort is famous for its opulent Sunday champagne brunch.

While water is the attraction for many, Havasu's arid side fascinates others. Especially in the spring the Sonoran Desert is alive with yellow creosote, red barrel cactus, brilliant orange-red ocotillo and the many-armed saguaros. Locals highly recommend an initial exploration with Outback Off-Road Adventures. Guests bounce along in a six-passenger Bronco 4x4 with a trained naturalist whose knowledge of plants and animals makes it possible to see life where none seems to exist.

A favorite excursion is a 20-minute ride across the lake on the Colorado River Express to the California side and Havasu Landing Resort and Casino. Because it is part of the Chemehuevi Indian Reservation, the resort can offer slot machines and electronic games of chance. Visitors often linger for lunch or supper at the casi-

Lake Havasu City, AZ

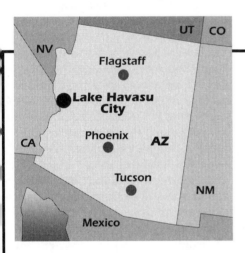

Population: 46,684 in Lake Havasu City, 147,529 in Mohave County.

Location: In the Sonoran desert on 45-mile-long Lake Havasu, created by damming the Colorado River. Founded in 1964, it sits on Arizona's boundary with California.

Climate:
	High	Low
January	67	43
July	110	83

Average relative humidity: 29%, but there are big seasonal differences. January averages 65%, June 15%.

Rain: 3.8 inches.
Extremely hot summers, moderate winters with an occasional freeze. Elevation 600 feet.

Cost of living: About average (specific index not available).

Average housing cost: $130,000 for a single-family home.

Sales tax: 7.85%

Sales tax exemptions: Groceries.

State income tax: For married couples filing jointly, graduated from 2.87% of taxable income up to $20,000 to 5.04% minus $2,276 on amounts over $300,000. For single filers, graduated from 2.87% of taxable income up to $10,000 to 5.04% minus $1,138 on amounts over $150,000.

Income tax exemptions: Social Security benefits and up to $2,500 on federal, state and local government pensions are exempt.

Intangibles tax: None.

Estate tax: None, except the state's "pick-up" portion of the federal tax, applicable to taxable estates of more than $1 million.

Property tax: $20.22 per $100 of assessed valuation, with homes assessed at 10% of market value. Taxes on a $130,000 home are about $2,629 a year.

Homestead exemption: None.

Religion: More than 30 churches represent 24 denominations.

Education: Mohave Community College, Lake Havasu Campus, offers degree programs and waives the $30 registration fee for students age 55 and older.

Transportation: There's no city bus service but an on-call van service delivers passengers door to door. The airport has commuter flights to Phoenix and Los Angeles.

Health: Havasu Regional Medical Center has a 99-bed, full-service acute-care facility and a 19-bed transitional-care unit. It's staffed by 70 physicians and visiting specialists and is state-certified as an advanced life-support base.

Housing options: Many single-family homes, apartments and condos and three mobile-home parks. Three-bedroom, two-bath single-family homes start at $80,000. **Queens Bay Condominiums** offers condos ranging from $160,000-$325,000. There are no planned retirement communities. Lots are generally sold individually or in small groups for development. Independent retirement apartment living with 24-hour assistance is available at **1221 Claremont**, (928) 855-4843, a retirement residence that provides three meals a day.

Visitor lodging: Havasu Dunes resort condominiums, (800) 438-6493, one-bedroom units start at $129 a night; London Bridge Resort, (800) 624-7939, double rooms with rates of $69-$349.

Information: Lake Havasu Area Chamber of Commerce, 314 London Bridge Road, Lake Havasu City, AZ 86403, (800) 242-8278, (928) 855-4115 or www.havasuchamber.com.

no lounge and restaurant.

A trip upriver to Topock Gorge and National Wildlife Refuge reveals another side of Havasu's aquatic nature. Via excursion boat or private craft, it's easy to spot many of the birds that are protected here. To those who are imaginative, the random shapes of surrounding cliffs, softened by centuries of river water, become an alligator, fish, dolphin, hippo and gorilla. Near the waterline, ancient Indian petroglyphs are clearly visible.

Havasu's arts calendar is filled with theater productions and art shows. The Lake Havasu Community Orchestra presents a number of yearly concerts featuring pops and the classics, and popular drama in a dinner theater setting is offered by the Drury Lane Repertory Players.

Recent Havasu Light Opera productions included "You're a Good Man, Charlie Brown." The 123-member Lake Havasu Art Guild sponsors a spring juried show, which attracts exhibitors from throughout the Southwest. Mohave Community College's Discovery Series presents talks, choral concerts, dance programs and other events. Residents go to Phoenix and Las Vegas for more cosmopolitan cultural venues.

The Lake Havasu Senior Center offers line-dancing classes, yoga, bingo and bridge and workout classes as well as noon lunches. Health-maintenance support includes blood pressure check and nutrition education. Writers, artists and entertainers frequently present programs and workshops.

Havasu Regional Medical Center provides 24-hour emergency care, surgical capabilities, a transitional-care unit and a home health-care agency. An extensive network of senior services may be accessed through the Interagency Council.

Many Havasu residents own houseboats, ideal for exploring the lake's placid waters and the coves and inlets along its irregular shoreline. These "floating condos" also are for rent. At 46 to 52 feet, or about the size of a large motor home, most houseboats have standard-size beds, completely equipped galleys, living rooms and barbecue areas on deck. Some can accommodate 10 to 12 guests. Houseboats also provide a base from which fishermen can pursue the wily trout, bass, bluegill, crappie and catfish.

The Aquatic Recreation Center is a good respite when lake waters are chilly or when summer's sun proves too intense. Colorful windsurfers float from the ceiling. "Surf" in the wave pool washes up on a cement "beach" that's fringed with frankly fake palm trees. Plastic coconuts periodically dump water on anyone underneath. A four-story water slide keeps kids busy, and a gently sloping shoreline-style entry is used for the aquatic wheelchair, available to anyone who needs it. A single admission to the center is $5.50, or $4.50 for seniors; yearly memberships are available.

Havasu is a planned community, taking the time to get things right. As chairman of the finance committee, Bob Ramsdell wrote the city's first budget and has served as mayor. When the Ramsdells moved here in 1977 there were 8,000 people. Now there are about 47,000, but "we still love it," Bob says.

Adds Jean, 75, "Since it was so small to begin with, shopping was a bit of a problem. We didn't have the stores we were used to." Now there are four major supermarkets, a Wal-Mart and dozens of other retail stores.

The Ramsdells say their taxes are much lower in Lake Havasu City — about $800 vs. more than $3,000 paid in "Taxachusetts," as Bob puts it. "We have a high electrical bill here, but when I add in the fuel costs from the other house to the electric bill, it's cheaper here," he adds.

Jean misses the colorful display of fall leaves they had in Massachusetts, but Bob says he misses nothing. "I gave up my two proudest possessions — my lawn mower and my snow blower."

Both the Ramsdells and the Augsburgers say that despite Lake Havasu City's growth, it still has the feel of a small town. "There's lots of gossip. With such an influx of people from all over the United States, I didn't expect that," says Oweita.

Pre-retirees considering Havasu should spend a summer there before making a year-around commitment, cautions John.

Bob advises retirees to reach out when they move to Lake Havasu City. "Go to the Senior Center, to your church, to town meetings, raise your right hand and they'll keep you so busy you'll never know that you're retired. And that way you develop friends, too," he says.●

Las Cruces, New Mexico

Multicultural population enriches oasis in southern New Mexico

By Judy Wade

Over the centuries, American Indians, Mexicans, Spaniards and pioneers discovered the fertile Mesilla Valley in the high desert country of southern New Mexico.

Settlers still come — now via east-west Interstate 10 and north-south Interstate 25 — and many of them are retirees looking for the modern-day oasis in that cultural crossroads, Las Cruces.

Proximity to Mexico — the border city of Juarez is less than an hour away — and centuries under the Mexican flag have left a strong Latino imprint. Rapid-fire staccato Spanish is as commonly heard as English, and Southwestern-style adobe is the dominant architecture.

Only 40 miles northwest of El Paso, TX, Las Cruces is New Mexico's second-largest city, a regional educational-medical center; yet, with about 74,000 residents, it's a comfortable size.

Retirees Herbert and Carol Anne Adams chose Las Cruces after retiring from Wisconsin to Bradenton, FL, in 1985. They left the No. 1 retirement state for several reasons.

Says Herb, 73, "I just felt crowded in Florida — all of the people, cars, burgeoning population. Then in winter, you superimpose on that the snowbirds."

They also grew tired of the humidity, the "no-see-ums" (little bugs) and living in a retirement community.

The Adamses ruled out California as too expensive. Carol, 50, adds, "Arizona is too hot and has too many retirees. Florida is too hot and has too many retirees."

After meeting a couple who had retired to Albuquerque, NM, the Adamses decided to check out the state.

"We bought a lot on our first visit (to Las Cruces), contracted to build a house and moved here when it was completed," says Herb.

The Adamses say they like the New Mexico climate but do miss being near the water — "but we lived within three-fourths of a mile of the Gulf of Mexico and there would be months on end between visits," he says.

Herb and Carol live in a small, 55-family subdivision in Mesilla (meaning "little table" in Spanish), a historic village adjacent to Las Cruces. Their community has just three winding streets along which tidy adobe-style homes are comfortably placed in desert surroundings. A fieldstone-walled yard is landscaped with native deer grass, pink Mexican primrose, silvercloud sage, purple verbena and other desert vegetation.

Las Cruces is framed by the dramatic spikes of the Organ Mountains on the east and the legendary Rio Grande on the west. It's named for "the crosses" that mark the burial place of a group of travelers killed here by Apaches in the mid-1800s.

Area residents appreciate the mosaic of cultures, fostering ethnic diversity in such celebrations as the annual Enchilada Festival, which culminates with the cooking of the world's largest enchilada.

The sun, the Rio Grande and a large supply of underground artesian water keep the Mesilla Valley green and productive. Groves of old cottonwood trees and agricultural fields make it seem like an oasis. Crops of cotton, chili peppers and pecans flourish with regular watering. Early on any given morning, elevated irrigation pipes on wheels roll slowly through the fields, delivering the nourishing mist.

An active cultural scene centers around New Mexico State University (NMSU), which promotes major concerts by popular artists at its Pan Am Center. The NMSU music department offers free jazz, classical and pop concerts.

Performing at the Music Center at NMSU, the Las Cruces Symphony has talented students, faculty and community musicians as its core and also hosts world-renowned guest artists.

The American Southwest Theatre Company brings classic dramas, comedies, musicals and original works to the University's Hershel Zohn Theatre. Enthusiastic non-professional players put on a full season of entertainment at the Las Cruces Community Theater, and diverse dance programs are performed by the Las Cruces Chamber Ballet.

The area's cultural diversity and the university were among the amenities that drew Bob Nelson, 66, and his wife, Alice, 59.

They considered Santa Fe — "loved the way it looks but too expensive and too crowded with tourists" — and Albuquerque before moving from Billings, MT, to Las Cruces.

The Nelsons also were attracted by the area's choice of outdoor activities year-round and its topography, the warm desert complemented with nearby mountains. In winter, there's alpine skiing at Ski Apache outside Ruidoso.

Volunteering and community involvement are sure-fire ways to integrate quickly with the lifestyle, say former teachers Winnie Jacobs, 58, and husband, Ed, 63. The couple moved from Reston, VA, after visiting Las Cruces for an Elderhostel program.

"We saw a house we liked across the street from the Good Samaritan Village, which was ideal for my 91-year-old mother who was in a nursing home in Maryland. It all just seemed to fit," she says.

The Jacobses became active with the American Association of Retired Persons, the League of Women Voters and as volunteers at a soup kitchen.

Bob and Alice Nelson are public radio station volunteers, and Alice is on the board of directors of the Academy for Learning in Retirement, which develops enrichment classes featuring speakers on various topics for seniors. Mini-courses cover topics ranging from local history to appreciating opera. A recent subject was Genetics in the Modern World, presented by an NMSU professor of agronomy.

Both Bob and Alice do regular 20- to 25-mile bicycle rides with the Las Cruces Bicycle and Chowder Club, which Bob describes as an informal organization "without a whole lotta structure, but with a whole lotta fun."

Herb and Carol became involved with the Las Cruces Symphony and the library, and Carol is active in the League of Women Voters.

Munson Senior Citizen Center is a hub of activity for card playing, arts and crafts, Olympic line dance practice (Dona Ana County holds Senior Olympics every April) and continuing-education classes on such subjects as creative writing and computer skills. It also provides noon meals.

A busy chapter of the Retired Senior Volunteer Program places individuals age 60 and older in volunteer jobs with non-profit agencies. Mesilla's Community Center also offers senior activities including noon meals.

From their home the Adamses often stroll the few blocks to the village of Mesilla for dinner and shopping. It is the area's historic centerpiece and was an important commerce center by the time the Gadsden Purchase made it officially part of the United States in 1854. Today a historic zoning ordinance restricts redevelopment and helps preserve buildings in the original adobe style.

At the heart of the village, St. Albino's church, established in 1851, overlooks a traditional plaza with a grassy park and gazebo. Unique shops and eateries open onto the plaza from behind the colorful doors of Mesilla's restored buildings. La Posta Restaurant occupies the old Butterfield stage building nearby, recalling a time when Mesilla was capital of the Arizona Territory and a stop on the Butterfield Overland Stage Route. Boutiques offer Navajo, Zuni, Hopi and Santo Domingo handmade Indian jewelry, folk art, decorative accessories and Southwest clothing.

While Las Cruces has definite ties to the past, it has a strong focus on the future, particularly through its association with research carried on at nearby

Las Cruces, NM

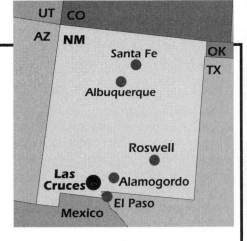

Population: 74,267 in Las Cruces, 174,682 in Dona Ana County.

Location: Mountain-ringed agricultural valley by the Rio Grande in high desert of southern New Mexico, about 40 miles northwest of El Paso, TX.

Climate:

	High	Low
January	57	26
July	98	70

Average relative humidity: 31%

Rain: 8 inches.

Snow: 3 inches. Four distinct seasons, with hot summer days that cool off in the evening. Late summer brings brief but heavy thunderstorms. Dust storms and sandstorms occur in spring. Elevation is 3,896 feet.

Cost of living: 95.3, based on national average of 100.

Average housing cost: $106,250

Sales tax: 6.375% (called a gross receipts tax).

Sales tax exemptions: None.

State income tax: For married couples filing jointly, graduated from 1.7% of taxable income up to $8,000 to 8.2% on amounts over $100,000. For single filers, graduated from 1.7% of taxable income up to $5,500 to 8.2% on amounts over $65,000.

Income tax exemptions: Individuals 65 and older are eligible for a deduction of up to $8,000 if joint income does not exceed $51,000 for married filing jointly or $28,500 for single filers.

Intangibles tax: None.

Estate tax: None, except the state's "pick-up" portion of the federal tax, applicable to taxable estates above $1 million.

Inheritance tax: None.

Property tax: $27.53 per $1,000 of assessed value, with homes assessed at 33.33% of market value. Yearly tax on a $106,250 home, less $2,000 homestead exemption, is $920.

Homestead exemption: $2,000 off assessed value.

Religion: More than 50 churches represent 31 denominations.

Education: For those age 65 and older, New Mexico State University has classes for $42 a credit hour (on a space-available basis) and Dona Ana Branch Community College, (505) 527-7500, also offers community education courses. The Academy for Learning in Retirement, (505) 527-7527, has enrichment classes at various sites, with programs costing around $20 and typically lasting two hours a day for four days.

Transportation: Roadrunner Transit of Las Cruces Transit Department has scheduled local bus service.

Health: The 286-bed Memorial Medical Center serves the region, offering advanced care, including coronary and cancer treatment. The city also has about 10 clinics and eight nursing homes.

Housing options: Single-family homes begin around $85,500 in a number of developments. One-bedroom furnished apartments begin at about $375 a month. **Sonoma Ranch**, (877) 700-7210, is a growing master-planned community with homes starting in the $180,000s. **Mesilla Farms** and **Desert Hills** are popular subdivisions where resale lots may be available; buyers contract with builders of their choice. Well-priced manufactured home communities are popular and plentiful.

Visitor lodging: Best Western Mesilla Valley Inn, $62-$92 double, (800) 327-3314; Las Cruces Hilton, $86 double, (505) 522-4300.

Information: Las Cruces Convention and Visitors Bureau, 211 N. Water St., Las Cruces, NM 88001, (800) 343-7827, (505) 541-2444 or www.lascrucescvb.com.

White Sands Missile Range. Much of the work is in partnership with the university and its Technological Innovation Center, physical science laboratory, and computer and plant genetic engineering departments.

Shopping opportunities are found at Mesilla Valley Mall, which has major department stores and smaller shops. Las Cruces Farmers and Crafts Market is open Wednesday and Saturday mornings in the downtown open-air mall. More than 200 artists, craftspeople and farmers offer antiques, homemade goods, fresh produce and herbs, artwork and typical Southwest decorative accessories at bargain prices.

Excellent health care is provided by Memorial Medical Center, a 286-bed county hospital, where coronary angioplasties and open-heart procedures are performed. Four Family Medical Centers provide quick medical care, and an eye clinic, hearing center and home health care all offer services. Military retirees can take advantage of medical care at William Beaumont Army Medical Center in El Paso, about 40 miles south.

A climate that encourages year-round outdoor sports also helps keep residents healthy. Area golf courses include Picacho Hills, a membership country club community. The Las Cruces Country Club Golf Course and the course at NMSU are open for public play.

Living costs are below the national average.

"Compared to Santa Fe, Denver or Southern California, it is very inexpensive here," says Alice Nelson, citing food, utilities and car licenses as being significantly less. For the Nelsons, real estate taxes are about half of what they were in Montana.

Many Las Cruces residents reduce utility bills by using evaporative coolers, known widely as "swamp coolers" along with air conditioning to keep their homes comfortable during the summer months. Evaporative cooling works on the principle of drawing air through moistened filters allowing natural evaporation to cool the air as a fan blows it into the home. They are much cheaper to run but may aggravate allergies as they do not filter outside air.

University Terrace Good Samaritan Village is a planned retirement area in Las Cruces. Individuals age 62 and older may rent studio and one- or two-bedroom apartments. There also is a 24-bed assisted-living facility. Adjacent to Memorial Medical Center, the village has emergency call buttons, local transportation, maid service and meals.

All couples stressed that a key to being happy in Las Cruces is to accept the town as it is.

"Don't try to change Las Cruces into what you came from," says Alice Nelson. "If you want ocean breezes, you should have figured out that we aren't going to get them here."

Carol Adams dislikes the wind and dust but finds those conditions preferable to the "constant oppressive heat" in Florida.

Carol reminds prospective residents that they are moving into an ethnically mixed community.

"If they are Anglo, they will be in the minority. There is a difference in the culture, and they just have to accept that fact. People (here) aren't going to change to suit their needs. They (newcomers) are going to have to change," she emphasizes.●

Las Vegas, Nevada

From affordable living to plentiful recreation, retirees find that this desert city has it all

By Adele Malott

Las Vegas Valley at night is a soup bowl of stars, an oasis of lights hugged up close by the Spring Mountains. For several decades this view has welcomed millions of vacationers arriving from throughout the world.

But for newcomers moving to the Las Vegas area each month, it now says "welcome home" to people like Ken and Marlene Rengert, who came to Las Vegas after Ken retired from the Air Force in Rantoul, IL. The Rengerts are great travelers — gone as much as 75 percent of the time some years — so the view of their new hometown from an airplane window when they return is one they know well.

Marlene Rengert says that when the plane crests the mountains, she likes to see the lights laid out beneath her. And when she's home, she tells her friends, "It's like having Christmas lights in the back yard all year long." The Rengerts chose a three-bedroom ranch home on Sunrise Mountain with views of the city lights for their retirement oasis.

Las Vegas did begin as an oasis for the Spanish and Mexicans who used the Old Spanish Trail to travel between Santa Fe and Southern California. These travelers named the area "Las Vegas," meaning "the meadows" — an image difficult to imagine when looking at the towers of neon and construction gantries that now dominate the skyline.

Las Vegas started to take shape in 1905 when the San Pedro, Los Angeles and Salt Lake Railroad (Union Pacific) auctioned off building sites for the spot it had chosen to change crews and get water for its trains. Another growth spurt pumped the city in the early 1930s when construction of Hoover Dam began, and again in the '40s when Bugsy Siegel built the Flamingo Hotel as a gaming spa for the mob, then in the 1960s when Howard Hughes came to town, and the '70s when the mammoth MGM Grand was built. Now, every third

or fourth year a new wave of construction adds to the skyline.

All the superlatives to describe Las Vegas have been used up as a tightening time-line spiral of boom and boom and boom has thrust the city repeatedly to the top of many different kinds of "fastest-growing" lists. So it is no surprise that people from all backgrounds, occupations and parts of the United States in search of a retirement home find what they want in Las Vegas. Retirees comprise the fastest-growing segment of Las Vegas' population, and the National Association of Home Builders predicts the city will be the most popular seniors housing market in the coming decade.

Many, like Terry and Claudia Culp, who moved to Las Vegas in 1998 from Buffalo, NY, are quick to emphasize that the Las Vegas in which they live is not the Las Vegas they were accustomed to reading about. Terry explains that the typical Easterner's view of Las Vegas "is a misinterpretation that assumes that all there is to do is to lay out in the sun or gamble. As it turns out, Las Vegas is totally different than what I envisioned," he says as he describes his discoveries. "Valley of Fire is absolutely gorgeous. I had heard about Lake Mead, but it is much bigger than I thought. Another surprise is Lake Powell — it's not that far away. And Hoover Dam is a little touristy, but you have to do it once, right?"

Perhaps one reason the Las Vegas Strip works so hard for the attention of visitors is that its glitter and glitz must compete with vast natural spectacles like Valley of Fire and Red Rock Canyon, places that could serve as God's own statuary gardens filled with sandstone creations named Elephant Rock and the Seven Sisters. These two geological parks are the east and west bookends for Las Vegas, and both draw millions of visitors annually.

Lake Mead National Recreation Area

is the massive playground that resulted from creating a needed flood- and drought-control project. With 822 miles of shoreline, Lake Mead offers a bonanza of water sports, as does Lake Mohave, created by the construction of Davis Dam nearly 50 years after Hoover Dam. Hoover was built to rein in the Colorado River's rampages and supply electrical power for much of the Southwest.

The enormous Hoover Dam construction project jump-started southern Nevada's economy in post-Depression years and today offers tourists a chance to take river rafting and excursion boat trips through Black Canyon at the base of the dam, which towers 726 feet overhead. River rafters are intrigued with often-told ghost stories that describe the moans and cries of construction workers trapped in the dam wall.

The Culps undertook methodical research to find their new home after they sold a family business in Buffalo and left 70-hour work weeks behind. They believed they would prefer the Southwest and began buying books and retirement publications to research their choices. Then they chose eight cities to look at critically during a 3,000-mile trek across the country: Lake Havasu City, Page, Phoenix and Tucson in Arizona, Santa Fe and Albuquerque in New Mexico, and Reno/Sparks and Las Vegas in Nevada. Each stop included visits with chamber of commerce officials and real estate agents. And once they decided on Las Vegas, they moved into an apartment to give themselves time to get a feel for the area until they found their 2,600-square-foot home in Henderson, southeast of downtown.

"There were a lot of pluses for each city we looked at, but when we boiled it all down, Las Vegas was the most attractive," says Terry Culp. "The small-town feel was a big advantage and, because Las Vegas is so easy and inexpensive to get in and out of, it was a good choice so our family and friends could visit." Terry laughs when he admits their decision was "sort of scientific" but also involved "our gut feelings."

Many of his views are seconded by Gail Imazaki, a nurse who retired to Las Vegas from Southern California in 1997. "You can live as quietly as you want, or you can get out and go to the clubs and shows," says Gail, who also researched a variety of locations, including Port Ludlow, WA, and Palm Desert and Roseville, CA.

Gail earned the crown of Ms. Senior Nevada in 1998 and was fourth runner-up

Las Vegas, NV

Population: 478,434

Location: In a broad desert valley in the southern tip of Nevada surrounded by mountains. The valley's elevation is about 1,200 feet, with surrounding mountains rising from 2,000 to 12,000 feet. Las Vegas is at the crossroads of I-15 (connecting southern California, Arizona and Utah), I-95 (from the northwest) and I-93/95 from the southeast.

Climate:

	High	Low
January	57	34
July	108	76

Average relative humidity: 31%

Rain: 3.8 inches.

Cost of living: 107, based on national average of 100.

Average housing costs: $155,455 for a new three-bedroom home of 1,800 square feet. Median sales price of an established home is $130,800. A 950-square-foot apartment rents for an average of about $700 per month.

Sales tax: 7.25%

Sales tax exemptions: Food for consumption at home, prescription drugs, vegetable plants and seeds, propane and fuel for home heating.

State income tax: None.

Intangibles tax: None.

Estate tax: None, except the state's "pick-up" portion of the federal tax applicable to taxable estates of up to $1 million.

Property tax: $2.04-$3.41 per $100 in assessed value depending on the taxing district within Clark County, with homes assessed at 35% of taxable value. The annual tax for a home valued at $155,455 would be $1,110-$1,855.

Homestead exemption: There is a property tax/rent rebate program for those 62 and older who meet specific income limits.

Religion: There are 584 churches serving the Las Vegas Valley.

Education: Two two-year colleges, Community College of Southern Nevada and Las Vegas College, and one four-year college, University of Nevada at Las Vegas. Those who are 62 or older can attend fall and spring semester credit classes at UNLV on a space-available basis without paying credit or tuition fees. Summer credit courses are offered at half-price. The Clark County School District offers a large number of adult education programs, as do area park and recreation departments.

Transportation: McCarran International Airport, 10 minutes south of the business district, is ranked in the top 10 busiest national airports with daily traffic of about 840 flights. Public bus transportation is provided by CAT (Citizens Area Transit). Trolleys also run along the Strip and from downtown to a mall and the Stratosphere Hotel. A recent project, the Senior Neighborhood Trolley Routes, stops at various senior centers and shops.

Health: About 10 hospitals boast a combined staff of 7,000 physicians and specialized care centers such as a bone marrow transplant facility, diabetes treatment center, coronary heart disease reversal program and a burn-care center. There are 2,313 licensed active physicians in Clark County.

Housing options: There is a vast array of housing choices available from townhouses, condominiums and apartment complexes to single-family homes (many of them on new golf courses). Nearby cities such as Henderson and Boulder City also are claiming their share of new residents. There are a number of active-adult housing developments. In Henderson, **Anthem** incorporates three types of neighborhoods: a gated country club community, an active-adult community for residents 55 and older, and a traditional neighborhood geared to families; call (800) 478-3763 for information. On the western rim of Las Vegas Valley, **Summerlin**, (800) 295-4554, is a 22,500-acre master-planned community currently comprised of about 15 villages in various stages of development and covering a broad range of housing styles and prices, including the age-restricted **Sun City Summerlin**. Plans call for a total of 30 villages. Still under development is **Siena**, (800) 856-7661, a guard-gated community with an 18-hole golf course, health and fitness center, and homes from the $140,000s.

Visitor lodging: Las Vegas has a huge inventory of hotels and motels with more than 100,000 rooms, including 12 of the 13 largest hotels in the world. In addition, the city offers long-term stay and corporate apartment facilities for those needing more than casual or vacation accommodations. Space can be at a premium during high-traffic conventions. For more information, call the hotel reservations hot line of the Las Vegas Convention and Visitors Authority, (800) 332-5333.

Information: Las Vegas Chamber of Commerce, 3720 Howard Hughes Parkway, Las Vegas, NV 89109, (702) 735-1616 or www.lvchamber.com. Ask for the biannual Las Vegas Relocation Guide. Las Vegas Convention and Visitors Authority, 3150 Paradise Road, Las Vegas, NV 89109, (702) 892-0711 or www.lasvegas24hours.com. Clark County Department of Comprehensive Planning, 500 S. Grand Central Parkway, No. 3012, Las Vegas, NV 89155-1741, (702) 455-4181. Aging Senior Division, Department of Human Resources, 3100 W. Sahara Ave., Suite 103, Las Vegas, NV 89102, (702) 486-3545.

in the national pageant, partly because of her dancing skills. A single senior, she now lives in a duplex on the eighth hole of Eagle Crest Golf Course in Sun City Summerlin, "with a spectacular view of the mountains that amazes me every morning when I wake up. I could never have afforded to live on the golf course in Los Angeles," she adds, noting that it is a location she enjoys even though she is not a player.

Gail ticks off the city's "pluses" in rapid order: "First, cheaper auto insurance; second, utilities much cheaper; third, no state (income) taxes." And then she laughs, "Another factor that swayed me were the inexpensive buffets. I rarely cook now, only microwave." But while Gail lists many good things about her choice, she admits Las Vegas is not perfect and worries that city amenities and services may not be able to keep up with rapid growth, especially in the area of health care.

The chance to spend more time dancing was one reason she decided to retire at age 60. As a registered nurse working on the open-heart surgery team at Good Samaritan Hospital in Los Angeles, Gail "was so busy I couldn't do my dancing." Now she practices in her dining room as well as attending recreation classes and serving as president of the Nevada chapter of the Cameo Club of Ms. Senior America, an alumni group.

Gail was persuaded to enter the Ms. Senior Nevada competition by Lori Sanchez, another Summerlin resident who claimed the Ms. Senior America title a few years earlier. The two met as performers putting on talent showcases at convalescent homes. Gail entered the Ms. Senior Nevada competition "with an attitude of meeting new ladies and for the experience — not to win," she says.

Representing Nevada also gave Gail a chance to "do some PR with senior citizens, to make sure they're well cared for. I can also help with referrals since a lot of seniors may not know about everything that's available to them in the way of services."

And there are many. Each Sunday's newspaper is filled with activities at dozens of senior facilities throughout the Las Vegas Valley, as well as news of health and financial assistance, discounts, volunteer opportunities, special continuing-education studies and seminars at the University of Nevada at Las Vegas. Terry Culp is enrolled in Spanish classes at the University of Nevada at Las Vegas and a computer class at the Community College of Southern Nevada.

Volunteering is part of what the Rengerts do, now that they are no longer in the military. Marlene Rengert helps at the hospital at Nellis Air Force Base, her church and as an AARP recruiter, while husband Ken is a tax aide volunteer for AARP.

When the Rengerts were moving from base to base during Ken's 30-year Air Force career, they learned about many areas in the United States. But Marlene Rengert says, "We fell in love with the desert and its warm, dry climate, which seems to make my rheumatoid arthritis less painful." While the weather was the top reason Las Vegas was right for the Rengerts, they also liked being close to a Veterans Administration hospital and connected to military roots at nearby Nellis Air Force Base.

Las Vegas is the kind of city that attracts more than the usual number of visitors, both friends and relatives of residents. But the Rengerts always look forward to visits from their grandchildren and say Las Vegas' many parks and libraries help them entertain their young guests. Other favorite stops are attractions like the Wet 'n' Wild water park and the highly interactive Lied (pronounced "leed") Children's Museum. Here kids of all ages can try out gadgets, work at solving problems and enjoy the performances and workshops of artists-in-residence who showcase arts from photography to puppetry and creative writing to sculpture.

If the man-made attractions weren't enough, the Rengerts point out that the Grand Canyon is nearby, and residents can ski on Mount Charleston and explore historic mining towns. "We could have chosen anywhere. But we often say, 'Didn't we make a good decision?' and pat each other on the back," says Marlene. "We think we did a really good job choosing."●

Lincoln City, Oregon

The jewel of the Central Oregon coast glitters with attraction for many

By Dana Tims

From signing the Emancipation Proclamation to delivering the Gettysburg Address to saving the Union, Abraham Lincoln is known to history for many acts of leadership. What the annals do not record about the 16th president, however, were his exploits in the Oregon Territory.

Why? Because he never had any. One can only ponder how Lincoln's life and the nation might have changed had he accepted an offer in 1849 to become governor of the newly formed Oregon Territory, a rough and wild section of country stretching from the West Coast to what is now Montana, Wyoming and Nevada.

A much different career path, one ultimately leading to Ford's Theater in Washington, DC, was chosen after his wife, Mary Todd Lincoln, told him that the untamed wilderness of the West was no place to raise children.

Lincoln City still is not for everyone, say members of the active senior community in the Oregon coastal town that bears the late president's name. But for those willing to put up with the boiling magnificence of a winter storm, summer breezes bending wildflowers low beneath stands of Sitka spruce and red alder on blustery Cascade Head, or a contemplative walk along more than seven miles of white-sand beaches, Lincoln City may be just the spot to call home.

Bounded on the east by scenic Devils Lake and to the west by the Pacific Ocean, Lincoln City long has been known as a haven for retirees. More than a third of the town's population of 7,437 residents, in fact, have pulled up stakes in other areas of the country and made the glittering Central Oregon coast their home.

George and Mary Jeffries had lived and worked in Chicago for six years before George retired in 1991 as director of workers compensation for CNA Insurance Co. Devotees of op-

era and theater, they loved the cultural accouterments available in a big city.

But when it came time to choose a retirement location, George and Mary gladly said goodbye to metropolis. The harsh winter weather, along with daunting daily traffic jams, had become too much. Having owned a small vacation cabin at Gleneden Beach, just south of Lincoln City, for years, they were well-acquainted with the area. Neither entertained thoughts of moving anywhere else. And they have not regretted their decision for a moment.

"We can't imagine having a better life," Mary says. "Everything we could ever want is right here in Lincoln City."

They immersed themselves in the area's abundant cultural and volunteer activities almost immediately. George, 65, fired up his long-dormant amateur acting career by building sets for Lincoln City's Theatre West. His love of literature landed him on the Friends of the Library board of directors, where he organizes weekly book sales that net enough money to buy such extras as a neon sign for the teen reading area and lighting to illuminate a stunning seascape painted and donated by another volunteer.

He also is an assistant gardener for the Connie Hansen Garden, a one-acre flowerfest of primroses, irises and perennials open to the public and named for the horticulturist who developed the parcel. In what little spare time he saves for himself, George painstakingly builds scale models of multimasted sailing ships.

"I wore suits for more than 40 years, and I just decided it was time to get rid of them," says George, who grew up in a small, informal town and still cherishes the ability to stump around Lincoln City's numerous art galleries and antique stores in casual clothes.

"When I was younger, going to the prom meant you had to wash your jeans. That's kind of how it is around here, too."

Mary, 64, wrote a seniors column for one of the town's weekly newspapers. Her topics included everything from tax-cutting ballot measures to the impact on local traffic and congestion from one of Lincoln City's newer attractions, the Chinook Winds Casino and Convention Center. "I'm not a gambler, but it's been a big shot in the arm for the city," she says of the casino, which is owned and operated by the Confederated Tribes of the Siletz Indians of Oregon.

An avid reader who always has at least three books going, Mary also is a member of the Friends of the Library board of directors. She augments her love of literature by working 10 hours a week in a cozy downtown bookstore.

When the couple moved to Lincoln City, they paid $115,000 for a comfortable two-bedroom house with an ocean view. They currently are looking for a residence with a garage to accommodate George's woodworking needs. Now asking $135,000 for their home, they hope to find something closer to the ocean, although they know it will be a little more expensive.

Patti Smith, an agent with Lincoln City's Pete Anderson Realty, says land and home prices never have declined in the decade she has been in the business. But with prices now tending to be more stable than in the past, she says there's a buyer's market featuring plenty of options and choices.

"We've got everything here that seniors could want, including shopping, great health-care facilities and a fantastic beach," she says. "Lincoln City is a retired person's paradise."

Lincoln City's housing market is dominated by two-story residences, which are preferred by homeowners seeking a coveted view of the Pacific Ocean. While a number of planned developments aimed specifically at seniors are springing up around the area, many seniors still prefer to buy single-family residences, which average $130,000 to $165,000 for a two-bedroom, two-bath house.

"Our seniors are the ones who keep this town alive and hopping," Patti Smith says. "Without them, I don't know where we'd be."

Bill and Mary Kacy, both 68, have seen some significant changes in Lincoln City since they moved here in 1982 from their longtime home in Austin, TX. Foremost has been the increase in traffic along U.S. Highway 101, the coastal highway that effectively cleaves the town down the middle.

Lincoln City, OR

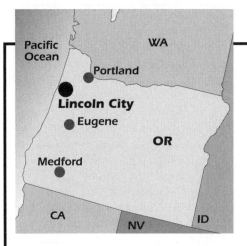

Population: 7,437 in the city, 44,479 in the county.

Location: Situated on the Central Oregon coast and bordered by the Salmon River to the north, Siletz Bay to the south and Devils Lake to the east. Lincoln City is 88 miles southwest of Oregon's largest city, Portland. Elevation is 11 feet.

Climate:

	High	Low
January	54	37
July	68	53

Average relative humidity: 62%

Rainfall: 71.8 inches.

Lincoln City has generally mild weather, with a winter storm season extending from mid-October to early March. Air quality is constantly refreshed with northwest winds in the summer and southwest winds in the winter.

Cost of living: 102.2 in Lincoln County, based on national average of 100.

Median housing cost: $160,000 for a single-family dwelling. Average rental $500 per month.

Sales tax: None.

State income tax: For married couples filing jointly, the rate is graduated from 5% of taxable income up to $5,000 to 9% on amounts over $12,600. For single filers, graduated from 5% of taxable income up to $2,500 to 9% on amounts over $6,300.

Income tax exemptions: Social Security benefits are exempt. Federal pensions are fully exempt for those who retired before October 1991 and may be partially ex-empt for retirement after that date. There is a retirement income tax credit of up to 9 percent of retirement income for those age 62 and older if they meet specified income limitations.

Intangibles tax: None.

Estate tax: None, except the state's "pick-up" portion of the federal tax, applicable to taxable estates of more than $1 million.

Property taxes: Rate ranges from $10 to $18 per $1,000 of assessed value. Homes are assessed at 100 percent of market value. The yearly tax on a $160,000 home would be approximately $1,600-$2,880.

Homestead exemption: None.

Religion: Twenty-six local churches and temples represent all major religious denominations.

Education: Oregon Coast Community College, with satellite branches in Lincoln City and nearby Newport and Waldport, offers more than 100 credit courses along with a variety of noncredit adult education courses. Seniors receive a 50 percent discount on community education tuition. Evening and weekend seminars are provided to accommodate the needs of business persons and busy retirees.

Transportation: Central Coast Connections is the county-sponsored bus transport that runs daily from Otis Junction, just east of Lincoln City, south along the coast to Yachats and east to Toledo and Siletz.

Health: North Lincoln Hospital in Lincoln City provides a full staff of physicians and nurses, along with 37 beds and units specializing in dialysis, strokes and neurological rehabilitation. In 1996, the hospital built a home health care building. The hospital maintains a 24-hour emergency room and a diversity of professional courses for staff and community members via satellite. In addition, the area is served by five medical complexes and two care facilities, which provide the latest in rehabilitation services, respite care and hospice care.

Housing options: Many retirees buy single-family homes in existing neighborhoods in the city. Prices range from $50,000 to $500,000-plus along the coast. Several retirement communities also are available. The **Dorchester House**, (541) 994-7175, is a restored historic hotel that now features 70 apartments for active seniors. Units rent for $1,475 and up for a 515-square-foot, one-bedroom apartment to $1,775 and up for a 672-square-foot, two-bedroom apartment. Services include weekly housekeeping and all meals. **Lincolnshire Retirement and Assisted Living**, (541) 994-7400, is a combination assisted- and independent-living facility overlooking quiet Devils Lake. It features 12 cottages and 55 studios and one-bedroom apartments. Monthly rents range from $1,895 for a studio to $2,450 for a one-bedroom unit, single occupancy (additional $500 for second occupant). Meals are provided and bus service is available to area medical and recreational facilities. **Hillside House**, (541) 994-8028, is an adult assisted-living facility with 33 units ranging from studios to one-bedroom apartments. Rents start at $1,500 per month for single occupants and go up, depending on the level of care. Additional occupants pay $650-$800 per month.

Visitor lodging: Lincoln City has a wide variety of overnight accommodations and features more than 2,000 rooms, the largest number of coastal motel and hotel rooms between San Francisco and Seattle. Among the options: Inn at Spanish Head, $159-$249, (541) 996-2161; Best Western Lincoln Sands Inn, $149 and up, (541) 994-4227; and Coho Inn, $65-$117, (541) 994-3684.

Information: Lincoln City Visitors and Convention Bureau, 801 S.W. Highway 101, Suite 1, Lincoln City, OR 97367, (800) 452-2151 or www.oregoncoast. org. Lincoln City Chamber of Commerce, P.O. Box 787, Lincoln City, OR 97367, (541) 994-3070 or www.lcchamber. com.

Area merchants, who for years opposed a proposed bypass around the town, now are supportive of the idea, especially since the town's 158,000-square-foot casino ensures that Lincoln City will never be without a steady influx of visitors. That shift of support, the Kacys say, could restore some of the charm lost to increased traffic.

However, both say that area seniors can manage very well, especially once they learn the side streets and shortcuts to such destinations as the county's quaint, turn-of-the-century covered wooden bridges, the North Lincoln County Historical Museum, the town's new senior community center, and North Lincoln Hospital with its state-of-the-art medical equipment.

The hospital serves the community with 37 beds, a full staff of physicians and nurses and units specializing in dialysis, strokes and neurological rehabilitation. Lincoln City also features five medical complexes and two care facilities providing services ranging from adult day care to hospice care.

Bill enjoys frequent rounds of golf at either Lakeside Golf Club's 18-hole course in Lincoln City or at the breathtaking ocean-view course at Salishan Lodge Golf Links just south in Gleneden Beach. "We have five courses within easy driving distance, and I can play all year around in a sweater," says Bill, who retired as regional director of public affairs for Union Carbide. "Our last year in Texas, it was over 100 degrees every day for two months. We could never go back to that."

He also has honed his computer programmer's skills by taking technology courses offered through Oregon Coast Community College. In addition, he volunteers at the hospital, where he serves on the board of directors.

The couple was forced to move from Texas because of Mary's respiratory problems. So while Bill remained behind to finish some last-minute work, Mary grabbed her Lhasa apso puppy, hopped in the car and headed solo to scout the West Coast. "I started at the southern end of Oregon and just drove north," says Mary, who managed the 25-story Westgate Building in Austin before retirement. "When I got to Lincoln City, I just knew I had found what I was looking for."

Mary, a freelance writer, has been published in a number of newspapers and magazines. She also helped city planners write Lincoln City's transportation master plan. For an artistic outlet, the rugs, colorful shawls and decorative place mats she weaves on a 36-inch loom are sold at area gift shops.

The couple still lives in the house Mary discovered on that first venture, a two-bedroom, two-bath residence tucked among the alder and spruce on Cascade Head, a stunning promontory that juts into the ocean and features both canopied and wind-swept hiking trails. A few houses and condominiums, some of them used only as vacation getaways, dot Cascade Head, which has earned federal designation as the Salmon River Estuary Scenic Research Area.

The home faces south, saving the Kacys a bundle on utility costs. Splashes of afternoon sun in the winter prompt Mary to throw wide the doors to avoid overheating, while gentle sea breezes ensure that there is no need for air-conditioning in the summer.

During afternoon walks with their dog, Rowdy, the Kacys often stumble across a herd of 30 massive Roosevelt elk. They also have spotted bald eagles, cougars, black bears, deer and graceful, swooping peregrine falcons.

"Every morning when I get up and look out, I just thank God I'm here," Mary says. "It's just so natural and exhilarating. There's a very spiritual feel to it."

For recreation, the Kacys further the love of sailing they developed in Austin on forays at Devils Lake. A popular swimming, boating and picnicking spot, the 16,000-year-old expanse of cobalt-blue water drains into the ocean through the D River, which at only 200 yards in length is touted as the world's shortest river.

Lincoln City's small-town size has not limited amenities such as shopping. One of the region's largest factory-outlet sites, with more than 65 brand-name stores, including the only L.L. Bean outlet on the West Coast, greets bargain hunters. Although the area's reputation as an artist colony has faded some-what in recent years, galleries and antique stores number in the scores.

"I'm afraid the word is finally getting out about us," says LoriAnn Sheridan, executive director of the Lincoln City Chamber of Commerce, noting that the town has been listed in two books profiling America's most desirable places to live. "But every word of it is true."

Joyce and Robert "Scotty" Scotton decided to retire to Lincoln City after spending the first of their retirement years in the Fiji Islands as Peace Corps volunteers. Both Joyce, a university-level home education administrator, and Scotty, a retired police officer, say they have found full and happy lives in Lincoln City.

Among the special attractions for them is the ever-present power of the Pacific Ocean. They regularly meet and make new friends during long walks along the beach. Joyce loves the beach so much that she has developed a standard reply any time a tourist traipses into the Lincoln City Visitors and Convention Bureau, where she volunteers, and asks what do to first in town. "I say, 'Have you got sand between your toes yet?' I direct them straight to the beach, and I've never had a complaint from anyone yet."

As for Abe Lincoln, well, the late president did make it to Lincoln City after all — sort of, anyway. A statue of Lincoln astride a horse graces the heart of town. One of only three works of its kind in the world, the statue by renowned sculptor Anne Hyatt Huntington captures the period of Lincoln's life just after he had turned down the governorship of the wild Oregon Territory.

Huntington, who broke the mold after she cast the three works, donated the statue to Lincoln City in 1965, but only after securing several key agreements from city and state leaders. Among these was a requirement that Lincoln would always face west.

So while in life the president may not have personally followed a path leading to Lincoln City's perch on the Pacific Ocean, increasing numbers of retirees are making some history of their own by doing just that. And ending up being glad they did.●

Longboat Key, Florida

Retirees bask in the casual lifestyle of this Florida isle

By Jay Clarke

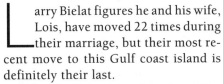

Larry Bielat figures he and his wife, Lois, have moved 22 times during their marriage, but their most recent move to this Gulf coast island is definitely their last.

"What do I like about Longboat? Everything," says Lois, 60. "I like the hot weather. I like the water. I like the people."

Larry, whose work as a college football coach took him to several Midwest schools during his career, agrees. "A friend got me interested in the area — said he figured living here would add 10 years to his life. So we vacationed here and really enjoyed it," says Larry, 62. The trip convinced the couple that this was where they wanted to spend their retirement years.

"The next summer we rented a place here and drove up and down the island, looking where we might want to buy," Larry says. They settled on the condominium complex where they now live, but it had no vacancies at the time. Two years later they learned that a couple living in the complex was thinking about moving into an assisted-living facility.

"I made a deal that they'd give me the first opportunity to buy when they were ready to go. A few months later, we moved in," Larry says.

Though retired, Larry still leads an active life. He maintains his contacts with Michigan State University, where he spent 10 years as a coach and alumni director. Every fall he returns to Lansing on weekends as a broadcast commentator for Michigan State home football games.

When he's not cruising the bay off Longboat Key in his 20-foot boat or dealing with problems as a member of the condominium board, he works with a neighbor on a new motivational book (he's written six others) that he says will be published soon.

"We love the area," he says. "We love boating and golf — there are 50 golf courses within a 45-minute drive. We

have access to airports in Sarasota and Tampa."

Another factor in the couple's decision to move to Longboat Key is its proximity to good medical facilities. Longboat is just a bridge removed from Sarasota and less than an hour from Tampa. "I have a cancer problem," Larry says, "but we have one of the top cancer centers at Moffitt Cancer Center in Tampa."

For other retirees like Art Golden, 77, it's the top-notch cultural scene in nearby Sarasota that convinces them to move to Longboat Key. "It's extremely good — amazing for a small town," says Art, who moved to Florida from Great Neck, NY. "We have the West Coast Symphony, the Asolo State Theater — there's just a lot going on. We wouldn't have come here without it."

A retired management consultant and corporate executive, Art says he doesn't miss New York. "We go north every year. What we do miss is the distance from our children. One is in Washington, one in Allentown (PA)."

But with the cultural connection cemented, making the decision to move to this elegant island was easy. "We'd been coming to Longboat for 10 or 15 years. And we wanted to be on the water," he says.

Longboat Key fit that criterion as well. Art and his wife, Eleanor, enjoyed boating in Great Neck, and they also have a boat here. And moving from the large house they maintained in Great Neck to the much smaller condo they occupy in Longboat also was no problem. "My wife wanted to downsize. Living here suits her fine."

Another relocated retiree, Annette Grishman, moved from Philadelphia to Longboat Key to satisfy a longtime dream of her husband's. "He loved Florida — always wanted to live in Florida," she says.

Planning retirement, they had looked at other Florida sites, notably Palm

Beach and Boca Raton on the state's east coast. "But I didn't like either one," Annette said. "When we came to Longboat, though, I said, 'Let's buy here.' And we did."

Like many others who have moved to Florida's west coast, she likes the friendliness of the people and the ease of living. "One thing I observed in this community is the openness to newcomers. People here are far more open, more receptive," she says.

Though she lived on Philadelphia's Society Hill for 35 years, she doesn't miss it. "I never felt rooted there," says the Chicago native. "When I go back to Philadelphia, I see great fear in the city. They (Philadelphians) are closed-off, not eager to meet new people."

To be fair, however, she does remember with some fondness the beat of the city in Philadelphia — its vitality and shopping. "It isn't a thing I miss much, though," she says. And while she likes cold weather, she doesn't miss that either, she says.

The Grishmans moved to Longboat Key seven years ago but, sadly, their idyll together lasted only a few years. Her husband died three years ago.

Nevertheless, Annette stays plugged into the pulse of the city. "I like to keep busy," she says. Annette serves on the board of Sarasota's symphony and opera, both of which she and her husband enjoyed. "Culturally, this is a marvelous community," she says.

She also plays golf and tennis and keeps in touch with her close-knit family. Her three children come en masse to visit her every June, "and each comes once during the winter," she notes.

While much of the growth of Longboat Key has come in recent years, another retiree, Dr. Robert Garber, 89, can remember when the island was far less populated. He first visited in 1961. "My wife and I loved it, so we kept coming back," he says.

When it came time to retire, the psychiatrist and his wife looked at a number of other sites, among them Phoenix, Tucson, Dallas, Mexico and San Diego. But they settled on familiar Longboat Key.

Like many other retirees, Robert found it easy to make friends here. Those friends sustained him when his wife died in 1987, and now, because an eye problem prevents him from driving, he relies on them to take him to his appointments. And after a lifetime of caring for people's minds, Robert has turned to caring for plants in retirement. At his condo complex, he has created and maintains a lovely garden with 27 rose bushes and 60 orchids.

At the opposite end of the age spectrum are Leo and Debbie Russo, who are unusual because they, too, are retired, but at a much younger age than most others. Leo, a New Jersey accountant, is just 45, and his wife is 43. They have no children.

The Russos vacationed in Longboat Key in 1995. "Once we crossed over the bridge, we fell in love with Longboat," Leo says.

They bought a condo two years later, and Leo says that "every day is para-

Longboat Key, FL

Population: 7,603 permanent, 12,000 seasonal. Median age of residents is 67.9 years.

Location: On Florida's Gulf coast, directly offshore from Sarasota. Longboat Key is 10.8 miles long and one-half to one mile wide, with elevation ranging from 3 to 18 feet.

Climate:

	High	Low
January	72	49
July	90	74

Average relative humidity: 88% in the morning, 58% in the afternoon

Rain: 53 inches per year.

Cost of living: Above average (specific index not available).

Average housing cost: Longboat Key is an upscale island. The average sale price in 2001 for a single-family home was $929,000. The average cost of a condominium was $529,000. Mix of housing is 40% owner-occupied, 6% renter-occupied, 44% for occasional use.

Sales tax: Longboat Key lies in two counties whose tax rates differ. The southern half of the island is in Sarasota County, where the sales tax is 7% and tax on transient rentals is 10%. The northern half of the island is in Manatee County, whose sales tax is 6.55% and tax on transient rentals is 9%.

Sales tax exemptions: Prescription drugs, groceries and medical services.

State income tax: None.

Estate tax: None, except the state's "pick-up" portion of the federal tax applicable to taxable estates of more than $1 million.

Inheritance tax: None.

Property tax: The town of Longboat Key's millage rate depends on which side of the island you live. In Manatee County, beachside property owners pay $19.995 per $1,000 of valuation while bayside owners pay $19.35. In Sarasota County, beachside owners pay $17.26 per $1,000, and bayside owners pay $16.62 per $1,000.

Homestead exemption: $25,000 off assessed value of primary, permanent residence.

Religion: Longboat Key has four houses of worship: an interfaith chapel, a Jewish synagogue and Roman Catholic and Episcopal churches.

Education: There are no schools on the key. Nearby is the University of South Florida (main campus in Tampa, New College campus in Sarasota). Community education courses are available at Longboat Center for the Arts and The Education Center.

Transportation: Longboat Key is connected to the mainland at the south end by New Pass Bridge to Sarasota, on the north by Longboat Pass Bridge to Bradenton. Public bus service connects the island to Sarasota. Sarasota/Bradenton International Airport is served by 13 airlines, some of them seasonally. Tampa International Airport, less than an hour away, is served by all major airlines year-round.

Health: The island has one medical center, but there are several hospitals in adjacent Bradenton and Sarasota: Blake Medical Center and Manatee Memorial Hospital in Bradenton, and Sarasota Memorial and Doctors Hospitals in Sarasota. Nearby Tampa has excellent medical facilities.

Housing options: Longboat Key has 1,701 single-family homes, 5,841 condos, 286 manufactured homes and 1,632 tourist units. Recent listings ranged from $84,500 to $5,470,000. A condo available recently for $525,000, just under the average condo price of $539,000, had two bedrooms and a pool on the waterfront. The Longboat Key Chamber of Commerce lists 17 member real estate agencies on the island with several more in Sarasota.

Visitor lodging: Major resorts are the Resort at Longboat Key Club, $175-$1,120, (800) 237-8821 or (941) 383-8821; The Colony, $195-$1,400, (800) 282-1138 or (941) 383-6464; the Longboat Key Hilton, $119-$410, (941) 383-2451 or (800) 282-3046; and the Longboat Key Holiday Inn, $143-$260, (800) 465-4436. There are also a number of smaller properties, among them the Silver Beach Resort, $70-$199, (941) 383-2434, and the Sea Grape Inn, $136-$248, (941) 383-2105. Vacation homes and condos also are available; one rental agent is Florida Vacation Accommodations, (800) 237-9505 or (941) 383-9505. Many lodgings can be rented by the week or month, and some properties impose minimum stays in season.

Information: Longboat Key Chamber of Commerce, 6854 Gulf of Mexico Drive, Longboat Key, FL 34228, (941) 383-2466 or www.longboatkey chamber.com.

dise." He also praises the island's casual lifestyle. "I've had a suit on only twice in the past five years," Leo says. He and Debbie walk the beach, do a little fishing and "wind down." He still does some accounting work for an old client.

Though Longboat Key is an elegant island, Leo says he finds the cost of living about the same as in New Jersey. The property taxes are a lot less, he says, but that is partly because he has downscaled his lifestyle.

Larry Bielat also finds no difference in the cost of living relative to his former home. "In a good restaurant, dinner for four may cost $125, the same as in Michigan," he says. Art Golden has found property taxes less here but, again, that's because of downsizing. "We had a big house in Great Neck," he says. The lack of a state income tax in Florida also helps, he says.

The island's popularity can cause some problems, though. Robert Garber can remember when Longboat Key was quiet and pristine. With the array of luxury condominiums and designer mansions that have risen in recent years, he admits, the island today is "pretty crowded — but that comes with growth. You learn to tolerate it."

Larry agrees. "From December to Easter, the traffic is extremely heavy. So you learn when to shop and when to get a haircut, and you stay off the road from 4 to 6 p.m.;" he says.

But what makes living on Longboat Key easy is that it is remarkably self-contained. Residents seldom need to leave the island. "We have just about all the facilities you need on the island — a grocery, two drug stores, a liquor store, plenty of golf and tennis," Robert says. The cultural venues are off-island, as are the movie theaters.

And island shoppers have money-saving options: They can make their big purchases in Bradenton near the north end of the island, where the sales tax is less because it is in Manatee County. Or they can hang it all and head south to adjacent St. Armands Key, home of elegant boutiques taxed at Sarasota County's higher rate.

Another attraction is that crime is minimal on Longboat Key. "The funniest reading we have every week is Cop's Corner, the police blotter report in the local newspaper," Larry says. The paper also keeps a running tally of police reports, among which are such gems are "dead turtles, 1; golf cart joyrides, 1; rude in restaurant, 1; picking toenails, 1; strange noises, 2; bizarre messages, 2; and loose iguanas, 0."

With problems rarely more serious than these, it's no wonder that many retirees consider life on Longboat a dream fulfilled.●

Maryville, Tennessee

Smoky Mountains town in eastern Tennessee attracts nature-loving retirees

By Richard L. Fox

Tucked in the foothills of eastern Tennessee's Smoky Mountains, Maryville's greatest asset is its enviable location.

Far from busy interstate highways and crowded urban centers, modern-day worries are forgotten — at least temporarily — when one is greeted daily by panoramic vistas of rolling, velvety slopes. A slower pace, small liberal arts college and abundance of outdoor recreation further add to the appeal of this quiet town of 23,120.

Maryville, the seat and geographical center of Blount County, cherishes its Smoky Mountains connection. Spring festivals celebrate regional heritage, wildlife and crafts, and in fall, residents and tourists alike take delight in a spectacular show of colorful foliage.

Many retirees, primarily attracted by the beauty of the mountains and lakes, live in rural planned developments outside Maryville and rely on the town for cultural, educational and social amenities.

"We love the isolation. We have bears, wild turkeys, deer and foxes roaming the area, and we live within walking distance of some wonderful hiking trails in the Great Smokies," says Bob Tiebout (pronounced Te-BOO). He and his wife, Lil, moved 22 times during his military career before settling in a gated community near Maryville in June 1994.

The Tiebouts began their search for a retirement town with a long list of requirements. "We wanted a planned community with plenty of space and facilities for outdoor recreation. We wanted a college town, quick access to air travel, and proximity to a military PX and medical facility. We got all of that — and a lot more," says Bob, 58.

The area's low cost of living and taxes that are among the lowest in the country were big incentives in their choice. "After spending our last two service years in Washington, DC, we were looking for economy," says Bob. "It's very economical here. Property taxes and utilities are very, very reasonable."

The Tiebouts found a home at Laurel Valley Country Club in Townsend. A scenic 16-mile drive south of Maryville, the 1,600-acre planned residential development backs up to Great Smoky Mountains National Park. There are approximately 360-370 homesites ranging in size from quarter-acre lots to 12-acre tracts. To date, nearly 250 homes have been constructed, with prices ranging from $120,000 to $1 million.

Laurel Valley offers a clubhouse, pool, restaurant and 18-hole golf course. Residents joke that the manned security gates are in place to keep out bears rather than criminals.

Opportunities for recreational activities abound throughout Blount County. Bicycling along lightly traveled roads is such a popular sport that the chamber of commerce offers a brochure with detailed descriptions of routes covering more than 100 miles.

For hiking, there are more than 125 miles of designated trails, including Greenbelt Park's two-mile lighted fitness trail and exercise course in the heart of Maryville.

Lakes Fort Loudoun, Tellico and Chilhowee and the Tennessee and Little Tennessee rivers form a semicircle to the west of Maryville. Sailboats, canoes, houseboats and cruisers ply these waters in search of fish, waterfowl and spectacular scenery.

To the south there is white-water rafting on the Nantahala and Ocoee rivers, and about 40 miles to the east is the Ober Gatlinburg Ski Resort.

Dr. Chuck and Jane Gariety vacationed in the Smoky Mountains for 15 years before moving permanently in 1992. "The mountains, climate and relaxed lifestyle that brought us here as vacationers keep us here as residents," says Jane, 64.

Formerly residents of Piqua, OH, the Garietys first bought property on Cherokee Lake northeast of Knoxville. After two years, the Garietys felt they had not formed strong attachments to that area. They also found that the glistening lake waters of summer nearly disappeared in winter when the Tennessee Valley Authority, which manages the lake, lowered the water level by 40 feet.

"If we had it to do over we would have moved here first," says Jane.

Like the Tiebouts, the Garietys moved to Laurel Oaks and appreciate its proximity to the national park. Chuck, 68, is a self-described do-it-yourselfer who enjoys woodworking and gardening. He took up golf after retirement and now lists it as his favorite recreational activity. Both Chuck and Jane love the mountainous landscape and the easy accessibility to area lakes.

As a bonus to Maryville's natural abundance, the urban trappings of several major cities are readily available. Travel from downtown Maryville to Knoxville is a quick 20 miles on the Pellissippi Parkway. Chattanooga is about 100 miles to the southwest, and Nashville is 194 miles west. McGhee Tyson Airport, the metropolitan Knoxville facility with more than 100 scheduled daily flights, is minutes away by car.

Maryville is off the major interstate highways, preventing heavy traffic from flowing through town. (From downtown Maryville, it is 17 miles to Interstate 40 and 22 miles to Interstate 75.) This has helped Maryville retain a peaceful and safe atmosphere, something retirees often cite as a factor in their decision to move here.

"We wanted to be close to a large

city, but far enough away not to be caught up in the traffic, crowds and crime," says Ed Crick.

Originally from Fort Washington, MD, Ed and his wife, Faye, ended a 10-year search for the right retirement town when they discovered Maryville. "We had looked all the way from Florida to Pennsylvania but couldn't find what we were looking for," explains Ed, 65, a retired federal auditor. "We visited Maryville for the first time in January 1993, left for two weeks, and came back and bought a lot. We've never second-guessed our decision."

Ed and Faye settled in Royal Oaks Country Club, a gatehouse-secure golf community within Maryville city limits. "It was a fairly new community with just 50 or 60 families at the time. We had an opportunity to get in on the ground floor and meet people as they came in. It now has around 160 households — mostly retired — and we know everyone who lives here," Ed says.

Faye, a former schoolteacher, serves on the official welcoming committee for Royal Oaks, and Ed is treasurer and on the board of directors for the property owners association. Ed also serves as a counselor for SCORE (Service Corps of Retired Executives), which advises small businesses. He does not plan to take on more activities any time soon: "I don't want to get so involved I don't have time for golf."

Maryville, TN

Population: 23,120 in Maryville, 105,823 in Blount County.

Location: In southeast Tennessee at an elevation of about 1,000 feet, within view of the Appalachian Mountains and Great Smoky Mountains National Park.

Climate:

	High	Low
January	47	30
July	87	68

Average relative humidity: 59%

Rain: 47 inches. **Snow:** 12 inches.

Cost of living: Below average (specific index not available).

Average housing cost: Approximately $130,000, according to the Blount County Chamber of Commerce.

Sales tax: 8.25%

Sales tax exemptions: Prescription drugs, professional services, hearing aids, prosthetic devices.

State income tax: None on earned income, but there is a state tax of 6% on interest and dividend income from certain stocks, bonds and long-term notes and mortgages. Interest from CDs, savings accounts and federal, state or local government bonds is exempt.

Income tax exemptions: Social Security benefits and private and government retirement pensions are exempt. The first $1,250 ($2,500 on a joint return) of taxable income is exempt, and individuals 65 or older with total annual income of $16,200 or less ($27,000 for joint filers) are exempt from the tax.

Intangibles tax: None.

Estate tax: None, except the state's "pick-up" portion of the federal tax, applicable to taxable estates of more than $1 million.

Inheritance tax: From 5.5% to 9.5%, based on amount of inheritance; spouse normally exempt. If under $700,000, there is no tax.

Property tax: $21.50 per $1,000 of assessed value, with homes assessed at 25% of market value. Yearly tax on a $130,000 home is about $699.

Homestead exemption: A reduced rate is available to homeowners age 65 and older.

Religion: There are 219 Protestant and two Catholic churches in Blount County.

Education: Maryville College is a liberal arts institution offering baccalaureate degrees in 33 majors. Pellissippi State Technical Community College has a campus in Blount County, and the University of Tennessee in Knoxville is about 30 minutes away.

Transportation: McGhee Tyson Airport (also called Metropolitan Knoxville Airport), only minutes from downtown Maryville, is served by eight major carriers and five commuter airlines with 120 scheduled flights daily.

Health: Blount Memorial Hospital is a 304-bed, acute-care facility with a trauma center equipped for all medical emergencies except neurological and cardiac surgery. Eight hospitals and medical centers in Knoxville include the University of Tennessee Medical Center, a full-service facility with a trauma center and complete range of specialties.

Housing options: Listings include a new two-bedroom, two-bath home in **Laurel Valley Country Club**, (865) 445-3300, for $169,900; a two-bedroom, two-bath log cabin in a rural neighborhood for $124,500; and new three-bedroom, two-bath homes for $60,900 and up in **Grand Vista**, a subdivision just outside city limits. **Royal Oaks Country Club**, (865) 984-2882, offers golf villas and custom single-family homes starting at $150,000 and up. **Rarity Bay**, (423) 884-3000, a 960-acre gated community southwest of Maryville on Lake Tellico, wooded homesites start at $60,000, golf course lots start at $75,000, and homesites on the waterfront are priced up to $350,000.

Visitor lodging: Rates at Airport Hilton-Alcoa are $79-$149, depending on the season, (423) 970-4300. Rates at Hampton Inn-Townsend are $50-$100 with continental breakfast, (865) 448-9000. The Inn at Blackberry Farm, a 1,100-acre retreat, provides three meals daily and use of all amenities for $395-$895, depending on season, per couple, per day, (865) 984-8166. Rustic cabins in secluded mountain settings are available in a wide range of prices; call the Smoky Mountains Visitors Bureau, (800) 525-6834.

Information: Blount County Chamber of Commerce, 201 S. Washington St., Maryville, TN 37804-5728, (865) 983-2241 or www.chamber.blount.tn.us.

Ed and Faye both took up golf soon after moving to Royal Oaks and say it is their favorite hobby. The community boasts two of the county's seven 18-hole golf courses and has single-family homes and golf villas situated around the greens. Villas start at 1,600 square feet and are priced from approximately $150,000. Custom homes on a lake, in the woods or on the golf course run about $150,000-$500,000.

There are housing options in Maryville for those not looking for gated, planned communities. New three-bedroom homes in town with 1,200-1,500 square feet are available for $72,900 to $89,900, while five-acre tracts in the suburbs can be purchased for $15,000 to $20,000.

A good hospital was high on the list of amenities Ed Crick sought in a retirement town. Health-care needs are met by 128 medical doctors and 464 registered nurses practicing in 304-bed Blount County Memorial Hospital. The hospital is equipped for all medical emergencies except neurological and cardiac surgery. In Knoxville there are more than 2,500 practitioners of every medical specialty and subspecialty.

Bob Tiebout, who used the facilities at famed Bethesda Naval Hospital while stationed in Washington, DC, is content with the local services. "We live within 20 minutes of Blount County Memorial and have access to Fort Sanders Regional Medical Center in Knoxville. We are more than satisfied with the health-care options in this area."

In the center of town stands the quiet, tree-lined campus of Maryville College. The liberal arts school with a Presbyterian Church connection was founded in 1819 and provided a way out of the mountains for many young people. Now it's one of the beacons attracting retirees to these mountains.

The 370-acre campus has 20 major buildings, including several listed on the National Register of Historic Places. With an enrollment of just 850, this small college contributes to the town's quality of life without dominating its pace and rhythms. The doors of its library are open to residents for study and browsing. Beautiful campus paths and serene wooded trails, easily accessible from downtown, are favorites among residents for walking, hiking and running.

The college's 1,200-seat Wilson Chapel and 400-seat Maryville College Playhouse theater offer orchestral and choral concerts and theatrical productions. Art gallery exhibits, the school's Appalachian Ballet Company and Division III NCAA athletic events add to the mix of activities available to the community through the college. There's also a series of non-credit courses designed for seniors.

The musically talented can toot their own horns by trying out for the Maryville-Alcoa College Community Orchestra. Made up of college musicians and residents of Maryville and nearby Alcoa, the orchestra performs six concerts a year.

Festivals are among the favorite rites of spring and fall in Maryville, and all conspire to foster an appreciation of the great outdoors. In April, the Appalachian Wildflower Celebration features garden tours, bird-watching walks, wildflower hikes and wildlife programs. At the end of the month, the eight-day Townsend in the Smokies Spring Festival offers food, music and the natural beauty of the Great Smoky Mountains. The Autumn Harvest Crafts Fair in October entertains the crowds who come to see the changing of colors that ushers in the fall season.

Civic organizations, many sponsored by the chamber of commerce, make an impact on the social, cultural and economic life of Maryville. Beautiful Blount, a group involved in beautification projects, recycling and litter education, and Blount County Partnership, a cooperative effort of four organizations, are among two dozen groups in town that work toward community improvement. Retirees work alongside civic leaders to recruit new industry, promote tourism, support education and develop cultural and philanthropic projects.

Maryville retirees find little to complain about. A few wish for better shopping and dining options, adding that Blount County is a "dry" county.

And though Bob Tiebout still misses the "camaraderie, and fervor of political drama" of military life in Washington, DC, he plans to stay in east Tennessee for the nature and the outdoor lifestyle he's come to enjoy.

"Every season has its own character, and all are beautiful," says Bob. ●

Mountain Home, Arkansas

Arkansas Ozarks reel in residents who love the lakes and quiet life

By Brenda Blagg

Lakes loaded with lunker bass, rivers teeming with trout and a feeling of peace and security — these are the lures to Mountain Home, an Arkansas haven for retirees seeking life at a slower pace.

As one man put it, this is not the place for people who want the hustle and bustle of big-city life. Instead, retirees find "country quiet" and "breathtaking scenery" in the Ozark Mountains.

Many retirees are first hooked on the region when they come for family vacations, centered around fishing, boating and other water sports on scenic rivers and the area's twin lakes, Norfork and Bull Shoals.

Located in north-central Arkansas near the Missouri border, Mountain Home has a little over 11,012 residents and is the seat of Baxter County, which touts itself as "a good place to grow up and a good place to wind down." The county claims a population of more than 38,386 citizens now, with one of three citizens age 64 or older.

Floyd Cannedy, 69, and his wife, Iola, 65, both originally from the Midwest, moved to Mountain Home in 1994 from Hattiesburg, MS. For a couple of years, they had looked at possible retirement places, including some in Florida. Avid campers, they were in Branson, MO, when a camping buddy suggested they look at Mountain Home, less than 100 miles away.

"We just fell in love with the place," says Iola, explaining that their first stop was the local Presbyterian church. They knew "not a soul" in the town, but on that first Sunday were invited to join an impromptu group of 25 people for lunch.

"That's an every-Sunday occurrence," adds Floyd, noting that restaurants are accustomed to throwing tables together for unscheduled gatherings.

The friendliness and that first "open-arms welcome" convinced them that moving to Mountain Home was "the thing to do," says Floyd, who was in the insurance business.

The only thing they would do differently is "just move here quicker," says Iola, noting a popular bumper sticker that says: "We weren't raised in Mountain Home but we got here as fast as we could."

The Cannedys say the cost of living is a trade-off, with some things higher than in Mississippi and some lower; both states are known for low living costs compared to other areas. Overall, the Cannedys say it's costing them less to live in retirement especially since life is so casual in Mountain Home.

"Church is about the only place you see people dressed up," Floyd says.

With no relatives in town, the Cannedys and other retirees "buddy with each other," Floyd says. He describes Mountain Home as "a great domino-playing town" with a wide range of activities for seniors, including a "very lively" senior center.

The first time the Cannedys left town on one of their camping trips, they returned to find their lawn had been mowed. They extend the same courtesy to their neighbors now. "Everybody just kind of looks after each other...it's wonderful to know people care," says Floyd.

The Cannedys have few complaints or cautions for others who might move to Mountain Home. Some areas of town have drainage problems and utility service is interrupted in bad weather, they say. Summer brings tourists and increased traffic, but a bypass has helped alleviate traffic problems. Otherwise, says Iola, "It's a wonderful place to live."

Mountain Home looks like many small Southern towns. Once centered around a courthouse square, development has shifted to highways that slice through the town, stretching either to the twin lakes or to transportation corridors. While the commercial strips look like almost any other town, the historic courthouse and older homes and buildings lend some distinct character.

Vernon Wolfram, 70, and his wife, Vivian, 68, moved south from their Detroit-area home in 1990, fulfilling a promise made when they married in 1948. At the time they both lived in St. Louis, his hometown, but Vivian had spent part of her youth in Fort Smith, AR. She exacted a promise from Vernon that they would return to Arkansas when they retired.

"I told Vern it would be in Arkansas someplace — we just had to find where," she says.

When retirement time came, they narrowed the search to three towns — Bella Vista, Rogers and Mountain Home, all in northern Arkansas. The couple spent a week in each, touring and looking at prospective homes.

On the last of their weeklong outings, the only time they visited Mountain Home before their move, the Wolframs shot video of a three-bedroom house they liked. Back in Michigan, they looked at the video night after night, then called the real estate agent to cut a deal on their "perfect" retirement home.

Vivian says, "The books we read led us to Mountain Home — for economy, for the beauty of the land." And "for (low) taxes," Vern adds.

"When we came and found out how great the people were and we found this house in this area," Vivian says, "we knew it was right."

Vern, a former plant manager for Ford Motor Co., actually retired twice. After almost 30 years with Ford, he took an early retirement but soon went to work for a Ford supplier and worked another 10 years. The couple downsized their lives, moving three times in the Detroit area as their four children completed their education and left home.

"It took us 10 years to get here," says Vivian.

Their home, in a wooded subdivision near Lake Norfork, sits on a "lot and a half," which is large enough to accommodate a big vegetable garden, one of Vern's passions. The site is well away from what Vivian calls the "busy-ness" of town, yet Vern says the neighborhood has plenty of action. Anytime he's outside, he discovers he must wave to everyone who drives by – if he doesn't they'll stop to see if he's OK.

Vern speaks of a sense of community that stretches down the block and to the next street, not just to the next house or two as in his Michigan experience. When the Wolframs moved in, the neighbors welcomed them with food; now the Wolframs do the same for others moving into the fast-growing subdivision.

They had planned to learn to fish when they got to Mountain Home, but they haven't had time. Both are busy volunteers, active in their church and pursuing hobbies in writing and crafts. Vivian has published three compilations of recipes and a collection of her thoughts on life. They also are in a boating club, one of many area organizations that match residents with common interests from politics to pansies, square dancing to china painting.

Vern says the most pleasant surprise in their move was paying taxes the first time. Taxes on the house, two cars and a boat, he says, were just $600.

The Wolframs' one-level home, originally purchased for $75,000 six years ago, is valued at $115,000 now, but it is definitely not for sale. They don't miss the stairs or the snow and ice they had in Michigan.

Mountain Home does get snow, but it usually doesn't last long.

Four distinct seasons and the opportunity to play golf and fish year-round were among the draws for Mid-

Mountain Home, AR

Population: 11,012 in town, 38,386 in Baxter County.

Location: In the Ozark Mountains of north-central Arkansas, 25 miles south of the Missouri border.

Climate:

	High	Low
January	46	24
July	91	67

Average relative humidity: 55%

Rain: 42 inches.

Snow: 8 inches.

Mild climate with four distinct seasons. Outdoor activities are possible most of the year. Snowfalls are usually light and melt quickly.

Cost of living: Below average (specific index not available).

Average housing cost: $90,614. Most homes under 10 years old in the area run $80,000-$120,000.

Sales tax: 7.125%

Sales tax exemptions: Medical/professional services and prescription drugs.

State income tax: For married couples filing jointly and single filers, graduated from 1% of taxable income up to $3,199 to 7% on amounts over $26,700.

Income tax exemptions: Social Security benefits and up to $6,000 on most public and private pensions is exempt.

Intangibles tax: None.

Estate tax: None, except the state's "pick-up" portion of the federal tax, applicable to taxable estates or more than $1 million.

Inheritance tax: None.

Property tax: In Mountain Home, $37.41 per $1,000 of assessed value, with homes assessed at 20 percent of market value. Yearly tax on a $90,614 home is $678. Also, specified personal property, including vehicles, livestock and farm equipment, is subject to tax at the same rate as homes.

Homestead exemption: A tax refund of up to $300 is available to homeowners. In addition, homeowners age 65 or older may have the value of their home frozen.

Religion: About 50 churches represent a wide range of denominations.

Education: Arkansas State University-Mountain Home has two-year university classes and occupational, technical and vocational programs. Seniors may attend credit courses tuition-free on a space-available basis.

Transportation: There is no local bus service. Baxter County Regional Airport has commuter service to St. Louis and Dallas, and there's long-distance bus service.

Health: Baxter County Regional Medical Center in Mountain Home has 372 beds, more than 100 specialized physicians and 24-hour emergency room service. Other features include a Radiation Therapy Institute, cardiac-care unit and physical therapy unit.

Housing options: A variety of housing is available in town, in nearby communities and on the lakes and rivers. There are no planned retirement communities. Areas popular with retirees include Village Green and Indian Creek, older neighborhoods in town; and High Ridge, a development at nearby Lakeview, where new homes begin at $92,000-$99,000. There also are independent-living facilities for seniors and six nursing homes.

Visitor lodging: Baxter Inn, (870) 425-5101, $50 for a double. Best Western Carriage Inn, (870) 425-6001, $65 for a double. Lakeside resorts are plentiful for around $500 a week, depending on amenities.

Information: Mountain Home Area Chamber of Commerce, P.O. Box 488, Mountain Home, AR 72653, (800) 822-3536 or www.mtnhomechamber.com.

westerners Joy and Merrill Eastman, both 69, who relocated from the Kansas City suburb of Overland Park, KS, in 1989. They settled in a community called Midway, on Route 5 midway between Mountain Home and Bull Shoals Lake.

They first planned to retire to Florida and had land there but "didn't want to fight the traffic in snowbird season," says Merrill, who had been general chairman for a railroad union.

A lower cost of living was a big factor in the Eastmans' choice of the area — including lower fees for golf, which Merrill enjoys, along with fishing. He keeps his boat in the water all year and considers a perfect day to be one in which he can fish half the day and golf the rest, or vice versa.

Joy misses the shopping opportunities they had in Kansas City and in Chicago, where they lived earlier. Mountain Home has no large malls so residents routinely make one-day outings to Springfield or Branson, MO, to shop and enjoy a wider range of entertainment.

Eugene Burroughs, 66, came home to Arkansas, bringing his wife Shirley, 45, and three youngest sons to Mountain Home after 14 years in California where he was a farm manager in the San Joaquin Valley.

"He wanted to fish. That was the main thing," says Shirley.

Eugene, who grew up in eastern Arkansas, had been thinking seriously about retiring for several years before settling on Mountain Home. Eugene always was provided a home by the farm management company, but he knew he wanted to buy his own place when he retired. "I started 20 years ago to plan for it," he says.

The Burroughs family moved in early 1995, and it's taking time for Shirley to adjust to being away from family in California, Nevada and Utah. She began volunteering at the local hospital and has made friends quickly.

Shirley and other retirees are proud of the town's medical services, the Baxter County Regional Hospital, a 372-bed facility with more than 100 active staff physicians.

Eugene considers Mountain Home a good choice for his retirement but warns those who need jobs that the wages are low. What he likes least about the place is that his sons "will have to leave here to go to work."

Elena and Victor Pollo moved from Chicago to Mountain Home more than 23 years ago. Both worked — he in watch and clock repair and she as executive secretary at Railway Express — but a heart problem soon forced Victor's early retirement. Now in their 80s, Elena and Victor are both retired but lead active lives.

Midwesterners make up a large portion of the retirees who have moved into the area. So many are from the Windy City itself that Mountain Home often is called "Little Chicago." The number of Illinois transplants in Baxter County is so high that the Mountain Home post office opens a special window to handle their business during the holidays.

Elena still misses the large department stores she rushed through to catch the commuter trains in Chicago, but she has no desire to go back to Chicago.

"You've got to understand this is different from a big city," says Elena. "It takes at least a year to make an adjustment."

Those who come here from urban areas will quickly note a lack of ethnic diversity in the community.

Like so many others, the Pollos connected with Mountain Home because of the fishing. Victor got his first glimpse of the region on a fishing trip years ago with friends. Later, when the couple visited, they happened onto what would become their retirement home.

In all their years in Mountain Home, the Pollos never considered a different house or a different town for retirement.●

Mount Dora, Florida

A century-old Florida town evokes New England charm

By Richard L. Fox

Scenic meandering pathways lead from downtown Mount Dora to the calm, blue waters of beautiful six-mile-long Lake Dora. For boat owners, the lake offers pleasant cruising waters as well as a popular shortcut to the city center from lakeside homes. It is connected by the Dora Canal to a chain of lakes leading to the St. Johns River and ultimately to the Atlantic Ocean, providing seagoing access that few inland towns can offer.

Bob and Mary Anderson had lived in rural Virginia 25 years when they discovered the small-town charm, convenience and historical legacy of Mount Dora. "We had built a room and porch on our house and planned to stay in Rockville," says Bob, 70. But then the couple planned a trip to Florida to help a neighbor who was moving in retirement, and Mary happened to see a newspaper article about Mount Dora.

"So we stopped by just for the fun of it, checked into Lakeside Inn, ordered a cocktail and watched the sunset over Lake Dora," says Bob, who retired from the office supplies industry. "The next day we drove home, sold our house and moved to Mount Dora."

Mount Dora — named for its 184-foot elevation in the generally flat Florida terrain — is an enchanting lakeside town of 9,418 residents, located 25 miles northwest of Orlando. It is characterized by its wide brick sidewalks, colorful outdoor cafes, and crafts and antique shops. Six pretty tree-shaded parks dot the town's landscape, and they are especially attractive to seniors who enjoy tennis, shuffleboard and lawn bowling. The Mount Dora Lawn Bowling Club is one of the largest in the United States, with more than 300 members hosting local and regional competitions.

"We moved here because it was small, 'antiquish,' and we liked the preservation, old houses, the historical aspects," says Mary, 68. Mount Dora predates a rail line that opened in 1887, bringing passengers and freight to a town that had two general stores, three hotels, two churches, a drug store and a carriage factory.

"It has a nice, relaxed atmosphere and provides great access to the beaches, Disney World and Miami," adds Mary, who worked for Signet Bank in Richmond. Bob also likes the convenience of living in town, even a small one like Mount Dora. "We had never lived in a city and were tired of going 15 miles to buy groceries, attend church and enjoy city amenities," he says.

They wasted no time getting actively involved in the social and civic opportunities of their new home. "We joined everything in sight," Mary laughs. Bob joined the chamber of commerce and serves on the membership committee, and he was appointed to the city's historic preservation board. He also is on the board of trustees of the United Methodist Church. "You have to be active in civic affairs to enjoy retirement here," he says.

The relatively recent discovery by retirees and young working families of this quiet haven just minutes from Greater Orlando has had its impact on Mount Dora's population and real estate prices. The 1990 census recorded an 11 percent increase in population in the 1980s, from 6,483 to 7,196 residents. Today's count is approaching 10,000, roughly a 25 percent increase in the last 10 years. Like many retirees who were drawn to the town by its small-town atmosphere, newcomer Ed Jones says in resignation, "I hate to see it grow."

Ed and Betty Jones, from Wilmington, DE, had lived in Vero Beach and Clearwater during their working lives but sought something smaller for their retirement. "The towns had grown so much that they had lost the small-town atmosphere we were looking for," says Betty, who was in sales prior to retirement. "We found it in Mount Dora, a

place where we felt we could belong. It has lots of clubs and organizations, a nice library and very friendly people."

Waterfront housing is available along Lake Dora and on smaller lakes within a mile of the city. The quiet, tree-lined streets adjacent to downtown, resplendent with beautifully restored Victorian homes, churches and landmark commercial buildings, are popular with those who savor the history of this century-old town and the convenience of living within walking distance of the village center. Several master-planned developments offer affordable, active lifestyles just a few minutes from downtown.

In the early 1990s, Mount Dora's homes sold for $50,000 to $300,000, with a median price of $80,400, according to local appraisers. The current average price of homes sold is $130,000, says Chuck Cox, broker-owner of Baker Street Realty. Several attractive condominium and townhouse developments recently offered homes for $70,000 to $190,000. Homes within walking distance of downtown sell for $80,000 to $275,000, while most lakeshore homes are priced from $175,000 to $400,000 and up. The Country Club of Mount Dora, a master-planned golf course development just minutes from downtown, has fairway homes and villas priced from the $150,000s to the lower $500,000s.

The Andersons chose a home built in 1955 on one of the smaller lakes in northwest Mount Dora, about a mile from downtown. Neighbors include residents in their 70s and 80s and young couples with children. Extensive renovations to the Andersons' home have paid off in substantial appreciation of their investment, but Bob doesn't like paying both city and county taxes — something he didn't have to do while living in rural Virginia. However, Mary claims that Virginia "had as many hidden taxes and 'gotchas' as Florida."

Though she wouldn't move "unless we win the lottery," Mary says she sometimes misses the peace and quiet of their home in rural Virginia. "Young people with loud car stereos can be a real nuisance," she says of life in Florida.

The Joneses also found a neighborhood they liked. "One reason we built in the Country Club of Mount Dora was its excellent tennis facilities," says Ed, 65, a retired engineering designer and one-time avid tennis player. Betty, also 65, enjoys the quiet, safe environment of her neighborhood, walks five days a week and spends her spare time volunteering at the chamber of commerce and the arts festival.

"There's always something going on downtown," adds Ed. Two dozen restaurants, mostly located within a six-block downtown area, range from casual sidewalk cafes and English-style tearooms to cozy, candlelit dining rooms with an international flair. These same streets harbor a dozen antiques and collectibles shops, and there's an annual Downtown Antique Extravaganza. Renninger's Twin Markets, just outside town on U.S. Highway 441, sponsors the Antique Extravaganza in January, February and November, with more than 1,500 dealers participating.

In fact, Mount Dora leads the state as the home of major festivals. The 24th annual February Fine Arts Festival at-

tracted almost 300,000 visitors, and the April Spring Festival, a celebration of music and literature, always packs the 300-seat Ice House Theatre, the 700-seat community building and every hotel in the area. A bicycle festival is the largest and oldest cycling event in the country, bringing hundreds of cyclists from across the nation in early October. Later that month, an annual juried craft fair displays the talents of some 250 skilled artisans, drawing about 150,000 visitors.

John and Billie Keenon visited popular retirement towns in six states before settling on Mount Dora. Both in their mid-60s, they had lived in Little Rock, AR, for six years when they read about

Mount Dora, FL

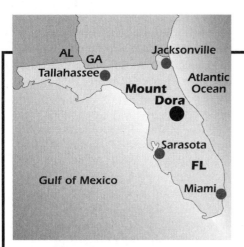

Population: 9,418
Location: In Central Florida, 25 miles northwest of Orlando.

Climate: High   Low
January   72   49
July   92   73

Average relative humidity: 85%
Rain: 54 inches.
Cost of living: Below average (specific index not available).
Average housing cost: $130,000
Sales tax: 7%
Sales tax exemptions: Prescription drugs, groceries and most services.
State income tax: None.
Intangibles tax: Assessed on stocks, bonds and other assets. Tax rate is $1 per $1,000 in assets. The first $20,000 in assets is exempt for individuals. For couples filing jointly, the first $40,000 is exempt. Those who owe less than $60 need not pay.
Estate tax: None, except the state's "pick-up" portion of the federal tax,

applicable to taxable of more than $1 million.
Property tax: The combined city-county tax rate is $21.99 per $1,000 of assessed value, with homes assessed at 100% of market value. The annual tax on a $130,000 home, with exemption noted below, is $2,309.
Homestead exemption: First $25,000 of assessed value on a primary, permanent residence.
Religion: One Catholic and 27 Protestant churches.
Education: There are no college or university campuses in Mount Dora. Lake Sumter Community College in nearby Leesburg offers two-year associate of arts and sciences degrees, plus many continuing-education and noncredit courses. Lake County Vo-Tech in nearby Eustis offers vocational training and a school of cosmetology.
Transportation: Orlando International and Daytona Beach Regional airports are approximately 60 minutes from Mount Dora. Amtrak's East Coast auto-train stops in Sanford, 20 miles east of Mount Dora.
Health: Florida Hospital Waterman, five miles north in Eustis, is a full-service facility with 182 beds, 24-hour emergency room and 195 physicians on staff. Leesburg Regional Medical Center, 25 miles away, has 414 beds and serves a three-county area.

Housing options: Newcomers have a choice of lakeside and lake-view single-family homes, condominiums and townhouses, many within a short walking distance of downtown, priced from $80,000 to $300,000. In-town historic and contemporary homes sell for $100,000 to $200,000. At the **Country Club of Mount Dora**, (800) 213-6132, fairway homes and villas are priced from $150,000 to the lower $500,000s. **Waterman Village**, (352) 383-0051, a 50-acre rental retirement community, has about 300 independent-living villas, 80 assisted-living units and a 120-bed nursing home. An additional 100 independent-living units have been completed. Prices range from $2,000-$4,500 a month for one person (add $500 for a second person), and include one meal a day, weekly housekeeping, security, scheduled transportation, emergency response system and events in the activities center.
Visitor lodging: Options include Lakeside Inn, $105-$235, (800) 556-5016 or (352) 383-4101, and Mount Dora Historic Inn, a restored 19th-century bed-and-breakfast inn located downtown, $100-$145, (800) 927-6344.
Information: Mount Dora Area Chamber of Commerce, 341 N. Alexander St., Mount Dora, FL 32757, (352) 383-2165 or www.mt-dora.com.

Mount Dora in *Where to Retire* magazine and decided to pay it a visit.

"Neither of us ever expected we would retire to Florida, but we fell in love with Mount Dora at first sight," Billie says. "And the people — real quality people — are so interested in the betterment of the community."

John, who spent his working years in the financial services industry, says he likes the wide assortment of activities and opportunities for participating in the community. He has served on the board of the Center for the Arts, the Mount Dora Chamber of Commerce and the Country Club of Mount Dora homeowners' association. "And I enjoy the concerts, Ice House Theatre performances and volunteering at the chamber of commerce," he says. His favorite recreational activities include golfing, boating and surfing the Internet.

"I play bridge, volunteer at the chamber, attend city council meetings and walk the dog," his wife, Billie, says. They describe their 2,200-square-foot contemporary home as light and airy with high ceilings. John feels it is appreciating in value. "They are still building and selling new homes, so it is likely prices are going up," he says.

Cost of living has not been a problem, all three couples say, agreeing that taxes in general are lower than in their previous home states. But there are plenty of opportunities to spend money, they say, citing the multitude of shopping, dining and entertainment outlets in the Greater Orlando area.

"In reality, the cost of living here is very reasonable," John Keenon says. "We still live the same lifestyle but eat out a lot more now." As for the Andersons, they credit financial planning with providing adequate income for their carefree retirement, along with one additional step taken some years ago. "We quit feeding our children money," Bob says with a laugh.

Although Mount Dora is sometimes called "New England of the South," thanks in part to some Victorian mansions near the downtown antiques district, the town is quintessential Florida when it comes to weather. Summers are hot and humid, with temperatures reaching into the 90s and humidity averaging 85 percent. Electrical storms are prevalent in late summer and early fall and winters are mild, with temperatures generally in the 50s to 70s.

Betty Jones misses the changing of seasons, but says, "Up North, there were a lot of gray, cloudy, rainy days. We don't get that much here." However, Billie Keenon doesn't like July and August in Mount Dora. "We try to go to Virginia to see our grandchildren in the summer," she says, "but sometimes it gets as hot there as here."

The Andersons are glad to put behind them the winter snowfalls back in Virginia. "Bob stood at the window and watched me shovel snow," Mary says of Virginia winters. "From November to April I hibernated," admits Bob.

Despite some misgivings about the hot summer temperatures, all three couples are glad they made the move and have no plans to relocate again. As John Keenon says, anyone considering Mount Dora as a retirement site "should put it on the top of their list."●

Myrtle Beach, South Carolina

Those who vacation in this South Carolina resort find reasons to return permanently

By William Schemmel

Myrtle Beach didn't get its city charter until 1957. But fueled by sun-seeking retirees, the hub of the 60-mile Grand Strand resort and residential area on South Carolina's northern Atlantic coast has boomed into a metropolis of 196,629 residents and about 12 million annual visitors.

The city takes the best of Nashville, Miami Beach and Disney World and blends them into a place where residents and visitors alike play year-round on 100 golf courses and enjoy 200 tennis courts, horseback riding, fishing, amusement parks, nature preserves and botanical gardens. They can unwind at trendy spots like Planet Hollywood, Hard Rock Cafe and NASCAR Cafe or showrooms featuring stars like Alabama, Kenny Rogers and the Gatlin Brothers. On another level, the entertainment calendar is crowded with touring Broadway musicals, plays and orchestra performances.

But for all these diversions, former New Jerseyites Charles and Betty Gary were won over by a tree.

"The huge live oak tree draping itself over our house was as big as anything in our decision to move to Myrtle Beach," recalls Charles, 78, a retired U.S. Army lieutenant colonel and former executive with New York Telephone Co. "I love that tree. I don't know what I'd do if anything happened to it."

The Garys bought their single-story, two-bedroom, two-bath house in Mount Gilead Place, a planned community in Garden City near the picturesque fishing village of Murrells Inlet. The community is a bonanza for fishermen because many homes sit along canals that lead into the inlet.

Population: 22,759 in Myrtle Beach, 196,629 in Horry (O-Ree) County.

Location: Extreme northeastern Atlantic coast of South Carolina, the hub of the 60-mile Grand Strand resort and residential area.

Climate:

	High	Low
January	60	40
July	90	70

Hot, humid summers tempered by ocean breezes. Mild winters with occasional below-freezing temperatures.

Average relative humidity: 57%

Rain: 50 inches.

Cost of living: 96.8, based on national average of 100.

Average housing cost: $127,820 for a 1,800-square-foot home with three bedrooms, two baths and two-car garage. Average rent is $568 for a two-bedroom, two-bath apartment.

Sales tax: 5%

Sales tax exemptions: Prescriptions, dental prosthetics and hearing aids. Motor vehicles are charged a maximum $300 sales tax. Persons 85 and older are exempt from 1% of sales tax.

State income tax: For married couples filing jointly and single filers, the rates are graduated in six tiers from 2.5% on the first $2,400 of taxable income to 7% on taxable income above $12,000.

Income tax exemptions: Social Security benefits are exempt. Retirees who are drawing income from qualified retirement plans may deduct up to $3,000 of that income.

Intangibles tax: None.

Estate tax: None except the state's "pick-up" portion of the federal tax, applicable to taxable estates above $1 million.

Property tax: Residential property is assessed at either 4% or 6% of actual appraised market value. For homes assessed at 4%, the tax rate is $152.90; for homes assessed at 6%, the rate is $239. The taxes on a $127,820 home would range between $782 and $1,833, depending on which percentage is assigned to the parcel by the assessor.

Personal property tax: Same rates as above. Applies to cars, motor homes and boats, which are assessed at 10.5% of market value.

Homestead exemption: Homeowners age 65 and older who have established a one-year residency are eligible for a $20,000 homestead exemption.

Religion: More than 100 churches and synagogues represent more than 20 denominations.

Education: Coastal Carolina University (4,965 students) offers a variety of full four-year programs and continuing-education courses. Full-time and part-time students enroll in evening classes at CCU's Wall School of Business. A high-tech two-way hookup with Winthrop University allows CCU students to earn nationally accredited MBA degrees.

Transportation: Coastal Rapid Public Transit Authority provides bus service in the Grand Strand area. Myrtle Beach International Airport is served by Delta, Air Tran, ASA, ComAir, Continental, Spirit, US Air and Vanguard. Conway-Horry County Airport and Grand Strand Airport are available to private and corporate aircraft.

Health: Columbia Grand Strand Regional Medical Center in Myrtle Beach is a full-service acute-care medical center, providing comprehensive cardiac care, 24-hour emergency care and diagnostic services. Georgetown Memorial Hospital, in neighboring Georgetown County, has a high-tech nuclear medicine department, magnetic resonance imaging (MRI) and cardiac catheterization. Loris Community Hospital offers emergency and nonemergency family health

"It's almost identical with our house in New Jersey," says Betty, 65, who retired as legal office manager for New York Telephone Co. "It has two great rooms, each opening into a sun room. We like to have our friends in, and it's large enough for a 50-person cocktail party."

Charles estimates that the house has appreciated in value about 15 percent since he and his wife purchased it in 1988. He says their property taxes are one-seventh what they paid on their former home in Lakehurst, NJ.

"We certainly feel safer here than we did in New Jersey," Charles adds. "We've never had any problems where we live in unincorporated southern Horry County. The city of Myrtle Beach, unfortunately, has a high crime rate, but most of it is concentrated in one part of town, and the city is taking steps to solve the problems in that area."

A downside, the Garys say, is traffic fueled by the Grand Strand's rapid development. But they add that traffic snarls, which are especially severe during the height of the summer tourist season, are mitigated by the opportunity to enjoy outdoor activities year-round.

"We used to do a lot of sailing, but we sold our sailboat when we moved here, so now we're walking, biking and golfing for exercise and recreation," says Charles.

"We miss the theater and music in New York City," he adds, "but cultural opportunities have improved tremendously since we moved here. And we certainly don't miss the cold weather in New York. The weather here is excellent. We get a taste of four seasons, and in the summer, the ocean breezes help cool things down."

They've also become active in local organizations, says Charles. "Along with Coastal Carolina University, we've hosted two Elderhostel programs at a local golf course. One of the first things we did after retirement was join the VISTA (Volunteers in Service to America) program. We're active in the chamber of commerce and Bike-the-Neck, a program to build a bike trail down to Georgetown. Betty is the board secretary for the Long Bay Symphony, and we're docents at Brookgreen Gardens."

America's oldest public sculpture garden, Brookgreen Gardens in neighboring Georgetown County south of Myrtle Beach was created in the 1930s. More than 450 19th- and early 20th-century sculptures grace formal gardens, alcoves, brick walkways, reflecting pools and fountains.

Also nearby are Huntington Beach and Myrtle Beach state parks, with protected beaches, fishing piers, campsites and other recreational amenities. North Carolina's hundreds of miles of Atlantic beaches begin at the state line a few minutes north of Myrtle Beach.

The Garys enjoy visits to historic

Myrtle Beach, SC

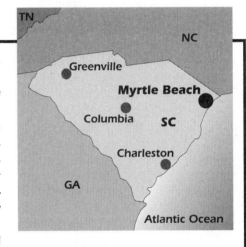

care. Conway Hospital has a trauma center, a minor emergency treatment center, maternity and pediatric care, mammography, cardiac rehabilitation and emergency and nonemergency services.

Housing options: The Grand Strand has many resort-style residential communities with golf courses, tennis courts, swimming pools, clubhouses and other amenities. There also are many condominium communities on the ocean and fairways. **Tidewater Golf and Country Club,** (800) 788-8433, has homes overlooking fairways, marshes and the Intracoastal Waterway, with prices from $115,000s. **The Park at Long Bay**, (843) 756-3111, eight miles from North Myrtle Beach, has manufactured homes from $30,000 and up. Also offering manufactured homes are **Ocean Pines/ Magnolia Grove**, at the southern end of the Grand Strand, and **Country Lakes**, near North Myrtle Beach. Homes are in the $60,000-$95,000 range. Residents, who must be age 55 or older, can take advantage of a clubhouse, swimming pool and organized activities. The communities are managed by Jensen's, (800) 458-6832. **The Tradition at Willbrook Plantation**, 18 miles

south on Pawley's Island, has homes for $180,000-$300,000. **Barefoot Resort**, (888) 996-4100, is a 2,300-acre golf community in North Myrtle Beach with homes from the $102,000s to the $400,000s. **Blackmoor**, (877) 603-2467, has homes for $163,000-$205,000. Prices include homesite; for information call (800) 572-0708. At **Pawleys Plantation Golf and Country Club** on Pawleys Island, (800) 367-9959, home sites start at $29,000. Two- and three-bedroom villas, $105,000-$249,000, overlook the fairways of the Jack Nicklaus-designed golf course. **Heritage Plantation**, (843) 237-9824, has homesites for $40,000-$325,000 and homes from $220,000. **Ocean Creek,** (800) 845-4102, offers 57 wooded acres with 2.5 miles of protected beach. Homes and villas are $99,000 to more than $1 million. Three-bedroom single-family homes at **Waterway Cove**, (843) 280-5370, start at $95,900. Three-bedroom homes with two-car garages at **The Oaks at Eastport**, (843) 272-8700, start at $133,500. **Legends,** (800) 552-2660, has two- and three-bedroom fairway villas from $250,000-$379,000 and single-family homesites from $40,000. Two- and three-bedroom condos at **The**

Moorings at Eastport, (843) 272-8700, begin at $89,900.

Visitor lodgings: The Grand Strand has 55,000 hotel and motel rooms and rental condos. Prices are seasonal, and rooms facing the ocean and golf fairways usually are higher than those without views. At Bermuda Sands, ocean-front rates for two people currently are $53-$295, (800) 448-8477. At Landmark Resort, ocean-front rate is $145, (800) 845-0658. At Beach Colony Resort, a suite with efficiency kitchen is $169, (800) 222-2141.

Information: Myrtle Beach Area Chamber of Commerce, P.O. Box 2115, Myrtle Beach, SC 29578, (843) 626-7444, www.mbchamber.com or www.myrtlebeachlive.com.

Charleston 95 miles down the coast, where they can satisfy their cultural appetites at the annual Spoleto USA Music Festival in May and June.

Like the Garys, many retirees appreciate the Grand Strand's increasing cultural opportunities — including Larry and Mary Ellen Osius. The couple had what amounted to a 20-year preview of their retirement during frequent visits to Myrtle Beach before they moved permanently.

"We'd been coming here since the '70s to play golf," Larry says, "and we built a patio home in North Myrtle Beach in 1980. We came down a lot for long weekends and never considered any other retirement sites."

The couple moved from northern Virginia in 1990, where they had lived for 25 years. Larry, 67, former editor and publisher of Electrical Magazine, had achieved his career goals, and "life in northern Virginia was getting to be more and more of a hassle."

"I got tired of planning my day around every appointment because of the traffic problems," adds Mary Ellen, 67.

The Osiuses moved first into a patio home and then into their present home in the Little River community, near the North Carolina border, in 1992. "Our development backs up to the Cypress Bay Golf Course," Larry says. "We have a beautiful fairway in our back yard, and we play it as our home course, but we don't have to pay to maintain it. We're going to stay here as long as our health allows."

Larry also likes Broadway at the Beach, a 350-acre entertainment complex with more than 100 retail stores, an IMAX theater, 20 restaurants (including Hard Rock Cafe and Planet Hollywood), and the 2,700-seat Palace Theater, which hosts everything from Broadway musicals like "Cats" to such country singers as Kenny Rogers.

In addition, the Osiuses enjoy outings at Barefoot Landing, an oceanside shopping complex with more than 100 specialty shops, 13 restaurants, a paddle-wheel boat and a 2,000-seat theater. Other entertainment is available at the Dixie Stampede, a Western-style indoor horse show owned by Dolly Parton's Dollywood Productions, and the Gatlin Brothers' 2,000-seat home base.

Larry and Mary Ellen both had good experiences with surgeries at Grand Strand Hospital. On the downside, Larry dislikes "the tackiness of commercial signage on U.S. 17," traffic problems and video gaming, which is popular along the Grand Strand. And while he appreciates that property taxes are lower here than in Northern Virginia, he says auto insurance is "outrageous."

"But this has been a satisfactory retirement place for us," says Larry, a member of the Community Choral Society, which gives four annual concerts. Larry and Mary Ellen both volunteer with North Strand Helping Hand, a cooperative effort of nine churches, the city and United Way to provide food, shelter, transportation and clothing for the needy.

Mary Ellen says their move to Myrtle Beach "worked out well. We were so familiar with the area and were within walking distance of the beach, grocery stores, the library and other places we enjoy." But she advises other potential retirees not familiar with the area to "visit and not break their ties until they're sure this is where they want to be."

That's what Gary and Marlene Stahley did when they moved from Columbia, MD, their home for 25 years. Before making their move in January 1994, the Stahleys visited the area three times. Their one-story, traditional-style brick home is in South Creek, an inland planned community next to the Myrtle Beach National Golf Course. "This is the best-built house we've ever had," Marlene enthuses. "We're not in a retirement community, although most of the residents are retired. It's like living in a small town where you know everybody. Shortly after we moved in, I had back surgery and our neighbors brought us food. They really take care of you here."

Their move also was influenced by the Grand Strand's moderate year-round climate. "I wanted a change of seasons in a warmer climate — warm, but not too hot," says Marlene, 60, a former office manager for a periodontist. "And we had some good friends who had already moved here and liked the area."

Gary, 60, a former computer analyst for the U.S. Department of Defense, believes their house has appreciated in value, although he has no plans to sell it. "We aren't too concerned about it because we plan to be here for a long time," he says.

"The Myrtle Beach area has a lot of things that we enjoy," he adds. "When we lived in Columbia, we always went to the beaches in Maryland and Delaware, and it was natural for us to move to an area where we could still enjoy the beaches. We couldn't have stayed much longer in the Baltimore-Washington area. It was too expensive and getting worse all the time. People complain about the traffic in Myrtle Beach, but it's nothing compared to the Washington, DC, area."

Even so, Marlene hopes the city will work to control "increased traffic resulting from the new golf courses, the live entertainment complexes and all the new developments." Gary worries about air pollution caused by open burning and auto emissions.

Among the things they like best about their new home, Marlene says, is that "you can never complain that you have nothing to do. We appreciate the culture that is here. There's always a show, or something going on at Coastal Carolina University. The local talent is amazing."

She also had a positive firsthand experience with local health-care facilities. "When I had my back surgery, the care at Grand Strand Hospital was marvelous. Many new medical practices are opening, and health care is fine and getting better all the time. I also feel safer here."

The Stahleys have become involved in many activities. Gary teaches a class in the Division of Extended Learning at Coastal Carolina University, giving them access to campus entertainment and other facilities. And there are courses of another kind. With all those tempting fairways designed by golf's biggest names, Gary has taken a serious interest in the game. Marlene also enjoys golf and is involved with her church and the South Creek community.

They recommend the area to other retirees. "I have no reservations about recommending the Grand Strand as a retirement place," Gary says. "But people have to understand that this is a tourist area and learn to live with it."●

Naples, Florida

With beaches, golf, culture and shopping, this chic town on Florida's southwest coast proves irresistible to retirees

By Karen Feldman

Palm Beach may have a higher profile, but the diminutive city of Naples holds its own in attracting the well-known and the well-to-do. Oozing savoir-faire, overflowing with sophisticated boutiques, restaurants and golf courses, and bounded by pristine beaches, Naples has plenty to attract visitors, swelling the town's population of 21,000 to twice that during the winter high season.

Its tony hotels — most notably the Ritz-Carlton Naples, frequently ranked among the world's 10 best resorts — attract celebrities seeking time in the sun without the glare of the limelight, including Tony Bennett, the Rolling Stones and Steve Forbes. Authors Robin Cook and Ben Bova call Naples home, as did the late Robert Ludlum.

Many area residents start by vacationing there. Then they buy a condo or house for the winters, hesitant to commit to staying through the hot and rainy summers. Finally, many settle in full time.

"It's the quality of life here that attracts them," says Mark Gianquitti, vice president of member services for the Naples Area Chamber of Commerce. "With the gorgeous beaches, the entertainment opportunities, the arts, some great restaurants and some first-class shopping, all of those tied in together make it irresistible."

Donald and Mary Moon lived in Kettering, OH, for many years before buying a condo in Naples in March 2001. The couple, whose spouses died several years ago, got married on the lanai of that condo three months after buying it.

"Florida is now our primary residence," says Donald, 70, a retired chiropractic physician. "We will probably spend the summers in Ohio. We're keeping our home there until we really see how we like spending the whole year in Florida."

Before buying their North Naples condo, the couple visited the area three times over six years, staying at a different condominium each time. "Every time we came down we loved the place," Donald says.

Bob and Christa Lederer lived in Leavenworth, KS, when they bought a condo in Naples in 1988. They vacationed in Naples four times a year until 1996, when they moved south full time.

Bob, 70, dreamed of retiring in Las Vegas during the 20 years the couple lived in Leavenworth, where he had an orthodontic dental practice. Meanwhile, 50-something Christa worked in her husband's office and envisioned life in Florida.

Bob's parents lived in Miami Beach, but Christa disliked the area. "We looked at the entire east coast (of Florida), but I told my husband, 'If we have to live on the east coast, I'll stay in Leavenworth.' The traffic was just awful."

Then they visited one of Christa's cousins in Naples on Florida's southwest coast. "The minute I drove into Naples, I said, 'This is it. We're buying a condo now,'" she says.

They bought one on the spot at Bay Colony, using it for five years. They put it on the market in early 2001. They plan to move to a new development, The Seasons at Naples Cay, in October or November of this year.

While property sales dipped somewhat following Sept. 11, activity picked back up in January, says Phil Wood, broker for John R. Wood Realtors in Naples. "It's been strong since the start of the year," he says. "There's a good inventory and a nice selection in a variety of price ranges."

Bob and Jo Ann Wasylenko lived in Naples for five years before selling their home and moving to neighboring Bonita Springs to live among a somewhat younger crowd (he's 64, she's 60). It took them only three weeks to sell their Naples property. It was Naples' cultural climate that attracted them in the first place.

There aren't quite as many cultural opportunities as there were in their hometown of St. Louis. But "the Philharmonic (Center for the Arts) is top-notch. Art galleries and exhibits are abundant and it isn't difficult to get to St. Petersburg or Sarasota for cultural events," Jo Ann says.

Culture notwithstanding, retirees considering a purchase in the Naples area "are mostly looking for one of two things — golf or gulf," John Wood says.

It's small wonder, considering that Naples boasts 11 miles of well-tended beach, including two beaches named to the Top 20 list by Stephen Leatherman, also known as Dr. Beach, director of the Laboratory for Coastal Research and International Hurricane Center at Florida International University.

The city has 50 golf courses and more under cstruction. Its courses attract not only amateurs but also the pros that compete at the Senior PGA Tour's ACE Group Classic and the Dodge Celebrity Invitational, among others. Even people who never picked up a club before quickly seem to get into the swing.

"When we moved here my husband didn't have a hobby and he was getting in my way," says Christa Lederer with a laugh. "Then I decided we were going to play golf. Neither of us had ever been on a golf course. We're playing now six or seven days a week. The people we meet on the golf course are now our best friends."

That's not the only thing that's changed since they left Leavenworth. "What's amazing to me is the wealth," she says. "It's mind-boggling to me: the size of homes and cost of homes. Coming from Kansas, I am shocked every day. When you ask someone here, 'How much is it?' they say 2.0, 5.9, 10, and that's always millions. It's something I can't comprehend."

Naples' reputation for style and sophistication is relatively new, but it's long been a haven for wealthy Northerners looking for respite from long, bleak winters. The city got its start in 1887, when the land on which it now sits was first surveyed, plotted and put on the market. It began as a small fishing village and beachside getaway for the affluent, which it remained for almost 80 years.

Millionaire Barron Gift Collier eventually acquired much of the land and was responsible for some of the area's early economic growth. He brought electric power, paved roads, telegraphs and other vital infrastructure improvements to the area. Among his most important projects was the Tamiami Trail (U.S. Highway 41), completed in 1928, running from the state's more developed east coast to Naples and north along the west coast. The county, of which Naples is the seat, is named Collier in his honor.

Development began in earnest in the 1960s and has ramped up steadily ever since. Collier County has seen a serious boom in growth in recent years. "We had a 65 percent growth in population from 1990 to 2000," Mark Gianquitti says. "From 2000 to 2001, it grew at about a 5 or 6 percent clip, about eight times faster than the national average."

Mary Moon, 65, is impressed by how the city is coping with its burgeoning population. "Take downtown Naples —

Old Naples — as an example. They have decided not to tear down the low buildings and put up high rises. It's a delicate balance they're trying to achieve, accommodating an influx of people, but at the same time keeping the characteristics that have been so attractive," she says.

A cornucopia of upscale housing options, as well as golf and water-related activities, provides much of the draw, but so do the entertainment options. Annual festivals and events run the gamut. There's the twice-yearly swamp buggy races in which the souped-up swamp buggies battle their way over the Mile O' Mud. The affair concludes with the winner tossing the swamp buggy queen in the mud.

Local residents also value the arts. The Philharmonic Center for the Arts, built in 1989 for cash, regularly hosts big-name shows, with performers such as Itzhak Perlman, Lyle Lovett and Mandy Patinkin appearing there. It's the west coast home

of the Miami City Ballet and the home of the Naples Philharmonic Orchestra.

Smack in the middle of the tony shopping and entertainment district along Fifth Avenue South in Old Naples is the Sugden Community Theatre, home of the Naples Players, an accomplished amateur troupe. The Naples Dinner Theatre produces musicals such as "Carousel" and "The King and I," as well as musical revues.

The city also boasts an impressive and diverse assortment of museums. The Naples Museum of Art hosts world-class traveling exhibitions. The Collier County Museum affords modern-day visitors a glimpse back at 10,000 years of the region's history. The Teddy Bear Museum is home to an international collection of 4,000 stuffed bears.

Bordered by three bodies of water — the Gulf of Mexico, Naples Bay and the Gordon River — Naples offers plenty of water-related activities, from a relaxing

Naples, FL

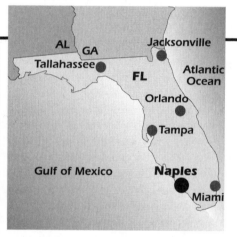

Population: 20,976 within the city limits, 251,377 in Collier County.
Location: Naples is the Collier County seat, located in southwest Florida about 110 miles west of Miami, 134 miles south of Tampa and about 35 miles south of Fort Myers.

Climate:	High	Low
January	74	53
July	91	75

Average relative humidity: 89% in the morning, 56% in the afternoon
Rain: About 52 inches.
Cost of living: Above average.
Median housing cost: $172,263
Sales tax: 6%
Sales tax exemption: Food, medicine and some services.
State income tax: None.

Intangibles tax: Assessed on stocks, bonds and other assets. Tax rate is $1 per $1,000 in assets. The first $20,000 in assets is exempt for individuals. For couples filing jointly, the first $40,000 is exempt. Those who owe less than $60 need not pay.
Estate tax: None, except the state's "pick-up" portion of the federal tax, applicable to taxable estates of more than $1 million.
Inheritance tax: None.
Property tax: All city residents pay $15 per $1,000 of assessed value. Some also are situated in special taxing districts for services such as street lighting. With a $25,000 homestead exemption, the annual tax on a $172,263 home would be $2,209.
Homestead exemption: $25,000 off assessed value of primary, permanent residence.
Religion: Dozens of houses of worship are located in and around Naples, representing all major denominations as well as many other faiths.
Education: Edison Community College, based in Fort Myers to the north, has a branch campus in Naples that offers a wide range of courses for credit as well as continuing education.

Among the continuing education courses available in the spring semester were feng shui, creative writing, Appalachian dulcimer, Shakespeare and computer use. Florida Gulf Coast University, situated midway between Naples and Fort Myers, also offers a mix of programs that lead to degrees and a variety of continuing-education classes.
Transportation: Southwest Florida International Airport in southern Lee County is served by more than two dozen major air carriers and is the region's primary airport. Naples Municipal Airport offers private charters, some commuter flights and some regularly scheduled flights. Naples Trolley Tours operates within the city, making many stops along the route and conducting guided tours. Taxi and limousine services are available from Southwest Florida International Airport. U.S. Highway 41 (also known as Tamiami Trail) is the main commercial route through the area, while Interstate 75 to the east of the city connects the region to Miami to the east and most of the state's west coast.
Health: Naples Community Hospital is a private, not-for-profit, acute-care hospital with 430 beds in the heart of the

sunbath on the beach to the always popular fishing off the Naples Pier to boating, water-skiing and swamp buggies.

While the city doesn't have a resident baseball team for spring training, it's less than an hour's drive to Fort Myers, where the Minnesota Twins and Boston Red Sox work out each February and March.

And the city still retains some of the classic attractions that amused visitors decades back. Caribbean Gardens is a prime example of an old-time attraction that has kept pace with the times. Its 52 acres include tropical gardens and an animal preserve. There are boat rides near islands with monkeys in a natural habitat and a variety of animal shows daily. On some Sundays during the winter, visitors can have brunch in the gardens.

As the population grows, so do the shopping opportunities. All the usual chains can be found in Naples, including most of the upscale ones, such as Saks Fifth Avenue, Williams-Sonoma and Talbots. But one of the city's enduring charms is its wealth of boutique shopping along well-groomed streets that draw visitors and residents alike. Third Street South and Fifth Avenue South in Old Naples — the city's historic district — are favorites of those seeking one-of-a-kind stores, art galleries and trendy restaurants.

Several of Naples' private art galleries include the works of big-name artists, including Robert Rauschenberg (who lives on Captiva, about an hour north of Naples), David Hockney and Pablo Picasso. During the winter, up-and-coming artists get a chance to show their works at monthly Art in the Park exhibitions sponsored by the Naples Art Association as well as at juried art shows.

The drawbacks of living in Naples are few, say the Moons and Lederers. Donald Moon hates the bugs, which include mosquitoes, gnats and beefy cockroaches, some of which fly. "We don't like the drinking water, either," he says, and traffic during the winter months seems to get worse every year.

Bob and Christa Lederer find the traffic annoying at times but say it's offset by the area's beauty and the quality of life they have there. To others considering a move to Naples, Christa says they should love to be outdoors. "A person who likes seasons cannot live in Naples."

Donald Moon cautions that newcomers should "make sure they have a decent income. It's a very expensive town." Before making a permanent commitment, Christa Lederer says, "the most important advice I can give is move here and rent for one or two years. Get familiar with the area, get familiar with the prices, get familiar with the different housing areas. Then you can make an educated decision."

For her, there's no going back to Kansas. "Bob wants to be buried in Leavenworth because his parents are buried there," Christa says. "I told him, 'Bob, I'm not going to your funeral. I'm not going back to Leavenworth!'" ●

---

city. North Collier Hospital is a 98-bed, not-for-profit hospital also offering acute-care services. The prestigious Cleveland Clinic has a 70-bed not-for-profit, acute-care hospital and clinic in north Naples. The David Lawrence Center offers psychiatric services for children and adults.

Housing options: Naples has a broad range of housing, starting at about $150,000 and rising to $30 million. In golf course communities, condominiums start at about $125,000, and homes on the golf course start at about $250,000. Waterfront homes start at about $300,000. In the Port Royal neighborhood, a long-established upscale area in which most homes are situated along lush waterways, seven-figure sales prices are the rule. There is no development office (individual builders construct custom homes), but the Port Royal Property Owners Association can be reached at (239) 261-6472. A sampling of the many housing options: **Bridgewater Bay** in North Naples, (877) 596-2619 or (239) 596-7020, offers homes for $130,000 to $400,000, which includes membership in the residents' club. **Bay Colony's Trieste**, (800) 924-2290 or (239) 598-3200, offers views of the Gulf of Mexico and the Ritz-Carlton Naples, with condos starting at about $1 million. Among the newest communities is **Tiburon**, (800) 924-2290 or (239) 593-9199, offering a 27-hole championship golf course designed by Greg Norman, with homes from $300,000 to more than $5 million. **Pelican Marsh**, (800) 256-5277 or (239) 597-5277, another golf course community, has homes starting in the mid-$200,000s to $3 million. **The Estates at TwinEagles**, (800) 281-9245, has estate sites starting in the high $200,000s, with homes starting at $1.2 million. **GreenLinks**, (888) 758-4653, is a condominium community with units priced from the $140,000s to the $200,000s; it has a Robert Trent Jones Sr. signature golf course, lighted tennis courts, fitness room and concierge service. **Tarpon Bay**, (888) 249-8889, offers beach access, a fitness center, tennis, putting green, boat slips and homes ranging from $152,990 to the $340,000s. **Cove Towers**, (888) 223-3215, is a high-rise community with units starting from $570,000. **The Colony Golf and Bay Club**, (800) 633-2180, in nearby Bonita Springs has single-family homes, villas and luxury high-rise condos starting from $485,000.

Visitor lodging: Regularly awarded five diamonds by AAA and five stars by Mobil, the Ritz-Carlton Naples has a prime gulf-front location, new spa, fine dining and a full range of services, $229-$1,059, (239) 598-3300 or (888) 856-4372. Just a few miles away is the Ritz-Carlton Golf Resort with 295 rooms and a Greg Norman-designed golf course, $189-$839, (239) 593-2000. The gulf-front Edgewater Beach Resort offers one- and two-bedroom suites, $155-$1,500, (239) 403-2000. Inn by the Sea is a bed-and-breakfast inn in a 1937 guesthouse two blocks from the beach and the downtown shopping and dining district, $94-$169, (239) 649-4124. Staybridge Suites Hotel by Holiday Inn has spacious studios as well as one- and two-bedroom suites at the northern end of the city, $67-$142, (239) 643-8002 or (800) 238-8000.

Information: Naples Tourism Alliance, 5395 Park Central Court, Naples, FL 34109, (800) 688-3600 or www.classic florida.com. Naples Area Chamber of Commerce, 895 Fifth Ave. S., Naples, FL 34102, (239) 262-6141.

Natchitoches, Louisiana

This historic town in north-central Louisiana works its charm on newcomers

By Honey Naylor

If you saw the 1988 movie "Steel Magnolias," you've already seen Natchitoches. Called Chinquapin in the film, Natchitoches was the boyhood home of Robert Harling, who wrote the smash-hit off-Broadway play on which the movie is based. The movie also was filmed here.

Natchitoches lazes on the banks of peaceful Cane River Lake, formed long ago when the Red River changed its course. (Since the waters don't flow, the 32-mile-long lake is not technically a river.) The green-grassy banks are shaded by ancient oak trees.

Front Street, in downtown Natchitoches overlooking the lake, is paved with brick laid around the turn of the century and is lined with small balconied structures decked in graceful wrought-iron trim. The town's 33-block historic district is on the National Register of Historic Places.

"We like the rolling hills around Natchitoches," says Ruth Malcolm, who with her husband, Leland, moved to the charming north-central Louisiana town in 1997.

Natchitoches (pronounced Nak-uh-tish) sits near the Kisatchie National Forest, a fit place for hiking and hunting, fishing and camping. Briarwood, nestled in the forest, was the home of Caroline Dormon, the first woman employed in forestry in the United States. She worked tirelessly with state and U.S. Forest Service leaders to establish the Kisatchie National Forest, now a nature preserve and the state's most complete botanical and wildlife sanctuary. In addition, the hill country around Natchitoches is virtually awash with lakes for boating, tubing and fishing — including Cane River Lake, Saline Lake, Black Lake, Clear Lake, Chaplin's Lake and Sibley Lake.

Ruth and Leland already were acquainted with the area and knew people here before moving. Both were born in south Louisiana — Ruth in the small town of Welsh near Lake Charles and Leland in Fenton. Both have family nearby, and after considering other places for retirement — Salt Lake City, Austin and Atlanta — they chose Natchitoches largely because of the proximity to their birthplaces and to family.

Ruth confesses that readjustment to a small town has been difficult — and for reasons that are a bit out of the ordinary. The Malcolms not only had to adjust to small-town living, they had to repatriate. For 12 years they lived overseas in Bahrain, where Leland was a facilities manager. They miss friends who still live in the Middle East and worry about them. "We don't miss the bullets or the bombs," Leland says.

Indeed, it seems the greatest danger for the Malcolms, both 57, now is the possibility of being hit by a golf ball. "Our house is on a lane right beside the golf course," says Ruth of the home they own in a 10-house planned community. Their development requires a 2,000-square-foot minimum home size and prohibits fences because, as Ruth says, "golfers have to be able to get to their errant balls."

With this kind of proximity to a golf course, Ruth and Leland both have taken golf lessons, and they also obtained real estate licenses and work part-time. They already owned rental property in Natchitoches prior to moving and buying a house here.

Another newcomer, Ken Bates, also is a native Louisianian. Ken, a retired U.S. Army major, and his wife, Donna, both attended Northwestern State University in Natchitoches and were acquainted with this area prior to relocating here in 1993 from New Cumberland, PA. Proximity to family also was a consideration for them, as Ken's mother lives in a nearby town.

Ken and Donna were stationed in Turkey when "Steel Magnolias" came out, but they've heard the many stories about the stars, the sets and the shoot since moving to Natchitoches.

That excitement has only slightly abated more than a decade later. Tour guides for Cane River City Belle Trolley and Cruises point out where the stars lived during the filming and where memorable scenes were shot. Almost everyone in town has a tale to tell about his or her part in making the film, no matter how small. Indeed, some had roles as extras.

The movie was a very big deal for this town of fewer than 18,000 people. During several months of filming, Natchitoches was home not only to Olympia Dukakis, Julia Roberts, Shirley MacLaine and Dylan McDermott, but to Dolly Parton, Sally Field, Daryl Hannah and Tom Skerritt, plus a sizable crew. The impact on the town was enormous, pumping millions of dollars into the local economy, and it was a shot in the arm for tourism. There now are 35 Natchitoches area bed-and-breakfast inns to help house tourists, many still drawn here by "Steel Magnolias."

They also come because of the area's rich history. That's another attraction for Donna Bates, who liked to explore Amish country when she lived in Pennsylvania.

Natchitoches is the oldest permanent European settlement in the Louisiana Purchase, a chunk of real estate that includes all of the territory between the Alleghenies and the Rockies. In 1682, the French explorer Robert Cavelier de La Salle followed the Mississippi River from Canada to the Gulf of Mexico and claimed for Louis XIV of France all of the land drained by the river.

In 1714, a young French Creole named Juchereau de St. Denis swashed and buckled his way to this site, which is named for the Natchitoches Indians. In 1803, President Thomas Jefferson bought the land from Napoleon Bonaparte, and the legendary Louisiana Purchase cost the young United States $15 million.

The Old Ducournau Building and the LaCoste Building are two 19th-century structures that form the core of downtown's Ducournau Square overlooking the lake. Their quaint carriageways lead from Front Street to courtyards in the rear, where small restored buildings once were stables or carriage houses. In the European style, the square's buildings have shops and restaurants at ground level and townhouses on upper floors.

Natchitoches sits on the cusp between south Louisiana, which was founded by the French, and north Louisiana, which was settled by English, Scots and Irish

Natchitoches, LA

Population: 17,865 in the city of Natchitoches, seat of Natchitoches Parish, which has a population of 39,080.

Location: Natchitoches is in north-central Louisiana, about 60 miles northwest of Alexandria. Natchitoches Parish is bordered on the southeast by the Red River.

Climate:

	High	Low
January	56	36
July	93	73

Average relative humidity: 73%
Rain: 50.32 inches.

Cost of living: Below average (specific index not available).

Average housing cost: A 1,500- to 1,600-square-foot, three-bedroom home is about $95,000. For a 1,300-square-foot, two-bedroom condominium or townhouse, the cost is about $70,000-$80,000, with maintenance about $300 per month.

Sales tax: Combined city, parish and state sales tax is 8%. Groceries are taxed at 7%, and prescription drugs are taxed at 4%.

State income tax: For married couples filing jointly, graduated from 2% of taxable income up to $20,000 to 6% on amounts over $101,000. For single filers, graduated from 2% of taxable income up to $10,000 to 6% on amounts over $51,000.

Income tax exemptions: Social Security benefits and federal, state and lo-

cal government pensions are exempt. There is an exemption for private pension or other retirement income of up to $6,000 for each taxpayer age 65 and older.

Intangibles tax: None.

Inheritance tax: Louisiana's inheritance tax will be phased out for deaths occuring after June 30, 2004. At this writing the following applies. Direct descendants, ascendants and surviving spouses are taxed at the following rate: Nothing is due on the first $25,000, 2% on the next $20,000, and 3% on the taxable amount in excess of $45,000. If the date of death occurred during the calendar year 1992 or thereafter, the total value to the surviving spouse is exempted from tax.

Estate tax: None, except the state's "pick-up" portion of the federal tax, applicable to taxable estates of more than $1 million.

Property tax: The tax rate in Natchitoches Parish is $106.32 per $1,000 of assessed value, with homes assessed at 10 percent of market value, and there's a $75,000 homestead exemption. Personal property is assessed at 15% of fair market value. In the city of Natchitoches, the tax rate is $17.03 per $1,000 of assessed value, with homes assessed at 10 percent of market value, and there's no homestead exemption. On a $100,000 home, you would pay parish taxes on $2,500 and city taxes on $10,000. Taxes due the parish would be $265.80, and taxes due the city would be $170.30, for a total bill of $436.10.

Homestead exemption: $75,000 on parish property taxes.

Religion: Natchitoches has more than 90 houses of worship representing 30 denominations.

Education: Northwestern State Uni-

versity, with an enrollment of approximately 7,000 students, offers community outreach programs, including continuing education, with courses and workshops on how to get out of debt, prelicensing real estate education, Cajun dancing, water aerobics and others.

Transportation: There is no public bus system, but the Council on Aging operates a van for seniors. Shreveport Regional Airport, 70 miles away, is served by 20 national airlines and major cargo carriers. Alexandria International Airport, 55 miles away, is served by three commercial airlines.

Health: The Natchitoches Parish Hospital, fully staffed with 33 physicians and specialists, has a 24-hour emergency room and services that include a long-term care unit, a senior care unit, a wellness program and Meals on Wheels.

Housing options: At **St. Clair Estates**, located between schools and the hospital, new homes are in the 2,000- to 2,500-square-foot range, priced from $155,000 and up. At **Chinquapin** subdivision, new homes are 1,600 to 2,000 square feet. Patio homes, featuring two bedrooms and two baths and 1,300 square feet for about $150,000, also are popular with area retirees, local builders say.

Visitor lodging: Some 35 bed-and-breakfast inns range in rates from $65 to $150 per night. Ask for a bed-and-breakfast brochure from the chamber of commerce. Other options include Ramada Inn, $50-$70, (888) 252-8281, and Comfort Inn, $70-$80, (800) 228-5150.

Information: Natchitoches Area Chamber of Commerce, 550 Second St., P.O. Box 3, Natchitoches, LA 71458, (318) 352-6894, www.natchitochescham ber.org or www.natchitoches.net.

immigrants. The Bateses, both 50, appreciate the cultural diversity afforded by the area and by Northwestern State University.

The Bateses' home, which they have owned for four years, is a two-story French chateau-style house in an upscale neighborhood on the opposite side of the lake from the historic district. Ken notes that property taxes are much lower here than in Pennsylvania, and that Louisiana does not tax military retirement.

Indeed, much of Natchitoches' appeal is due to its affordability. The town offers a low cost of living and reasonably priced homes, and state and local taxes are below average.

Another recent newcomer, David Graham, says that the lower cost of living, along with the mild climate, was a factor in his move from Tennessee to Natchitoches. David, who says he's been thinking about possible retirement places "all my life," moved here with his wife, Carolyn, in 1997.

For 25 years the Grahams had lived in Germantown, TN, where David, 67, owned an insurance agency and Carolyn was an insurance claims administrator and a schoolteacher. They live in a one-story traditional house with gingerbread trim in a riverfront residential neighborhood. They enjoy participating in the cultural aspects of the area when not baby-sitting their 10 grandchildren.

The Grahams also had old friends here when they moved. But Carolyn echoes the Bateses, saying, "It's easy to make new friends if you join groups and become involved with the church."

The Grahams share a love of music: He sings in the church choir and she plays in a hand-bell choir and also plays piano and saxophone. In addition to music, Carolyn, 62, enjoys historic preservation and belongs to the Natchitoches Historical Society. David, a member of the Lions Club, plans to volunteer with the chamber of commerce.

"Natchitoches has so much more to offer," says David, referring to their choice of Natchitoches over Hot Springs, AR, another town they had considered. "There's so much to do, and there's a festival almost every week."

Indeed, there are festivals aplenty. Natchitoches is known in these parts for its Christmas Festival of Lights, when the downtown area is festooned with twinkling lights, and some 150,000 visitors come to see it. The festival kicks off with spectacular fireworks, parades both on and off the water, and a street fair with food, games, rides and music.

In October, historic homes are open to the public for a fall pilgrimage, and a jazz festival livens things up in the spring. An annual fiddlers championship is held at the nearby Rebel States Commemorative Area in Marthaville, and the annual folk festival is held on the campus of Northwestern State University in July.

A few miles south of town, Melrose Plantation, a national historic landmark, hosts the Melrose Plantation Arts and Crafts Festival each June. Some 25,000 people attend the festival, which features top-quality hand-crafted baskets, pottery, dolls, sculptures, jewelry and other items. The plantation, open for tours throughout the year, was the home of the late Cammie Henry, a patron of the arts who welcomed writers to come to Melrose to live and work.

Lyle Saxon and Sherwood Anderson are among the writers who have stayed in this handsome mid-19th-century house, which also was the home of the late primitive artist Clementine Hunter. Among her works on display is a mural she painted on the interior walls of African House, one of the outbuildings included in the tour.

Melrose is one of several plantation homes open to the public south of Natchitoches. The Kate Chopin House bears the name of the 19th-century author of "The Awakening" who lived here with her husband. Chopin also wrote "Bayou Folk," a book about the people of this region, and a first-edition is displayed in a museum in the house.

Magnolia Plantation, whose stunning main mansion dates from the mid-18th century, is a national bicentennial farm. An antiques-filled bed-and-breakfast inn, as well as a still-working plantation, Magnolia is a part of the Cane River National Heritage Area. Like Magnolia, nearby Beau Fort Plantation is a bed-and-breakfast inn with a wonderful collection of 18th- and 19th-century antiques.

In town, Northwestern State University offers symphony, ballet and theater, plus a raft of sports activities that ranges from football and baseball to rodeoing and rowing. In the spring, Cane River Lake attracts rowing teams from across the nation for practice and competition.

Donna Bates says she misses the change of seasons in Pennsylvania, and Ken misses the mountains — the highest point in all of Louisiana is just 520 feet above sea level. But they agree that it's hard to find friendlier people than the folks in Natchitoches. And Leland Malcolm has only one word of advice to retirees considering a move to charming Natchitoches: "Hurry." ●

New Bern, North Carolina

Northern transplants find a warm welcome in this historic North Carolina port town

By Lan Sluder

Here's a formula for falling in love with a small town: Plan to arrive in the early evening. Come in over the high-rise bridge across the wide curve of water where two rivers meet the sound, where you can watch sailboats head back to the marina at day's end. Look as the setting sun frames the historic district on the waterfront and the twinkling lights of a bustling downtown. Catch a glimpse of expansive riverside homes with championship golf out the back door. Enjoy, even in deepest winter, a hint of warmth in the air and the soft gray of Spanish moss on oak trees, thanks to the moderating impact of the Gulf Stream not far away.

This is New Bern, NC, at its best. The first view of this picturesque port town in Craven County, 105 miles southeast of Raleigh, is capturing the hearts of more than a few retirees, and its agreeable combination of riverfront living, mild four-season climate, affordable housing, strong and diversified economy, interesting history, welcoming locals and wide-ranging recreational opportunities is winning them as full-time residents.

"My husband and I had made various trips, checking out towns, and when we drove into New Bern in 1997, we just looked at each other and said, 'We like this town — this is it,'" says Betty Ann Walker, who with her husband, Bill, decided to move to New Bern from Naples, FL.

Bill, 74, and Betty Ann, 53, spent just one day with a real estate agent, looked at only a half-dozen houses and quickly bought one, a 1970s-vintage brick rancher on a creek. Within a short time, the Walkers (they are nearly newlyweds, having been married less than three years) turned the house into a showplace, says Pam Michel of Coastal Homes Real Estate.

"We got twice the house here for the money than you could in Naples," says Betty Ann. Originally from Ontario, Canada, she had lived in Naples for 25 years.

Bill had lived in Illinois before moving to Naples, where he spent 11 years. "Half-backs" from Florida, those who moved to Florida from the Northeast or Midwest and then decided to move "half the way back," represent a growing group in towns like New Bern.

"In Naples we lived in a gated golfing community where everyone was over 65, and 80 percent of the residents left in the summer," says Betty Ann. In her neighborhood in New Bern, ages range from 4 to 94, and everybody lives here full time, she says.

The Walkers travel, garden, exercise and, like many retirees in the New Bern area, tool around the usually benign waters of the Neuse and Trent rivers and Pamlico Sound in their "yacht" — in this case, a 13-foot Boston Whaler.

"We were looking for a small town that didn't advertise itself on postcards," says Betty Ann. With the buzz New Bern is enjoying these days, the town may not need to do much advertising. The second-oldest town in North Carolina (Bath in Beaufort County claims to be the oldest incorporated town in the state) is suddenly one of the hottest retirement destinations in the region.

"Most of the retirees we get here, and we're getting a lot of them, are from the North — especially New York, New Jersey, Pennsylvania, the Washington area and from as far west as Ohio and Indiana," says Bob Bartram, co-owner of Century 21 Action Associates. "They're looking for a warm area, but not too warm," he says, noting that New Bern has four distinct seasons.

The average retiree pays around $200,000 for a home in New Bern, Bob says, though the range is wide, from around $75,000 to $700,000. Neighborhoods and communities around New Bern offer all types of housing options, from the country club environs of Trent Woods to houses from three centuries in the historic district and golf-oriented developments such as Taberna, developed by

Weyerhaeuser, where lot and home packages start around $140,000. There are waterfront projects such as Fairfield Harbour, which has two 18-hole golf courses, a 250-slip marina and housing options from condos to custom homes from $20,000 to $450,000, and there are timeshares, manufactured housing subdivisions and rural trailer parks.

Jeanne and Curt Collison are fairly typical of retirees from the North. Jeanne, 59 (her name is pronounced Jeanie), grew up on Martha's Vineyard, MA, and Curt, 60, in Rhode Island and New York. During the years when Curt worked for Ocean Spray, eventually becoming senior vice president, and Jeanne worked as a registered nurse, becoming charge nurse at a hospital emergency room, they lived in various towns in Massachusetts, Rhode Island, Connecticut and New Hampshire.

Following a stroke in 1992, Curt took early retirement, and the Collisons made a list of 16 things they felt were important in a retirement location. Among the most important were a warm climate with four seasons, proximity to a river or lake and within 25 miles of the ocean (but not directly on the ocean), a small town with history and fewer than 25,000 year-round residents, a location within a day's drive of the couple's three sons, and a place that's hospitable to Northern transplants.

Among the finalists were several small towns in eastern North Carolina, including Edenton, Bath and Beaufort. But after spending a week in New Bern, the town just "felt right for us," Curt says.

"We're antiques nuts and old house nuts," says Curt, so he and his wife were impressed with New Bern's vibrant 56-square-block downtown historic district. Founded by Swiss and German settlers in 1710 and named for Bern, Switzerland (Bern means bear in German, and a stylized bear is the town's omnipresent symbol), New Bern celebrates its past in a variety of historical attractions, most notably Tryon Palace. The Georgian-style palace, with 14 acres of gardens, is a reconstruction of the 18th-century residence of British colonial governor William Tryon. Most of the original structure, considered one of the grandest public buildings in the young country, was destroyed in a 1798 fire. New Bern also had the first printing press and the first newspaper in the state.

History lessons in New Bern needn't be stuffy, though. As proud as they are of the area's pre-Revolutionary history, residents appear equally proud that Pepsi-Cola was invented by pharmacist Caleb Bradham in New Bern in 1898. The "birthplace of Pepsi" at the corner of Middle and Pollack streets, now a gift shop with a soda fountain, is one of New Bern's most popular tourist attractions. New Bern's many B&Bs and motels stay busy year-round, and a new convention center complex on the riverfront doubtless will add to the attraction of the area for visitors.

In the heart of the historic district, the Collisons in late 1992 bought a three-story, 4,000-square-foot home, dating from 1817 with two later additions. In 1994 they began renovating it, a job that, while mostly completed, has continued to the present.

The Collisons say they love their historic home, described in New Bern promotional brochures as Federalist-Greek Revival with Victorian embellishments. "We especially love living in the historic district," says Curt. "It is a real tight community, including all ages, where you can sit on your front porch and know 90 percent of the people who walk by."

Active in the local preservation league, in antiques organizations and other groups, the Collisons say they have felt exceptionally welcome as lifelong Northerners in this Southern town. "We haven't even come close to seeing any anti-Yankee feeling — many of our closest friends were born and brought up here," he says.

Another couple who found their retirement paradise in New Bern are Dan and Vicki Larimer, who moved here in 1998 from the town of Jim Thorpe in Pennsylvania. Dan, 59, was an English professor at a community college, and Vicki, 58, ran the college's nursery school. The Larimers had become familiar with this part of North Carolina when they camped on the Outer Banks with their two daughters.

The Larimers bought in Taberna, a Wey-erhaeuser development with golf course carved out of an area near the Croatan National Forest, a 155,000-acre national forest southeast of New Bern. Avid boaters, the Larimers own a 20-foot yawl that they sail on the Neuse and Trent rivers. They also are birders and have joined the local birding club. The Larimers say they enjoy the cultural activities available locally, including a Shakespeare festival, a concert series and an excellent library. They also enjoying biking or driving to visit the many quaint small towns around New Bern, including Swansboro, Oriental and Beaufort.

As with many retirees, weather and the water were the reasons Clair and Dorothy Smith chose New Bern. They began looking at the area in 1985, doing a lot of research, and eventually moved from Michigan to New Bern in 1993. They call it "a fabulous place to live." They chose a patio home at Greenbrier, a planned community with a golf course. Though boatless at present, the Smiths belong to a sailing club. Clair says he volunteers at the North Carolina Maritime Museum in nearby Beaufort, helping build and repair wooden boats.

New Bern, NC

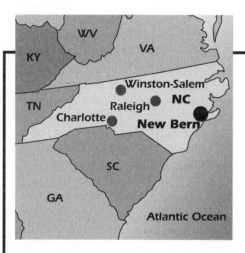

Population: 23,128 in New Bern, 91,436 in Craven County.

Location: New Bern, the county seat of Craven County, is at the confluence of the Neuse and Trent rivers in eastern North Carolina, about 105 miles (a little over two hours by car) southeast of Raleigh and about 35 miles (45 minutes by car) from coastal beaches.

Climate:

	High	Low
January	54	34
July	88	70

New Bern has a mild, four-season climate, with average mean daily temperature of 62, although summers are warm with highs in the upper 80s. Hurricane season is June-November.

Average relative humidity: 57%

Rain: 53 inches.

Cost of living: Average (specific index not available).

Average housing cost: The average residential sale in Craven County is $127,000. However, local real estate agents say retirees moving to the area are likely to spend $150,000 to $250,000 or more for a newer home in a desirable neighborhood. One- and two-bedroom apartments in desirable areas typically rent for $400 to $750 a month.

Sales tax: 6.5% (4.5% state and 2% local).

Sales tax exemptions: Prescription medicine, eyeglasses, some medical supplies and most services.

State income tax: For married couples filing jointly, the rate is graduated from 6% of taxable income up to $21,250 to 8.25% on amounts over $200,000. For single filers, it is graduated from 6% of income up to $12,750 to 8.25% on amounts over $120,000.

Income tax exemptions: Social Security benefits are exempt. Up to $2,000 of distributions from private retirement benefits and IRAs (up to the amount reported in federal income taxes), or up to $4,000 of government pensions may be exempt. Total deductions may not exceed $4,000 per person.

Intangibles tax: None.

Estate tax: None, except the state's pick-up portion of the federal tax, applicable to taxable estates above $1 million.

Property tax: $5.80 per $1,000 of assessed market value in Craven County. New Bern residents pay an additional $4.70 for a total of $10.50 per $1,000 of assessed value. Annual tax on a $150,000 home in New Bern would be about $1,575.

Homestead exemption: $20,000 or 50% (whichever is greater) off assessed value of permanent residence for those 65 or older with annual income of less than $18,000.

Religion: The metropolitan area is home to about 225 churches and synagogues of more than 40 denominations.

Dorothy, who goes by the nickname Dottie, is a bridge player, member of a chorus and active in volunteer groups. She credits the local newcomers club, with some 400 members, as opening doors for her and other retirees. Although newcomers can stay in the club for only three years, they can graduate to an alumni group and stay in it indefinitely.

A different kind of club — "Uncle Sam's Club" — is the reason why another large group of retirees selects the New Bern area. About 18 miles away in Havelock is Cherry Point, the largest Marine Corps Air Station in the United States. At Jacksonville, about 36 miles from New Bern, is Camp Lejeune Marine Base, where new recruits go through the rigors of Marine boot camp. Career Marine and Navy personnel who have served at one of these bases often return here in retirement.

There's no scarcity of outdoor recreational activities in New Bern. Big-time fishing and boating abound on area rivers and sounds, with at least 10 marinas serving boaters. The Neuse River, a mile wide at New Bern and several miles wide downstream of the town, is more like a big bay or lake than a river. New Bern is home to eight area golf courses.

Good swimming beaches are a short distance from New Bern at Emerald Isle, Atlantic Beach, Hammocks Beach State Park and Topsail Beach. Only about 45 miles by car and a short ferry ride away is the Cape Lookout National Seashore. The island of Ocracoke, one of the jewels of the North Carolina Outer Banks, is 75 miles and a two-and-a-half-hour ferry trip away.

While New Bern isn't for the shop-'til-you-drop crowd, the suburbs have the usual array of Wal-Mart, Target, Kmart and other national stores. There's a small mall, Twin Rivers, anchored by J.C. Penney and Belk department stores. Downtown has an eclectic mix of antique and junque shops, boutiques and galleries. For serious shoppers, regional malls in Raleigh are about two hours away, and Wilmington is even closer.

If there's a serpent in this Eden, it's the possibility of hurricanes, say retirees here. Two hurricanes hit coastal North Carolina in 1996 and another in 1998. In 1999, record heavy rains resulting from Hurricane Floyd and other storms caused billions of dollars of damage in the state, although New Bern and the immediate area have been spared serious damage. Flooding is possible in New Bern, but severe storm surges — the killers in most hurricanes — are unlikely here because of New Bern's average elevation of 12 to 18 feet above sea level, the presence of barrier islands east of Pamlico Sound and the sheer distance of New Bern from the open ocean.

However, many retirees say the snows back home were twice as bad as the potential for hurricanes in eastern North Carolina. The infrequent snowfalls in New Bern rarely stay on the ground more than a day or so, although it did snow two to three inches on two occasions early this year, around the time a fluke storm dumped nearly two feet of snow on Raleigh, two hours away.

Some retirees say they also had to adjust to the heat and humidity of summers in New Bern. However, Bill Ball, 60, who with his wife, Judy, 58, relocated from Weirton, WV, in 1994, says the upside is that the warm climate helps his arthritis. "Spending three or four months walking around in 35 degrees and wet, I'd start having a personality change," says Bill. Now, while he's not cured of his arthritis, he no longer has black circles under his eyes from lack of sleep. "We like the basic mildness of the winter, and being hill people tired of hills, it's a pleasure to drive on flat land," he says.●

Education: Retirees can take courses at a community college, Craven Community College, and at a campus of a four-year college, Mount Olive College. About 40 miles away in Greenville is East Carolina University, part of the University of North Carolina system and one of the largest universities in the state.

Transportation: Craven Regional Airport, a small but modern airport, is served by US Airways Express, offering flights to US Airways' hub in Charlotte, and Midway Airlines, with service to Raleigh-Durham. U.S. highways 70 and 17 are the major highway arteries. I-95 is the nearest interstate, 80 miles away.

Health: Craven Regional Medical Center in New Bern is a 313-bed, acute-care facility with more than 180 physicians on staff, supported by some 1,300 other staff. About two and a half hours away in Durham is Duke University Medical Center, one of the nation's leading hospitals.

Housing options: The New Bern area offers a wide choice of housing options, from 18th- and 19th-century homes in the downtown historic district ($100,000 to $500,000) to rural mobile home parks to riverfront and golf-course living in planned communities. Among the planned communities in the area are: **Taberna**, (800) 367-1278 or (252) 636-3700, with a private golf course and canoe dock on Brice's Creek and homesites from $47,000 to $175,000, or $140,000 to $750,000 for home and lot; **Evans Mill**, (800) 622-6297 or (252) 633-6100, country-style living on large lots, with lots from the mid-$20,000s, lots and homes from $175,000; **Greenbrier**, west of New Bern with a noted golf course, The Emerald, and homes from around $185,000 to $400,000; **Fairfield Harbour**, (800) 317-3303 or (252) 638-8011, about 10 miles from New Bern on the Neuse River, with two golf courses and a marina, condos and homes from $120,000 to $450,000. Among local real estate firms serving retirees moving to New Bern are **Coastal Homes Real Estate**, (888) 831-2620 or (252) 635-6500 and **Century 21 Action Associates**, (800) 521-2780 or (252) 633-0075. Retirement specialist Whit Morgan at **New Bern Real Estate** leads prospective residents on a free three-hour tour of New Bern and the surrounding area. For information call (800) 636-2992 or (252) 636-2200.

Visitor lodging: New Bern has seven bed-and-breakfast inns and a six motels. The 172-room Sheraton Grand, $79-$299, is New Bern's lodging leader, with a prime waterfront location near the new convention center, renovated rooms and many upscale amenities, (800) 326-3745 or (252) 638-3585. Comfort Suites, $87-$97, has a lovely Riverfront Park location, (800) 228-5150 or (252) 636-0022. The Airie, $79-$109, is a seven-room B&B in a converted Victorian home in the downtown historic district, complete with player piano in the parlor, (800) 849-5553 or (252) 636-5553.

Information: Chamber of Commerce of New Bern, 316 S. Front St., P.O. Drawer C, New Bern, NC 28560, (252) 637-3111 or www.newbernchamber.com. The chamber offers a relocation guide for $6.

Ocala, Florida

Retirees like rural setting, warm weather with seasons

By David Wilkening

Ocala's not your normal Florida scene — and that's one reason it's increasingly popular with retirees.

It's a small city in a rural setting, not a flashy coastal town. The terrain is hilly, perfect country for the many horse farms clustered in this north-central part of the state.

Palm trees are greatly outnumbered by sprawling old oak trees that shade homes and streets. Frame houses that conjure images of Northern residences add variety to the concrete-block structures so common in Florida. Although modern malls have brought in chain stores, Ocala still has a traditional downtown square that lends charm to the community.

With its somewhat sleepy atmosphere, plus a low cost of living and good climate, Ocala has attracted many retirees in recent years.

"We like the slow pace, and the people are friendly," says Julia Tierney, 57, who moved to Ocala from Washington, DC, with her husband, Francis, 67.

While many retirees have migrated here from the North, Ocala also is drawing retirees who've become disenchanted with other parts of Florida, particularly the southern area where congestion and crime are rising problems.

Marvin and Jean Van Merton, 71 and 60 respectively, retired from Oak Forest, IL, to Fort Myers first. She likes to joke that she prefers Ocala over the coast because "the cars don't rust like they do on the ocean." But there are more serious reasons for their move to Ocala.

"The coast was too crowded. There was too much traffic," says Jean. The Van Mertons like the more rural lifestyle Ocala offers. "We haven't found a better place to be," Jean says.

Ocala has become one of the fastest growing cities in the country. With a population of about 46,000, it is the largest city in Marion County, which has a population of 258,916.

Newcomers are quickly absorbed, in part because they are so common, according to the area's economic development council. Half of all residents have lived in the county less than 10 years, and a demographic profile of the county shows 24.5 percent of its residents are 65 or older.

Lester Crull, 72, and his wife, Marjorie, 60, moved here in 1990 from Waco, TX, but had lived much of their lives in Michigan. The Crulls like Ocala's country atmosphere and the variety of opportunities to do volunteer work, in hospitals and in programs to help shut-ins.

"We had gone past Ocala during other Florida trips," he says. "We knew it was more laid-back and a little cheaper than a lot of areas."

Indeed, the town is less costly than many other parts of Florida. Low cost of housing is a major reason that Ocala is more affordable. In 2001, home sales started at $72,000, according to the economic development council. Apartments also are reasonable, with recent figures showing the average monthly rent at $450 for one bedroom and $575 for three bedrooms.

"There's a lot of varied housing. You can find just about anything you want," says Jean. The Van Mertons looked at several options before choosing a custom homebuilder.

Many retirees favor the more traditional-style homes familiar in the North, but here they come with pools, sun decks and other extras that reflect the active outdoor lifestyle.

Ocala's average property tax is in the middle range for the state, says Villie Smith, Marion County's assistant property appraiser.

While Ocala boasts the traditional sunny Florida weather, it has an added attraction: a sense of seasons.

Joseph C. Finzer, 77, came here 22 years ago from his job in research-engineering at Eastman Kodak in Rochester, NY. He wanted to escape the snow.

"Ocala is somewhat like the North in that there are four seasons," he says, adding that the changes are more subtle than up North but more distinct than in southern Florida. Ocala is drawing retirees from southern Florida, many of them transplants who fled Northern climates, then decided they missed seasonal changes. But they don't want severe winters.

In Ocala, winter is short and mild. In January the average low temperature is 43 degrees, and in summer, the average high is 91. The annual mean temperature is just about perfect, at 70.

Along with its attributes come some drawbacks.

Residents bemoan a lack of public transportation but note that the problem is common in smaller cities throughout the country.

The area is short on fine dining opportunities but does have many reasonably priced, family-style places where dinners start at $5.95. On the upper price end, dinner entrees start at $11.

Summers can be humid, even sticky hot. Some retirees have problems with allergies they didn't have elsewhere and complain about bugs that, like humans, thrive in the balmy climate.

Ocala, like other cities its size, can't offer the cultural smorgasbord possible in metropolitan areas. The Tierneys, for example, miss the cultural amenities of their native Washington, DC, but say Ocala is expanding its offerings.

"Just in the short time we've been here we've seen changes, such as the enlargement of the civic theater," says Julia.

Its Appleton Museum of Art has more than 6,000 pieces and has been praised by directors of the National Endowment for the Arts as being "a major museum that would be impressive in any community."

The Crulls think Ocala's cultural pursuits aren't as good as their previous residence, a college town, but they think it has other advantages.

Ocala, an Indian name, was Florida's

southernmost tourist center for years until railroads began laying the tracks that would take visitors all the way down the coast.

In modern times, it's emerged as a cattle- and horse-breeding area. Today, 400 of the state's 600 horse-breeding farms are here, according to the state's Thoroughbred breeders association.

The area is also famous for its huge, 388,315-acre Ocala National Forest, a major recreation area for tourists and residents who enjoy fishing, hunting and camping.

Two other popular getaways are nearby. The Juniper Springs Recreation Area offers a tropical setting, with a huge rustic waterwheel churning 8 million gallons of cool spring water a day. At Silver Springs, glass-bottom boats take visitors over natural springs that have

been bubbling for centuries. A 350-acre nature park at the attraction has been the setting for "Tarzan" and "James Bond" movies.

A drawing factor for Ocala is that it's centrally located, on major highways, but not in the midst of too much action. For instance, beaches are only 75 miles away on the Atlantic side and 40 miles on the Gulf side. And Orlando with its many family attractions is about 100 miles away.

In health care, Ocala has two full-service hospitals, as well as psychiatric and drug and alcohol centers. Shands Hospital in Gainesville, 35 miles north, offers outstanding specialized care.

Florida as a whole attracts many retirees because of its financial and physical climate. The state long has granted a $25,000 homestead exemption on taxes

for property owners of all ages. The state has no personal income tax and no property tax on automobiles. It does have a sales tax of 6 percent, but groceries, medical and professional services and prescription drugs are exempt.

Whether they are seeking lower taxes or snowless winters, there are numerous reasons retirees are choosing to relocate here. Some reasons may be subtle, at least for Northerners who fled the cold but didn't want to totally escape their past.

"The good part about Ocala," says Finzer, "is that if you lived up North, it'll make you think a little about where you're from. But the good thing is that we don't get snow here."

Well, not usually, at least. It did snow briefly a few years ago. Finzer didn't mind — since it was only a flurry.●

Ocala, FL

Population: 45,943 in Ocala, 258,916 in Marion County.

Location: In north-central part of state, with hilly terrain that's become a center for Thoroughbred horse-breeding. Close to Ocala National Forest, with its hot springs parks.

Climate:

	High	Low
January	67	43
July	91	71

Average relative humidity: 55%
Rain: 53 inches.
Moderate climate. Mild winters; hot, humid summers.

Cost of living: 97.2, based on national average of 100.

Housing cost: In 2001, home sales ranged from $72,000 to $250,000.

Sales tax: 6%

Sales tax exemptions: Groceries, med-

ical services, prescription drugs.

Intangibles tax: Assessed on stocks, bonds and other assets. Tax rate is $1 per $1,000 in assets. The first $20,000 in assets is exempt for individuals. For couples filing jointly, the first $40,000 is exempt. Those who owe less than $60 need not pay.

Estate tax: None, except the state's "pick-up" portion of the federal tax, applicable to taxable estates up to $1 million.

Property tax: $21.22-$23 per $1,000 of assessed value, with homes assessed at 100% of market value. Taxes on a $100,000 home would be about $1,592 - $1,725 with homestead exemption.

Homestead exemption: First $25,000 of assessed value on primary, permanent residence.

Religion: 135 Protestant churches, 5 Catholic churches and 3 synagogues in the Ocala area.

Education: Classes are available at Central Florida Community College in Ocala and the University of Florida in Gainesville.

Transportation: No public transportation is available, residents rely on cars. The nearest airport is Gainesville Regional Airport, 40 miles away.

Health: Ocala has two full-service hospitals, Ocala Regional Medical Center and Munroe Regional Medical Center. The

county has three hospitals and seven nursing homes.

Housing options: A number of communities geared to retirees have been developed. **Lake Diamond Golf and Country Club**, (888) 907-5253, is a gated community with championship golf course, 43-acre lake, RV and boat storage, and homes from the low $160,000s. **Colonnades at On Top of the World**, (800) 421-4162, offers two 18-hole golf courses and a recreational center equipped with two pools, tennis courts and fitness center. Homes in the gated community start at $89,900. **Cherrywood Estates**, (800) 880-9050, has homes from $69,900 and such amenities as a heated pool, fitness center and tennis courts. **Oak Bend**, (800) 354-3636, offers manufactured homes from about $20,000 to $40,000. **Oak Run Country Club**, (800) 874-0898, or (800) 342-9626 in Florida, has homes from $98,000 to $207,000. **Ocala Palms Golf & Country Club**, (800) 872-7256, has single-family homes from $120,000 to $220,000. The area also has several retirement centers.

Visitor lodging: Ocala Holiday Inn, doubles $79, (352) 629-0381.

Information: Ocala-Marion County Chamber of Commerce, P.O. Box 1210, Ocala, FL 34478, (352) 629-8051 or www.ocalacc.com.

Ojai, California

Retirees find Shangri-La in a peaceful Southern California valley

By Mary Lu Abbott

In the evening, a cool hush descends on the valley. Traffic on the main street of Ojai dwindles to a few cars and pickups, and shops and galleries shut their doors. The tree toads and crickets strike up a chorus as the hour tolls from the Spanish bell tower downtown. The last rays of the sun illuminate the Topa Topa Mountains guarding the upper end of Ojai. At first a warm gold bathes the high ridge, then it blushes pink, briefly blessing the valley with a rosy glow until eclipsed by night.

It's the "pink moment," residents say. It's one of the treasures people take time to enjoy in this quiet valley in Southern California, only about 90 minutes northwest of the sprawling mega-lopolis of Los Angeles.

"This place has magic, something special. It's hard to put a finger on it," says Richard Sumner, 63, who retired here in late 1999 from the San Francisco Bay Area with his wife, Billie, 50.

Maybe it's the mountains, maybe the coastal air, maybe the groves of oranges, lemons and avocados, or the rose gardens that bloom year-round, or the romantic Spanish Mission architecture, or the huge old oak trees that form canopies over roads, or the evening smell of wood-burning fireplaces. Maybe it's the community spirit that embraces the young and the old, values the small-town life, supports local merchants and vows to limit growth and keep the valley pristine.

A family of artists, the Sumners first came here in the mid-1990s after Billie read a book by Beatrice Wood, a noted Ojai ceramic artist whose studio they wanted to visit. They never met the artist, but they fell in love with Ojai that spring when the orchards were in bloom.

"All the orange blossoms — it smells like going into an Oriental tea shop. The smell is incredible, especially in the evenings when it's warm. It fills the whole valley. It's very dreamy," Richard says.

Another couple who moved to the valley in retirement is Jim Christiansen, 57, and his wife, Fran, 54. Both lawyers, they retired early and moved here from Fresno in 2000. Jim already had a mental image from the 1950s, when as a young boy he

---

Population: About 32,000 in Ojai Valley, including Ojai, Meiners Oaks, Mira Monte, Oak View and Casitas Springs. Population of Ojai is about 7,862.

Location: The mountainous valley, about 85 miles northwest of Los Angeles, runs 14 miles inland from Ventura and is about 35 miles from Santa Barbara. Adjacent to Los Padres National Forest, the town of Ojai spreads across the upper end of the valley beneath the Topa Topa Mountains, which rise slightly above 6,000 feet.

Climate:

	High	Low
January	67	37
July	90	55

A Mediterranean-like climate contributes to a lush valley with orange, lemon and avocado orchards, rose gardens, bougainvillea and cactus. Days are sunny and warm, and nights are cool, even chilly in winter. Summer highs can top 100 but other seasons are mild. Air conditioning is needed a minimum number of days. Rain usually comes in winter; summer and fall are quite dry. Elevation ranges from about 750 feet in the Lower Valley to 1,500 feet in the Upper Valley.

Average relative humidity: 53%

Rain: 21.25 inches.

Snow: Rare in the valley, but mountain peaks are snowcapped in winter.

Cost of living: Above average, except for heating and air conditioning, which are needed only minimally.

Housing cost: Median in 2001 was about $380,000.

Sales tax: 7.25%

Sales tax exemptions: Food products, prescription medicines and services.

State income tax: For married couples filing jointly, graduated from 1% of taxable income up to $11,496 to 9.3% on amounts over $75,450. For single filers, graduated from 1% of taxable income up to $5,748 to 9.3% on amounts over $37,725.

Income tax exemptions: Social Security benefits and railroad pensions are exempt.

Intangibles tax: None.

Estate tax: None, except the state's "pick-up" portion of the federal tax, applicable to taxable estates of more than $1 million.

Inheritance tax: None.

Property tax: 1.062177% of value in incorporated areas of the valley (Ojai), 1.036500% to 1.078481% in unincorporated areas (other communities adjacent to Ojai). Property value is considered to be the purchase price the first year and then escalates about 2% a year. Taxing jurisdictions can add special assessments (for instance, for flood or pest control). In an incorporated area, basic tax on a $380,000 home would be about $3,962 with the exemption noted below. The state's homeowner assistance program reimburses up to $356 to those who are 62 or older (or blind or disabled) and have an income of no more than $35,251.

Homestead exemptions: $7,000 off the value for those who live in their home.

Religion: The valley has about 20 denominations represented among places of worship and several spiritual centers, including Krishnamurti Library, Krotona Institute of Theosophy and Meditation Mount.

Education: HELP, an extensive program for seniors, has numerous arts, crafts and self-enrichment classes at its center in Ojai. Adult education classes also are available at the University of California at

was captivated by an article in a sports magazine. It had a picture of a young woman tennis player against a backdrop of beautiful foliage. The setting was the public courts in the center of Ojai.

"So I associated Ojai with that beautiful picture. It (Ojai) is a very pretty word to say, and I had this beautiful sort of imagery about it, a real positive association going back to the '50s," Jim says.

For Jim and Fran, beauty was a high priority in relocating, and Ojai won out over the Pacific Northwest and the Santa Fe area. "Even after a year here, when I get in the car and drive into Ojai, I like to take the back road along the creek. I always appreciate how beautiful it is here," Fran says.

It is Shangri-La — indeed, the Shangri-La envisioned in the 1930s movie "Lost Horizon." In the valley's East End, Highway 150 winds up a string of switchbacks to Dennison Grade, where at 1,248 feet you gain the same view as in the movie.

It's a broad valley, most of the floor carpeted in velvety green citrus trees neatly planted in rows. It's protected by hills and mountains rising to 6,200 feet, the chaparral-covered slopes a brownish gray-green in the dry days of late summer, more vivid green after the winter rains.

Even now, more than six decades after the movie, serenity surrounds the valley, particularly the town of Ojai at the East End. A Chumash Indian word, Ojai (pronounced oh-hi) has been interpreted as "moon" and as "nest." For years, artists, writers, actors, movie producers and others in creative fields have settled here, finding inspiration and relaxation in an area that feels like Old California.

Considered a healing place since early times, it has spas, retreats and spiritual centers. Off Highway 150, Reeves Road climbs to a ridge known as Meditation Mount, a favorite spot to soak in the beauty of the land at sunset and gather for full-moon meditations.

The valley lies inland about 14 miles from Ventura and 35 miles from Santa Barbara on two roads off coastal U.S. Highway 101. Highway 150 twists over the mountains past sparkling Lake Casitas, which has 60 miles of shoreline along dozens of coves only minutes from valley communities. Highway 33, the more direct route over the valley floor from Ventura, is multilane several miles, then narrows to two lanes as it comes into the communities of Casitas Springs, Oak View and Mira Monte. It joins Highway 150 eastward past Meiners Oaks and into Ojai, which has a population of about 7,862.

Along the lower part of Highway 33, a few "praying mantis" pumpers still work the land. "Oil oozed from the hills. The pumpers used to be thick as ants, but there aren't near as many now," says Sandy Townsend, who works at the charming Hummingbird Inn of Ojai. Its namesake birds hover by feeders, and, like many homes here, the motel has

Ojai, CA

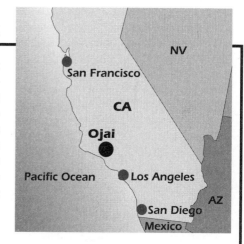

Santa Barbara and at its Ventura Center, and at Ventura College.

Transportation: During the day, the Ojai Trolley operates two routes, one an hourly circuit of Ojai and the other round-trip from Ojai through Meiners Oaks and Mira Monte. Fare is 25 cents; ages 65 and older ride free. Cab service is available. South Coast Area Transit (SCAT) runs buses from Ojai through the valley to Ventura. It is possible for residents of the town to get to major services and activities without a car. Residents and visitors are encouraged to use a park-and-ride lot and take the trolley into town to ease traffic along the two-lane main street, which also is Highway 150/33 through the valley to U.S. Highway 101. Highway 33 to Ventura can be slow-moving at peak hours.

Health: The Ojai Valley Community Hospital, on the edge of Ojai and Meiners Oaks, is a 110-bed modern facility, providing acute care and continuing care. General physicians and specialists of nearly all fields serve the valley, and practices in Ventura and Santa Barbara augment care. Alternative health-care options also are readily available.

Housing options: The valley does not have country club, golf or planned active-adult communities. Most homes are resales because there's limited new construction, though some individual lots are available. Homes are available in neighborhoods and small subdivisions in towns. On the outskirts, such as the East End of Ojai, homes usually are set on two to five acres. Overall, homes tend to be more expensive in Ojai, lower in Oak View, Mira Monte and Meiners Oaks, though expensive housing is scattered throughout the valley. While the median price is $350,000, the **Hitching Post** and **Creekside** developments have condominiums for $250,000 to $300,000. Small two-bedroom homes may be available for under $200,000, and there are a number of manufactured-home communities, with pools and clubhouses, with housing for under $80,000. **Whispering Oaks**, (805) 646-5809, is a retirement community with independent-living apartments for rent, and **St. Joseph's Health and Retirement Center**, (805) 646-1466, has accommodations amid citrus groves.

Visitor lodging: The Hummingbird Inn of Ojai, (800) 228-3744, is a small motel with fountains, gardens, a hammock, pool, mountain views and hummingbirds. It has comfortable rooms starting at $80 with continental breakfast; rates are higher in summer. There is a AAA discount. The Ojai Valley Inn and Spa, (800) 422-6524, which has a golf course and other activities, has deluxe rooms from $279, with some less-expensive weekday packages. The valley also has some B&Bs and chains.

Information: Ojai Valley Chamber of Commerce and Visitors Bureau, 150 W. Ojai Ave., Ojai, CA 93024, (805) 646-8126 or www.the-ojai.org.

gardens with rose bushes that bloom nearly continuously. A hammock on the lawn invites guests to slow down and relax.nearly continuously. A hammock on the lawn invites guests to slow down and relax.

"It's really peaceful here," Richard Sumner says. Adds Billie, "We found what we were looking for."

A fifth-generation resident of the San Francisco Bay Area, Richard traces his ancestry back to explorers of 1740. He owned several Bay Area framing galleries for three decades, and Billie was in the high-tech business, but they grew weary of the scene in the 1990s.

"The whole environment in the Bay Area was too much — the traffic, the overcrowding. Everyone was becoming a millionaire, and greed was rampant. There was a kind of frenzy we wanted to escape," Billie says.

They left at the height of the real estate market and dot-com companies, Richard says. They briefly thought about retiring in Mexico. They looked around Healdsburg in Sonoma County north of San Francisco but decided it was getting congested. They also thought about moving to the Santa Cruz Mountains near their home.

"Nothing was as beautiful as this, not even close," Richard says. So they started looking for a home in Ojai. "We came down about five times. We couldn't find any with a view of the mountains that were in our price range," he says.

A serendipitous question led to their new home. While consulting with their real estate agent, they frequently parked on an empty lot, admiring the mountain views. One day they asked if the land was for sale — and it was. So they bought it, found an architect and built a Spanish/Tuscany-style home on the two acres in the East End, outside the main part of the town.

They liked the area particularly for its low stone walls, many laid by Chinese laborers. "Some of these are hand-stacked, no mortar. They were built 100 years ago. They're five feet thick," Richard says. The Sumners followed suit, building a stone wall on their property, too.

They picked an architect who had grown up here — "he's more an artist," Richard says — and had him design a small house: a master bedroom, a guest bedroom and a "great room" with living and dining areas and a kitchen. Their stucco home has an open-beamed ceiling in the great room, with tall picture windows overlooking a high peak. During the year of construction, Richard came down once or twice monthly to check on the home. They also built a separate studio where he paints, makes prints and custom frames and teaches art and printing to friends.

"Our property is a work in progress. Little by little we want to landscape it ourselves. We're going to plant grapes. We have seven olive trees. I've pickled the olives once and they're delicious," Richard says.

On their acreage they also have three goats, one lamb and two wild burros. "We've always liked animals but never had a place to keep nondomestic animals. Goats are affectionate, intelligent, curious, just like dogs," Billie says. Their small border terrier, Chloe, keeps watch over Richard's activities during the day. Billie works for a firm specializing in employee safety.

Residents of Fresno for 30 years, Jim and Fran Christiansen started looking for a place to retire in 1995. They came to Santa Barbara frequently, visiting friends and a daughter in school there, and considered Santa Fe, Seattle and Washington's San Juan Islands for retirement. While all fit their desire for a beautiful place, Fran was hesitant to leave California, and they liked this area's climate best.

"Here you have this wonderful Mediterranean climate," says Jim, adding that it does get quite warm, though. "When we were leaving Fresno, which is one of the hottest parts in the state, one of our neighbors warned us about how hot Ojai is in the summers. But Fresno doesn't cool down at night, and here it does, and that makes a dramatic difference. We're a little cooler (in Oak View) — maybe five degrees — than Ojai proper because we're closer to the ocean," Jim says.

Though summer temperatures can top 100 degrees, the Christiansens and Sumners say they've needed their air conditioning only a few days of the year.

The Christiansens had targeted the Santa Barbara area for relocating but found it too pricey and came to the valley. Finding something in Ojai proved difficult because property was selling so quickly. When Jim was en route to see a listing, it sold before he got there. Then the agent suggested a home in Oak View, one of the unincorporated areas a couple of miles from Ojai. He liked it, the owner held it until Fran could come down, and they bought it. They sold their home in Fresno within a few days of listing it.

Jim liked the Spanish architecture with tile roof and felt they would be able to downsize comfortably into the home. Fran liked the open floor plan, the mountain views from the deck and the bonus — apricot, plum, apple, tangerine, orange and lemon trees in the back yard. The property also has huge, sprawling oak trees in the front yard.

"I love trees. I love the shade provided, the shadowy effect and watching them move in the wind. It's all very relaxing to me," she says.

The climate — "and grandchildren" — brought Marilyn Hefner, 66, to Ojai from Bend, OR. A native Oregonian, she grew "tired of slipping and falling on snow and ice" and moved here in 1998 after a daughter and family relocated south, also for the climate. She's not retired yet but figures this will be her choice when she does quit work. She was able to find a job in two weeks.

"Real estate prices are horrendous here," Marilyn says. The median in the first half of 2002 was running $380,000, but Marilyn found a viable alternative: a manufactured-home community. There are quite a few in the valley, many with clubhouses, pools and views. Marilyn bought a resale two-bedroom, two-bath home with a carport, air conditioning and heat.

"It's very nice and comfortable. The home was really taken care of. I have great neighbors. Everyone looks out for each other. There are young families and older people, a real mix," she says.

The climate encourages outdoor recreation year-round, with abundant choices only minutes from home. Hiking trails lead to peaks, canyons, creeks and waterfalls in the coastal mountains and adjacent Los Padres National Forest. Walkers, joggers, cyclists and equestrians take to the Ojai Valley Trail, which winds all the way to Ventura, with only a slight grade and frequent shade. Lake Casitas offers a beautiful mountainous setting for fishing and boating, and there are several campgrounds nearby.

Golfers tee off at Soule Park, an 18-hole public course in Ojai, and the renowned

Ojai Valley Inn and Spa has a noted championship course. Public courts in downtown Ojai's Libbey Park are the proving ground of champions, the site of the Ojai Tennis Tournament, the oldest annual amateur competition in the country.

California beaches are within 20 minutes, too. For Jim Christiansen, the proximity of the ocean has led to a new hobby: surfing. He had tried the sport briefly after high school, then in 1998 spent a week at a surfing camp.

"When we moved here, I took up surfing with a vengeance. It's a very popular surfing area," he says, noting that he frequents beaches between Ventura and Santa Barbara, where he encounters all ages who love the sport. Jim is so enthusiastic about surfing that he has written a book about retiring and taking up a totally new venture.

"The most heartwarming aspect is the bond between surfers that just cuts across all those lines that divide people frequently," Jim says. "For example, if I go into a surf shop and start talking with some kid behind the counter, who may be 15 or 20, there's none of that generational conflict where the kid is patronizing or talking to me as anything other than a surfer. There's just an acceptance. The person realizes I've got the same enthusiasm for the sport he or she does. There's a bond, and it's really a beautiful thing.

"People I've surfed with have been great, very friendly, nice, enthusiastic," he says.

While he made new friends surfing, Fran got to know people in the community when she volunteered to assist with the first Ojai Film Festival. That work led to her appointment to the board of the Ojai Film Society, which regularly screens foreign and independent films at the local playhouse. Fran says there are many volunteer opportunities.

One of them is HELP, a nonprofit seniors center that has been providing senior services for 35 years. It attracts retirees as both participants and volunteers. It has activities, self-enrichment classes and trips, and it provides volunteers for museums, schools, libraries and an after-school program. More than 700 people volunteer through HELP.

"Everyone is extremely friendly and welcoming. It has a wonderful sense of community," says Billie Sumner.

The Sumners' neighbors include a number of movie stars and people in the film industry. "Anthony Hopkins was living around the corner, but he has moved. We see Larry Hagman all over the place. He's like a pillar of strength here, a community supporter. I almost ran into Ellen DeGeneres in her car. They (the stars) are just like part of the community," Richard says, noting that residents respect their privacy.

One reason people, especially those from large cities, are drawn here is the quality of life. For all its modern amenities, Ojai feels like a flashback to a small town of another era. Residential areas shaded by huge live and coastal oaks and sycamores fan out from Ojai Avenue, the main street. Kids ride their bikes everywhere.

Along Ojai Avenue, the focal point and meeting place is the post office tower, a Ventura County landmark of Spanish Mission architecture, where bells toll the hour. Adjacent is Libbey Park, named for Edmund Libbey of Libbey Glass, a major benefactor of the town. The park's outdoor arena hosts summer concerts, the Ojai Music Festival and Shakespeare in the Park.

Across the street, gift shops, art galleries, a tearoom, cafes, a bookstore, ice cream parlor and other businesses are joined under a Spanish-style arcade. In the adjoining block, a 1919 Mission-style chapel now serves as the Ojai Valley Museum.

Culturally, besides film, music and drama events, there's an active arts community with frequent exhibits and tours of private studios. In addition, Santa Barbara and Ventura have other venues, and the attractions of Los Angeles are within an easy drive, the couples say.

"If someone comes to Ojai and is bored, it's only because they haven't stepped outside their door," says Teddy Schneider, a broker with Prudential Ojai Realty.

A large part of the valley remains agricultural or open space, and residents want it to stay that way. Building permits are limited, and oaks, sycamores and mature trees are protected. Residents cannot cut down such trees or even significantly prune them without a permit. Where the Sumners live, most homes have acreage with grass, and Richard says that authorities are strict about keeping the grass cut because of the danger of wildfires in the mountains.

"People here really revere the environment and are very determined to keep it nice. There are all kinds of environmental groups, and they do a good job of monitoring what's going on. You're not going to see explosive residential growth or commercial growth," Jim says.

"The tree-huggers and extreme conservatives are all together on some ideas, to preserve the area and keep it peaceful," agrees Richard.

"In general, we have an antigrowth environment in Ojai," says Daniel Singer, Ojai city manager. The housing market is tight, mostly with resales as there are no planned communities with new homes. The area has limited land open to development, and vacant lots or acreage may not be zoned for housing.

Retirees interviewed have few complaints. They all note the high price of housing. While the Christiansens think the overall costs are higher here, the Sumners feel the cost of living is somewhat less than in the Bay Area. The retirees find the health care good, though not as extensive as the larger cities in which they lived.

They're satisfied with area dining-out options, but Billie says items for ethnic cooking are hard to find, though available in Los Angeles. They caution that July and August usually bring days with 100-degree heat.

The Sumners did find a surprise: "Coyotes are everywhere. They come down the street sometimes. We have to keep them away from the animals (pets). At night, you can hear them," Richard says.

Rains normally come in winter and can be heavy, leading to flooding of creeks and the Ventura River. Traffic in morning and evening can move slowly on the two-lane highway from Ojai to Ventura, but the city manager points out that it's minor compared to metropolitan congestion.

The Christiansens think the valley appeals to active retirees who like the outdoors and those who want to participate in the community. Richard says it's for "a person who doesn't mind a little hot weather and a quiet place. By 9 or 10 (p.m.), it's locked down."

"What I like above all is that it's a kinder-spirited area," Jim says. "I think there's a very humane spirit that runs through the Ojai Valley."

For Richard its treasures are "mostly the stillness, the quietness, the peace. It's incredibly peaceful."●

Ormond Beach, Florida

Once a haven for the rich, this Florida community offers affordable housing

By David Wilkening

Nestled next to one of the world's most famous and busiest beaches is a quieter area that became known in the early part of the century as a winter home to many of America's richest families — including the Vanderbilts, the Astors and the Fords. Local lore has it that John D. Rockefeller settled here only after his staff spent five exhaustive years searching for the country's best retirement area.

Today you'll find that the small seaside town of Ormond Beach (population about 35,000) is home to many year-round residents. They may not be as famous or rich as those early settlers, but they like it here just the same.

Many of them shared with Rockefeller a desire to find the perfect retirement home. And many must have agreed with the oil tycoon's conclusion, because the area now has a large contingent of retirees from out-of-state.

"Ormond Beach was more residential and less touristy than other areas we looked at in Florida," explains Ruth Alvord, a 61-year-old widow who moved here from Buffalo, NY, in 1968 with her husband when he began receiving a disability pension.

"We liked the beauty of the location and the small-town flavor," she says. "I'm also near the river and the ocean. And I'm able to do things outdoors all year around."

Ormond Beach's fortunate geographical accident is to be on the Atlantic Ocean, about eight miles north of Daytona Beach and 90 miles south of Jacksonville. Orlando — the world's most popular tourist destination — is an hourlong ride by car. Historic St. Augustine is only a 30-minute drive.

Nearby Daytona Beach makes the news each year with its colorful auto racing and motorcycle madness, but Ormond Beach is better known for its tranquillity. It is a city in a parklike setting of tree-lined streets with residents often living in small houses only a few minutes by car, or even a few minutes on foot, from the ocean.

With sometimes-stiff ocean breezes helping keep the temperature at an annual average of 70 degrees, Ormond Beach offers a pleasant climate with many recreational opportunities near the water.

There are six golf courses — four public and two private — in Ormond Beach and many others within easy driving distance. Tennis enthusiasts have at their disposal two tennis complexes as well as 22 municipal courts popular with keenly competitive retirees. The city also operates baseball, soccer and football fields, picnic sites, horseshoe and shuffleboard courts and an extensive jogging trail.

All of this helped attract retirees like Joe and Patricia Lipscomb. Joe preferred what he saw in Ormond Beach to the many cities he visited throughout the world while traveling as a consulting engineer.

Joe, 68, had lived here in the 1950s before his job took him traveling. "Our children were born here. It was like coming home for us," says Joe, who was so eager to get here that he and his wife, Patricia, left their Pennsylvania home and headed for Florida on the very day that he retired.

They say they like the generally laid-back and slower-paced suburban lifestyle of Ormond Beach. They also like the variety of available housing. High-rise condos offering views of the Atlantic Ocean can cost upwards of $105,000 (the average area condo is $125,000), but Joe and others say that smaller homes only two or three blocks from the ocean still can be found for $60,000 to $70,000. Manufactured homes can be bought for even less. The average price for a single-family home is $124,000.

Retirees like Joe Lipscomb who like to fish can choose between the Atlantic Ocean and the Halifax River, which are only about two blocks apart. "I do pretty well fishing, though I don't go out and slay them," he jokes. "At least I get to stand in the water and cool off."

Joe fishes in the Halifax for game fish, trout and mangrove snapper. He sometimes ventures a few blocks to fish the glistening blue waters of the Atlantic, where cavorting dolphins can sometimes be seen from the shoreline.

He readily admits that Ormond Beach does not have as much culture as would be found in a larger northern city. But he points out that for a smaller area, there's a surprising amount of high-toned activity. The London Symphony, for example, comes for an extended visit every two years. It's an event that the entire community embraces with unbridled enthusiasm.

The Ormond Beach Performing Arts Center sponsors children's theater, a school of dance, touring theatrical productions, community theater and a concert series. There are big-name concerts in Daytona Beach, and other regularly scheduled events such as summer's Jazz Matazz festival also offer a variety of entertainment.

The Seaside Music Theater in Daytona Beach brings in a variety of distinguished actors and directors and produces many popular plays. The Memorial Art Museum showcases rotating exhibits of Florida artists, and the nearby Museum of Arts and Science has a planetarium. A local landmark and restaurant can be found at the Ponce de Leon Lighthouse, built in 1887 and still offering a panoramic view of the entire area.

Another Northerner who liked what she saw when she first visited was Mary Panny, 71, who lives in a manufactured-home community with her husband, Ed, also 71. They like "the easy availability of everything," says Mary. "We're close to a lot of things, such as the beach and shopping."

They also are close to regional shopping malls and Walt Disney World in Orlando, about 60 miles away. So many visiting relatives have wanted to see the land of Mickey Mouse that the couple bought an annual pass to the theme park.

Still another couple, Vera and Charles Hood, moved from Birming-ham, AL, soon after Charles, an executive with the telephone company, retired just over a decade ago. "We had visited my son, who lives here, and we thought this area was quieter and more residential than Birmingham," Charles explains.

In common with most residents, the Hoods like the proximity of the beach, as do John and Nancy Goss, 74 and 68 respectively. The Gosses, who were lifelong residents of New York City, considered Melbourne and Key West before retiring to Orlando. But then they were lured to Ormond by its beaches and climate.

"Ormond Beach is about three to four degrees cooler than Orlando because of its proximity to the ocean, which gives us a nice breeze," says John. Summers can be muggy, but residents say that ever-present air conditioning helps keep them cool.

If anyone gets a little hot under the collar in the dog days of summer, the near-perfect climate of winter months makes up for it. In January, for example, the average temperature is 63

Ormond Beach, FL

Population: 36,301

Location: Bordering the Atlantic Ocean and bisected by the Halifax River. About 90 miles south of Jacksonville, just north of Daytona Beach, and about 60 miles from Orlando.

Climate:

	High	Low
January	68	47
July	90	73

Average relative humidity: 61%

Rain: 49 inches.

Cost of living: Below average (specific index not available).

Housing costs: Average home price is $124,000.

Sales tax: 6.5% levied by the state.

Sales tax exemptions: Groceries, medicines, some professional services.

State income tax: None.

Intangibles tax: Assessed on stocks, bonds and other assets. Tax rate is $1 per $1,000 in assets. The first $20,000 in assets is exempt for individuals. For couples filing jointly, the first $40,000 is exempt. Those who owe less than $60 need not pay.

Estate tax: None, except the state's "pick-up" portion of the federal tax, ap-plicable to taxable estates above $1 million.

Property tax: $22.29 per $1,000 of assessed home value, with homes assessed at 80 percent of market value. Taxes on a $124,000 home are $1,654 with homestead exemption.

Homestead exemption: First $25,000 of assessed value on primary, permanent residence, plus $500 exemption for widows and widowers.

Religion: More than 250 houses of worship serve many faiths in Volusia County.

Education: Inexpensive adult-education courses ranging from fishing to water-color painting to yoga are available at The Casements, former home of John D. Rockefeller. The Ormond Beach Senior Center has exercise and dance classes, computer instruction and foreign-language courses, among others. Daytona Beach Community College, a two-year school, also offers a variety of classes, including an especially popular adult-education course on how to write mystery novels. It's taught by local authors.

Transportation: Daytona Beach International Airport has 27 daily departures, with nonstop flights to Atlanta, Charlotte, Jacksonville, Miami, Newark, Orlando, Philadelphia and Raleigh-Durham. Scheduled airlines include Continental, Delta, Gulfstream and USAir. There are nearby municipal airports at Ormond Beach, DeLand and New Smyrna. Orlando International Airport, about 60 miles from Ormond Beach, has daily nonstop flights to more than 64 U.S. and 14 international cities.

Health: Hospitals include Memorial Hospital-Ormond Beach, with 205 beds, more than 300 physicians and Volusia County's only cardiovascular center performing open-heart surgery. Radiation therapy for cancer also is available. Other facilities in the area include Halifax Medical Center in Daytona Beach, which has 402 doctors and 748 nurses.

Housing options: The Falls at Ormond, (386) 673-2333, is the area's first manufactured-home community with such features as 24-hour security, clubhouse, pools, tennis courts and nine lakes. Homes start at $35,000. A newer manufactured-home community by the same builder is **Aberdeen at Ormond Beach,** (800) 898-5541, where homes start at $58,999. Another option is **Ormond in the Pines,** (386) 676-7463, located in a parklike setting with 214 apartments that are owned and operated by the nationally known Holiday Retirement Corp. It offers independent, assisted and supervised living options. Rent starts at $1,300 a month, which includes three sit-down meals a day, housekeeping services and paid utilities. The facility has a activities director and offers organized events.

Visitor lodging: Ormond Beach's newest hotel is the seven-story, 98-unit Coral Beach, (800) 553-4712. Ocean-view rooms generally are $50-$160 a night. Prices can go higher during special events.

Information: Ormond Beach Chamber of Commerce, 165 W. Granada Blvd., Ormond Beach, FL 32174, (386) 677-3454 or www.ormondchamber.com.

degrees, compared to 82 degrees in July. The average annual rainfall is almost 49 inches, much of that coming between June and October, usually in the form of afternoon showers that cool the beaches before giving way to sunny skies.

Larry and Olive Gorman, both 70, moved to Ormond Beach for health reasons. He was in the computer business and she was a teacher in Albany, NY, before they retired first to a small town near Sarasota on Florida's Gulf Coast.

"It was very quiet and there was not much activity. At that time, there were hardly even any restaurants," Larry recalls. But the final straw came when he experienced heart problems and lost confidence in the local hospital.

"My wife didn't feel safe living there anymore. We happened to talk to a real estate agent who told us the hospital in Ormond Beach was world-famous for its heart specialists," says Larry. He later had successful heart surgery at Memorial Hospital-Ormond Beach, a 205-bed facility that is the county's only cardiovascular center performing open-heart surgery.

Larry also likes the wide selection of area restaurants. There are inexpensive hamburgers and milkshakes at the 1950s nostalgia-rich Doo-Wop-A-Doo. More sedate and upscale surroundings are found at such longtime favorites as Julian's Restaurant, known for its prime rib and live music.

The Gormans and others say Ormond Beach is retiree-friendly. There are early-bird dinner specials at affordable restaurants, and many merchants offer special senior discount days.

There are a few drawbacks, but local retirees don't seem to mind the noisy two-wheelers that sometimes venture into Ormond Beach from Daytona Beach, where motorcycle racing is becoming increasingly popular. "The motorcyclists are these people who like to sometimes run around in the woods and watch girls wrestle in coleslaw and stuff, but they go their way while we go ours. They don't really bother anybody, other than they make some noise," says Joe Lipscomb.

Like many Florida communities, Ormond Beach was little more than a settlement as recently as a century ago. It began to appear on the map when the East Coast Railway was extended in 1886. Two years later, the once-stately but now abandoned Ormond Hotel opened to cater to such society travelers as the Astors and the Rockefellers, who began migrating down from the North.

Situated in Volusia County, about 90 miles south of Jacksonville, Ormond acquired the no-longer-used nickname of "gateway to the tropics." In common with its more flashy big sister, Daytona Beach, Ormond also was popular with early auto enthusiasts.

Just after the turn of the century, Ransom Olds and Alexander Wilton, two early manufacturers of "horseless carriages," challenged each other to an auto race on the hard-packed sand of Ormond Beach. Each clocked an identical 57 miles per hour, yielding no victor but inaugurating a tradition of racing that continues today at world-famous Daytona International Speedway.

For some 60 years, owners and manufacturers of the world's best-known motor vehicles — Olds, Ford, Chevrolet and Kaiser — endeavored to set speed records on the wide beaches of Ormond and Daytona. A new motor sports attraction, Daytona USA on the grounds of Daytona International Speedway, chronicles this rich auto history.

Beach racing is a thing of the past, but motor vehicles (with some restrictions) still are allowed to drive along much of Volusia County's 43-mile stretch of hard-packed beaches. There are inevitable complaints, and it's likely that the vehicles eventually will be banned for safety and environmental reasons, though polls taken by the *Daytona Beach News Journal* generally have shown the local population to be evenly divided on the issue of driving on the beaches.

What would John D. Rockefeller have made of the evolution of Ormond Beach from a wealthy winter home of racing enthusiasts to a suburban-style community popular with retirees? It's hard to say, but one thing seems certain. The notoriously tight-fisted Rockefeller would almost certainly approve of Ormond Beach's tax rate, one of the lowest in Volusia County.

Yes, Rockefeller might still think this was the best place to retire.●

Oxford, Mississippi

A rich cultural and literary tradition enriches this unique Mississippi town

By Linda Herbst

If you ever tour the Deep South, make time to visit one of its jewels — Oxford, home of the University of Mississippi. Located on the picturesque route through the Mississippi Delta from Memphis to Natchez and New Orleans, Oxford has long been a favorite stopover for travelers meandering through the historic South.

Just an hour south of Memphis, the gracious curves of the area's rolling hills slope to level stretches of grassy valleys and pastureland. On the way into town, travelers often stop at the gates of one of the farmhouses that line the road. This particular one belongs to one of the nation's most popular writers, John Grisham, and is just one of Oxford's many literary landmarks. Beginning with Pulitzer and Nobel Prize winner William Faulkner, Oxford was the home and inspiration of nationally renowned novelists, poets, photographers, artists and musicians for the greater part of the 20th century.

It is its literary tradition, however, that sets Oxford apart from other arts meccas. Writers as diverse as Faulkner, Willie Morris, Larry Brown, Barry Hannah, Cynthia Shearer, John Grisham, Donna Tartt and Mary Hood have lived and worked in Oxford. Nearly every week world-renowned writers and poets visit Oxford and the university to read from their work and revel in what nearly all have called its "literary mystique." Residents and visitors alike have a hard time pinning down exactly what that mystique is all about, but one thing is for sure: The creative atmosphere here is intoxicating.

Once a year, usually in April, Oxford and the University of Mississippi host the Oxford Conference for the Book, a weeklong conference attended by the nation's foremost publishers, novelists, short story writers and journalists. The nonacademic conference is generally free and open to the Oxford community, and the whole town gets into the spirit of celebrating books. In August, the university hosts one of the most respected and longest-running literary conferences in the world, the Faulkner and Yoknapatawpha Conference.

Despite the Southern summer sun, the town seems to burst at its seams with distinguished Faulkner scholars from around the world, and once again the city revels in the excitement of being part of this important tradition. In many ways, Oxford is the manifestation of Faulkner's words: "The past is never dead. It's not even past." This is true of both the city of Oxford and the University of Mississippi, known as "Ole Miss," whose homes and public buildings house the sorrows and joys of the people who lived here during its frontier days, through the Civil War and the turbulent '60s. In its own way, Oxford's heritage is a story about the South from a perspective unparalleled in Southern history.

Aside from its literary traditions and historical value, Oxford's charms are so numerous that it is hard to choose the singular aspect that has placed it at the top of great places to settle for retirement. The overwhelming majority of retirees living in Oxford, however, are quick to point out that while Oxford is a great place to retire, it's not a retirement community.

"By that, I mean Oxford's a real place with a multigenerational population. It's not a controlled environment at all," says Bill Gurley, who with his wife, Clair, retired to Oxford several years ago from Greenwood, MS. Bill, a former bank president, maintains that the word "retirement" has great latitude. "For us, it doesn't necessarily mean strictly a time of leisure. Just because you don't have a job anymore doesn't mean you don't work," points out Bill, who has become a sales associate with a local real estate firm.

Bill and Clair's raised Louisiana cottage was completed in 1996. They were lucky to have found a lovely lot in an older, established neighborhood within easy walking distance of the town square. One of the most charming features of their three-bedroom home is its wraparound porch, which the Gurleys have decorated with ceiling fans and small groupings of easy chairs and cocktail tables. Bill and Clair can be seen nearly every nice afternoon enjoying the ease of this wonderful porch, and neighbors and friends are likely to join them.

Several years ago Clair Gurley was diagnosed with a heart problem, so quality of health care was a primary concern when it came time to decide on a retirement location. Baptist Memorial Hospital-North Mississippi, a 204-bed acute-care facility, has more than 70 medical and surgical physicians representing more than 30 specialty areas. It is one of the region's fastest-growing hospitals, serving a population of 200,000 in an eight-county area. Current expansion plans include an outpatient surgery center, cancer center and wellness and rehabilitation center.

The Gurleys also wanted to live in a college town. "The university and all that it offers — open-mindedness, continuing education, performing arts — were very important to us," says Clair. And with two daughters and two grandchildren living out of state, the Gurleys were pleased that Memphis International Airport was only 70 miles north of Oxford. The airport is located in the southernmost area of Memphis, so driving there doesn't require big-city traffic nerves.

Most of Oxford's retirees share Bill's energetic attitude toward retirement. Rev. Frank Poole and his wife, Mary, retired to Oxford in the summer of 1999 from Baton Rouge, LA. As part of the United Methodist tradition, Frank and Mary have made a lifelong commitment to ministry through music. They joined the Oxford-University Methodist Church and immediately became involved in its music traditions.

Frank and Mary love the atmosphere of small towns. In Oxford, they feel safe and independent from the constraints a larger place would put on them in terms of safety. Traffic can be hectic at times, but Mary says that because the weather is mostly nice, she and Frank feel safe enough to walk at any time of the day or night. Frank and Mary have moved into their newly constructed home but continue to add the finishing touches, and they also appreciate the level of trust they have with their contractor and the workmen who come and go at their home.

Mary's mother and father, Dr. and Mrs. A.B. Lewis, live directly behind them. The Lewises, both in their late 90s, have full-time sitters and house-

Oxford, MS

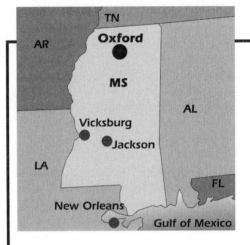

Population: The population of the city is 11,756, and enrollment at the University of Mississippi is about 14,500.

Location: Oxford is located in the hilly section of north Mississippi, 75 miles from Memphis, TN, and 165 miles from Jackson, MS, the state capital. Elevation is 380 feet.

Climate:

	High	Low
January	55	36
July	91	72

Average rainfall: 54 inches.

Average snowfall: 3 to 4 inches.

Cost of living: Below average (specific index not available).

Median housing cost: $125,000 for a single-family, three-bedroom home.

Sales tax: 7%

Sales tax exemptions: Prescription drugs.

State income tax: For married couples filing jointly and single filers, the rate is graduated from 3% of taxable income up to $5,000 to 5% on amounts over $10,000.

Income tax exemptions: Social Security benefits, public and private pensions, IRAs and annuities are exempt. There is an additional $1,500 personal exemption for residents age 65 and older.

Income tax exemptions: Qualified retirement income is exempt, including Social Security benefits, public and private pensions, IRAs and annuities. There is an additional $1,500 personal exemption for residents age 65 and older.

Intangibles tax: None.

Estate tax: None, except the state's "pick-up" portion of the federal tax, applicable to taxable estates above $1 million.

Property tax: Property and automobiles are subject to ad valorem taxes. Automobiles are assessed at 30% of market value, and 6% of the assessed value is used as a tax credit. Residential property in Mississippi is assessed at 10% of its market value. A house valued at $125,000 would be assessed at $12,500. Based on the local tax rate of $69.10 per $1,000, the yearly tax would be $864, without the exemption noted below.

Homestead exemption: There is a homestead exemption in the form of a tax credit of up to $240 for all homeowners. Residents age 65 and above can claim the first $864 of assessed value or $60,000 of market value as exempt from all ad valorem taxes.

Religion: The Oxford area represents, supports and conducts services for a wide variety of beliefs including Protestant, Catholic and Jewish faiths.

Education: The University of Mississippi focuses on seven major schools of study: liberal arts, engineering, education, law, pharmacy, business and medicine. Masters and doctoral degrees are offered. Ole Miss is a participant in the Elderhostel program, and planning has begun on an institute for lifelong learning.

Transportation: Memphis International Airport is 70 miles north of Oxford and provides service to all major cities.

Health: Baptist Memorial Hospital is a 204-bed acute-care facility. It has more than 70 medical and surgical physicians representing more than 30 specialty areas. Leased by one of the largest not-for-profit health care systems in the country, Baptist Memorial Health Care Systems of Memphis, the hospital provides a full range of comprehensive medical care to all ages.

Housing options: Housing sites in the historic neighborhood are few, and houses generally cost more in that neighborhood. However, housing sites are available in newer housing developments that dot the county. At **St. Charles Place**, one mile south of Oxford Square, most homes have three bedrooms and two baths and range in price from $150,000 to $200,000. For more information, call Kessinger Real Estate, (662) 234-5555. **Grand Oaks** is set among rolling hills, with family homes that range from $400,000 to $750,000 on one side of the golf course development and three-bedroom golf villas ranging from $180,000 to $200,000 on the other side. For more information, contact Kessinger Real Estate, (662) 234-5555. At **Azalea Gardens**, an independent and assisted-living facility, services include transportation, activities, dining, housekeeping, beauty shop, massage therapist, exercise rooms, performances, arts and crafts, a full-time nurse and personal emergency response system. These services are available both to residents of the main facility as well as homeowners on the property. Popular new cottages for sale on the grounds have two bedrooms and range from $130,000 to $145,000. For a monthly fee, the management also takes care of 24-hour security, trash pickup and yard maintenance. For more information about Azalea Gardens, call (662) 234-9600.

Visitor lodging: There are eight hotels with more than 400 rooms, including three bed-and-breakfast inns. A sampling includes the Downtown Inn, $60-$85, (800) 606-1497; Oxford Days Inn, $59-$65, (662) 234-9500; Comfort Inn, $65-$125, (662) 234-6000; and Oliver-Britt House, $55-$85, (662) 234-8043.

Information: Oxford-Lafayette County Chamber of Commerce, 299 W. Jackson Ave., P.O. Box 108, Oxford, MS 38655, (800) 880-6967, (601) 234-4651 or www.oxfordms.com. The chamber has a retiree attraction program director. Oxford Tourism Council, 115 S. Lamar Blvd., Oxford, MS 38655, (662) 234-4680. For information about Hometown Mississippi Retirement, call (800) 350-3323.

keepers, and Mary says it is a joy and a privilege to spend these last years with her parents. Dr. Lewis is the retired dean of liberal arts at the University of Mississippi. He and his wife have lived in Oxford for 40 years, so Oxford has been a second home to Frank and Mary in many ways.

One of the many aspects of Oxford and the university that the Pooles enjoy is the frequency and quality of concerts and theater performances on campus each season. From opera and Shakespeare to visiting symphonies and dance companies, the university's "artist series" is an affordable entertainment option.

"I was made for retirement," says Frank. "I have so much time now to concentrate on music."

"Some of the nicest evenings we've had here in Oxford have been those in which we've had a light supper, then walked to campus to a performance or concert," adds Mary. The Pooles live less than a quarter-mile from the university, which isn't necessarily a rarity in Oxford. Many retirees have chosen to live near the university and historic Oxford Square, and one can see the over-60 crowd walking side-by-side with coeds on any nice afternoon.

Aside from concerts and theater performances, the university offers an array of continuing-education classes, including wine tastings, music lessons, language classes, computer workshops, painting and sculpture lessons and cultural excursions to the Mississippi Delta and Memphis.

Usually, when asked, Oxford retirees either claim the wealth of cultural opportunities, the presence of the University of Mississippi, the literary heritage or the overwhelming sense of history as Oxford's biggest draws. "But don't forget the shopping and dining," says Clair Gurley.

Oxford's historic town square has a lively year-round festive atmosphere. The community boasts more than 50 restaurants, many of them unique to Oxford — gourmet coffeehouses, fine dining, Memphis-style barbecue and down-home cafes. In the spring and fall, students and residents dine on balconies overlooking the square, shop in the multitude of boutiques, gift and antique shops, or just pause for a neigh-borly chat on one of the square's strategically placed park benches. Oxford's centrally located department store, Neilson's, is privately owned by an Oxford family and is considered the South's oldest store, established in 1848.

"Let's just say it fits every criteria for a retirement choice," says Shirley Perry, one of Oxford's newest retirees. "In doing my research, I found that Oxford was literally the only place that actually fit every criteria I had on my list — and the list was long, I can tell you."

Shirley retired to Oxford in September 1999, making the move from her longtime home in Boston, where she was a consultant to pharmaceutical and biotech industries in business development. "I had been thinking of where to retire for quite some time," says Shirley. "I literally subscribed to every magazine about the subject. I went to the library; I made calls and attended conferences. My criteria were very specific.

"It had to be a town versus a city, for one — someplace easy to negotiate, as well as one with a defined sense of community," she says. "It had to have regularly organized cultural events, since I've always loved community theater. It also had to have a sense of history and achievement. When I discovered that Oxford had all that and more — a university, a great health-care community and a low cost of living — my decision was made."

Shirley's traditional brick house is in a lovely new neighborhood called South Oaks. Just three miles from the charm of the town square, South Oaks features spacious, wooded lots. Shirley's new four-bedroom home is built in what Shirley calls "Mississippi modern" style and sits on a half-acre corner lot. The one-story home has an imposing gabled roof, and the rooms are light and airy with high ceilings.

Writing and bicycling are two of Shirley's favorite hobbies. Despite the hills, Shirley finds cycling in Oxford a pleasure. The streets are safe and bicycle-friendly, she says, and there are many cyclists, young and old, on the streets. Plans are underway to create a bike path along the old railroad track that runs through town.

For most of her professional life, Shirley worked for the Central Intelligence Agency in Europe. She plans to begin work on her memoirs as soon as her house is completed, and she finds the literary community and the many writers' groups and classes stimulating.

Small, safe, friendly, beautiful and cultural usually add up to expensive, but that's not necessarily true in Oxford. While the real estate market has boomed in the last few years, with values on some properties growing 100 percent or more, deals are still available. The average three-bedroom home is $125,000. Generally, properties at this price won't be located in the historic district, but Oxford has many welcoming neighborhoods, new and old. There are virtually no empty lots for sale in the historic part of town.

Occasionally there are houses for sale that can be remodeled or demolished and rebuilt. Homes in the historic area range from $300,000 and up.

New housing developments are abundant, however. These include St. Charles Place, designed in the mode of a small harbor town or New Orleans neighborhood; Grand Oaks, an upscale neighborhood on a lovely 18-hole golf course; and Azalea Gardens, an independent and assisted-living retirement community.

The average cost of living in Mississippi is 10 percent below the national average, and Mississippi residents benefit from the lowest per capita tax burden in the nation. In addition to low taxes in general, retirees living in Mississippi benefit from additional tax breaks. Social Security is not taxed, regardless of total income. Retirement income from IRAs, 401(k)s, Keoghs and qualified public and private pension plans are not taxable. The state welcomes, and even recruits, relocating retirees.

"I actually received an invitation to retire in Mississippi," says Shirley Perry, referring to the state's active retiree recruitment program, Hometown Mississippi Retirement. "I'd always heard about Southern hospitality, but now I'm experiencing it first-hand."

"We love the mixture of young and old, as well as the mixture of cultures here," says Frank Poole. "It's a small, but cosmopolitan town — all the benefits of a city without the negative side. We're having a great time enjoying our freedom together here."●

Palm Coast, Florida

This quiet, clean community on Florida's Atlantic coast boasts affordable housing and ample recreation

By Karen Feldman

When Bill and Mary Ilavsky started looking for a place to retire in the early 1990s, they wanted a locale more temperate than Rockaway, NJ, their home of 30 years. Their search led them to Palm Coast, a small city that is quietly thriving between St. Augustine and Daytona Beach on Florida's northeast coast.

They first considered the Sunshine State's southwestern coast, but Palm Coast won their hearts. "There seems to be a lot less traffic up this way," says Mary, 63. Besides that, they like having something of a change of seasons, she says. "We get winter here, and we have to wear our coats and gloves sometimes — but it doesn't last."

With virtually year-round boating weather, the Ilavskys enjoy living on a canal. They dock their 19-foot Sea Ray motorboat behind their house, where it's easily accessible for a spur-of-the-moment ride. A favorite excursion is taking a leisurely hour-long ride up the Intracoastal Waterway to St. Augustine for lunch and back. Along the way, they share the water with dolphins, manatees, herons, egrets and pelicans.

"It's nice for when the children come, and it doesn't cost us a fortune," Mary says.

Still another plus is Palm Coast's location in the northeasternmost part of the state close to Interstate 95, which makes it easier for the couple's 10 children and eight grandchildren to visit than if they lived farther south.

Fewer crowds, great weather and a prime location make Palm Coast appealing to many retirees. Population figures indicate that 45 percent of the city's 33,000 residents are 55 and older.

"We're in a key location," says Bob Sgroi, 63, who retired to Palm Coast in 1995 with his wife, Barbara, 64. "We border Daytona to the south, St. Augustine to the north. The beach is close by, and we have seven or eight golf courses."

The couple from Sayville, a community on Long Island, NY, bought a condo in Palm Coast in 1984 and vacationed there every year for a decade. When they retired — he as commissioner of real estate for Suffolk County, and she from a job with the Federal Aviation Administration — they never considered living anywhere but Palm Coast.

The city has grown considerably since the Sgrois and Ilavskys arrived, a boom that has its roots in the 1970s. That's when ITT Community Development Corp. moved into Flagler County and purchased a huge swath of the county for a planned community, says Chuck Warren, owner-broker of Prudential Warren Real Estate in Palm Coast.

"Basically ITT came in the '70s and created 48,000 lots," he says. "They had the deep pockets to be able to entirely put in all the infrastructure — roads,

---

Population: 32,732 in Palm Coast.

Location: On Florida's northeast coast, Palm Coast is the largest city in Flagler County. It's 68 miles south of Jacksonville, 31 miles south of St. Augustine and 24 miles north of Daytona Beach.

Climate:

	High	Low
January	63	38
July	90	72

Average relative humidity: 53%

Rain: 48 inches, most of which falls from June through October.

Cost of living: Below average (specific index not available).

Average housing cost: $101,500

Sales tax: 7%

Sales tax exemptions: Food, some services and medicine.

State income tax: None.

Intangibles tax: A tax of $1 per $1,000 is assessed on stocks, bonds and other assets. The first $20,000 is exempt for individuals. For couples filing jointly, the first $40,000 is exempt. Those who owe less than $60 need not pay.

Estate tax: None, except the state's "pick-up" portion of the federal tax, applicable to taxable estates of more than $1 million.

Inheritance tax: None.

Property tax: $18.75 per $1,000 of assessed value. With a $25,000 homestead exemption, the annual tax on a $101,500 home would be $1,434.

Homestead exemption: $25,000 off assessed value of primary, permanent residence.

Religion: Within Flagler County, there are five Roman Catholic churches, 33 Protestant churches, one Orthodox church and a synagogue.

Education: A satellite campus of Daytona Beach Community College offers two-year degrees as well as adult and community education programs and lifelong learning.

Transportation: Major airlines serve Daytona Beach International Airport, the nearest commercial facility. Corporate jets and small aircraft can use the Flagler County Airport. Jacksonville International Airport is about an hour's drive north. The city is convenient to Interstate 95. The East Coast Intracoastal Waterway, which bisects the eastern portion of Flagler County, is navigable from the St. Lawrence Seaway to Miami.

Health: A plentiful supply of doctors and dentists, Memorial Hospital (81 beds, located in Bunnell) and two 100-bed nursing homes provide for the health needs of residents in the city and the rest of Flagler County. Nearby facilities include Flagler Hospital in St. Augustine, 30 minutes north, and Halifax Medical Center and Columbia Medical Center, 30 minutes south in Daytona Beach. A new Memorial Hospital and Memorial Medical Park are under construction and

water, sewer, power," Warren says. They also designated space for government buildings, a library, schools and the fire department.

Dick Morris, executive director of the Flagler County Palm Coast Chamber of Commerce, says that after building the roads and infrastructure, ITT marketed the area as a prime retirement spot, selling parcels of lots to Northeasterners as well as investors from Europe, South America, Russia and Japan.

Fewer than 8,000 people lived here in 1980, but the developers envisioned bigger things to come. They built golf courses, designed communities with individual themes and included amenities such as tennis courts and restaurants.

The completion of an interchange onto Interstate 95 made Palm Coast more accessible. The pace of building began to accelerate, exploding between 1990 and 2001. The population swelled by more than 76 percent, despite the departure of ITT in the mid-1990s when it decided to concentrate on other aspects of business.

Nonetheless, the city continues to expand, imbued with something many Florida locales lack: room to grow. "Today Palm Coast consists of roughly

20,000-plus homes and condos and roughly 30,000 vacant lots," Warren says. "It's not even half built out."

When the Ilavskys built their three-bedroom home on the canal, there weren't any homes on the island on the other side. Nine years later, a gated community called The Sanctuary is under construction, with 167 lots and homes priced from $350,000 to $1 million.

Housing options are wide-ranging both in styles and prices. "Houses are cheap," says Bill Ilavsky, 70. "You can get a house on the water very inexpensively."

The availability of waterfront land places Palm Coast among a precious few Florida communities. About 30 percent of the lots in Palm Coast are on water, says Morris. A large number sit along the city's 23 miles of navigable saltwater canals, where homeowners take to the water on everything from kayaks to 60-foot yachts.

Adding to the city's appeal are many bike paths, numerous parks, tennis facilities and golf courses. A golf magazine has dubbed Ocean Hammock, the newest course, "the Pebble Beach of the East Coast," with at least eight holes

overlooking the Atlantic Ocean.

Warren says there's a lot of affordable property for two reasons: "The city never had to spend money on the infrastructure. It was deeded over to them, so they don't have the issues of deferred maintenance or expansion of services. Another reason is that with all these vacant lots, they are making a contribution to the tax base, yet virtually no services have to be supplied to them."

At the low end, he says, quarter-acre lots are available for as little as $5,000, although $10,000 to $15,000 is more common. It's possible to build a 1,200-square-foot home with three bedrooms, two baths and a two-car garage on a quarter-acre lot for $90,000, he says.

There are at least six condominium complexes in the city, providing a mix of one-, two- and three-bedroom units ranging from about 750 square feet to about 1,700 square feet. Prices range from the mid-$50,000s through the mid-$100,000s, Warren says.

While the choice of lots remaining on saltwater canals is limited, homes periodically come up for sale, ranging from two-bedroom, two-bath houses built in the mid-1970s that might sell for about $150,000 to larger, more contemporary

Palm Coast, FL

expected to open by the end of 2002. The new hospital will offer all private rooms, a larger emergency room and the Memorial Heart Institute, Memorial Cancer Care Center and outpatient services. Acupuncture, chiropractic and hospice care also are available.

Housing options: Palm Coast offers a wide range of housing opportunities, from compact condos to sprawling waterfront homes. A basic quarter-acre lot costs $5,000-$15,000. One-, two- and three-bedroom condos are available at several complexes, ranging from the mid-$50,000s to the mid-$100,000s. Single-family homes range from about $80,000 on a standard interior lot (one that doesn't back up to a golf course or canal) to about $1 million for a spacious waterfront home. **Centex Homes**, one of the nation's largest builders of single-family homes, has new homes in several architectural styles in Palm Coast. For information, call Palm

Coast Real Estate Co., (800) 441-3044 or www.palmcoastrealestate.com. Bordered on the east by the Intracoastal Waterway and on the west by a 4,000-acre wildlife preserve, the new **Palm Coast Plantation** will be developed as an upscale, gated community anchored by a 120-acre spring-fed freshwater lake. Waterfront lots start at $99,880, and water-view sites start at $69,880. For information, call (888) 473-8700 or visit www.palmcoast plantation.com. **Grand Haven**, also nestled between the Intracoastal Waterway and the nature preserve, encompasses 1,350 wooded acres and features a Jack Nicklaus golf course. Buyers can choose from seven builders. For information, call (800) 957-0213 or go to www.grandhavenfla.com.

Visitor lodging: Palm Coast Golf Resort sits along the Intracoastal Waterway and has five championship golf courses, tennis and a marina, $79-$350, (800) 571-8793

or (386) 445-3000. The Hampton Inn is close to I-95, $69-$239, (800) HAMPTON or (386) 446-4457. Palm Coast Villas Motel was built in the 1930s of native coquina shell and has 22 modestly furnished units, $49-$89, (386) 445-3525.

Information: Flagler County Palm Coast Chamber of Commerce, 20 Airport Road, Bunnell, FL 32110, (386) 437-0106 or (800) 881-1022. The chamber Web site is www.flaglerpcchamber.org.

homes that sell for $250,000 to more than $500,000.

Gated communities, which have mushroomed in Florida over the past decade, are just beginning to crop up in Palm Coast. According to Warren, prices start in the mid-$100,000s and climb up to about $1 million-plus at the area's gated neighborhoods.

While the Sgrois began life in Palm Coast in the condo they'd owned since the early 1980s, four years ago they bought a 2,200-square-foot ranch home in Indian Trails with three bedrooms, two bathrooms and a swimming pool. The house sits on a freshwater canal that leads to Bird-of-Paradise Lake.

The Ilavskys' waterfront home in the Palm Harbor neighborhood has three bedrooms and two bathrooms designed in a split plan so they and their guests have some privacy. They have a spacious Florida room and a Jacuzzi in a screened enclosure next to it that faces the saltwater canal bordering their back yard.

They enjoy their home as well as the neighborhood in which they live. "We have very nice neighbors," Mary says. "We're all there for one another. If we go away, we can say, 'keep an eye on our house,' and they'll help water the plants."

The Sgrois had visions of kicking back and relaxing when they retired. "We thought we'd do some fishing, take trips, go on cruises," Bob says. But that's not how it turned out.

Initially they made friends at the condominium complex in which they lived, then joined the Elks as well as the New York and New Jersey social clubs. These days they are involved in the Citizens Observation Patrol, a volunteer group that patrols neighborhoods each evening, lending a hand to stranded motorists, directing traffic when signals malfunction and alerting the sheriff's department when a deputy is needed.

Barbara Sgrois does volunteer work at the Flagler County Humane Society, the American Red Cross and the local chapter of the National Audubon Society. Bob serves on the city's planning board, the housing authority and the architectural review board. He ran for mayor a couple of years ago, placing third out of nine candidates. He says he's been asked to run for the county commission in November and is considering it.

Outside of their extensive volunteer work, both have hobbies. He likes to fish while she gardens and enjoys the area's abundance of birds and other wildlife. "There's so much to do," Barbara says. "It's easy to make friends."

When they moved to town, the Ilavskys didn't think they knew anyone in the area but quickly discovered otherwise. "When we first went to church, one of the deacons was a good friend of Bill's from New Jersey," Mary says.

From there it was easy to meet new people. "Friends at church introduced us to the whole community," Bill says. "And I made friends on the golf course."

Bill and Mary keep busy. He golfs, runs and enjoys cutting stained glass, a hobby he began after retiring from his job as an engineer for the Department of the Army. Mary, who retired from a post as legislative aide to a New Jersey state senator, has taken up line dancing and is teaching herself to play the accordion. They like to walk and bicycle together, making use of the city's extensive system of bicycle paths.

They both volunteer at a soup kitchen in nearby St. Augustine and mentor children at the school run by the Catholic Church, to which they belong. Mary also helps run a Rainbows program, a support group for children dealing with death or divorce in their families. Bill devotes two mornings a week to Habitat for Humanity, helping to build homes for those who cannot afford to buy one on their own

"It's a nice balance," Mary says. "You have to be involved in activities you're happy with. No one can be bored here unless they choose to be."

Dick Morris estimates there are more than 200 clubs and civic organizations in the city. "If you can't find something to do here, you don't want to do anything," he says.

Palm Coast is the largest community in Flagler County, which is named for Henry Morrison Flagler, the famed industrialist who also helped found the Audubon Society with John James Audubon. The county follows in that tradition of encouraging clean industry while nurturing the area's abundant natural resources. Its extensive parks and recreation system have won accolades.

Among its natural crown jewels is Princess Place Preserve, a 1,500-acre natural resource and heritage park. The Princess Estate Lodge, which sits on the property, is listed on the National Register of Historic Places.

Another preserved treasure is Washington Oaks State Gardens, which began as part of a plantation owned by a militia general who led troops during the Second Seminole War. It sprawls across 400 acres of coastal land between the Atlantic Ocean and the Matanzas River. There are tidal marshes, a beach and hammock and coquina outcroppings that have worn into odd shapes. Its pristine state appeals to birds and forest animals as well as people seeking to commune with nature.

There are formal gardens as well, containing exotic plants from around the world. Guided tours take place on weekends. The many attractions of two popular tourist destinations, St. Augustine and Daytona Beach, also are nearby.

St. Augustine, believed to be the oldest continuously occupied European settlement in the United States, has all sorts of historical sites, including the Castillo de San Marcos National Monument, a huge Spanish masonry fort that dates to 1672. In Daytona, the famed Daytona International Speedway hosts eight weekends of racing each year, including the Daytona 500 in February and the Pepsi 400 in July. Something else that's unique to Daytona: Cars can drive on many of the hard-packed sand beaches during the day.

After living in Palm Coast for nine years, the Ilavskys would heartily recommend it to others as a good place to retire. "It has all you could look for in a retirement community, but it's not a retirement community per se," Mary says. "There are lots of young, active residents."

For those thinking about retiring to Palm Coast, Bill Ilavsky advises: "Get involved." His wife elaborates: "Especially for women who leave family behind, you have to do things you're happy doing. The days go by very fast, and your children will come down to see you," she says. ●

Palm Desert, California

A warm, dry climate and casual lifestyle draw retirees to this Southern California valley

By Mary Lu Abbott

Beyond San Gorgonio Pass, the sky becomes bluer, the air fresher, the mountain views clearer and the lifestyle more relaxed as Interstate 10 descends into broad Coachella Valley east of Los Angeles.

State Highway 111 veers off the fast lanes and angles its way through communities that blend one into another for more than 30 miles. At the heart sits Palm Desert, the cultural and retail hub of a growing resort complex that began with Palm Springs and has carpeted the desert eastward to Indio.

Hollywood couldn't improve on the setting — thousands of tall, skinny palm trees standing like sentinels and a half-dozen mountain ranges guarding the desert floor in all directions. The jagged San Jacinto Mountains, topping 10,000 feet, form a protective ridge to the west and southwest and may wear a cape of snow in winter. A defining presence, the mountains continually attract your eyes, whether you're playing golf, shopping, dining al fresco or simply sitting on your patio. In the light of predawn and in late evening, the peaks take on a velvety blue hue, and during the day, shadows add tone and color.

"The view of the mountains is impressive," says Rich Davidson, 58, who retired to the Sun City Palm Desert community in 2000 with his wife, Dianne, 56. Ticking off what she likes best in the Palm Desert area, Dianne cites "the mountains, the blue sky, the colors, the red sunsets." Dawn's illumination of the mountains and valley is so pretty that, she says, "I get up just to watch the sunrise."

Andy and JoAnn Macek, who lived in Simi Valley in the Los Angeles area and used Where to Retire magazine in their search for a retirement spot, agree on the beauty of Palm Desert. "The mountains sometimes look like a painting," says Andy, 66, who retired in 1999. JoAnn, 65, adds, "Every place we went, we compared to Coachella Val-

ley. No place is as pretty." Its attractions are far more than what first meets the eyes, she says, noting that it has all the shopping, dining and cultural amenities that active retirees want and all the health facilities that might be needed later.

For the Davidsons, the climate was a major factor in their decision to move here from San Jose in Northern California. Turned by man into an oasis with 100 golf courses where waterfalls and lakes accent expansive greens, the Coachella Valley nonetheless is part of the Colorado Desert, with the great Mojave Desert bordering to the north. It is sunny, warm — perhaps hot is the better word — and very dry here, with an average annual rainfall of less than 5 inches.

Dianne has arthritis and allergies, particularly to ragweed and pine. "I need to be in a dry, dry climate — the drier the better. We used to come here every August for many years and it would dry out my allergies. My allergies have improved immensely being here," says Dianne, who has met others who moved to the area from Northern California to escape the damper climate.

The decision to move south wasn't easy, despite Southern California being her childhood home. A daughter and grandson live in Northern California, so Rich and Dianne began looking for retirement sites closer to San Jose. They discovered the Del Webb communities at Roseville and Lincoln Hills, both near Sacramento. They liked the active-adult lifestyle that Del Webb provides with its golf courses, clubhouses, fitness centers and group activities.

They looked in Nevada and Arizona and visited other active-adult communities, but they found themselves returning to the Del Webb communities and finally settled on the one in Palm Desert.

"We did a lot of research. For the

money, the best buy is here. We needed to stretch our dollars. I like the accessibility, too. You get off the freeway and you're here," Dianne says. Because Sun City Palm Desert is a large community, with about 6,800 current residents and a projected total of 9,000, the monthly association fees are comparatively low, about $125 a month.

Rich says they found similar homes for $50,000 to $70,000 less in Arizona, but they didn't want to move there. They feel that for California residents who want to stay in the state when they retire, Palm Desert is one of the less-expensive options.

"We fell in love with this community," Rich says. Unlike some retirees, they didn't downsize and chose one of the largest home plans, with nearly 3,000 square feet and three bedrooms with a den. They wanted space for their family, including a son in college, to visit.

They decided on a lot and model in the fall of 1999, although Rich wasn't retiring until the following summer. He told the builder he didn't want to start construction until April, "and they held off driving the first nail," says Rich, noting that allowed him to get everything in order for retirement from TRW, the automotive, aerospace and information technology giant, where he was an engineer.

Their best-laid plans went awry, though, when they put their San Jose home on the market and a buyer wanted it before their planned moving date in August. The buyer offered an extra $10,000 if the Davidsons could be out by June 27.

They took the deal and rented a house in Palm Desert until their home was ready. "We spent two months buying furniture and having an eight-week vacation," Rich says.

Originally from Cleveland, OH, the Maceks yearned to live in Southern California, where they had visited friends. When his company offered a transfer in the 1970s, they happily moved to Simi Valley, and Andy later started his own tool business.

The Maceks fell in love with the Coachella Valley on a visit about 30 years ago and bought a second home in Palm Desert in the early 1990s. They weren't sure they wanted to retire here, though, and they considered other places in the Southwest, including Pahrump, outside Las Vegas, NV, where they have property, and Carlsbad, NM.

"Every time we looked elsewhere, we said we would have to give up this or that. Down the line we don't want to have to drive 45 minutes to find a decent medical center. Yes, you have Nevada where you don't have a state (income) tax, but there are trade-offs. I sort of planted my feet and said, 'I really like this area.' It's a beautiful, well-taken-care-of city and has all the services you might need. It's so geared for seniors," JoAnn says.

They decided that for retirement they needed a larger place than their second home. They wanted extra space for Andy's mother to live with them and a garage where he could pursue his hob-by of restoring old cars. Andy found his dream place, but it took awhile to convince his wife. "JoAnn said, 'I don't like this,' and I said, 'Isn't this great?'" recalls Andy, who particularly liked the large workshop out back.

The house and garage occupied a quarter of an acre of land — and "in California, that's big. Out here you usually walk out your door and shake hands with somebody," Andy says, noting that homes normally are built quite close to lot lines. The house also had a bedroom and bath that would afford privacy for his mother, 88.

JoAnn finally agreed to the purchase if she could have the house remodeled to her specifications. "I said, 'Not a problem.' So now she says we bought a workshop with a house attached to it," Andy says. They tore out the entire front of the home and redid it. She now has her favored butterfly motif everywhere, and he has room for seven cars.

The Maceks did not want to live in an all-adult community. "I do like a mix in my neighborhood. I like the young, the middle-aged and the seniors together. I enjoy seeing the kids," says JoAnn, who has not retired yet. She's executive di-rector of the Specialty Advertising Association of California and works from her condo in the West Hills area of Los Angeles. She commutes to Palm Desert most weekends, leaving her office on Thursdays, and stays extended periods during holidays.

On the other hand, the Davidsons wanted an active-adult community for several reasons. "I didn't want to move to a community not knowing that there were 12 teenagers in the next house or something like that. The quiet serenity here is just fantastic," Rich says of their home at Sun City Palm Desert. "I can sit outside on the chaise longue at night, especially in summertime, and it's so peaceful and quiet. I like that."

They also wanted activities available. Dianne notes that her husband was worried that she might get bored. "I can kick back, but Dianne needs activity," Rich says. "You can be active all day here if you want, or you can be contemplative." He's trying to write a novel, something he had always wanted to do. While he works on his book, Dianne can go her own way.

While Sun City Palm Desert has about 80 clubs and a large roster of activities,

---

Population: About 41,155 permanent residents and an additional 31,000 in winter. About 330,000 people live year-round in the Coachella Valley communities, increasing to more than 500,000 in winter.

Location: About 125 miles east of Los Angeles (about three hours) and 15 miles southeast of Palm Springs, adjacent to I-10. It's in the Coachella Valley, which extends about 40 miles in desert terrain surrounded by mountains. Palm Desert is the cultural and retail hub of several desert communities lining the valley, including Cathedral City, Rancho Mirage, Indian Wells, La Quinta and Indio.

Climate:

	High	Low
January	70	41
July	107	74

The valley has a sunny, dry climate with warm days and cold nights in winter and hot days with pleasant evenings in summer. Daytime temperatures often top 100 degrees from June into September and can exceed 110 degrees, but low humidity makes the heat more tolerable.

Rainy season usually is mid-October to mid-February. Elevation ranges from about 250 feet in Palm Desert to 8,516 feet at the Mountain Station of the Palm Springs Aerial Tramway in the San Jacinto Mountains.

Average relative humidity: 26.5%

Rain: 3.38 inches.

Snow: Rare in the valley, but mountain peaks are snowcapped in winter.

Cost of living: Above average (specific index not available).

Housing costs: In first quarter of 2002, the median was $240,000, including single-family homes and condos.

Sales tax: 7.75%

Sales exemptions tax: Food products, prescription medicines and services.

State income tax: For married couples filing jointly, graduated from 1% of taxable income up to $11,496 to 9.3% on amounts over $75,450. For single filers, graduated from 1% of taxable income up to $5,748 to 9.3% on amounts over $37,725.

Income tax exemptions: Social Secu-rity benefits and railroad pensions are exempt.

Estate tax: None, except the state's "pick-up" portion of the federal tax, applicable to taxable estates of more than $1 million.

Inheritance tax: None.

Property tax: Homes are assessed at either 100% of market value or purchase price plus 2% per year, whichever is lower. The rate varies by area, and there may be special assessments added by various taxing jurisdictions. Basic tax on a $240,000 home with the exemption noted below would be about $2,586 at a rate of 1.11%. The state's homeowner assistance program reimburses up to $473 to those who are 62 or older (or blind or disabled) and have an income of no more than $35,251.

Homestead exemptions: $7,000 off the value for those who live in their home.

Religion: The city has about 30 churches, synagogues and temples, augmented by places of worship in adjoining

Dianne says she had some trouble finding her niche. Because of her arthritis, Dianne, 46, retired early from teaching. While the community has a large number of people who are in their 50s, many of them still work.

Friendly and outgoing, Dianne says she went through a lonely period because she had not made friends among her age group. "I didn't know anybody. Everyone sort of has their attachments and you have to work your way in," she says.

At a first-time luncheon for baby boomers in the community, she met 19 other residents and was off and running "with a new project." She has organized the group, which now has more than 150 members in the Sun City community. "We had a '50s-'60s dance and 190 people showed up," she says. "I was surprised at how fast the boomer group came together and how many nice friends I've met."

Both Dianne and Rich have taken their time about getting into groups rather than rushing to try a host of activities. Rich says he's not a club join-er but has no problem partnering for golf a couple of times a week. If he doesn't find someone to play with by phone, he can join threesomes at the course.

"The community is very friendly," says Rich, noting that residents walking or driving their cars or golf carts greet each other with a wave. He meets people playing bocce and ping-pong, and such associations have led to couples meeting for dinner or a glass of wine.

JoAnn says town residents also are quite friendly, noting that it's easy to strike up conversations at the grocery store. "People in California tend to stay to themselves, but here people are more open, maybe because the pace is slower. We've developed a circle of friends and socialize," she says.

Her husband has made friends through his car restoration hobby, joining clubs for Thunderbird, Crosley and Buick owners. "I'm working on a '56 Thunderbird, and have a '52 Crosley Super Sport convertible and a '65 Buick Riviera that I bought from a man at the senior center. He was the original owner," Andy says.

Andy is active at the Joslyn Senior Center of the Cove Communities in Palm Desert. He started bringing his mother to the center on Thursdays for potluck and bingo. When the center needed someone to run bingo, he volunteered. He's now on the board of directors of the center, which serves Palm Desert, Rancho Mirage and Indian Wells residents.

A social, recreational, education and health center, Joslyn bustles with activities, attracting about 400 people daily to programs that run the gamut from salsa dancing to Tibetan meditation. About 140 volunteers assist with operations.

"Everything you need is in Palm Desert — all the retail shopping from Target to Macy's to Home Depot, to high-end jewelers, galleries and shops at El Paseo, and plenty of restaurants and theater," says Michael Barnard, executive director of the Joslyn Senior Center. "It's a very stable city with strong civic leadership. It puts a lot of money

Palm Desert, CA

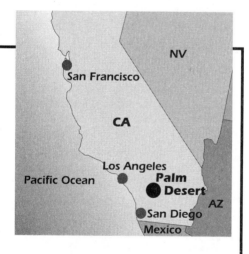

communities. All faiths are represented.
Education: Adult education classes are available at the two-year College of the Desert, and California State University at San Bernardino is constructing a Coachella Valley Campus in Palm Desert, which will become a separate branch of the CSU system.

Transportation: From Palm Desert, Palm Springs International Airport is about 25 minutes away. Of the Los Angeles airports, Ontario and John Wayne are closest, at slightly under two hours by car. Los Angeles International Airport is about 2.5 hours away. Palm Desert runs a free Shopper Hopper bus to major shopping areas, and the SunLine Transit Agency has a SunBus serving towns throughout the valley at low fares.

Health: The valley has outstanding medical facilities and physicians in all specialties. The three major facilities are the Eisenhower Medical Center in neighboring Rancho Mirage, the Desert Regional Medical Center in Palm Springs and the JFK Memorial Hospital in Indio.

Housing options: Sun City Palm Desert, a Del Webb planned active-adult community with about 6,800 residents of an expected 9,000 total, (800) 847-0754, is the major neighborhood of new homes in Palm Desert. It has three clubhouse recreation centers, two 18-hole championship golf courses, a fishing lake and walking and biking trails among its amenities. Homes start in the mid-$100,000s. Palm Desert has a number of gated and country-club communities with resale homes available, and there are new developments in neighboring **Rancho Mirage** and **La Quinta**. The desert communities meld together.

Visitor lodging: The town has 15 resort hotels and other accommodations, including Marriott's Desert Springs Resort and Spa, from $275 nightly in high season and $99 in low season, (800) 331-3112, and Vacation Inn Resort, from $155 in high season and $69 in low season, (800) 231-8675. For those considering buying a home in its retirement community, Sun City Palm Desert offers vacation villas from $119 nightly in high season and $89 in low season, (800) 533-5932.

Information: Palm Desert Visitor Information Center, 72-990 Highway 111, Palm Desert, CA 92260, (800) 873-2428 or www.palmdesert.org. Palm Desert Chamber of Commerce, 73-710 Fred Waring Drive, Suite 114, Palm Desert, CA 92260, (760) 346-6111 or www.pdcc.org. Joslyn Senior Center of the Cove Communities, 73-750 Catalina Way, Palm Desert, CA 92260, (760) 340-3220.

back into the community. We have a huge park with an amphitheater and baseball fields. It's the nicest in the valley."

He says Palm Desert has attracted all ages, with young families as well as retirees. According to visitor bureau statistics, the average age is 48. It's an easy city to navigate, with broad streets, clear signage and many roadways marked with lanes for electric golf carts. To be driven in traffic, the carts have to be street-legal, with mirrors and horns on them. Andy says he sees many handicapped retirees using the golf-cart lanes to go all over town.

Throughout the valley, Gerald Ford Drive, Ginger Rogers Road, Gene Autry Trail, the Bob Hope Chrysler Classic golf tournament and the Frank Sinatra Celebrity Invitational pay homage to the many celebrities who have frequented or lived in the area and contributed to its growth.

Palm Desert itself has 150 tennis courts and 32 golf courses, including the city-owned Desert Willow Golf Resort, which has two championship courses recognized for both their play and their environmental design using desert vegetation and reclaimed water to keep fairways green.

The city's McCallum Theatre for the Performing Arts hosts touring musicals and other cultural attractions, and free movies and concerts are staged throughout the summer in the Civic Center Park, where the valley scenery adds to the show. The city's innovative Art in Public Places program has brought 96 artworks to parks, street medians, public facilities and business buildings, with 19 sculptures displayed in the upscale El Paseo shopping district.

El Paseo, with its landscaped median, al fresco cafes and classy boutiques, evokes a promenade ambiance and serves as a downtown. The city has a dozen more shopping centers, and on the western edge of the valley along I-10, the large Desert Hills Premium Outlets has good buys from such retailers as Anne Klein, Ralph Lauren, Giorgio Armani, Barneys New York, Gucci and Tommy Hilfiger.

The Davidsons like the casual lifestyle. "To be able to go to a nice restaurant and not have to wear a coat and tie is really good," Rich says.

When family and visitors come, there's no shortage of things to see and do. The city adjoins the Santa Rosa Mountains National Scenic Area with wilderness hiking. The Living Desert Wildlife and Botanical Park showcases area plants, animals and history. Scenic Highway 74 will take you from the desert into the mountain pines in less than an hour.

The valley is noted for its health-care facilities, including the major Eisenhower Medical Center in neighboring Rancho Mirage. While the Maceks don't need all the medical services now, the proximity of care and the focus of facilities on the older generation were important in their decision to retire here.

"If it's good enough for Bob Hope, it's good enough for me," Rich says of the valley's medical care. The beloved star lives in the valley.

The hot summers, though, are a drawback. Daytime temperatures usually top 100 degrees from June into September and may exceed 110 degrees in July and August. Low humidity is a mitigating factor.

Neither the Davidsons nor the Maceks mind the heat. In fact, both couples cite the weather as a major attraction for them. "We love the dry heat. That's why we moved here," Dianne says. Rich adds, "Eight months, we have perfect weather. Four months, it's hot, but we don't worry about it."

Andy says it's really hot only about two months, in August and parts of July and maybe September. "What people don't realize is that 120 degrees in dry heat here is like 70 or 80 degrees back East with humidity," he says.

Andy does caution that hot summer temperatures raise the monthly electric bills because of air conditioning. "Our high bill was $450, but in the winter it's down to $70 or $80. We're looking into a new air-conditioning system with better efficiency that could save up to 50 percent," he says.

"The only thing we don't like is the growth, which is almost every place, though," Andy says. "They keep building golf courses and gated communities with lakes, and the more lakes, the more humidity."

Highway 111, the main route through the towns, can get congested at peak times and has some ongoing widening projects that slow traffic. Rich doesn't complain, though, because he escaped congestion in San Jose that made his 25-mile commute take about 90 minutes each way.

Rich wishes he knew more Spanish because there are so many Spanish-speaking residents, and he's learning the language. Dianne misses seeing her daughter and grandson in Monterey and experiencing the change of seasons.

Andy thinks the area is especially well-suited for those who enjoy sports, particularly golf.

"The whole city is well-planned and has wonderful services, very in tune to seniors' needs," JoAnn says. "We have friends who just can't handle living without changes of season, but for people who love the desert, keep an active lifestyle and want to have everything close by, this is a wonderful place to live."

"I think this is the place to live," says Andy.●

Paris, Tennessee

Friendly people and four-season climate give Tennessee community all-American charm

By William Schemmel

Nine years ago, when they began thinking seriously about retiring, Al and Mary Walker surveyed the country from Chesapeake Bay to the Arizona desert. Among their stacks of literature, they found a retirement guide that gave high praise to an unexpected place. It was their old hometown of Paris, TN.

The Walkers grew up in this western Tennessee town of less than 10,000 people. But for 33 years, Al's career as a nuclear energy engineer had moved the family to Philadelphia, Boston and Pittsburgh — and as far as Saudi Arabia and South America. The Walkers traveled around the world.

"The retirement guide made Paris sound so good, we decided we'd better come down and look it over," says Al. "We did a survey of the area. We talked to banks and people we still knew here. We liked what we saw, but we wondered whether we could fit in again after being away all these years. So, we decided to buy a house and give it a try for two years."

Now, the Walkers can't imagine living anywhere else. "The safety factor is one of the things retirees should look at closely," says Mary. "Paris and Henry County have a very low crime rate. We also have a wonderful four-season climate. And, unlike many small towns, our downtown courthouse square is very stable, with hardly any vacant storefronts."

Housing costs and property taxes are other retirement pluses, say the Walkers. Their 2,800-square-foot home on a wooded one-acre lot cost $70,000. Yearly property taxes on a home valued at $70,000 are about $760.

And there are other advantages. Paris has plenty of ways to keep active retirees like the Walkers as busy as they want to be.

"This is a very active community,"

says Mary. "You can belong to civic clubs, garden clubs, political clubs and charitable organizations. You can get involved with chamber of commerce programs. The Arts Council produces a couple of plays a year, and they also bring in plays and performers from Nashville and Memphis."

"The people here are very open to newcomer participation," adds Al. "But you have to circulate and show an interest. If you sit back and wait to be called, you'll probably mold over."

Kentucky Lake, 16 miles east of downtown Paris, is easily the area's biggest attraction. The waterway was created by a Tennessee Valley Authority dam on the Tennessee River. Its 2,100-mile shoreline is a happy hunting ground for fishermen and a major playground for boaters, swimmers and water-skiers. It's separated from equally impressive Lake Barkley, on the Cumberland River, by Land Between the Lakes, a recreation-rich, 270-square-mile peninsula administered by the National Park Service.

All this fishing naturally calls for a celebration. Each April, more than 90,000 visitors come from all over the United States for what's billed as the world's biggest fish fry. During the weeklong festival, more than 13,000 pounds of Kentucky Lake catfish, bass and crappie are dispatched. Other highlights include parades, car shows, arts and crafts and a rodeo.

Unlike the Walkers, Lois and Pat Smith had never heard of Paris until they stopped here on their way home to Chicago. They ended up buying a house and have been Parisians for nine years.

"The years have just flown by," says Lois. "We love living here, and we can still drive back to Chicago in less than a day."

The Smiths' three-bedroom, ranch-style house is valued at about $120,000. The 2,000-square-foot

home sits on a three-acre lot, with plenty of space for Pat's flourishing vegetable garden. It's in Country Club Estates, a neighborhood of well-spaced, meticulously kept homes developed about 20 years ago.

Avid golfers, the Smiths are a two-minute golf cart ride from Paris Country Club's nine-hole course. When they need a change of fairways, they drive 15 minutes to Paris Landing State Park. On Kentucky Lake, the 841-acre park's 18-hole course is the equal of many private courses. Seniors play free all day Monday. They can purchase a $300 annual pass for unlimited play on state park courses all over Tennessee. The resort-style park also has an inn with 100 motel-type rooms, a conference center, restaurant, swimming pools, tennis courts, marinas, fishing docks, picnic areas and other amenities.

Paris is about 40 miles north of Interstate 40 — the main east-west route between Nashville and Memphis — and about 60 miles west of Interstate 24, a busy route that links Nashville with freeways into St. Louis and Chicago. Residents say the area's location off the interstate highways is a mixed blessing. It keeps out "strip development" but sometimes discourages new business and industry.

Locally, small family-owned stores on the courthouse square are complemented by Wal-Mart and other chain stores. Most Parisians drive to Nashville (110 miles east) for heavy shopping, entertainment and air transportation. Airfares from Nashville, they say, are generally less expensive than from Memphis (133 miles west). Large regional shopping malls in Nashville's western suburbs are less than two hours by car.

Nashville's restaurants also are an attraction for Paris newcomers accustomed to fine dining. Prohibition of mixed drinks limits Paris restaurants mainly to small establishments specializing in steak and seafood. Package liquor, beer and wine are available.

Like Pat and Lois Smith, many Paris retirees are Midwesterners who originally came for vacations at Land Between the Lakes. Others come on business with industrial plants that the area has attracted in recent years.

"My wife and I came down on business in 1984," says former Detroiter Art Nellen. "We were staying out at Paris Landing State Park when my wife became ill. We were treated so well, we started thinking it would be a nice place to live."

Paris boasts a full-service hospital, the 142-bed Henry County Medical Center, with a 24-hour emergency room and facilities for nuclear medicine, cardiac/intensive care, outpatient surgery, physical therapy and other specialized treatment. A helicopter is available around the clock to fly patients to larger hospitals in Nashville and Memphis.

"The people here are wonderful and very accepting of outsiders," says Art. "I keep myself busy by going to the lake, working in my yard and doing projects for the chamber of commerce."

He helped organize a "Paris USA Convention" that attracted representatives of nine American cities named for the French capital, which also sent an official. (Chartered in 1823, Tennessee's Paris was named in tribute to the Marquis de Lafayette's aid to the American Revolution. Henry County was named for patriot Patrick Henry.) As a lasting landmark of the convention, the engineering school at Christian Brothers College in Memphis built a 65-foot scale model of the Eiffel Tower. It now sits in Paris' Memorial Park.

Other newcomers are military families assigned to nearby Fort Campbell, KY. About 1,200 Army officers retire from Fort Campbell every year, and many of them make their permanent homes in Paris and elsewhere in western Tennessee and Kentucky.

With its growing retirement community, Paris is experiencing a short-

Paris, TN

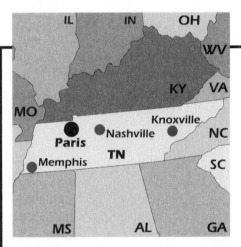

Population: 9,763 in Paris; 31,115 in Henry County.

Location: On Kentucky Lake in western Tennessee, 110 miles west of Nashville and 133 miles east of Memphis.

Climate:

	High	Low
January	45	26
July	90	70

Average relative humidity: 60%

Rain: 50 inches.

Snow: 11 inches.

Winters are moderately cold; summers are warm and humid. Most rainfall arrives in winter months.

Cost of living: Below average (specific index not available).

Average housing cost: $125,000 for a new three-bedroom in the lakes area. Homes in town average about $75,000.

Sales tax: 8.75%

Sales tax exemptions: Prescription drugs, professional services, hearing aids, prosthetic devices.

State income tax: None on earned income, but there is a state tax of 6% on interest and dividend income from certain stocks, bonds and long-term notes and mortgages. Interest from CDs, savings accounts and federal, state or local government bonds is exempt.

Income tax exemptions: Social Security benefits and private and government retirement pensions are exempt. The first $1,250 ($2,500 on a joint return) of taxable income is exempt, and individuals 65 or older with total annual income of $16,200 or less ($27,000 for joint filers) are exempt from the tax.

Intangibles tax: None.

Estate tax: None, except the state's "pick-up" portion of the federal tax, applicable to taxable estates above $1 million.

Inheritance tax: From 5.5% to 9.5%, based on amount of inheritance; spouse normally exempt. If under $700,000, there is no tax.

Property tax: Residents in the city pay $36.50 per $1,000 (a combined rate of $12.10 for the city and $24.40 for the county). Homes are assessed at 25% of market value. The tax on a $125,000 home in the city is about $1,140, and in the county about $763.

Homestead exemption: Homeowners age 65 and older with a household income of $10,000 or less are eligible for a state tax relief credit.

Religion: About 100 Protestant churches and one Catholic church in Henry County.

Education: Four-year colleges at nearby Clarksville and Jackson, TN, and Murray, KY.

Transportation: No public transportation. 100 miles to Nashville International Airport.

Health: 142-bed Paris/Henry County Medical Center. Helicopter ambulance to hospitals in Nashville and Memphis.

Housing options: Affordable housing includes new and older homes in the city and in unincorporated areas of the county and a small selection of rental homes and apartments. Many retirees prefer living in one of many developments on Kentucky Lake and smaller lakes, where single-family homes and condominiums are available for $125,000 to $500,000 and higher.

Visitor lodging: Best Western Travelers Inn, $44 double, (800) 528-1234 or (731) 642-8881; Paris Landing State Park, from $60 double off-season (November-February) to $65-$70 in season, (731) 642-4311.

Information: Paris/Henry County Chamber of Commerce, P.O. Box 8, Paris, TN 38242-0008, (800) 345-1103, (731) 642-3431 or www.paris.tn.org.

age of available housing in some price ranges. Lois Smith says the shortage is especially acute in large $80,000-$90,000 houses that many retirees want. But she adds that there is a good supply of smaller houses in the $40,000-$50,000 range. Most of those are older homes inside the city. On the upper end, large homes on spacious lots in the new Country Woods area are $125,000 and up.

Many retirees want to live on Kentucky Lake. Originally from Wisconsin, Bill and Dot Jerstad were living in Jackson, TN, just 60 miles south of Paris, when a realty company invited them to look at lots on the lake.

"That was in 1959," Bill recalls. "The lots they showed us were on a ridge where you couldn't see the water. But we saw two other lots overlooking the water. We paid $1,400 for each of them, and in 1988, we built our home here."

Bill says they recently were offered $250,000 for their spacious one-level house, which is surrounded by gardens and lake-view patios.

To accommodate newcomers who want to live on Kentucky Lake, Buchanan Resort, a 50-year-old recreation area owned by a local family, has built a 70-unit lakeside condominium complex called Pleasant Place. The 1,800-square-foot, three-bedroom condos run from $150,000 and up, plus a monthly $150 maintenance fee. Each condo has a large outside deck overlooking the lake. Amenities include marinas, swimming pool, tennis courts and a restaurant.

The rolling, heavily wooded farmland around Paris is attractive to retirees like Grace and John Underwood. John, originally from Illinois, and Grace, a Henry County native, met while they were students at nearby Murray State University in Kentucky. They taught in western Tennessee public schools for 38 years.

"Family was one of the big reasons we decided to retire around Paris," says John, a former school principal. "At the time, one daughter and her husband lived just across the road and another daughter lived in Paris. Along with that, we've always enjoyed a rural atmosphere. Living conditions here are great. We have a definite change of seasons, and taxes and the cost of living are reasonable."

The Underwoods built a 1,600-square-foot "Tennessee tenant-style" house with most of the living space downstairs. An upstairs loft serves as Grace's workroom and a dormitory for visiting children and grandchildren.

"Before we started building, we studied our previous house to see what was really necessary," Grace says. "We wanted a house that was comfortable, functional, easy to clean and inexpensive to heat and cool."

To stay active and bring in added income, Grace specializes in restoring plaster picture frames, which were popular in the 1920s. John restores antique furniture in a workshop behind the house. They operate booths in downtown antiques stores. Their neighbors in the rural Palestine community, about 15 minutes from downtown, include 70 Mennonite families who relocated from Kentucky.

Unlike many small American towns, downtown Paris is alive and well. Small department stores, apparel, jewelry, sporting goods, drug and antique stores, banks and restaurants ring the tree-shaded Henry County Courthouse. Many of the buildings have been returned to their original 1890s look, with freshly painted facades and awnings. Parking is free on the street and in two city-owned lots.

Early in the morning, retirees gather around tables on the courthouse lawn for lively games of dominoes and pitch, a popular card game. When the weather is bad, they have a "reserved" room in the courthouse basement.

"We attribute the square's prosperity to two things," says Bryant Williams, editor emeritus of *The Post-Intelligencer*, Paris' daily newspaper. "First, the Downtown Merchants Association is very strong. They put pressure on the building owners to restore their turn-of-the-century look. They compete strongly with the shopping centers that have robbed so many small towns of their livelihood.

"Secondly, when the courthouse got into bad disrepair, we organized the Paris/Henry County Development Corp. as a non-profit organization so gifts would be tax-deductible. We raised about $75,000 to build brick sidewalks, new lawns and lighting fixtures. The county then got in the action and refurbished the courthouse inside and out. It's the second-oldest working courthouse in the state, and now it looks very much as it did when it was new in 1897."

To many residents, the downtown square symbolizes a way of life in Paris.

"We especially like the easy pace of life," says Art Nellen. "The climate's perfect, the cost of living is reasonable and you can be as active or inactive as you want to be."●

Pensacola, Florida

Colonial Spanish appeal adds to sparkling beaches of Florida's Panhandle

By Constance Snow

From Spanish galleons to the high-flying Blue Angels of Pensacola Naval Air Station, ancient and modern mariners have been attracted by the natural beauty of the coast of the Florida Panhandle. Clear turquoise waters lap at glistening sugar-white sand (99 percent pure quartz) on 40 miles of shoreline from Perdido Key to Navarre.

The first snowbirds to relocate in Florida hit Pensacola's beaches in 1559, establishing the state's earliest European settlement several years before St. Augustine, the oldest city in the United States. Pensacola was settled permanently in 1698.

Three centuries later, retirees are finding the same stunning natural attractions, now augmented by a town that's a Creole charmer. Old Pensacola's early Spanish cottages surrounding oak-shaded Seville Square have been converted into smart restaurants and shops. Nearby, New Orleans-style lacy ironwork decorates Spanish renaissance buildings of the Palafox Historic District. And, the North Hill Preservation District, with more than 500 houses in 50 blocks, is a living museum of Queen Anne, neoclassic, Tudor revival and Mediterranean architecture.

When Bill and Carol Ross wanted to retire from their jobs in Hong Kong with IBM, they found that Pensacola had the spark of cultural energy they had enjoyed in their years of living around the world. They also had worked in Atlanta and Washington, DC, and were eager to settle into a less hectic community for retirement.

"I moved 29 times with IBM, so I didn't really have roots anywhere," says Bill, 62, who was drawn to the "small-town amenities and friendly, honest people" of Pensacola. "It's sort of an easygoing lifestyle where the clerks in the stores really try to help you — not just sell you something."

Their search for a new home began with a map and a list of towns.

"When they (IBM) talked to Bill about the early retirement package," Carol says, "we sat down and started making a list of the things we wanted in a retirement community — a full university, close to water, a nice-sized town but not too big."

They decided to visit Pensacola first, then make day trips to Mobile, AL, and Panama City and Tallahassee, FL, before investigating other sites.

"We looked around for a week and we kept saying, 'We ought to drive over to Mobile one day' or 'We ought to drive over to Panama City one day,' but we never drove anywhere," says Carol, 48. "We liked it so much that we never went to the other places. We started looking for a house."

An ever-growing population of transplants from larger cities supports a booming arts colony that flourishes in the seaside village atmosphere. The historic Saenger Theatre, which hosts Broadway road shows from September through May, also is home to the Pensacola Symphony Orchestra, First City Dance, the Choral Society and the Pensacola Opera.

The downtown Civic Center seats 10,000 for concerts, sports, conventions and other major programs. Community productions are staged by the Pensacola Little Theatre, and the University of West Florida produces Artists in Residence Summer Theatre. Pensacola Junior College sponsors its own theatrical season as well as a lecture series.

A quirky setting in the former city jail (complete with iron-barred cells and looming stairwells) keeps the mood light at Pensacola Museum of Art, a regular stop for national touring exhibits. Local painters and craftspeople create the stock and man the sales desk at Quayside, the largest cooperative art gallery in the South. And each fall, the Greater Gulf Coast

Arts Festival attracts more than 100,000 visitors.

Meanwhile, the cultural calendar is peppered with a lively collection of other special events: the Fiesta of Five Flags, Fourth of July in Old Seville, Homecoming for the Blue Angels (the U.S. Navy's precision flight team), a chili cook-off, a jazz festival, a seafood celebration and much more.

Like many area retirees, the Rosses are members of a thriving network of community volunteers.

Bill serves on the Advisory Council for the College of Business at the University of West Florida and sets up guided tours at the National Museum of Naval Aviation. Enthusiastic gardeners, Carol and Bill both pitch in with landscaping and carpentry for the local chapter of Habitat for Humanity, a nationwide "barn-raising" organization that helps elderly and low-income residents build their own houses.

The Pensacola area is rich with affordable housing. A typical 1,600-square-foot, single-level house (with two or three bedrooms, two baths and a garage) costs $96,000, with average property taxes of about $1,500.

Apartments average $550 per month, rental homes $700. Monthly rates for condominiums on Pensacola Beach range from $750 to $1,200 per month. And more than 25 retirement and life-care communities are located in the area, many with on-site medical facilities.

The Rosses worked with an architect for three years to create their own custom-designed house on a small, relatively undeveloped island where friendly porpoises swim right up to their front yard.

The intricate coastline of the Panhandle zigzags along bays, sounds and inlets, providing plenty of waterfront home sites. But efforts by local preservationists have established safeguards against the high-rise blight that plagues South Florida.

The Gulf Islands National Seashore is a 150-mile strip of barrier islands, natural harbors and submerged land, most of which is located in Pensacola. It was created in 1971 to protect and conserve the natural beauty of more than 100,000 acres of land and water for future generations and to defend the area against overdevelopment. On Santa Rosa Island and nearby mainland areas, 19th-century coastal defense forts and World War II batteries remain, and archaeological sites at Naval Live Oaks are a link to earlier settlements.

Jim and Janet Hess wrote "big water" on the first line of their wish list when they began planning his retirement from a bank in Muncie, the landlocked Indiana city where they had lived for 30 years.

An initial scouting trip to the Carolinas was rerouted because of bad weather. Then their southern detour to visit friends in Fort Walton Beach came to an abrupt halt about 40 miles up the Florida Gulf Coast.

"We took the three-mile bridge to Pensacola Beach and went no farther," says Janet. "We knew we had found home. The emerald-blue water and snow-white sand clinched it for us."

Self-described "water people," the Hesses spend many of their days swimming and exploring the shoreline. They have moved three times in the Pensacola area, and now divide their time between Muncie, caring for Jim's 91-year-old mother, and their new condo on Pensacola Beach.

From the western tip of Perdido

Pensacola, FL

Population: 56,255 in Pensacola, 294,410 in Escambia County, 117,743 in Santa Rosa County.

Location: In the Panhandle on Florida's Gulf Coast. Pensacola and Pensacola Beach are in Escambia County, but the peninsula between them is in Santa Rosa County. Terrain is sandy beaches, salt marshes, Southern mixed forest. A series of natural harbors and waterways are protected by a necklace of tiny islands. Elevations vary from sea level to more than 300 feet inland.

Climate:

	High	Low
January	62	45
July	89	74

Average relative humidity: 73%
Rain: 60 inches.
Mild winters, hot and humid summers. Annual rainfall peaks with summer thunderstorm season. Snow is rare.
Cost of living: 98.4, based on national average of 100.
Average housing cost: $109,500
Sales tax: 7.5%
Sales tax exemptions: Groceries, prescription drugs, medical services.

State income tax: None.
Intangibles tax: Assessed on stocks, bonds and other assets. Tax rate is $1 per $1,000 in assets. The first $20,000 in assets is exempt for individuals. For couples filing jointly, the first $40,000 is exempt. Those who owe less than $60 need not pay.
Estate tax: None, except the state's "pick-up" portion of the federal tax, applicable to taxable estates above $1 million.
Property tax: $24.85 per $1,000 of assessed value downtown, $22.85 elsewhere in the city, $18.54 in unincorporated areas of the county. Assessment is based on 100% of market value. Yearly tax on a $109,000 house in the city is about $1,919 with the homestead exemption noted below.
Homestead exemption: $25,000 off assessed value on primary, permanent residence.
Religion: More than 370 churches of various denominations and two synagogues.
Education: University of West Florida and Pensacola Christian College offer full four-year programs. Pensacola Junior College and George Stone Vocational College also serve the community.
Transportation: Escambia County Transit Authority's city buses offer routes and schedules with reduced rates for senior citizens. The Pensacola Regional Airport is served by several major airlines and commuter flights, and Amtrak stops en route between Los Angeles and Miami.

Health: Baptist Hospital (546 beds) has an emergency/trauma center and an electrophysiology laboratory for the diagnosis of heart disease. West Florida Regional Medical Center (547 beds) and Sacred Heart Hospital (431 beds) offer full-service acute care. Hospitals at Pensacola Naval Air Station and Eglin Air Force Base treat military retirees. Lifeflight Helicopter is a 24-hour air ambulance.
Housing options: Wide range of housing includes patio home subdivisions, townhouses and condos starting in the $40,000s. Waterfront property available on gulf, bay, sound, bayou and river. **Marcus Pointe**, (850) 429-1490, and **Champions Green**, (800) 445-2507 or (850) 932-9228, are two of many area golf course communities. **Sandy Key**, (800) 233-4469 or (850) 492-4469, and **Perdido Sun**, (800) 227-2390 or (850) 492-2390, are gulf-front condominium high-rises. **Azalea Trace**, (800) 828-8274 or (850) 478-5200, and **Homestead Village**, (800) 937-1735 or (850) 944-4366, are retirement communities.
Visitor lodging: On Pensacola Beach, Clarion, $99-$179 for one-bedroom suite with kitchenette, (800) 874-5303; Best Western, $134-$162 double with kitchenette, (850) 479-1099. There are more than 7,300 rooms available.
Information: There is a retirement/relocation specialist on staff at the Pensacola Area Chamber of Commerce, 117 W. Garden St., Pensacola, FL 32501, (850) 438-4081 or www. pensacolachamber.com.

Key to the long barrier island of Santa Rosa (a skinny sandbar shared by the neighboring resorts of Navarre Beach and Pensacola Beach), Pensacola's clear waters are a boater's paradise.

Private and public marinas are plentiful. Snorkelers and scuba divers can paddle along natural reefs or venture into numerous wrecks, such as the USS Massachusetts, a 350-foot World War I battleship that sank in 1927 in just 30 feet of water.

Nearby, the spring-fed wilderness streams of the Coldwater, Blackwater and Sweetwater/Juniper creeks crisscross the "canoe capital" of Florida. Fishermen will find inexpensive charters as well as several public fishing piers. Hikers can tramp through Big Lagoon State Recreation Area or Bay Bluffs Park, where an elevated boardwalk descends Florida's only scenic bluffs, formed more than 20,000 years ago. More than 10 area golf courses are uncrowded and affordable.

The Hesses are actively recruiting their Northern friends — four other families have relocated to Pensacola because of their endorsement — but the couple has made many new friends as well. Janet is vice president of the women's group at St. Francis of Assisi Church, and Jim paints children's faces for the city's annual Cinco de Mayo Celebrations. Both help out with preparations for tongue-in-cheek extravaganzas staged by the flamboyant Krewe of Wrecks each Mardi Gras.

"One of the reasons we haven't been more involved is that Jim suffered a heart attack shortly after we moved here," says Janet, 59. "He had to have triple bypass surgery and has completely recuperated."

"I feel like a million dollars," agrees Jim, 60. "We have complete confidence in the Pensacola medical facilities and doctors, due to an excellent experience during this time."

Five hospitals with a total of 1,696 beds are serviced by Lifeflight Helicopter, a 24-hour air ambulance. The 546-bed Baptist Hospital boasts a state-of-the-art emergency and trauma center. One of 10 Florida facilities designated for the treatment of acute spinal cord injuries, it also operates the area's only electrophysiology laboratory for the diagnosis of heart disease.

Major hospital and commissary facilities are located at Pensacola Naval Air Station and Eglin Air Force Base. The Pensacola Naval Hospital was cited for superior care and treatment of retirees and dependents.

Area bases also offer clubs, boating, camping, golf, bowling, swimming and other amenities for military retirees, and several active associations welcome new members.

Those support services were a big part of the attraction for Ed Maddock, 71, a retired Navy commander, and wife Gloria, 70, a former library assistant. They had been stationed here in the early 1950s and returned in 1989, following a 23-year residence in Annandale, VA.

The Maddocks are history buffs who both volunteer at the National Museum of Naval Aviation. Gloria also works with the Corry Station Library. They left Virginia to escape cold weather and traffic congestion.

"After retirement," Ed says, "I got a job in downtown DC, only 10 miles from home, but it took an hour and a half to commute one-way." He enjoys Pensacola's easy driving, three seasons (spring, summer, fall), seafood and low cost of living: "I like sitting and watching my bank account grow."

Gloria says she likes this "small town with friendly people," although she's not too crazy about "the humidity in July and August. The temperatures are OK, but not the humidity."

The Rosses and Hesses also warn against Florida's muggy climate, as well as Pensacola's rather sketchy zoning laws. "I think there is a lack of community pride associated with taking advantage of the natural beauty," Bill Ross says. "You really run into some areas that look unattractive because of that, and then you run into some magnificently attractive areas."

"There will be a lovely house and then a dump beside it," Janet Hess agrees, noting a prevailing carefree attitude that is an attraction for many to the coastal resort. "The people are more laid back than I thought. If you have to get someone to do service work and the surf is up — forget it!"

Humidity and institutionalized laziness go with the territory in a beach town, but a citizens committee, appointed to promote Northwest Florida as a retirement location, has renewed emphasis on zoning and growth management. Their report calls for mandatory garbage pickup, additional funding for programs that improve community appearance and increased support for Pensacola's Clean and Green Program.

It seems a manageable goal for a town that already has been rated highly in several national surveys, including No. 2 in the nation for quality of life in a study of 130 U.S. cities by Joseph Gyourdo, a Wharton Business School finance professor at the University of Pennsylvania. Perdido Key is among America's top 20 beaches, according to a study by Stephen Leatherman of Florida International University that considered aesthetics, swimming conditions, weather, pollution and other factors.

And don't forget the city's stunning, albeit tastefully restrained, victory as the "sixth most-polite city in the nation," according to Marjabelle Young-Stewart, also known as the "empress of etiquette."

"That's up from No. 7 in my last survey," she says, "so it's getting better all the time." ●

Petoskey, Michigan

Bay-front Michigan town satisfies retirees who like "cool" living

By Dixie Franklin

The waters of Lake Michigan often settle to a glassy stillness as the evening hours approach, offering front-row seats to spectacular sunsets. The shore along Little Traverse Bay is backed by forests of pine, spruce, hemlock and mixed northern hardwood that blaze crimson and gold in autumn. Hills climb to Michigan's prime ski slopes when winter blankets the landscape.

In the bend of the bay is Petoskey, whose year-round population of 6,000 triples when summer residents return to their cottages and second homes. Petoskey could almost be a state of mind shared with the nearby communities of Bay View and Harbor Springs.

"The communities are in step with each other, and always have been," says Stafford Smith, who owns restaurants in all three.

Retirees have long found Petoskey attractive, drawn here by its natural beauty, support services and a growing number of peers. Retired executives, especially from Detroit, Chicago, Indianapolis and cities in Ohio, come first as vacationers, then build second homes and eventually retire here. The area draws more retirees from the region than from distant states.

"There's an easy flow of everyday living," says Dick Wise, who retired here twice. "You get to know almost everybody in town."

Wise and his wife, Betty, moved here in 1971, "looking for a better way of life" after he spent 20 years as an engineer for Ford Motor Co. in the Detroit area.

"Betty's heel marks are still on I-75 from when I dragged her up here in 1971, but now she wouldn't leave," Wise says.

He started a business, retired again eight years ago and now volunteers for the local Service Corps of Retired Executives (SCORE), sponsored by the Small Business Administration.

"A group of eight to 10 of us works with young entrepreneurs to help them get off to a good start," Wise says.

Petoskey is a mix of old and new, with lovely old churches and active service clubs. Street scenes in the Gaslight District along Lake, Howard and Bay streets include old-fashioned lampposts, flower boxes bursting with blooms and benches that encourage genteel loitering.

The Gaslight Shopping District has close to 60 shops and restaurants. Along its tree-lined streets are galleries, boutiques and gift shops. One of them, Symons General Store, is a nostalgic shop of charming clutter under high tin ceilings, with merchandise spilling out the door and onto the sidewalk.

One local gathering place is the Virginia McCune Community Arts Center, still known to many longtime residents as "the church" even though it has been years since Allen McCune bought the idle church building and donated it to the city in his wife's name. The art center hosts changing exhibits, with theater and arts and crafts. On Thursday evenings in June, July and August, women of the Epsilon Jazz Band liven up the stage of the First Presbyterian Church in performances reminiscent of old New Orleans. Most are seniors.

Down the hill past Symons General Store, a tunneled walkway runs under U.S. Highway 31 to a park on the harbor. Mauve banners line the park and marina, adding a splash of color to the boats along the docks. A stage built into the hillside hosts outdoor programs and evening performances.

Pink concrete sidewalks and curbs distinguish Bay View, formed in the 1800s as a Methodist Bible camp. Its personality has changed since its Bible camp days, but it still is primarily a summer community. Outstanding Victorian homes with decorative gingerbread trim, turrets and swirls are reminiscent of turn-of-the-century styles and helped put the town on the National Register of Historic Places.

Around the bay is Harbor Springs, primarily a second-home community for retirees whose main residence is farther south — although a few skiers and winter sports enthusiasts do stay to enjoy the snow. The year-round population is about 1,600.

Retirees seeking homes in the area naturally look first to the waterfront, but property facing the bay is very expensive, easily topping $400,000. Less-expensive alternatives, in the $175,000 range, can be found on the nearby inland lakes of Walloon, Burt and Crooked and the river systems that feed them, according to associate broker Gary Phillips of Re/Max Real Estate of Petoskey.

Many retirees choose homes in Petoskey neighborhoods, where good buys can be found for under $200,000. Single-family homes are more common than condominium units. Most construction is wood, and basements are common.

"Very rarely do I have a home listed with air-conditioning," Phillips says. "With the Northern air and the big lake to keep us cool, there may be one week of the year when we are a bit too warm."

Water recreation is a main attraction in the summer. Residents sail, boat and fish for lake trout and Coho salmon on Lake Michigan. Inland lakes and streams can produce nice catches of rainbow trout, walleye and bass.

Other popular activities include golf and tennis, bike riding and beachcombing along the waterline for Petoskey stones, which wash up on the shores of Lake Michigan. The hexagon-shaped green stone, a fossilized coral, has a distinctive flowerlike pattern that is easy to spot when it is wet or polished. Every pleasant evening finds couples out for a stroll, especially along the waterfront.

The Friendship Center offers 46 senior services, including transportation.

Many retirees find time to work as volunteers through the Northern Michigan Hospital Auxiliary in Petoskey.

Retirees both take and give comfort at the hospital, which works closely with Burns Clinic, a nationally recognized regional referral facility. The 229-bed hospital has a medical staff of more than 125 physicians, including those affiliated with the clinic.

"Every major medical and surgical specialty is represented here, including a health information and physician referral program," says Diane Murray, public affairs manager at the hospital. She says patients often tease that their hospital rooms have better sunset views over the bay than local hotels do.

Herman and Mary Jo Tilly, originally from Indianapolis, volunteer at the hospital up to three times a week. He makes pharmacy runs, helps discharge patients and handles errands while Mary Jo works in the gift shop operated by the auxiliary.

"I was an engineer, and Mary Jo was a speech pathologist in the public schools. We have dealt with people all our lives and felt a need to continue," he says. "We get more out of it than we put in."

Other seniors volunteer their services at the Little Traverse Historical Society, housed in an 1892 railroad depot. While much of the museum contains typical regional historical collections, the display of Petoskey stones is outstanding. There also is a large collection of Ernest Hemingway memorabilia. Hemingway spent many summers at nearby Walloon Lake.

Some retirees stay year-round, but about 60 percent of them leave for at least part of the winter. Favorite getaway months are "the mud months of November and April," says Dave Williams, a retiree who is active as a volunteer in several organizations.

Winter snowfall is abundant with an annual average of 121 inches. But the winters that drive snowbirds south are eagerly anticipated by senior skiers. Downhill skiers head for the slopes at Boyne Mountain, Boyne Highlands and Nubs Nob ski resorts. There is an active over-70 ski club.

"Cross-country skiing is big with the older crowd," says Williams. "This is a very active group of seniors."

Not all retirees who stay for the winter are skiers; some simply enjoy the seasonal differences. In winter, without all the vacationers, the communities take on more of a hometown flavor. The landscape is beautiful in snow, and getting around isn't too difficult because roads are well-maintained.

"We're not great winter sports people, but we enjoy the holiday time of the year up North," Wise says. "The community goes all out for the holidays." ●

Petoskey, MI

Population: 6,080 year-round, 25,000 during the summer.

Location: In the northern part of Lower Michigan on Little Traverse Bay of Lake Michigan. The terrain is gently rolling. The city, which was founded in 1895, was named for Chippewa Chief Pet-O-Sega.

Climate:

	High	Low
January	28	15
July	76	59

Average relative humidity: 60%

Rain: 32 inches.

Snow: 121 inches.

Idyllic summer days with lake breezes; cold winters with abundant snowfall.

Cost of living: Above average (specific index not available).

Average housing cost: $240,000 in the city, but substantially higher for lakefront and waterfront property. Condominiums average $125,000.

Sales tax: 6%

Sales tax exemptions: Groceries, prescription drugs, medical services.

State income tax: 4.2% of taxable income, based on federal adjusted gross income with modifications.

Income tax exemptions: Social Security benefits and federal, state and local government pensions are exempt. There is an exemption for private pensions of up to $36,090 for each taxpayer. For taxpayers age 65 and older there is a deduction of $8,048 in interest, dividends and capital gains.

Intangibles tax: None.

Estate tax: None, except the state's "pickup" portion of the federal tax, applicable to taxable estates above $1 million.

Property tax: $35.95 per $1,000 of assessed value, with homes assessed at 50% of market value. On a $240,000 home, taxes would be $4,434 a year.

Homestead exemption: Up to $1,200 tax credit, depending on property tax paid in proportion to income.

Religion: 36 churches, one synagogue.

Education: North Central Michigan College, a community college, waives tuition for students age 60 and older.

Transportation: No city bus service, though Friendship Center has transportation service for seniors. Pellston Regional Airport, about 20 miles away, provides commuter service.

Health: 229-bed Northern Michigan Hospital; 125 physicians.

Housing options: Most popular choice is a single-family home in Petoskey or one of the neighboring towns. There are no planned retirement communities. **Birchwood Farm Estate**, an upscale development north of Harbor Springs, attracts many retirees; the average price of a three-bedroom home with two-and-a-half baths is about $275,000. Homeowners who spend part of the year elsewhere can contract for year-round maintenance.

Visitor lodging: Apple Tree Inn, $75-$165, (231) 348-2900; Comfort Inn, $35-$350, (231) 347-3220.

Information: Petoskey Chamber of Commerce, 401 E. Mitchell St., Petoskey, MI 49770, (231) 347-4150 or www.petoskey.com.

Pinehurst, North Carolina

This 105-year-old town in the North Carolina Sandhills is closely linked to the game of golf

By Lan Sluder

If golf, golf and more golf is your idea of paradise, Pinehurst may be your cup of, er, tee. The area has more than 40 golf courses, all playable virtually year-round in this mild climate, and a plethora of golfing communities, gated and otherwise. Yet unlike faster-growing golfing neighbors such as Myrtle Beach in South Carolina, Pinehurst retains a true small-town ambiance. The local newspaper is published only three times a week, and the airport has an honor system for parking.

"The pace of life, running in low gear rather than flat out in high gear, attracted us," says Paul Kauffman, 63, a retired IBM engineer who, with his wife, Amy, moved to Pinehurst from Northern Virginia in 1992. Golf also was a deciding factor for the Kauffmans. A 14-handicap golfer, Paul plays four or five times a week.

Golf undeniably is a big deal here. "There are a lot of things for the non-golfer, but many, many people's lives revolve around golf," says Bill Graning, an employee of Ford Motor Co. for 33 years. Bill took early retirement and moved here in 1996 from Plymouth, MI, and now lives on the 11th hole of the Holly course at Pinewild Golf Club, a gated community in Pinehurst. Bill, 62, has a 15 handicap, and his wife, Barbara, a 36. "We have had no second thoughts about moving here and couldn't be happier," he says.

Pinehurst is in southern Moore County, about 70 miles, or 90 minutes by car, southwest of Raleigh. With other towns in the area, including Southern Pines and Aberdeen, Pinehurst is part of the Sandhills region of North Carolina.

The Sandhills take their name from the region's sandy soil, which results from a prehistoric seashore, although the Atlantic Ocean now is about 100 miles away. The sandy soil isn't ideal for most farm crops, aside from peaches, but there are three benefits. First, the sand absorbs water quickly, reduc-

ing breeding places for mosquitoes and other noxious bugs, so you'll spend less time slapping and swatting than in most other parts of the Eastern Carolinas. Second, the soil, along with the 500-foot elevation, contributes to a lower-than-average humidity for the Southeast, making even hot Southern summer days a little more bearable. Finally, for those with a yen for gentleperson farming, the soft earth is kind to the hooves of horses, so the Sandhills area, like Aiken, SC, has horse farms, riding events and stables. A harness racing track in Pinehurst has recently undergone restoration.

Pinehurst owes its existence to a New England drug store entrepreneur named James Walker Tufts, after whom Tufts University in Boston is named. Exhausted from his job as head of the American Soda Fountain Co., Tufts left Boston in 1893 on a trip to Florida in search of a place with fresh air and a healthy environment. He didn't much care for Florida, finding the hotels of the time overpriced and of poor quality, but in the Sandhills he came upon 6,000 acres of pine-barren land, recently cut for its timber. Tufts bought the land for less than $1 an acre and soon undertook to build a resort that he hoped would become "America's winter playground."

Beginning in 1895, Tufts turned over his Boston business interests to his son so he could concentrate on developing the resort first called Tuftstown and later Pinehurst after a planned development on Martha's Vineyard where Tufts had a cottage. He hired Frederick Law Olmsted, the landscape architect of New York's Central Park and fresh from the grounds of the grand Biltmore estate in Asheville, NC, to develop a plan for the new resort.

Olmsted came up with a plan patterned after a New England village, right down to the village green and rambling narrow side streets. He planted nearly 250,000 cedars, hollies, pin oaks, sy-

camores, maples and other trees and shrubs to go along with the remaining native longleaf and loblolly pines. For his part, Tufts moved swiftly to build first the Holly Inn, a small jewel of a hotel still in business today in the Village of Pinehurst, and then the Carolina Hotel, at the time the largest frame hotel in North Carolina. It also is still in existence, now the Pinehurst Hotel, part of the Pinehurst Resort and Country Club. He called the Carolina Hotel the "queen of the South."

The story goes that Tufts was introduced to golf when dairy farmers in the area complained to him that his hotel guests were hitting their cows with little white balls. However true that may be, a Scots golf pro named Donald Ross, who came to be regarded as one of the world's greatest golf course designers with some 600 courses to his credit, was brought in to design and build the first courses at Pinehurst. His second local effort, Pinehurst No. 2, was destined to become one of the most famous of all courses, home to myriad golf tournaments over the years, including the U.S. Open in 1999. The Open will return to Pinehurst No. 2 in 2005.

Ross eventually made his home in Pinehurst and died there in 1948. His golf course designs emphasize tricky greens and strategic layouts that test even the best of golfers. His early courses had sand greens and few water hazards, and one of his guiding principles was that Mother Nature should direct the design, with the golf course following the natural lay of the land. That's true of the three courses he designed at Pinehurst from 1898 to 1910, and in some ways also true of the other five courses at Pinehurst Resort and Country Club. Tom Fazio designed three of them (4, 6 and 8), and the No. 7, a Rees Jones par-72 that was under renovation at press time, has been rated as among the top courses in America along with No. 2.

Pinehurst — that is, the golf courses and hotels in the Village of Pinehurst — was operated as a resort by the Tufts family from 1895 to 1970, then for several years as a real estate development company owned by Diamondhead Corp. After financial problems in the late 1970s, the resort was purchased by Club Corporation of America, which still operates it today. Though it paid only about $15 million for the property, Club Corp. has invested a reported $100 million or more in restoring and improving the hotels and golf courses. A ninth course, on land off Highway 5 between Pinehurst and Aberdeen, with the design by Rees Jones, is under way.

But retirees who have moved to Pinehurst say they were attracted by the small-town atmosphere as much as by the golf. They like the lack of traffic, the slower pace of life and the fact that they fast get to know their neighbors.

Most people in Pinehurst are "very gracious, friendly and outgoing," says Arvilla Sheron, who moved here in 1998 with husband Dick from Newport Beach, CA. Trained as a psychologist, Arvilla was a real estate agent in Newport Beach, and Dick was a regional sales manager for several national companies.

"It's incredible the amount of friends we've made here in a short time — we've been to more parties here in one year than in 10 years in California," she says. Dick, a 9-handicap golfer until a hip replacement slowed him down a little, discovered Pinehurst while entertaining clients on a golf trip. Arvilla says she "tries to stay 39 years old" and has a 32 handicap. The Sherons, like the Kauffmans, ended up at Pinewild, which is predominantly but not exclusively occupied by retirees. Their house,

a 3,000-square-foot rancher on the fourth green of the Holly course, cost about $350,000 and has appreciated, according to Arvilla.

Thanks to the fact that Pinehurst and Southern Pines get hundreds of thousands of golf vacationers each year, the area also has more than its fair share of good restaurants. "We like the small-town atmosphere and lack of traffic and congestion, but we also like the larger city amenities such as good restaurants," says Bill Graning, the former Ford employee.

Of course, the area also has a few drawbacks. Residents point to a lack of "big shopping" opportunities. The Pinehurst/Southern Pines area has upscale grocery stores along with a 24-hour Wal-Mart and Kmart, a Belk department store, a Talbots and a number of boutiques. But for mall shopping, resi-

Population: 9,706 in Pinehurst, 74,769 in Moore County.
Location: Pinehurst is located in the Sand-hills region of south-central North Carolina, about 70 miles southwest of Raleigh.
Climate:

	High	Low
January	55	44
July	91	68

Pinehurst has a moderate four-season climate.
Rain: 51 inches.
Snow: 6 inches.
Cost of living: About average (specific index not available).
Average housing cost: The average residential sale in Moore County was $189,632 in 2001. However, real estate prices vary greatly, ranging from under $90,000 for a small condo to more than $500,000 for a large home in an exclusive golf community or in the Village of Pinehurst. Homes on an interior lot in a golf community average about $180,000. Homes fronting golf courses average about $275,000. Local real estate agents say retirees moving to the area typically spend $175,000-$225,000. Building costs average about $100 per square foot. Two-bedroom apartments rent for $300-$1,500, averaging about $550.
Sales tax: 6.5%

Sales tax exemptions: Prescription medicine, eyeglasses, some medical supplies and most services are exempt.
State income tax: For married couples filing jointly, the rate is graduated from 6% of taxable income up to $21,250 to 8.25% on amounts over $200,000. For single filers, it is graduated from 6% of income up to $12,750 to 8.25% on amounts over $120,000.
Income tax exemptions: Social Security benefits are exempt. Up to $2,000 of distributions from private retirement benefits and IRAs (up to the amount reported in federal income taxes), or up to $4,000 of government pensions may be exempt. Total deductions may not exceed $4,000 per person.
Intangibles tax: None.
Estate tax: None, except the state's pickup portion of the federal tax for estates over $1 million.
Property tax: The basic tax rate for Moore County is 59.5 cents per $100 valuation, including 5 cents for paramedic services. Property is assessed at market value, and the next countywide assessment is scheduled for 2003. In addition, municipalities in the county levy taxes at varying rates, with Pinehurst being among the lowest at 35 cents per $100. A $200,000 home would be taxed at about $1,890 annually.

Homestead exemption: Homeowners age 65 and older, or disabled, living in the home and earning $18,000 or less per year qualify for an exemption of $20,000 or 50% of the value of the home, whichever is greater.
Religion: The area is home to several dozen churches and synagogues representing most religions and denominations.
Education: Some 13,000 students take courses through the Division of Continuing Education at the two-year Sandhills Community College, located on a 250-acre campus near Pinehurst. Within a two-hour drive are four top-rated national universities: Duke University in Durham, the University of North Carolina in Chapel Hill, North Carolina State in Raleigh and Wake Forest University in Winston-Salem.
Transportation: Pinehurst has a small, modern airport with service to Charlotte, a major hub for US Airways via US Airways Express. Many Pinehurst residents drive 90 minutes to the Raleigh-Durham airport for jet service. Interstate 95, the East Coast's major north-south interstate, is about 45 minutes east of Pinehurst near Fayetteville. Amtrak provides passenger rail service with a station in Southern Pines.
Health: Moore Regional Hospital is a

dents usually drive 90 minutes to Raleigh or 45 minutes to Fayetteville, where Fort Bragg Army Base and Pope Air Force Base, one of the largest military complexes in the world, are located.

Many residents who travel frequently drive to the Raleigh-Durham airport or to Greensboro or Charlotte. But Moore County does have a first-rate regional hospital. Moore County Regional Hospital serves 14 counties with state-of-the-art care. A new cancer center has recently been completed, and retirees say the presence of quality medical care was a chief factor in their decision to come here. "Good medical care and the weather were probably our two main criteria for choosing Pinehurst," says Bill Graning.

The prospective Pinehurst retiree will find plenty of choices in homes, lots and retirement communities. Many of the golf courses were developed as a way to generate sales for the real estate around the courses, and there are dozens of choices in golf communities. Real estate agents say as much as one-half of their buyer clients are people considering retirement in the area.

Real estate choices range from homes and lots on Pinehurst Resort and Country Club's eight courses — the No. 6 course alone has some 1,400 lots — to upscale private developments such as the National Golf Club to midpriced golf developments such as Talamore and Seven Lakes. In rural areas of the county, options include smaller single-family homes and mobile homes.

The Pinehurst area offers some "real bargains," according to George McManus, a broker who sells Pinewild Country Club and other properties. Pinewild has around 500 completed homes. Eventual build-out is likely to be around 700 homes, he says. Most Pinewild newcomers buy a lot of around three-quarters of an acre for about $40,000 (interior) to $70,000 or $80,000 (for a golf-front lot). The price includes a $20,000 membership fee.

But while no one is ready to put Pinehurst real estate brokers on the welfare rolls, the area is not as hot a real estate market as some other parts of the state, such as Raleigh, Wilmington and Asheville. Local brokers say many listings are on the market about six months, above average for the state and the re-

Pinehurst, NC

400-bed, acute-care, not-for-profit facility serving a 14-county region. With a medical staff of about 130 physicians, a professional staff of nearly 2,000 and more than 500 volunteers, the hospital has a reputation for excellence in cardiology, cancer care and other specialties.
Housing options: The Pinehurst area offers a wide range of housing choices, from large luxury homes in the "old town" area of the Village of Pinehurst for $1 million or more to small houses or mobile homes for less than $75,000. Among area developments: **National Golf Club** in Southern Pines, (800) 471-4339, offers single-family homes from $350,000 and golf course lots from $85,000. **Pinehurst Resort and Country Club** has golf course lots for $100,000-$200,000. **Pinewild Country Club of Pinehurst**, (800) 826-7624, has golf course lots from around $70,000, including a $20,000 golf club membership fee. At **Whispering Winds at Whispering Pines**, homesites with views of the golf course and pond start from the mid-$20,000s and 16 townhomes start from $165,900. **Beacon Ridge at Seven Lakes West**, (800) 200-4653, surrounds Lake Auman and features homes from $170,000 to over $2 million. Homesites start at $16,500, including country club membership. **Foxfire**,

(888) 295-2997, offers homes in the middle $100,000s, and **Talamore Villas**, (910) 692-7207, has two-bedroom furnished condos from around $150,000. **Longleaf of Southern Pines**, (800) 522-9426, has townhomes from the low $200,000s and single-family homes with golf course views from the upper $200,000s. The Pinehurst area also has several assisted-living communities, including **Belle Meade Retirement Resort**, (910) 246-1000; **Quail Haven Village**, (910) 295-2294; and **Manorhouse**, (910) 695-0011.
Visitor lodging: Accommodations range from historic inns to modern motels. The rambling 222-room, wood-frame Pinehurst Resort and Country Club retains the charm of its early days as the Carolina Hotel. Rates are $182-$436, depending on season, including breakfast and dinner. High season is March-May and September-November, (800) 487-4653. The Holly Inn, also in the Village of Pinehurst and affiliated with the Pinehurst Resort and Country Club, is smaller, with 77 rooms and eight suites, but even more charming, with rates of $326-$480, including breakfast and dinner, (800) 487-4653. Another small hotel, with 11 rooms, is the Magnolia Inn, also in the Village of Pinehurst. Packages including breakfast and dinner and green

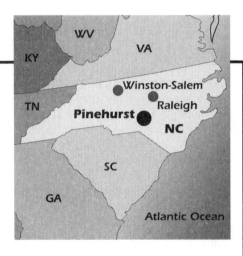

fees at selected courses are $205-$380, double occupancy, for two nights, (800) 526-5562. Among chain motels in the area are Hampton Inn, $69-$89, (800) 333-9266, and Springhill Suites by Marriott, $69-$79, (910) 695-0234. Many golf developments offer packages that include greens fees and short-term condo rentals from $140 per night, double occupancy. For information: Pinehurst Area Realty, (910) 295-5011; Tin Cup Golf and Travel, (888) 465-3857; or First Tee Golf Packages, (800) 781-1165.
Information: Pinehurst Area Convention and Visitors Bureau/Chamber of Commerce, P.O. Box 2270, Southern Pines, NC 28388, (800) 346-5362 or www.homeofgolf.com. It concentrates mostly on golf information for visitors but can provide limited retirement information. Sandhills On-line (www.sandhills.org) has information about the area and links to local businesses.

gion. "I would say strong is overstating the market. It's a growing market, not a strong one," says Paul Shaffer, broker in charge of ERA Realty One in Pinehurst, though he says his own business has increased every year since he began working in real estate here in the early 1990s.

It's mainly a matter of supply and demand. There's simply too much supply, especially in golf-oriented communities, say local developers and brokers. When you visit Pinehurst and Southern Pines, a short drive will disclose a number of golf developments with large inventories of unsold lots and few homes under construction. This situation is exacerbated by the perception of some prospective retiree homeowners that Pinehurst is a one-dimensional golf destination.

Also impacting the market is that golf as a sport has been flat for the past three or four years. The number of golf courses in the United States has increased by 15 percent during the past decade, but the number of golfers hasn't grown. In the South Atlantic states, a region that includes North Carolina, the number of golf rounds played in 1999 was down 2.6 percent from 1998. Some courses in the Pinehurst area also have reported lower rates of play. One course, Legacy in Aberdeen, reported a 3.8 percent drop in rounds played in 1999.

But if you're into horses and hounds, you'll also feel at home in the Sandhills. Each fall, owners from the North and Midwest bring their jumpers, hunters and dressage horses to the Pinehurst/Southern Pines area to take advantage of the mild winter climate and soft sand footing. Thanksgiving Day traditionally marks the opening day of the local hunt season, which culminates with hunter trials in March. The Pinehurst Harness Track, on the National Register of Historic Places, has been the winter home for standardbreds for more than 50 years.

Beyond horses and golf, there are other places of interest in the Pinehurst area. The Malcolm Blue Farm in Aberdeen is an example of the small farms of Scottish immigrants who settled the area in the 19th century. Weymouth Center in Southern Pines is the site of the North Carolina Literary Hall of Fame. Weymouth Woods Nature Preserve is a 571-acre wildlife reserve with hiking trails and a pond in Southern Pines.

About 35 miles northwest of Pinehurst is Seagrove, renowned for its pottery. In Colonial times, potters from England were attracted to this area because of its deposits of fine potting clay. Now, nearly 100 pottery studios are scattered along U.S. Highway 220, and the North Carolina Pottery Center has exhibits of pottery from around the state.

Asheboro, 50 miles northwest of Pinehurst, is home to the North Carolina Zoo. This 1,500-acre zoological park has 1,600 animals and 60,000 exotic plants. Pinehurst is about two hours from Myrtle Beach and the Wilmington area, the closest beaches. Real estate agents say they lose some prospects who want to live on the coast but gain others seeking to avoid the threat of hurricanes. The North Carolina coast has been hit hard by hurricanes in recent years, and residents have had to evacuate several times. Only Hurricane Fran in 1996 had any recent impact on Pinehurst, and that was mainly in the form of downed trees and branches.

At an elevation of around 500 feet, Pinehurst has some low rolling hills, but the nearest mountains are three to four hours away in the western part of the state. Surprisingly, last winter Pinehurst got more snow than the mile-high mountains of Western North Carolina. A freak storm dropped 22 inches of snow around Pinehurst, closing down everything for days and destroying tens of thousands of trees, which snapped under layers of ice and snow. Normally Pinehurst gets little snow, and it usually disappears by the next day, residents say.

But the Millers looked at a number of areas before selecting Pinehurst, including several places in Arizona, Southern California, Florida and coastal South Carolina. "They were all too crowded, too hot, too flat, too expensive or too something," says Jim, 63, who was an engineer with Boeing before he retired.

And that brings up one of the things that Jim says he especially likes about Pinehurst. He says residents are accepted for what they are now, rather than what they did before retirement. Jim, a 13-handicap golfer, and other retirees say it's rare for anyone even to ask what they did before they retired.●

Port Townsend, Washington

A sense of history lingers in this 19th-century seaport on Washington's Olympic Peninsula

By Stanton H. Patty

Port Townsend always has been a dreamscape. Back in the 1890s, the picturesque seaport in the northwestern corner of Washington state boasted that it was on the way to becoming the "New York of the West." That was when city fathers were certain that a railroad northward from the Columbia River would bypass Seattle and roll into Port Townsend. It never happened.

But later, as big-city residents began searching out quiet zones for their retirement years, dreams did come true in old Port Townsend. "We live in paradise," says Helen Cleveland, a Port Townsend resident since 1995. "But, shhh, we don't want everyone to know what a wonderful place this is."

Helen and her husband, Robert, moved to Port Townsend from Minneapolis by way of adventurous working years in Australia, Singapore and Manhattan. Robert, 64, retired from a career in merchant banking and sales. England-born Helen, 60, was a librarian and office manager. Now they have a 2,300-square-foot home near Port Townsend's airport, with a splendid garden of rhododendrons and azaleas — and what Helen describes as a "knock-dead" view of 10,778-foot-high Mount Baker across Puget Sound in Washington's Cascade Range.

Another happily retired couple in Port Townsend is Richard and Anne Schneider, who built a vacation home in Port Townsend in 1993. For the next three years Dick Schneider split his time between Port Townsend and his investment-business office in Southern California.

"Then one day I had a great revelation," Dick recalls. "I asked myself, 'Why am I leaving this great place?' Right then, I decided to retire, and here we are."

The Schneiders have a waterfront home on two acres of property — plus a 48-foot boat for cruising through British Columbia and other destinations. They didn't wait for their Social Security years to retire — Dick is 59, and Anne is 58 — and they thoroughly researched their options. "We spent 10 years looking for a retirement place," Dick says. "This is it."

Another couple who took special care in choosing a retirement community was Bobby and Rose Morrison, who both were working in the California prison system when they began methodical retirement planning. That was in 1987, and they already had set 1996 as their retirement date.

Bobby, 62, was based in Sacramento, in the central office of the California Department of Corrections, implementing wheelchair access and other such facilities for disabled inmates. Rose, 54, was a nurse consultant, helping to oversee medical care for a dozen prisons.

"We had a target," says Rose. "We're planners. First, we made individual lists of key things we wanted in a retirement place. Then we merged our lists and prioritized."

Among their prime factors: a close-to-nature saltwater setting, adequate medical facilities, a quality library system, strong cultural assets and proximity to a major city for shopping and the arts. Port Townsend, population 8,334, met all the requirements for the Morrisons and many of their retired neighbors.

The retirees also are aware that they reside in one of the Pacific Northwest's history-rich communities. Port Townsend was founded in 1851, six months before settlers reached nearby Seattle. Farming, logging and seafaring were the first industries.

Because of its commanding site at the entrance to Puget Sound, the United States government soon designated Port Townsend as headquarters of a busy customs district. The stampede to the Klondike gold fields was under way. A steady procession of vessels steaming to and from Alaska — through the waters of neighboring Canada — were required to check in with customs inspectors at Port Townsend. There also was a growing trade between Puget Sound and Asia.

Saloons, brothels and assorted other nefarious enterprises crowded Water Street, the main drag. Port Townsend was a brawling port with a reputation almost as wicked as that of San Francisco's Barbary Coast. Proper families built fine Victorian homes on a bluff above the harbor, and stairways linking the bluff with downtown were declared "off limits" to the soiled doves of Water Street.

Just as the 19th century was ebbing, Port Townsend had high hopes of connecting to a major railroad out of Portland, OR. Speculators framed Water Street with showy buildings built of brick. Promoters laid 25 miles or so of railroad track toward Portland. Property values soared, and boosters dubbed Port Townsend "the inevitable New York."

But the dream crashed in 1904 when civic leaders were handed a telegram with the news that the Union Pacific Railroad had decided to go to Seattle instead. Downtown construction projects halted so suddenly that carpentry tools were found years later in the upper stories of unfinished business buildings. Perhaps half of the town's 7,000 or so citizens departed over the next year.

Port Townsend survived — frozen in time as a museum of a town — until a few years ago when it was rediscovered by city dwellers. Now most of this treasure of a town on Washington's Olympic Peninsula is preserved as a national historic district. The sturdy brick buildings along Water Street are restaurants, galleries and offices. Many of the elegant Victorians on the virtuous bluff are bed-and-breakfast inns.

And retirees such as Bob and Helen Cleveland are happy to be a part of this contented community. "The only way they will ever get me out of Port Townsend is feet first," vows Helen.

The Clevelands and many of their friends are active in Centrum, a thriving, nonprofit center for the arts at adjacent Fort Worden State Park. Retirees volunteer as ushers, for office work and other chores. Centrum features workshops and festivals that range from jazz to classics, from writers' conferences to teacher training.

Maybe you remember seeing Fort Worden in the movies. The former military post was the setting for "An Officer and a Gentleman." But Port Townsend's transplants didn't need directions from Hollywood to find Port Townsend. "I call it serendipity," says Anne Schneider.

The Schneiders had considered several areas for retirement, including Arizona, New Mexico, Colorado and California. Then one day in 1990, while on vacation, they happened to drive through Port Townsend on the way to catch a ferry to nearby Whidbey Island.

"Suddenly, we realized Port Townsend was what we had been looking for," Dick Schneider remembers. "We stopped at a real estate office and asked them to show us some properties. Right after we returned home (to Dana Point, CA), I went to my office and called the Realtor in Port Townsend and arranged to buy a waterfront lot."

Among Port Townsend's assets, the Schneiders say, are fascinating people. "It's an eclectic mix of successful, well-traveled people who have chosen to be here — just great people," Dick says.

Anne Schneider puts it this way: "There's a heart and soul to this town."

Jefferson General Hospital, Port Townsend's only hospital, offers excellent care, Dick says, and the stylish community is attracting talented young physicians. Also available, for critical-care patients, are air-ambulance helicopter flights to medical centers in Seattle. "But our hospital can handle a lot of heavy-duty stuff," Dick says.

Dick Schneider stays busy with boating and gardening and as a board member of Port Townsend's Marine Science Center. Anne Schneider is president of the Centrum board and serves with Working Images, an organization that provides appropriate clothing for women leaving the welfare rolls for the work force. Somehow the Schneiders still find time to travel. Next winter they will participate in a study cruise to the Antarctic.

Port Townsend, WA

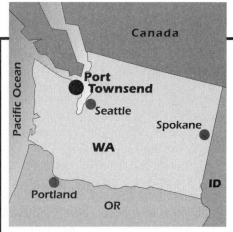

Population: 8,334 in the city, 25,953 in Jefferson County.

Location: On Puget Sound in the northeastern corner of Washington state's Olympic Peninsula, about 52 miles by highway and ferry north and west of Seattle. There are views of the Cascade Range to the east and the Olympic Mountains to the west. Elevation in the Port Townsend area ranges from sea level to 350 feet.

Climate:

	High	Low
January	44	35
July	71	51

Weather is mild because the city is sheltered by the "rain shadow" of the Olympic Mountains.

Average relative humidity: 60%
Rain: 16 inches.
Snow: Rare.
Cost of living: Generally average, but food prices tend to be higher than in Seattle because of transportation costs.
Average housing cost: $176,261 in Port Townsend in 2001, $204,573 in Jefferson County.
Sales tax: 8.2%
Sales tax exemptions: Food items at grocery stores.
State income tax: None.
Intangibles tax: None.
Estate tax: None, except the state's "pick-up" portion of the federal tax, applicable to taxable estates above $1 million.
Property tax: The city tax rate is $11.31 per $1,000 of assessed valuation. The tax on a $176,261 home in the city is about $1,993.
Homestead exemption: Homeowners age 61 or older, with a gross household income of $30,000 or less, are eligible for certain property tax exemptions.
Religion: Several denominations are represented, with at least 30 places of worship in the Port Townsend/Olympic Peninsula region.

Education: Port Townsend has a branch of Peninsula Community College, which has its headquarters in nearby Port Angeles. Washington State University has a branch campus in Port Hadlock, about six miles southeast of Port Townsend. Both offer programs for older adults.

Transportation: Jefferson County International Airport is served by air-taxi operators with charter flights to Seattle, Washington's San Juan Islands, Vancouver and Victoria in neighboring British Columbia and other points. There is no scheduled air service to or from Port Townsend. Jefferson County Transit is an integrated system serving Jefferson, Clallam and Kitsap counties for transportation around the Olympic Peninsula. Within Port Townsend, there is free shuttle service between the port area and the city's historic districts. Washington State Ferries operates between Port Townsend and Keystone on Whidbey Island, with crossings taking about 35 minutes each way. The most direct way to reach Port Townsend from Seattle is

Bob and Helen Cleveland are among Port Townsend's more adventurous retirees. In 1969, they went to Australia as migrants, at a time when Australia was seeking newcomers with strong skills. They stayed six years.

"We went without a position, but the odds were good for Americans," Bob recalls. Soon Bob was named an assistant to the chairman of a merchant bank in Sydney.

It was on the way to Australia that the Clevelands met a couple from Vancouver, British Columbia, who suggested they visit Port Townsend. "We did, and we liked it instantly," says Helen Cleveland. "This definitely is God's country."

Both volunteer at Centrum events. They hike and camp through the Olympic Peninsula, including outings in nearby 897,000-acre Olympic National Park. Bob is a fly-fishing enthusiast who finds productive catch-and-release waters in the area's streams and lakes.

Their travel schedule also is full. "We're just back from Nepal, India and Japan," Helen says. "Next will be Ireland."

Bobby and Rose Morrison hope to visit Europe next year, but they might have a difficult time tearing themselves away from Port Townsend for a few weeks. "There are two deer walking around here as I am talking to you," Bobby says. "It's a great sight — as long as they don't eat my azaleas."

The Morrisons have a three-bedroom house with a 10- by 40-foot outdoor deck that overlooks a serene half-acre of trees and shrubs. "We hear birds and know that there are four-footed types out there," Bobby says. "This is special."

The Morrisons consider their neighbors special, too. "The people here are very nice, very honest, very open and intelligent," Bobby says. "They are willing to accept ideas and to express opinions. I guess we are 'closet hippies.'"

There isn't much time for loafing on the Morrisons' schedule. Rose Morrison volunteers at the Port Townsend Visitor Center and at Centrum. The couple also tries to walk at least two miles a day, often with a dachshund named Mischief. "Sometimes, on gray days, we miss the sunshine," admits Bobby Morrison. "Then we toss another log on the fire and cuddle up and everything's OK."

Capt. George Vancouver, the English navigator, put Port Townsend on the map when he sailed by in 1792 aboard the HMS Discovery. Vancouver sighted what he described as "a very safe and capacious harbor." He named it Port Townshend for his friend, the marquis of Townshend. American settlers dropped the "h," and that's the way it stayed.

George Townshend, the marquis, never saw his namesake town. But his younger brother, Charles, certainly left his mark on America. It was Charles Townshend who was responsible for imposing the detestable tax on tea and other goods that resulted in the Boston Tea Party.

"There's a real sense of history here," says Bobby Morrison. "And it's just a darned nice place." ●

---

to ride the Bainbridge Island ferry (Washington State Ferries) from downtown Seattle to Bainbridge Island, then take State Route 305 northwest about 13 miles, past Poulsbo, to State Route 3 and follow signs for seven miles to the Hood Canal Bridge. Cross the bridge and turn left. About one-half mile later, there is a sign pointing toward Port Townsend. About five miles after that, turn right on State Route 19. Continue about 22 miles to the town of Chimacum and to a four-way stop on State Route 19. Route 19 joins State Route 20 about seven miles south of Port Townsend. Follow Route 20 into Port Townsend. The trip normally takes one and a half to two hours.

Health: Jefferson General Hospital, with 42 beds, is Port Townsend's only hospital. Air-ambulance service to medical centers in Seattle is available through Jefferson General. At last count, the Port Townsend area had 32 physicians and 15 dentists. Kah Tai Care Center in Port Townsend is a nursing home with 84 beds. Victoria House, (360) 379-8223, close to downtown Port Townsend, is an assisted-living facility with 39 apartments for residents needing various levels of care. Studio apartments at Victoria House rent for $2,200 to $3,000 a month; one-bedroom apartments range from $2,500 to $3,000. Other assisted-living facilities are situated in the town of Sequim ("skwim"), a major center for retirees, about 28 miles west of Port Townsend.

Housing options: Popular with Port Townsend retirees are the Kala Point and Cape George neighborhoods. **Kala Point**, about four miles south of the city center, near the airport, has a mix of single-family dwellings, townhouses and time-share and for-sale condominiums. Amenities include beach access, walking trails, tennis courts and boat launching. Prices range from about $170,000 for a two-bedroom house to $1 million for a waterfront home with generous acreage. Three-bedroom condominiums are priced at about $300,000. **Cape George**, on Discovery Bay some eight miles west of Port Townsend, features beach access, a marina, swimming pool, community club, a workshop for hobbyists and views of the Olympic Mountains. Cape George is divided into three zones — first is The Colony, a residential area with single-family homes priced from about $200,000 to $500,000. A second zone, The Village, has less expensive properties, ranging from about $60,000 to $150,000. Some modular and mobile homes are permitted in The Village. The third zone is in forested property behind The Colony and The Village. Home prices in that zone range from about $150,000 to $300,000.

Visitor lodging: Accommodations include hotels, motels and bed-and-breakfast inns. Options include the 48-room Port Townsend Inn downtown, with rates from $78 to $158 a night, double occupancy, (800) 216-4985. Bishop Victorian Hotel has 15 suites downtown, with rates from $99 to $200, (800) 824-4738. Blue Gull Inn, a six-room B&B in Port Townsend's historic district, has rates from $85 to $125 year-round. (888) 700-0205.

Information: Port Townsend Chamber of Commerce and Visitor Information Center, 2437 E. Sims Way, Port Townsend, WA 98368, (360) 385-7869 or (360) 385-2722. On the Internet, visit www.ptguide.com.

Prescott, Arizona

This cool retreat is set high in the pine-clad mountains of central Arizona

By Ron Butler

It doesn't take long to discover why people from back East and up North are settling in Prescott, and why well-heeled Silicon Valley residents are building second homes and retirement homes in the piney oasis of ponderosa that surrounds town like a shimmering green shawl.

You may have to give it a few days, but it soon will become obvious why this mile-high town of 33,938 people in central Arizona is growing so rapidly as a retirement destination, as is its next-door neighbor, Prescott Valley. At first glance, Prescott probably won't knock your socks off. There are too many boxy homes going up amid magnificent old Victorian houses, and too many weathered wooden structures that should be abandoned or torn down.

But list climate among the attractions. Midway between the state's lowest desert and its highest mountains, Prescott offers four distinct seasons. Many newcomers attracted to Arizona's laid-back lifestyle find the scorching desert summers too hot to handle, and Prescott is the perfect alternative.

That's what sold Bill and Lola Jolly, 75 and 70 respectively, who moved to Prescott in 1991 from Fullerton, CA, where Bill was a retail furniture executive and Lola worked as a real estate agent. They had been coming to Prescott for years to visit California friends who had settled there. "We were never here when the weather wasn't perfect," says Bill. "Even when it snows, the snow disappears in a couple of hours. We have snow chains for our car but have never had them out of the box."

The Jollys live in a three-bedroom home in a planned development in the Antelope Hills area on the Prescott-Chino Valley border, not far from the Prescott Airport (catering to small, private and light craft) and immediately adjacent to the Antelope Hills Golf Course, a 36-hole public course. Also in Prescott are two private golf courses,

the Prescott Golf and Country Club and Quailwood Greens. An avid golfer, Bill's retirement present from his firm was a golf cart.

Thus, about eight miles from downtown Prescott, Bill and Lola can look through the large picture windows in their living room and see lush green fairways in one direction or track light aircraft gliding through dense blue sky in another. Scenes from "Planet of the Apes" were filmed in the rocky outcropping of nearby Granite Dells.

But they don't spend that much time at home. "The fine arts department at Yavapai Junior College offers marvelous entertainment," says Lola. "There are good museums, antique shops, a fine library and several good bookstores. I think we've eaten at every restaurant in town."

Lola and Bill both volunteer one or two days a week at the downtown visitors center. There also are special classes for adults at Yavapai College and an active community bridge club. Bill, a fighter pilot in Hawaii during World War II, adds the action at Bucky's Casino and seasonal horse racing to the entertainment mix. The casino, located on a hilltop in what formerly was a Sheraton Hotel, is operated by the Yavapai Prescott Indian tribe.

For many, Prescott's strong sense of history is a major selling point and the inspiration, perhaps, for its city slogan, "Everybody's home town." The Palace Bar on historic Whiskey Row no longer has gambling tables and painted ladies, but it has lost little of its frontier flavor over the years, and the sound of spurs is as common as the jingle of pocket change.

Outside on its central pediment, the Palace Hotel wears the Great Seal of the Territory of Arizona. When President Lincoln named Arizona a territory in 1864, Prescott was declared its capital by order of the first territorial governor, former congressman John N. Good-

win. Arizona's seat of government moved to Tucson in 1867, back to Prescott 10 years later, and finally to Phoenix in 1889.

As frequently happened during the days of the early West, a time when towns were constructed almost entirely of wood, Prescott was devastated by fire. In its heyday, Whiskey Row had more than 20 saloons going full blast, 24 hours a day, filling the glasses of thirsty miners and cowboys. Three local breweries helped meet the demand. In 1900, a drunken miner knocked over a kerosene lamp in a boarding house and the resulting inferno destroyed five hotels, 25 saloons and more than 50 downtown businesses. When the flames came swooping in, undaunted patrons at the Palace lifted the massive bar, carried it out the door and across the street, and set it up on the courthouse lawn, where libations continued to flow.

Prescott also is where the rodeo was born. Cowboy competitions were common during the early days of the American West. By matching roping and riding skills, ranch against ranch, the hard-working cowboys let off steam and had themselves a ball doing what they did best. As part of its Independence Day celebration in 1888, Prescott sponsored a cowboy competition, the nation's first, making it a signature community event. The Prescott Frontier Days Rodeo has been a July Fourth weekend tradition ever since, now the oldest continuous celebration of leather and sweat in existence and one of the most popular.

Thousands of cowboys and cowboy types — tourists, vagrants, "buckle bunnies" (young women who follow the rodeo cowboys) and other assorted revelers — come pouring into town, filling the hotels and spilling over into the hills beyond. They sleep in pickup trucks, camp trailers and in bedrolls and sleeping bags just off the highway. The rules of the rodeo have been refined and standardized over the years, but little else has changed since the very first one was staged in Prescott. The dust and enthusiasm are still blinding.

More local history can be explored in 525 buildings that have been placed on the National Register of Historic Places. The town plaza, shaded by cotton-woods, is the star attraction. Its historic white granite Yavapai County Courthouse, built in 1916 in handsome Neoclassic Revival style, represents the justice and order that eventually came to the wild and bawdy West.

Among Prescott's legendary lawmen was George Ruffner, who was Arizona's oldest peacemaker when he died in 1933 at the age of 71. A local newspaper wrote of Ruffner, the first Arizonan elected to the Hall of Great Westerners at the Cowboy Hall of Fame: "He possesses nerves of steel, utmost calm in moments of danger, and his name has become a terror to the outlaws and

Prescott, AZ

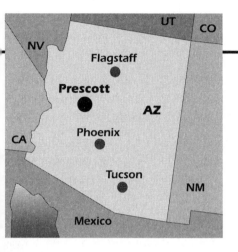

Population: 33,938 in Prescott, 167,517 in Yavapai County.

Location: Prescott is located in central Arizona amid the largest stand of ponderosa pine in the world. The community is 96 miles northwest of Phoenix and 90 miles southwest of Flagstaff.

Climate:

	High	Low
January	50	22
July	89	57

Rain: 19 inches.
Snow: 21 inches.
Cost of living: Above average (specific index not available).
Average home price: $185,200 in Prescott.
Sales tax: 8.35%
Sales tax exemptions: Groceries and prescription drugs
State income tax: For married couples filing jointly, graduated from 2.87% of taxable income up to $20,000 to 5.04% minus $2,276 on amounts over $300,000. For single filers, graduated from 2.87% of taxable income up to $10,000 to 5.04% minus $1,138 on amounts over $150,000.
Income tax exemptions: Social Security benefits and up to $2,500 on federal, state and local government pensions are exempt.
Estate tax: None, except the state's "pick-up" portion of federal tax applicable to taxable estates above $1 million.

Inheritance tax: None.
Property tax: Residential property is assessed at 10% of market value, with average property taxes at about 1.3% of the assessor's full cash value. Taxes on a $185,200 home would be about $2,408.
Homestead exemptions: None.
Religion: Prescott has dozens of houses of worship, representing virtually every denomination.
Education: Yavapai Community College is a public two-year institution offering both university transfer credits and occupation education. Prescott College is a four-year liberal arts college. Embry-Riddle Aeronautical is a four-year university offering bachelor degrees in the fields of aviation and engineering.
Transportation: Interstate 17 is 36 miles east of Prescott via Highway 69 or 169. Prescott is 52 miles south of Interstate 40 via U.S. Highway 89. Local bus service, Greyhound connections and shuttle to Sky Harbor International Airport in Phoenix are available.
Health: Yavapai Regional Medical Center has 117 beds and is fully accredited. Northern Arizona Veterans Administration Health Care System offers 150 beds, plus 208 beds for domiciliary care and a 60-bed nursing home care unit and long-term care facilities. Other area facilities include Las Fuentes Care Center, Peppertree Square of Prescott, Prescott Samaritan Village, Meadowpark Care Center, Mountain View Manor, Center for Adult Care, Mi Casa Care Home Group and Margaret Morris Center (for Alzheimer's care).
Housing options: Medium-priced and luxury condominiums, townhouses, patio homes and ranch-style homes, plus other styles of one- and two-story single-family homes, are all available, as are mobile homes. Among new-home developments is **Pinon Oaks**, (877) 829-

4150, a development planned for 2,650 homes. Eleven builders are constructing homes in Pinon Oaks, and a recent home selection ranged from 1,800 to 2,500 square feet in size and $204,000-$330,000 in price. At the **Viewpoint at Prescott Valley**, (928) 775-2000, homes by more than a dozen builders range in size from 1,300 to 2,500 square feet and start in the low to mid-$100,000s. Luxury custom homes at the 1,000-acre **Ranch at Prescott**, (888) 778-2766, are built on lots that range from the $60,000s to the $120,000s, depending on view.

Visitor lodging: SpringHill Suites by Marriott, within walking distance of the Prescott plaza, is conveniently located in a retail center near restaurants, stores and a supermarket, (888) 287-9400 or (928) 776-0998. Rates for double occupancy are $79 Sunday-Thursday and $99 Friday-Saturday, including buffet breakfast, free local calls, a pool and workout facilities. The renowned Hassayampa Inn, (800) 322-1927 or (928) 778-9434, opened its 200 guest rooms in 1927 right off the plaza. Meticulously maintained, it offers the romance and luxury of a bygone era, highlighted by its gourmet Peacock Room for elegant dining. Rates for standard double occupancy range from $99 to $139, depending on season, including a full breakfast in the Peacock Room. Other hotels include the Antelope Ridge Resort, Hampton Inn, Ramada, Prescott Resort and Conference Center and Super 8. In total, Prescott offers 1,300 rooms in 32 hotels and motels and 19 bed-and-breakfast inns.
Information: Prescott Chamber of Commerce, 101 S. Cortez, P.O. Box 1147, Prescott, AZ 86302-1147, (928) 778-2193 or www.prescott.org. Prescott Area Coalition for Tourism, (800) 266-7534 or www.visit-prescott.com.

toughs that infest the territory."

Bucky O'Neill was another Prescott hero who wore a badge. Sheriff, mayor and one-time newspaperman, he helped organize the famous Rough Riders during the Spanish-American War, rode alongside Teddy Roosevelt and died in combat on a Cuban hillside. An equestrian statue, erected on the square by the State of Arizona in 1907, honors O'Neill. These days the statue overlooks square dances and band concerts held on warm summer evenings.

No one views Prescott with more of a sense of communal purpose and pride than Don and Annette Schiller, both 62, who moved from Irving, TX. Originally from California, Don, whose background includes cable television management and production as well as alarms and security systems, bought property in Prescott in 1989 and eventually built a two-story, three-bedroom home, all gables and picture windows — "I wanted to bring the outside inside" — in what's now known as the Timber Ridge development.

Since arriving in Prescott, Don has immersed himself in community activities — Rotary Club and the chamber of commerce as well as youth group activities such as the Youth Exchange, Chamber of Commerce Youth Division, Boy Scouts and Big Brothers/Big Sisters. For the past five years he has appeared as Santa Claus, raising money for the Prescott Big Brothers organization. During our interview, his cell phone rang incessantly.

Don's wife, Annette, is a retired schoolteacher who now enjoys teaching nature studies to young children at the Highlands Center for Natural History. She is a past president of the American Association of University Women. Don and Annette both like to travel in Scotland and the Philippines, and they frequently hike in the woods near their home. Their son, Brad, is a lighting designer and programmer in Texas. He and his wife, Margaret, have a 3-year-old son, Matthew.

The arrival of Ginny, 48, and John Van Vliet, 57, was more circuitous. They came by Winnebago after traveling around the country for two years, from Mississippi to Southern California, before deciding to settle in Prescott. "It met our budget, wants and needs," says Ginny, who previously worked as a sign language interpreter for General Motors. Husband John was human resources director for the Miller Brewing Co. and worked briefly as a Harley Davidson representative in Milwaukee. Both now own Harleys and frequently ride around the countryside or "90 miles down the hill to Phoenix." The growing number of Hell's Angels bikers in town gives more bark than bite, says Ginny.

The Van Vliets live in a single-family subdivision in the Yavapai Hills east of Prescott. Their three-bedroom home has huge picture windows and decks. The Flying U Court, where they live, is adjacent to the Bar Circle A ranch, which belonged to early cowboy film star Tom Mix before he was killed in a car accident in Florence, AZ.

John likes to golf, and Ginny belongs to a ladies luncheon group. Since settling in Prescott three and a half years ago, they've been to glitzy Las Vegas seven times. The casinos and restaurants in Las Vegas, 268 miles away, counter limited options in Prescott, says Ginny.

As for Lola Jolly, the former California real estate agent, she notes that the local junipers "are killers for anyone with allergies" when asked about drawbacks, but she says that buyers can get twice as much for their real estate dollar.

And Don Schiller, affiliated with the Prescott Chamber of Commerce on a volunteer basis, can find nothing at all on the downside. "Every time I drive back from town through that beautiful pine forest, I can't help but be thankful that I'm not on those choking freeways in Texas or Los Angeles," he says.●

Punta Gorda, Florida

Florida city offers a sense of the past and an eye to the future

By Karen Feldman

When Spanish explorer Juan Ponce de Leon set sail in search of the fountain of youth, he made his way to Florida's shores, starting at the northeast in St. Augustine and wending his way down to Southwest Florida.

At Charlotte Harbor, he encountered the Calusa Indians and, judging from the fierce defense of their territory, became convinced that this was where the magical fountain must be. Why else would the Calusas fight so hard?

For Ponce de Leon, what is today Punta Gorda proved not to be the site of eternal youth, but of untimely death in 1513, when the Calusas killed him in battle.

Both the Calusas and the search for the fountain of youth are history. But many of the city's 14,344 residents find that simply living in this waterfront city, with its historic brick streets, miles of canals, manicured parks and golf courses, can be curative in itself. For those 50 and older, who comprise more than 65 percent of the city's population, it can come close to heaven.

Harriet Mielke, 62, moved to Punta Gorda from Detroit with her husband, Leonard, in 1992 and now volunteers at the chamber of commerce for Charlotte County, of which Punta Gorda is the county seat. "When I talk to prospects who visit the chamber, I tell them we have found Utopia," the former Detroit Public Schools employee says.

"It's a really diverse community," says Julie Mathis, executive director of the chamber. Recent publicity has focused attention on the area, drawing the curious who "come here and fall in love with it," she says.

It's a common occurrence. Bob and Jackie Meatty, both retired from the U.S. Department of State's Foreign Service, moved to Punta Gorda in 1995 from Alexandria, VA. They had seriously considered retiring in Charleston, SC, and checked out spots all along the Atlantic Coast from North Carolina on down.

After one visit to Punta Gorda, they decided it was where they wanted to be. They rented for five months, then purchased a single-family home with a large family room on a canal in Punta Gorda Isles, an upscale community where many homes are built on a multitude of canals that offer direct access to Charlotte Harbor and, beyond that, the Gulf of Mexico.

For Bob Meatty, 59, it was the "climate, lifestyle, ease of water access and a home on a canal" that convinced him. For 62-year-old Jackie, it was all those things as well as a lower cost of living. Jackie misses some of the cultural opportunities of the Washington, DC, area but happily lives without the metropolitan traffic.

As for Bob, "I don't miss anything." Low crime, moderately priced housing, lots of outdoor activities and a subtropical climate are the main attractions for them and for other Northerners looking for their place in the sun.

Although no one is sure of the exact spot at which Ponce de Leon landed, the city lays claim to the explorer and maintains Ponce de Leon Park on a choice piece of unspoiled land that looks out on Charlotte Harbor. His statue stands sentry over the park's entrance. Each March, the town celebrates his landing — with men dressing up as conquistadors and crossing Charlotte Harbor by boat to claim the city.

Other than the Calusas, most found the area inhospitable with its almost impassable crush of plants and ferocious mosquitoes. Eventually the English found their way to the region, settling a bit north of the harbor along the Peace River. In 1885, Col. Isaac Trabue from Kentucky bought the land from the British and named it Trabue. When the city incorporated in 1887, it returned to the more popular Spanish name, Punta Gorda. Trabue Cottage, the colonel's home, still stands.

Today, the city's downtown area has won recognition as a state historic district, and the city's Streetscape program is restoring its Old Florida look by adding to the historic red-brick streets, planting more trees and installing street lamps, benches and brick planters. Old wooden homes are being restored and have become highly sought real estate.

The city's residents are content to leave the busier pace and commercial development to Port Charlotte, its neighbor to the north across Charlotte Harbor. In Punta Gorda's downtown, cozy shops and restaurants share space with City Hall and the soon-to-be-replaced county courthouse.

In Punta Gorda Isles, just west of downtown, almost everyone has a car but also is likely to have one or more other forms of transportation: boats, bicycles and golf carts. It's not uncommon to see residents tooling along neighborhood streets in their golf carts, whether or not they are headed to the golf course.

For the Mielkes, it was their interest in boating through which they initially made friends. The Detroit couple didn't know a soul in Punta Gorda when they moved.

"The first year was very hard," Harriet Mielke says. "Once we joined the yacht club, though, we met a lot of people." After that, they made still more friends through tennis and golf. "This is a place where you can get up in the morning and find 10 people to play golf with," she says. "It's a great party town."

Punta Gorda, FL

Population: 14,344 in Punta Gorda, 141,627 in Charlotte County.

Location: On the southwest Gulf coast 100 miles south of Tampa.

Climate:

	High	Low
January	74	53
July	91	75

Average relative humidity: 56%

Rain: 52.55 inches.

Cost of living: Below average (specific index not available).

Average housing cost: $90,492 in the county. About $180,000 in the city.

Sales tax: 7%

Sales tax exemptions: Most food items, prescription drugs and professional services.

State income tax: None.

Intangibles tax: Assessed on stocks, bonds and other assets. Tax rate is $1 per $1,000 in assets. The first $20,000 in assets is exempt for individuals. For couples filing jointly, the first $40,000 is exempt. Those who owe less than $60 need not pay.

Estate tax: None, except the state's "pick-up" portion of the federal tax, applicable to taxable estates of more than $1 million.

Property tax: $19.29 per $1,000 in Punta Gorda, with homes assessed at 100% of market value. Annual tax on a $180,000 home is about $2,990 with the homestead exemption noted below. The rate in unincorporated Charlotte County is $17.12 per $1,000, excluding special taxing districts in some areas.

Homestead exemption: $25,000 off assessed value of permanent, primary residence.

Religion: There are 20 churches and one synagogue in Punta Gorda and 40 churches and one synagogue in neighboring Port Charlotte.

Education: Edison Community College offers two-year associate degrees on the Punta Gorda campus. Florida Southern College Charlotte-DeSoto in Port Charlotte, a satellite of Florida Southern College in Lakeland, offers a bachelor of liberal arts degree, with some credit given for life experiences. The program is geared to students 40 and older. Florida Gulf Coast University is about 40 miles south in Fort Myers. It offers undergraduate and graduate degrees.

Transportation: Interstate 75 runs through the east side of the city, with access about a mile from downtown. Southwest Florida International Airport is about 35 miles south and easily reached via I-75. Charlotte County Airport, just east of the city, is a general aviation airport for smaller planes but no commercial lines.

Health: Charlotte Regional Medical Center is a 208-bed hospital offering 24-hour emergency care, a cardiac care unit, sports medicine and rehabilitation, two wellness centers, diabetes and sleep disorder centers, and treatment for psychiatric and chemical dependency disorders. In nearby Port Charlotte are Columbia Fawcett Memorial Hospital, a 254-bed full-service, acute-care hospital with 24-hour emergency treatment, and Bon Secours-St. Joseph Hospital, a 212-bed not-for-profit facility with 24-hour emergency services, a women's center and an affiliated nursing home, hospice care and assisted living.

Housing options: Single-family homes are the primary form of housing with prices ranging from $60,000 in modest neighborhoods to $1 million for more lavish dwellings that sit along the edge of Charlotte Harbor. There also are manufactured-home communities, where prices start in the $40,000s. **Punta Gorda Isles**, (800) 445-6560, just west of downtown, is a community that began in the early 1960s and continues to grow today. Most of the homes are on canals. Prices start at about $75,000 for an older two-bedroom home. New waterfront homes start at about $250,000 and go up to about $1 million. Downtown Punta Gorda, a state historic district, features mainly wooden structures, many of which have been refurbished in recent years. Convenient to downtown shops, waterfront parks and I-75, these in-demand properties range from $100,000 to about $400,000. **Burnt Store Marina**, south of the city, has a spectacular location on a wide stretch of Charlotte Harbor. This gated community offers waterfront condominiums from the $400,000s and single-family homes from the $300,000s. Less expensive resale homes are also available, (800) 237-4255 (Florida Design Communities). There's a large marina, tennis courts and a restaurant on property. **Burnt Store Meadows**, south of Burnt Store Marina, has more modest homes, with lots starting at about $10,000. **Blue Heron Pines**, a golf-course community for those age 55 and older, offers manufactured homes starting in the $50,000s. Amenities include a clubhouse, exercise room and heated pool, (800) 635-4834. **Burnt Store Colony**, a manufactured-home community, also is geared to those 55 and older, with a newly renovated clubhouse, pool, tennis courts and shuffleboard. Prices start in the low $70,000s for new homes and the $30,000s for resale homes, (800) 445-0943 or (941) 639-4009. On the east side of the city is **Ventura Lakes**, which offers manufactured homes starting in the $60,000s, a security gate, tennis courts, shuffleboard and clubhouse, (941) 575-6220 or (888) 575-6220.

Visitor lodging: Best Western in downtown Punta Gorda overlooks Charlotte Harbor, $79-$134 with discounts for AAA and AARP members, (800) 525-1022 or (941) 639-1165. Days Inn just off Interstate 75, $44-$150, (941) 637-7200. Other options include Punta Gorda RV Resort, $23 per day, $138 weekly, (941) 639-2010; Fisherman's Village Resort Club, $99-$121, (941) 639-8721; and Burnt Store Marina and Country Club Resort, $89-$99 summer, $150-$195 winter, (800) 859-7529.

Information: The Charlotte County Chamber of Commerce, 326 W. Marion, No. 112, Punta Gorda, 33950-4417, (941) 639-2222 or www.charlottecounty chamber.org.

Ed and Barbara Ring found much the same thing 12 years ago when they moved to Tropical Gulf Acres, a rural subdivision about seven miles south of the city limits. Their early friendships came through church and the Tropical Gulf Acres Civic Association, recalls Ed, 65.

But, even before that, Barbara, 63, says, "While we were building our home, our neighbors came by to chat."

The Rings had spent the better part of their married life traveling as Ed rose through the ranks in the U.S. Marines. They moved first to Port Charlotte but, after a couple of years, decided they "wanted a slower, quieter lifestyle," Ed says.

They were drawn to Tropical Gulf Acres because it was still relatively undeveloped and, as a result, most of their neighbors were birds and other wildlife. Their two-acre parcel sits on the banks of a pond.

Barbara says, "To me it's home — what we have been looking for after a nomadic military life. We have a bass in our pond that grew from a few inches to a foot long since we moved here and now follows us as we walk the bank of the pond. We feed him Cheerios."

The subdivision's 39 lakes attract osprey, ring-necked ducks "and a hawk that takes baths in the pond" behind the house, she says.

Nature's not far off even for those who live in more populated portions of the city. It's not uncommon to see fish leaping gracefully out of the water in backyard canals, or to see large turtles plodding along the roadside or sunning on a sea wall. Tiny lizards, called anoles, scamper about on sidewalks and climb screens around most homes.

Manatees, lumbering but docile sea mammals, make their way into the harbor and canals during cold weather, seeking warmer waters and the tons of sea grasses they need to eat to survive. Dolphins leaping about in the harbor, or playing in the wake of powerboats, are familiar sights. So are osprey, eagles, pelicans and all sorts of other birds.

Even the less-welcome alligator makes an occasional appearance, posing loglike in a canal, sunbathing in grasses along the shore or, once in a while, getting disoriented and scurrying for cover under a car in the driveway. Feeding gators is illegal — the more accustomed they become to being fed by humans, the bolder they grow and the more likely they are to become aggressive. Those that venture too close to homes are picked up by wildlife officials.

Parks are numerous, too. Punta Gorda has six city parks, and there also are 34 county parks, four state facilities, and a federal wildlife refuge. There also are 15 public beach access sites, although none are in Punta Gorda itself. There's a small beach on Charlotte Harbor in Port Charlotte and, on the northwestern end of the county, access to the Gulf of Mexico in Englewood. South of Englewood is Boca Grande, an upscale island from which some of the world's best tarpon fishing takes place.

About 45 miles south, off the coast of Fort Myers, are the renowned beaches of Captiva and Sanibel islands. Sanibel is ranked one of the top three places in the world for shell collecting. There are several excellent public beaches and many places to dine and stay.

While residents describe Punta Gorda as on the sleepy side, there are quite a few things to see and do when not boating, fishing, playing golf or tennis.

There are lots of shops downtown and still more at the waterfront complex Fisherman's Village, which also has a marina and restaurants. For more extensive shopping, the Port Charlotte Town Center has department stores, 100 specialty shops and a food court.

The Florida Adventure Museum contains four exhibit galleries and offers traveling exhibits from around the country. The focus is on Florida-related themes. For artists and those who would like to be, the Visual Arts Center offers classes, programs, workshops and exhibits.

Babcock Wilderness Adventures consist of swamp buggy tours high above the waters of the 8,000-acre Telegraph Cypress Swamp and elsewhere on the 90,000-acre Crescent B Ranch, where visitors will see unspoiled Florida interpreted by well-trained guides.

The Charlotte Harbor Environmental Center offers environmental education and recreation, including guided tours of four miles of nature trails. And the Peace River Wildlife Center in Ponce de Leon Park protects and preserves native wildlife that has been orphaned, displaced or injured. Visitors are welcome.

Annual events include the aforementioned observance of Ponce de Leon's Landing in March. This also is the height of the tourist season and the month when the boys of summer head to the state for baseball spring training. The Texas Rangers train at the $6 million Charlotte County Stadium a few miles northwest of Port Charlotte. The Boston Red Sox train in Fort Myers, and the Minnesota Twins play just south of Fort Myers.

In April, the two-day Florida International Air Show swoops above and into Charlotte County Airport, featuring expert aerobatic and ground displays. The U.S. Navy Blue Angels and Army Golden Nights are frequent participants.

May brings warmer temperatures and fewer visitors, but the fun continues with the annual Charlotte Harbor Fishing Tournament and the annual Chili Challenge for Charity, which benefits the YMCA. At Christmas there's the Peace River Lighted Boat Parade and Holly Days, when Punta Gorda businesses hold open houses.

Volunteer opportunities abound at places such as the Charlotte County Chamber of Commerce, the Visual Arts Center, the Florida Adventure Museum, Port Charlotte Cultural Center and Charlotte Regional Medical Center. At the hospital, golf-cart driving volunteers give visitors lifts from their cars to the hospital entrance.

While Charlotte County is no longer the fastest-growing county in the nation, about 3,000 people a year continue to move in, far outstripping the numbers who leave.

The Meattys, the Mielkes and the Rings have no plans to relocate. "We like living where we are," Ed Ring says. "There's no place nicer."●

Reno, Nevada

The "biggest little city" is a winner with retirees

By Adele R. Malott

Although loudly dressed in neon, Reno's casinos are no match for nature's compelling colors arrayed along the banks of the Truckee River as it travels from Lake Tahoe in the soaring Sierra Nevada through the heart of town and on to Pyramid Lake. The Truckee's route is one that was used by hundreds of thousands of emigrants on their way to the riches they hoped to find in California's gold fields. A few stayed on in the lush green valley now called the Truckee Meadows, which eventually became Reno and the neighboring city of Sparks.

Reno — known as the "biggest little city" — now often seems a secret closely held by its residents. Nearly everyone in the United States will recognize the city's name, but few could tell you much about it beyond historic references to easy divorce, prizefights, gaming or the beauty of nearby Lake Tahoe.

Today the Truckee's banks are marked by walking and biking paths and provide a venue for cultural events like big band dances, the symphony, opera and ballet. Artists' studios can be found in the restored Riverside Casino. Festival events are held nearly every month of the year, and a downtown skating rink adjoins the river in winter. Beyond downtown, theaters, community centers and parks decorate the river.

Reno's downtown has been freshened up with streetlights, banners and markers to help visitors find their way. The Nevada Museum of Art, a small museum just a few years old, is in the process of being replaced by a spacious new facility that is under construction. A new hotel-casino with the look of Tuscany, the Siena, sits on the Truckee River adjacent to the National Automo-

bile Museum.

And there is a buzz about what might be planned for the river's-edge site of the historic Mapes Hotel, where the likes of Marilyn Monroe stayed while filming "The Misfits." Ideas range from a market square like Seattle's Pike Place to an indoor skating arena.

Festivals give Reno the feeling that a party is always going on somewhere in town. Among the more popular are Hot August Nights, a tribute to 1950s music, cars and culture; Artown, 30 days of music, dance and art, mostly free each July; a hot-air balloon festival; food festivals like the Best of the West Rib Cook-off in Sparks; and ethnic festivals honoring the Greeks, Italians and Basques.

The Basques, who migrated to states like Nevada from the Pyrenees Mountains of Europe, have left a special lega-

---

Population: 179,000 in Reno and 67,000 in neighboring Sparks, with an estimated population of 335,000 in the metropolitan area.

Location: Tucked into the rain shadow of the Sierra Nevada, Reno and Sparks are located in Washoe County. Often referred to as the Truckee Meadows, the area is a circular green valley at an elevation of 4,500 feet. Some 530 miles to the east is Salt Lake City, 120 miles west is Sacramento and 450 miles south is Las Vegas.

Climate:

	High	Low
January	45	21
July	92	51

The moderate year-around climate offers four distinct seasons with golf possible most of the year and winter skiing within an hour at any of Lake Tahoe's many ski resorts. Temperatures may vary 30 to 40 degrees in a 24-hour period, virtually guaranteeing cool nights summer and winter.

Average relative humidity: 31%

Rain: 7.5 inches.
Snow: 25.3 inches.
Cost of living: 108.7, based on national average of 100.
Housing cost: Median home price is $162,800, while an average two-bedroom apartment rents for about $715 per month.
Sales tax: 7.25%.
Sales tax exemptions: Prescriptions, groceries, utilities and domestic fuels.
State income tax: None.
Estate tax: None, except the state's "pick-up" portion of the federal tax, applicable to taxable estates of more than $1 million.
Property tax: All property tax is assessed at 35% of appraised or market value. The state limits the rate of property tax to $3.64 for each $100 of assessed value. The rate is $3.59 per $100 in Reno, $3.42 in Sparks and $2.69 in Washoe County. Tax on a $162,800 home in Reno would be $2,046; in Sparks, $1,949; in the coun-

ty, $1,533.
Homestead exemption: Nevada offers a property tax rebate program for seniors as well as property tax exemptions to veterans and widows.
Religion: Choices range from nondenominational congregations to those representing faiths from around the world.
Education: The University of Nevada at Reno, a land-grant college established in 1862, is within 10 minutes of Reno's downtown. In addition to offering nearly 175 degree programs, UNR also has the nation's only judicial college for the training of trial court judges. It also offers a lifelong learning program called Elder College, with extensive lectures and enrichment programs for seniors and discounted tuition.
Transportation: 10 airlines serve Reno, as do Amtrak and various bus lines. Citifare provides local service throughout the metropolitan area. Cit-

cy in the number of family-style restaurants in Reno and surrounding communities. Always popular, the meals are a bargain. Many a savvy newcomer will take the opportunity to find out more about Reno by visiting with tablemates during a Basque dinner.

Reno is populated by independent people who are careful and conscientious in reaching decisions about their city's future and not easily swayed by crowd preferences or what Las Vegas, nearly 500 miles south, is doing. Many neighborhoods have mature trees offering shade to popular walking areas like the milelong circle around Virginia Lake and the Crooked Mile along the Truckee. New areas are following suit by incorporating walking paths in their design.

New residents — many of whom arrive as a result of word-of-mouth recommendations from friends and family — quickly become Reno advocates. Wanda Dingwall, a widow who moved to Reno from Denver the day after she retired in 1999, says Reno simply is "more manageable" than most places. She points to attractions being within an easy distance of one another — most within 15 minutes — and with little traffic to interfere.

Reno is "just right" in many ways for Wanda, who cites its "perfect size, mild climate, wonderful people" and a "vast array of cultural activities." The bonus for Wanda is that Reno is a "fantastic place to grow roses." Indeed, Reno has a comprehensive municipal rose garden in Idlewild Park along the river. Aficionados share expertise on pruning and soil preparation at workshops held each spring.

Wanda chose Reno in part because her daughter lives here and "really likes it." Wanda selected a single-family home in a new golf course community on the east side of Sparks where a fitness center and social club are available to her.

Reno was just one possibility when Wanda began looking for a place to relocate. So was the Four Corners area where Colorado, New Mexico, Arizona and Utah meet. In evaluating the two, she felt Four Corners was too isolated for her needs and, she says, "I really needed some culture." Wanda is now urging her sister to make the move to Reno, too.

Judy and Ken Heitzenrader lived in San Marino, CA, and then bought a home in Palm Desert for retirement. When they found they didn't care for that area, they looked north to Reno, where their son lives, and chose a model home on the west side of Reno. Reno has "all kinds of recreational options, cultural activities, nature trails. It fills all our needs," Judy says. As president of the Reno-Sparks Newcomers Club, she sees up to 20 new members join the club every month.

"Reno reminds us of Fresno, where we lived when we were younger," Judy says. "It has the medical facilities that we'll need — and it has a Costco," she laughs. It also has the desert lights and shadows that her artist husband covets in his painting. And the city's central location provides rich opportunities for the couple to discover assets in nearby areas, such as Nevada's mining history in Virginia City, the Gold Country in Auburn, CA, and the snowy peaks of the Sierra Nevada range that surround beautiful Lake Tahoe.

Reno, NV

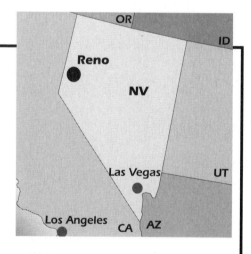

ilift serves the elderly and handicapped.

Health: Some 1,500 hospital beds in 12 medical and psychiatric facilities — including three major medical centers and a Veterans Administration hospital — are available in the Reno-Sparks area. There are a number of skilled-nursing facilities.

Housing options: Nearly 30 specialty retirement and life-care communities are available to seniors, including **Promenade on the River**, (775) 786-8853, one of Reno's newest independent living communities for seniors with 44 different model apartments at a riverfront location. Rates, which cover all costs from three daily meals to a day spa, range from $1,595 to $4,400 a month, depending on number of bedrooms. Another new senior community for independent seniors is **Sky Peaks**, (775) 747-9555, in the northwest section of Reno, with monthly rents averaging around $2,000 for all services except telephone. **Toscano at D'Andrea** in Sparks, (775) 331-4646, is an active-adult gated community of 480 single-family homes. Amenities range from a 12,000-square-foot recreation center with indoor and outdoor pools, hiking and walking trails, and discounted green fees at the nearby golf course. Prices range from $155,000 to $290,000.

Visitor lodging: Hotel-casinos and motels are available throughout the metro area. For hotel facilities, availability and rates, call the area's reservations line at (800) 367-7366 or visit www.renolaketahoe.com. Reno's rates vary with the season and reflect heavy bookings during popular festivals and weekends. Among favorites of residents are the Atlantis, (800) 723-6500, near the new convention facility, where a tower room is priced at about $70 for two in early fall. John Ascuaga's Nugget in Sparks, (800) 648-1177, has a rate of around $100 in its tower, while the downtown Siena, (877) 743-6233, quotes about $70. The Marriott Residence Inn, (800) 228-9290, charges $114 for one bedroom with kitchen.

Information: Reno-Sparks Chamber of Commerce, P.O. Box 3499, Reno, NV 89505, (775) 337-3030 or www.reno-sparkschamber.org. A relocation package is available for $10, including shipping. An extensive list of senior resources also is available. Reno-Sparks Convention and Visitors Authority, P.O. Box 837, Reno, NV 89504, (888) 448-7366 or www.rscva.com.

The area around Reno is a treasure trove of things to do and see. A drive north on Nevada Route 447 leads to Pyramid Lake with good fishing and views of a robin's-egg-blue lake surrounded by a landscape that changes with the passing clouds. It was Pyramid Lake that Charlton Heston parted as the Red Sea in the film, "The Ten Commandments."

It also is home to the Anaho Island National Wildlife Refuge, a white pelican rookery. Fascinating for city folk is the fish hatchery operated by members of the Paiute tribe, which is trying to save the prehistoric cui-ui (pronounced kwee-wee) from extinction. The tribe also has a new museum and visitors center that provides insights about the area's past. Beyond Pyramid Lake is the Black Rock Desert.

To the southeast, modern-day explorers can discover the adobe remnants of Fort Churchill State Park, built in 1860 as an outpost to protect settlers and Pony Express riders and to house the U.S. Army during the Civil War, making it a prime site for Civil War re-enactments today. To the south is Carson City, with its silver-domed state capitol building and a good museum in what was once the U.S. Mint building. History buffs will seek out the city's fine old homes and the State Railroad Museum for glimpses of the past and insights into the lives of such early residents as Mark Twain's brother, once secretary of the state of Nevada.

To the east is Lake Tahoe, a year-round playground for those who love the outdoors. A skier's paradise with 15 alpine and 13 cross-country ski areas in winter, Tahoe transforms itself into a summer beauty offering water sports, boating and fishing in the deep-blue alpine lake. The Great Tahoe Rim Trail, 150 miles around the lake, was started in 1984 and is within steps of being completed by the determined volunteers who have cleared the path for hikers.

Four major casinos serve up gaming with special events like slot machine tournaments along with variety shows and name stars for entertainment. Scattered throughout the area are historic towns like Virginia City with surrounding mountains veined with silver and gold, and Genoa, Nevada's first settlement, as well as signature golf courses designed by the likes of Arnold Palmer and Jack Nicklaus.

Fred Sennewald, who retired 11 years ago, is a practical man who watches the numbers. He worked as a civil engineer with Redwood City, CA, for 15 years and decided "people didn't know how to enjoy life." As a result, he retired early and went to San Jose State University for a master's degree in leisure studies. Since then he has been teaching classes in retirement strategies and how to "live smarter, not harder."

Fred confesses he had marked off everything on his "to do" list except to start a workshop about enjoying life. So he began looking for a two-bedroom apartment that would accommodate an office. Rents quoted in the Silicon Valley were "not in the cards," so he visited Reno and found an apartment in a complex with an extensive fitness center, tennis and swimming facilities.

But he didn't really want to move away from his grandkids at the time, so he stayed put. He later renewed his interest in Reno when he discovered that the apartment complex he had originally chosen had increased its rents only $25 in five intervening years, making it a value. Now he travels to San Jose frequently to visit his grandkids.

"You have to want to get involved" in your community, Fred says. He didn't know anyone in Reno, but he joined the Reno Singles Club, worked on a Veterans Day Parade and signed up for the RSVP Clown Arounds, a group of volunteers who entertain at community events.

"Besides all the events and activities going on here all the time, you can get to them without being stressed out and park free, too," says Fred, who is content with his choice. One of the spots for these events and activities is the University of Nevada at Reno, where new buildings seem to pop up like mushrooms to house burgeoning programs, including a wide selection of lectures and programs available free or at a low fee to Reno's mature residents.

Crowded conditions and the hectic pace were what sent Judy and Howard Lenfestey looking for something different. While they moved to Reno from Los Altos, CA, in 1998, they had started to think they "wanted out" of the San Francisco Bay area a couple of years earlier. They had opportunities to visit Reno for many years and had seen the city in its different seasons and moods, watching it develop and add more amenities.

While a less-expensive housing market and tax conditions were appealing, the low-stress atmosphere and the leisure outdoor opportunities available were more important to the Lenfesteys. They admit they did not get involved in community activities right away. That was delayed as they cared for sick family members. But when they joined the Newcomers Club, they began to build a network of friends through several of the 50 different interest groups.

Judy Lenfestey is amused at the reactions of disbelief when she tells old friends that she and her husband retired to Reno. But it isn't long before she finds those friends impressed when they come to visit and see all the activities available, particularly those tied to the arts and outdoors.

The Reno-Sparks Chamber of Commerce says the information they mail goes to seniors at a three-to-one ratio. And many new residents, eager to keep Reno their very own secret, joke about building fences at the California border as one way to keep Reno a manageable, low-stress place to live. ●

Rio Grande Valley, Texas

Retirees find inexpensive living, friendly neighbors and a bicultural ambiance in sunny South Texas

By Mary Lu Abbott

If the words "Texas" and "tropics" seem at odds in your mind, then picture this: green parakeets screeching in palm trees, red-crowned parrots flocking in brush lands and butterflies painting gardens a myriad of bright colors. Add to that rosy and purple bougainvillea tumbling over adobe walls and the scent of oranges, grapefruit and lemons wafting through the air.

Welcome to the Rio Grande Valley, at the very southernmost tip of Texas. Draw a line across the Gulf of Mexico and you're on similar latitude as Miami and the Florida Keys. Sunny and warm — some might say hot — year-round.

At a junction of temperate and subtropical ecological systems and on two migratory flyways between North and South America, the Valley rewards its residents and thousands of bird-watching visitors with sightings for the record book. More than 500 species of birds and 300 species of butterflies have been seen in the Valley, the number and variety of spottings drawing birding enthusiasts from all over the world. Many of the birds, including some found nowhere else in North America, live here year-round while others are seasonal visitors.

Likewise, retirees have discovered that the Rio Grande Valley is a good place to call home. Many seniors first come here seasonally, enjoying winters when daytime temperatures normally in the 60s and 70s allow golfing, fishing, birding and other outdoor pursuits.

After experiencing its other attributes, retirees often resettle here year-round. Besides the weather, the Valley has a favorable economic climate with a cost of living that is considerably lower than average. It has colleges, cultural attractions and extensive health facilities. Its cities and small towns welcome retirees, catering to them with a variety of programs and services. And, Mexico is literally the next-door neighbor, creating a bilingual, bicultural environment throughout South Texas.

Encompassing four counties, the area known as the Valley stretches along the Rio Grande from the towns of Roma and Rio Grande City eastward to Brownsville and South Padre Island on the Gulf of Mexico. Numerous small towns dot the area, some melding into the larger cities of Brownsville, McAllen and Harlingen. Many who retire in the Valley are from the Midwest — the area was settled by Midwestern farmers in the late 1800s — and the warm climate often is the deciding factor for them.

Former residents of St. Louis, Jim and Hope Golliher considered the mountains of the Carolinas and places in Arkansas and Florida for retirement. They found property in the Carolinas too expensive and winters too disagreeable in Arkansas, and Hope didn't care for Florida. While in the Air Force, Jim had been stationed in Harlingen and remembered that he liked it, so they came to visit and found it suited them best.

Besides the weather, they liked the small-town atmosphere, the stable economy, economical cost of living and proximity of medical facilities. But there was something more: "I didn't want any place you couldn't grow palm trees," says Jim, 65, a former stockbroker. "We have 23 palm trees in our yard." The Gollihers moved in the fall of 2000 to a home in Harlingen Country Club, a golf-course community with a clubhouse.

Hal and Sandy Schultz settled in the Valley in 1988 when he took early retirement; both were with the U.S. Postal Service. At first they split their time between the Valley and their home in Eagan, a suburb of St. Paul, MN. By 1997 they tired of moving twice a year and moved permanently to their home in Mission, in the McAllen metropolitan area.

"We liked to travel and had been to every state. In Florida, Arizona and Texas, we looked for retirement locales," says Sandy, 60. "Florida was too humid. We wanted to be near a college town for theater, cultural and sporting events."

They came to check out Austin but encountered a cold winter and went to the Valley. "The weather was gorgeous. We decided then that this was the place for us," Sandy says.

Hal, 62, says they first rented a place in Weslaco, between Harlingen and McAllen, then explored the area and decided that the upper Valley — the McAllen area — had more amenities and activities they sought after being urbanites. The McAllen-Edinburg-Mission metropolitan area, one of the fastest-growing in the country, had a population of 569,463 in the 2000 census. McAllen, with about 110,000 residents, is the financial, retail and health center of the Valley. Mission has about 45,000 residents but is adjacent to McAllen and seven miles from Edinburg, site of the largest university in the area, the University of Texas-Pan American.

The Valley's weather, friendly people and abundant fresh produce brought Bill Miller, 76, a former salesman, and his wife, Jean, 72, to Edinburg in 1994. Formerly residents of Gurnee, IL, between Chicago and Milwaukee, WI, the Millers had considered retiring in Kentucky, Tennessee, Florida, New Mexico, Arizona and Austin, TX.

"We spent a month at a time in different places. We saw so many people leave the North and come south and then in a year be back home because they didn't like it," says Jean, a former teacher. "We read a lot and traveled."

They bought a mobile home and lived in the Valley a year before making a final decision to sell their home in Illinois. "This just fit our niche," Jean says. "We like a town with activities. Edinburg is the county seat and has a university, a wonderful campus. There's symphony and theater. McAllen has a civic center, too.

"Prices are at a level retirees can handle," says Jean, noting that eating out is quite inexpensive. For instance, a neighborhood restaurant offers a breakfast of two eggs with bacon, ham or sausage, hash-brown potatoes or refried beans and a biscuit for $1.69.

Jean notes that health factors also were a consideration in their move. "I'm an asthmatic, and I haven't been to an allergist since we moved here," Jean says.

One of her greatest joys is having citrus outside her door. "I can go out and pick oranges and grapefruit. I have six grapefruit trees, three oranges and one lime in my yard," she says. Jean and Bill have a manufactured home in Orange Grove RV Park, a master-planned community with about 500 units, a clubhouse and a pool.

Retirees note that farmers markets and roadside fruit stands sell fresh produce at low prices, and with several growing seasons, there nearly always are good selections. The Valley's renowned Rio Star red grapefruit is considered sweeter than Florida grapefruit by many people, and the farms produce a number of varieties of oranges, Hal says.

"After a harvest, a lot of produce is left in the fields. Many of us go out and glean the fields (pick up remaining produce). We take a percentage to the homeless shelters and keep some for ourselves and neighbors. Some neighbor is always coming by offering cabbage, carrots or something. Maybe hundreds go out to the fields," Hal says.

The Valley has been ranchland since Spanish colonial days. Reynosa, in Mexico across the river from McAllen, was settled in 1749; Laredo to the north in 1755; and Matamoros, across the river from Brownsville, in the late 1700s. After Texas won its independence from Mexico in 1836, a dispute arose over the new border, with Texas claiming the Rio Grande and Mexico declaring the boundary farther north at the Nueces River, which flows into Corpus Christi Bay.

After the Republic of Texas became a state in 1845, Fort Brown was built by the Rio Grande, setting off battles that led to the Mexican-American War. The American victory enlarged the United States by one-third, bringing in territory that today stretches from West Texas to California and north to Wyoming.

Around Fort Brown, Brownsville grew as a major port and industrial center along with its Mexican neighbor Matamoros, a heritage that remains true today with the increased commerce across the border fostered by the North American Free Trade Agreement. The remaining buildings of old Fort Brown today are part of the University of Texas at Brownsville and Texas Southmost College campuses.

With the realization that the area was a fertile delta, the Valley became heavily agricultural around the turn of the 20th century as Midwest farmers were drawn by the long growing season. Today more

Population: The 2000 Census shows more than 978,000 residents in the Valley's four counties. The largest metro area is McAllen-Edinburg-Mission with about 569,463 residents. The Brownsville-Harlingen-San Benito area has about 335,227 residents. McAllen has an estimated 110,000 residents, Brownsville about 140,000, Harlingen about 59,000, Edinburg about 48,000 and Mission about 45,000. With the populations of Matamoros and Reynosa across the Rio Grande in Mexico, the region has 2.2 million residents.

Location: The area known as the Rio Grande Valley is a delta along the river, extending about 100 miles from South Padre Island on the Gulf of Mexico inland to the town of Roma. From Brownsville, on the river border with Mexico, U.S. Highway 83 links the towns westward. At the southernmost tip of Texas, the Valley is 272 miles south of San Antonio.

Climate:

	High	Low
January	69	50
July	93	76

Average relative humidity: 63%
The subtropical climate fosters growth of palm trees, aloe vera, groves of citrus trees and fields of vegetables. Freezes are rare, though winter can bring some cool weather. Summers are hot and humid, and September is usually rainy.

Rain: 27 inches.

Snow: Extremely rare.

Cost of living: Below average (93 for Harlingen and 94 for McAllen, based on a national average of 100). Food and housing costs are particularly low.

Housing cost: The average cost is about $90,000 in Harlingen, $96,600 in the McAllen metro area ($84,000 in Edinburg, $115,000 in Mission) and $96,450 in Brownsville.

Sales tax: 8.25% in most places.

Sales tax exemptions: Groceries, prescriptions and over-the-counter drugs, medicines and dietary supplements, professional services.

State income tax: None.

Intangibles tax: None.

Estate tax: None, except the state's "pick-up" portion of the federal tax, applicable to taxable estates above $1 million.

Property tax: Taxes range from about $24 to $28 per $1,000 valuation with homes assessed at market value. Besides city, county and school taxes, levies may be assessed by road, fire and irrigation districts.

Homestead exemptions: Harlingen (Cameron County), Edinburg and Mission (both in Hidalgo County) give a homestead exemption of $15,000 off valuation for the school taxes for owners who live in their homes. City, county and school taxing entities give homeowners age 65 and older additional exemptions ranging from $4,000 to $12,000 off valuations.

Religion: There are numerous places of worship throughout the Valley, representing all faiths.

Education: The University of Texas-Pan American in Edinburg is the largest campus, with about 13,000 students and numerous cultural programs and events. The University of Texas at Brownsville and Texas Southmost College have about 10,000 students. South Texas Community College has several sites in the Valley, and Texas State Technical College is located in Harlingen. Continuing-education programs are available. Also, the Harlingen Chamber of Commerce sponsors a Center for Creative Retirement with programs for those 55 and older.

Transportation: Airports at Brownsville, Harlingen and McAllen serve the Valley. Valley Transit Company buses serve towns in the area. Brownsville and McAllen have city bus services.

than 40 crops are raised in the area. Though perhaps best known for its citrus, the Valley also has large acreage in cotton and grain sorghum and produces many vegetables, among them the noted sweet Texas 1015 onion.

The Valley stretches for about 100 miles, with U.S. Highway 83 threading the towns along the Rio Grande. Mexico is paces away, accessible via a number of international bridges. Increased trade across the border over the last few years has re-energized the Valley, contributing to a more urbanized environment. An expressway links the major towns, and large shopping centers with name retailers have located along the route.

Because of the heritage of exchange between the borders, the population of the Valley is about 85 percent Hispanic. None of the three couples interviewed speak Spanish, though some have taken Spanish lessons. But they all enjoy the bicultural lifestyle.

"The Valley people are very, very friendly. It's like when you were a child and knew all of your neighbors. You can go to the supermarket and come home with a new friend," says Jean Miller. "You would expect cultural differences, but we get along very well with everyone. The Hispanics are hard-working, family-oriented people."

Jim Golliher calls the Hispanics in the area "the most polite and generous people of any nationality I have ever known. Just the other day, for the second time in my life, I ran my car out of gas, loaded with groceries and a dog. Just as I pushed it off the road, a gentleman came along and gave us a ride home. He couldn't speak a word of English."

Jim and Hope often cross the border. "At the place I get my hair cut now (in Nuevo Progreso), they have asked us to come down along with all their customers and have dinner in their home," Jim says.

The area still attracts many Midwesterners. Hal Schultz says Mission has a small-town atmosphere. "Aladdin Villa, our development, is very tight-knit and friendly. Most of the residents are from the upper Midwest. If you don't go to church, they will call to find out if you're OK. Our roof needed work, and a neighbor insisted on going up on the roof and worked on it all day. That sort of thing is normal here," Hal says.

Hal and Sandy first bought a small home in Aladdin Villa, a 55-and-older retirement community, and recently built a slightly larger home on one of the last lots available there. The community of about 800 residents has a pool, woodworking shops, ballroom and outdoor

Rio Grande Valley, TX

The Harlingen-San Benito Express is an urban demand response system providing transportation mainly for seniors and the disabled to medical facilities, shopping centers and other businesses on a reservation basis.

Health: State-of-the-art health-care facilities are available from Brownsville to McAllen, and the area is served by emergency helicopter. A new center under construction will have a medical school, research facility and public health institute at different sites in the Valley. McAllen and Harlingen have medical complexes with several hospitals, and Brownsville has a regional medical center and other hospitals. Several smaller towns also have hospitals. All fields of medicine are covered.

Housing options: A wide range of options is available, from manufactured housing communities to country club estates. Among the choices: **South Padre Island Golf Club**, which hosts the Texas Senior Open tournament, (956) 943-3622, is a gated residential community in Laguna Vista, between Brownsville and South Padre Island. Condos start in the $90,000s, townhomes about $102,000 and homes in the $130,000s. **Impact Properties**, (956) 425-7098, handles homes in several

country club and golf course communities in the Harlingen area. **Stuart Place Country Club** in Harlingen, (956) 428-1000, is an active-adult community built around 11 lakes, with a clubhouse and executive golf course; smaller patio homes start at $69,000 and larger homes at $100,000. In Mission, **Bentsen Lakes**, (956) 792-6001, is a new gated community with homes from $170,000s, and **Sharyland Plantation**, (956) 585-9595, has nine communities. There are assisted-living and continuing-care communities.

Visitor lodging: Throughout the Valley are lodgings in all price ranges, including several hundred RV parks and many apartments for six-month rentals ($350-$600). South Padre Island has many condos. Among options: Renaissance Casa de Palmas, a historic hotel in McAllen, (956) 631-1101, from about $80-$100. The Inn at Chachalaca Bend in Los Fresnos, (888) 612-6800, from $100, including breakfast. Note: The Valley, particularly South Padre Island, is a favorite escape for high school and college students at spring break during March and into April.

Information: The Rio Grande Valley Partnership/Chamber of Commerce,

P.O. Box 1499, Weslaco, TX 78599, (956) 968-3141 or www.valleychamber.com. Brownsville Chamber of Commerce, 1600 E. Elizabeth, Brownsville, TX 78520, (956) 542-4341, and Brownsville Convention and Visitors Bureau, P.O. Box 4697, (800) 626-2639 or www.brownsville.org. Harlingen Area Chamber of Commerce, 311 E. Tyler, Harlingen, TX 78550, (800) 531-7346 or www.harlingen.com. McAllen Chamber of Commerce, 10 N. Broadway, McAllen, TX 78501, (956) 682-2871, (877) MCALLEN or www.mcallencvb.com. South Padre Island Chamber of Commerce, 600 Padre Blvd., South Padre Island, TX 78597, (956) 761-4412 or www.spichamber.com, and South Padre Island Convention and Visitors Bureau, 600 Padre Blvd., South Padre Island, TX 78597, (800) OK-PADRE or www.sopadre.com.

games.

"We had no trouble selling our home. A San Diego couple who's retiring bought it. They're square dancers and had met someone who lived at Aladdin Villa," Hal says. The McAllen area is known as the square-dance capital of the world. Each February, the annual Texas Square Dance Jamboree draws more than 2,000 dancers, and on any given day enthusiasts will be able to swing their partner at some dance in the area. While none of the three couples interviewed are square dancers, some assist with the jamboree as one of their volunteering activities.

All are active in community work. "This is a volunteering community. Everything is done by volunteers. It's a primary hobby of many people," Hal says. He and his wife are McAllen Chamber of Commerce "Amigos," working at the chamber information desk. They also participate in HOSTS, Help One Student To Succeed, an elementary school program that pairs adults on a one-to-one basis with children with learning problems. They act "as a mentor, as a teacher, as a friend — it's been very successful," Sandy says.

Jim and Hope volunteer at the Creative Retirement Center, established by the Harlingen Chamber of Commerce to provide learning opportunities for those 55 and older. Jim serves as program director and Hope is the hospitality chairperson. Monthly lectures and excursions include such offerings as "Report Card on NAFTA," a look at how the trade agreement functions today; "Water, Agriculture and Ranching in South Texas;" "History and Culture of a Shared Border;" and "Habitat and Birding in the Rio Grande Valley." The Gollihers also volunteer at the Loaves and Fishes food kitchen.

Bill and Jean give their time and talents at the McAllen Chamber of Commerce and help greet newcomers to their neighborhood.

There's no lack of things to do in the Valley, particularly nature-oriented outings. There are more than 30 birding areas, including about a half dozen wildlife refuges from dry brush country to wetlands. A new World Birding Center, a network of nine sites, is taking shape along a 120-mile stretch of the historic river road.

Golfers have a choice of about 30 courses, and both freshwater and saltwater fishing are less than an hour's drive from most places. There's a professional baseball team with a new stadium at Edinburg. South Padre Island, a major resort with a long stretch of beautiful beach on the Gulf of Mexico, is within easy reach, about 25 miles east of Brownsville and about 70 miles from McAllen.

There are historical museums, two vintage airplane collections, the acclaimed Gladys Porter Zoo at Brownsville, a cultural arts center and several theaters and other entertainment venues for ballet, symphony and visiting performers.

Jean Miller says they miss some of the entertainment they had in Chicago and Milwaukee, "but we have community concerts here, a band and productions at Pan Am University."

Hope Golliher, 46, likes the variety of restaurants available. "It's like a mini-St. Louis in terms of ethnic restaurants. We didn't lose a lot when we moved here," says Hope, who previously worked with a brokerage firm.

All agree that health-care facilities are on par with the urban areas where they previously lived. There are extensive medical facilities throughout the Valley. The Regional Academic Health Center under construction in Harlingen will have an upper-level medical school and is part of a Valley-wide system planned to include a public health institute and a medical research facility. McAllen has three major hospitals and a cancer center, and Harlingen has a medical complex with three hospitals and another medical center under way. Brownsville has three hospitals, and Edinburg, Mission and a couple more towns have at least one hospital each.

For the Schultzes and the Gollihers, the lower cost of living was a factor in choosing the Valley, and while the Millers didn't think about it at the time they moved, they now appreciate that their money goes further here.

None of the couples finds much fault with the area, but it's not without some problems. In Mission, a current controversy centers on the presence of toxic chemicals found in some property near an abandoned chemical warehouse complex that was found to be polluted and underwent cleanup by the Environmental Protection Agency. Residents are awaiting the results of more testing, but a lawsuit already has been filed.

The couples note that with the border so close, there is some drug trafficking and theft. FBI reports show that towns in the Valley do have higher-than-average crime rates, but none of the couples felt unsafe or considered the crime a serious problem. Many of the crimes are larceny-theft, such as shoplifting or taking bicycles or motor vehicle parts, without the threat of violence or use of force.

None of the couples seems to mind the warm weather. The hot, humid summers can seem stifling to some people unaccustomed to the weather here, but the Valley does have strong breezes. "The summer here is better than the winter there," Hal says of the Valley heat versus the Minnesota cold.

With its proximity to the Gulf, there's a threat of hurricanes. Hal says one reason he chose Mission is that the town is about 70 miles inland and would not bear the brunt of a hurricane.

The Valley gets two major influxes of tourists. Thousands of "Winter Texans," many of them retirees in RVs, come in late fall to escape the cold in the North. Spring brings large numbers of high school and college students on break, mainly heading to South Padre Island for sun and suds and across the border to Matamoros.

Hal says roads are busier in winter, although it still doesn't take him long to get anywhere, but Bill Miller says highway expansion sometimes can make getting around more difficult. Traffic can be heavy along the U.S. 83 expressway, which still is under construction in some areas.

Bill adds that there's considerable dust in the air when fields are being plowed and the wind blows, and Hope Golliher doesn't like it when the sugar cane fields are being burned.

The couples consider the Valley the paradise they wanted. "It's just about the perfect place. The quality of life is at a high level," Bill says.

"Small-town Northern residents feel very comfortable here — and those looking for year-round golfing," Hal says, also noting it's a good place for bird and butterfly enthusiasts and square dancers. His wife, Sandy, adds, "Movers and shakers, jet-setters would be bored here."●

St. Augustine, Florida

With a 400-year history, this Florida town boasts a colorful past

By Ruth Rejnis

With a history dating back more than 400 years, St. Augustine isn't your usual Florida boom town.

Its narrow streets, garden courtyards, a plaza and massive fort attest to a long Spanish colonial heritage. Add to that touches of British, Greek and Italian influence and a legacy as one of Florida's turn-of-the-century fashionable resorts.

The result is a congenial town of 11,592 that mixes the New World with the Old World.

St. Augustine is historically significant as the nation's oldest permanent European settlement. It was visited by Ponce de Leon in 1513, and in 1565 was claimed for Spain by adventuresome conquistador Pedro Menendez de Aviles.

A major tourist spot on the Atlantic side of north Florida, it attracts guests to its 144-block historic district, an area enshrined in the National Register of Historic Places. Although most of the original colonial Spanish buildings have succumbed to ravages of the ages, reconstructions help capture the spirit of old Spain that gives St. Augustine much of its appeal.

The city lies between the St. Johns River on the west and the Matanzas River and Bay (also the Intracoastal Waterway) to the east, two miles from the ocean. The quarter-mile Bridge of Lions links the downtown area to a string of small beach communities on Anastasia Island along coastal Highway A1A, the first of which is St. Augustine Beach.

Ron and Dot Firster, retired teachers from Butler, PA, were tourists for many years before taking up permanent residence.

"I spent most of 1945 here in the military," Ron, 67, recalls, "and I always planned to retire here. This was our favorite vacation spot, and we came here many times over the years."

Dot, also 67, says that they were attracted by the climate and the city's homey atmosphere.

While the area is popular as a retirement site, only a sixth of St. Johns County residents are age 65 and older. Retirees say it's easy to meet other seniors, though, through church, volunteer projects, bicycling, walking and other outdoor activities encouraged by the benign climate.

"One of the things I like about the town is its good civic spirit," says Norman Baker, a retired chamber of commerce executive from Columbus, OH, who moved here in 1984. "There's such a wide range of activities," he notes. "If you want to do it, it's here."

Norman, 76, and his wife, Jane, also 76 and a retired nurse, say they're kept as busy as they want to be with church and civic organizations. Both are tutors in Learn-to-Read of St. Johns County and have served on that association's board of directors.

Bob and Louise Ebbinghaus, who moved to St. Augustine from Port Chester, NY, also are active volunteer tutors. They put in several hours a week at local schools as part of the state-sponsored Retired Seniors Volunteer Program.

"We help teachers correct papers, help kids and do whatever else needs to be done," says Louise, 70, a former personnel assistant. She and her husband were recognized for their service with a state education award a few years ago.

The city's senior center has an active program schedule, and St. Augustine's historic attractions and programs staged with tourists in mind offer a busy year-round calendar. For example, Menendez Day each spring celebrates the conquistador's settling of the area, and summer brings Spanish Night Watch 1790, a torchlight procession through the Spanish Quarter by people in period dress. During

the holidays, visitors and residents look forward to 18th-century Christmas caroling.

Flagler College, a four-year liberal arts institution, adds to St. Augustine's cultural core. When oil magnate Henry Morrison Flagler developed a good deal of St. Augustine in the 1880s, he opened Ponce de Leon Hotel, now the college. The pink, vaguely Moorish complex is considered a Spanish Renaissance masterpiece.

Local real estate agents divide St. Augustine into three sections: houses in the historic district, those outside the district and homes at the beach.

"Houses in the historic district start at about $140,000 for a fixer-upper," says Janice Johnson of Johnson-Farrell Realty in St. Augustine. "They go up to $750,000. The average price is $250,000 for a moderate-quality historic home." Those houses are typically wood-frame. There are no condominiums in the historic district.

Elsewhere, homes range from around $115,000 for a condominium to more than $1 million for an oceanfront single-family house.

All three couples interviewed live in St. Augustine Shores, a 2,500-unit planned community on the Matanzas River about eight miles south of downtown and two miles from the beach. The subdivision features single-family homes and condominiums, a golf course, clubhouse and pool.

Norman Baker estimates about 40 percent of the residents are retired. The lineup of social events at the clubhouse, he says, is a good one.

"You'd have to be a hermit not to make friends here," adds Bob Firster.

Cost of living in this part of Florida is lower than in the southern part of the state and is considerably below living costs in the Northeast or on the West Coast. It was the relatively inexpensive lifestyle that attracted the Ebbinghauses.

"We just couldn't afford to live in New York on a fixed income," says Bob, a 73-year-old former letter carrier. "It would have cost us $1,000 a month to rent a three-room house up there."

Louise adds, "We were happily surprised at the low taxes (in St. Augustine). The $25,000 (statewide) property tax exemption was a pleasant shock."

The climate enticed all three couples, they say. Hot summers are relieved by ocean breezes. By fall, temperatures cool down. Deciduous trees lose their leaves, although with the large number of palms, firs and other greenery, there is never the stark, bare look associated with areas that winter treats more harshly.

Shirt sleeves usually are adequate at midday during winter months, but morning and evening temperatures can drop to the 30s. That doesn't deter sunrise walkers and joggers, though, who simply bundle up in jackets, gloves and knit caps. Snowfall is rare.

Ocean swimming in winter is strictly for members of the Polar Bear Club, although lazing on the beach is certainly possible on sunny days.

"My daughter can come down here from New York in December and dash off to the beach when it's in the 60s, and I'm freezing," says Louise Ebbinghaus.

Hurricanes are a possibility, but the last big wind to hit St. Johns County

St. Augustine, FL

Population: 11,592 in St. Augustine, 4,683 in St. Augustine Beach, 123,135 in St. Johns County.

Location: About 90 miles south of the Florida-Georgia border and 50 miles north of Daytona Beach.

Climate:

	High	Low
January	70	47
July	89	71

Average relative humidity: 72%

Rain: 52 inches.

Cost of living: About average (specific index not available).

Average housing cost: $140,000 for a single-family home in St. Johns County.

Sales tax: 6%

Sales tax exemptions: Medical services, prescription drugs, groceries.

State income tax: None.

Intangibles tax: Assessed on stocks, bonds and other assets. Tax rate is $1 per $1,000 in assets. The first $20,000 in assets is exempt for individuals. For couples filing jointly, the first $40,000 is exempt. Those who owe less than $60 need not pay.

Estate tax: None, except the state's "pick-up" portion of the federal tax, applicable to taxable estates above $1 million.

Property tax: Rates are $22.77 per $1,000 of assessed value in St. Augustine and $18.27 in St. Augustine Beach, with assessments at 100% of market value. Yearly tax on a $140,000 home with the homestead exemption noted below is about $2,619 in the city, $2,101 at the beach. Both areas have a solid waste tax of $65 per household per year.

Homestead exemption: $25,000 off assessed value for primary, permanent residence.

Religion: The town and beach areas have more than 80 churches and synagogues.

Education: Flagler College, a four-year liberal arts institution, is in the heart of St. Augustine. The town also has a branch of St. Johns River Community College, based in Palatka, about 30 miles southwest of St. Augustine. Various adult education courses are offered by the public schools.

Transportation: No public services. Jacksonville International Airport is about one hour away.

Health: Flagler Hospital is a 230-bed community hospital. It's augmented by more than a half-dozen hospitals and medical centers, including a branch of the Mayo Clinic, in Jacksonville, 25 miles north of St. Augustine.

Housing options: There's a wide range of houses and condominiums but few rental units in the area. **Coquina Crossing**, (800) 446-0699, has custom-manufactured homes from the $70,000s. **St. Augustine Shores**, a planned community on the Matanzas River eight miles south of the historic district, features single-family homes and condominiums starting in the $100,000s. The subdivision, which still is adding new homes, offers a clubhouse, golf, pool and tennis courts. Sales and resales are available through local realty agencies. At St. Augustine Beach, **Commodores Club**, is a lakeside patio-home community within walking distance of the beach and about six miles south of the downtown historic area. Homes are $125,000-$175,000. **Marsh Creek**, (904) 471-4343, at St. Augustine Beach, overlooking the marsh lands along the Matanzas River about six miles south of downtown, offers single-family and patio homes for $350,000-$1 million, with complete country club amenities. Luxury condominiums in **The Residences at World Golf Village**, (800) 279-1743, start in the low to mid-$300,000s. **Anastasia Dunes**, (866) 461-7080, is a beach-side gated community that eventually will have 138 homes set amid 20 acres of conservation areas. Lot prices range from the low $100,000s to the high $150,000s.

Visitor lodging: Accommodations are available in all price ranges. Comfort Inn, (904) 824-5554, three blocks from the beach, is $79. Bed-and-breakfast inns in the historic district begin at about $80. Furnished time-share beach apartments are available for short-term rental. Call Resort Rentals of St. Augustine, (800) 727-4656, or Ocean Gallery Properties, (904) 471-6663. Rates are generally higher during the summer.

Information: St. Augustine & St. Johns County Chamber of Commerce, 1 Riberia St., St. Augustine, FL 32084, (904) 829-5681 or www.staugustinechamber.com.

was Hurricane Dora in 1964.

St. Johns County, which extends 43 miles along the east coast of Florida at its northeastern corner, is growing. The St. Johns Development, a 6,300-acre complex eight miles north of downtown, features homes, shops, the PGA Golf Hall of Fame and a golf academy. The airport, situated about five miles north of downtown, completed a $50 million expansion.

A number of large shopping malls serve St. Augustine, including an outlet center with 90-plus stores. Jacksonville, about 40 minutes by car, offers an even greater selection. In St. Augustine's downtown area, cobblestone St. George Street is lined with small shops and boutiques.

The area has a surprising number of good, well-priced restaurants, residents say. "We can afford to eat out a couple of times a week," says Louise Ebbinghaus. "Not at the best restaurants, but up there (in New York), we could eat out only about once a month."

St. Augustine offers engaging sightseeing to visitors from home. Grandchildren are delighted by the oddities at Ripley's Believe It or Not, the Castillo de San Marcos fortress, Potter's Wax Museum, the "authentic" old jail, the Fountain of Youth, and other attractions in the downtown area.

Marineland of Florida, the noted oceanarium, is just a few miles south of St. Augustine Beach. The St. Augustine Alligator Farm is at the beach. And for everyone, the St. Augustine Amphitheatre at the beach stages "The Cross & Sword," a colorful play depicting the settling of the city.

Retirees to St. Augustine say there's no shortage of company. Louise used to lead guests around, she says, "but now we sometimes just point them to downtown and give them the brochures about all they can see."

The city's geographical location is a plus for some. "I like the accessibility to major cities," says Bob Ebbinghaus. "You can get to New York (by car) with just one overnight stay." St. Augustine's historic district is about six miles east of Interstate 95, which runs from Florida to Maine. U.S. Route 1 runs through the town.

At the county's northern tip is Ponte Vedra Beach, an upscale community of about 25,000 where Sawgrass, the noted residential/recreational resort, is home to the national headquarters of the Professional Golf Association. The Players Championship, which features the top players in professional golf, is held there in March. The Association of Tennis Professionals international headquarters and facilities also are at Ponte Vedra Beach.

All three couples say that crime is no worse in St. Augustine than in their previous communities, and some say things are even a little better. Ron Firster expresses an awareness of areas prone to burglaries and muggings, but says those areas are easy to avoid.

What is an issue, though, is traffic, which even those most in love with the town concede can be dreadful at times.

"When we came here, you could walk down the middle of the streets," says Bob. "It doesn't seem possible it has gotten so busy in 10 years."

Besides the influx of cars brought by winter visitors, the community also has horse-drawn carriages and open-air sightseeing trams offering guided tours of the historic district. Limited downtown parking and frequent congestion can cause frustrating delays. City leaders are grappling with the problem.

The city also is trying to determine the most efficient and best use for its historic area.

"I don't think enough is being done to capitalize on the natural beauty of St. Augustine," notes Norman Baker. "They could do a better job of putting a good face on the city."

The town's multifaceted past encompasses a melange of styles. Along with structures of both wood and shellstone from the Spanish colonial period, the era of Henry Flagler left its mark with grand public buildings. Flagler, the dominant figure in opening Florida to tourism at the turn of the century, built two major hotels in St. Augustine and headquartered his Florida East Coast Railroad here. Another major landmark besides Flagler College is Lightner Museum, the former Alcazar Hotel that opened in 1888.

Add to this mixture numerous shops selling T-shirts and souvenirs and the end result, according to some residents, doesn't blend as well as it could. Civic leaders are looking at the successful historic district in Charleston, SC, to learn how such a mix can work.

But the smattering of problems is not a worry to residents. Says Norman Baker, "I think it's a rare person who wants to move out of St. Augustine." ●

St. George, Utah

"Utah's Dixie" blends history with a spectacular setting

By Jerry Camarillo Dunn Jr.

St. George exerts an attraction that's like love at first sight. Falling for St. George is as easy as one-two-three. First, the town has a gorgeous setting in southwestern Utah. Overhead, the sky is bonnet blue, with high clouds streaming like white ribbons. Behind town, the sandstone cliffs look like pleated skirts of red wool.

Second, there's the green patchwork created by the area's nine golf courses — a huge lure for retirees. Some people call St. George "the other Palm Springs."

Third, there's the climate of this high desert hot spot. Just ask John and Audrey Castle, both 76, who moved here in 1992 from Midland, MI. "We have sunshine at least 300 days a year," exults John, his native English accent coming as a surprise in the wild West. "We love the lack of rain and snow."

Well, yes, he admits, summer days do drive the thermometer well above 100 degrees. "But it's very dry heat, so it doesn't bother you. If you stood out in the middle of the street, of course, you'd get plenty hot — you'd probably get killed, too! But you have air-conditioning in your home and in your car."

As for winter, St. George is blessedly mild, with daytime temperatures of 55 to 65 degrees. "It's a long way from an English winter," says John. "Thank goodness!"

Before retiring, John was in the "education racket" as he jokingly calls it, teaching business administration at Michigan's Northwood University. Audrey worked at a daycare center. When they decided to retire, it didn't take the Castles long to decide on St. George, even after touring other appealing places in their search for the perfect retirement spot.

"We flew in on Friday and bought our house on Saturday," John recalls. "We just said, 'This is it.'" And they weren't alone: Between 1990 and 1995, St. George's population grew by two-thirds. Retirees make up 30 percent of the residents.

The Castles purchased a three-bedroom townhouse in a Southwestern-style condominium complex in the Green Valley district. On their patio they enjoy barbecuing and looking out at Pine Valley Mountain, whose peaks

---

Population: 49,663 in St. George, 90,354 in Washington County.

Location: St. George lies at 2,880 feet above sea level in a valley in far southwestern Utah, six miles from the Arizona border. Red sandstone cliffs form a backdrop for the city. St. George is 120 miles from Las Vegas and 305 miles from Salt Lake City, Utah's capital. Zion National Park is 43 miles away.

Climate:

	High	Low
January	54	27
July	102	69

St. George has approximately 300 days of sunshine each year.

Rain: 8 inches, primarily in April and May.

Snow: About one snowstorm per year, lasting only a few hours.

Cost of living: 96, based on national average of 100.

Average home price: A single-family, three-bedroom, two-bath house costs an average of $154,195. A two- or three-bedroom condominium costs an average $109,654. An average homesite sells for $63,837.

Sales tax: 6.25% in Washington County (which includes St. George).

Sales tax exemptions: None.

State income tax: For married couples filing jointly, graduated from 2.3% of taxable income up to $1,726 to 7% on amounts over $8,626. For single filers, graduated from 2.3% of taxable income up to $863 to 7% on amounts over $4,313.

Income tax exemptions: There are exemptions in pensions and taxable Social Security benefits of up to $4,800 for each taxpayer under age 65 and up to $7,500 for those age 65 and older if they meet specified income limitations.

Inheritance tax: None.

Estate tax: None, except the state's "pick-up" portion of the federal tax applicable to taxable estates above $1 million.

Property tax: $11.148 per $1,000 valuation, with primary residences assessed at 55% of market value. Annual tax on a $154,195 home would be $945.

Homestead exemption: None.

Religion: While St. George's population is about 70 percent Mormon (Church of Jesus Christ of Latter-day Saints), two dozen other churches are active, including Assembly of God, Baptist, Catholic, Christian Science, Episcopal, Lutheran, Methodist and Presbyterian.

Education: Founded in 1911, Dixie State College, (435) 652-7500, is a comprehensive community college serving 5,500 students. The college's Institute for Continued Learning, (435) 652-7670, specifically for retirees and pre-retirees, offers classes ranging from archaeology and Spanish to bridge, along with field trips, discussion groups and special events. For a $45 fee, seniors can take classes all year.

Transportation: Interstate 15 links the city to Las Vegas (two hours south) and Salt Lake City (four hours north); there are three exits in St. George. Local bus and taxi services are available, as well as transportation services for those who need assistance with medical appointments. For air travel, SkyWest offers six departures daily to

tower more than 10,000 feet high. The condo complex has a swimming pool where John and Audrey often spend an hour or so exercising under radiant blue skies.

Those skies also spread over some of southwestern Utah's most stunning canyonlands scenery — particularly Zion National Park, just 43 miles east of St. George. Zion is a place of big fundamentals — rock, water and sky — where everything seems exalted. Even the names on the map spell out glories: Angels Landing, East Temple, Great White Throne.

On a 6.5-mile scenic drive into the heart of the canyon, one stop is Weeping Rock, where a seep of water on a vertical cliff creates a hanging garden of scarlet monkey flowers and ferns.

Nearby, the easy Narrows Trail follows the Virgin River, the liquid force that carved the canon. Motorists also stop at the visitors center to hear informative talks about local geology and wildlife. ("If you could unhinge your jaws the way a rattlesnake does to swallow a mouse," a park ranger tells a mesmerized crowd, "you could gulp down a watermelon.")

Another popular drive from St. George is the two-hour trip on Interstate 15 to Las Vegas. "If we want to live it up, we just get in the car and go," John Castle says. "We make three or four trips a year."

Glittering Las Vegas offers a strong contrast with homespun St. George, which has about 50,000 residents. "St. George is reasonably small, with a slow pace of life and not much traffic, yet it still retains some of the advantages of a bigger city," John says. "The shopping, for instance, is pretty good here."

In fact, St. George is the regional shopping hub. The enclosed Red Cliffs Mall boasts more than 50 stores and shops, while Zion Factory Stores and The Promenade offer an equal number of stores selling everything from sporting goods and discounted name-brand clothes to books.

Speaking of books, says John Castle, "The public library is very good here. We can always get any book we want."

Another factor in the Castles' decision to move to St. George was the town's low crime rate. A possible explanation for the civic tranquility: "St. George is heavily influenced by the Mormons, who make up about 70 percent of the population," John says. "Their influence is very beneficial, especially their family values and good, clean living."

Not surprisingly, the history of St. George has a lot to do with Mormons. The town got its start in 1861 when Brigham Young, president of the Church of Jesus Christ of Latter-day Saints (Mormons), sent a group of 309 pioneer families to grow cotton and wine grapes in this unlikely terrain. Other products included silk, dried fruit, molasses and pecans. Because so many of the settlers hailed from the South, the region was nicknamed Dixie. The St. George area is still known as "Utah's Dixie."

St. George, UT

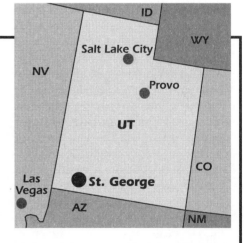

Salt Lake City, and the St. George Shuttle makes seven daily round trips to McCarran Airport in Las Vegas.

Health: Dixie Regional Medical Center, (435) 634-4000, is a 137-bed comprehensive community hospital; it will open a second facility in 2003. Other health-care services include the Snow Canyon Clinic, Color Country Health Express, IHC Health Center and the St. George Medical Clinic. Services available include cardiology, behavioral medicine, cancer treatment, radiology, rehabilitation, intensive and critical care, pediatric care, obstetrics, chronic wound healing, home and hospice care, outpatient surgery and treatment and 24-hour emergency service.

Housing options: Housing comes in a variety of sizes and styles, with home prices in St. George and nearby communities ranging from $85,000 to more than $3 million. At **Entrada at Snow Canyon**, (800) 368-7232 or (435) 656-5600, a Southwestern-style development with a top-rated golf course, prices vary from $275,000 for patio homes to more than $600,000 for villas; home lots range from $42,900 to more than $200,000. **SunRiver St. George**, (888) 688-6556 or (435) 688-1000, is a new active-adult golfing development where homes begin at $114,900; there is an indoor pool, fitness center, tennis courts and lawn bowling. **Coral Canyon**, (435) 688-1500, is a golf-oriented community on 2,700 acres, with model homes starting at $98,990 and home sites starting at $75,000. There is a trail system for hiking and biking. St. George's assisted-living facilities include **Sterling Court**, (435) 628-1400; **PeachTree Place**, (435) 628-1117; and **The Meadows**, (435) 628-0090.

Visitor lodging: In the downtown historic district, Greene Gate Village Historic Bed and Breakfast Inn is a cluster of restored 1870s pioneer homes, $79-$139, (800) 350-6999 or (435) 628-6999. The Green Valley Spa offers one-bedroom condos by the night at $110, and a spa stay (accommodations, full meals, fitness instruction, guided hikes) requires a three-night minimum and is priced for double occupancy from $1,100 per person (spa treatments are extra), (800) 237-1068 or (435) 628-8060. St. George's other accommodations include national chains (Holiday Inn, Quality Inn, Hampton Inn, Best Western, Sheraton Super 8, Motel 6) and several bed-and-breakfast inns.

Information: St. George Area Chamber of Commerce, 97 E. St. George Blvd., St. George, UT 84770, (435) 628-1658 or www.stgeorgecham ber.com. Other helpful Web sites: www.sgcity.org, www.southernutah. com and www.utahsdixie.com.

Young also saw the health benefits of the warm climate — he suffered from rheumatism — so the Mormon leader became St. George's first snowbird, leaving Salt Lake City and building himself a tidy winter home with a white picket fence. Today new residents enjoy looking at the house's historic furnishings, including a piano hauled across the plains in a covered wagon, silverware forged from melted-down coins and a wooden rocking chair made by Brigham Young himself.

As you gaze across the townscape, it's hard to miss the gleaming white St. George Temple, which the Mormons completed in 1877 at a cost of $800,000. Unless you're a church member, you'll find it buttoned up tighter than a starched shirt. There is a visitors center, however, where earnest church members are on hand to discuss their faith and educate people about the temple, the first one west of the Mississippi River.

A few blocks away stands the St. George Tabernacle. To build the walls, huge slabs of limestone were brought from local quarries, while wooden trusses were made of logs hauled from the mountains 32 miles away.

Another hub of local history is the Jacob Hamblin Home in the adjacent community of Santa Clara. Built in 1862 by a Mormon missionary to the Paiute Indian tribe, this stone-and-timber homestead played host to Saturday night dances and Sunday school classes alike. Spread on the wooden floor are mountain lion and buffalo skins once used as blankets and rugs in pioneer days.

Local history is something you'll learn about if you drop by St. George's Chamber of Commerce Visitors Center, which is partly staffed by retiree volunteers like Curt and Ann Olson, both 64, who moved here from Decorah, IA. "There are lots of opportunities to volunteer in St. George," says Ann, a former junior high school library and computer lab supervisor. Retirees donate their time at the Dixie Regional Medical Center, usher for a concert series and volunteer to help out at the annual Huntsman World Senior Games.

"These games are attended by retired people from all over the world," explains Curt, who managed an insurance association before his retirement. "They compete at just about everything — basketball, tennis, golf, bowling, racquetball, swimming, and track and field. They play softball and even bridge."

The Olsons themselves play bridge at the Elks Club every Monday night. On Tuesdays they have a standing golf date with another couple. "Golf" is a magic word in St. George. Eight of its courses lie within 15 minutes of each other, and they include several of Utah's top-rated links, known for challenging designs, scenic features, careful maintenance and year-round play. During winter, balmy temperatures make it a breeze to play a full 18 holes.

"Golfing is also more affordable here than in Phoenix or Las Vegas," Ann points out. "And on city courses, local residents can buy a punch card that really reduces the fees. It gives you 20 rounds of nine holes for just $120 in summer and $160 in winter.

"There are courses for every kind of golfer," she says. "If you're learning and don't hit a very long ball, you'd feel quite comfortable playing a course like Dixie Red Hills. The St. George Golf Club is flat and easy. And the front nine at Southgate Golf Club is very easy for someone who's not very good yet."

Sunbrook is tougher. It was rated by a national golf magazine a few years back as Utah's top course. A challenger is the area's newest course, Entrada. Designed by Johnny Miller, it features rolling dunes, black lava beds and winding arroyos.

SunRiver St. George, a 50-plus community, is built around a golf course that has views of red rock cliffs and Pine Valley Mountain. At Coral Canyon, the challenges range from a labyrinth of dry washes to red rock outcroppings.

Besides golf, another popular outdoor activity takes place in October — the famous St. George Marathon. A qualifying race for the Boston Marathon, it winds through high desert terrain and attracts about 5,000 runners, including a number of retirees.

All year around, the St. George Recreation Center provides locals with a fitness room, racquetball courts and a new gym, while the Sand Hollow Aquatic Center has both competition and leisure pools.

All that exercise builds up an appetite, and St. George offers more than 50 restaurants. "If you come from San Francisco, you might not find St. George up to your dining standards," cautions Ann Olson. "We don't have gourmet restaurants with the wine and the atmosphere, although we do have several very nice restaurants."

Utah's strong Mormon influence has created liquor laws different from those in most places, she explains. Unless you eat something, you can't order a drink in a restaurant. And many restaurants don't have liquor licenses, period. "If you like to relax with a cocktail and then go in to dinner, you won't find that available," Ann says. "And if you like beer with your pizza, you're out of luck. There's no beer at any pizza place in St. George.

"One nice thing about all this is that we don't have bars," she says. "So St. George doesn't have the type of atmosphere where people go sit in a bar and stagger out at midnight."

Churchgoers find that all the major denominations are thriving in St. George. And Ann likes the fact that the town has plenty of things to keep residents busy night and day. The $25 million Tuacahn Center for the Arts in nearby Snow Canyon — named for a family called Snow, not for icy weather — presents Broadway plays. "You sit outdoors in a beautiful red rock amphitheater, and the performances are very good," she says.

During summer, "St. George Live" offers tours of historical sites led by local residents costumed as pioneers. Besides these offerings, there are nearby state parks, ghost towns and canyons. The Olsons like to hook up their fifth-wheel trailer and camp at Zion, Snow Canyon or Panguitch Lake. And Curt regularly goes fishing in local reservoirs stocked with trout. "I've been catching my limit," he says happily.

Like many retirees, the Olsons also enjoy touring throughout the West. "We've been roaming for the past eight years, from Reno to Phoenix," Curt says. "And you know what? In all that traveling, we haven't found anyplace we like better than St. George." ●

San Antonio, Texas

A colorful history and international flavor add spice to this Texas city

By Julie Cooper

It was March 6, 1836, when 189 valiant defenders of the Mission San Antonio de Valero fell at the hands of Mexican General Santa Anna and his troops, giving rise to the independence battle cry, "Remember the Alamo," as the fort is better known. More than 17 decades later, the Alamo and its poignant past are remembered fondly by thousands of visitors who annually pay homage to the most famous historical site in Texas.

For Ray and Barbara Clark, those fond feelings extended to the entire Alamo City, where they were stationed early in Ray's military career.

They couldn't forget the life they once had in San Antonio and finally fulfilled a dream to move back in retirement.

"We'd been trying to get back to San Antonio for 25 years," Barbara confesses. When Ray retired as an Air Force master sergeant in the mid-1970s, the couple was set to move to nearby Austin, where Ray had a job lined up with Texas Instruments. But family obligations took them back to Barbara's hometown of Evansville, IN.

The couple owned and operated a number of businesses in the Evansville area, including the 11th Frame Lounge and Cross-Eyed Cricket family restaurant. When retirement finally did dawn, the Clarks once again turned their eyes to the Lone Star State.

The eighth-largest city in the United States, San Antonio has one of the lowest costs of living among major cities. The seat of Bexar (pronounced Bear) County, San Antonio has a population of 1.14 million. The population of the metropolitan statistical area, which includes Bexar, Comal, Guadalupe and Wilson counties, is 1.59 million.

Whether they live in outlying Converse, Universal City or Garden Ridge, communities popular among newcomer retirees, most residents say they're from San Antonio. The city is about a three-hour drive from the Texas Gulf Coast and about four hours to the Mexico border. San Antonio is in south-central Texas and enjoys an average temperature of 68.7 degrees. Its proximity to the Texas Hill Country, with its rich history of 19th-century German settlements and wildflower-dotted pastures and roadsides in spring, is a big draw for Texas residents.

San Antonio ranks No. 1 with Texans as a vacation destination. Four interstate highways, five U.S. highways and five state highways make getting there a snap. The San Antonio International Airport serves the city and surrounding area and is just 13 miles from the downtown River Walk, an area along the San Antonio River that is packed with restaurants, clubs and shops. City attractions also include historic Market Square, museums, theme parks and scores of savory Mexican restaurants.

Before settling near San Antonio, the Clarks spent two years crisscrossing America in a 34-foot recreational vehicle. They found their 1,800-square-foot dream house in Carolina Crossing, a new gated community in Schertz, a booming community of 18,700 just north of San Antonio in Guadalupe County. The Clarks thought about a condo or garden home but wanted a small yard for their schnauzer, Shotzie. They bought a model home the same day it went on the market in February 1996

"We saved a good $1,200 to $1,300 a month by moving to San Antonio," says Barbara, 68. Ray, 67, estimates that the neighborhood includes about 30 percent active military and 30 percent retirees. Military retirees can use the exchange, commissary and pharmacy at Randolph Air Force Base in nearby Universal City.

The military presence in south-central Texas is a big plus with retirees. Lackland, Kelly (which is being phased out) and Brooks Air Force bases lie on the south side of town, while Randolph Air Force Base sits on the northern edge. Fort Sam Houston, northeast of downtown, has been an Army base since 1845.

If they so choose, the Clarks could use the medical services at Brook Army Medical Center, but they prefer to use an HMO to supplement Medicare. "The medical facilities are tremendous," Ray says. Major hospital systems include Baptist, Methodist, Christus Santa Rosa, Southwest General and Nix Medical Center, among the 36 hospitals serving the area.

The Air Force is part of the reason that Schertz has seen its population jump from 10,500 in 1990 to 18,700, according to city manager Kerry Sweat. "The large number of persons retired from the military is really how Schertz began," says Sweat of the town once called Cutoff by the railroads. "We have a lot of the advantages of the big city. We're close enough to enjoy it and still be a small town," he says.

Part of what they enjoy about San Antonio is a history that is a colorful draw for vacationers and residents alike. In 1718, Father Antonio Olivares, a missionary in south Texas, helped establish Mission San Antonio de Valero (the Alamo) and Villa de Bexar, the military outpost. The missions continued to grow as the Franciscans moved to convert the local Native Americans to Christianity. These missions still stand today along the historic Mission Trail and are active Catholic parish churches.

The flavor of Mexico is very much in evidence in multicultural San Antonio. In April, San Antonio holds its biggest party of the year when it celebrates Fiesta, a nine-day festival commemorating the area's rich history and cultures. Parades, parties, special exhibits, concerts and coronations are just some of the activities.

Fans of Western movies — whether it is John Wayne's "The Alamo" or Errol Flynn's "San Antonio" — won't be disappointed in the cowboy history that the area retains. Each February the city immerses itself in all things Western with the San Antonio Rodeo and Stock Show.

Trail riders and chuck wagons make a journey from all parts of South and Central Texas to meet up for the start of the

16-day rodeo, fair and livestock show.

Lascelles Wisdom, 55, doesn't have to wait for February to enjoy saddles

San Antonio, TX

Population: 1.14 million in San Antonio, 1.4 in Bexar County.

Location: In south-central Texas at the edge of the Gulf coastal plains, about 140 miles north of the Gulf of Mexico, 78 miles south of Austin, 270 miles south of Dallas and 197 miles west of Houston. Elevation is 701 feet.

Climate:

	High	Low
January	63	39
July	94	69

Average relative humidity: 50%

Rain: 28 inches.

Cost of living: 88.6, based on national average of 100.

Median housing cost: $104,000 for a new home.

Sales tax: 7.75%

Sales tax exemptions: Food and produce, pharmaceuticals and some agricultural services.

State income tax: None.

Intangibles tax: None.

Estate tax: None, except the state's "pick-up" portion of the federal tax, applicable to taxable estates above $1 million.

Property tax: Paid to the city, county, local school districts and a host of other special taxing districts. Taxes are assessed at 100% of the current market valuation. Rates are .320756 per $100 valuation in Bexar County, .578540 in San Antonio, .3825 in Schertz and .5600 in Converse. There are 13 school districts in Bexar County with tax rates from 1.5 to 1.76 per $100 valuation.

Homestead exemption: Each taxing entity caps exemptions for homeowners 65 and older at a differ-

ent amount, the highest being the city of San Antonio at $60,000. Bexar County exempts the first $50,000, and the Alamo Community College District exempts $30,000. Guadalupe County exempts $10,000 of the appraised value of a residential homestead. For homeowners under age 65, there is a $3,000 flood exemption and a $15,000 school district exemption; other exemptions may be available, depending on the neighborhood in which you live.

Religion: More than 1,200 churches represent every denomination. There are nine synagogues.

Education: There are four campuses in the Alamo Community College District: Northwest Vista College, Palo Alto College, St. Phillip's College and San Antonio College. The University of Texas at San Antonio was established in 1973 as part of the UT system. Trinity University is a top-rated liberal arts school established in 1869. The University of Incarnate Word is a Catholic university with a current enrollment of 3,312. St. Mary's University is the oldest and largest Catholic University in Texas with three undergraduate schools, one graduate level and the only law school in San Antonio. The UT Health Science Center at San Antonio includes medicine, nursing, dental, allied health sciences and graduate-level bio-medical science. Our Lady of the Lake University offers undergraduate degrees in more than 40 areas, master's degrees in nine programs and a doctorate in psychology. The National University of Mexico also has a downtown campus offering classes in Spanish, English as a second language, Mexican arts, history, literature and computers.

Transportation: Via Metropolitan Transit serves the metropolitan area. Funded through a .5 percent sales tax, VIA operates a fleet of 529 buses. Bus fare is 75 cents and there are discounts for senior citizens and people with disabilities. The Park & Ride system serves special events such as Fiesta, Spurs games and events at

the Alamodome.

Health: The San Antonio area has more than 35 hospitals, including three military hospitals, mental health centers and rehabilitation centers. The Cancer Therapy and Research Center, a joint venture with UT Health Science Center, is dedicated to the cure and prevention of cancer and offers outpatient treatment and clinical research. The 700-acre South Texas Medical Center is the largest in Texas and represents a combined annual budget of $2.6 billion. The Center has more than 25,000 full-time employees.

Housing options: There are more than 145,000 rental housing units, including apartments, townhouses and duplexes in all sections of the metropolitan area. San Antonio's hottest area is in the northwest. Newer developments include **The Ridge at Carolina Crossing**, from $110,000; **The Springs at Stone Oak**, from $160,000; and **Mainland Square**, from the $90,000s. There also are build-to-suit sites of one-half to five acres starting in the mid-$40,000s. There are more than 47 retirement and life-care communities, which include assisted living, residential care and Alzheimer's care.

Visitor lodging: There are 25,000 rooms in hotels, motels, resorts and bed-and-breakfast lodgings. The Westin La Cantera offers room rates of $199-$269. A sister hotel, the 474-room Westin Riverwalk, opened in November 2000; rates start at $119, (800) WESTIN-1. Historic hotels on or near the San Antonio River Walk include the Menger Hotel, La Mansion del Rio, Fairmount and St. Anthony Wyndham Grand Heritage.

Information: San Antonio Convention and Visitors Bureau, 201 E. Market St., San Antonio, TX 78205, (800) 447-3372 or www.sacvb.com. The San Antonio Chamber of Commerce, P.O. Box 1628, San Antonio, TX 78296, (210) 229-2100 or www.sachamber. org. The chamber has a Guide to San Antonio retirement package for $15, plus $4 postage and handling, (888) 242-3068.

and spurs. The recent retiree from Long Island, NY, has indulged his love of horses by purchasing eight thoroughbred racehorses. He stables them at Retama Park Racetrack, a new facility 15 minutes northeast of downtown San Antonio that offers thoroughbred racing July through October.

Lascelles and his wife, Netilda, 64, moved to San Antonio just last October. The Wisdoms had checked out Florida and South Carolina, where many of their friends had moved, as likely retirement spots. They chose Texas in part to be close to their daughter, Lorraine Smith, and her family.

Retirement came early for Lascelles when he accepted a buyout from Long Island Lighting Co. after 26 years as a welding engineer. He says he and his wife never considered staying in New York. "It is very expensive to retire and live in New York," Lascelles says. "My house was paid for, but the taxes were $8,200 a year."

The Wisdoms traded a five-bedroom "high ranch" for a newly built four-bedroom home in Converse in the northeast part of Bexar County. Netilda, who retired as an assistant rehabilitation aide in a nursing home, has tentative plans to do volunteer work. Currently, though, she's busy furnishing her new home. The Wisdoms left much of their furniture in New York rather than move it.

The median selling price for new homes in San Antonio is $104,000. The average monthly rental rate on a two-bedroom, two-bath unit is $710.

"I used to visit Lorraine and fell in love with San Antonio," Netilda says. "The people here are, let me say, different. The people here are friendly," she says with added emphasis.

There is an international flavor that permeates San Antonio. According to 2000 census figures, 59 percent of the population is Hispanic, 32 percent is Anglo and 7 percent is African-American. The low number of African-Americans among the populace does not bother the Wisdoms, both natives of Port Antonio, Jamaica.

"Where I lived in Jamaica, we were one people," Netilda says. "When we moved to Long Island, about 2 percent of the population was black," Lascelles adds.

Other recent retirees also have found San Antonio to be a friendly place to live.

"It's amazing how friendly the people are," says Nan Birmingham, 75. A former contributing editor for Town & Country magazine, Nan was ready to say goodbye to the New York winters and find a slower pace of life. She moved to San Antonio in 1998, partly to be closer to her only grandchild, Caitlin. Caitlin and her parents live 25 minutes away.

"I've finally stopped looking over my shoulder," Nan says, chuckling about the "innate suspicion" that many New Yorkers have for passers-by when it comes to crime. "I'm getting over it now," she says.

Nan sold her townhouse in the Bronx and opted to rent a spacious one-bedroom apartment in the Meridian, a gated complex near San Antonio's Quarry Market. Her ground-floor apartment borders the green space that backs into the complex. Nan estimates that a similar apartment in New York City would go for $3,500 a month — a far cry from the $1,270 a month she pays, and that includes use of a pool, health club, security and party room.

"I figure I've cut my overhead probably in half," says Nan, who likes to breakfast on her plant-filled terrace. She has turned half of her expansive kitchen into an office with computer and couch.

A native of California, Nan says she briefly considered San Francisco for retirement, and she watched a number of her friends retire to Florida and New Mexico. Besides traveling, which she does two to three months of the year, Nan enjoys the San Antonio Museum of Art, where she holds museum membership. One of the top art museums in Texas, SAMA is home to the Nelson A. Rockefeller Center for Latin American Art.

Other art draws include the McNay Art Museum, where admission is free but the art is priceless. The museum is housed in a Mediterranean-style mansion built in 1927. It holds Cezanne, Mondrian and bronzes by Rodin. And the Southwest School of Art and Craft is the place for learning the arts. Classes include photography, painting, ceramics, weaving and carving. The school is housed in the Old Ursuline Academy, begun in the late 1840s.

Both Nan Birmingham and the Clarks pitch Central Market as a fun spot to go near downtown. "It's my favorite place," Nan says. "When everyone said, 'Oh, you have to try the Central Market,' I envisioned Texas pickup trucks and fresh vegetables in an outdoor setting." She was surprised to find valet parking at a store once dubbed "Gucci B" by San Antonians. Central Market is part of the HEB Grocery Co., which has its corporate headquarters in San Antonio. A cooking school that offers weekly classes is another reason that Nan, a former cooking instructor, likes Central Market. And, "the price is right," she says.

The Clarks, who have authored a cookbook, frequently make the 20-mile drive from their home to Alamo Heights for a special shopping foray at Central Market. The longer growing season and proximity to Mexico mean more fresh fruits and vegetables at good prices almost year-round in San Antonio stores.

But if eating out is on the menu, there is more to the city than tacos and tamales. Former restaurateurs, the Clarks admit to a love affair with TexMex food and appreciate the spicy stuff. "We eat out about three times a week," says Barbara, noting that she and Ray usually stop for lunch when they are running errands. The early influences on the city's restaurants were Mexican and German, but the wide variety today boasts American, Continental, Chinese, Italian, Vietnamese, Indian and steakhouses too numerous to count.

On the negative side, what do retirees find to complain about? "The standing joke is we're running a B&B," Barbara says. The Clarks find their home popular among vacationing friends and relatives, but Barbara and Ray like to travel as well. They made five or six trips to Mexico in 1999 — "especially when friends come to visit," Barbara says.

Three months into their retirement, the Wisdoms were still adjusting to the way Texans drive. "I've got to get used to the driving in the center lane — those arrows are turning left and right and I don't know where to go," Lascelles says.

The Clarks are busy counting their blessings. "There's hardly a day that goes by that one of us doesn't say, 'I love Texas' or 'I love my house,' " Barbara says with a laugh. "I love Texas," Ray quips in agreement. "I love the attitude of the people here, and the patriotism," he adds.●

Sanibel, Florida

Retirees enjoy unspoiled natural beauty and a casual lifestyle
on this tranquil Florida island

By Karen Feldman

While many Florida beachfront communities have been all but overrun with high-rise condominiums and commercial development, Sanibel Island stands out for its steadfast refusal to go with the flow. This barrier island off the Southwest Florida coast has fewer than 6,200 permanent residents, miles of well-tended bike paths and thousands of acres of unspoiled nature sanctuaries teeming with wildlife. The residents are careful to cultivate culture as well as nature, supporting playhouses, art centers, galleries, boutiques, restaurants and hotels.

What's missing? Not much, other than traffic lights, beachfront high-rises and all except one of the usual fast-food franchises. So it's not surprising that a move to Sanibel is the retirement dream of — and logical step for — many people who vacation there year after year.

That was the case for full-time residents Bob Hanger and William (Bill) and Tina Hillebrandt. Bob's first trip to the island was by car ferry from the mainland in 1962, to visit his first wife's aunt. He fell in love with the island, and when he retired from his sales job with Merck & Co., the decision to move came easily.

"We knew we were going to come here. We had already bought a lot here," says Bob, 81. "We never considered retiring anywhere else."

He and his wife moved south in October 1981, driving over the causeway and settling into a three-bedroom home with swimming pool. When his wife died, Bob remained, eventually remarrying.

In 1986, the Hillebrandts were looking for a quiet getaway from their home in Omaha when a friend told them about Sanibel Island. "We'd never heard of it," says Tina, 43. "We had no idea what we were coming to. It was magical."

They arrived after dark. "When we walked out the door in the morning, it

took our breath away," says Bill, 58, a retired freight transportation executive.

They rode bicycles around the island for a few days and bought a condo before they left. "We borrowed against my retirement plan," Bill says. "We really went out on a limb."

They visited a few weeks each year until they moved full time in 1992. As is the case for many who move to the island, cost wasn't their primary consideration. "We were paying the same amount of taxes on the house we owned in Omaha at the time," says Tina.

What really sold them, says Bill, was "the natural philosophy of the community, the preservation, the conservation." In the 1970s, the county commission approved a measure that would allow a total of 90,000 people to live on the island. Residents balked. They held a referendum, incorporated as a city and promptly reduced the maximum allowable population to 9,000.

That sort of active environmental concern draws a lot of residents, says Keith Trowbridge, executive director of the Sanibel-Captiva Chamber of Commerce. "Sixty-five percent of the island is sanctuary," he says. "It's tranquil and serene. There are a lot of community activities and three live theaters. People are retiring earlier today; they're healthy, 50 or 55, and have 30 years to look forward to. They'd better get busy doing something."

Finding ways to stay busy on Sanibel is not difficult. Activities, classes and cultural and volunteer opportunities abound. Because of its roomy beaches along the gentle gulf, Sanibel is a popular vacation destination for Americans and Europeans. That, in turn, has created a wealth of well-stocked boutiques and galleries as well as a sophisticated dining scene.

Despite the inevitable reduction in pace to island time that occurs when crossing the causeway, residents also like the fact that their peaceful getaway

is close to the rest of the world. Southwest Florida International Airport is growing rapidly, with more flights going to more cities, many nonstop, including Frankfurt and London.

Add in low crime and that no-nonsense attitude toward growth control, and its appeal as a retirement haven looms large. And many people aren't putting off the dream of an island lifestyle until the traditional retirement years.

"We're seeing a lot of early retirees, people in their 40s and 50s, many of whom have made their money in the stock market," says Pam Pfahler, a real estate agent with John Naumann Associates on Sanibel. "We're also seeing some with younger families who are able to locate their homes anywhere and work from their home office." With real estate appreciating at a nice clip, it's an attractive market for those with money to invest.

Count Debbie and John Friedlund among that younger group who couldn't wait for retirement to relocate. They vacationed on Sanibel more than 20 years ago and found returning to the Chicago area very difficult. "We tried to like winter but we just didn't," Debbie Friedlund says. "On that vacation in 1979 we talked to Realtors and never looked back."

Although they would continue working, they knew they wanted to live out their retirement years on Sanibel. Today, at 49, the couple recently sold their island motel and Debbie has retired, although John still works. While she has no paying job, she keeps busy.

"There are lots of organizations here depending on volunteers, like the library, the chamber of commerce and CROW (Clinic for the Rehabilitation of Wildlife)," she says. "They all have training programs in place; you know what's expected of you. You feel like you're needed and really making a difference. I have to be careful not to overdo it."

She devotes time to CROW, a rehabilitation center for injured native animals, such as burrowing owls, hawks, snakes and turtles. She also helps the Sanibel-Captiva Conservation Foundation with beach patrols, a summer ritual during which volunteers help protect nesting sea turtles and their eggs and help guide hatchlings to the sea.

The Hillebrandts do turtle patrols, too, and early one morning last summer happened on a huge endangered loggerhead turtle laying her eggs. "I was late for tennis, but I didn't care," Bill says.

With the advent of mosquito control and air conditioning, today's residents live a far more comfortable existence than their forebears did. Researchers believe people lived on Sanibel Island 2,500 years ago, not long after it became an island, rising from the sea as a persistent ridge of sand. Archaeologists have found evidence of the prehistoric Calusa Indians, who eventually died out. Later, Cuban and Indian mullet fishermen came next, living in thatched structures.

Eventually, settlers on the island and wealthy cattle farmers across the bay requisitioned a lighthouse, a 104-foot tower built in 1884 that still stands today. The beach around that structure is one of the island's most popular, with broad expanses of sand, lots of shells washing up with the tides, sprawling

Sanibel, FL

Population: 6,138 permanent residents and as many as 12,000 part-time (mostly winter) residents.

Location: A barrier island off the coast of Fort Myers in Southwest Florida, Sanibel Island is 145 miles south of Tampa and 158 miles west of Miami.

Climate:

	High	Low
January	72	52
July	91	73

Average relative humidity: 52 percent

Rainfall: 53 inches.

Cost of living: Above average (specific index not available).

Median housing cost: $480,000

Sales tax: 6%

Sales tax exemptions: Food, some services and medicine.

State income tax: None.

Intangibles tax: Assessed on stocks, bonds and other assets. Tax rate is $1 per $1,000 in assets. The first $20,000 in assets is exempt for individuals. For couples filing jointly, the first $40,000 is exempt. Those who owe less than $60 need not pay.

Estate tax: None, except the state's "pick-up" portion of the federal tax, applicable to taxable estates of more than $1 million.

Inheritance tax: None.

Property tax: In 2002, Sanibel residents paid $18.69 per $1,000 of assessed value, with homes assessed at 100% of market value. Yearly tax on a $480,000 home with homestead exemption below is about $8,504.

Homestead exemption: $25,000 off the assessed value of a permanent, primary residence.

Religion: There is one synagogue as well as several churches on the island, including multidenominational, United Church of Christ, Catholic, Episcopal, Unitarian-Universalist and Christian Scientist. Other religions meet on neighboring Captiva Island and on the mainland in Fort Myers.

Education: There's only an elementary school on the island, but the Sanibel Community Center and BIG Arts hold a variety of classes and seminars, including various types of art, music and current events. On the mainland, Edison Community College in Fort Myers offers a variety of two- and four-year degrees as well as adult education classes. Also in Fort Myers is Florida Gulf Coast University, the state's newest university. It offers distance learning, many degree programs and special events.

Transportation: There is no public transit system operating on Sanibel Island. A number of shuttle services transport passengers to and from Southwest Florida International Airport in Lee County. Taxi service also is available.

Health: There are no hospitals, but numerous physicians have offices on Sanibel, including dentists, internists, ophthalmologists and other specialists. HealthPark of the Islands services many of the medical needs of the community, from routine check-ups to emergencies and minor surgery. Lee Memorial Health System's HealthPark Medical Center on the mainland about five miles from the causeway offers a full range of services in a well-appointed structure as well as seminars, senior services and discounts.

Housing options: Housing along the beaches is in demand and hard to come by. A four-bedroom, three-bath home on the beach starts at about $2.2 million ($2 million on the bay) while beachfront condos start in the high $300,000s for one bedroom, mid-$400,000s for two bedrooms. Inland homes are selling for upwards of $200,000, with most averaging in the $400,000s. Lots start in the $100,000s inland and run to about $2 million on the beach.

Visitor lodging: Because of the island's popularity as a vacation destination, there are dozens of choices. Rates are highest from Christmas to Easter. Among the options are: Best Western Sanibel Island Beach Resort, a beachfront motel, $135-$439, double occupancy, (800) 528-1234. Brennen's Tarpon Tale Inn offers cottages and motel rooms within walking distance of the beach, $79-$199, (941) 472-0939. Casa Ybel Resort is a beachfront all-suites resort, $190-$495, (800) 276-4753. Holiday Inn Beach Resort is a beachfront hotel, $149-$250, (800) 443-0909. Song of the Sea is a beachfront European-style inn, $160-$449, (800) 231-1045.

Information: Sanibel and Captiva Islands Chamber of Commerce, 1159 Causeway Road, Sanibel, FL 33957, (941) 472-1080 or www.sanibel-captiva.org.

sea grape trees and gnarled driftwood facing an aquamarine gulf.

In the 1920s, the island began drawing famous visitors looking for a place to get away from it all. When his isolationist views earned Charles Lindbergh the public's scorn, he and his wife, Anne, became regular visitors. Thomas Edison sailed from his winter home in Fort Myers to study native plants and savor the beach. Poet Edna St. Vincent Millay vacationed there in the 1930s.

In 1935, Pulitzer Prize-winning political cartoonist Jay Norwood "Ding" Darling began the first of many winters on the island and its neighbor, Captiva, which is still more sparsely developed and more expensive than Sanibel. A staunch conservationist, he campaigned for federal protection of the fragile and unique environment on Sanibel. The result is the 6,000-acre J.N. "Ding" Darling Wildlife Refuge, which occupies a third of Sanibel Island.

Take a walk, bike, car or tram ride along the five-mile Wildlife Drive in the refuge and come upon alligators sunning themselves, raccoons and possums foraging for a snack, and a host of birds, including roseate spoonbills, great white egrets, Florida scrub jays, white ibis, ospreys, red-shouldered hawks, bald eagles, cormorants and herons.

Long renowned as one of the top three areas in the world for shell collecting, Sanibel takes its reputation seriously. Every spring for 65 years, the Sanibel Community Association has held the Sanibel Shell Fair and Show. It began as a small affair on someone's porch with a few islanders displaying their prized finds. Over the years it's outgrown the community center, spilling out onto the grounds as well.

The Bailey-Matthews Shell Museum bills itself as the only museum in the United States devoted entirely to the shells of the world, featuring exhibits of shells and shell-related subjects, shells in tribal art, and a collection of tree snails. There's even a name for that telltale posture struck when the urge to reach down and pick up a beautiful shell from the beach becomes irresistible. It's called the Sanibel Stoop, and it can be seen on every beach on the island at all times of the day.

The island is fast becoming as culturally well-endowed as it is environmentally appealing. BIG Arts (Barrier Island Group for the Arts) is in its third decade of promoting arts on the island, offering concerts, workshops, films, lectures, discussion groups and a Thanksgiving weekend arts and crafts fair.

The Old Schoolhouse Theater is a cozy little structure built in 1896 and transformed into a theater in 1964. With 90 seats in which pioneer children once learned reading, writing and such, it now offers an intimate approach to live theater. The Pirate Playhouse at the J. Howard Wood Theatre houses a professional regional theater company, bringing actors, directors and designers from throughout the country for drama, classics and comedies.

Tina Hillebrandt has been a board member there, although she's had to cut back because of illness in the family this year. She remains active in the church. A certified massage therapist, she also donates massages to women who pay for them by doing something nice for someone else.

In November Bill will finish his term on the city council, and he is past president of the conservation foundation board and remains active in the organization. "There are so many wonderful, legitimate things to do around here — not busy work," Bill says. "We get a chance to give back because we've been given so much."

Tina says, "We've got life down to three questions: Can you live where you want to live, be with people you want to be with and do what you want to do? If you can get one out of three, you're living a good life. Bill and I are living a dream. We have all three."

Tina and Bill Hillebrandt started making friends on that very first visit in 1986 and still socialize with some of those people today. They both play tennis, bicycle and enjoy boating. One of their favorite activities is watching the sunset every night.

"There's something to be said for sitting, periodically taking that daily pause," Bill says. "There are lots of nice places just to pause — on the beach, on the bay, in the middle of "Ding" Darling (refuge), you can pause and look up anywhere and see beautiful things."

They've moved five times, first from condo to condo, then two houses on the beach and now to a three-bedroom home with a dock on the bay, which seems the best fit so far. "We didn't know it at the time, but when we bought our first condo we got into the Sanibel real estate market at a pretty good time," Bill says. "Our investment then made it possible for us to be here now."

As for their old life back in the Midwest, "that was then and this is now," he says, adding that they stay in touch with family and old friends. "It's amazing how many more people come to see us in Florida than in Omaha."

If there's anything about their current life that's bothersome, it might be the traffic during the busy winter months. "Like Tina says, traffic and no-see-ums (gnats) are God's reminders that we're not in paradise," Bill quips. But he adds, "It's a choice. The community wisely made the decision to keep the road two lanes, relatively rural. We've lived in small towns and big cities. Sanibel is another small town; it's just surrounded by water. But that's part of its charm."

To those considering a move there, Tina kids, "The bugs are big, there are live animals roaming the streets and you really should consider Montana." Her husband adds: "The traffic is terrible; the taxes are outrageous. But other than that, we'd love to see you."

Joking aside, they caution that the life they love on Sanibel isn't for everyone. "When the sun goes down, it really gets dark," says Bill. "There are no street lights, no traffic lights. People half-kiddingly say that 9 p.m. is Sanibel's midnight, but it's true that there's not much going on after that. For a lot of people, it's not their bag. But we found it appealing."●

San Juan Capistrano, California

A deep sense of history permeates this Southern California town

By Mary-Ann Bendel

San Juan Capistrano, established in 1776, is the oldest community in a state that prides itself on being first with the latest trends. "This is a very special city," says Mayor Collene Campbell. "I think our city motto, 'Preserving the Past to Enhance the Future,' says it all."

The city welcomes retirees and has no trouble attracting them with its near-perfect climate. With the Pacific Ocean only a mile away, air conditioning is not needed and the winters are full of sunshine.

Much of the city centers around Mission San Juan Capistrano, considered the most romantic and the jewel in the chain of 21 Franciscan missions that are situated from San Diego to Sonoma. If you arrive in the early morning after a rare night of rain, the gardens will smell like they must have to followers of Father Junipero Serra, who founded the mission in 1776. It's also likely that you will find retiree Al Ravera and other volunteers working in the gardens to keep them beautiful. The 30 volunteers call themselves the Gardening Angels.

"We have to save this mission. It's a big part of California's history," says Al, who moved with his wife, Gloria, to San Juan Capistrano from Orange, CA, where he was director of city services. Like many seniors here, they are involved in volunteer work at the mission. "This is a very friendly community with a strong preservation mode," says Al, noting that people come from all over the world to see the mission's famous arches, hear the tolling of its bells and walk its time-worn paths.

When the Spanish missionaries arrived, local Native Americans helped build the mission and work the farms, make candles and soap and do the weaving and tanning. Adobe homes were built for families with ties to the mis-

sion. With the Mexican independence of 1821, mission lands were divested, and land grants put large "ranchos" in the hands of a few powerful families. With its location halfway between San Diego and Los Angeles, San Juan Capistrano became an overnight stage stop on the way to newly discovered gold fields in Northern California. But the Capistrano Valley developed as an agricultural center with a tight-knit group of farm families and merchants. They were relatively untouched by the explosion of development to the north and south.

All this history can be viewed at the San Juan Capistrano Historical Society in the O'Neill Museum, located in a Victorian-era home across from the railroad depot. The society has 4,000 photos dating to 1870, and a docent program helps visitors interpret the photo display on weekends. Don and Mary Tyron retired to the city 10 years ago, from San Pedro, CA, and they both volunteer a day each week at the society. "Most of us who work here are seniors," says Mary. "We talk to fourth graders and dress them up in old costumes. It's fun."

But San Juan Capistrano probably is best known for the return of the swallows to the mission every spring. The swallows migrate between San Juan Capistrano and Goya, Argentina, traditionally arriving in San Juan Capistrano on March 19, St. Joseph's Day. A festival has evolved around the swallow migration.

The Swallows Festival, or Fiesta de las Golondrinas, is a two-month-long celebration beginning in late February with a Taste of San Juan reception. In mid-March, Swallows Week kicks off with a ball followed by a full calendar of events. The annual Swallows Day Parade is famous as the largest nonmotor-

ized parade in the United States. Horses and riders in old California costumes and marching bands make for a gala event.

"My father was a good friend of Gene Autry, who wrote a song about the swallows returning to San Juan Capistrano," says Gil Jones, a retiree who was born in Texas and raised in Oklahoma. That song inspired him to visit San Juan Capistrano, and he and his wife, Millie, moved here from Lake Forest, CA, in 1980. Although Gil and Millie say they are retired, Gil operates a minifarm complete with pony rides, a petting pen and an outdoor picnic area, and Millie teaches china painting classes in her home. "I've made many friends here through that endeavor," she says.

The busy couple believes San Juan Capistrano has attractions particularly amenable to seniors. "The city council here has always held seniors in high regard," says Gil, a former mayor. "There's a bond between the community and older residents not always found in other communities. There's a great deal of pride in the community, and it's a very small community, but you can go anyplace in the world and people have heard of it," he says. "It's very easy to become involved and be heard. Other towns are a little envious of how we operate and of our success at controlling growth and maintaining a large percentage of open space."

With a current population of 34,000, the plan is to expand to 40,000, and that will be the end of residential development. San Juan Capistrano's city government is committed to this plan to prevent the overbuilding that has impacted much of Southern California. It is a conscious decision by city government to preserve open land and protect beautiful ridge lines from development. "We are pretty close to build-out now," says city engineer Tony Foster, who believes San Juan Capistrano "is one of the more mellow places to live in Orange County."

Another retired couple enjoying life here is Les and Marie Blair, who had lived in the same house in Downey, CA, for 40 years before they decided to move. They always had wanted to live near the ocean, so six years ago they researched favorite coastal cities, chose San Juan Capistrano and never looked back. They bought a three-bedroom stucco home in an 8-year-old, 96-home planned community that encompasses all ages. One mile from downtown, their hilltop home overlooks the mission and downtown San Juan Capistrano. Married 58 years, Les will be 79 this summer and feels 50.

Both he and Marie jog and swim every day.

Les says San Juan Capistrano reminds him of Broken Arrow, OK, where he grew up. Marie adds, "I love this town, the mission and the history here."

They have had no trouble making friends. Because of their jogging, they meet a lot of people — and dogs. "We know some of the dogs better than their owners," Marie says with a laugh.

They also have found volunteering basic to their new life here. Les was assigned aboard the USS Pennsylvania in Pearl Harbor when it was attacked at the outset of World War II. He survived 17 naval battles in the Pacific and now visits local schools to share his experiences with young people. He also works

with Alzheimer's patients, makes deliveries for Meals on Wheels and has served as president of the Seniors Club. One of his proudest possessions is the Olympic torch he got to keep when he ran in the Olympic torch relay on the Pacific Coast Highway in 1996. Both he and Marie work with the Special Olympics and answer children's letters to Santa Claus. They dance West Coast swing, line dance and participate in dance contests, often winning.

Les believes their home has appreciated in value about $100,000 since they bought it six years ago, but Gil Jones says housing still is available at all income levels. "You can still get a two-bedroom condo for $80,000 — or a million-dollar mansion," he says.

San Juan Capistrano, CA

Population: 33,826

Location: The city is in southern Orange County in a picturesque coastal valley approximately 1.5 miles inland from the Pacific Ocean midway between Los Angeles and San Diego. San Juan Capistrano is 62 miles south of Los Angeles and 65 miles north of San Diego. Altitude is 104 feet above sea level.

Climate:

	High	Low
January	65	50
July	89	73

Average relative humidity: 65%
Rain: 10 inches.
San Juan Capistrano enjoys pleasant summers and moderate winters with offshore breezes prevailing.
Cost of living: Above average (specific index not available).
Median housing cost: $295,000
Sales tax: 7.75%
Sales tax exemptions: Food products, prescription medicines and services.

State income tax: For married couples filing jointly, graduated from 1% of taxable income up to $11,496 to 9.3% on amounts over $75,450. For single filers, graduated from 1% of taxable income up to $5,748 to 9.3% on amounts over $37,725.
Income tax exemptions: Social Security benefits and railroad pensions are exempt.
Estate tax: None, except the state's "pickup" portion of the federal tax, applicable to taxable estates above $1 million.
Property tax: The most common rate is 1.067% of appraised value (the range is 1.0604% to 1.2%). The annual tax on a home valued at $295,000 would be about $3,148, using the most common rate.
Homestead exemption: None.
Religion: Most denominations are represented locally or in nearby communities.
Education: Options include Saddleback Community College in Mission Viejo, Irvine Valley College in Irvine, Orange Coast College in Costa Mesa, University of California at Irvine and California State University in Fullerton.
Transportation: Orange County Rapid Transit, Dial-a-Ride and Senior Van offer local transportation, and taxi service also is available. Amtrak and Metrolink make daily rail stops. John Wayne Airport is 20 miles north, Los Angeles International Airport is 65 miles north, and Lindberg

Field in San Diego is 65 miles south.
Health: San Clemente Medical Center, Mission Hospital in Mission Viejo (the regional trauma center), South Coast Medical Center in Laguna Beach (an acute-care hospital) and Saddleback Memorial Medical Center in Laguna Hills are within 10 miles of San Juan Capistrano. All are highly rated medical facilities.
Housing options: Mobile home options include **Capistrano Valley Mobile Estates**, (949) 493-4411, and **El Nido Mobile Home Estates**, (949) 493-2666. **The Seasons at San Juan**, (949) 487-0210, is an income-restricted apartment complex for seniors, with one-bedroom apartments renting for $801 a month. **Marriott Brighton Gardens**, (949) 248-8855, offers assisted living. **The Fountains at Sea Bluff** at Dana Point, (800) 846-4440, is a full-service condominium retirement development with prices from $146,000 to $600,000.
Visitor lodging: Best Western Capistrano Inn, $89-$99, (949) 493-5661. The Mission Inn Motel, $135-$185, (949) 234-0249. Ritz Carlton in Dana Point, $295-$595, (949) 240-2000. Blue Lantern Inn in Dana Point, $170-$500, (800) 950-1236.
Information: San Juan Capistrano Chamber of Commerce, P.O. Box 1878, San Juan Capistrano, CA 92693-1878, (949) 493-4700 or www.sanjuan chamber.com.

As visitors drive around residential areas, they can't help but notice the preserved open spaces and ridges that are left natural. But there is a wide range of housing options, including rent-controlled apartments, luxury townhouses, affordable condominiums and planned developments. "People who retire here are happy campers," says Tom Hriber, a broker with Re/Max Real Estate Services. "San Juan Capistrano gives seniors a wide variance of home prices."

The city is attractive to seniors because it cares about their quality of life, says Tom Tomlinson, San Juan Capistrano's planning director. "In the late 1970s, the city established a cap on rent increases," he says. That offers assurance to seniors that they won't be forced out of their housing because of rate increases.

The Seasons at San Juan is an income-restricted apartment complex for active seniors 62 and older. To live here, residents cannot have an income of more than $31,740. Rent is based on ability to pay, with the average one-bedroom apartment renting for $801 a month. With 112 units, the seven-building garden apartment complex is attractive and affordable. "Seniors here call it paradise," says Jesse Talmo, property manager at the Seasons at San Juan.

For seniors who need physical assistance, options include the Marriott Brighton Gardens assisted-living development. It includes nursing and rehabilitative services as well as a special care center for people with Alzheimer's disease and related memory disorders. There also are full-service condominium buildings like the Fountains at Sea Bluff at Dana Point, which overlooks the Pacific Ocean. Fees of $2,000-$2,500 a month include meals and transportation. One-bedroom units are priced from $146,000 to $286,000, and two-bedroom units are $240,000 to $600,000. "We spoil our residents in a resortlike atmosphere," says Meg Righton, marketing director at the Fountains at Sea Bluff.

There are several mobile home parks, including El Nido Mobile Home Park, which has about 150 homes that range from $120,000 to $250,000. Single-family homes run the gamut from historic adobes to elegant hillside estates. A number of single-family options usually can be found for $250,000 to $300,000.

Virgene and Jack Heath live in a mobile home in Capistrano Valley Mobile Estates, and they are more than satisfied with their 1,700-square-foot home. With a garden in back, life is good here, they say. Jack moved to San Juan Capistrano in 1973 while he still worked at an advertising job in Fullerton, CA, and decided to stay after he retired. "I fell in love with the coast," he says. He and Virgene take art classes together and walk at the nearby Dana Point Marina. They travel on cruises to places like the Panama Canal, Alaska and the Mississippi River.

Now 80 years old, Jack started an association for residents of his mobile home community and works with other retirees to keep large chain stores out of the city. San Juan Capistrano is determined to stave off the influx of development that has impacted much of Southern California. Intense development pressures in the early 1970s prompted citizens to create a general plan for the city that preserved historic resources and open space, limited development density and provided for ridge-line preservation. These measures, adopted in 1974, put San Juan Capistrano years ahead of many other California communities in terms of planning and should ensure the unique heritage of San Juan Capistrano for many years to come. Most retirees want to keep the quiet, rural atmosphere they now enjoy.

That rural atmosphere also helps make San Juan Capistrano popular among equestrians of all ages, and the horse population is one of the things Les Blair says he likes best about the area. San Juan Capistrano boasts eight stables and about 2,000 horses, a unique feature of this small city. There are 30 miles of trails on 1,400 acres of public lands that also are open to hikers and mountain bikers.

Besides riding, there is an opportunity for seniors to volunteer at the Fran Joswick Therapeutic Riding Center. The center provides therapeutic horseback riding in an effort to help disabled children and adults improve their cognitive, physical and psychological abilities. More than 200 volunteers help with lessons, office work, fund raising and maintenance of the stables.

"We have clients ranging in age from 2 to 82 with a wide range of ability level. Seniors are always welcome to help us," says Dana Butler, executive director of the Fran Joswick Center.

Another perquisite of this city is a recently built community center for all ages, from kids to seniors. The gym has volleyball courts, badminton courts and a basketball court that can go from college basketball dimensions to a court for 6-year-olds. The senior center there is a hub of activity, with bright activity rooms for a variety of interests. The center works with the Ruby Gerontology Center at Cal State-Fullerton in programs to improve neuromuscular strength and flexibility, thus cutting down on the risk for falls. The center also offers Saddleback College Emeritus Institute classes in sketching, nutrition, yoga and cooking for one or two. There are classes in film, history, law for the layman, literature and music at various locations in the community. "It warms your heart to see the joy here," says Elaine Tracy, senior citizen program coordinator for the city.

Even though the city is small, there is a lot to do. There are restaurants like El Adobe, President Nixon's favorite when he lived in San Clemente. The Depot at the train station is charming and a local favorite. The Dana Point Marina is a bike ride away. Besides many shops and restaurants, it has the new Orange County Marine Institute, another volunteer possibility.

In addition, the La Sala Library was designed by architect Michael Graves in 1983, and has received worldwide acclaim as the first structure of a new design genre, neoclassicism. The Los Rios Historic District comprises the oldest neighborhood in California, including three adobe homes built in 1794. It's a good area to stroll, shop and have a meal, and guided walking tours are available.

Lee Howard, a 73-year-old former professional ballplayer with the Pittsburgh Pirates, moved to San Juan Capistrano 14 years ago. "It's the only place in the world to live," he claims. Agrees Marie Blair, "I haven't had a bad day since moving here. The air is so clean. There's always a beautiful breeze."

Adds her husband, Les, "Come on down!" ●

San Juan Islands, Washington

Low-key and secluded, these islands in northwest Washington boast charming villages and spectacular scenery

By Stanton H. Patty

In the San Juan Islands, the times seem perpetually kinder and gentler — sort of like the old "Happy Days" television show, say David and Sondra Bayley, who were vacationing from the Los Angeles area when they found the spot they thought was perfect for retirement.

Other retirees found equally compelling reasons to move here. Richard and Victoria Baker retired from high-voltage jobs in Southern California to become innkeepers. Jim and Carolee Maya took early retirement from California teaching careers — and then Jim

became known as Captain Jim, skipper of a whale-watching charter boat. Ron and Carol Duke retired, rented a truck and moved their belongings from the hectic Seattle area to a place where "people really care about people."

All of these retirees set a course for the San Juan Islands, a string of saltwater pearls in northwestern Washington state. Canada's British Columbia is a near neighbor across the water. "It's a great place to live," says Captain Jim. "I have this incredible feeling of safety and peacefulness."

At last count (depending on whether tallies were made at high or low tide) there were more than 700 islands and islets in the archipelago. Only 40 or so are inhabited, some by lone occupants. Most of the islands' 14,200 residents live on four islands: San Juan, Orcas, Lopez and Shaw. The principal islands are as different as Chinook salmon and Dungeness crab, favorite bounties of the San Juans.

San Juan Island (population 6,500), home of the islands' largest community, Friday Harbor, is where most retirees have settled. And it's where most visitors go ashore from island-hopping ferries, floatplanes and fast catamaran shuttles from Seattle. There are no high-

way connections to the San Juans. The only way to reach the islands is by water or air. And that's just fine with most of the contented islanders.

"I like the ferry — I like the distance that it creates," says Sondra Bayley, 66, former owner of a court-reporting agency in the Los Angeles area. Sondra and her husband, David, 58, a retired community college instructor, built their retirement home 12 miles northwest of Friday Harbor.

Friday Harbor (population 2,098) is the seat of San Juan County, which covers all of the islands. It's a snug harbor where sailing yachts, powerboats and commercial fishing vessels are moored almost hull to hull in summer. There's a merry fugue of whistle toots as ferries arrive and mewing gulls wheel overhead. Cyclists pedal off the ferries and go exploring on country roads to catch views of killer whales (orcas) prowling the waterways.

Orcas Island (population 4,500) is the largest of the San Juans with almost 57 square miles of charming hamlets and dazzling scenery. The commercial center is Eastsound, which actually is on the north end of the island. (Yes, one needs a compass to navigate in the San Juans.) Hikers and cyclists on Orcas challenge

2,047-foot Mount Constitution, highest point in the San Juans, for summit views that sweep from British Columbia to Washington's Cascade and Olympic mountain ranges.

Lopez Island (population 2,100) is another favored destination for cyclists because of its mostly flat terrain, uncrowded beaches and cozy bed-and-breakfast inns. Lopez residents still wave greetings at each passing car and bicycle.

Shaw Island (population about 230) has a small county park with limited

camping and picnicking facilities. Most of the eight-square-mile island is private property. Members of a local order of Catholic nuns have been operating the ferry landing there for more than 15 years.

The San Juans have been attracting visitors ever since Capt. George Vancouver, the English navigator, sailed by in 1792. Vancouver described the islands thusly in his log: "The serenity of the climate, the innumerable pleasing landscapes, the most lovely country that can be imagined . . . "

Sailors, pirates, smugglers, soldiers and a few pioneer settlers followed. Soon villages took root. Then boaters from Seattle and other Puget Sound cities made the San Juans a popular rendezvous. One visit to these getaway islands today and a traveler might be tempted to settle in the San Juans forever.

But island life may not be for everyone, retirees caution. "If you come here, you need to be comfortable with yourself, comfortable with your partner," David Bayley says.

Sondra Bayley suggests that newcomers rent awhile before building or buying an island home.

"Some people come with unrealistic expectations and are soon out," she says. The Bayleys visited Mexico "and all the pretty places people go in the West" before considering retirement in the San Juans. In 1988, well before they actually retired, they made a down payment on a lot. They returned the following two years and camped on their property, "experiencing it," David recalls. Then it was time to build.

The lifestyle also attracted Richard and Victoria Baker, the proprietors of Wildwood Manor, a three-story bed-and-breakfast inn that crowns a wooded knoll on the northeast side of San Juan Island.

Opening the B&B was a dramatic lifestyle change for the former Californians. Richard, 65, is a retired Los Angeles fire chief. Victoria, 59, used to be a deputy sheriff in Los Angeles County.

They decided to "check out" the San Juans after friends, who had honeymooned in the area, brought home enthusiastic reports. "We came to visit, saw the property we wanted, and that was it," Richard says.

Victoria, who had studied architecture after retiring from police work, designed their 4,500-square-foot, Queen Anne-style Victorian. Now Wildwood Manor, looking like a small castle in the wilderness, offers three guest rooms and a smashing saltwater view across San Juan Channel to the Cascade Mountains. The top floor is reserved for the Bakers' children and grandchildren when they visit from California and Colorado.

Volunteerism is a major activity for Friday Harbor-area retirees. Victoria is a past president of the local Kiwanis service club. Richard served as presi-

San Juan Islands, WA

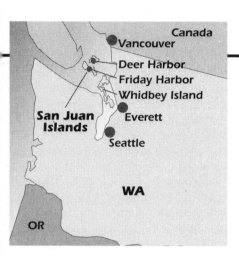

Population: 14,200 total on all islands; 6,500 on San Juan Island, including 2,098 in Friday Harbor, 4,500 on Orcas Island and 2,100 on Lopez Island.

Location: In northwestern Washington state, about 80 air miles north of Seattle. Only four islands — San Juan, Orcas, Lopez and Shaw — are served by Washington state ferries.

Climate[1]:

	High	Low
January	43	35
July	70	50

(The above figures are averages. Temperatures and rainfall vary from island to island.)

Average relative humidity: 40%
Rain: 20.98 inches.
Snow: Up to 6 inches some years, depending on location.
Mild climate with warm, sometimes breezy, summers and cool, often damp, winters. The sun shines an average of 247 days a year. Severe windstorms are rare.

Cost of living: Slightly above average (specific index not available). Most goods are shipped to the islands by ferries or by air. Gasoline arrives by barges.

Median housing cost: $320,000 on San Juan Island for a home with three bedrooms, two and a half baths and a water view. Waterfront homes fetch considerably higher prices.

Sales tax: 7.7%
Sales tax exemptions: Food items at grocery stores, medical services and drugs.
State income tax: None.
Intangibles tax: None.
Estate tax: Washington claims part of federal taxes due on amounts above $1 million.
Property taxes: They range from a low of $5.1780 per $1,000 of assessed valuation to a high of $9.1762, depending on levies approved by voters for schools and other programs. Friday Harbor has the highest tax rate. Property is assessed statewide at 100% of market value.
Homestead exemption: None, except for those age 61 or older (or disabled) with household income less than $30,000.
Religion: Eight places of worship on the four main islands, representing Protestant and Roman Catholic denominations.
Education: Skagit Valley College, based in Mount Vernon, a mainland neighbor, operates the San Juan Center campus in Friday Harbor. The center offers a two-year liberal arts degree and has a variety of classes designed for seniors. Senior courses include genealogy, literature and history. In addition, seniors (age 60 or older) are able to audit regular classes for only $5 per course. Several classes are taught by retired academics. Additional information: San Juan Center, (360) 378-3220.
Transportation: Access from the mainland mostly is by state ferries and air taxis. There is no public transit system in the islands. However, the San Juan County Health and Community Services

Department has senior centers on San Juan, Orcas and Lopez islands, and these centers operate vans for both on-island and off-island trips. There also is van service for twice-weekly lunches at the senior centers, and lunches are delivered to shut-ins.

Health: There are emergency/primary care clinics on San Juan, Orcas and Lopez islands. The Friday Harbor clinic, the largest, has four physicians on staff. Top-rated paramedics are on duty aboard the three islands. Serious cases are transported by helicopter or ferry to hospitals in mainland cities.

Housing options: Most islanders buy or build single-family homes that usually include some acreage. A few condominiums are available in Friday Harbor and in Roche Harbor, both on San Juan Island. Prices range generally from $167,000 to about $450,000.

Visitor lodging: In Friday Harbor, Inns at Friday Harbor, $59-$510, (800) 752-5752. Hillside House Bed and Breakfast, $80-$250, (800) 232-4730. On Orcas Island, Orcas Hotel, $79-$198, (360) 376-4300. Rosario Resort, $259-$399, (800) 562-8820. On Lopez Island, Lopez Islander Resort, $80-$260, (360) 468-2233.

Information: San Juan Islands Visitor Information Service, P.O. Box 65, Lopez Island, WA 98261, (888) 468-3701 (toll free) or (360) 468-3663, or visit www.guidetosanjuans.com. Other sources: San Juan Island Chamber of Commerce, (360) 378-5240; Orcas Island Chamber of Commerce, (360) 376-2273; Lopez Island Chamber of Commerce, (360) 468-4664.

[1]Temperatures vary from island to island. These figures are for the only official weather station in the San Juans, at Olga on Orcas Island. Rainfall also varies, even on each island.

dent of the Lions Club. He also is a past commander of the Friday Harbor Power Squadron, an educational organization that promotes boating safety. "We've met a lot of wonderful people here," he says.

First-rate medical care is a priority for San Juans residents. Seniors make up 26 percent of the county's population, the highest percentage in Washington. There are no hospitals in the San Juans, but three islands — San Juan, Orcas and Lopez — have emergency clinics and paramedic units.

Richard Baker, who had two open-heart surgeries before moving to San Juan Island and knows about skill levels from his years as a firefighter, gives the local paramedics and volunteer fire department "excellent" ratings. The Inter-Island Medical Center on San Juan Island (Friday Harbor) is staffed by four physicians. There also is a family physician in private practice on the island. Patients requiring care beyond the island clinics' capabilities are transported to hospitals in nearby cities — Anacortes, Mount Vernon and Bellingham — or to more distant Seattle.

Anacortes (Anna-COURT-ess), about 80 highway miles north of Seattle, is where most San Juans-bound visitors board Washington state ferries. It, too, is on an island, Fidalgo, but it is connected by bridges to the Washington mainland. Mount Vernon is on Interstate 5, on the way to Anacortes. Bellingham, also on I-5, is some 90 miles north of Seattle.

All three are "off-island" shopping destinations for San Juans residents. Bellingham also is the southern terminus of the Alaska Marine Highway, the state of Alaska's seagoing ferry system.

"This is a fabulous place to retire," says Wendy Stephens, director of senior services for San Juan County's Department of Health and Community Services. "Our retirees are fabulous peo-

ple. They are creative and resilient folks who have had rich experiences through the Great Depression and world wars. We love working with them." There are additional senior centers on Orcas and Lopez islands.

Transportation is another major concern for San Juans retirees. They depend mostly on the state ferries that cruise to and from the islands from the Anacortes gateway. The ferries that carry islanders and their vehicles also bring tourists, sometimes swarms of visitors that crowd the ferries. The result can be aggravating boarding delays, especially in Friday Harbor and over on Orcas Island.

Canny residents bound for "off-island" excursions have devised a way to beat the crowds. They park their cars in a waiting line along a pier as soon as a fully loaded ferry departs, then go home to have breakfast or lunch until shortly before the next scheduled ferry is due to arrive.

"It's difficult to be resentful of tourists," says Victoria Baker. "After all, most of us came here as tourists."

In fact, Jim Maya, 63, a retired high school theater teacher, has a new career that caters to tourists: whale watching. It is a business, but for Maya it's pure joy as he pilots his 22-foot charter boat, Annie Mae, on whale-watching trips from Friday Harbor in search of killer whales.

Pods of resident killer whales, known around the Northwest as orcas, voyage through the San Juans. At times the local orcas are joined by transient whales bound for distant waters. "It's a very exciting time out there," Captain Jim says. "Those whales are about the most magnificent creatures on earth — wild, intelligent and beautiful."

The Mayas retired early to move in 1990 from Gilroy, CA, to the San Juans. "We could have stayed in California and retired at 62 or 63 to get the max out of our retirement, but we just wanted to live here," Jim says. Jim also orga-

nizes San Juan Island's annual Santa Ship program. Santa, you see, reaches salty Friday Harbor by boat, not with reindeer.

It would be nice, the Mayas say, if San Juan Island had a shopping mall and department stores. But they don't miss smog, traffic congestion and what they remember as the "frantic" pace of California. "The tradeoffs have been incredible," Jim says. "I can be in my boat in 15 minutes, catching salmon. This is the dream spot of the United States for a boater."

Another couple who came first as tourists were Ron and Carol Duke, frequent visitors to the islands before moving from the Seattle area in 1998. Ron, 64, had been a mailer at a Seattle newspaper. Carol, 62, is a retired history teacher.

They were attracted to San Juan Island by what Carol describes as the "warm and welcoming people here." An added incentive was that their son, Andy, operates a sporting goods store in Friday Harbor.

"We had heard that it takes a long time for people to accept you in a small town, but we haven't found that to be true at all," Carol says. "We have a grandson, Henry (14 months old), and when I take him for walks everybody knows Henry and they say, 'Hello, Henry.' It's nice."

The Dukes built a modest 1,870-square-foot home on a hillside two miles north of Friday Harbor. It's not waterfront property, but does have a saltwater view. Their advice to couples who are thinking of retiring to the San Juans: "Come and rent for a year. See if this is the lifestyle you want."

But you may not want to wait too long to try the San Juans. Waterfront property at appealing prices is in short supply. "Mother Nature is not making new islands," warns Jim Knych, a Friday Harbor real estate agent.●

Santa Fe, New Mexico

The creative spirit thrives in New Mexico's multicultural capital

By John Villani

Nestled along the southern flanks of the Rocky Mountains, the arts mecca of Santa Fe presents a unique experience for retirees. Some refer to it as small-town life with all the trimmings, while others venture into philosophical discourses about the region's tricultural heritage and high-desert environment. But everyone agrees on the alluring charm of this city of 62,203 residents.

In recent years, Santa Fe has matured into a community of individualists, a place where people from across the globe have decided to put down roots and share in whatever magic it was that inspired Georgia O'Keeffe's masterful paintings. While there are several golf courses and two country clubs, Santa Fe's attractiveness as a place for retirement seems to transcend qualities that define other locales. It's for good reason this place is known as "the City Different."

Even though its charms have gotten national publicity, many visitors assume Santa Fe's climate is comparable to places like Scottsdale or San Antonio, which is not the case. While residents revel in plenty of year-round sunshine, Santa Fe's 7,000-foot elevation translates into four distinct seasons. Winter's first snowflakes fall in late October and reappear without fail through late April. That's why fireplaces are a common, and practical, feature in adobe homes and snow shovels are kept in garages.

In 1998, Santa Fe celebrated the 400th anniversary of its founding by Spanish conquistadors, which means that before an English-speaking colony of Europeans ever set foot on Plymouth Rock, a Spanish-speaking colony of Europeans was flourishing in New Mexico. Today, Santa Fe and the rest of northern New Mexico remain predominantly Hispanic, and Spanish is commonly spoken on the streets and in supermarkets, government offices and local schools. In Santa Fe, Spanish culture and traditions are celebrated as the most important pieces of the American pie.

Native American traditions also are given the same deference as Hispanic culture. Eight Native American pueblos (known elsewhere as reservations) are located in northern New Mexico, some close enough to Santa Fe to allow pueblo residents to commute to jobs in the city. In this part of the country, people of European origin who are not Spanish are referred to as Anglos, an all-purpose term that conveniently lumps together Catholics, Moslems and Jews as well as Russians, Irish and Australians.

While Santa Fe's first artists were the Spanish santeros who created religious paintings and sculpture for the Catholic Church, it wasn't until the Santa Fe Railway's publicity campaigns in the years following World War I that this area began developing a reputation as an arts colony. Sent here to paint the landscape and Native Americans, some of those early 20th-century artists scratched out a living selling paintings to local businessmen and tourists or trading their work to settle up restaurant and bar bills.

After developing its reputation as an arts colony, Santa Fe began attracting a technicolor populace of eccentrics, renegades and visionaries that solidified its reputation as a place where alternative lifestyles were accepted. Today, as is the case in places such as Key West, FL, and Carmel, CA, Santa Fe is home to a large and economically powerful gay and lesbian community of all ages whose influence and input is woven into the town's fabric of daily life.

For those considering retirement to Santa Fe, becoming comfortable with the city's weather, culture and eclectic population is an absolute must. This is an exceedingly informal place where great restaurants combine with a diverse cultural life in a high-desert environment, creating an ideal climate for forming new friendships and expanding one's horizons. It's a heady mix that appeals to an urbane and culturally attuned retiree populace ready to wrap their lives around a part of the world that is culturally distinct.

"I find the adobe architecture to be very peaceful, and I really enjoy the way residential and commercial buildings fit in with the landscape," says Ted Meredith, a 55-year-old retired publishing executive who moved here with his wife, Nancy, in 1993. Nancy, 55, who had been in real estate as well as publishing, initially visited Santa Fe with Ted on the advice of their son, Douglas.

"At first we missed our friends back in Indianapolis and Connecticut, but after we moved to Santa Fe they all started visiting us... and have come back more than once," she says.

Ted, who lists among his recent achievements visits to the Los Angeles Dodgers fantasy camp, a car-racing course in Laguna Seca, CA, with the Skip Barber Racing School, and a motorcycle trip around the South Island of New Zealand with son Douglas, says that making new friends since moving to Santa Fe has been easy.

"We took out a membership at Las Campanas golf club, and that turned out to be a terrific meeting ground," he says. "There's so much to do here that I've even gotten used to not having the season tickets for professional hockey, football and basketball that we had when we lived near large cities."

For Nancy, an art lover who once volunteered her time at the Eiteljorg Museum, a renowned museum devoted to Native American art in Indianapolis, relocating to a community loaded with more than 200 art galleries and nearly a dozen art museums has been a rewarding experience.

"Santa Fe just brought us a wonderful opportunity to focus our interests in art," she says. "I've pursued my interest in Australian aboriginal art by taking a trip Down Under, and I have made friends with artists from Taos to Tasmania. I especially enjoy taking Australian artists around northern New Mexico when they're visiting here for an exhibition at Dreamtime Gallery."

David R. Anderson, a retired attorney, moved to Santa Fe from Washington, DC, in 1992 with wife Phoebe Girard. Politically involved and an avid collector of art, he wants to "be a good neighbor and friend with people who are from a different cultural tradition." He and Phoebe, who works for United Way, describe resulting friendships they've made as very rewarding.

A nine-year board member of Arena Stage Theatre in Washington, DC, David, 64, admits to having an abiding love for the arts. These days he divides his creative energies between writing short stories and serving as a board member of Shakespeare in Santa Fe, a professional summer theater company. "Santa Fe is a small town where there's lots to do and where people are grateful for the efforts of volunteers like myself who have a natural bent toward community participation," he says.

"It's a distinctive and interesting place to live, and every morning when I go outside to get my newspaper, I look up at the sky and immediately feel like I'm living in a resort. If there are any drawbacks to living here, it's the extremely dry climate and the constant sunshine, which take a toll on my skin."

Santa Fe, NM

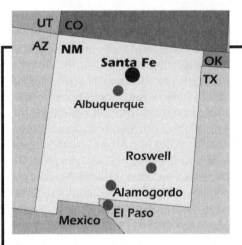

Population: 62,203 in Santa Fe, 129,292 in Santa Fe County.

Location: Northern New Mexico at 7,000 feet in the Sangre de Cristo Mountains.

Climate:

	High	Low
January	40	19
July	82	57

Average relative humidity: 30%
Rain: 14 inches.
Snow: 32 inches.
Cost of living: 114.2, based on national average of 100.
Median housing cost: $268,000
Sales tax: Called a gross receipts tax locally, the rate is 6.45% in the city and 5.75% in the county.
Sales tax exemptions: Prescription drugs.
State income tax: For married couples filing jointly, graduated from 1.7% of taxable income up to $8,000 to 8.2% on amounts over $100,000. For single filers, graduated from 1.7% of taxable income up to $5,500 to 8.2% on amounts over $65,000.
Income tax exemptions: Individuals 65 and older are eligible for a deduction of up to $8,000 if joint income does not exceed $51,000 for married filing jointly or $28,500 for single filers.
Intangibles tax: None.
Estate tax: None, except for the state's "pick-up portion" of the federal tax applicable to taxable estates of more than $1 million.
Property tax: $17.70 per $1,000 of assessed value, with homes assessed at one-third of appraised value. The annual tax on a $268,000 home, with exemption noted below, is about $1,530.
Homestead exemption: There is a head-of-household exemption of $2,000 off the assessed value of a primary residence.
Religion: Predominantly Catholic with every major religion represented along with Buddhist, Baha'i, Latter Day Saints, Quaker, Greek Orthodox and nondenominational congregations.
Education: Santa Fe Community College offers degree courses as well as noncredit adult-education courses both for day and night students. St. John's College and the College of Santa Fe are four-year institutions offering undergraduate and graduate degree programs.
Transportation: Santa Fe Trails, the city's transit system, uses buses powered by compressed natural gas in covering its 10 routes. Fare is 50 cents and most routes are operated six days a week. Santa Fe Airport is primarily used by private aircraft, but Great Lakes Aviation has several daily flights on twin-engine planes to and from Denver. Albuquerque International Airport is served by major airlines and is one hour south by car or shuttle.
Health: St. Vincent's Hospital, a full-service facility, is licensed for 268 beds and has 250 physicians on staff. The hospital also has a cardiac care unit and cancer treatment center.
Housing options: Las Campanas, (505) 989-8877, a gated community featuring two golf courses, stables and clubhouse, has homesites starting at $140,000 and homes from $550,000 and up. **Shadowridge Apartments**, (505) 988-1919, offers a range of apartment sizes from $689 to $829. **El Castillo**, (505) 988-2877, a continuing-care retirement community, offers housing with entrance fees from $50,000 to $180,000.
Visitor lodging: El Rey Inn offers spacious motel rooms for $85-$135, (505) 982-1931. Adobe Abode has bed-and-breakfast accommodations in a historic downtown Santa Fe residence for $135-$215, (505) 983-3133. La Fonda, another historic downtown hotel, offers rooms for $209-$249, (800) 523-5002 or (505) 982-5511.
Information: Santa Fe County Chamber of Commerce, P.O. Box 1928, Santa Fe, NM 87504, (505) 983-7317 or www.santafechamber.com. Santa Fe Convention and Visitors Bureau, 201 W. Marcy St., Santa Fe, NM 87504-0909, (800) 777-2489 or www.santafe.org.

Retired university professors Sarah Lanier Barber and Gloria Donadello moved to Santa Fe after spending their professional lives in New York City, sharing a classic loft apartment in the Soho neighborhood. "We fell in love with Santa Fe immediately, especially for its strong arts scene, its cosmopolitan, yet informal, friendliness, and its great restaurants," says Gloria. "We were looking for a multicultural place that was gay-friendly and someplace where we wouldn't have to turn on the air conditioning in February."

Since arriving here in 1991, Gloria and Sarah have been active in Santa Fe's community affairs, serving as co-founders of Hope House, a residence for people with AIDS. Sarah, 62, also is a founder and co-chairperson of the Lesbian and Gay Community Funding Partnership, while Gloria, 72, served as co-chairperson of Santa Fe Festival Ballet. Like many other New York professionals who retire to Santa Fe, this couple has discovered that even in retirement their appointment books stay filled with music lessons, aerobics classes, social gatherings, art openings and evenings at the Santa Fe Opera.

Their comfortable adobe home has a spectacular view of the Sangre de Cristo Mountains and is filled with art collected primarily from local galleries. Sarah, who has spent the past five years mastering the cello, says that the cultural composition of northern New Mexico took time to understand. "I taught students from all over the world during my career, and I had lots of exposure to Puerto Ricans, Dominicans, Ecuadorians and other Latino people," she says. "But until I moved here, I had never had any contact with New Mexico's Hispanic culture, and I sure didn't know much about Native Americans."

"Santa Fe is an easy place to make friends, but it's also an expensive place to live and a place where the cultures tend to be more segregated than what we were used to in the city," says Gloria. "But on the other hand, it's culturally rich, you get great movies, and the people you meet are willing to extend themselves out to you in a deep and meaningful way. Without our being able to participate in the life of this community, our retirement experience wouldn't have been as rich as it is."

Bob and Bridget Nurock, who moved to Santa Fe from Philadelphia in 1993, surprised themselves when they "immediately bought a home in Santa Fe after spending a week's vacation here in April 1993. We couldn't believe it ourselves, but our feeling for the town was instantaneous," says Bridget, 52, a clinical social worker specializing in care of the elderly.

Bob, 60, a semiretired investment consultant specializing in stock market strategies for institutional investors, says that since moving to Santa Fe, he's reduced his workload "to about a seven on a scale of 10, and I'm fast headed in the direction of a low five. The main interest in my working life right now is painting, and I'm taking courses and working on my technique every day," he says.

Bob and Bridget both are avid skiers who enjoy living within a half-hour of Santa Fe Ski Area's 12,000-foot heights. They also are serious collectors of works by such artists as Santa Fe landscape painter Phyllis Kapp and serve on the boards of local organizations such as the Native American Preparatory School.

"Santa Fe is the kind of place that has so many activities going on that you never have any problems meeting people," says Bob. "Our shared interest in art has resulted in lots of friendships with artists and gallery owners, and we both enjoy the tricultural composition of this community. We're not necessarily country club-type people, so what matters for us is living close in to town, getting involved with the community, and sharing the love we have for the outdoors and for art. The best advice I have for anyone thinking of retiring here is to make up your mind that you're going to get involved in the life of this community."

"We dove into this place and don't have any regrets," says Bridget. "But if you're thinking of having a home built for you in Santa Fe, I promise you're going to learn about a whole new way of being patient."

That's a sentiment echoed by Jim Van Sant, a retired businessman from St. Louis who moved to Santa Fe in 1987 and now is the opera critic for Santa Fe's daily newspaper. "This place is hellishly expensive for just about all goods and services, and you're continually at the mercy of craftsmen of all kinds. Most folks I know need a couple of months away from here in midwinter, especially to places like San Miguel de Allende (in Mexico), which is much cheaper, yet still has a great cultural life," he says.

"I probably should add that one of the more curious things about retiring to Santa Fe is that you always have to protect yourself from having too many house guests. On the other hand, when you travel away from here, you come to realize that you have a certain status simply by virtue of having decided to live in Santa Fe. People listen to you a bit more, and I find it fun to live in such a high-profile small town."●

Sarasota, Florida

Vibrant city on Florida's Gulf Coast has an impressive cultural scene

By Karen Feldman

The lure of almost any Florida community includes a mild climate and countless opportunities for outdoor fun, but Sarasota boasts that plus something more: culture. Lots and lots of culture. Opera, ballet, theater, film festivals and the visual arts flourish in this small, sophisticated city on the state's southwest coast.

Much of the credit for this bounty goes to circus magnate John Ringling, who in 1927 decided to base his famed circus in Sarasota. Today his legacy lives on in many ways. John and Mable Ringling's estate, which includes the Ringling Museum of the Circus, the Ringling Museum of Art and his 30-room mansion, Ca'd'Zan (Venetian dialect for "House of John"), are resplendent treasures situated along Sarasota Bay in the heart of the city.

Although best-known for his circus success, Ringling made a fortune through shrewd investments in oil, railroads and real estate. Many of his business associates and acquaintances found their way to Sarasota, bringing their money, influence and desires for the finer things of life along with them. Today the Ringling estate remains a cultural hub of the city, and its influence radiates out in many directions.

Add to that 35 miles of pristine beaches along the Gulf of Mexico, five dozen golf courses, year-round fishing and a location convenient to Tampa and Orlando, and Sarasota weighs in as a serious contender even against much larger Florida cities.

"It's one of those rare special places that has big-city amenities without the hassle of being in a big city," says David May, former president of the Greater Sarasota Chamber of Commerce.

It was just that combination that attracted Sam and Susan Kalush here in 1993, when they decided to move south from Michigan. The retired cardiac surgeon and his wife, an interior designer, considered the central Piedmont and Research Triangle regions of North Carolina and many other Florida towns. After several visits to Sarasota, they were sold.

Why? "The warm climate, and it was large enough to offer the amenities of culture, entertainment and good restaurants," says Sam, 58, who also cites its proximity to Tampa and the ocean. "You are not overwhelmed by a big urban environment with urban center problems," he says.

"It has the feel of a small town," agrees Susan, 56.

The city's population stands at about 52,715, with another 273,260 in the rest of the county. Development, which has thrived for more than a decade, continues at a brisk pace. With the growing population comes "a wide range of retail establishments and restaurants that make it an interesting place to live and to entertain," says David May.

For Joe and Lolly Hascal, the move from Louisville, KY, to Sarasota was a foregone conclusion. Joe, 75, had owned a condo on Siesta Key, a barrier island along Sarasota's western flank, and visited regularly for 17 years. After retiring from the men's retail clothing business, he and Lolly, 71, a mental health counselor and educator, bought a duplex in the 125-unit Crestwood Villas. They moved in November 1994, quickly and easily making friends at the community's pool and clubhouse.

When it comes to housing, the options are many, including cozy, rambling old neighborhoods and sleek, well-manicured new ones. There are waterfront and country club communities and options downtown among the art galleries and cafes or away from it all on large tracts with a country feel.

"There's housing here to meet all tastes, from apartments to a whole variety of single-family housing, villas and condos. There's a very good housing stock," says David May. "People used to paying housing costs in the Northeast or large communities like the Chicago metropolitan area will find it to be a very affordable market."

Renee Eppard, a broker with ReMax Properties in Sarasota, agrees. "We have so many choices here it's unbelievable," she says. "Prices range from $60,000 for a 1,000-square-foot older condo to $8 million homes on the bay. And there's everything in between."

In order to take time to consider their options, the Kalushes first rented a home for about four months. They ended up buying a house in the development where they'd rented — Bent Tree, a subdivision of about 600 homes with an 18-hole golf course. Their home is 3,200 square feet, an open, split plan with guest rooms on one end and the master suite on the other. It has a lakeside lot and a lanai, swimming pool and large open family room. "We spend a lot of time and eat a lot of meals outside on the lanai and around the pool," Susan says.

In general, Renee Eppard says, a new three-bedroom, two-bath home with a pool and a two-car garage runs $200,000 to $250,000 but can climb as high as $8 million for a beachfront location.

Many retirees prefer something smaller or want to skip the lawn and pool maintenance, so they choose a condominium development. Here again, prices range widely. From the basic older model that starts in the low $60,000s, prices rise to the $125,000-to-$600,000 range and up for a 2,500-square-foot luxury villa. Condos on Siesta and Lido keys start at about $250,000, while those on Longboat Key start at $500,000. Enjoying a resurgence in popularity is the Sarasota Bayfront downtown, where luxury condos start at about $400,000.

Another plus for retirees, David May says, is "a whole range of assisted-living options. New projects have come on line to cater to the middle-income-and-up retiree who has the means and desire to live a good lifestyle."

That already has occurred to the Hascals. "When we get too feeble, they have gorgeous retirement places here," Lolly says.

Wherever they live, Sarasota residents have lots of reasons to leave their homes in pursuit of any number of interests. "For those who want to be active, there is an almost unlimited number of orga-nizations that need talented volunteers," David May says.

Both the Kalushes and the Hascals have answered the call for volunteers. Sam volunteers his cardiology expertise at Senior Friendship Center, which of-fers low- or no-cost medical care and other health services to seniors by uti-lizing the retired medical community. He also instructs Red Cross courses on cardiopulmonary resuscitation and first aid. Susan volunteers at Doctors Hospi-tal and serves as a tour guide at the Sarasota Florida House, an environmen-tally friendly house that serves as a model for the public. She's also the chairwom-

Sarasota, FL

Population: 52,715 in the city, 325,975 in Sarasota County.

Location: On the west coast of Florida, 60 miles south of the Tampa-St. Peters-burg area. Easily accessible via Interstate 75 as well as the Sarasota-Bradenton International Airport and Tampa Inter-national Airport.

Climate:

	High	Low
January	72	50
July	91	72

Average relative humidity: 52%

Rain: About 60 inches annually.

Cost of living: 109.1, based on nation-al average of 100.

Median housing cost: $167,600 for existing homes, according to first quar-ter 2002 report by the National Associa-tion of Realtors.

Sales tax: 7%

Sales tax exemptions: Food, some services and medicine.

State income tax: None.

Intangibles tax: Assessed on stocks, bonds and other assets. Tax rate is $1 per $1,000 in assets. The first $20,000 in assets is exempt for individuals. For cou-ples filing jointly, the first $40,000 is exempt. Those who owe less than $60 need not pay.

Estate tax: None, except the state's "pick-up" portion of the federal tax, ap-plicable to taxable estates of more than $1 million.

Property tax: $14.05 per $1,000 in Sarasota, with homes assessed at 100% of market value. The annual tax on a $167,600 home, with exemption noted below, is $2,004. Additional taxes vary depending on location and may include water management, lighting and other special assessments.

Homestead exemption: $25,000 off the assessed value of a permanent, pri-mary residence.

Religion: All major religions and many smaller ones are represented in the 150-plus churches and synagogues in Sara-sota County.

Education: There are several colleges, including the University of South Flori-da, New College, Eckerd College, the Ringling School of Art and Design and the University of Sarasota. These colleg-es offer a variety of degrees ranging from associates to doctorates. Noncred-it courses for adults also are available.

Transportation: Sarasota-Bradenton In-ternational Airport provides service to many U.S. cities with a combination of major air carriers and commuter carri-ers. Sarasota County Area Transit pro-vides local bus service.

Health: There are two primary health-care hospitals: Doctors Hospital offers a full range of services, including emer-gency treatment, radiology, pain man-agement, chest pain care, hyperbaric medicine, a women's unit and a mature adult community center, and Sarasota Memorial Hospital offers urgent and emergency care, rehabilitation, chest pain treatment, cardiac care (including open-heart surgery), joint replacement, gerontology, outpatient surgery, a nurs-ing facility and more, including a 24-hour line for health questions and phy-sician referral. In addition, there are sev-eral licensed nursing and congregate-care facilities.

Housing options: Apartments, condo-miniums, patio homes and single-family residences abound in the city and its metropolitan area. There are waterfront, downtown and country club communi-ties to choose from, as well. Prices range from the low $60,000s to $8 million.

Lakewood Ranch, (800) 30-RANCH, a 5,500-acre community, offers two 18-hole golf courses, a private country club and housing by several builders, rang-ing from modest condos from the $100,000s to estate homes over $3 mil-lion. Many communities have both inde-pendent and assisted-living options. Among those are **Bay Village**, (941) 966-5611; **The Fountains at Lake Pointe Woods**, (941) 923-4944; and **Kabernick House**, (941) 377-0781.

Visitor lodging: This popular tourist destination offers a wealth of hotels, motor inns and resorts. In or near down-town Sarasota are Hampton Inn Sarasot-ta-Bradenton, $64-$110, (941) 351-7734; Inn by the Bay, $69-$109, (941) 365-1900; and Hyatt Sarasota, $99-$240, (941) 953-1234. On Siesta Key: The Palm Bay Club, $125-$220, (941) 349-1911, and The Turtle Beach Resort, $180-$365, (941) 349-4554. On Long-boat Key: The Colony Beach and Tennis Resort, $195-$1,400, (800) 282-1138, and the Longboat Key Hilton Beach Re-sort, $119-$410, (941) 383-2451 or (800) 282-3046. Rates are per night, double occupancy, and are lowest from mid-April through mid-December, rising 20% to 60% from Christmas through Easter.

Information: The Sarasota Visitor Infor-mation Center, 655 N. Tamiami Trail, Sarasota, FL 34236, (941) 957-1877, (800) 522-9799 or www.sara sotafl.org. The Greater Sarasota Chamber of Com-merce, 1819 Main St., Suite 240, Saraso-ta, FL 34236, (941) 955-8187 or www.sarasotachamber.org.

an of a social group at the country club. Joe volunteers at Senior Friendship Center as well, delivering meals, picking up groceries, running errands and visiting shut-ins. Lolly uses her training as a mental health counselor to lead a weekly support group and lectures once a month.

When not volunteering, Lolly also likes to folk dance and work on her computer while Joe shops and takes walks on the beach. Both enjoy swimming. For the Kalushes, golfing, fishing, boating, walking and bicycling are favorite pastimes.

David May says it's natural that most people think of the beaches and golf courses when they picture Sarasota, but he suggests exploring farther inland as well. "We have the largest state park (Myakka River State Park), beautiful inland waterways and wetlands that really make this area special for people who enjoy being outside," he says.

About nine miles east of Interstate 75, the park is easy to reach. Among its inhabitants are 200 species of birds, alligators, deer, feral pigs and bobcats. There are nature trails, observation decks, airboat and guided tram tours available. For yet another perspective, the state plans to add a rope walkway at treetop level, much like those found in rain forests.

Many current residents were once tourists looking for a warm-weather getaway. They found Sarasota and liked it so much that they eventually relocated. The many qualities that attract tourists are among those that appeal to residents, too.

The area has lots of Gulf access along the barrier islands of Lido Key, Longboat Key and Siesta Key. There's also lots of activity along the shoreline of sparkling Sarasota Bay.

The Ringling Estate, which overlooks the bay, sprawls over 66 acres, much of which is open for visitors to enjoy the trees, gardens and statuary. Within the Ringling Museum of Art, built in Italian Renaissance style, is a garden courtyard filled with reproductions of famous statues, including Michelangelo's "David." The estate is at its most startling each year during a Renaissance festival held in early March that fills the grounds with knights, wizards, ladies fair and other medieval characters.

Not far south along the water are the Marie Selby Botanical Gardens, nine lush acres filled with huge banyan trees, massive stands of bamboo, water lilies, cypress trees, orchids and Amazonian bromeliads. An elevated boardwalk winds through a mangrove swamp.

Tucked on a spit of land between Longboat and St. Armands keys, the Mote Marine Aquarium lets the public in to see the shark tank, sea turtles, a large touch tank and other marine exhibits. It also is headquarters for a group of marine researchers studying matters such as why sharks are immune to cancer and how that might aid humans in battling the disease.

St. Armands Circle houses a collection of shops, galleries, restaurants and night spots arranged in a large circle ideal for browsing and dining. In downtown Sarasota, a number of art galleries, theaters and restaurants now draw crowds, too.

Greyhound racing takes place from late December to mid-April at the Sarasota Kennel Club. The Cincinnati Reds spend March and early April in spring training camp at Ed Smith Sports Complex. The Royal Lipizzan Stallions offer free shows from January through March at Col. Hermann's Ranch in neighboring Manatee County. There are also all the requisite water activities: fishing, canoeing, water-skiing, kayaking, dolphin watching, wildlife tours and swimming.

The city also is home to the Asolo Theatre Co., The Players, Sarasota Opera, the Sarasota Ballet of Florida, the Florida West Coast Symphony and a number of vocal and chamber ensembles. Big names in entertainment often appear at the Florida State University Center for the Performing Arts and the purple-hued Van Wezel Hall.

About an hour away are St. Petersburg and Tampa, home to the Salvador Dali Museum, Florida International Museum, The Florida Aquarium, the Museum of Fine Arts, the Tampa Bay Performing Arts Center and Busch Gardens. Orlando is about two hours east.

After living in the city for several years, neither the Kalushes nor the Hascals have plans to move. Their advice to others who are thinking about relocating and considering Sarasota: "It's an excellent choice," Sam says.

"I hate to encourage others," Susan adds. "It has gotten busier and busier in the last five years. When we first got here, we were very pleased because it wasn't so crowded. But I think it's still one of the prime places on the Gulf Coast."

Lolly Hascal expresses a similar sentiment: "You will love it." But, she jokes, "Wait 'til we leave."●

Scottsdale, Arizona

A Phoenix suburb blends Southwestern and Mediterranean architecture with beautiful desert scenery

By Ron Butler

Forty years ago, Scottsdale was little more than a dirt road and a couple of saloons — Lulu Belle's and the Pink Pony. Then word got out and Scottsdale was swept up in the phenomenal Arizona population explosion that today makes the Phoenix-Scottsdale area one of the fast-growing urban centers in the country.

Just being in Scottsdale is an event — imagine living there. Situated seamlessly between Phoenix, Paradise Valley, Carefree and Tempe, Scottsdale's population is now near 203,000. Known for its outstanding architectural and landscape design, the impressive city also has impressive numbers — about 125 art galleries (the biggest art center this side of Santa Fe), four libraries, 32 indoor theaters, one outdoor theater, 28 parks, four bowling alleys. There are three municipal swimming pools, 30 golf courses, 20 tennis parks, five museums, a civic center, baseball stadium, a Center for the Arts and the Scottsdale Community College.

Its downtown Civic Center Senior Center is groundbreaking in concept. "As part of the city of Scottsdale, we give our community a place to have fun, a place to be safe, and help to enhance the quality of life, especially for our senior population," says Human Services spokeswoman Cathie McDaniel. The center looks like a bank or office building outside, but inside there's a wide variety of social and recreational programs, health screenings, special events, organized outings, discussion groups and classes in everything from computer techniques to Spanish language. Only the special classes and concert and theater outings require fees. Everything else is free.

Throw in gorgeous desert scenery with proud mountain landscapes and a near-perfect climate, and it makes

you wonder why Nancy and Ned Benedict, 52 and 59 respectively, took so long to move there. They came from San Francisco three years ago. Ned spent 32 years as a career pilot for Federal Express. Nancy, his co-pilot if you will, is a homemaker.

The Benedicts live in a sprawling five-bedroom, three-and-a-half-bath ranch-style home in a gated, master-planned community north of town called Terravita, meaning harmony of life and land. Frequent visits to relatives in the area made them forsake San Francisco for the Arizona desert.

Golf is a big priority with the Benedicts. (Membership fee for the Terravita Club is $50,000. Greens fees for guests range from $30 to $100, depending on season.) The couple also enjoys excursions into the desert and trips to towns such as Tucson, Bisbee and Douglas in the southern part of the state to soak up all that Western ambiance. They enjoy eating out, with Roy's Pacific Rim Cuisine their current favorite, offering seared lemon grass-crusted salmon with watercress-ginger sauce, and grilled spiny lobster with bean thread noodles and macadamia nuts.

Eating out also is a favorite activity of Dr. Melvin Breeze, 85, and his wife Elizabeth, 84, who moved to Scottsdale from Portland, OR, five and a half years ago. They count 44 restaurants within walking distance of their Forum Pueblo Norte senior living community, and have tried them all.

Melvin is a retired pediatrician and gynecologist; Elizabeth was on the home economics staff at Oregon State University. Married in 1937, they have five children and five great-grandchildren.

It was a medical convention at the Wigwam resort in nearby Litchfield and subsequent conferences in the area that introduced Melvin to the

glories of desert living. He liked the people and loved the climate. He and Elizabeth have taken two apartments in the Forum, a Marriott retirement property, and combined them to make one large apartment with four bedrooms, a guest room and possibly the largest-screen TV set this side of the big sports bar on Scottsdale Road.

The Forum also has its own health-care center and an assisted-living community. Services include one meal a day, downtown shuttle service, weekly housekeeping, free local calls, utilities, maintenance, heated swimming pool, shuffleboard and a putting green along with a wide range of organized social and cultural activities. The Breezes are members of the Scottsdale Arts Center and enjoy a full active life outside the Forum as well.

Norman and Cathy Arthur, 63 and 52 respectively, gave up the good life in Hawaii for the good life in Scottsdale and now reside in a gated community in the mountain foothills in the north part of town. He's a retired civil engineer; she's a computer consultant who still takes part-time assignments. They enjoy the desert scenery and often are part of it, taking long hikes and jogging 10 miles a day. They're often thrilled to spot a coyote or a bobcat or a pair of javelinas (wild pigs) along the way. They enjoy several challenging trails among the sheer red cliffs of Camelback Mountain, the area's best-known landmark, and they also play tennis but have an aversion to golf.

Their tastefully decorated home, with four bedrooms and three baths, is filled with Western artifacts and art — Hopi Kachina dolls, desert paintings, Indian blankets. The Arthurs also have a cabin in the summer recreation area of Pinetop, but it was primarily economic considerations that made Scottsdale a retirement choice. The cost of living in

Scottsdale is about half of what it was in Hawaii, and there are all those pesky volcanoes.

They have a 17-year-old son living at home and another at school. The community has no age restrictions, so the Arthurs enjoy an eclectic group of neighbors, ranging from empty-nesters to retirees and even a couple of newlyweds on their second and third marriages. They like to read so it's not unusual to find them browsing the shelves at the fine downtown bookstores such as the Antiquarian Shop. Here serious collectors can pick up a signed, first edition of John Steinbeck's "In Dubious Battle" for $8,000, a first edition of Ernest Hemingway's

Scottsdale, AZ

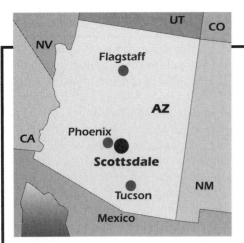

Population: 202,705

Location: In south-central Arizona, bordered by Phoenix, Paradise Valley, Carefree and Tempe in the legendary Valley of the Sun.

Climate:

	High	Low
January	65	39
July	105	80

Humidity: 23%

Rain: 7.05 inches of rain per year.

Cost of living: Above average (specific index not available).

Median housing costs: Home prices range from $120,000 to $6 million, averaging about $200,000. Apartments averaging 950 square feet with two bedrooms and one and a half to two baths rent for about $1,000-$2,000 a month, excluding utilities.

Sales tax: 7.1%

Sales tax exemptions: Groceries and prescription drugs.

State income tax: For married couples filing jointly, graduated from 2.87% of taxable income up to $20,000 to 5.04% minus $2,276 on amounts over $300,000. For single filers, graduated from 2.87% of taxable income up to $10,000 to 5.04% minus $1,138 on amounts over $150,000.

Income tax exemptions: Social Security benefits and up to $2,500 on federal, state and local government pensions are exempt.

Estate tax: None, except the state's "pickup" portion of federal tax, applicable to taxable estates of more than $1 million.

Property tax: $11.55 per $100 assessed valuation, with homes assessed at 10% of market value. The annual tax due on a $200,000 home would be about $2,310.

Homestead exemptions: None.

Religion: Scottsdale has hundreds of churches and synagogues representing virtually every denomination.

Education: Scottsdale Community College offers an associate degree with credits transferable to university levels and technical degrees. A wide range of continuing-education classes and community service programs also are available. Arizona State University, the state's largest university with an enrollment of more than 40,000, is located in the neighboring community of Tempe.

Transportation: Nearly everyone in Arizona drives, but those who don't will find Scottsdale taxis among the most expensive anywhere. Figure about $1 a mile in this sprawling area. The Scottsdale Connection provides wheelchair-accessible bus service throughout Scottsdale with connecting service to major Phoenix and other regional transportation routes. Ollie the Trolley offers free transportation throughout downtown Scottsdale from mid-November to May. Dial-a-Ride is a low-cost transportation program operating in Scottsdale and Tempe for persons 65 and older. Proof of age (Medicare card or photo identification) is required. The Scottsdale Municipal Airport, one of the busiest single-runway facilities in the country, accommodates business and recreational flyers.

Health: Scottsdale is home to one of the three branches of the Mayo Clinic, a multispecialty outpatient clinic with more than 297 physicians and a medical support staff of more than 1,500. Scottsdale Healthcare is the largest single employer in Scottsdale with more than 4,000 staff members and 1,350 active physicians.

Housing options: Medium-priced and luxury condominiums, townhouses, patio homes, ranch-style homes and two-story homes are all available in Scottsdale, making housing options one of its most attractive features. Of the more than 86,000 dwelling units currently occupied in Scottsdale, approximatly 70 percent are owned and 30 percent are rented. Scottsdale has several nationally recognized planned communities, such as **McCormick Ranch, Gainy Ranch, Scottsdale Ranch, Desert Highlands, Grayhawk, Desert Mountain, Troon, Terravita, McDowell Mountain Ranch** and **Scottsdale Mountain**. For information, call Neighborhood Resource Guide, (480) 312-7251.

Visitor lodging: Options range from glittering five-star resorts like the world-famous Phoenician, $195-$309, (480) 941-8200, and the Fairmont Scottsdale Princess, $159-$509, (480) 585-4848, to short-term rentals like the Abode Apartment Hotel, (480) 945-3544. Days Inn Fashion Square, (480) 947-5411, is immediately adjacent to Scottsdale's most prestigious shopping mall and offers rates ranging from $49 for a standard room in low season to $70 for a suite in high season. For visitor information online, see the Scottsdale Convention and Visitors Bureau site at www.scottsdalecvb.com.

Information: Scottsdale Chamber of Commerce and Convention and Visitors Bureau, 7343 Scottsdale Mall, Scottsdale, AZ 85251, (866) 475-0535 or (480) 421-1004. Arizona Office of Senior Living, 3800 N. Central Ave., Suite 1500, Phoenix, AZ 85012, (602) 280-1300, provides out-of-state retiree prospects with free relocation information. Web sites to check out include www.scottsdalechamber.com.

"Death in the Afternoon" for $4,000 or Arthur Conan Doyle's "Hound of the Baskervilles" for $4,000.

Victor and Ann Phillips, 72 and 70 respectively, gave up Ohio's frigid winters to worship El Sol in Scottsdale 12 years ago. They lived in Oxford, a charming little town of cobbled streets and unique shops where both were affiliated with Miami University, he (following a 24-year military career) in business and she in library arts. They raised four children.

Today, home is a comfortable, art-filled, two-bedroom casita in the Classic Residence of Scottsdale, a senior living community by Hyatt and the Plaza companies that offers virtually all the amenities of a luxury resort. These include 24-hour concierge service, one meal a day (lunch or dinner), weekly housecleaning and linen service, shuttle service and a wide variety of health and fitness programs.

The scenery is all mountains and lofty saguaros. Ann, who keeps busy with volunteer church, library and bilingual school classes, complains that a persistent family of javelinas has been eating her flower garden, roots and all.

With their obvious love for art (their home is filled with Western oils, bronzes and tie-dye prints), the Phillipses couldn't have settled in a more compatible community. Scottsdale's art scene is world famous. Sculptor Bob Parks' magnificent downtown fountain with four life-sized Arabian stallions frolicking about — the most photographed landmark in Scottsdale — sets the tone.

For the past 20 years, Scottsdale galleries have treated visitors and locals to Thursday night Art Walks, the oldest such art event in the United States. Many of the best-known galleries are concentrated along Marshal Way and Main Street (the arts and antique district), with others clustered in the Fifth Avenue shopping area and Old Town. Buck Saunders Gallery on East Camelback Road was the first major gallery to feature the work of the late Ted DeGrazia, Arizona's best-known, most-loved artist, and was long his exclusive representative. Now many of the local galleries, most notably Anthony's, feature the works of this world-known painter.

For the downside of living in Scottsdale — ah, and you thought there wasn't any — progress seems to be the main culprit. Nearly everyone echoes the same complaint — too many people, too much traffic, limited bus service, too much building and banging. "There's so much work," says Ned Benedict, the former Federal Express pilot, "that many unqualified workers are filling the work force, taking forever to show up for a job when you call them, and then doing shoddy work."

Yet for all of its glitz and development, there's something about Scottsdale that calls to mind the small towns in Italy or Spain where old men spend their time sitting around the town square, sipping coffee or wine and discussing the cares of the day. You see the same men in downtown Scottsdale — but they're at trendy outdoor cappuccino bars, and they dress better.●

Seaside, Florida

An upscale new town sports an old-fashioned look in the Florida Panhandle

By Karen Feldman

Florida's Panhandle is an unlikely place to find a development that has set the standard for a new kind of community, one that blends the best features of old-fashioned villages with modern conveniences and environmental awareness. Yet the Panhandle, with its honky-tonk towns that sprawl along the edge of the Gulf of Mexico, is where the community of Seaside has flourished.

Most of the Panhandle's Gulf Coast developed helter-skelter as entrepreneurs crammed in as many motels, surf shops, eateries, and tattoo and piercing parlors as the market would bear. Apparently it will bear a lot, as the solid mass of commercial development along U.S. Highway 98, the main route along the Gulf, reveals.

But turn onto County Road 30A, and the development becomes less dense, the beach widens and palms line the roads of upscale condo communities. The scene sets the stage for Seaside, a testament to what can happen when one man with conviction turns his vision into reality.

That's what developer Robert Davis has proved with his creation of Seaside. While Seaside may not be a household name, anyone who has watched "The Truman Show," a movie starring Jim Carrey, has seen the idyllic 80-acre town with its pastel-hued cottages and white picket fences lining red-brick streets.

What Davis had in mind was a new type of community created by culling the best aspects of towns of the past. To find out what those were, Davis and his wife spent two years driving around Florida studying towns, their architecture and the qualities that gave them character. He and his team of architects then compiled the features that were to become the basis for this model town. Among these were white picket fences of varying designs around each home, screened porches with large overhangs, galvanized metal roofs, dirt footpaths and native landscaping.

What started as a couple of cottages built for about $65,000 each now encompasses 325 homes with prices that start at $280,000 and go upwards of $3 million. There are a dozen restaurants, an amphitheater for community events and a town center to which people walk for shopping and socializing. Across the highway is a large expanse of sugar-sand beach upon which the Gulf of Mexico laps gently.

Begun in 1982, Seaside is a teenager, both chronologically and in terms of maturity. Virtually all the empty lots have been sold and most have been built upon. Besides restaurants, there are shops, a gourmet supermarket, a bank, a post office, a fitness club and a small charter school. Yet to come are a chapel, a full complement of medical services and a significant number of full-time residents. Right now, about 10 percent of the homeowners occupy their cottages year-round, and another handful is in residence about half the year. Most homeowners spend a few weeks there annually and rent their homes to beach-loving vacationers the rest of the time.

Carroll and Felton Temple consider Seaside their primary residence, although they spend half the year in Charlotte, NC. Carroll, 67, is a retired medicinal chemist who worked for the Southern Research Institute in Birmingham, AL. Felton, 66, is a medical transcriptionist who still works when she chooses.

During the 43 years in which they lived in Birmingham and raised a family, the Temples took many trips to Florida's Panhandle. It was during one of those trips in 1983 that they happened upon Seaside. Even then the fledgling community caught their eye. "There were three or four cottages here," Felton recalls. "I screamed for my husband to stop. I tried to get my husband interested in building a house, but he wouldn't do it."

Instead, they spent at least one vacation a year at Seaside, renting cottages owned by others. After eight years, Carroll came around. When they couldn't find an existing house to suit them, they built the four-bedroom cottage they

dubbed Blue Heaven. The name comes from the University of North Carolina at Chapel Hill, where Carroll did his graduate work. The school's colors are blue and white and are referred to as Blue Heaven.

Blue also happens to be Felton's favorite color. Not surprisingly, the cottage is painted blue outside and "has a blue theme running more or less inside," Felton says. "One bedroom is blue with peach, another is blue with yellow, and so on."

While the couple's home is larger than many of the so-called cottages at Seaside, its whimsical name and decor are typical of the community's ambiance. Each cottage has a name neatly posted on the white picket fence or near the door, along with the homeowners' names, including those of their children and sometimes pets as well. The cottages have names such as Salad Days, Dreamweaver, Hakuna Matata, Freckles, Plum Lazy, Sunkissed and Ooh-La-La.

Felton says the couple didn't look anywhere else when they decided to build a second home. "We never considered any other place but Seaside. The Gulf is so beautiful. I liked the concept of little Victorian houses and cobblestone streets. You can't describe how pretty it is to anybody. They have to see it for themselves," says Felton, who notes that they put their cottage into the Seaside rental program during the summer, when it's too hot there for their tastes, and head north to Charlotte.

Charles and Sarah Modica discovered Seaside in much the same way as the Temples. In 1983, when they were vacationing at Panama City Beach, they drove out to see Seagrove Beach, just down the road from Seaside. From the road, they "saw a man sitting on the porch of a red house with his two dogs on his lap," Charles recalls. "That was Robert Davis and he was talking about what the city would look like."

At the time, Seaside consisted of two cottages on an unpaved street. "I said,

'Sarah, this man is crazy. Let's go,'" says Charles, who also thought the asking price of $65,000 for a house was on the high side back then. But his wife had other ideas, and the Modicas bought a lot and built the home they still occupy on Tupelo Street. Although it was to be a summer home, a respite from their grocery business in Alabama, Davis encouraged them to start an ice cream and sandwich shop on the beach. Sarah stayed and ran it while Charles continued to operate their grocery store in Alabama.

Seaside continued to grow and 10 years ago, Davis persuaded the Modicas to open a gourmet grocery store there. Charles, who was 61 at the time, objected that he was too old to start a new business, but Davis persisted. So the Modicas traveled around to see gourmet establishments in New Orleans and elsewhere, then opened their store, Modica Market, which is stocked floor-to-ceiling with everything from basics like toilet paper and onions to high-end wines, gourmet breads, cheeses and fresh seafood. Their son, Charles Jr.,

is now part of the business as well.

Although Charles Sr., now 71, and his 67-year-old wife had visions of retiring at Seaside, he can't foresee that day coming. The business, open seven days a week, is booming. He walks to work and enjoys his customers, including the children whose parents set up accounts at the store so the kids can go in and buy what they want on their own. "It's a close community," Charles says. "They take care of one another. It's like living in paradise."

While Seaside can't yet be considered a

Seaside, FL

Population: During summer, the population averages 1,500. During winter, it ranges from 300 to 500.

Location: On Florida's northwest Gulf Coast between Panama City and Destin, 140 miles west of Tallahassee and 300 miles southwest of Atlanta.

Climate:

	High	Low
January	61	42
July	89	74

Average relative humidity: 49%

Rainfall: 60 inches.

Cost of living: Well above average (specific index not available).

Median housing cost: $1 million

Sales tax: 6%

Sales tax exemptions: Food, some services and medicine.

State income tax: None.

Intangibles tax: Assessed on stocks, bonds and other assets. Tax rate is $1 per $1,000 in assets. The first $20,000 in assets is exempt for individuals. For couples filing jointly, the first $40,000 is exempt. Those who owe less than $60 need not pay.

Estate tax: None, except the state's "pick-up" portion of the federal tax, applicable to taxable estates of more

than $1 million.

Property tax: $13.9174 per $1,000 in Seaside, with homes assessed at 85% of market value. The annual tax on a $1 million home, with exemption noted below, is about $11,482.

Homestead exemption: $25,000 off the assessed value of a permanent, primary residence.

Religion: There is a small nondenominational chapel in Seaside. In neighboring cities, houses of worship include Episcopal, Lutheran, Presbyterian, Roman Catholic, United Methodist, Unity, Jewish and interdenominational.

Education: The Seaside Institute is a nonprofit organization devoted to expanding the concept of town planning and living. It sponsors intellectual and cultural events throughout the year. The Seaside Neighborhood School is a charter school offering classes for about 90 students in grades 6 through 8.

Transportation: The self-contained community encourages foot and bicycle traffic only. The airport shuttle provides service to the Bay County Airport/Fanin Field in Panama City, 35 miles east of Seaside; Okaloosa County Airport in Fort Walton Beach, 45 miles west of Seaside; Pensacola Airport, 80 miles west of Seaside; and Tallahassee Airport, 140 miles east of Seaside. US Airways and Atlantic Southwest Airlines/Delta serve all four airports; Northwest Airlink serves Bay County, while Northwest flies into Okaloosa and Pensacola. American and Continental also serve Pensacola.

Health: Seaside's health-care facility has a resident physician and visiting specialists. Nearby are the Bay Medical Center and the Emerald Shores Medical Center. The closest hospital is in Panama City, about a 30-minute drive.

Housing options: Structures range from one-bedroom penthouses, which sell for $280,000 to $500,000, to four-bedroom cottages that cost upward of $3 million.

Visitor lodging: The Seaside Cottage Rental Agency, (800) 277-8696 or www.seasidefl.com, serves as the agent for more than 270 privately owned rental cottages. Rental options range from one-bedroom cottages that sleep two or four to a six-bedroom house that sleeps 15. Rentals are least expensive in winter, rising in spring and fall and highest in summer. Many cottages must be rented for a minimum of three days. The three-night rate for a one-bedroom cottage is $448-$715 in winter, $553-$925 in the summer. Beachfront Cottages offer couples a view of the Gulf starting at $333 per night. Beachside Cottages also have a Gulf view, accommodate small families and rent from $250 a night. The Seaside Motor Court offers old-fashioned motel accommodations with a nostalgic 1950s decor. Rooms rent for $142 a night. Josephine's French Country Inn, (800) 848-1840 or (850) 231-1939, offers bed-and-breakfast accommodations for $200-$250.

Information: Seaside Community Realty Inc., P.O. Box 4730, Seaside, FL 32459, (888) SEASIDE or www.seasidefl.com.

retirement town, it has the potential to become one. Most Seaside homebuyers now are well-heeled baby boomers with families who are looking for an investment or ensuring themselves a retirement place in the sun in a few years.

"If you look at fairly recent research on what people want out of a retirement community, what the plurality want is a small town with urban amenities," says developer Robert Davis. "College towns fit that bill rather well, and so does Seaside, with the added benefit of having a beach and warm weather, unlike Hanover (NH) and Amherst (MA)."

Davis, whose iconoclastic approach to development initially was ridiculed, only to later win high praise and many awards, is blunt about his dislike for the growing trend of adult-only housing developments spreading across Florida and other retirement states. "What people are looking for, I think, at least in this generation of preretirees, is a place very unlike the summer camps for the elderly," he says. "These concentrations of one age group, I think it's unhealthy for us as a culture and unhealthy for people who are so concentrated."

Davis, who is 55 and owns a home in Seaside, says, "I don't know many of my friends who picture themselves going off to live with our own age group. I would find it completely deadly. Yet I know a lot of people go to these places even if they don't want to segregate by age because the suburban environment where we have spent most of our lives is so completely unsupportive of people without driver's licenses.

"Seaside represents a place where people without driver's licenses can do just fine," he says. "They can walk to most of the things they need on a daily basis, and there's a van that will run errands for them, take them to the airport — basically, there's no reason that they need a driver's license to live comfortably."

Comfortable living without a car is what Seaside is all about. Even those who can drive are encouraged to park their cars at their cottages and leave them there for the duration of their stay. As a result, pedestrians, bicyclists and skaters have the streets to themselves.

The heart of the community is Central Square, where much of the commercial element is clustered. There's the MM Fitness Studio, an attorney's office, clothing stores, art galleries, a real estate broker, a wine bar and the Seaside Institute, a nonprofit organization that offers educational and cultural programs. Modica Market is nearby.

An outdoor amphitheater provides a communal gathering spot for a variety of activities, such as concerts, a summer film series and storytelling. There are wine festivals twice a year, architectural tours, a conference for writers and other cultural events.

Across the highway are more shops and eateries. PER-SPI-CAS-ITY, an open-air market like those found in Italy, features stalls with all sorts of clothing and accessories. There's also Piazza Nancy Drew, an open area with shops on which the fanciful paintings of well-known designer Nancy Drew create festive fronts. Bud & Alley's bistro and rooftop bar overlook the Gulf and feature rustic coastal cuisine such as crab cakes and seafood stew.

Among Seaside's most distinctive features are the nine beach pavilions that frame the entrances to the beach, providing access over the high dunes as well as bathroom facilities and yet another opportunity for architecture to shine. The pavilions, each designed by a different architect, also are popular gathering spots for watching the sun set. All lead to a smooth beach virtually devoid of shells. Big blue beach umbrellas shading lounge chairs line up like so many sandpipers facing the water. Besides the beach, amenities include three swimming pools, six tennis courts and a croquet lawn.

The town is divvied up into various smaller neighborhoods, such as Ruskin Place Artist Colony, where artists can create and sell their works on the ground floor, while townhomes with a New Orleans flavor occupy the upper floors. And although it was the town's beauty and location that prompted the Temples to build there, there's no disputing that it was a good investment. "Our house has more than doubled in value since we built it — almost tripled," Felton says.

Jacky Barker, real estate broker for Seaside, says property values are climbing fast. "We've averaged 10 percent appreciation a year, but in the last couple of years it's run between 12 and 15 percent," she says.

When Robert Davis' grandfather, Birmingham department store owner J.S. Smolian, bought the remote 80-acre property in 1946, his family considered his $100-an-acre investment foolish. Davis inherited the land in 1978, and in the early 1980s, the most expensive lots ran about $20,000. "Those lots today would probably sell for $220,000 to $250,000," Barker says.

One-bedroom penthouses sell for $255,000 to $358,000, and townhouses run from $695,000 to $1.6 million. Cottages start at about $542,000 for a one-bedroom house with room to add on and rise to about $2 million for a four-bedroom dwelling that overlooks the water. Most cottages have three bedrooms and run $700,000 to $850,000, says Barker.

"People buy here because there is a sense of community," Barker says. "A lot of the folks have been renting here and their families just love it. They get to know other families. The children can roam the streets here without the parents having to worry about it."

When they do put their properties up for sale, there's very little flexibility in the price. "Some have more than one property," Barker says. "Their attitude is, 'If I'm going to sell it, this is what the price is going to be.'"

While they may be trailblazers, the Temples find Seaside almost ideal for retirement living. The only drawbacks, Felton says, are that "it's a little hot in the summer and they don't have very extensive medical facilities yet."

The Temples find plenty to keep themselves occupied, even in the winter when there are only about 300 people in residence. Felton likes to read and do needlepoint. Carroll likes to paint. They both like to take long walks around the town and along the beach.

"We also like to try out the different restaurants," Felton says. "The facilities for eating seafood around here are wonderful." To others considering retiring in Seaside, she only has one piece of advice: "Just do it."●

Sequim, Washington

Retirees find homes with views on Washington's Olympic Peninsula

By Richard L. Fox

The 8,000-foot peaks of the Olympic Mountains and the picturesque Strait of Juan de Fuca captivate many first-time visitors to Sequim. Unlike some better-known towns in this part of Washington's Olympic Peninsula, Sequim (pronounced "Skwim") is defined not so much by man-made structures as by its location, topography and congenial residents.

At the northern edge of the peninsula, the town of Sequim is clean and open, unpretentious and uncluttered. No tall buildings mar its skyline. It does not have a defined downtown; rather, shops, restaurants and motels are strung along a two-mile stretch of U.S. Highway 101 (called Washington Street in town), interspersed with art galleries, antique stores and gift shops. Among the shoppers and browsers are tourists who discover that Sequim's main street is the only available route to destinations farther out on the peninsula — a boon for shopkeepers but a matter of some concern for local drivers during peak season.

Byron and Barbara Nelson moved to Sequim in 1995 from Covina, CA, their home for 22 years. Going from the urban environment of Southern California to the peaceful surroundings of Sequim was a big change, according to Byron, a former police chief in Azusa, CA. "I don't hear sirens. I don't hear traffic noise. I don't see smog. I don't hear gunshots. Your home is safe. You can walk downtown any time of day or night without fear," he says.

Barbara, 56, was taken by the "fresh air, outstanding scenery, a slower pace, serenity and friendly people." For the Nelsons, the area's natural beauty is without parallel. "After retirement we took a six-week, 10,000-mile camping tour of the United States. New England (and) the East

Coast were beautiful in the fall, (but) when it was over, we agreed there was not a prettier place in the United States than where we were going to live," says Byron, 57.

The growing community boasts an active cadre of volunteers. The Retired Senior Volunteer Program advertises for grade-school tutors, aides for the courthouse information desk, senior center assistants and naturalists for the Dungeness Spit, the world's largest natural sand hook. Volunteers also staff the New Dungeness Lighthouse, a historic structure that has guided ships through the Strait of Juan de Fuca since 1857.

More than 160 organizations enlist the help of retirees such as Bryce and Gail Fish, both 56, who moved to Sequim from Madison, WI, in 1990.

Bryce and Gail knew the area before retirement, having lived near Seattle for three years during the 1960s. They visited several times, and after selling their lumber business, moved here permanently.

With longtime friends not far away in Bellevue, the Fishes settled quickly into their new community. Bryce serves on the boards of several clubs and service organizations, including the Citizens Advisory Committee for Schools and the Boys and Girls Club. Gail, a retired registered nurse, is a volunteer and well-loved fixture at the visitor center.

Most Sequim residents travel to Seattle for big-city shopping, dining and entertainment. Although the trip takes two to three hours, getting there can be infinitely more rewarding than an ordinary excursion to the mall. The quickest, most popular route starts with a slow-paced drive through small villages and thick virgin forests to Bainbridge Island, followed by a 30-minute ferry ride to Seattle.

The most scenic way to return home is to drive south to Olympia on Inter-

state 5, then north along Hwy. 101 between Olympic National Forest (keeping watch for deer and elk) and the Hood Canal (where you might spot a U.S. Trident submarine or aircraft carrier) and finally past Sequim Bay (where gray whales sometimes stray off-course during their Pacific coast migration).

Five airports offer daily flights out of the north Olympic Peninsula; those at Port Angeles and Port Townsend connect with Seattle-Tacoma International Airport (SeaTac) and several Canadian destinations, including Victoria and Vancouver in British Columbia.

"We enjoy going into Seattle," says Agnes Bell, 69, who moved with her husband, Bob, from Hamburg, NJ, in 1989. Before their move, "going into town" meant going into New York City. "We didn't want to do that anymore," says Bob, 70.

Bob and Agnes exchanged the hill country of western New Jersey for the hilly Sequim prairie and found that much of the environment looked comfortingly familiar. "One of our sons came out to visit us after we moved and said, 'I know why you're here. You're still living in Sussex County, NJ'," jokes Bob, a former postmaster.

"New Jersey is the home of my birth," adds Agnes, a retired executive secretary. "I lived there most of my life, but I must say I feel just as much at home here as I ever did there.

"I appreciate the weather here more because the highs and lows aren't as extreme," she continues. "I don't miss the ice and snow at all. I don't miss the mosquitoes, or the hot, hot summers with high humidity. We don't have that here."

Sequim's dry, sunny weather is an appreciated anomaly in the region. Thanks to the Olympic Mountains, which block rain clouds as they pass over the peninsula, Sequim tallies considerably more sunshine and less rain than towns just a few miles away. While Sequim averages 16 inches of rain a year, neighboring Port Angeles counts up to 25 inches, Seattle records around 30 inches, and the rain forests 60 miles west are deluged with more than 200 inches.

The low annual rainfall can be a two-edged sword — nice and dry for golfing, hiking and horseback-riding, but woefully short for meeting water supply and agricultural needs.

In 1895, the residents of Sequim and surrounding Dungeness Valley built flumes and irrigation ditches to bring water from the Dungeness River to the parched prairie surrounding it. Today more than 100 miles of irrigation ditches water the valley's farms and pastures, bringing agricultural prosperity (and a large herd of elk) to the area. The Sequim Irrigation Festi-val, which recently marked its 105th anniversary, is the town's biggest celebration and Washington's oldest continuing festival.

Housing options are plentiful, in locales from the shores of the Strait of Juan de Fuca to the southern hills. Choices include manufactured-home parks, established single-family neighborhoods, townhomes and condominiums, three-acre estates and five-acre minifarms.

Prices range from $39,500 for a double-wide manufactured home to $450,000 for a home on a large lot with a great view of the mountains or the strait. A two-bedroom condo may go for $66,500, a three-bedroom townhouse for $189,500, and a large custom home on a golf course for $225,000.

One-acre lots with views of the mountains or water start at more than $20,000. Water-view lots at Diamond Point by the bay are priced from $34,900 to $59,500, and lots on the strait start at $79,000.

At Bell Hill, just south of Sequim, lots start at $50,000. It's a popular place for retirees to settle, offering views of the strait with its parading tall ships, military and commercial vessels and occasionally the distant lights of Victoria twinkling across the water. Most of the time Bell Hill affords a bird's-eye view of downtown Sequim, surrounding residential neighborhoods, golf courses, parks, marinas and the waterfront Dungeness Recreation Area and Dungeness Spit.

Some residents warn that Bell Hill often is cloaked in clouds during winter months when dense fog settles in the higher elevations. As the day heats up, the clouds usually dissipate, but

Sequim, WA

Population: 4,334 in Sequim, 23,000 in Dungeness Valley.

Location: In western Washington state, nestled between the Olympic Mountains and the Strait of Juan de Fuca on the north coast of the Olympic Peninsula. Elevation is 180 feet.

Climate:

	High	Low
January	46	32
July	71	52

Average relative humidity: 77%

Rain: 16 inches.

The area boasts 300 sunny days a year and moderate temperatures.

Cost of living: Above average (specific index not available).

Average housing cost: $182,000

Sales tax: 8.2%

Sales tax exemptions: Prescription drugs, groceries and medical services.

State income tax: None.

Intangibles tax: None.

Estate tax: None, except the state's "pick-up" portion of the federal tax, applicable to taxable estates of more than $1 million.

Property tax: In Sequim, $10.21 per $1,000 of assessed value, with homes assessed at 100% of market value. Tax on a $182,000 home in Sequim is $1,858.

Homestead exemption: Homeowners age 61 or older, with a gross household income of $30,000 or less, are eligible for certain property tax exemptions.

Religion: Twenty-one Protestant and two Catholic churches serve the Sequim-Dungeness Valley area.

Education: Peninsula College in Port Angeles is part of the state community college system. It offers associate degrees, Elderhostel, continuing education and public service programs. Senior citizens can choose from a variety of courses at reduced fees.

Transportation: Clallam County Transit Authority offers bus service between Olympic Peninsula towns. Ferry service provides access to Victoria, Whidbey Island, the San Juan Islands and Seattle. Fairchild Airport in Port Angeles (25 miles) and Jefferson County International Airport in Port Townsend (22 miles) provide daily connections with SeaTac International Airport south of Seattle.

Health: Olympic Medical Center, 17 miles west in Port Angeles, is a 126-bed, full-service facility with 24-hour emergency service. Seventy-seven physicians practice 20 medical specialties, with additional specialists from Seattle making regular local office visits.

Housing options: A wide variety of housing is available. Double-wide manufactured homes in adults-only parks are listed for $39,500-$100,000. One- and two-bedroom condos with clubhouse privileges are $99,000-$240,000. New three-bedroom townhomes with two-car garages on a golf course are priced at $189,500. Three-bedroom, two-bath custom homes in new developments start at $175,000. The 3,500-square-foot custom homes in Sunlands Country Club are priced from $225,000 and up. On Bell Hill, three-bedroom, two-bath homes on one or two acres go for upward of $450,000.

Visitor lodging: Sequim Bay Lodge, $63-$149, (360) 683-0691. Ramada Limited Sequim, $44-$99, (800) 683-1775.

Information: Sequim-Dungeness Valley Chamber of Commerce, P.O. Box 907, Sequim, WA 98382, (360) 683-6197 or www.cityofsequim.com.

some newcomers have been known to move after one winter on Bell Hill.

Byron and Barbara Nelson built their home in Happy Valley, a rural area on the back side of Bell Hill that boasts views of the strait, valley, mountains and Vancouver Island. "At night you can see the lights of ships on the strait from our house," says Barbara. With a stable and pasture on five acres of land, the Nelsons have plenty of room to accommodate their horses and indulge their favorite recreational activity — riding.

Happy Valley provided the first proof that man hunted the mastodon in North America 12,000 to 14,000 years ago. Artifacts and fossils from the area are on display at the Museum and Arts Center, lending credence to theories that hunters chased the animals across land bridges over the Bering Strait.

Bob and Agnes Bell found a house in the early stages of construction in the Sunlands Country Club and Golf Course development and bought it before completion. "I love the view, the snow on top of the mountains. Every time I go out, I see a different view," says Agnes. "It's never the same."

Gail and Bryce Fish bought what Bryce calls a "country rambler in need of some TLC, with 20 acres of land." Located four miles west of Sequim between Highway 101 and the water, the home has an unobstructed view of the Olympic Mountains.

Bryce and Gail love hiking in the Olympic Mountains and sailing the waters of Sequim Bay and the strait, the latter a carry-over from their days in Wisconsin when they sailed the Great Lakes. There is snow skiing within a four-hour drive.

With some 300 sunny days and temperatures rarely above the low 80s, being outdoors is a way of life for most residents. Boating, bicycling, fishing and golfing are among the traditionally popular activities, but the uniqueness of Dungeness Spit makes it a popular site for hiking, bird-watching, beachcombing and crabbing. The bay formed by the spit is famous as the home of the Dungeness crab.

There are trails for horseback riding in parts of the Dungeness National Wildlife Refuge and Dungeness Spit. The spit is about five miles long and accessible only by foot; at low tide, hardy hikers like to make the 10-mile round-trip walk to New Dungeness Lighthouse at the end of the spit.

Agnes Bell is one of the inveterate walkers seen in the area on a regular basis. "It's only a mile from our house to the strait, and I walk it every day."

Agnes also is a member of MEOW (Machine Embroiderers of Oregon and Washington) and spends time with the group traveling and sewing. She also describes herself as a cyberspace granny. "I e-mail my grandchildren regularly," she says.

The nearest hospital is 126-bed Olympic Memorial, 17 miles west in Port Angeles. Sequim Medical Plaza has a medical staff practicing 22 specialties as well as facilities for surgery, radiology, laboratory technology, physical therapy and nutrition counseling.

Agnes credits the area's medical care as partly influencing their decision to move to Sequim. "We knew that as we got older we would need good medical attention," she says. "The very best doctors in Seattle come over to the medical center and see patients on a regular basis."

Bob goes to cardiac rehabilitation three times a week, and both he and Agnes use the facilities at the Sequim Aquatic Recreation Center to stay fit.

Bryce Fish has some advice for anyone considering a retirement move to Sequim. "You need to be financially secure since there aren't many jobs here to supplement income. You need to be able to entertain yourself. This is a natural environment that doesn't offer a lot of planned activities."

Says Gail Fish, "If you're planning on eating every meal out, don't come. There are some good restaurants, but not many." Shopping facilities also are modest by Madison standards, though Gail feels they're adequate.

"There are times when you need something that's not available, and you have to go to a larger city to find it," says Byron Nelson.

Bob Bell, mindful of the town's escalating growth rate, says with a mirthful smile, "Everyone should have as nice a retirement as we're having. But do it somewhere else!"●

Sierra Vista, Arizona

Arizona town has military ties and an affinity with nature

By Judy Wade

Sierra Vista defies the image of most Southern Arizona towns, owing its existence neither to mining nor cattle ranching. Rather, it grew up around the U.S. Army's Fort Huachuca, established in 1877 as a cavalry post to safeguard settlers.

Sierra Vista developed initially as a place to live for those supplying support services to the Army. Now there are about 11,700 military and civilian employees at the fort, with another 11,200 military family members living in town. Military retirees are attracted to Sierra Vista because of base privileges and medical facilities there.

The city's low cost of living and hometown personality have made Sierra Vista popular with other retirees as well. Its senior population increased by more than 200 percent during the last decade, and about a quarter of the city's residents consider themselves retired.

Chamber of commerce marketing efforts picture a happy couple with salt-and-pepper hair that have escaped to "the nicest little town under the sun." Yet big-city shopping and culture is readily accessible in Tucson, 70 miles to the northwest.

For Frank and Sally Solano, 65 and 68 respectively, moving to Sierra Vista was a homecoming of sorts. They retired to Sierra Vista from Cleveland, where Frank worked with the National Aeronautics and Space Administration and Sally was a homemaker. "Frank, who went to high school in nearby Douglas, AZ, worked as a student at Fort Huachuca in 1959," says Sally. "Sierra Vista wasn't even a town then. But he remembered the clean air, pristine atmosphere and lovely four-season climate. When we came back, we were shocked to see this little town here."

The Solanos live in an area of custom homes on large, open lots where deer, antelope, coyotes and quail roam freely. Sally says wild turkeys sometimes come in from the canyons south of town. "We can see mountain peaks in Mexico from here. In the Huachucas, we can see snow on Miller Peak, which is about 9,600 feet high, until Mother's Day," she says.

Situated on the eastern slope of the Huachuca Mountains overlooking the San Pedro River Valley, Sierra Vista's name means "mountain view" in Spanish. It is surrounded by the Mule, Dragoon and Whetstone mountains. Reliably good weather averages 75 degrees in summer and 50 degrees in winter.

The town itself, population 37,775, is low-key but with a sophistication created by relatively high income and educational levels among its residents.

The Sierra Vista Symphony performs regularly, and an annual concert series features nationally known artists. A Thursday evening summer series at Veterans Memorial Park includes blues, jazz, pop and rock ensembles.

More than 75 restaurants create an eclectic dining-out scene. Residents have kiddingly dubbed Fry Boulevard, the town's main street, "French Fry Boulevard" because of the number of fast-food outlets strung along its length. But they are complemented by such restaurants as Ricardo's, which serves Mexican food, and the Mesquite Tree, with patio views of the Huachucas. Fine dining is offered at The Grille at Pueblo del Sol Country Club, where gourmet fare is presented in the evening and breakfast and lunch features inventive, well-priced menus.

Many shopping needs are met at the 400,000-square-foot Mall at Sierra Vista, which is anchored by Dillard's, Sears and a 10-screen cinema. Major retailers such as J.C. Penney, Kmart, Wal-Mart and Target are located elsewhere in the city.

Jan and Bob Cole, 56 and 68 respectively, moved from Phoenix where Bob owned a business-forms company. "We hardly feel retired because we volunteer with the Red Cross doing disaster relief all over the state and also with the chamber of commerce," says Jan. "It really keeps us busy."

Originally they bought property in Sedona, north of Phoenix, but discovered that the traffic and fast-paced lifestyle weren't what they wanted. "Everyone thinks about going north. They don't realize we're at more than 4,000 feet here, which creates a wonderful four-season climate," says Bob. Both say they like Sierra Vista's open spaces, mountain views and especially the supportive small-town ambiance.

Winterhaven is Sierra Vista's only master-planned, age-restricted (55 plus) community of single-family homes. Located within Country Club Estates, an existing golf-course community, Winterhaven has single-story homes bordering the mature, 25-year-old course and along winding streets. An RV park with hookups and storage will be completed at the edge of the property early this year.

Bob Strain, 64, a widower, lived in Sierra Vista for 10 years before he chose a Winterhaven home. "I trusted the alliance of the developers, Castle & Cooke, who are working with KE&G Homes, a local builder. And the opportunities for appreciation look good," he says. He chose an 1,831-square-foot floor plan with 10-foot ceilings, walk-in closets, two bedrooms and a den. Other plans with two to four bedrooms also are offered.

Even though he doesn't play golf, proximity to a course helped influence Strain. "It's kind of like being in the paratroops. You don't really like to jump out of airplanes but you like to hang out with people who do," he smiles. "And the golf community is a part of the ambiance that makes quality of life that much nicer."

Keith and Linda Howver, ages 63 and 50, lived in Mesa, AZ, before building their cul-de-sac home in Winterhaven. "We wanted to move someplace cooler, and we wanted more of a small town. At our age we like being in a retirement area, yet across the road there are all different ages," says Linda.

"Our lot has mountain views that will never be blocked," she says. The Howvers chose a floor plan and customized it, adding a fireplace to the master bedroom and bath, opting for ceramic tile rather than carpeting throughout.

The market for resale homes is booming, according to Jeanne Milczarek, a real-estate agent with Coldwell Banker. "Our average single-family-home listing is about $102,000," she says. "Condos run the gamut from $42,000 to well over $100,000, with manufactured homes and lots, depending on location, averaging $75,000 to $80,000."

Mack McCabe, a real-estate agent with Sierra Vista Realty, says that for the past 18 months the local multiple listing service reports a total of 1,236 sales of condominiums and single-family and manufactured homes with $90,150 the median sales price and $98,157 the average. "By far the greatest number are single-family homes. Our market is definitely in a good place right now, with prices sliding upward," he says.

But retiree Bobbie Snyder, 70, who moved to Sierra Vista with husband Joseph in 1983, is not so sure she likes the growth pattern that she sees. "In the 14 years we've lived here, our taxes have more than doubled, she says, adding that their original property taxes were only about $400 per year.

The new Buena High School is the home of the Buena Performing Arts Center, the venue for community presentations that attract regional audiences. Hot tickets have included the Count Basie Orchestra, the Kingston Trio, Ink Spots and the Lettermen. Other series feature classical performers. The center has wheelchair access for guests and facilities for the hearing-impaired.

"Education Row," of which the high

Sierra Vista, AZ

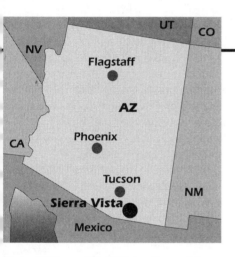

Population: 37,775 in Sierra Vista, 119,281 in Cochise County.

Location: In southeast Arizona, 70 miles southeast of Tucson among the Dragoon, Mule and Whetstone mountains at an elevation of 4,623 feet.

Climate:

	High	Low
January	58	34
July	89	66

Average relative humidity: 32%
Rain: 14.6 inches.
More than half of Sierra Vista's rain falls in July and August when monsoon conditions are right. Dustings of snow in December and January rarely last longer than half a day.

Cost of living: 91.2, based on national average of 100.

Housing cost: $90,150 median, $98,157 average.

Sales tax: 7.5%

Sales tax exemptions: None.

State income tax: For married couples filing jointly, graduated from 2.87% of taxable income up to $20,000 to 5.04% minus $2,276 on amounts over $300,000. For single filers, graduated from 2.87% of taxable income up to $10,000 to 5.04% minus $1,138 on amounts over $150,000.

Income tax exemptions: Social Security benefits and up to $2,500 on federal, state and local government pensions are exempt.

Intangibles tax: None.

Estate tax: None, except the state's "pick-up" portion of the federal tax, applicable to taxable estates above $1 million.

Property tax: $117 per $1,000 of assessed value, with homes assessed at 10% of market value. Annual taxes on a $100,000 home are about $1,170.

Homestead exemption: None.

Religion: More than 30 churches and places of worship represent about 20 denominations.

Education: College-level courses are offered at the University of Arizona's Sierra Vista campus. Cochise Community College, Chapman College and Golden Gate University offer courses in a variety of fields.

Transportation: Sierra Vista Public Transit System has a 50-cent senior fare anywhere in the city. Scheduled bus service goes to Tucson, and America West Express, operated by Mesa Airlines, flies to Phoenix for connections to world destinations.

Health: Recently updated Sierra Vista Regional Health Center has 24-hour emergency care and a complete range of facilities. Hacienda Rehabilitation and Care Center offers physical, occupational, speech and respiratory therapy as well as Alzheimer's care. Fort Huachuca also has a hospital.

Housing options: Winterhaven, (800) 837-6841, a Castle & Cooke development, is the city's only master-planned, age-restricted, active-adult community. Homes range from $103,990 to $240,000 including lot. Custom homes begin at $159,990 not including lot. Resale manufactured homes at **Sierra Vista Mobile Home Village**, (520) 459-1690, are $42,000-$75,000 with a $240-$287 per month assessment that includes garbage pickup, water, cable television and recreation center facilities.

Visitor lodging: Best Western Mission Inn, $64, double occupancy, with senior discount, (800) 528-1234. Ramsey Canyon Inn, $121-$145, (520) 378-3010. For prospective buyers, Winterhaven offers three days and two nights in an on-site home for $166, double occupancy, (800) 837-6841.

Information: Sierra Vista Chamber of Commerce, 21 E. Wilcox Drive, Sierra Vista, AZ 85635, (800) 288-3861, (520) 458-6940 or www.sierravistachamber.org.

school is a part, also includes a branch of the University of Arizona where seniors can take courses at no charge on a space-available basis. Cochise College offers two-year degree programs. Elderhostel opportunities include birding, hiking and bicycling trips.

The Oscar Yrun Community Center has an extensive senior program that includes noon lunch for a nominal fee. Monthly Dine-A-Nites allow older residents to try a variety of local restaurants. Recent bus outings have included Tucson's Gaslight Theater, an excursion on the San Pedro train through the National Riparian Conservation Area, a four-day trip to Mexico and a weeklong Branson, MO, sojourn. A new 31,000-square-foot public library opened next to City Hall in spring of 1999.

Sally Solano particularly likes Sierra Vista's proximity to Ramsey Canyon, a Nature Conservancy preserve at the hub of one of the country's finest birding areas. The 300-acre arroyo is a unique biological crossroads where more than a dozen species of hummingbirds gather from spring until early autumn.

The annual four-day Southwest Wings Birding Festival held in August attracts birders from all over the world and includes field trips, workshops, history and archaeology tours and other programs. It is so popular that field trips fill up two months in advance and local hotels are completely booked.

The town's age diversity is a valued community asset, according to chamber of commerce representatives, who say that some retirees are practically "professional volunteers." The community relies heavily on the senior population to work with elementary-school children in reading and enrichment programs and with local youth clubs. A mediation and arbitration group sponsored by the county superior court includes close to 100 certified mediators and arbitrators, many of whom are retirees.

Former Iowa resident Roberta Dillig, 79, volunteers as the choreographer for the Rickety Rockettes, a dance group made up of women ages 58 to 86 who perform locally and in nearby cities. She recently competed in the Miss Senior Arizona Pageant where she exhibited her tap-dancing talent. "I was second runner-up. The two who beat me were only 62," she laughs.

The Sierra Vista Regional Health Center has been renovated, adding new equipment and services that include a helicopter landing pad, a 51-bed medical/surgical department, intensive care and telemetry unit and 24-hour emergency department. A new ambulatory surgery center was recently completed. Many seniors volunteer with the hospital auxiliary. A second hospital is located at Fort Huachuca.

City government, a manager/mayor system with six council members, keeps a close eye on situations affecting this high desert community, such as the water supply, which is an ongoing issue. Sierra Vista sits on its own aquifer that is recharged twice a year, once by snow melt and once by a summer monsoon during which rainfall can total almost 14 inches. Some claim the aquifer has remained at approximately the same level over the last century, a contention vehemently denied by others.

"There is plenty of water for the city's growth," says Sierra Vista Herald managing editor John Moeur, "as long as it is a maintained and reasonable growth. What effect that will have on the San Pedro River, which is a key riparian habitat, is under debate, and no one has a lot of great answers."

The Herald, a daily newspaper, is an excellent source of information regarding annexations, city council proceedings, Fort Huachuca information and club meetings that include Rotary, Kiwanis, Veterans of Foreign Wars, Elks and bridge and chess clubs.

A projected population of 50,000 may be as big as Sierra Vista ever gets, simply because it is bordered on two sides by Fort Huachuca, on another side by the San Pedro Riparian Area preserve, and on another by the Huachuca Mountains. There isn't a lot of space in which to expand.

And many residents like it that way.●

Siesta Key, Florida

It's a slow, casual lifestyle on this Florida Gulf Coast island

By Karen Feldman

If ever there were a town whose name perfectly suited its nature, it's Siesta Key. Laid-back, casual and short on pretension, the barrier island community prides itself on its soothing pace.

Its beach extends the entire 8-mile length of the island, much of it a broad expanse of what's been voted the finest, whitest sand in the world. It, too, beckons visitors to settle in and chill out.

The island just southwest of the city of Sarasota is home to 12,000 residents year-round and twice that many in the winter. They are joined by some 350,000 tourists a year.

It's not uncommon for visitors to become residents.

"A lot of people stay for the winter season and buy a place before they leave," says Jean Kelly, a real estate associate with RE/MAX on the key and a Siesta Key resident for 43 years.

Diane Spencer, former executive director of the Siesta Key Chamber of Commerce, says that while some area communities tend toward formality, "Siesta Key is laid-back. The people are more free-spirited. We have a lot of independent thinkers, a lot of artists and musicians. These are people who have lived elsewhere, suffered the slings and arrows of life and ended up here."

For some, Siesta Key is their choice after considering a number of possibilities. For others, it's an annual vacation destination that eventually becomes a retirement home.

Bob and June Wood vacationed on Siesta Key for 23 years. Nine years ago, they left Lincoln, MA, and bought a gulf-front condo on the key.

"We had been coming for so long, it was like a second home," says June, 70. "We felt very comfortable here."

They had considered Honolulu and Southern California, but "kind of backed into the choice" of Siesta Key, says Bob,

70, who was with Polaroid. "We decided we couldn't afford to live in California and the distance from our family was too great in Honolulu."

Siesta Key was the only place that Jerry and Kathy Groom considered retiring. Jerry, 65, and Kathy, 60, had been fleeing to the island to escape the brutal Illinois winters for about five years before moving to their Siesta Key condo.

They enjoy the island lifestyle. "It's casual," says Jerry, who was with Levi Strauss. "It has a small-town atmosphere. We have the best of two worlds: Sarasota and Siesta Key."

Groom, recently inducted into the College Football Hall of Fame for his career as a Notre Dame center and linebacker, still works at keeping his 6-foot-4-inch frame in shape. He walks on the beach, swims and regularly exercises Murphy, the couple's 4-year-old Lhasa apso.

They scaled down from a four-bedroom home to a two-bedroom condo. Their sixth-floor unit has a broad view of the Gulf of Mexico and the public beach on the other side of Midnight Pass Road, one of the island's main thoroughfares.

"It's easy to travel out of a condo," says Jerry. "You just shut it up and go."

Don and Jan Metzler searched a 100-mile swath of the Florida Gulf Coast before relocating to Siesta Key from Utica, MI.

They liked Bonita Springs, a waterfront community south of Fort Myers, but opted for Siesta Key "because of the arts and culture," says Jan, 55, a professional artist. "Any day of the week, you can go to a show or art event."

The Metzlers bought a 3,000-square-foot home on a canal in a secluded neighborhood and spent a lot of time renovating it. Canals — some 50 miles of them — meander through the island community and lead to the Intracoastal Waterway, Sarasota Bay

and the Gulf of Mexico.

Waterways and their accompanying beaches may draw people to Siesta Key, but what clinches it for many visitors is the wealth of culture available in Sarasota, just east of Siesta Key.

Circus magnate John Ringling built his own bayfront estate at Sarasota in the mid-1920s and invested heavily in the area. His home, Ca'd'Zan (Venetian dialect for House of John), the Italian Renaissance Ringling Museum of Art, the 18th-century Asolo Theater and a circus gallery are run by the state and are among the city's top tourist attractions.

A bigger Asolo Center for the Performing Arts, a $10 million playhouse, houses an official state theatrical troupe and is also on the 38-acre Ringling estate. It presents a variety of plays throughout the year.

Nearby is the Van Wezel Performing Arts Hall, a lavender scallop-shaped landmark designed by Frank Lloyd Wright, which attracts nationally known artists and local productions with its high-quality acoustics.

The city also has its own ballet company, opera company and symphony. The downtown is chock-full of art galleries, restaurants and boutiques, which draw lots of shoppers during the winter season. So, too, does nearby St. Armands Key, which features a large circle of upscale shops and restaurants.

The Marie Selby Botanical Gardens, on the Sarasota bayfront just east of St. Armands Key, sprawls over 14 acres of lush property. It specializes in ecological preservation, has a world-class collection of orchids and other bromeliads, a museum of botany and arts, lots of plant sales, classes and special events.

Mote Marine Laboratory, just north of St. Armands, has tanks displaying plants and animals native to the bay and gulf, a 135,000-gallon outdoor shark tank and a 30-foot touch tank.

Among the region's best known annual events is the French Film Festival, which has drawn increasing national attention for the number of high-quality French films that make U.S. debuts there.

Siesta Key residents like knowing that culture is just a short drive away, but many also like not having to leave the island for much of anything else.

"You could really stay on the island if you wanted to," says Kathy Groom. "There are filling stations, banks, groceries, most of the places you need."

Most of these are clustered at the heart of the island in the shopping district, a busy center filled with restaurants, boutiques and T-shirt and tourist-ware emporiums.

There are tennis and volleyball courts and an exercise track at the public beach. People rollerblade and bicycle along the island's streets, and it's not unusual to see groups moving through graceful tai chi routines on the beach.

Diane Spencer likes to kayak in the gulf, renting equipment from a local shop. "The dolphins come up right beside me," she says. "I've been out several times and I'm a grandmother.

It's wonderful."

Barrier islands always have been Florida's prime real estate. That's as true in Siesta Key as the rest of the state. While properties cost more than in many mainland communities, many people find them affordable when compared to their previous residences, particularly in Northern states.

Jerry Groom is still kicking himself for not buying the condo next door when he could have snapped it up for $45,000 several years ago. Units in the small complex sell for about five times that now, and there's a waiting list of interested buyers.

Siesta Key, FL

Population: 12,000 year-round, 24,000 in the winter.

Location: A barrier island on the Gulf of Mexico along the southwest Florida coast a few miles southwest of Sarasota.

Climate:	High	Low
January	72	51
July	92	75

Average relative humidity: 70%
Rain: 47 inches.

Subtropical climate is hot and humid May through October, temperate and drier November through April with short-lived freezes possible. Hurricane season is June 1 to Nov. 30; most severe storms usually occur in September and October. Siesta Key is vulnerable to hurricanes, particularly in the Gulf of Mexico, but has not experienced damage recently.

Cost of living: Above average (specific index not available).

Median housing cost: $500,000 for homes; condos about $475,000.

Sales tax: 7%

Sales tax exemptions: Medical servic-

es, prescription drugs, groceries.

State income tax: None.

Intangibles tax: Assessed on stocks, bonds and other assets. Tax rate is $1 per $1,000 in assets. The first $20,000 in assets is exempt for individuals. For couples filing jointly, the first $40,000 is exempt. Those who owe less than $60 need not pay.

Estate tax: None, except the state's "pick-up" portion of the federal tax, applicable to taxable estates above $1 million.

Property tax: Rate is $14.43 per $1,000 of assessed value, with homes assessed at 100% of market value. The yearly tax on a $500,000 home with $25,000 homestead exemption is about $6,854.

Homestead exemption: First $25,000 of assessed value of primary, permanent residence.

Religion: There are Episcopal, Catholic and Presbyterian churches on the island; all major religions and many smaller ones are represented in Sarasota.

Education: The University of South Florida offers those age 60 and older the opportunity to audit classes (no credit, no tests) without charge on a space-available basis.

Transportation: The Siesta Key Trolley runs the length of the island, making stops at many condos and restaurants; it also goes to downtown Sarasota. The Sarasota County Area Transit buses cover a similar route but with fewer stops. Sarasota-Bradenton International Airport is about 20 minutes away.

Health: There are no hospitals on Siesta Key, but next-door-neighbor Sarasota offers extensive medical services. Sarasota Memorial Hospital is a 952-bed, not-for-profit hospital with a full range of medical care. Its SeniorCare program has 16,000 members 50 years and older who receive health education, access to a senior care adviser, assistance completing health claims, discounts and physician referrals. Doctors Hospital, a private facility offering many services, moved into a new 168-bed complex including a medical office near the access route to Siesta Key. The hospital participates in the national Senior Friend program, offering discounts and special programs for a $10 annual fee.

Housing options: Condominiums and single-family homes are available, many of which have views of the gulf or bay. One-bedroom condos start at about $200,000 on the bay side and at about $400,000 on the gulf side. Houses start at $350,000 and top out at $11 million.

Visitor lodging: Best Western Siesta Beach Resort, (800) 223-5786, has rates starting at $144 from mid-December through mid-April and $89 the rest of the time. Many condo and apartment complexes rent units on a weekly or monthly basis. Contact the chamber of commerce or RE/MAX on the Key, (800) 486-4557, for information.

Information: The Siesta Key Chamber of Commerce, 5100 Ocean Blvd., Unit B, Siesta Key, FL 34242, (941) 349-3800 or www.siestakeychamber.com.

The island's real estate market differs from much of the state because vacant land is scarce. In some cases, the land is worth more than the structure standing on it; as a result, some buyers are tearing down existing structures to build new homes.

Property values are on the rise all over the island. For instance, the Metzlers estimate that their canal-front home has doubled in value since they bought it seven years ago.

Houses on the Intracoastal Waterway start at about $400,000. In the Sandaling Club, a gated community of single-family homes, there's a $5 million house and maybe a few for as little as $400,000. Most run about $1 million or higher.

On the bay side of the island, one-bedroom condos start at about $200,000, with larger units running upward of $600,000. On the gulf, a one-bedroom condo is likely to run from $400,000 to $1 million.

But you can pay substantially less, as the Grooms did, by buying on the other side of the street from the waterfront. They've still got a prime view of the water, but at about half the price.

As a comparison, you can go just across the bridge to the mainland and get a one-bedroom condo for $75,000 at Casa del Mar, from which you can walk across the bridge to the beach.

Realtor Jean Kelly says the average age of a Siesta Key condo is about 17 years, but that virtually all of them are well-kept. She also says her agency has fewer condo listings now than it's ever had. "People are holding on to them because prices are going up," she says.

Many people buy condos and rent them out during the winter season. With only one motor inn on the island, there's a big market for condo rentals, with about 6,000 units available on the key. The going rate for a well-appointed, two-bedroom condo on the beach is about $1,500 a week.

Many retirees, particularly those coming from the North, find the cost of living here is less. Don Metzler, 57, who was a college professor, says,

"What we paid in taxes alone there (in Michigan) would pay all taxes, utilities and insurance here."

The Grooms say their cost of living is lower than it was in Illinois mainly because of moving from a large home into a 1,300-square-foot condo. Both avid golfers, the Grooms found they could join two golf clubs in Sarasota for what it cost them to join one up north.

The retirees find little fault with the area.

"Even the rain isn't bad," Jerry says. "At least you don't have to shovel it."

Most residents do voice one complaint, though: During the winter season, traffic on the island's two main thoroughfares is painfully slow and congested.

But that, too, depends on your perspective.

"You do have to allow extra time to get most places in the winter," Kathy Groom says. "It's bad, but it's not as bad as Chicago."

And what's the rush? After all, this is Siesta Key.●

Tallahassee, Florida

Oak-canopied lanes lend Southern ambiance to this Florida capital city and university town

By William Schemmel

Bordering southwestern Georgia, the Tallahassee area has a Southern accent with piney woods, azaleas and dogwoods instead of the palmettos, palms and bougainvillea that visitors expect to see elsewhere in Florida. Canopy roads are Tallahassee's "beauty mark." Originally created as dirt and sand trails linking the county's cotton plantations, the paved, two-lane roads pass through leafy tunnels of live oak and laurel oak that are draped in Spanish moss. To preserve 65 miles of these roads from the pressures of development and transportation, a city ordinance officially designated five Canopy Roads and established a city-county agreement to maintain and preserve them.

It is this beauty, plus opportunities to stay active in a youthful population, that attracts retirees. "Tallahassee is a great place to retire if you like to keep busy," Edward Northcutt says cheerfully. More than 15 years after retiring as a marketing director of Eastern Airlines, Edward, 76, maintains a work ethic that keeps him in vigorous mental and physical health. The important difference in his working career and retirement life is that now it's all volunteer.

"On Mondays and Thursdays, my wife (Martha, 75, a retired real estate agent) and I deliver meals-on-wheels and do other work at Elder Care Services, a wonderful organization that does so much for people in this area who are too old or too disabled to do things for themselves," says Edward. "On Tuesdays I go to Kiwanis, on Wednesdays I'm a tour guide at the Florida State Capitol, and on Fridays I'm a docent at Pebble Hill, a historic hunting plantation at Thomasville, GA, 30 miles from Tallahassee," he says.

"If you want to sit around a golf course all day, then Tallahassee probably isn't the place for you," he adds, "but if you want to keep busy volunteering, there's plenty for you to do."

When they're not volunteering, the Northcutts keep fit by power walking in their northeast Tallahassee neighborhood and taking day trips to Florida Gulf Coast beaches and nature preserves an hour or two away.

The Northcutts lived in Florida's capital city in the late 1940s, then moved to Miami and on to Orlando, where Edward worked for 15 years as Eastern Airline's marketing manager at Walt Disney World. Eastern was then Disney World's "official airline."

"When I retired in 1985, my wife and I wanted to get out of the tourist market," he says. "We'd lived in Tallahassee before, and it felt like home, so we decided to move back. We haven't regretted it. It's a beautiful area, more like south Georgia than many other places in Florida," says Edward.

"It's the state capital, so government is really the main industry. Then we've got two major universities, Florida State University (31,000 students) and Florida A&M University (12,000 students), and Tallahassee Community College (10,700 students) and several smaller colleges, that offer opportunities for continuing

---

Population: 150,600 in Tallahassee, 239,450 in Leon County.

Location: Northwest Florida panhandle, 475 miles northwest of Miami, 165 miles west of Jacksonville and 257 miles northwest of Orlando. Florida's Gulf of Mexico coast is an hour south of the city.

Climate:

	High	Low
January	62	38
July	91	71

Tallahassee has hot, humid summers with frequent thunderstorms, and mild winters with occasional frost. Spring and fall are delightful.

Average relative humidity: 68%

Rain: 55 inches.

Cost of living: Above average (specific index not available).

Average housing cost: The average cost of a 2,000-square-foot home is $130,000.

Sales tax: 7%

Sales tax exemptions: Food, some services and medicine.

State income tax: None.

Intangibles tax: Assessed on stocks, bonds and other assets. The tax rate is $1 per $1,000 for assets. The first $20,000 in assets is exempt for individuals. For couples filing jointly, the first $40,000 is exempt. Those who owe less than $60 need not pay.

Estate tax: None, although there is a "pick-up" portion of the federal tax applicable to taxable estates of more than $1 million.

Inheritance tax: None.

Property tax: $21.44 per $1,000 valuation, with property assessed at 85% of market value. Annual tax on a $130,000 home, with homestead exemption listed below, is $1,833.

Homestead exemption: $25,000 off assessed value of primary, permanent residence.

Religion: More than 300 churches represent all major faiths.

Education: Florida State University (31,000 students) and Florida A&M University (12,000 students) offer a comprehensive choice of day and evening credit and noncredit courses, as well as cultural, entertainment and athletic opportunities. Tallahassee Community College (10,700 students) has two-year programs in the arts and sciences.

Transportation: TalTran, Tallahassee's public bus service, has more than 50 routes in the city.

Health: Tallahassee Memorial Health Care and Tallahassee Community Hos-

education, as well as sports and other activities in which the community can participate," he says.

With a population of 150,600 — 239,450 in Leon County — Tallahassee has almost a small-town feeling compared with Miami (475 miles), Tampa-St. Petersburg (275 miles), Orlando (257 miles), Jacksonville (165 miles) and other Florida metropolitan areas. The city defies many Sunshine State stereotypes. For example, with nearly 60,000 college students, thousands of state government workers and young professionals, Tallahassee has a higher proportion of younger residents than most Florida cities. It's the perfect Florida destination for retirees who want to live in a community of all ages.

A temperate four-season climate is another big contrast with the rest of the state. "We're not stuck with hot weather all the time," Edward Northcutt says. "We have definite spring, summer, fall and winter."

Hot and humid in midsummer, with frequent afternoon thunderstorms, Tallahassee and the rest of Florida's northwestern Panhandle get a brisk taste of fall. In January and February, occasional frosts and rare snow flurries wrap residents in sweaters and topcoats. Spring is glorious, with tens of thousands of azaleas, dogwoods, forsythia and other colorful plants brightening parks, gardens and roadways.

Like many other newcomers, the Northcutts relocated to northeast Tallahassee, the city's most popular residential area. "We bought (the late sportscaster) Red Barber's four-bedroom, three-bath house. It's a solid brick house in pretty much the same area where we lived before. This is one of the most desirable areas in Tallahassee. The annual property taxes on our house run about $2,000, which is about what we paid in Orlando," Edward says.

You can probably beat Tallahassee's real estate prices, admits Edward, but "you can't beat the lifestyle."

Large homes in Betton Hills, Bobbin Brook, Golden Eagle Plantation, Killearn Estates, Waverly Hills, Woodgate and other northeast quadrant communities range in price from the $200,000s to $650,000 and up, with some selling for $1 million or more. Area residents have easy access to upscale shopping, dining and recreation areas. Alfred B. Maclay State Gardens showcases 150 varieties of camellias and 50 types of azaleas. Maclay's Lake Hall recreation area has a boat ramp, swimming, fishing and picnic grounds.

Tallahassee's public park system includes several golf courses, tennis, basketball, racquetball and volleyball courts, swimming pools and softball and baseball fields. The cultural calendar is enliv-

ened by local theater, dance and musical companies, touring performers and Broadway musicals. Art galleries are plentiful, and a number of city, state and privately operated museums are devoted to fine arts, science, history and natural history.

Fifty sites in Leon County are on the National Register of Historic Places. Now a historical museum, the domed Old State Capitol has been restored to its 1902 appearance. In the 1970s the seat of government moved to the adjacent, 22-story "new" capitol building. Hernando DeSoto State Historic Site, less than a mile from the capitol, is the only place in North America confirmed as a site connected with the Spanish explorer's 1539-1540 trek through the Southeast.

Only a few years ago, housing prices in Florida's capital city were considerably below the state average, but home prices have been rising and now are considered above average. The average price of a 2,000-square-foot home in Tallahassee is $130,000.

"You can find affordable homes," says Michael Parker, Tallahassee's housing and community development director, "but you have to look for them." He defines affordable homes as equal in price to 80 percent or less of the city's median family income, times two, about $100,000.

Tallahassee, FL

pital have complete acute-care services with a full range of surgical specialties, including 24-hour emergency care and outpatient services. Leon County has 536 licensed physicians.

Housing options: The city's northeast quadrant is the most preferred residential area. Resale homes in **Killearn Estates**, a golf-course community, average about $200,000. **Killearn Lakes**, a newer development, has lots starting at $20,000. Other prestige subdivisions are **Betton Hills**, **Bobbin Brook**, **Woodgate** and **Eastgate**, with homes from about $212,000 to $400,000. With its large student population, the city has hundreds of apartment and condominium complexes and mobile home parks. In northwest Tallahas-

see, homes in **Huntington Woods**, **Hartsfield Woods**, **Settlers Creek**, **Lakeview** and other neighborhoods average about $115,000. **Westminster Oaks**, (850) 878-1136, Tallahassee's only continuing-care retirement community, has homes and assisted- and independent-living apartments.

Visitor lodging: Holiday Inn Capital, near the state capitol and universities, has double-occupancy rates from $77 in January to $149 in summer and fall, (850) 877-3171 or (800) 465-4329. Amenities include a fitness center, pool, voice mail and data ports. Other major chain hotels are Best Western Pride Inn, (850) 656-6312; Courtyard by Marriott, (850) 222-8822; and Days Inn University Center, (850) 222-3219. Double-occupancy rates at the Wakulla Springs

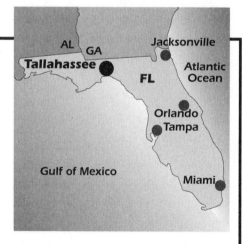

State Park Lodge, (850) 224-5950, are $69-$90. Amenities include cable TV, phone and private bath.

Information: Tallahassee Area Chamber of Commerce, 100 N. Duval St., P.O. Box 1639, Tallahassee, FL 32302, (850) 224-8116 or www.talchamber.com. A relocation package for new residents is $18.

Detached single-family homes are the most popular type of housing, making up 47 percent of all units that have received construction permits since 1990, and 59 percent of all constructed housing units overall in Tallahassee (not counting mobile homes). Single-family homes are especially prevalent in the northern and eastern areas of the city. Mobile homes, which make up about 20 percent of the housing market, are most popular in the southern and western areas of the city.

College students looking for off-campus housing have created a strong demand for all types of housing. That also has helped increase rents and purchase prices.

Another retired couple, Bill and Della Kell, moved from Atlanta to the Bear Creek subdivision in northeast Tallahassee two years ago. They've also lived in St. Petersburg and spent 10 months in Iran when Bill, 79, was a telephone company executive. Homes in their neighborhood sell for $175,000-$250,000, Della says. The Kells pay about $2,000 in property taxes on their custom-designed, 1,700-square-foot home.

Like the Northcutts, the Kells keep active by volunteering with Elder Care Services. Bill also has volunteered with Habitat for Humanity. Other organizations that welcome retiree volunteers include Leon County Volunteer Services, Retired Seniors Volunteer Program and Tallahassee-Leon County Shelter. Retirees are invited to join clubs that include the Florida Daffodil Society, the Rose Society, Amateur Radio Society and others that foster bridge, stamp collecting, model railroads, computers, investing, birding and preservation of vintage vehicles.

"We looked at some other areas for our retirement," says Della, 72, "but we chose Tallahassee for several reasons. We're within a day's drive from our daughter, who lives in Huntsville, AL, which is very important to us. And Tallahassee has a much more relaxed pace than other places we've lived. It has everything that big cities have, but it's just so much more convenient. We fell in love with it — it's a beautiful place, and we have wonderful neighbors. Many of the streets in Tallahassee have canopies of trees where you feel like you're in

a forest and not a city."

Tallahassee's scenic beauty also attracted Charles and Mary Lou Watford back to Tallahassee in the mid-1980s after 13 years in Miami. "We're both from this area, and we both graduated from FSU, but we moved all around when Charles was with the telephone company," says Mary Lou, 63, a former schoolteacher. "When we decided to take early retirement, we came back here by choice. After living in Miami, I've really enjoyed not being in a big city," she says.

"Tallahassee is a beautiful place," says Mary Lou. "When my sister and her husband were visiting us from Mississippi, they marveled at all our wonderful trees."

The Watfords designed their 2,800-square-foot home in northeast Tallahassee, with ample room for Charles to enjoy his hobby, growing camellias. There's also ample room for their children, who return frequently for football games and other activities at FSU.

"In the fall, our population increases by about 62,000 students, says Mary Lou, "but they're over on the west side, away from us. FSU and Florida A&M have all kinds of programs of which people who live in the area can take advantage. We can attend football and basketball games, and go to concerts, film and lectures, and they have courses in everything imaginable." The problem with all those students, Mary Lou laughs, "is they love this area so much, when they graduate, they don't want to go home."

The Watfords also participate in programs at the Tallahassee Senior Center. "We played a lot of bridge when we were younger, and recently took a refresher course at the senior center to get back into it. It's great mental exercise, especially for Charles, who's recovering from a stroke," says Mary Lou. She also suggests churches as an excellent way for local retirees to meet other people and to keep busy. "Our Baptist church has a very active senior choir and other programs for older adults," she says.

Many retirees, including the Watfords, spend free time exploring nearby state parks, wildlife refuges and Gulf of Mexico beaches. Tallahassee isn't a beach community, but the Gulf Coast's blinding white sands and tur-

quoise waters are only about 90 minutes by car from the city. St. George Island State Park, consistently top-ranked nationally, is a big favorite of Tallahasseans. Recreational amenities on the island's nine miles of sandy shores include swimming, sunbathing, camping, fishing, hiking and nature study. It's also happy hunting grounds for shell collectors.

St. Joseph Peninsula State Park, also ranked highly among beaches, is a 2,516-acre park surrounded by the Gulf of Mexico and St. Joseph Bay. Birdwatchers come to the park to observe some 209 species. While they're here, they enjoy the park's miles of sandy beaches, camping, fishing, hiking and boating.

Last fall, Mary Lou and Charles Watford and their visiting relatives drove down to the St. Marks National Wildlife Refuge, south of Tallahassee, to observe the annual migration of monarch butterflies heading south to Mexico for the winter. When the monarchs aren't the main attraction, the 67,000-acre sanctuary attracts flocks of birders. Seventy-five miles of marked trails are ideal for spotting more than 270 species of waterfowl, shore birds and long-legged waders.

The 16-mile Tallahassee-St. Marks Historic Railroad State Trail is another popular day outing. Once Florida's oldest operating railroad line, the abandoned roadbed has been transformed into an outdoor mecca for bicyclists, hikers, joggers, in-line skaters and horseback riders.

And at Edward Ball Wakulla Springs State Park and Lodge, between Tallahassee and the Gulf, retirees enjoy nature trails and brisk dips in 70-degree spring water. Glass-bottom boats provide views deep into the crystal-clear spring. Wildlife observation boats cruise into wilderness sections of the Wakulla River. Tallahassee residents can make an overnight or weekend trip of it at the historic Wakulla Lodge, which has a full-service restaurant.

It's among many attractions that are drawing more and more retirees to Tallahassee. "I've felt all along that retirement is going to be one of the biggest factors in this area's growth — but I don't want too many people to discover this place," laughs Mary Lou Watford. ●

Temecula, California

Retirees enjoy a small-town ambiance amid
vineyards and rolling hills in Southern California

Carole Jacobs

Sue and Jerry Turek still can't believe their luck. This time last year they were shoveling snow in suburban Chicago. Today the 60-year-old active retirees are living the good life in Rancho Vista, an upscale community in Temecula, where they both work part time as freelance consultants.

"We live so much nicer here than we ever lived there," says Sue, whose mission is to get all her friends to move to this sage-scrubbed Shangri-La located 60 miles north of San Diego. "I send them brochures of our historic downtown and beautiful wine country and they can't believe their eyes. I see flowered hillsides in February and I can hardly believe it myself," she says.

"We could never have afforded a house like this in Los Angeles," says Linda Cole, who with husband Bill, formerly with AT&T, moved to Temecula from Redondo Beach, a seaside community outside Los Angeles. "We went from a dinky 900-square-foot house to a 2,400-square-foot single-family home in Rancho Highlands," an upscale development with a pool and tennis courts, she says. "From the size of our house to the quality of our life, everything went up except the cost."

A Midwest native, Linda says Temecula's small-town friendliness and four-season climate feels more like home than Redondo Beach ever did. "We lived there for more than 20 years and didn't know people who lived a few doors down. We've only been in Temecula a year and already it feels like we know everybody," says Linda, who didn't waste any time getting involved in community life. She currently chairs the Senior Golden Years Club — a sort of brat pack for seniors with more than 200 members.

Crystal-clear air, picture-perfect weather sans bugs, a low crime rate, quality medical care, a small-town atmosphere with big city-amenities, a wide variety of affordable housing, a state-of-the-art senior center with a politically active membership, plus a wine country that's giving

Napa a run for its Riesling — it's easy to see why Temecula is the 10th-fastest growing city in California. The population increased by 7 percent to nearly 58,000 residents in 2000, and retirees now account for about 9 percent of Temecula's overall population.

"We're really not what you'd consider a retirement mecca," stresses City Manager Shawn Nelson. Most of the growth is the result of young and middle-aged families moving in from San Diego and Los Angeles counties — a fact that makes what former Mayor Jeff Stone calls the town's "enormous investment in our seniors" even more remarkable.

Ringed by rolling hills that are Bonanza-brown in summer and Brigadoon-green in winter, Temecula inhabits a unique microclimate not unlike Tuscany — a mild, dry climate that is as ideal for wineries as for retirees. Pacific breezes whip up through the canyons and Temecula's aptly named Rainbow Gap and collide with drier desert air that results in thunderstorms. The clouds scoot off to reveal an Oz-land where double rainbows ring emerald hilltops and arch gracefully across the valleys to snowcapped peaks. It was this breathtaking natural phenomenon that inspired Temecula's first inhabitants, the Luiseno Indians, to name it Temecula, which means "where the sun breaks through the mist."

Call it love at first sight (they do), but it was largely the bucolic climate and scenery that inspired Dick and Fran Handley to abandon the Detroit heat, cold and gridlock 20 years ago and retire to Temecula. "We moved into a mobile home community and have been living in the land of wine and roses ever since," says Dick, formerly with the Detroit Department of Traffic.

Just one look was also all it took to encourage Rosemary and Richard Parsons to pull up roots in suburban Chicago and settle into an affordable senior housing community in Temecula. "We flew out one weekend, picked out a house,

packed up and moved," says Richard, a retired paratrooper with the U.S. Army who has lived all over the world. "When it's 85 in Chicago, you're ready to fight," quips Richard. "In Temecula, it can be 100 degrees out, but you're never uncomfortable, and the nights are always cool." Adds Rosemary, "All my life I wanted to live in California near the ocean. Now we're only an hour away."

Norma Matkovich, 75, moved to Temecula in 1984 after having lived all over the world with her ex-husband, a military man. After her divorce, she wanted to live in a small town where she could make friends and feel like a part of the community. She chose Temecula for its natural beauty and small-town charm and has never looked back. "In Long Beach (her last stop before moving to Temecula) the only people you met were at work — you never ran into anyone you knew when you went shopping at malls," she says. "In Temecula, you have to get dressed in the morning because you never know who you're going to run into."

Ask retirees what they do for fun and a sense of community and it's not long before the recently expanded Mary Phillips Senior Center comes up. "I've been all over the world and I've never seen anything like what our senior center offers," says Richard Parsons. "We have friends in Chicago who can't wait to retire and move here," he says, "and our son and two daughters already have. Not only is Temecula wonderful for retirees, but it's also a great place to raise grandkids."

Adds Dick Handley, "We were a little worried about not knowing anyone when we first moved here, but it was never a problem. With the senior center, it wasn't long before we made our own nuclear family." With a free daily lunch program plus Meals on Wheels, potlucks, dinner dances, far-flung field trips and a daily exercise schedule that could make Jane Fonda wilt, there's rarely a dull moment at the center. "Aerobics, weight lifting, swing dance, line dance, hip-hop, field trips to

Las Vegas, classes in everything from Spanish and nutrition to driving and health insurance — they wear me out," says recreation director Candice Flohr of the seniors who frequent the center.

The center includes a recent 3,000-square-foot expansion housing a full kitchen, a billiards room, a library and three additional classrooms. It was named after the late Mary Phillips, "a feisty lady who pestered city council until they agreed to gut the old bus depot and turn it into a senior center," recalls Norma Matkovich, who lent her energies and "loud mouth" to the cause. Since then, Norma has served in a variety of capacities at the senior center and is currently treasurer of its Senior Golden Years Club. When the Golden Yearers, as they call themselves, aren't raising funds for the less fortunate or donating holiday fruit baskets, they're likely to be gallivanting around Old Town terrorizing small restaurants, chuckles Dick Handley. "They see 27 of us coming at once and they just about tear their hair out," he grins.

Temecula also is an ideal place for single. seniors to start anew, says Norma Matkovich. "One couple met here, married and took 55 of us with them on their honeymoon to Las Vegas," she says.

Still single herself, Norma says "there are enough men here to keep me busy. But I haven't met anyone yet I want to take home." She adds, "My married friends put up with me, and there's so much to do. And even with all the growth, Temecula still feels like the country."

In fact, Temecula appears to be expanding on all fronts. Beyond the beehive of the senior center lies Historic Old Town, Temecula's recently redeveloped nine-block historic district. Front Street, with boardwalks and lantern-style streetlights, is lined with shops, antiques dealers, art galleries, Western-style restaurants and saloons (one still has a hitching post). A year-round farmer's market is open on Saturdays. Festivals celebrate the town's colorful past as a stop on the Butterfield Stage route and location for Hollywood westerns as well as its more recent claim to fame as Califor-

nia's "other" wine country. Festivals include Old Town Western Days in April, a wine tasting and arts festival in May, an old-fashioned Fourth of July celebration, a film festival in September, the Temecula Tractor Race in October and a Christmas festival and parade.

Outside the time warp of Old Town lies modern-day Temecula, a sprawl of green where the sparkling Promenade Mall offers 110 specialty shops, major department stores, cinemas and a cluster of restaurants. Trendy baby boomers weren't far behind the retirees in moving to Temecula.

Other attractions include the five-acre Temecula Duck Pond, nine championship golf courses, the 6,000-acre Skinner Lake Recreation Area (for camping, fishing, boating, picnicking, horseback riding, hiking trails and outdoor swimming in a half-acre swimming lagoon), the 8,300-acre Santa Rosa Plateau Ecological Reserve and the century-old Glen Ivy Hot Springs spa, where you can slather yourself with local mud or ease into a bubbly

Population: 57,716

Location: The Temecula Valley is located in Southern California, 85 miles south of Los Angeles and 60 miles north of San Diego. Elevations range from 1,980 feet in the east to 2,600 feet on the west.

Climate:

	High	Low
January	69	46
July	92	61

The weather is comparable to the Napa Valley, with warm, dry days and cool evenings. Although separated from the Pacific Ocean by the Santa Rosa range, the Rainbow Gap funnels a mild beach climate into the valley.

Average relative humidity: 25%

Rain: 24 inches.

Cost of living: Above average (specific index not available).

Median housing cost: $208,000

Sales tax: 7.75%

State income tax: For married couples filing jointly, graduated from 1% of taxable income up to $11,496 to 9.3% on amounts over $75,450. For single filers, graduated from 1% of taxable income up to $5,748 to 9.3% on amounts over $37,725.

Income tax exemptions: Social Security benefits and railroad pensions are exempt.

Estate tax: None, except the state's pickup portion of the federal tax, applicable to taxable estates of more than $1 million.

Inheritance tax: None.

Property tax: 1.3%-1.4%, does not include special assessments in some parts of the city. The state reimburses up to $300 in property taxes for those 62 years or older, or those who are blind or disabled and with federal adjusted gross income of $37,000 or less.

Homestead exemption: Up to a maximum of $7,000 of assessed value.

Religion: Most denominations are represented locally or in nearby communities.

Education: Temecula is within commuting distance of 22 private and public colleges and universities with a combined enrollment of more than 139,000 students. This includes nationally known private liberal arts schools like the Claremont Colleges and the University of Redlands. Impressive scientific work is being conducted at Harvey Mudd College, California State Polytechnic University at Pomona and the University of California at Riverside. Loma Linda University boasts

a renowned medical school. The University of La Verne School of Law is located in Ontario. Cal State San Marcos in nearby San Diego County offers classes in Temecula as does UCR Extension and the University of Redlands. There are five community colleges in the region, including Mount San Jacinto Community College, which also offers classes in Temecula.

Transportation: Riverside Transit Agency operates Dial-a-Ride, which provides curb-to-curb transportation for the elderly and disabled. Fixed-route bus service operates along major streets. Senior Van offers local transportation to and from the Mary Phillips Senior Center. Temecula is 55 minutes from San Diego International Airport, 45 minutes from Ontario Airport, and 90 minutes from Los Angeles International Airport. Van and limo service to the three airports is $70-$95, $65-$85 and $125-$165, respectively.

Health: The 80-bed Inland Valley Regional Medical Center in Wildomar and the Rancho Springs Medical Center in Murrieta, a 96-bed facility, both have radiology and oncology departments. Inland Valley also is the regional trauma

pool fed by natural hot springs.

Then there's Temecula's burgeoning wine country. Scattered in the rolling hillsides, it is home to more than 15 wineries ranging from small ma-and-pa establishments to grandiose estates featuring wine-tasting rooms, patio fountain cafes, gourmet restaurants and herb gardens. Almost a city unto itself, the wine district en toto and individual wineries host fetes galore, from barbecue suppers with hayrides to candlelight gourmet dinners, jazz concerts under the stars and even wine-stomping events where you can help press the grapes.

While housing developments expressly for the 55-and-older crowd have been limited in Temecula in recent years, a current senior housing boom will add hundreds of units of affordable living within the next few years, says Gloria Wolnick, marketing coordinator for the City of Temecula. Housing options for seniors currently range from quality apartment units and luxury condominiums to single-family homes, she says. Vicki MacHale, activities director for the Vintage Hills Planned Community Association, says nearby Sun City and Banning also offer a wide variety of senior housing for all income levels.

Temecula real estate agent Gene Wunderlich, president of the Southwest Riverside Association of Realtors, predicts that a wider range of housing options for retirees, from inexpensive mobile home parks and senior housing facilities to upscale golf communities and acres for custom estates, will encourage even more people to consider Temecula as their retirement home.

"With one of the best affordability indexes in a state notorious for high-priced real estate, 50 percent of Temecula's residents can afford a medium-priced home," says Wunderlich, adding that Temecula is especially a bargain for retirees who move from more upscale areas of neighboring Orange and San Diego counties. "They can sell their homes there and buy a palace out here," he says.

Sue and Jerry Turek agree. Their new four-bedroom home with backyard pool cost $298,000 – and that's $50,000 less than what they got for their smaller 70-year-old home in Chicago.

All Temecula residents are benefiting from a recent tax cut, while a new recreational tax approved by residents is paving the city with lush greenbelts and regional parks stocked with tennis, basketball and squash courts, baseball fields and swimming pools.

"It's a win-win situation," says Wunderlich. "From volunteering to drive unarmed patrol cars to raising money for charities, our seniors are a highly visible and vibrant part of the community. I've had people in their 70s and 80s tell me they don't want to live with a bunch of old people. They want to contribute to the community and be appreciated, and in Temecula, they really are."●

Temecula, CA

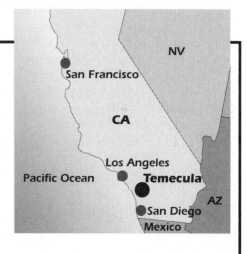

center, with 13 beds devoted to emergency care and two for trauma.

Housing options: The Fountains at Temecula, (909) 506-1579. This gated community has 244 apartment homes plus a fully appointed clubhouse with planned activities, a pool and therapeutic spa, library, computer learning center, putting greens and covered parking. In fall 1999, developer K. Hovnanian opened **Four Seasons at Temecula Valley,** (888) 257-1271. The active-adult community has 524 homes with prices starting in the mid-$200,000s. Recreation facilities will include a swimming pool, tennis courts, walking and jogging trails, putting green, driving range and amenity-filled community center. Other properties for seniors only include **The Colony** in neighboring Murrieta. Built in the mid-1980s, the golf community includes nearly 300 single-story houses in Spanish or Southwestern architecture priced from $230,000 and up. Another option is **Murrieta Hot Springs,** a 30-year-old golf and retirement community for residents age 55 and over, just outside Temecula on the grounds of the former Murrieta Hot Springs Resort. Housing ranges from condos and manufactured homes to vacant lots where you can

move your own mobile or manufactured home. A clubhouse with swimming pool serves as the community's social hub. Prices for mobile homes start at $80,000, and condo prices start at $75,000. **Temeku Hills Golf Community,** (909) 693-1440, is a California mission-style community of single-family homes set in rolling hills at the 72-acre Temeku Hills Country Club. The community is popular with active retirees and features special senior recreational and service programs at its clubhouse. Prices for four-bedroom homes start at $350,000. Assisted-living communities include **Chancellor Place of Murrieta,** (909) 696-5753, which offers independent living in large studio and one-bedroom suites with full baths and kitchenettes for older seniors who require assistance. The property overlooks a golf course and is within walking distance of a shopping center. Prices for studios start at $2,495 per month and vary widely depending on level of care; prices for one-bedroom suites start at $3,195 per month. **Sterling Senior Communities,** (909) 506-5555, is a new 179-unit senior apartment complex on 21 acres. The community has an independent-living complex of 52 apartments, an assisted-living complex of 74

apartments and an Alzheimer's complex of 53 beds. The independent-living quarters range from studios at $1,950 to two-bedroom apartments up to $4,625.

Visitor lodging: Options include Best Western Country Inn, $78, (800) 528-1234; Comfort Inn, $90, (909) 296-3788; Embassy Suites, $99-$189, (909) 676-5656; Loma Vista B&B, $120-$199, (909) 676-7047; Temecula Creek Inn, $185-$205, (909) 694-1000; and Temecula Supreme Hospitality, $80-$99, (909) 699-2444.

Information: Temecula Valley Chamber of Commerce, 27450 Ynez Road, Suite 124, Temecula, CA 92591, (909) 676-5090 or www.temecula.org.

Thomasville, Georgia

An idyllic town draws retirees to the red hills of southern Georgia

By Mary Lu Abbott

Spring days are heady experiences around the Georgia town of Thomasville. A morning mist caresses rolling meadows and old moss-laden live oak and magnolia trees shading gracious plantations, most of which still are privately owned and enjoyed as leisure retreats. Fuchsia, scarlet and white azaleas and dogwood blossoms give way to roses perfuming the air in preparation for the town's annual rose show, celebrated since 1921.

Colorfully painted Victorian storefronts house several dozen shops and restaurants facing brick-paved streets downtown, where parking is free and only steps from the stores. A cool breeze snaps U.S. flags and bright banners along Broad Street that proclaim Thomasville a Great American Main Street award-winning town, one of five recognized last year for exceptional achievement in revitalization programs.

Ralph Fort recalls one spring when he and his wife came from Little Rock, AR, to visit their daughter in Thomasville. "We thought this had to be the prettiest town in the U.S.A. We thought it would be great to retire here," says Ralph. And, they did relocate here.

Norman and Ruth Smith were searching for an alternative retirement spot from their home in Leesburg, FL, when they visited Thomasville. "I walked down Main Street and thought to myself, 'Boy, this is beautiful,' " says Ruth. They decided to build a home here.

Hollywood couldn't dream up a more idyllic hometown than Thomasville. It is modern, yet exudes a lifestyle reminiscent of yesteryear. Residents go downtown to shop, eat and visit, greeting strangers as well as friends strolling along the sidewalk. While many downtown renovations have resulted in mainly tourist-oriented shops, Thomasville blends traditional and new businesses. Wander along Broad, Jackson, Madison and adjacent streets, and you will find children's, women's and men's clothing stores, shoe stores, jewelry shops, a lingerie boutique and a tailor, music and book shops, hardware, home furnishings and antique stores, a soda fountain and a drugstore, the latter in business since 1881. All are locally owned, not chains.

Adjacent to downtown are churches and neighborhoods with shaded sidewalks passing dozens of homes that date from antebellum through Victorian eras, most of them still occupied and lovingly preserved. Only a block off Broad Street, branches of a giant sprawling oak tree extend so far over the street that signs warn of low clearance. The oak is more than 300 years old.

"Thomasville has something special about it — its own personality. It's real Southern but yet very progressive — sometimes those two things don't go together," says Marjorie Fort, who was born in a nearby Florida town and retired to Thomasville from suburban Philadelphia.

Thomasville's size and location add to its appeal. It has about 20,000 residents, neither too small nor too large, and it's in a scenic pocket of pine forests known as the red hills, easily accessible yet removed from the fast-lane life. About 35 miles northeast of Tallahassee, FL, it is located on three not-too-busy U.S. highways, including a section of U.S. Highway 19 known as the Florida-Georgia Parkway. Still a farming center, it has one of the largest fresh produce markets in the state.

From its early days, Thomasville has been a prosperous community. Founded in 1826, it developed into an agricultural, commercial, social and political center, with cotton plantations fueling a major part of its growth. "There has always been money here," says Tom Hill, a Thomasville native and curator of the Thomas County Historical Society, which operates the Museum of History. He says the area attracted second sons of well-to-do families, the boys who would not inherit the home estate but were well-educated and had the backing to start businesses.

While the Civil War crippled the economy, Thomasville suffered far less than other Southern towns as it tapped a new industry: tourists. In the 1870s, wealthy Northerners were seeking resorts to escape for the winter and discovered Thomasville, a railroad terminus about 60 miles from the Gulf of Mexico. Its altitude of 273 feet kept it from being malaria-infested like much of Florida at the time, and the mild climate and pine-scented air had earned it a reputation as a health retreat.

Rather than turning their backs on the Northerners, local businessmen who had come through the war with some cash built large, blocklong hotels. Entire families arrived, often with servants, in late fall and stayed through spring. At the 400-foot-long Piney Woods Hotel, rooms were a princely sum of $4 a night with meals, but if you wanted a private bath, the rate jumped to $11. Among the names on the register: Mr. and Mrs. Cornelius Vanderbilt. Called "the best winter resort on three continents" by Harper's Bazaar in 1887, the town once boasted as many as 15 hotels and 25 boarding houses.

Many visitors liked the area so much that they built "winter cottages" in town or bought plantations or land at bargain prices where they established grand hunting estates. A staff of servants tended to the home, grounds, dogs and horses year-round, and the owners came seasonally, from November to March to hunt duck and quail, socialize and later play golf when a private course opened in 1896. Now part of the Glen Arven Country Club, it's one of the oldest continuously played private courses in the South.

With the taming of malaria, Florida began to siphon the tourist flow after the turn of the century, causing the demise of the Thomasville hotels, but many who had built homes here continued to come "for the season," and their descendants still do today. Within a 35-mile, three-county area stretching southward, there are 71 plantations covering about 300,000 acres, most of them originating in the antebellum period.

Hill says the plantations are unusual in several respects, including that so many still exist. Noting that most surviving plantations elsewhere have become tour homes and museums because residents could no longer afford their upkeep, Hill says owners still live in most of these plantations, coming to enjoy "fox hunting, tea at four and dressing for dinner" during the winter.

Today's tourists can glimpse into the lifestyle of the rich and famous here at Pebble Hill Plantation, a 3,000-acre complex with everything from stables and kennels to a dog hospital, log-cabin school and main house with 43 rooms and 26 baths. It was donated by its owners to be open to the public.

Established in the 1820s by an early settler, it was purchased in 1896 by the

Thomasville, GA

Population: 20,000. Thomasville is the largest community in Thomas County.

Location: In the southern red hills of Georgia, Thomasville is about 45 miles west of I-75 and Valdosta, GA, and about 35 miles northeast of Tallahassee, FL, and I-10. It's on U.S. highways 19, 319 and 84.

Climate:

	High	Low
January	63	39
July	92	71

Fall and winter are mild, spring brings a profusion of colorful blossoms, and summer is hot.

Average relative humidity: 50%

Rain: 52 inches.

Cost of living: Below average to average (specific index not available).

Average housing cost: $120,000 for a home, $400-$475 a month for a two-bedroom apartment.

Sales tax: 6%

Sales tax exemptions: Prescription drugs, medical services and some groceries.

State income tax: For married couples filing jointly, graduated from 1% of taxable income up to $1,000 to $340 plus 6% on amounts over $10,000. For single filers, graduated from 1% of income up to $750 to $230 plus 6% on amounts over $7,000.

Income tax exemptions: Social Security benefits are exempt. Up to $14,000 in retirement income is exempt for each taxpayer age 62 and older. Up to $4,000 of earned income can be included in the $14,000 exemption.

Intangibles tax: None.

Estate tax: None, except the state's "pick-up" portion of the federal tax, applicable to taxable estates above $1 million.

Property tax: Thomasville residents pay a combined city-county rate of $29.03 per $1,000 valuation, with homes assessed at 40% of fair market value. Rates for county residents range from $20.26 to $35.25 per $1,000 in assessed value. Yearly taxes on a $120,000 home would be about $1,335 in town, $932-$1,622 in the county, including the $2,000 exemption noted below.

Homestead exemption: $2,000 off the 40% assessment value for permanent residents. Residents age 62 and older may qualify for further exemptions based on age and income.

Personal property tax: Same tax rates and assessment ratio apply to pleasure boats, but there's no $2,000 exemption.

Religion: There are several dozen places of worship, including Jewish, Protestant and Catholic.

Education: Thomas College, with about 800 students, offers four-year degrees, continuing-education classes and special seniors programs.

Transportation: There's no public transportation system. The local airport serves private aircraft 24 hours a day. Commercial flights are available from Tallahassee, 35 miles southwest.

Health: The hub of a regional health-care system of five hospitals and four nursing homes, the John D. Archbold Memorial Hospital in Thomasville has 264 beds and about 100 physicians in 35 specialties. Its extensive services include trauma, cancer, cardiac and rehabilitative care. The community has four nursing homes.

Housing options: Within the town and county are numerous choices in housing, from historic to modern homes at reasonable prices. Homes in convenient neighborhoods in town run from the $85,000s to $120,000s. Also in town, Lake Eagle is a new adult neighborhood with townhomes and free-standing houses starting at about $100,000. In the county, two popular developments are Tall Timbers with homes for the $90,000s to $130,000s and Tall Pines with prices in the low $100,000s to $175,000s. The Fairways, with condominiums from the $120,000s and higher-priced custom homes, is among developments near the Glen Arven Country Club, dating to the turn of the century. There's limited availability of rental housing in the area. For information on housing, contact a real estate agency; the largest is First Thomasville Realty, (229) 226-6515.

Visitor lodging: The area has about a dozen bed-and-breakfast inns, most of them in historic homes. Most notable is Melhana Plantation Resort, four miles outside town, which has luxury accommodations starting at $285 a night, (888) 920-3030 or (229) 226-2290. Other lodging in the area starts at about $75.

Information: Thomasville and Thomas County Chamber of Commerce, P.O. Box 560, Thomasville, GA 31799, (229) 226-9600, www.thomasvillechamber.com. Thomasville Welcome Center, 135 N. Broad St., Thomasville, GA 31792, (800) 704-2350, www.thomasvillega.com.

prominent Hanna family, industrialists in Cleveland, OH, and expanded into a renowned sporting retreat for hunting and polo. In the 1920s, the owners spent $1 million on a new dairy and stables complex, and when most of the country was reeling from the Great Depression of the 1930s, the main house was rebuilt in the grand style seen today after a fire destroyed the older home. A staff of 36 was required to run the estate. President Dwight Eisenhower was among guests who came to hunt and play golf, and formal balls still are held at the home about five miles outside town.

At the neighboring Melhana Plantation, also once owned by the Hanna family, visitors can overnight in luxury and indulge in an updated estate lifestyle, strolling through gardens with peacocks, riding horses under a magnificent cathedral of oak and magnolia trees or lounging in a restored 1930s pool house. Turned into an elegant country-manor resort by local owners Charlie and Fran Lewis, Melhana has fine dining, spa services and 19 beautifully appointed rooms, with more accommodations planned as other historic buildings are renovated.

In town, the prized "winter cottage" is the 1885 Lapham-Patterson House, a whimsical golden-colored Queen Anne mansion unique in several architectural respects, most notably because it was built without any right angles or symmetry. Shoe merchant Charles Willard Lapham had suffered lung damage in the great Chicago fire of 1871, and at the time, the asymmetrical design was thought to be more like nature and thus healthier. Each of the 19 rooms has at least one door to the outside, and there are 53 windows. The Lapham-Patterson House is open for tours, and other homes can be seen on a self-guided walking and driving tour of the historic areas.

A century ago, Thomasville merchants and city leaders catered to their wealthy residents with upscale shops, good restaurants and an active cultural scene, and that tradition carries through today. "We're a high-end retail center," says Sharlene Celaya, executive director of Main Street development and tourism. "Downtown flourishes even though Thomasville has a mall. We used to go down to Tallahassee (to shop), but that trend has reversed. Now Tallahassee res-idents are tired of the traffic down there and come up here to shop. They like the hospitality and service of our merchants."

Fran and Charlie Lewis echo the praises of downtown merchants, who get to know their customers, call when preferred merchandise arrives and gather a selection of clothes for a customer to take home, select from and pay for later.

The arts also are a priority. Local residents rescued a 1915 school with $3.3 million in private funds and turned it into the Thomasville Cultural Center, where a local theater group and dance troupe perform and two annual concert series bring in major artists. Thomas College, which has four-year degree programs, also serves as a cultural venue.

Over the years, wealthy winter visitors contributed greatly to the community, most notably in establishing the Archbold Medical Center, based in Thomasville and providing state-of-the-art health care to a 13-county area of Georgia and Florida through five hospitals, four nursing homes and other services. With about 1,400 staff and workers in Thomasville, it is one of the largest employers in the county.

While the last decade has brought numerous changes, they've been on the plus side, says Marjorie, who settled here after living 44 years in the Philadelphia area. When she and her husband, Harry Fisher, decided to retire, they wanted warmer weather, looked at sites in Florida where she has relatives, came to Thomasville and decided it was right for them. When he died a few years later, Marjorie remained in Thomasville, staying active in volunteer work with youngsters.

Ralph and Lois Fort also moved here in the 1980s, and Ralph, an engineer, became an avid tennis player. His wife died in 1991. Though the Forts and the Fishers had not known each other, a mutual friend tried to play matchmaker for Ralph and Marjorie, but plans for meetings always fell through, Ralph recalls. "I picked up the phone one night, called Marjorie, told her we were grown folks and why didn't we just go out and have dinner and meet each other ourselves. That started our romance," he says.

"I felt like the Lord brought us together. We felt so at home with each other right off," says Marjorie. They were mar-ried in 1993.

Norman and Ruth Smith decided to stay in Leesburg, FL, when his water-pollution control company was sold and he retired, but they grew discontented with their golf-course community. "The only thing people talked about was the club and how good or bad the food was. We didn't like that and started looking for a real community," says Ruth. They considered Tallahassee but found it too busy and moved to Thomasville in the late 1980s because it was "beautiful and a nice size," she says.

Chet and June Ledford had bought a farm in Ohio when he retired as an insurance agent, but after a number of years they decided it was more work than fun. They had come to the Thomasville area frequently to play golf. "We always liked the town and decided to move here," he says.

While all three couples say Thomasville residents are warm and friendly, some newcomers say that it can take time to become part of the social scene. "We found that people have lived here for generations, and it's not so easy to get acquainted as it is in Florida (where many residents are newcomers). It takes longer," says Ruth. But she calls Thomasville "a wonderful community" with a good art guild and numerous cultural events, and she and her husband have joined in community work.

Ralph and Marjorie made new friends through neighbors and their churches, and the Ledfords say the church and garden club served as their main entrees into local society.

The Ledfords often yearn for the rolling hills of Ohio. June says she was surprised that "the summers are too hot to grow iris and peonies" in Thomasville, and Chet dislikes "the pine straw dropping all the time — we use it for mulch and still have to carry it off." Ralph and Marjorie miss the colorful falls at their previous homes, and the Smiths sometimes wish for the easy lifestyle in Florida but are happy to be away from the heavy traffic.

Overall, the couples find the cost of living here about the same or easier on the pocketbook. They all would recommend that others consider Thomasville for retirement. "Come see it and talk to the people," says Marjorie. "I can't imagine anyone not liking Thomasville." ●

Tucson, Arizona

A touch of the Old West mingles with urban sophistication in this Arizona oasis

By Ron Butler

"Geronimo Slept Here," proclaims a popular Tucson travel poster indicative of an allure that harkens to the Old West. With its 480,000-plus population, Tucson is one of the country's fasest-growing communities, a city that revels in the joy of its desert and its lively Western heritage.

This is the flavor that brought Roger and Edie Harvey, 65 and 63, respectively, to Tucson from their former home in Reno, NV, where Roger was an electrician and Edie was personnel director for a medical supply company. Tucson's Western ambiance — plus fabulous weather, easy prices and, considering that both Roger and Edie are avid golfers, its hole-in-one potential — is what lured the couple to Sun City Vistoso, a retirement community about 30 minutes from downtown Tucson.

A genuine feel of the Old West, with its galloping wide-open spaces and dusty bravado, still exists in Tucson and in neighboring places like Bisbee, Benson, Tombstone and Yuma, all within easy driving range. It exists in honky-tonks like the Maverick, where the two-step is the dance of choice. Cowboys and cowgirls, often wearing matching shirts, glide around the dance floor as though on roller skates, perhaps minus a wheel or two. Bean burritos and cold beer still comprise a breakfast standard, and the city's Sun Tran bus drivers all wear cowboy hats, although some modern-day local cowboys sport gold neck chains and boots that have never stepped in mud.

The Harveys, who have relatives in the area, visited Tucson regularly for six years before making the move, attracted in part by the lay of the land. The city's grid is surrounded by mountains: the Santa Ritas, the Catalinas and the Rincons, all subliminal landmarks for motorists. On rare rainy days when clouds hang low in the sky like a tarpaulin to obscure the details of the mountains, drivers often lose their sense of direction, driving south instead of north, east instead of west. But usually the weather is glorious, and sunglasses are sold by corner street vendors the way umbrellas are peddled in Seattle or New York City.

At night the city lights are kept at a dim twinkle, not to conserve energy but out of consideration for the scientists and astronomers at the Kitt Peak National Observatory, where the world's most powerful solar telescope peers into the galaxies. In the telescope's shadow, Yaqui, Pima and Tohono O'Oodham Indians still consult tribal medicine men for their aches and pains and harvest the desert for cactus fruit and building materials.

Golf is a year-round activity in Tucson, and Roger, with a 17 handicap, and Edie, who won't divulge hers, are on the course almost daily. The first thing visitors are likely to notice at their home is a golf cart loaded for bear. Membership at Sun City Golf Club is $4,350 for two; guests pay $38-$62 for greens fees and cart.

Sun City Vistoso contains more than 2,500 homes, many with 12-foot ceilings and three-car garages, and most are in the $122,000-$400,000 range. Tucson has numerous housing options, including 10 retirement communities, 17 parks for recreational vehicles and mobile homes, and more than 25 active-adult retirement apartment complexes in addition to facilities for retirees needing assisted-living services.

In their retirement community, the Harveys have access to all kinds of social and community groups, travel clubs, a volunteer library and an easy, relaxed atmosphere that's conducive to making friends. But they also take advantage of Tucson's wealth of cultural activities. With two major learning institutions, the University of Arizona and fast-growing Pima College, there's something going on all the time — lectures, theater, dance, name entertainment and local talent.

Edie, an avid reader, is particularly impressed with the number of successful writers in Tucson. Authors such as Charles Bowden ("The Blue Desert," "Desierto") and Richard Shelton ("Going Back to Bisbee") follow a course set by the late naturalist Joseph Wood Krutch and writer Edward Abbey ("The Brave Cowboy," "Desert Solitaire") in defining, preserving and protecting the stark, awesome landscape. Top-selling writers such as Barbara Kingsolver ("The Poisonwood Bible," "The Bean Trees"), Tom Miller ("Trading With the Enemy," "The Panama Hat Trail") and Byrd Baylor ("Desert Voices") also call Tucson home. Larry McMurtry ("Lonesome Dove") spends almost enough time in Tucson to qualify as a local.

Also drawn to Tucson by its spectacular scenery, fabulous weather and laid-back Western ambiance are Warner and Liesel Zimmt, 77 and 60-something respectively. He's a Berlin-born chemist and archaeologist, and she's a retired office manager from Los Angeles. They were married just a year ago.

Zimmt, who has five degrees and all but speaks in equations, finds Tucson's academic atmosphere appealing. He volunteers several days a week at the University of Arizona in various research departments and as a research associate with the Arizona State Museum. He also works one day a week as a volunteer attendant at the Metropolitan Tucson Convention and Visitors Bureau information booth downtown.

The Zimmts live in a large two-story home in the Sabino Canyon area, not far from the eastern section of

Tucson's Saguaro National Park, formerly classified as a national monument before it became the country's 52nd national park. It contains thousands of acres of candelabra-shaped cactuses that annually attract more than 700,000 visitors. Many of the towering plants, some more than 60 feet high, have stood tall in the desert since before the time of Coronado.

Columnar, lofty and majestic, their limbs raised to the heavens as though in prayer, the saguaro is the very symbol of the Arizona desert. No Tucson travel advertisement is complete without one, nor is any Hollywood Western. They've even been transported to Spain and Italy to authenticate the scenery for "spaghetti Westerns."

Saguaro National Park actually consists of two sprawling sections of the Sonoran Desert east and west of town, about 30 miles apart. Designated driving loops offer a close-up look at the towering plants that grow in such profusion nowhere else in the world.

Within its dry sierras, canyons and mesas, Tucson and its southern Arizona boundaries contain 27 varieties of cactuses and a wide assortment of flora, wildlife and birds. Desert walks are popular, especially at sunrise.

The Southwest desert was long considered a scourge of man, arid and untamable, but now more and more people see in its raw, awesome beauty

Tucson, AZ

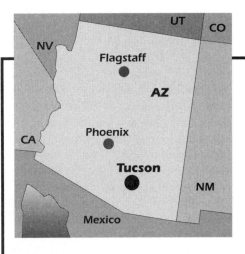

Population: More than 486,699 in Tucson, 843,746 in Pima County.

Location: Tucson is located in south-central Arizona 60 miles north of the Mexican border.

Climate:

	High	Low
January	64	38
July	99	74

Average relative humidity: 25%

Rain: 11 inches.

Cost of living: 100 (national average is 100).

Median housing cost: $117,700

Sales tax: 7.6%

Sales tax exemptions: Groceries and prescription drugs.

State income tax: For married couples filing jointly, graduated from 2.87% of taxable income up to $20,000 to 5.04% minus $2,276 on amounts over $300,000. For single filers, graduated from 2.87% of taxable income up to $10,000 to 5.04% minus $1,138 on amounts over $150,000.

Income tax exemptions: Social Security benefits and up to $2,500 on federal, state and local government pensions are exempt.

Estate tax: None, except the state's "pick-up" portion of federal tax, applicable to taxable estates of more than $1 million.

Property tax: Approximately $15-$17 per $100 of assessed value depending on the school district. Residential property is assessed at 10 percent of market value. The annual tax on a $117,700 home would be $1,766-$2,001.

Homestead exemption: None.

Religion: More than 1,500 churches and synagogues represent virtually every denomination.

Education: Student enrollment at the University of Arizona is 35,747, and the university is the county's largest employer with a staff and faculty of more than 10,000. Pima Community College is the fifth-largest multicampus community college in the nation with more than 72,000 credit and noncredit students enrolled in more than 2,000 classes annually. The University of Phoenix, the largest private business school in the country, has a campus in Tucson. Prescott College has an adult degree program in Tucson, attracting older students who are continuing their educations or hoping to start over in a new career.

Transportation: Sun Tran offers bus service throughout Tucson. Fare is $1 (40 cents for passengers 65 and older).

Health: Tucson has 14 major hospitals, more than 1,500 doctors and more than 400 dentists. Tucson has the state's only medical school and is home of the Arizona Cancer Center and the University Medical Center. University Medical Center's transplant program is one of only nine in the nation.

Housing options: Apartments, condominiums and townhouses are available in all sections of the metropolitan area.

Tucson has more than 25 adult retirement apartment complexes and 17 parks for recreational vehicles and mobile homes. **Civano,** (888) 224-8266, is an 818-acre community that merges traditional neighborhood concepts with conservation-focused building methods. Styles include bungalows, adobe-inspired homes and contemporary Southwest designs. Townhomes start in the mid-$160,000s, and single-family homes range from the low $100,000s to the high $200,000s. **Sunflower** by Del Webb, (888) 833-5932, is a 245-acre active-adult community about 12 miles northwest of Tucson. Ten floor plans are available, with prices from the $100,000s. Residents can enjoy tennis, a fitness center and a Village Center that houses art and crafts, a game room and meeting rooms. Other active-adult retirement communities include **The Cascades,** (520) 886-3171; **Copper Crest,** (520) 883-6670; **Quail Ridge Estates,** (520) 825-9088; **SaddleBrooke,** (520) 825-3030; and **Villa Compana Retirement Residences,** (520) 886-3600.

Visitor lodging: There are about 13,000 rooms in hotels, resorts, motels, bed-and-breakfast inns and guest ranches in the metropolitan area. About 2,000 rooms are in resort and luxury accommodations, including Sheraton El Conquistador, $114-$285, (800) 325-3535; Loews Ventana Canyon, $80-$375, (520) 299-2020; and Westward Look Resort, $99-$340, (520) 297-1151.

Information: Tucson Metropolitan Chamber of Commerce, 465 W. St. Marys Road, Tucson, AZ 85701, (520) 792-1212 or www.tucsonchamber.org.

the last vestige of America's wilderness. For Warner and Liesel Zimmt, it represents the very essence of Tucson's lifestyle.

Also celebrating the desert is the Arizona-Sonora Desert Museum, an internationally known zoo in the 16,000-acre Tucson Mountain Park 12 miles west of town. Founded about 40 years ago, its "cages" are sand dunes, water holes, dry washes, rock caves, shrubs and trees. Glass-panel viewing allows visitors to watch otters and beavers cavort underwater.

The museum maintains the precise natural habitat of the animals, fish, birds and insects it houses and protects, from mountain lions to tarantulas and javelinas to rattlesnakes. The result is a zoo that seems not to be a zoo at all — always the best kind.

Along with the wildlife exhibits, underground limestone caves can be explored. They're part of the Earth Sciences Center, which also includes meteor and mineral displays. Visitors are encouraged to examine the stones and even study them under magnifying glasses. The Arizona-Sonora Desert Museum is one of the most popular tourist attractions in the state, second only to the Grand Canyon.

Tucson's informal entrepreneurial style — a throwback to frontier days — makes total retirement difficult. Many newcomers opt to open small businesses such as gift shops, bed-and-breakfast inns, restaurants and the like. Among them are Eve and Gerry Searle, 63 and 75, respectively. Eve was raised in Czechoslovakia and India, where her family moved to escape life under a communist dictatorship. In 1948 her family moved again, this time to Sydney, Australia, where Eve worked as a pilot and flying instructor.

While visiting Tucson, Eve thought a cattle roundup might be fun. That's where she met Gerry, a guy on a horse who looked to Eve like a movie star, and she wasn't far wrong. Gerry worked as a stuntman and rider on such Western hits as "High Chaparral," "Heaven With a Gun," "Dirty Dingus Magee" and "Monte Walsh" and was Lee Marvin's double in several films.

Eve and Gerry married and now own and operate the Grapevine Canyon Ranch at the base of Dragoon Mountain, some 85 miles southeast of Tucson. There's nothing else around for miles except mountains, canyons, mesquite, oak and manzanita. At an elevation of 5,000 feet, no lofty saguaros stab at the sky. There's only brush, small trees and crumbling adobe, the remains of early homesteads.

Eve is fascinated by the area's history. East is the Chiricahua Mountain Range, which includes Fort Bowie, the Chiricahua National Monument, Rucker Canyon in the Coronado National Forest, and Turkey Creek. The Chiricahua Mountain Range was the setting for Elliott Arnold's classic novel, "Blood Brother," about the friendship between Cochise and American scout Tom Jeffords. It was made into the film "Broken Arrow," with Jeff Chandler playing Cochise and Jimmy Stewart as the scout.

The Searles consider Grapevine Canyon Ranch as their nest egg and retirement home, which they share with numerous visitors. Many of them check out the stark, stunning landscape, spotting a lion or a bobcat off in the distance, or watch a hawk flying overhead in wide, watchful circles. It's the kind of vista that makes guests think that, heck, Tucson might not be a bad place to retire.

On the debit side, the outspoken Warner Zimmt finds Tucson bus service abominable for a city its size. Residents complain that service is too infrequent, the buses don't go far enough out of town, and hours are limited. Two lines, the Broadway and Speedway, whose buses run every 20 minutes or so, are praised, but the city's once-an-hour cross-town lines draw criticism.

Traffic in general also is a topic of concern to numerous Tucsonans. While city traffic hasn't reached the gridlock proportions of Phoenix, its sprawling sister city to the north, it continues to worsen. At press time, Tucsan had the sixth highest automobile theft rate in the country. Cars parked at Tucson shopping centers seem especially attractive targets and sometimes are found across the border in Mexico. The border town of Nogales is only 60 miles to the south.

But when asked if there was anything about Tucson they didn't like, Roger and Edie Harvey had to think about it over tea and brownies in the living room of their spotless desert home filled with Indian and Mexican prints by a nationally known local artist, the late Ted DeGrazia. "I don't like snakes," says Edie, hard pressed for an answer.●

Venice, Florida

This Florida town's popularity with retirees dates to 1925

By Richard L. Fox

Take a casual stroll, drive or bicycle ride along Venice Avenue from downtown west to the Gulf of Mexico beaches, and you are struck by the charm, grace and beauty of Venice. Draped in tropical vegetation and shaded by huge oaks, Florida pines and palms, and built in the architectural styles of the canal city of northern Italy, this picturesque village exudes the trappings of a retirement paradise.

Blossoming orange trees, crape myrtles, azaleas and bougainvillea bring diverse fragrances and vivid colors to the wide median of this popular boulevard, which serves as a main conduit to many small parks and sporting venues for a growing colony of retirees. Legions of active, health-conscious seniors, numbering more than half the total population, frequent the tennis courts, lawn bowling greens and shuffleboard lanes within walking distance of their homes.

"There is a wonderful sense of community," says Gay McCarthy, who vacationed in Venice for several years from her home in Massachusetts before moving to Southwest Florida in retirement with her husband. "The people are extremely friendly."

The town's popularity with retirees has a long history. It was selected by the National Brotherhood of Locomotive Engineers as its retirement city in 1925 and has been building on that image ever since. A historic district and architectural review board were created to ensure that the city's original Northern Italian Renaissance architectural styles will be maintained, and plans for new construction or exterior renovation must meet this critical objective.

Its designation as a Florida Main Street City reinforces the preservation of its heritage. Downtown Venice is a safe, clean, visitor-friendly collection of gift shops, boutiques, art galleries, museums and restaurants, many housed in buildings listed on the National Register of Historic Places.

Casually dressed visitors and residents stroll palm-lined sidewalks, barely aware of passing traffic on its lightly traveled cobblestone streets. These same quiet avenues transition westward into elegant neighborhoods of small parks, manicured lawns and attractive, well-kept homes before arriving at water's edge.

When the Gulf Coast Intracoastal Waterway was constructed in 1963, downtown Venice was spared separation from the Gulf — an affliction of many coastal towns that requires extensive bridge networks. With the major north-south highways, Highway 41 (Tamiami Trail) and Highway 41

Bypass located east of downtown, an uninterrupted beach connection enhances local traffic flow, especially pedestrian traffic. Neighborhood growth patterns east of these arteries also have benefited, with less intrusion by nonlocal traffic into residential communities, and easy access to the interstate highway.

John and Betty Moody, natives of England, spent three years in the United States and abroad searching for a place to retire. Included in this odyssey was a winter in a 400-year-old cottage in England, three months on Longboat Key in Florida, and shorter stays in Oceanside and Carlsbad, CA, before settling in Nokomis, a tiny coastal enclave across Roberts Bay from Venice. John, 75, and Betty, 63, had lived a number of years in South Africa, Kenya and Zimbabwe and 12 years in Santa Barbara, CA, but they found what they were looking for on a secluded bay in Southwest Florida.

After service in the British Royal Navy in World War II, John settled in southern Africa in 1947. First engaged in real estate, he later manufactured travel trailers in Bulawayo, Zimbabwe, then trailers, pickup campers and motor homes in Durban, South Africa. Before marrying Betty in 1972 and moving to California in 1977, he manufactured mobile homes and developed retirement mobile-home parks in South Africa.

"We have four children in Georgia, New Hampshire and Maine, and they all love Florida," Betty says. "But the thing that brought us to Venice is its feeling of community. Sarasota (18 miles north) is a beautiful city, but I don't get the same feeling of community. Venice fits our interests and has the amenities we like. We love the climate and relaxed way of life."

They bought a "Florida home with all sliding glass doors opening into the pool area" in one of the "secret little neighborhoods" that make Venice so appealing, Betty says. Their home is on Hidden Bay, which flows into Shakett Creek, which becomes Dona Bay, eventually bisecting the Intracoastal Waterway before emptying into the Gulf of Mexico. By boat they navigate this three-mile passage in a matter of minutes. By automobile, they can cover the two miles from their home to Interstate 75 in five minutes.

Larry and Gay McCarthy owned a condominium in Venice for seven years and visited the area regularly from their home in Falmouth, MA, before moving here in 1994. Gay's late parents were longtime residents of Venice, and there was never any doubt about where she and Larry would live in retirement.

After 31 years in banking, the opportunity came shortly after the New World Bank of Cape Cod, where Larry, 56, was president, was acquired by another bank. A change of climate was a strong motivation for the move, Larry says, coupled with a lower cost of living and the fact that Florida has no state income tax.

They built a new home two years ago in Capri Isles, a master-planned subdivision three miles east of downtown. Gay describes it as "a typical Florida home" built on a former horse-riding farm.

Larry is a member of the Venice Rotary Club, sits on the Venice Foundation board and is a director of their homeowner's association. He also serves as chairman of the Senior Outreach Committee of the Venice Area Chamber of Commerce.

When he isn't busy volunteering, Larry enjoys landscaping and recently took up golf — "I never had time to play before retirement" — at the urging of his sons, who enjoy golfing with him when they visit Florida.

Gay, 55, likes "the beauty of the town, its beaches and Gulf waters." When she isn't playing tennis, swimming, practicing aerobic exercises, walking, bicycling or gardening, Gay serves on the board of the Friends of Venice Art Center and as a member of Courtside Tennis Club and the YMCA.

Housing options are plentiful in the area. Many retirees choose older homes in tree-shaded neighborhoods within walking distance of downtown and the beaches. Some pick property on a canal or the bay in one of the quiet, unincorporated communities — Nokomis, Laurel, Osprey and South Venice — that encircle Venice. Still others prefer modern Florida ranch homes in upscale, gated, golf-course subdivisions like Waterford, Capri Isles, Calusa Lakes and Venice Golf and Country Club on the outskirts of the city.

Resident-owned condominiums vie with resort accommodations, yacht clubs and marinas for prized land on the Gulf. Cost-conscious retirees find that manufactured-home communities run the gamut from upscale, grandly designed Bay Indies to less-expensive sites.

For retirees who want health-care options, Village on the Isle, a non-profit continuing-care retirement community, has 211 independent-living apartments, 95 assisted-living units and a 60-bed skilled nursing facility. There is a one-time entrance fee and a monthly service fee. A pri-

Venice, FL

Population: 25,144 in Venice (the population doubles in winter) and 325,957 in Sarasota County.
Location: Florida Gulf Coast between Sarasota and Fort Myers.
Climate:

	High	Low
January	73	52
July	91	72

Average relative humidity: 62%
Rain: 47 inches.
Cost of living: Above average (specific index not available).
Average housing cost: Average price of single-family home sales is $195,000.
Sales tax: 7%
Sales tax exemptions: Food, medicine and professional services.
State income tax: None.
Intangibles tax: Assessed on stocks, bonds and other assets. Tax rate is $1 per $1,000 in assets. The first $20,000 in assets is exempt for individuals. For

couples filing jointly, the first $40,000 is exempt. Those who owe less than $60 need not pay.
Estate tax: None, except the state's "pick-up" portion of the federal tax, applicable to taxable estates above $1 million.
Property tax: In the city, the rate is $17.46 per $1,000 of assessed value, with homes assessed at 100% of market value. In Sarasota County, the rate is $14.05 per $1,000. The yearly tax on a $195,000 home in Venice is $2,968 (with $25,000 exemption noted below).
Homestead exemption: First $25,000 of assessed value on primary, permanent residence.
Religion: 88 Protestant churches and a Jewish synagogue.
Education: Manatee Community College, eight miles east of Venice, offers more than 90 fields of study. The University of South Florida, Nova University and the Ringling School of Art and Design offer a broad range of courses in Sarasota, 18 miles north.
Transportation: Sarasota County Area Transit (SCAT) provides bus service within the county. Sarasota-Bradenton International Airport is 25 miles north; Southwest Florida International Airport is 56 miles south.
Health: Bon Secours-Venice Hospital has 342 beds and is a full-service facility

with 24-hour emergency service. There are 158 physicians on staff.
Housing options: Gulf-view condominiums are listed from $200,000 to $1 million. **Bay Indies,** a manufactured-home community with excellent amenities, has resales from $15,000 to $96,500, (941) 485-5441. **Pelican Pointe Golf and Country Club,** a gated community, has homes from $250,000 to $600,000, (941) 496-4663. **Calusa Lakes** has lake-front and golf course locations. Maintenance-free homes are $200,000 to $300,000, and custom homes range from $389,000 to $800,000, (941) 484-6004. **The Venice Golf and Country Club** has detached maintenance-free patio and custom single-family homes from $150,000, (941) 493-3100. **Village on the Isle** is a continuing-care retirement community, (941) 484-9753.
Visitor lodging: Veranda Inn, $52-$142 depending on season, (941) 484-9559. Best Western Sandbar Beach Resort, $109-$399, (800) 822-4853. The Quarterdeck Resort Condominiums, $610-$780 per week (depending on season) for a one-bedroom unit, (800) 845-0251.
Information: Venice Area Chamber of Commerce, 257 Tamiami Trail N., Vence, FL 34285-1908, (941) 488-2236 or www.venicechamber.com.

ority program permits applicants to reserve the apartment of their choice for $1,000, which is applied to the entrance fee when residents move in. New residents must be at least 62 and in good health.

The McCarthys and Moodys rate health-care facilities equal to or better than those in their former hometowns. The 342-bed Bon Secours-Venice Hospital, a full-service facility with 24-hour emergency service, requires all of its medical staff to be board-certified in their specialties. But residents in the extreme north and south may have faster access to hospitals in one of the neighboring cities.

Sarasota Memorial, approximately 20 miles north of Venice, is a 845-bed regional center, the second-largest nonprofit public hospital in Florida. It ranks among the top 25 in the country in the number of open-heart surgical procedures performed annually and is among the top 10 in joint replacements performed each year.

Englewood Community Hospital, about 20 miles south, has a 24-hour emergency care center, a cardiac care center, and helicopter port for quick transport of critically ill patients to better-equipped nearby hospitals.

The community offers many options for volunteers. Volunteer Center South, a nonprofit United Way agency, organizes and coordinates placement of volunteers in 70 organizations in the area and publishes a yearly "wishbook" listing the specific needs of these groups in terms of tax-deductible material donations, volunteering time and help with special projects.

Culturally, Venice may not receive the acclaim of its more famous sister city, Sarasota, but it boasts an impressive array of cultural arts organizations, including a community the-ater, dinner theater, opera and theater guilds, ballet company and symphony orchestra. The Venice Little Theater enjoys national renown with a full schedule of musicals, one-act plays and summer children's theater.

The Venice Art Center hosts year-round exhibits, sells original artworks, and offers classes for adults and children. Venice Community Center downtown seats more than 700 and is the main venue for cultural activities.

But Floridians like to spend most daylight hours outdoors, and Venetians are no exception. Fourteen miles of soft white-sand beaches from Osprey to Manasota Key draw sunbathers, swimmers, shell collectors and beach strollers. A sand replenishment project completed in 1996 widened a three-mile stretch along Venice Beach up to 300 feet deep, correcting an erosion problem and providing acres of additional space for beach-front activities. For those who prefer inland activities, 13 public and semiprivate golf courses in the greater Venice area are available to challenge the skills and endurance of the most inveterate golfers.

The highlight of the summer season is the Sharks Tooth and Seafood Festival, an annual event that takes place at the Venice Fishing Pier on the second weekend in August, attracting thousands of visitors from all over Florida. In addition to sharks-tooth hunts and culinary delights prepared by more than 25 area restaurants, this festive occasion features a juried display of original works by artists and craftsmen from around the state, and popular educational displays from the Mote Marine Laboratory of Sarasota and the Pelican Man's Bird Sanctuary, which rescues and rehabilitates injured pelicans and oth-er wild birds.

In January, February and March, a series of senior street dances is sponsored by the Parks and Recreation Department, and the Sunset Serenade Concert Series January through April brings out large numbers of visitors and locals alike at the Gazebo in downtown Venice.

The Venice Area Chamber of Commerce sponsors a year-round program of wellness walks that feature free continental breakfasts, door-prize drawings and guest speakers in addition to the one-mile walk. Health-conscious retirees are well-represented at these events.

Continuing-education courses for retirees are available at the South County Adult and Community Education Center, and Manatee Community College eight miles east of Venice. The latter enrolls more than 1,500 full- and part-time students in more than 90 academic fields of study. Advanced courses are available at the University of South Florida and the Ringling School of Art and Design in Sarasota.

Betty Moody, who spent a number of years in executive positions with Max Factor, was surprised to find 18 members in the local chapter of the Daughters of the British Empire when she joined upon moving to Venice. Betty says she and her husband both enjoy walking, swimming, fishing and boating, but her favorite pastime is "assisting with line dancing in the Venice Senior Center."

Mustering all of the diplomacy for which the British are noted when asked what she likes least about Venice, Betty Moody grudgingly confides, "One would not be mean enough to say, 'the winters, when all the visitors come,' but I can think of nothing else." ●

Vero Beach, Florida

Strict rules protect land, water at Florida Atlantic Coast community

By Jay Clarke

Herman and Judith Niebuhr Jr., both professors at Temple University in Philadelphia, knew they wanted to retire in Florida. Their problem, as with many people approaching retirement age, was choosing just where in Florida to settle.

They checked out the Keys, West Palm Beach and Melbourne. Then they drove into Vero Beach.

"Once we saw it, it took us about 20 minutes to decide to move here," says Judith Niebuhr. "It's beautiful. It's like living in a park. And it turns out it's a great community as well."

People turn on quickly to Vero Beach. It's a tight little community with an upscale bent, an orderly place with strict rules to protect its land and waters and to keep development in line. It also offers a wealth of recreational opportunities, from boating, fishing and golf to Grapefruit League baseball, theater and active volunteerism.

That kind of ambiance has special appeal to retirees, especially when it is set in a caring community attuned to the needs of its older residents. In addition to its variety of housing options for retirees, Vero Beach has good supportive programs.

The not-for-profit Council on Aging, for example, maintains a senior center and offers a wide range of help and activities, from shuffleboard and art classes to transportation and meals for the elderly. The city has three accredited hospitals, a new library and excellent cultural facilities.

For many retirees, though, a large part of Vero's appeal lies in its opportunities for active lifestyles. The Niebuhrs are passionate about movements that help retirees put more activity and purpose in their lives.

"Research shows that if you keep an active, questing mind moving, you're apt to live longer," notes Herman "Reck" Niebuhr, 66. "Yet I see one guy pacing on his balcony of his condo all day long. And, you know, we've got retired CEOs living in John's Island who are worth a couple million bucks or so, and a third of them are going bananas.

"They live in a gilded cage, bored silly, looking for something to do — so they've gotten involved in what we're trying to do."

Reck is coordinating a Volunteer Action Center, a non-profit group sponsored by the Junior Service League. The center recruits and trains volunteers and fosters a sense of purpose that sometimes is lacking in the lives of retirees.

"And with so many single parents, or homes where both parents work, we have also developed a 'neighborhood grandparents' concept where we get involved with kids in the neighborhood," he says.

Keeping busy also is something Howard and Joyce Brand strive to achieve, but in a different way. Formerly of Wisconsin, the Brands, like the Niebuhrs, immediately were impressed with Vero Beach.

"It was such a clean little city. The ocean was right there with good access to inlets. We like to fish and boat. There were good golf courses close by. We have never been disappointed," says Howard.

They had wintered once in Lakeland and canvassed other locales in Florida before visiting Vero Beach one weekend. "That was it," says Howard. "We went back to Wisconsin, sold our home, loaded up the car and came back to Vero Beach."

The Brands, ardent boaters, keep busy setting up excursions for the Grady Bunch, a group of Grady White boat owners who travel together four or five times a year on trips around Florida. Both have been commodores of the Vero Beach Boat Club.

"It is hard to think about leaving your children and grandchildren, but we have been so busy we hardly have time to think about them. People here are awfully friendly. We really feel part of the community," says Joyce.

The Center for the Arts, Vero Beach's outstanding cultural facility, stages national and international exhibitions and has the largest museum art school in the state. Sports fans can watch major league baseball every spring when the Los Angeles Dodgers come to town. The Dodgers have taken spring practice in Vero Beach since 1948, when they were the pride of Brooklyn.

Dodgertown, their practice ground, is a sprawling complex that includes a convention center, a golf course (open to the public), a stadium, practice diamonds and rentable rooms and apartments, each with a street lamp whose globe is shaped like an outsized baseball. Roads in the complex are named after famous Dodger players, among them Jackie Robinson, Roy Campanella, Pee Wee Reese and Sandy Koufax.

Those are the most recognizable names one is likely to come across in Vero Beach, which likes to keep a low profile. More than just a way of life, it is a literal fact: By law, no building in the county can rise higher than three stories (five stories in town). Except for two grandfathered structures, Vero allows no high-rises, even on valuable beachfront property. Strict setbacks, square-footage requirements and high impact fees discourage rampant development.

That's quite a change from the Vero Beach of half a century ago, when one of its most prominent citizens was an eccentric who built three of the city's most unusual structures. Waldo Sexton, using no blueprints and simply shouting instructions to workers, incorporated driftwood, stone, odd lumber, mastodon bones and anything else that suited his fancy into his

Driftwood Inn, which the New York Times once described as "the damnedest place you've ever seen."

He furnished it with eclectic items he acquired abroad or bought at estate auctions — among them Tiffany lamps and other items from Palm Beach mansions, and ship's bells from wherever he could get them. In one of the inn's rooms is Fanny Brice's couch; on the facade of another building is an original della Robbia.

Sexton died years ago, but his legacies live on. The weather-beaten Driftwood Inn still stands on the beach, and a block away is another of his unusual buildings, the Ocean Grill, one of the area's prime restaurants. The third structure, the Patio Restaurant, also survives in town; a mantle from the estate of car magnate Horace Dodge is among the decor.

In Sexton's day, the Driftwood and Ocean Grill were about the only developments on the beach. Today, the main beach road, Highway A1A, is lined with condominiums, resorts, tony housing developments and dozens of upscale businesses like stock brokerages and trendy boutiques.

The area's poshest developments lie on A1A. Places like John's Island, the Moorings, Sea Oaks, Sea Grove and Riomar are plush havens for retired nabobs of industry and commerce, and new ones are being developed. Windsor, a Galen Weston and Abercrombie & Kent project, attracts an international clientele. General Electric has put together Bermuda Bay, and Disney chose Vero Beach as the site for its first oceanside resort.

On the mainland side of the Indian River, the lagoon that extends for 156 miles on Florida's east coast, Vero has many less-pricey housing developments as well as continuing-care facilities and nursing homes for those

Vero Beach, FL

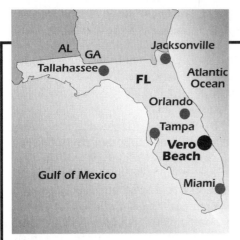

Population: 18,000 in Vero Beach, 115,700 in Indian River County.

Location: On the Atlantic Coast in mid-Florida, about halfway between West Palm Beach and Cape Canaveral.

Climate:

	High	Low
January	72	52
July	90	72

Average relative humidity: 60% Dry season runs from November to May, wet season June to October. A breeze from the ocean makes the summer heat more bearable.

Rain: 50 inches.

Cost of living: 99, based on national average of 100.

Median housing cost: The average sales price of a single-family home is $137,500. Average sale price for homes on the barrier island is $350,000.

Sales tax: 7%

Sales tax exemptions: Groceries, prescription drugs, medical services.

State income tax: None.

Intangibles tax: Assessed on stocks, bonds and other specified assets. Tax rate is $1 per $1,000 in assets. The first $20,000 in assets is exempt for individuals. For couples filing jointly, the first $40,000 is exempt. Those who owe less than $60 need not pay.

Estate tax: None, except the state's "pick-up" portion of the federal tax, applicable to taxable estates of more than $1 million.

Property taxes: About $19.3 per $1,000 of assessed value. Homes are assessed at 100% of market value. Yearly tax on a $137,500 home is about $2,171, with the homestead exemption noted below.

Homestead exemption: $25,000 off assessed value on primary, permanent residence.

Religion: The county has more than 100 churches of various denominations.

Education: Indian River Community College in Fort Pierce has a branch campus in Vero Beach. Florida Institute of Technology is situated in Melbourne, about 35 miles north.

Transportation: Community Coach bus system provides transportation through the Council on Aging. The nearest airport is Melbourne International Airport in Melbourne, 35 minutes away.

Health: Indian River County is served by two general hospitals and one rehabilitation hospital. The largest is Indian River Memorial Hospital, just north of Vero, with 347 beds. Sebastian River Medical Center has 133 beds. Both offer critical care. Treasure Coast Rehabilitation Hospital near Indian River Memorial has 70 beds.

Housing options: A wide range of housing styles are available, including **Isles of Vero Beach**, a retirement community of apartments for rent, (561) 778-7888, and **Vista Properties**, which has several condominium developments in the area, (561) 569-3416. **The Village of Sea Oaks,** (888) 732-6257, is on a barrier island north of Vero Beach and has tennis, a clubhouse with private beach, and fitness center. **Indian River Estates** is the area's largest continuing-care facility, (561) 770-0058; a smaller facility is the 24-bed **Orchid Island Manor**, (561) 567-6769.

Visitor lodging: Vero Beach attracts more than 500,000 visitors a year and has 1,700 rooms beachside and on the mainland. Moderate examples include the beachside Vero Beach Inn, $79, (800) 227-8615, and Comfort Inn in town, $49-$71, (561) 569-0900. Rates increase December through April.

Information: Vero Beach-Indian River County Chamber of Commerce, P.O. Box 2947, Vero Beach, FL 32961, (561) 567-3491 or www.vero-beach.fl.us/chamber.

in less robust health.

Single-family homes in Indian River County run $30,000 to $3 million. The average price for a single-family home is $137,500. Homes on the barrier island are more expensive, with an average price of $350,000.

Also on the mainland is downtown Vero, which is sprucing up its look for tourists. The newly restored Heritage Center is of some historical interest; it is where William Jennings Bryan, "the Great Commoner," made his last public appearance in 1925.

Causeways cross the Indian River to connect the mainland with Memorial Island, site of the Center for the Arts and the Riverside Theater, an equity playhouse, and with the beach, which enjoys national renown.

But the Indian River itself, which is really not a river but an estuary lagoon, is one of Vero's prime attractions. Its brackish waters are home to some of America's best game fish — bluefish, cobia, grouper, king mackerel and tarpon among them — and the surrounding lands harbor almost 1,500 kinds of plants and 310 species of birds.

Running through the middle of it is the Intracoastal Waterway, the boat highway that runs from Florida to Maine. That waterway makes it easy to reach Sebastian Inlet State Park, the state's most popular state park 14 miles north of Vero, and nearby Pelican Island, America's first federal wildlife refuge.

Some towns that make a fine first impression sometimes lose their luster after a while. But Vero's sheen seems to last.

If the Brands had it to do over, would they do anything differently? "Yes," says Joyce. "We'd come down 10 years earlier."

The Niebuhrs also are happy with their move and have no plans to look elsewhere.

"We're done," says Reck Niebuhr. "It doesn't get any better than this."●

Vicksburg, Mississippi

Ole Man River sets the tone in this easygoing port city

By Bern Keating

In the spring, camellias, azaleas, banksia and peach trees grace the gardens of Greek Revival antebellum mansions in this slow-paced city of about 29,000 residents, a time capsule perched on the bluffs of the Mississippi River midway between Memphis and New Orleans.

Vicksburg's gracious Southern hospitality and Civil War landmarks are attractions to thousands of tourists each year, but an unsurpassed friendliness is what attracts newcomers like Jim and Sarah Pilgrim to relocate to Vicksburg in retirement. Jim, 62, moved to Vicksburg after retiring from his post in Little Rock, AR, as a regional official for an interstate electric power company.

"Of the 20 moves we made during my career from lineman to management, we enjoyed by far the widest circle of friends during our short stay in Vicksburg," says Jim, backed by Sarah's nods of agreement. "We remembered that when it came time to pick a spot for the rest of our lives."

Like seaports, river ports are traditionally more mixed ethnically, educationally and socially than inland cities, says Jim. Because of the constant comings and goings, residents tend to be less frightened of newcomers in port towns, he says.

And there are plenty of comings and goings in Vicksburg. Besides the port, the Vicksburg National Military Park attracts hordes of tourists from around the world. They come to walk the 1,800 acres of the magnificently preserved site of the 47-day siege that played a large part in the outcome of the Civil War.

"Also, the huge U.S. Army Corps of Engineers station here promotes a steady changeover of highly educated professionals who contribute their sophisticated leavening to the mixture," adds Jim.

Visitors to the small city are so numerous that they support 80 stylish restaurants and more modest cafes. There are 22 motels and hotels of major international and national franchises.

And there are 12 bed-and-breakfast inns lodged in stunning landmark buildings, like Anchuca, an 1820 Greek Revival mansion where Jefferson Davis, president of the defeated Confederacy, made a speech from the second-story balcony. A Union cannonball remains lodged in the parlor of Cedar Grove, built in 1840. Another bed-and-breakfast inn, Duff Green Mansion, served as a hospital for soldiers on both sides of the Civil War.

Other recent Vicksburg newcomers include James Bowman and his wife, Barbara, who both retired from the U.S. Army Medical Corps — James, 50, after 30 years of service and Barbara, 47, after 20 years. The Bowmans are African-American, and James admits he initially was dubious about moving to Mississippi. He worried they might not feel welcome, but his fears have been more than assuaged.

Two years before retirement from their post in Germany, James flew back to the states to investigate possible retirement locations. Still looking for a home, the South Carolina native accompanied his wife on a visit to her 11 siblings in Vicksburg — and found an astonishing friendliness that sold him on the city.

James located a lot on an upscale street east of town. After their retirement ceremony in Germany, the Bowmans moved into the impressive red brick house they built in a new development in Vicksburg.

"Soon after we moved in, I gave myself a 50th birthday party on our lawn," James remembers. "A crowd of 110 came to wish us well. All my neighbors were there."

Even Mississippi's scorching summer heat and humidity didn't discourage James. "After eight years of German snow and ice, this Vicksburg sun is just beginning to thaw me out," he chuckles.

Vicksburg's climate is, indeed, warm. July noontime temperatures average 92 with high humidity. But universal air conditioning has come to the rescue. Winters are almost semitropical, and years pass between snowfalls. Northerners are amused that schools and public offices close in panic when less than an inch of rapidly melting snow accumulates on the ground.

In the Edwards family, it was wife Edna, 63, who dragged Sam, 64, around the country in a recreational vehicle looking for a more solid home than a campsite on wheels. Though she hails from the highly touted retirement spot of Cape May, NJ, she didn't like the tourist hordes that she says have taken over the beaches there. And she thought Vicksburg was the friendliest spot they had found.

When Sam retired from his trucking job in Richmond, VA, Edna put the pressure on her husband to move to the Mississippi city. Sam had grown up in Yazoo City, MS, a small town near Vicksburg, and at first was not enthusiastic about moving back to his home state, fearing that Mississippi might not have kept pace with the times.

But Edna's arguments were persuasive. "Vicksburg has music, libraries, schools, art shows, theater. The town is spruced up and clean," says Edna. Shortly after moving into her suburban home, she was certain she had picked the right place when she spotted deer in her yard and a half-grown bobcat crossing the road in front of her house.

Medical facilities finally convinced Sam, a disabled veteran of the Korean War, that Vicksburg was a good move. The Veterans Administration Hospital is only 42 miles east in Jackson, also the home of University Medical Center, which enjoys world renown for its surgical procedures. Vicksburg itself has two hospitals and about 100 doctors in all major specialties. There also are five long-term care facilities, four home health agencies, one personal care home and three clinics.

Vicksburg is one of 20 certified retirement cities in the state's official retiree attraction program, Hometown Mississippi Retirement. Sam Edwards and Jim Pilgrim volunteer at the Retirement Development Center, where they provide information to relocating retirees. Jim also is readying himself for a new career as a student at the Hinds Community College branch campus in Vicksburg, where he is eyeing woodworking classes.

James Bowman has embarked on a second career with the school system. When he went to enroll his daughter at her new school, the principal quizzed James about his military career. The next thing James knew, he was the new instructor of the Reserve Officers Training Corps. James also is president of the nonprofit Magnificent Seven, a group of men who teach reading and writing to students, and has progressed from

Vicksburg, MS

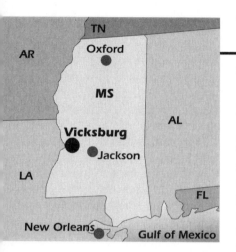

Population: 29,100 in Vicksburg, 50,871 in Warren County.

Location: In western Mississippi on the bluffs of the Mississippi River, 220 miles south of Memphis, 220 miles north of New Orleans and 42 miles west of Jackson. Elevation is 200 feet.

Climate:

	High	Low
January	56	33
July	92	71

Average relative humidity: 58%

Rain: 55.37 inches.

Cost of living: 92.2, based on national average of 100.

Average housing cost: Cost of a new 2,000-square-foot brick home on a half-acre lot is about $150,000. Average cost of an established home is $80,000-$90,000.

Sales tax: 7%

Sales tax exemptions: Prescription drugs.

State income tax: For married couples filing jointly and single filers, the rate is graduated from 3% of taxable income up to $5,000 to 5% on amounts over $10,000.

Income tax exemptions: Social Security benefits, public and private pensions, IRAs and annuities are exempt. There is an additional $1,500 personal exemption for residents age 65 and older.

Intangibles tax: None.

Estate tax: None, except the state's "pick-up" portion of the federal tax, applicable to taxable estates above $1 million.

Property tax: $116.58 per $1,000 of the assessed value of a primary residence. Taxes are assessed on 10 percent of the home's value. Taxes on a $150,000 home would be $1,749, or $874 with the homestead exemption noted below.

Homestead exemption: There is a homestead exemption in the form of a $300 tax credit for all homeowners. Homeowners over age 65 are exempt from property taxes on the first $75,000 of the value of a primary residence. Persons with disabilities also can apply for homestead exemptions.

Religion: There are more than 100 houses of worship serving 30 denominations and faiths in addition to a Jewish temple.

Education: The Vicksburg campus of Hinds Community College is the largest vocational-technical facility in the state and offers courses to retirees. At the U.S. Army Corps of Engineers Waterways Experiment Station, retirees can study for academic credit and graduate degrees granted by such cooperating universities as Louisiana State, Mississippi State and Texas A&M. Retirees willing to commute 42 miles east to Jackson can avail themselves of options at Belhaven College, Jackson State University, Millsaps College and the University of Mississippi Medical Center.

Transportation: Nearest commercial airport is Jackson International, 50 miles east. It is served by Delta, TWA, American Eagle, Southwest, Northwest Airlink and Continental Express. Delta Bus and Greyhound offer service through Vicksburg.

Health: Vicksburg Medical Center and Parkview Regional Medical Center merged in 2002 to create the River Region Health System, the largest hospital building project in the state. It includes 215 patient beds, a 27-bed emergency wing, cardiac catheterization, magnetic resonance imaging (MRI), inpatient dialysis services, physical therapy and the state's first digital mammography equipment. Forty-two miles east in Jackson is the 155-acre University Medical Center campus, home of the prestigious University of Mississippi School of Medicine. It is especially known for its heart and kidney transplant units.

Housing options: Carlton Place is Vicksburg's first gated community. Another new community is **Turning Leaf**, which has four lakes, sports fields, walking trails and a 10-acre common area. Patio homes are available at **Mill Creek**, and housing in established neighborhoods is available in all price ranges, says Mike Davis, chairman of community relations on retiree relocation for the chamber of commerce and an agent with the 100-year-old **Century 21 P.L. Hennessey**, (601) 634-1921. Apartments are available, but house rentals are scarce.

Visitor lodging: Twenty-two hotels and motels and three campgrounds are available to visitors. Among the options are casino hotels and antebellum bed-and-breakfast mansions, including Cedar Grove Mansion Inn, $100-$190, (800) 862-1300; Anchuca, $95-$175, (888) 686-0111; and Duff Green Mansion, $95-$125, (800) 992-0037. At Harrah's Vicksburg Casino, rates start at $79-$109 weeknights (Sunday-Thursday) and $89-$129 weekends (Friday-Saturday), (800) 427-7247.

Information: Vicksburg-Warren County Chamber of Commerce, P.O. Box 709, Vicksburg, MS 39181, (888) VICKSBURG or visit www.vicksburg.org on the Internet. Another helpful site is www.vicksburgliving.com. Ask for a free Mississippi Living guide from Hometown Mississippi Retirement, P.O. Box 849, Jackson, MS 39205-0849, (800) 350-3323 or visit www.mississippi.org on the Internet.

deacon to associate pastor at Mount Zion Baptist Church.

Other Vicksburg retirees work for the Red Cross and Salvation Army and in shelters for the abused and homeless. Some help with literacy and tutorial programs to help faltering students, and a prison ministry offers drug and alcohol counseling and assists families of prisoners with transportation and clothing. The Community Council provides daily hot meals at home for the frail elderly and transportation to group meals.

Between volunteer tasks, retirees find plenty to keep busy. The first job of a newcomer is to explore the sprawling beauty of the Vicksburg National Military Park, which nearly surrounds the city with its 1,300 state and regional statues and monuments to soldiers of both the Confederate and Union armies. After watching an 18-minute movie about the Siege of Vicksburg at the visitors center, the amateur historian can follow the course of the battle by walking in the very footsteps of the soldiers who stormed and defended the fortifications, now beautifully maintained.

Vicksburg offers several other museums, including the Old Court House, where the Confederate flag came down and the Stars and Stripes went up on July 4, 1863. At the Gray and Blue Naval Museum is the world's largest collection of Civil War-era gunboat models. Other museum stops include the Southern Cultural Heritage Center, where both Confederate and Union armies barracked during the Civil War; Jacqueline House, dedicated to the preservation of African-American culture; and Yesterday's Children Antique Doll and Toy Museum. The Biedenharn Museum of Coca-Cola Memorabilia celebrates the bottling of the first coke there in 1894, and you can get an ice-cream float at its old-fashioned soda fountain and candy store.

A hydrojet boat trip with Mississippi River Adventures takes visitors past Civil War fortifications as well as the four major 24-hour casinos — Harrah's, Isle of Capri, Ameristar and Rainbow — that profoundly affected the local economy and considerably enlivened nightlife after they opened in 1993-94.

Jim Pilgrim is among retirees who list hunting and fishing as hobbies. The forests around Vicksburg teem with deer and turkey, and annual dove and duck hunts keep outdoorsmen in the fields for long hours.

The Vicksburg Country Club has an 18-hole golf course as well as a driving range, putting green, tennis courts, swimming pool, pro shop and clubhouse. The Clear Creek Golf Course, with a clubhouse and golf shop, is open to the public. The city owns a swimming pool that it plans to cover for year-round use, and there are many tennis courts and soccer, softball and baseball facilities throughout the county.

A highlight of local festivals is the two-week Spring Pilgrimage in mid-March, when a dozen historic houses are open to the public. The city's nationally known melodrama, "Gold in the Hills," is performed during Spring Pilgrimage, and the audience is encouraged to cheer the hero and pelt the villain with peanuts. Run Through History, a road race, walk and fun run through Vicksburg National Military Park, is in March, and there's a spring arts and crafts show and three-day Riverfest street party in mid-April. A reenactment of the Vicksburg siege is in early July.

All are superbly equipped for making retirement fun. But Jim Pilgrim says it again: "Vicksburg is big enough to provide modern services and entertainment but small enough so the clerks in the stores call you by your first name. It is that friendliness that counts." ●

Viera, Florida

This young, master-planned town in eastern Florida puts residents close to Atlantic beaches and big-city amenities

By Karen Feldman

It was faith that motivated Don and Patti Sabin to leave their home of years in Nashville, TN, and retire to Viera.

"Viera is Slavic for faith," says Patti, 60. "It's the first thing that hit me. I'm a faithful person."

It seemed like a serendipitous match and, three years later, it appears the couple's faith in their new community was well-founded. "I'm so happy here, I can't believe it," Patti says. "It's the most perfect place I've ever lived. It's so easy to make a lot of friends and acquaintances. Everybody wants to be friendly. Everybody says 'hi.'"

While many Florida communities bear names that reflect the surrounding flora and fauna, Viera's name mirrors its hopeful beginnings. An unincorporated community in central Brevard County, Viera once was a sprawling tract of farmland owned by Czechoslovakian immigrant Andrew Duda. His company, A. Duda and Sons, grew to be a large and thriving agricultural operation that ran a successful sod and cattle ranch where Viera now stands.

In the 1980s, Duda's descendants shifted gears, choosing to grow a community that eventually will cover 38,000 acres with a total of 18,000 homes. By 2015, planning experts expect the population to climb to 40,000.

Right now it's considerably smaller, with about 3,000 homes and roughly 7,000 residents, appealing to those who want proximity to Florida's major attractions without having to live in their midst.

"It's like a country lifestyle, but it's not," says Lee Bohlmann, president of the Melbourne Palm Bay Area Chamber of Commerce. "You really have lots of open space. It's very common to have many ponds with ducks, canoes and paddleboats. It's very high-quality living with a lot of attention paid to ambiance."

Homes range in price from the low

$100,000s to about $600,000, says Viera Corp. vice president Steve Johnson. The large master-planned community has no condominiums, but it does have some apartments available, as well as a variety of villas and duplexes. There are some resales to be had, Bohlmann says, but "you'd better put your offer in fast. Anything that's already up sells in less than a month."

Builders such as Lennar, Pulte, Barber, Holiday and Damar are among those constructing homes in Viera. Most of the town's commercial development is clustered along the main thoroughfare, Wickham Road, "with shopping opportunities and some grand restaurants so the neighborhoods truly are very secluded and quiet," Bohlmann says. "With older cities, you're very likely to have a grocery store in the middle of your block. That's not the case in Viera."

That's what attracted the Sabins, who bought their Viera home in the fall of 1997 and moved in 18 months later. They knew they wanted to live in Florida and had checked out other communities, including Destin and Fort Walton Beach, but settled on Viera and the model home they purchased from the developer.

"It's a small community with big-city amenities," says Don Sabin, 66, a retired vice president of human resources with Universal Tire Co.

"We were impressed with the salespeople and its proximity to Orlando, the beach, the King Center (for the Performing Arts)," Patti says. "It's an exciting community that is building up unbelievably."

When they first moved in, they had to travel four or five miles to a supermarket or retail store. That's no longer the case. Over the past three years, Kash N' Karry and Publix supermarkets have opened, as has Lowe's home improvement store. There's a thriving strip center, and Wal-Mart is building a super-

store with five acres of air-conditioned space that should open this summer, making it the county's largest Wal-Mart.

According to Johnson, the development company has gotten county approval for some three million square feet of office space and an equal amount of retail space, ensuring the community will have a solid commercial base.

Also in the works is a town center, known as The Promenade, that will serve as a gathering spot for residents. Johnson says it will include a 16-screen stadium theater as well as restaurants, retail shops, a residential area and lots of open space. The company hopes to open it in the spring of 2003.

Bohlmann says one of the unique features of the proposed town center is Cobblestone, a complex designed to accommodate the needs of disabled people, their caregivers and parents.

Despite Viera's rapid growth, the neighborhoods remain peaceful, lushly landscaped and well kept. The Sabins immediately liked the ambiance, amenities and the people. "It was not a senior citizens' community," says Patti, a retired office manager with Abbott Labs.

That's appealing to many retirees who want to live among a diverse population. "Hundreds of retirees move to Viera for that kind of laid-back lifestyle," Bohlmann says. "This is a section of Florida where water is a great part of our lives. Many of these people have water recreation crafts, whether it's a very large boat or a canoe or kayak they put in on the river or creek. That is a huge part of living here."

The community was designed so that most properties don't back up to other homes. Instead they look out over open space or water, giving the feeling of being worlds away from civilization even though the town is just minutes from Melbourne and an hour southeast of Orlando.

It was that happy combination of ambiance and location that attracted Wilson and Tiny Butler. In the year before Wilson retired after 39 years with the federal Securities and Exchange Commission, the couple considered a number of possibilities, including San Francisco, Raleigh, NC, and Myrtle Beach, SC.

It was Viera that proved irresistible and, after visiting once, they bought a house and moved from Waldorf, MD, in February 1999.

"The warm people, warm climate, its convenience to cruises and travel and golf opportunities" all played a part in their decision, says Wilson, 62. They decided to build in the Viera East Golf Club neighborhood, and Tiny, 54, kept a close eye on the project.

"The first call I got was that the house would not fit on the lot, and they were just going to make it fit," recalls Tiny. "I flew down and bought another lot. If they were out of tile or needed another sink, I drove to Kmart or Home Depot and bought it."

Her diligence paid off. "Tiny supervised construction," Wilson says. "She stayed down here and visited the site daily from her motel room. The laborers were asking her regularly how she wanted things to be done."

Once they moved in, the rest was easy. They made new friends just walking around the circle of homes in their neighborhood, Tiny says. They also made a point of attending community gatherings. "Residents use any excuse for a party," Wilson says.

Both Wilson and Tiny enjoy golfing, a hobby they took up only after retiring. They also eat out often, walk and dance. Tiny likes to bowl, too.

The Sabins found the same convivial atmosphere in their neighborhood. "We took the dog and walked the streets," Patti says. "Everyone here is friendly." Golf, church and volunteering — both volunteer at Wuesthoff Hospital and have served on their homeowners association board — broadened their social circle still further.

The Sabins decided they didn't want the hassle of building a house from afar, so they bought a model home and leased it back to the developer for 16 months until they were ready to relocate.

It's a 2,100-square-foot house with

Viera, FL

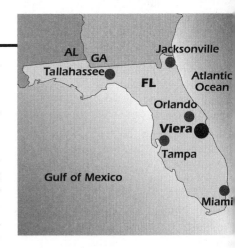

Population: About 7,000.
Location: Viera is south of Cocoa and north of Melbourne in Brevard County on Florida's east coast.
Climate:

	High	Low
January	71	51
July	90	72

Rain: About 46 inches.
Average relative humidity: 62%
Average housing cost: About $225,000
Cost of living: Average (specific index not available).
Sales tax: 6%
Sales tax exemptions: Prescription drugs, groceries and some services.
State income tax: None.
Intangibles tax: A tax of $1 per $1,000 is assessed on stocks, bonds and other assets. The first $20,000 is exempt for individuals. For couples filing jointly, the first $40,000 is exempt. Those who owe less than $60 need not pay.
Estate tax: None, except the state's "pick-up" portion of the federal tax applicable to taxable estates of more than $1 million.
Inheritance tax: None.
Property tax: $19.41 per $1,000 in taxable property. A $225,000 home with a $25,000 homestead exemption would be assessed $3,882 annually.
Homestead exemption: $25,000 off the assessed value of primary, permanent residence.

Religion: Local houses of worship include Lutheran, Roman Catholic and Jewish. In addition, Brevard County is home to dozens of denominations, including Buddhist, Baptist, Quaker and Unitarian.
Education: Florida Institute of Technology in Melbourne is an independent scientific and technological university with a main campus in Melbourne and satellite campuses throughout the county. Brevard Community College is based in Cocoa but has a Melbourne campus and offers associate of arts and science degrees. Keiser College in Melbourne offers associate of science and arts degrees.
Transportation: Melbourne International Airport is served by several commercial airlines as well as charter and air freight companies. Space Coast Area Transit provides public bus transportation throughout the county with a fixed bus route, transport for those who are disabled or disadvantaged and van pool programs.
Health: Two full-service hospitals are located about 20 minutes from Viera. Wuesthoff Hospital, in the town of Rockledge, offers such services as emergency, cardiac, mental health, hospice care and fitness centers. Holmes Regional Medical Center is in Melbourne, offering cardiac care and air ambulance service for emergency care, among oth-

er medical services.
Housing options: A variety of homebuilders operate in Viera, offering a range of villas, duplexes and single-family homes. Many have golf-course views or are situated on freshwater lakes. Prices range from about $110,000 to $600,000, with some priced higher.
Visitor lodging: The Crane Creek Inn Waterfront Bed and Breakfast is a 1924 home with Florida decor overlooking Crane Creek, $90-$150, (321) 768-6416. Another option is Holiday Inn Melbourne Oceanfront, $60-$90, (321) 777-4100.
Information: Viera, 7380 Murrell Road, Suite 201, Viera, FL 32940, (800) 238-4372 or www.viera.com. Melbourne Palm Bay Area Chamber of Commerce, 1005 E. Strawbridge Ave., Melbourne, FL 32901-4740, (321) 724-5400 or www.melpb-chamber.org.

three bedrooms, two baths, a large lanai and pool. All the rooms have 12-foot ceilings and most have sliding glass doors that open to the pool area. "It's a great house to party in," Patti says.

Their community of Heron's Landing also has an Olympic-size swimming pool and numerous bike and walking trails. While Viera has adult communities, such as Grand Isle, the Sabins wanted to live among a mix of retirees and younger families with children. The couple often travels around the neighborhood in their golf cart.

They also enjoy golfing, playing three or four times a week. "I'm a pathetic golfer, but I love it," Patti says.

In her 2001 Christmas letter to friends and family, she wrote: "Don and I still struggle with our golf games ... but the course is magnificent and even if we're not playing good golf, you can't help but enjoy the beauty. There are giant turtles, coveys of birds and an alligator sits in the water watching us hit off the tee. Sandhill cranes dare you to hit them. They know they own the course." The abundant wildlife is a large part of what makes life in Viera so satisfying, Patti says.

Richard and Seena Fox get close to nature via a freshwater lake behind their home. The couple had lived in Scarsdale, NY, for more than 30 years when they literally stumbled upon Viera while vacationing.

"I had no idea of retiring," says Richard Fox, 69. "My son had a friend who had a condo on Melbourne Beach. We came down and liked it so much that we used it the following two years."

When his hands began to bother him, he retired from his dental practice earlier than he had planned. Although Richard had once entertained a move to Maine, Seena, 70, wanted to live someplace warmer. That's when the couple decided to move to Florida.

"We liked the Melbourne area so much that we didn't look at other parts of the state," Richard says. "I have friends who live farther south. The best thing about visiting them is leaving."

"I wanted a new community where everybody was new and looking for new relationships," says Seena, a retired secretary. They bought their three-bedroom, two-bath house on a lake and moved in July 1996. They remain happy with their decision. "The people are courteous, quiet, polite," Richard says. "It's a good pace of living."

Viera is situated inland, in the central portion of Brevard County, which sprawls 72 miles from north to south with a population close to 600,000. The region has a thriving mix of high-tech and natural resources.

At the technological forefront is the National Aeronautics and Space Administration (NASA), which has launched rockets from Cape Canaveral since the 1950s. That history led to the region being dubbed the Space Coast. Today, the space shuttle hurtles into the heavens from Kennedy Space Center several times a year, its trail clearly visible throughout the area, particularly during night launches.

The Kennedy Space Center's Visitor Complex welcomes more than 2.5 million visitors a year and chronicles America's efforts to explore the heavens. Nearby, the Astronaut Hall of Fame tells the stories of individual astronauts. The American Police Hall of Fame and Museum plans to relocate from Miami to its new center near the Astronaut Hall of Fame in May 2003.

Citrus and fishing remain two of the area's industries, and numerous cruise ships set sail from Port Canaveral. Popular as a tourist destination, it also appeals to those who want a temperate climate and things to do that make the most of the good weather.

There are more than 160 parks and two dozen golf courses throughout the county. The Indian River Lagoon, which runs through the heart of the county east of Viera, is home to more than 3,000 species of animals and plants.

Bohlmann says Crane Creek is a popular place for canoeing. "I recently saw six manatees while I was canoeing there," she says. "There are parts of that

creek where you see nothing but nature. You'd think you were in Africa."

The Brevard Zoo, home to more than 400 animals, attracts close to a quarter-million visitors each year and continues to expand its exhibits. Every March and April, the Florida Marlins conduct spring training at the Carl Barger Baseball Complex at Space Coast Stadium in Viera, vying in preseason competition with other major league teams that hold spring training in Florida as part of the Grapefruit League. From November through April, the Melbourne Greyhound Park has live performances.

While the Sabins, Foxes and Butlers would prefer more cultural activities, the area is far from a wasteland. The King Center for the Performing Arts attracts a variety of big-name performers throughout the year, such as Itzhak Perlman, Natalie Cole, Dan Fogelberg, Kenny Rogers, "Godspell," Pilobolus Dance Theatre, the Peking Acrobats and comedian Bob Newhart.

There are numerous museums in the region as well, including the Valiant Air Command Warbird Museum in Titusville, which houses warplanes predating World War II on up to a present-day F-14; the Air Force Space and Missile Museum, which explores the early unmanned space program; the Brevard Museum of History and Natural Science in Cocoa; the Brevard Veterans Memorial Museum; and the Brevard Museum of Art and Science in Melbourne.

The town is about an hour's drive from Orlando and its many attractions, including Walt Disney World, Universal Studios Florida and Sea World. Viera is also relatively close to the beaches and about 2.5 hours north of Miami Beach, so residents have a broad range of choices in virtually any direction.

"Come here and experience it, and it will sell itself," says Don Sabin to others considering Viera. Adds Wilson Butler, "You're welcome. If you want the fullness of retirement, Viera is the place to be." ●

Waynesville, North Carolina

A mountain town in western North Carolina shows strong community spirit

By Richard L. Fox

Lodged on a plateau between western North Carolina's Great Smoky Mountains National Park and the Pisgah National Forest, Waynesville has many of the ingredients of a great vacation destination — except hordes of tourists. This slow-paced mountain hamlet is populated by working families and a growing cadre of relocated retirees lured by scenic vistas, outdoor recreation, a four-season climate and a safe environment.

Viewed from a nearby mountainside, Waynesville's eight-block downtown is marked by five church spires, lending an air of serenity to the otherwise busy central marketplace. The tree-lined sidewalks are alive with pedestrian activity as shoppers, diners and gallery-goers pass in and out of more than 100 establishments clustered along Main Street. Others are content to relax on benches in the shade, enjoying the measured hustle and bustle of the street against the calming vistas of the surrounding Balsam, Blue Ridge and Great Smoky mountains.

One always-busy downtown destination is the three-story, neoclassically styled Haywood County courthouse. Built in 1932, it stands as a symbol of stability and authority, fronted by an inviting entrance and surrounded by large trees. It is the fourth courthouse to occupy the site; the first was constructed four years after Haywood County was carved out of sprawling Buncombe County in 1808.

Originally called Mount Pleasant, Waynesville flirted with tourism early. For a brief time, the area gained some renown as a health resort after the construction of the White Sulphur Springs Hotel, the town's first lodging, in 1850. Despite advertising a healthy climate and an abundance of pure, cold spring water, the idea of down-to-earth Waynesville as a health resort never caught on.

Today, visitors who find their way to Waynesville are likely to have come from other parts of western North Carolina, like Maggie Valley, Cherokee or Highlands. The Folkmoot International Dance Festival, Church Street Art and Craft Show, Apple Festival and other annual events bring several thousand visitors to Waynesville for short stays or day trips.

A sign in Waynesville displays the often-used sentiment, "I was not born here, but I came as fast as I could." It's good advice for anyone considering a retirement move, says Bob Bottoms, 68, who with wife Virginia, 67, moved to Waynesville in 1994 after making six visits in five months.

Their first retirement move in 1983 took them from Pittsburgh, PA, to Hilton Head, SC. After 10 years, though, they felt that Hilton Head had become "too touristy, crowded and expensive," says Bob.

During the search for a new town, the Bottomses say they considered just about every southeastern state and even thought about retiring to New Zealand or Tahiti. But for now, Bob and Virginia have no plans to move again. "We have a 360-degree view of the mountains from our home, outstanding weather and the most beautiful mountain golf course I have ever seen," says Bob, retired general manager of international sales at U.S. Steel.

Waynesville's 2,658-foot elevation plays an important part in the town's popularity. In summer, pleasant warm days and invariably cool nights attract "lowlanders" seeking relief from humid, sweltering Augusts. Winters generally are mild, with infrequent snowfall rarely measuring more than one or two inches. In the surrounding higher mountain elevations, ski slopes are filled with skiers November through March.

"The year-round climate is wonderful, with only February a time to get away to Florida," says Barbara Bennett, 52, who moved here with husband John, 74, from Princeton, NJ, in 1991.

"Princeton is a working man's community. We wanted a retirement community," says John. About two years after John retired as chief executive officer of a computer software company, the Bennetts moved to Waynesville.

They chose a site on a mountainside about 1,000 feet above Waynesville. Their custom-built home takes maximum advantage of the breathtaking vistas of the town and mountains beyond. Barbara, an interior designer, selected a floor plan and window placements for the best views.

In 1983 John and Erika Elshoff bought a home overlooking Waynesville that was 5,280 feet above sea level, and they came every summer from Treasure Island, FL, to enjoy the cool temperatures.

"I first laid eyes on Waynesville in the early 1960s and fell in love with it then," says John. When he retired as chief executive officer of a horticultural company in 1993, they moved to Waynesville full time, selling the vacation home and buying another place not quite so high up the mountain. "That (high elevation) is fine when you come here for the summer, but not for year-round living," says John, 64.

The Elshoffs' current home at 3,500 feet has six acres of land, a waterfall and trout pond. Erika says the beauty of the area and its climate strongly influenced her desire to relocate from the sunny Florida flat lands to mountainous, sometimes chilly, Waynesville. The "more tranquil pace of life, free of worry about crime" also was a big draw for her.

As more retirees settle in Waynesville, the town itself is changing to accommodate them. Residents anticipate some minor growing pains, but at the current population of 9,687, it is the epitome of small-town living.

A sense of community is one of the elements that Virginia and Bob Bottoms sought when they chose Waynesville. "When we moved to our new home, it was very easy to make friends, mostly through the country club," says Virginia.

John Elshoff advises seeking out friends. "There are two ways to come

to the mountains. If you are so inclined and don't want to make any effort, you can become a recluse. Or, you can reach out to people and not wait for them to come to you," he says.

"We found a lot of transplants looking for new friends, so it was easy," says Erika.

The relocating retiree population in Haywood County is far from reclusive, according to Kay Dossey, executive director of the Greater Haywood County Chamber of Commerce. "Retirees have had a tremendous impact

on quality of life in this area. Barbara Bennett's fund raising has become legendary among the business community and major contributors in Haywood County," Dossey says.

Barbara credits others. "I like the fact that there are so many people willing to make the effort to come together and work for the improvement of the town. These efforts have made a big difference in just the few years we've been here."

The opportunity for involvement was Barbara's main incentive when the Bennetts selected Waynesville. "I

Waynesville, NC

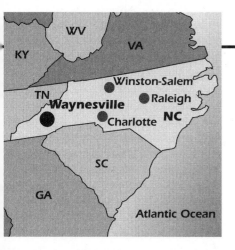

Population: 9,687 in town, 54,033 in Haywood County.

Location: In mountainous western North Carolina, bordered by Great Smoky Mountains National Park to the north and Pisgah National Forest to the south. The town's elevation is 2,658 feet.

Climate:

	High	Low
January	47	23
July	82	58

Average relative humidity: 58% in Asheville, about 30 miles away (figures for Waynesville not available).

Rain: 47 inches.

Cost of living: 94.4, based on national average of 100.

Average housing cost: $145,300

Sales tax: 6.5%

Sales tax exemptions: Prescriptions, services and automobiles.

State income tax: For married couples filing jointly, the rate is graduated from 6% of taxable income up to $21,250 to 8.25% on amounts over $200,000. For single filers, it is graduated from 6% of income up to $12,750

to 8.25% on amounts over $120,000.

Income tax exemptions: Social Security benefits are exempt. Up to $2,000 of distributions from private retirement benefits and IRAs (up to the amount reported in federal income taxes), or up to $4,000 of government pensions may be exempt. Total deductions may not exceed $4,000 per person.

Intangibles tax: None.

Estate tax: None, except the state's "pick-up" portion of the federal tax, applicable to taxable estates above $1 million.

Property tax: $10.40 in the city ($6.10 in the county) per $1,000 of assessed value, with homes assessed at 100% of appraised value. The annual tax on a $145,300 home in Waynesville is $1,511 without exemptions.

Homestead exemption: $20,000 or 50% (whichever is greater) off assessed value of permanent residence for those over age 65 with annual combined income of $18,000 or less.

Personal property tax: Same rate as real property, on the depreciated value of cars, boats, mobile homes and airplanes.

Religion: One Catholic and 50 Protestant places of worship. Lake Junaluska Assembly, a worldwide religious group, is located here on a 250-acre lake.

Education: Haywood Community College, with an enrollment of more than 2,000, offers associate degrees in 30 disciplines and continuing-education

courses; senior citizens pay no registration fees in the continuing-education program. The University of North Carolina at Asheville is 30 miles east, and Western Carolina University in Cullowhee is 25 miles southwest.

Transportation: No local bus service. Interstate 40 and four U.S. highways provide excellent highway access. Asheville Regional Airport, served by jets and commuter aircraft, is a 30-minute drive away.

Health: Haywood Regional Medical Center is a 200-bed, full-service, regional facility with 24-hour emergency service and a staff practicing 24 medical specialties.

Housing options: A variety of choices from large estates to small farms, mountainside chalets to rustic and remote log cabins, contemporary, custom-built country club homes to condos and townhomes. **Maggie Valley Resort and Country Club**, about 10 miles from Waynesville, has new two- and three-bedroom condos starting at $184,800.

Visitor lodging: Best Western Smoky Mountain Inn, $49-$139, (828) 456-4402. Waynesville Country Club Inn, $85-$294 with golf package, (828) 456-3551. Comfort Inn-Maggie Valley, $49-99, including continental breakfast, (828) 926-9106.

Information: Haywood County Chamber of Commerce, P.O. Drawer 600, Waynesville, NC 28786-0600, (828) 456-3021 or www.haywood-nc.com. Visitor information, (800) 334-9036.

wanted to be part of a growing town where I could make a contribution to the quality of life," she says.

Barbara volunteers her time and efforts to the Haywood County Arts Council. The council sponsors a diverse offering of cultural activities, such as free Sunday afternoon concerts in the public library and an annual two-week rehearsal residency by the Atlanta Ballet. The Folkmoot-USA program, part of International Festival Day, features dance troupes from around the world and brings thousands of spectators downtown. Stemming from the Folkmoot Festival, a new international school for ballet and dance opened four years ago.

The Haywood Arts Repertory Theatre, an amateur theater company offering four productions annually, celebrated the opening of a new $1 million, 250-seat theater recently. The Folk Art Center, youth theater, a museum and galleries showcase local talent.

As strong as the cultural movement is here, Waynesville is not an arts community in the tradition of Santa Fe, NM. Erika Elshoff cautions newcomers: "You can't come with a high-society attitude. It helps to love nature and outdoor activities."

National parks and forests comprise nearly 40 percent of Haywood County. More than 200 miles of hiking trails, including large sections of the Appalachian Trail, entice residents to the outdoors. Camping, canoeing, mountain biking, fishing, hunting, horseback riding, skiing and golf all are available.

North Carolina's oldest ski resort, Cataloochee Ski Area in Maggie Valley, can be reached in minutes, and white-water rafting outfitters are in nearby Nantahala, Asheville, Bryson City and Almond. The much-ac-claimed, much-visited Blue Ridge Parkway eight miles southwest of town leads to many quaint villages, good for same-day exploration.

Laurel Ridge Country Club, a private course rated as one of the best in the country by *Golfweek* magazine in 1993 and 1994, and the 27-hole Waynesville Country Club course are among seven courses (six public and one private) in the county.

The influx of retirees has been cited as the cause of rising home prices in Waynesville. "Waynesville has become such a popular living area that housing costs have really gone up in recent years," says Marty Prevost of Main-Street Realty. "There is a real shortage of nice homes in the $100,000-$150,000 price range — the price most downsizing retirees are looking for," she adds.

According to Prevost, the Waynesville Country Club area — one of the nicer, established neighborhoods — is built out, but resales sometimes are available in the $150,000-$295,000 range. She also notes that custom-built homes start at $125 per square foot, depending on amenities, and a new 1,800- to 2,000-square-foot home on three-fourths to one acre of land likely will be priced at $200,000-$500,000.

Retirees seeking luxury living may want to take a look at Smoky Mountain Sanctuary, an upscale gated community with underground utilities, clubhouse, helicopter landing pad and other perks. Two- to six-acre home sites are priced approximately $100,000, and a new five-bedroom, three-bath home has an asking price of $495,000.

The Haywood County Hospital Foundation is responsible for creating the new $900,000 Woman's Care Center and raised $5 million for the construction of a 50,000-square-foot health and fitness center.

Barbara Bennett is chairwoman of fund raising for the hospital foundation. With the foundation's help, Haywood Regional Medical Center, a 200-bed, full-service facility and the largest hospital west of Asheville, hired 27 new physicians during the last few years. The hospital also acquired new diagnostic equipment, including an MRI and CT scanner, and established a home health-care facility. In Asheville, Memorial Mission Medical Center (503 beds) and St. Joseph's Hospital (331) offer advanced medical technology and most specialties.

Among indications of the town's growing appreciation for its retirees are the special offerings for seniors at Haywood Community College. With an 83-acre main campus and 320-acre "teaching forest," it offers no-registration-fee continuing-education courses for senior citizens in clay, fiber, jewelry-making and woodwork. Higher-education courses are available at Western Carolina University in Cullowhee and the University of North Carolina at Asheville, each about 30 minutes away.

Downtown shops and area shopping centers provide for basic needs but are no substitute for the major malls and giant department stores in large urban areas. But Virginia Bottoms credits local merchants with serving the community well. "The shops on Main Street are nice, friendly places with quality merchandise," she says. And though John Elshoff cites the lack of upscale stores as a drawback, he adds upon reflection: "It's not a big deal."

When Erika Elshoff is asked if she'll ever move out of Waynesville, she says, "There are no hurricanes, no flooding, no fires, no earthquakes. Where else can you live and not have one or more of these conditions?" ●

Whidbey Island, Washington

Retirees find a place to pursue their dreams on this pretty Pacific Northwest island

By Stanton H. Patty

Up a country road on Washington state's Whidbey Island, there are clusters of purple heather, a ramshackle barn that may not last another winter, and the studio of one of the Pacific Northwest's celebrated artists. There you might find Georgia Gerber shaping a life-size sculpture of a little girl dancing with a playful bear and other critters.

"What's the story?" asks a visitor. "Whatever you want it to be," Georgia replies. "Let your imagination go."

Dr. Herb McDonald understands that invitation. The retired cardiologist, felled by heart disease a few years ago, has found a new life on this quiet island, only an hour or so from Seattle's smothering traffic. Now he is writing short stories about what he calls "slices of life" on Whidbey Island. Many of the stories involve the four dogs that share a saltwater-view home with Herb and his wife, Susan, a retired nurse. "I've always enjoyed creative writing," says the 65-year-old physician. "Now I have time to do it."

Another couple, Dick Curdy and Lynn Geri, also followed a dream to Whidbey Island. They moved to the island to open a bed-and-breakfast inn. Dick, 65, had been a high school English teacher for 24 years in Bellevue, a Seattle suburb. Lynn, 61, worked in counseling with several corporations. "We're having a great time, meeting wonderful people who come to stay with us," Lynn says.

Also having a wonderful time are Ed and Marie Parr, who conducted a methodical search of Northwest communities before deciding to settle on Whidbey Island. "We looked at many places with a critical eye," Marie recalls. The Parrs had decided in advance that their retirement spot should be near a major airport (Seattle-Tacoma International, in this case), have adequate medical facilities (Whidbey General Hospital), offer a first-rate golf course (Useless Bay Golf and Country Club) — and be more or less snow-free.

"I shoveled snow when we lived in Colorado. Now I don't have to do that anymore," says Ed, 74, a real-estate consultant and developer in Berthoud, CO, north of Boulder, before he retired. Marie, 74, was a full-time mother of five and also held a real-estate license.

Whidbey Island, anchored in Puget Sound just north of Seattle, is a favorite weekend retreat for the high-voltage Microsoft crowd. They come to browse the island's country towns and gardens, to go sea kayaking and beachcombing, to find blissful serenity. And some return to stay for good.

Whidbey's dazzling scenery, its mild climate and the appeal of slow-tempo living have peopled the 45-mile-long island with painters, potters, sculptors, writers — and now dozens of contented retired couples. "This is a place where people care about each other," says Georgia Gerber.

Georgia gave the island one of its top attractions, a beloved sculpture in the seaside village of Langley. "Boy and Dog" is the title. In the scene, a lifelike youth, in bronze, leans on a railing, daydreaming and looking toward distant, snow-streaked mountains. There is a bronze dog at his feet. Someone left a leather leash beside the bronze dog a few weeks ago, and there was speculation that it might have belonged to a visitor's pet that had died.

Georgia's eyes mist when told about the leash. The dog portrayed in the sculpture was her longtime companion. "I still miss him," says Georgia, who moved from Seattle in 1982 to build her studio on the island.

Langley, near the southern tip of Whidbey, is the magnet for most visitors aboard this seahorse-shaped island. The town of only 1,000 residents offers stylish inns, art galleries and award-winning restaurants — all within one cozy square mile. "It's all about tranquility here," says Karen Davis, assistant manager at Langley's Saratoga Inn. "We don't hear traffic. We hear birds and squirrels and chipmunks. We're on 'island time.' Things move a little slower here, and we like it that way."

So do Whidbey Island's retirees. Marie Parr tells of daily breakfast gatherings at Sapori, a Langley cafe and bakery. "We laugh a lot," she says. "We're all retired — authors, artists, musicians, business executives, lawyers, engineers and airline pilots. It's a wonderful mix. We share experiences, and then we go our own ways."

The Parrs discovered Whidbey during their first visit to the Northwest. They rented a car in Seattle and went exploring for a possible retirement site. While Ed Parr searched for his golf course, Marie was on the lookout for an easy-maintenance home. Marie had been injured seriously in an automobile accident before moving to Whidbey Island, and the crash caused her to give up golf — and their 40-acre ranch in Colorado. "The ranch was too much to handle," she says. "It was time for a change of lifestyle."

Once the decision was made to move to the Langley area, they bought and remodeled a two-bedroom home with a smashing view of Saratoga Passage, the scenic waterway between Whidbey and neighboring Camano Island. Do they feel isolated on an island where residents depend mostly on ferries to reach the mainland? "Not really," Ed says. "We have a good hospital and clinics here. If it were an extreme emergency, we could be airlifted to hospitals in Seattle."

The Parrs have traveled extensively in Europe and are planning a trip soon to Scotland and Italy. Ed has his heart set on playing Scotland's historic St. Andrews golf course. But they always are eager to return home to Whidbey Island. "This is just a very nice place," says Ed.

Dr. Herb McDonald, the cardiologist, was advised to retire about four years ago after undergoing coronary artery bypass surgery in El Paso, TX. His wife, Susan, then was working as a nurse in El Paso. "It was time, what with the stress and long hours," Herb says.

Herb knew Seattle from his days as a medical student at the University of Washington, and he also had attended school in Spokane in eastern Washington, so they decided to settle in the Northwest. They focused first on Washington's Olympic Peninsula communities, including Port Townsend and Sequim, before choosing Whidbey Island.

"One thing we knew for sure is that we didn't want to be in a big city," says

Whidbey Island, WA

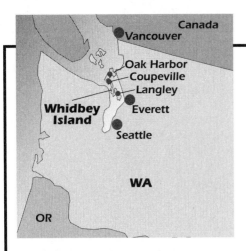

Population: 7,558 in Island County, which includes both Whidbey Island and neighboring Camano Island.

Location: In Puget Sound, about 35 miles north of Seattle by highway and ferry. There are three incorporated cities on Whidbey Island — Langley in the South Whidbey area, Coupeville in Central Whidbey, and Oak Harbor in North Whidbey.

Climate:

	High	Low
January	46	36
July	73	51

Average relative humidity: 40%-90%, depending on location.

Rain: 18-35 inches, depending on location. Whidbey benefits from being sheltered in the "rain shadow" of the Olympic Mountains.

Snow: Rare.

Cost of living: Slightly higher than average because of transportation costs. Specific index not available.

Housing costs: Ranging from about $150,000-$212,000 in North Whidbey, $139,000-$212,000 in Central Whidbey, and $160,000-$260,000 in South Whidbey. Highest prices are for waterfront property on Puget Sound.

Sales tax: 8.3%

Sales tax exemptions: Food items at grocery stores, prescription drugs

State income tax: None.

Intangibles tax: None.

Estate tax: None, except the state's "pick-up" portion of the federal tax, applicable to taxable estates over $1 million.

Property tax: Averages about 1% of assessed value. Tax on a home valued at $100,000 would be about $1,000.

Homestead exemption: Available to low-income senior citizens and disabled persons.

Religion: Whidbey Island has 64 churches representing many denominations.

Education: There are no four-year colleges or universities on Whidbey Island. Skagit Valley College, a community college, has a small campus in Oak Harbor (North Whidbey) and a satellite facility in Langley (South Whidbey) that offers limited classes. Four-year degrees are offered through Chapman University's Academic Center at Whidbey Naval Air Station.

Transportation: Whidbey Island is served by Washington state ferries from the mainland port of Mukilteo north of Seattle, and from Port Townsend on Washington's Olympic Peninsula. Ferries from Mukilteo call at Clinton in South Whidbey. Crossing time is about 30 minutes. Ferries operating from Port Townsend call at Keystone in Central Whidbey. Crossing time is about 45 minutes. The Deception Pass Bridge at the north end of the island, near Oak Harbor, connects Whidbey Island to Washington's highway system. Harbor Air offers scheduled commuter service between Oak Harbor and Seattle-Tacoma International Airport. Flight time is about 25 minutes. Island Transit, a free public bus system, operates on all of Whidbey's main roads.

Health: The 51-bed Whidbey General Hospital in Coupeville (Central Whidbey) has a 24-hour emergency room. Specialties include surgery, critical care, home health care, childbirth, physical and sports therapy, cancer care and diagnostic imaging services. There also are community clinics in Oak Harbor (North Whidbey) and Langley (South Whidbey). In addition, Naval Hospital Oak Harbor offers inpatient and outpatient services for active-duty military personnel and their families and for eligible retired military personnel and their eligible family members. Paramedic-staffed ambulances serve all points on Whidbey Island.

Housing options: Most island retirees live in single-family homes. There are few apartments for low- to moderate-income residents. A popular upscale development is Useless Bay Colony near Langley on the west side of the island. The colony has about 20 condominiums, with prices beginning at about $200,000, and some 200 single-family homes, priced from about $160,000 to $300,000. Features include a golf course and tennis courts.

Visitor lodging: Langley area: Harbour Inn, $61-$90, (360) 331-6900, and Saratoga Inn, $110-$275, (360) 221-5801. Coupeville area: Coupeville Inn, $70-$115, (360) 678-6668 or (800) 247-6162 in Washington, and Anchorage Inn, $80-$130, (877) 230-1313. Oak Harbor area: Acorn Motor Inn, $44-$89, (800) 280-6646.

Information: Langley Chamber of Commerce, 124½ Second St., Langley, WA 98260, (360) 221-5676 for general information or (360) 221-6765 for lodging information, or www.whidbey.com/langley. Central Whidbey Chamber of Commerce, P.O. Box 152, Coupeville, WA 98239, (360) 678-5434 for recorded information or www.islandweb.org. (Note: The Central Whidbey Chamber does not return long-distance calls.) Greater Oak Harbor Chamber of Commerce, 5506 Highway 20, Oak Harbor, WA 98277, (360) 675-3535 or www.islandweb.org.

Susan. "And we didn't want to live in a retirement community. We wanted to be in a place that had kids and adults, people younger and older than we."

The McDonalds reside in Coupeville, a picturesque Victorian town in the central section of Whidbey Island. Coupeville was founded in 1852 by a sea captain who made his fortune by shipping the Northwest's tall timber to booming California. Coupeville's old-fashioned main drag, Front Street, is a favorite setting with Hollywood movie-makers. Celebrities and other travelers gather there to dine on just-harvested mussels at Toby's Tavern.

The McDonalds built a 2,300-square-foot house on 10 acres that overlook Penn Cove, where the tasty mussels are grown. The property is decked with madrona trees and Douglas firs and stretches down to the shore of the salt-water cove. "We have six children, so we also built a guest house," Susan says.

The McDonalds describe Coupeville as a vibrant community with a rich cultural menu and volunteer organizations that welcome newcomers. Susan is a board member of Concerts on the Cove, a group that sponsors a summer series of musical events running the scale from symphony to bluegrass. Always open to ideas, Concerts on the Cove staged a rock concert for students at Coupeville High School's Performing Arts Center a few weeks ago.

Meanwhile, when he isn't writing short stories or meeting with fellow members of a local group of writers, Herb serves on Whidbey Island's Community Health Advisory Board. The board's aim, he says, is to "stay ahead" of problems. Current projects include support for positive programs involving young persons and seniors.

Whidbey Island's only public hospi-tal is the 51-bed Whidbey General Hospital in Coupeville. There also is a military hospital at Naval Air Station Whidbey Island, adjacent to the city of Oak Harbor near the northern end of the island. Herb McDonald rates Whidbey General as "good and getting better." He is especially pleased with the hospital's Patient First program that gives patients more involvement in treatment decisions.

Susan McDonald was a nursing supervisor at Whidbey General for a while after moving from El Paso, then retired to begin a new career in real estate. Much of the McDonalds' travel schedule involves trips to visit their children. They also go "off island" to Seattle about once a month to attend theater performances and to shop at Seattle's famed Pike Place Market with its array of fresh produce and seafood.

Last fall Susan traveled to Cuba with the Seattle Peace Chorus. "It was a fabulous trip, a real awakening," she says. The McDonalds say they have no regrets regarding their decision to snuggle into Whidbey Island. "Every time we come home, we know in our hearts that we made an excellent choice," says Susan.

Lynn Geri and Dick Curdy are the proud proprietors of the Brierly Inn, a bed-and-breakfast inn near the South Whidbey town of Clinton. Vehicle and passenger ferries commute between Clinton and the mainland city of Mukilteo north of Seattle. "It was nothing but a brier patch when we first looked at the property in 1998," says Dick in explaining how the inn got its name.

Lynn and Dick, partners for 14 years, bought that brier patch along with a 16-year-old Tudor-style manor house on five acres and opened their B&B. It's a peaceful place, they say, with towering cedars, meadows and a garden bright with rhododendrons, roses and other blossoms. There is a Web site, too: www.brierlyinn.com.

It's quite a change for Dick, the former schoolteacher, and Lynn, the former corporate counselor. "We were looking around for a business to buy," Lynn recalls. "There was a deli for sale on the island, but that didn't interest us. Then we found this beautiful house in a real-estate flier. Sometimes now we soak in the guest hot tub and ask ourselves: 'Do you know how lucky we are?' We just love it here."

The couple also considered Washington's sunny San Juan Islands before deciding on Whidbey. But, says Lynn, they wanted to be closer to their Seattle-area children — and they were concerned about being wholly dependent on ferries that serve the San Juans. That holiday archipelago has no highway connection to the Washington mainland. Whidbey Island has ferry service between Clinton and nearby Mukilteo, and a ferry that operates between Keystone on Whidbey Island and Port Townsend on the Olympic Peninsula. But there also is a highway connection to the mainland by way of the Deception Pass Bridge on the north end of Whidbey.

Now Dick spends quite a bit of time in the Brierly Inn's garden. He became a master gardener after moving to Whidbey Island, taking 65 hours of classes offered by Washington State University and the Island County Extension Service. Now, between chores at the inn, he volunteers at the acclaimed Meerkerk Gardens near the Whidbey community of Freeland and helps neighbors solve their gardening problems during clinics at weekend farm markets.

"It's a different tempo for us now," says Lynn Geri. "And we are counting our blessings every day." ●

Wickenburg, Arizona

A once wild and woolly mining town is now
a top retirement retreat

By Ron Butler

Phoenix takes its name from the legendary bird that rises from its own ashes. But the name also could apply to Wickenburg, a tiny community 50 miles to the northwest of Arizona's capital that also shows remarkable rejuvenating powers.

Wickenburg (named after Austrian settler Henry Wickenburg) has survived one mule kick after another throughout its history. It was once a hot spot for gold. The Vulture and 80 other such mines sparked a $30 million boom that made Wickenburg the third-largest city in Arizona. Then the gold ran out.

Wickenburg (named after Austrian settler Henry Wickenburg) has survived one mule kick after another throughout its history. It was once a hot spot for gold. The Vulture and 80 other such mines sparked a $30 million boom that made Wickenburg the third-largest city in Arizona. Then the gold ran out.

But Wickenburg's near-perfect climate, its proximity to Phoenix and its wide-open spaces made it an ideal setting for a Western resort boom, and it prospered again. Boasting a dozen major resorts, it became renowned for its dude ranches. Then that concept fizzled as well.

Vacation trends change, and the idea of sleeping under the stars, washing in a tin basin and accepting the bruises and hardships of cowboy life in order to escape big-city hassles once may have seemed romantic. But Wickenburg's surfeit of dude ranches has shrunk to three. Gone, too, is Merv Griffin's venerable Wickenburg Inn Tennis and Golf Ranch, now a school for girls.

However, with the same features intact that once attracted cowboys and well-heeled dudes from back East, Wickenburg is now thriving as one of Arizona's leading retirement destinations. It is still tiny, although its permanent population of 5,000 doubles in the winter. But that is part of its tremendous appeal.

"We're 40 percent retirees and 60 percent regular people," says the home-grown executive director of the Wickenburg Chamber of Commerce, Julie Brooks, part den mother and part cheerleader for the impressive number of retired volunteers who help with office duties and the many annual citywide events such as Gold Rush Days in February, the Bluegrass Festival in November and Christmas decorations and Cowboy Poetry Festival in December.

Wickenburg, at an elevation of 2,100 feet, is slightly cooler than some of its neighboring desert communities. The air is fresh and the people are warm and friendly. There's a historic downtown section with interesting shops, two major supermarkets, a hospital, several banks, restaurants, a movie theater, library and a world-class museum.

Wickenburg holds proudly to its Old West heritage. Downtown Frontier Street contains a number of vintage wood and brick buildings, including an old-time train depot that now houses the chamber of commerce. Horses are a common sight. Behind the town hall is a steam locomotive and tender from the old Santa Fe line. The Hassayampa, once the town's leading hotel (named after the almost perpetually dry Hassayampa River that runs south of town) now contains office space. It was originally built to serve overnight railroad passengers and early tourists to the area.

Before the local jail was constructed, the nearby Jail Tree was used to chain criminals, not one of whom ever escaped. Today the famous 200-year-old mesquite at Tegner and Wickenburg Way is behind the local Circle-K convenience store. Even the town's newest motel, a Super Eight, has a wood-paneled facade in keeping with downtown's Old West spirit.

It's not surprising that Harry Thurston, 72, who began his career in ranching and saddle-making near the Grand Canyon area, and his wife, Nancy, 62, a former school teacher, chose Wickenburg as the place to retire. Harry had worked for many years as a saddle and pack expert with H. Porter's, one of the leaders in the field for gear and westernwear. It was a period in his life when he got to know and pal around with some of Hollywood's top Western stars, including Ben Johnson, Slim Pickens, Richard Farnsworth and Alex Cord. When his eyes began to give him trouble, he decided to pull up stakes.

Now he has a five-acre ranch-style home on the outskirts of town, where he cares for six show horses, including his wife's two Arabian stallions. Nancy Thurston was one of the earliest members of the Arizona Arabian Horse Association.

From his on-premise saddle shop, a place where the smells of leather and polish are strong and talk is of bits and fast horses, Harry still does custom assignments. For relaxation he trail rides, camps out, participates in rodeo events and hangs out with the boys at the Custer Cowboy Cafe downtown, where entrees are generally too big for Easterners and the walls are festooned with rodeo memorabilia, framed championship belt buckles and photos of bronc and bull-riding events.

Wickenburg has art galleries, museums and saloons such as La Cabana, scene of rousing good times. During the day, the thing to do is get a car or a four-wheel-drive vehicle and head for the backcountry in search of abandoned mining camps, wind-rattled ghost towns, lonely pioneer cemeteries and boulders marked with ancient Indian petroglyphs.

"For someone as much into horses and the West as I am," Harry says, "this is about as close to Paradise as you can get. Whenever I go off for an early morning ride in the desert, I half expect to run into John Wayne or John Ford setting up a scene."

Fourteen rugged miles west of Wickenburg is the Vulture Mine — ghostly, abandoned, guarded by ominous, gray Vulture Peak. For a fee, visitors can take the self-guided walking tour through the ramshackle town that's little-changed since mining operations ceased in 1942. The quarter-mile loop includes an assay office, a school, a hanging tree, the 2,000-foot main mine shaft and the bunkhouse where long johns and rotted Levis hang on a rusted bed frame. Legend contends that the Vulture Mine was so named because a vulture felled by a gunshot landed near a gold nugget.

This is the same old-time Old West ambiance that appealed to Dick and Hazel Conklin, both 74, who moved from the small town of Richland in southeast Iowa. They had been visiting friends in Phoenix for years, falling in love with Arizona a little more each time. Finally when Dick decided to give up his hair-styling business and retire, he and Hazel, who worked as a bookkeeper for a grain company, picked Wickenburg.

It was close to Phoenix but without the traffic and pollution. Because they came from a small town, they wanted to retire to a place that had the same small-town atmosphere to which they were

Wickenburg, AZ

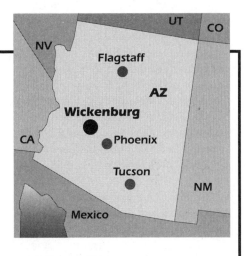

Population: 5,000. Another 2,000 to 4,000 people live outside the town limits or are winter residents.

Location: In south-central Arizona in foothills on the northern edge of the Sonoran Desert, 50 miles northwest of Phoenix, in Maricopa County. Elevation is 2,100 feet.

Climate:

	High	Low
January	65	39
July	105	80

Rain: 10.77 inches.

Cost of living: Above average (specific index not available).

Average home price: $185,000, with prices ranging from $100,000 to $1,500,000.

Sales tax: 6.7%

Sales tax exemptions: Groceries and prescription drugs.

State income tax: For married couples filing jointly, graduated from 2.87% of taxable income up to $20,000 to 5.04% minus $2,276 on amounts over $300,000. For single filers, graduated from 2.87% of taxable income up to $10,000 to 5.04% minus $1,138 on amounts over $150,000.

Income tax exemptions: Social Security benefits and up to $2,500 on federal, state and local government pensions are exempt.

Estate tax: None, except the state's "pick-up" portion of the federal tax, applicable to taxable estates of more than $1 million.

Inheritance tax: None.

Property tax: Maricopa County property taxes are $10.06 per $100 in assessed valuation. Homes are assessed at 10% of fair market value. Annual tax on a home valued at $185,000 would be approximately $1,861.

Homestead exemptions: None.

Religion: Many denominations serve Wickenburg residents. A "Guide to Wickenburg Churches" is available at the chamber of commerce office.

Education: Arizona State University West and Glendale and Estrella community colleges are within an hour's drive. Courses also are available through Rio Salado Community College, a member of Maricopa Community College District that has no traditional campus.

Transportation: If you don't own or rent a car, you'll have difficulty getting around in Wickenburg. There is no public transportation and only limited taxi service. Greyhound makes one daily stop from Phoenix, arriving in the early morning hours. Shuttle service from Sky Harbor Airport in Phoenix is limited and expensive. Try VIP Airport Express, (928) 684-0925. For municipal airport information, call (928) 684-5690.

Health: The Wickenburg Regional Medical Center has 23 beds for acute care, 57 for extended care and a medical staff of seven physicians and visiting specialists directing surgery, laboratory, radiology, cardiopulmonary and physical therapy, along with 24-hour emergency care. The fully accredited Del E. Webb Memorial Hospital and Boswell Memorial Hospital are 30 miles south of Wickenburg. The city also has a number of wellness and addiction centers, including the renowned Meadows, treating addictions to alcohol, drugs, sex, gambling, work and compulsive eating disorders. Wickenburg operates a volunteer ambulance service staffed by paramedics and emergency medical technicians. It is supplemented by Lifenet helicopter service to Phoenix hospitals.

Housing options: Housing types include single-family homes, investment properties and ranches. Medium-priced and luxury condominiums, townhouses, patio homes and ranch-style homes are all available, as are mobile homes. Construction is typically Southwestern stucco homes with tile roofs or territorial Santa Fe-style homes.

Visitor lodging: Because tourism has long been an important industry, numerous guest facilities are available, ranging from luxury resorts such as the famous Rancho de los Caballeros, (928) 684-5484, to motels, hotels, bed-and-breakfast inns, RV parks and campgrounds. Among the newer facilities is the Los Viajeros Inn, which offers in-room refrigerators, private balconies or patios, large heated swimming pool and hot tub and free continental breakfast. Rates for double occupancy range from $78 in the summer to $83 in the winter, (800) 915-9795. The new Super 8 Motel boasts a convenient downtown location and offers continental breakfast. Rates per double are $60, (928) 684-0808.

Information: Wickenburg Chamber of Commerce, 216 N. Frontier St., Wickenburg, AZ 85390, (928) 684-5479 or www.wickenburgchamber.com.

accustomed — and which Wickenburg offered. In 1991, they built a ranch-style house on the edge of the desert on a cul-de-sac in a 27-home development known as Sunset Terrace. Their home is all white — walls, carpets, drapes, furnishings — a decorative theme broken only by the colorful relics and remnants of a lifetime of travel: paintings, folk art, baskets and statues from Russia, Europe, Central and South America and the United States.

Both are active with the Wickenburg Chamber of Commerce, which entails everything from stuffing the monthly newsletter into envelopes to marshaling at the annual rodeo parade. Dick belongs to the local 600-member Elks Club (which offers fish fries and dancing on Friday nights) and both, avid golfers, belong to the semiprivate Wickenburg Country Club. Membership is $1,200; monthly dues $135 per couple. Golf is also available at the Los Caballeros Golf Club and at the public Salome Heights Golf Course.

"There's a small-town friendliness here that's rather surprising in a state that's so upscale and trendy," Dick says. "But it's not overpowering. If you want to be alone, nobody bothers you."

Four years ago, Roger and Betty Clodt, 68 and 62 respectively, left Temecula, CA, and headed their 36-foot RV motor home toward Wickenburg. They knew the way. Roger's sister lives in Scottsdale and they visited often. Now, home is a custom Santa Fe-style house in the Desert Hills area three miles west of town. The decor is Western — paintings, Kachina dolls, Indian baskets — with large picture windows bringing the blue sky inside.

Active and gregarious (Roger was formerly in sales promotion), the Clodts enjoy going to first-run movies at the Saguaro Theatre and to the more formal offerings at the spectacular new Del Webb Center for the Performing Arts on Vulture Mine Road, now in its inaugural season, which includes everything from the big band sounds of the Jimmy Dorsey Orchestra to Dancing on Common Ground, a rousing 12-dancer ensemble of tapping, clogging and Irish step dancing. The Clodts also do regular volunteer work at the chamber of commerce and their church.

"I hardly consider myself a gourmet cook," Betty says, "but I was immediately impressed here with the variety of spices and unique food items available, reflecting the area's diverse cultures — Mexican, American Indian — and, of course, all the locally grown fruits and vegetables.

"The diversity is also reflected in the wide range of restaurants for a town this size," she says. "Our favorites are Anita's Cocina, a modest two-room place just a block off the main drag, for giant taco salads and other spicy Mexican delights, and the Sizzling Wok on Wickenburg Way, a longtime favorite for Chinese specialties. Also on Wickenburg Way is the House of Berlin. You can't get much more German than that."

On the minus scale, the Clodts find Wickenburg's increasing traffic a downer, especially during rush-hour periods, a problem proportionately compounded in larger cities in everburgeoning Arizona. Also, the summer heat is a bit much, which is why June, July and August often find them on the road in their mobile home heading for Vancouver or Alaska.

Mounting traffic and the city's growth also trouble Harry Thurston, who recalls that when he first bought his property, its boundaries were marked by barbed wire fences. Now it's at the confluence of two major highways.

Wickenburg's showstopper attraction for residents and visitors alike is the Desert Caballeros Western Museum, an impressive two-story structure that covers the history of Wickenburg and its surroundings with displays of Indian and early frontier artifacts, cowboy gear, miniature dioramas and a life-sized reproduction of a turn-of-the-century town. The paintings on its gallery walls pay tribute to Western masters Charlie Russell, Frederic Remington, Thomas Moran, Maynard Dixon and numerous others, a collection that outshines those in cities many times its size.

At the museum's entrance is a poignant life-sized bronze statue by sculptor Joe Beeler called "Thanks for the Rain." It depicts a cowboy kneeling beside his tired horse. The work has pretty much been appropriated as a symbol of Wickenburg, appearing in numerous ads and brochures. It seems an appropriate icon for Wickenburg's remarkable talent for survival and growth.●

Williamsburg, Virginia

Colonial heritage and college-town appeal draw retirees to Virginia Peninsula

By Mary Ann Hemphill

It's not all fife and drums and horse-drawn carriages in Williamsburg. Although the heart of the city is Colonial Williamsburg, a major tourist attraction, the community also is a vibrant, rapidly growing town, home of the College of William and Mary and an area increasingly attractive to retirees.

The heritage of a Colonial past, the energy of a college and the warmth of a small town make an ideal blend. For Sandie and Tom House, it was love at first sight. Longtime residents of the Washington, DC, area, the Houses had thought of retiring to the West Coast. But before making the move, they wanted to see more of the sights on the East Coast.

In September 1987, they went to Williamsburg, spent the weekend in Ford's Colony, a planned community that offered hotel accommodations — and bought a house. They moved to Williamsburg on a part-time basis later that year, then full time in 1989 after Tom's retirement. Tom, 76, had been the president of the Frozen Food Institute, and Sandie, 58, was a dietician in the Navy Reserve when they moved to Williamsburg.

Mac and Marty MacDonald's decision was more deliberate. Mac, 75, was head of government sales activities for General Motors. Marty, 73, had worked part time in a nursery. They'd lived in Potomac, MD, for 14 years and had considered Maryland's Eastern Shore for retirement. They also had looked all along Route 17 north of Hilton Head, always mindful of their desire to live in a small college town.

Passing through Williamsburg in January 1987, Mac picked up the local newspaper while Marty browsed the shops. "I saw an ad for the Kingsmill area and called the real estate office there. Once we received the material, I told Marty, 'We've got to check this out. It looks terrific.'"

They visited Kingsmill and Mac was instantly convinced that it was where they should retire. "It was an affair of the heart, not of the head," Mac says. Marty took a little longer to decide it was the right choice. "I had not considered a gated community or a golf area. I had played golf maybe once in my life," says Marty, who now plays twice a week.

Golf is a major attraction in Williamsburg. *Golf Digest* ranked Williamsburg 24th among the 50 greatest golf destinations in the world in 2000. There are almost 20 public and private courses, several of them in three planned communities.

Tom House hadn't played golf in 25 years, and Sandie never had played. Yet, "we said that golf would be the deciding factor," Sandie says. "If we liked it, we would stay. Otherwise, we would sell the Williamsburg house and move elsewhere." Obviously, golf clicked.

"Once we were here, we happily discovered the other benefits of the area," Tom says. "We liked the atmosphere of a college town, the ease of attending a football game, and the historical aspects of Colonial Williamsburg, Jamestown and Yorktown."

The many facets of Williamsburg's personality come together in Merchants Square, a two-block area (one block closed to cars) of shops, restaurants and outdoor dining patios. Here you'll find tourists resting on benches and students jogging, grabbing a sandwich or stocking up at the college bookstore. Adding to the mix are local residents shopping, dining or enjoying a summer evening concert.

In one direction from Market Square is Colonial Williamsburg, and in the other is the College of William and Mary, one of the top-ranked small public universities in the country. The college educated U.S. presidents Thomas Jefferson, James Monroe and John Tyler.

Colonial Williamsburg Historic Area ("CW" in local jargon) is 173 acres with 88 restored and scores of reconstructed buildings where character actors and talented craftspeople bring 18th-century Virginia to life. It is one point of the Historic Triangle, which also includes Jamestown, site of North America's first permanent settlement in 1607, and Yorktown, where the final major battle of the American Revolution was fought in 1781. Williamsburg also is well-located for access to other attractions.

Dudley Hughes, who relocated to Williamsburg in 1985, notes that the town has "access to the beach and to the mountains." Her husband, Tommy, adds, "It's three hours to Wintergreen for skiing, an hour to Virginia Beach for swimming, and two hours to Washington, DC." Norfolk and Richmond each are an hour away.

Making new friends was not a problem for Tommy and Dudley. They were part of a group of 12 couples who eventually relocated to Williamsburg from Chappaqua, NY, where Tommy had been vice president of sales for General Foods. Tommy, 83, and Dudley, 80, visited friends who had moved to Kingsmill. They liked the area and the people they met, so they bought a lot in 1983 and started building their home in 1985.

Marty MacDonald knew "not a soul" when she moved to Williamsburg. Mac's interest in golf resulted in their first friends locally, and Marty joined the Kingsmill Women's Club, as most newcomers do. Marty calls their wide range of friends "just a great bunch of people." Sandie House says, "Ford Colony's Newcomers Club immediately plunges you into the social scene. Add an activity or two, and suddenly your dance card is full. If you're bored, it's your choice."

Kingsmill-on-the-James, Ford's Colony and Governor's Land at Two Rivers are planned golf course communities with households of families and retirees. Kingsmill is 2,900 acres of gently rolling hills, woods and ponds along the James River. Five minutes from Colonial Williamsburg, Kingsmill is both a prime residential area and a world-class resort. It has three golf courses, including the River Course, which hosts the October Michelob Championship at Kingsmill on the PGA Tour.

After several trips to look at the options in Kingsmill, the MacDonalds bought a single-family home in 1987. Eleven years later it was, in Mac's words, "time to get rid of the lawnmower," so they moved to a townhouse in the Wareham's Point neighborhood in Kingsmill.

Both the Hugheses and the Mac-Donalds extol Kingsmill. "We're just spoiled rotten here. We live in a beautiful setting with the bonuses of three golf courses, tennis, marina, restaurants and sports club with its fitness and spa facilities," Marty says. As for Tommy and Dudley Hughes, they moved 20 times in their first 21 years of marriage. "Of all the places we have lived," Tommy says, "Kingsmill people are the best. They go out of their way to be nice."

The Houses are equally ecstatic about Ford's Colony. Sandie is convinced that "there is no place we would rather live than Ford's Colony, and all of our friends here agree." Their house has a breathtaking panoramic view over a lake to the golf course.

But Sandie notes that you don't have to be a golfer to enjoy life at Ford's Colony. A multitude of special-interest groups includes calligraphy, tennis, computers, biking, travel and gardening. "If your particular interest is not among these, then let it be known and we'll probably start offering it," Sandie says.

Many cite the impressive Caring Neighbors program. Volunteers register to provide various services, including transportation for medical services, loan of cribs or rollaway beds for visiting grandchildren or guests, an information network on medical conditions and meal preparation for those needing help because of a family illness or death.

Ford's Colony has three golf courses, jogging trails, a 200-acre wildlife preserve and a AAA five-star restaurant on its 2,800 acres. There are about 1,500 to 1,600 homes now, with build-out planned at 3,500 homes.

With just 734 home sites on 1,428 acres, Governor's Land is less densely developed than the other two planned communities. About 70 percent of this land will remain open, and there are four miles of riverfront on the James

Williamsburg, VA

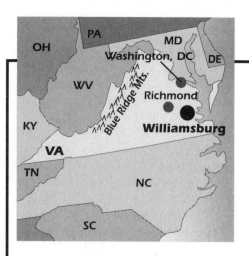

Population: 11,998 in Williamsburg (approximately 6% of the residents are over 55), plus a student population of about 7,600. Population in James City County is 48,102 (28.3% of the residents are 55 or older). The county's population has grown by 38.3 percent since 1990, making James City County the eighth-fastest-growing locality in Virginia.

Location: On gently rolling hills of the Virginia Peninsula, midway between Norfolk (45 miles away) and Richmond (50 miles). It's 150 miles from Williamsburg to Washington, DC.

Climate: High Low

	High	Low
January	48	31
July	83	65

Average relative humidity: 70%

Rain: 45.22 inches

Snow: 7.6 inches

Cost of living: 97.4, based on national average of 100.

Average housing cost: $252,000 for a new home

Sales tax: 4.5%. There is an additional 4% food tax in restaurants, bringing the tax on a restaurant tab to 8.5%.

Sales tax exemptions: Prescription and nonprescription drugs, some medical equipment, home heating fuels, utility services and most other services. Reduced sales tax rate on groceries.

State income tax: For married couples filing jointly and single filers, the rate is graduated from 2% of taxable income up to $3,000 to 5.75% on amounts over $17,000.

Income tax exemptions: Social Security benefits are exempt. There is an $800 personal exemption for residents age 65 or older. There is a $6,000 deduction per person from adjusted gross income for residents age 62-64, and a $12,000 deduction per person for residents 65 and older.

Estate tax: None, except the state's "pick-up" portion of the federal tax, applicable to taxable estates of more than $1 million.

Property tax: In the city of Williams-

burg, $5.40 per $1,000 of assessed value. James City County, $8.70 per $1,000 of assessed value. Homes are assessed at 100 percent of market value. Tax on a $252,000 home would be $1,360 in the city and $2,192 in the county. Personal property tax for cars: In the city of Williamsburg, $35 per $1,000 of assessed valuation. James City County, $40 per $1,000 of assessed valuation.

Religion: There are more than 40 churches of varying denominations, as well as one synagogue.

Education: Founded by Royal Charter in 1693, the College of William and Mary is the second-oldest continuous institution of higher education in the country after Harvard.

Transportation: Williamsburg is just off Interstate 64. Amtrak serves Williamsburg with a train from Washington, DC, and the nearest airports are in Richmond and Norfolk. James City County Transit provides local bus service for $1 per ride (transfer fee is 25 cents), and passengers over 60 can ride for half-price. Door-to-door Paratransit service, also $1, is available to anyone who can't ride a regular bus because of disability. Residents can also take advantage of the Relax and Ride system that provides ser-

and Chickahominy rivers. In addition to the private country club with its golf privileges on the Tom Fazio-designed course, plus tennis courts, swimming pools and dining facilities, there is the Two Rivers Harbor and Yacht Club with private boat slips.

According to Tessa Louer, a real estate agent with Prudential McCardle, any homes close to Colonial Williamsburg's historic area are very desirable, "regardless of condition." She says that the average sales price in the Williamsburg area is $200,000. Mentioning Piney Creek as an example, Tessa notes that there are several small communities with good builders where buyers can get a brick house for well under $300,000.

Set in the Virginia countryside near Williamsburg is Brickshire, a golf community tucked amid gently rolling, wooded hills. It features an 18-hole Curtis Strange course, swimming and tennis, walking paths and equestrian facilities. Situated just off Interstate 64 midway between Williamsburg and Richmond, the community has homesites starting in the $50,000s and custom homes from the $300,000s.

Colonial Williamsburg's Good Neighbor program gives local residents free admission to all sites and discounts admission tickets for friends visiting residents. Like most newcomers, the Hugheses "did all there is to do at first," but they still like to return with their guests. Marty MacDonald can't get enough of CW's gardens and Abby Aldrich Rockefeller Folk Art Museum.

Under the auspices of the College of William and Mary, the Christopher Wren Society offers a wide range of classes to those over 55 years of age. Sandie says she is "always taking something here," most recently classes on Theodore Roosevelt and on the 2002 Congressional elections. The $75-per-semester fee covers attendance in two courses. Marty has signed up for classes in art history and literature and takes advantage of William and Mary's program of letting those who are over 60 and who have lived in Virginia for a year audit classes at no charge.

Williamsburg's cultural scene is rapidly expanding. In addition to the folk art museum, Colonial Williamsburg has the DeWitt Wallace Decorative Arts Museum. The Muscarelle Museum of Art at William and Mary has permanent and changing exhibits of fine paintings and sculpture. The music scene is especially rich, including the 70-voice Chorale Guild and the Williamsburg Symphonia. Each presents three major concerts during the year.

Tommy and Dudley Hughes have season tickets to the Williamsburg Players. "They are all local talent, and they are outstanding," Tommy says. Marty MacDonald volunteers at This Century

vice between local hotels, motels, attractions and shopping centers. An all-day pass is $1 for those 60 and older. This service is seasonal, running May 25-Sept. 3.

Health: The nearest hospital is the 139-bed Williamsburg Community Hospital, which is considering moving to a new site seven miles from its current site. Specialized care is available at the 576-bed Riverside Regional Medical Center in Newport News at the Medical College of Virginia in Richmond.

Housing options: Kingsmill's residential options include single-family homes, cluster homes, townhouses and condominiums. Prices for townhouses, resale homes and condos range from the low $200,000s to well over $1 million, (800) 392-0026. Building sites are sold out. Resale prices for those depend upon location; those with pond or creek views cost $200,000 to $300,000. In **Ford's Colony**, townhomes begin at $189,000 and single-family homes range from $240,000 to $700,000. Home sites, depending upon their size and location, range from $79,000 to $450,000, (800) 334-6033. (Check out the cost-of-living calculator at www.fordscolony.com.) **Governor's Land** has no condos or townhouses. Homes range from $400,000 to more than $1 million and lots begin at $74,900, (800) 633-5965. **Brickshire**, (888) 655-5263, has homesites with views of the golf course, lake or wooded scenery from the $50,000s and custom homes starting in the $300,000s. Townhouses at **Counselors Close**, just three blocks from Colonial Williamsburg, are $200,000 to $400,000. **Port Anne**, also near Colonial Williamsburg, is a moderately priced neighborhood. **Holly Hills**, also in the city, has homes built within the past five years, with prices ranging from $400,000 to more than $1 million. Contact real estate agents regarding resales at Counselors Close, Port Anne or Holly Hills. Several communities offer a mix of independent and assisted-living facilities. The newest is **WindsorMeade**, (877) 582-6385. Built on 106 acres, it has 75 independent living villas and 175 apartments, including private licensed nursing beds and a memory support section. Its community center has bed-and-breakfast accommodations for visiting guests. **Williamsburg Landing**, (800) 554-5517, has cottage neighborhoods for independent living, assisted living and memory-impaired illnesses facilities and a 58-bed nursing center. A fitness and wellness center will open there in summer of 2003. **Chambrel at Williamsburg**, (800) 868-4654, also offers independent and assisted living. **Patriot's Colony**, (800) 716-9000, is an active retirement and assisted-living facility for retired military officers and senior government officials.

Visitor lodging: More than 10,000 rooms are available in local resorts, hotels, motels and bed-and-breakfast inns. For reservations, call the Williamsburg Hotel and Motel Association at (800) 899-9462. Colonial Williamsburg's Colonial Homes, which are former taverns, kitchens, offices and shops in the historic area, feature antique and reproduction furnishings and 21st-century amenities such as air conditioning and cable TV, $175-$230. The Woodlands Hotel and Suites is a new 300-room, contemporary hotel near the Colonial Williamsburg Visitors Center, $115-$145. All accommodations in Colonial Williamsburg can be booked at (800) 447-8679.

Information: Williamsburg Area Convention and Visitors Bureau, P.O. Box 3585, Williamsburg, VA 23187-3585, (800) 368-6511 or www.visitwilliamsburg.com.

Gallery, which sells works in all media by local artists as well as those from outside Virginia. Classes at this gallery inspired her husband, Mac, to resume acrylic painting.

These retirees also work seriously at keeping fit. All except Dudley are golfers. The Hugheses and Marty MacDonald regularly work out at Kingsmill's sports club. Physical fitness is always on the Houses' agenda, with daily walks and extensive work in their yard.

Despite the regular fitness routines, there's sometimes a need for medical care. Dudley recently had a knee replacement. Unlike husband Tommy, who had to go to Richmond when he needed both knees replaced several years ago, Dudley was able to have this done locally, thanks to the presence of a new orthopedic surgeon in Williamsburg. Those needing major cardio procedures, such as a bypass, must go to Richmond or Newport News.

Tom House, who was hospitalized in late 2001, praises the Williamsburg Community Hospital. "All was expertly done, with up-to-date care and excellent professionalism," he says.

Shopping opportunities, however, are limited despite an abundance of outlet malls. "Coming from DC, where we had everything, shopping in Williamsburg was a shock," Sandie says. Marty echoes Sandie's opinion. "There's no department store. We have to go to Richmond or Norfolk for the better stores," she says. Dudley handles the problem by doing a lot of catalog shopping. "There is no place around Merchants Square to get ordinary things, such as a pair of pajamas," she says.

Dining is a mixed scene with, as Marty MacDonald says, "lots of tourist places and just a few good restaurants." But in his years here, Tom House has noticed a big improvement, with more upscale restaurants opening.

Of Williamsburg's four seasons, summer, with its heat and high humidity, is the toughest – especially for the Hugheses. But Sandie House loves the heat and humidity. "It beats running around DC in a coat and tie in the summer," agrees her husband, Tom. "I can just put on shorts and a golf shirt." The MacDonalds escape into air-conditioning.

All agree with Mac MacDonald that growing pains are the area's biggest negative. "The traffic is getting worse, and highway construction is not keeping up with the growth because the state government is suffering a budget crunch. We worry where the water is coming from," Mac says.

But there are more than enough attractions to offset any drawbacks, local retirees say. Sandie House loves the area's beauty — "the water, the trees, the architecture."

"The cost of living is less than many other places, certainly less than New York," says Tommy Hughes. "It's a wonderful place to retire," says Tommy, who remembers when Williamsburg was "a sleepy little Southern town."

"Despite the growth, this is still a beautiful town," says Dudley Hughes. "Come on down — you'll love it."●

Wilmington, North Carolina

A university, historic homes and a Hollywood presence
lend star quality to this coastal North Carolina city

By Jim Kerr

It was only a few years ago that the city of Wilmington, a coastal port steeped in history and Southern traditions, awoke from relative obscurity to discover that it had become not only a major draw for tourists and retirees, but Hollywood film crews as well.

Suddenly the city, which was blockaded by the Union in the Civil War, found itself up to its azaleas in film producers. Along with the celebrities and film crews in the 1990s came increased numbers of college students, investors, real estate developers and thousands of retirees and tourists bent on enjoying the area's attractions.

Uppermost on the minds of visitors and retirees were the beaches along the nearby Cape Fear coast, where mild winters and hot summers had always been a regional lure. Other high-ranking attractions included traditional Southern ambiance, historic houses and the friendliness of the townsfolk.

What revolutionized the complexion of the place, energizing the city from a somewhat sleepy port into the seventh-largest city in the state, was the completion of Interstate 40 at the end of the 1980s. It connected the former railhead center with Interstate 95, the major corridor between cities of the Northeast and to vehicular arteries to the Midwest as well. License plates from Ohio and Michigan began to mingle with those from the Carolinas, Virginia, New York and New England.

Within a decade, the city's population ballooned from 55,000 to 90,000, a 62 percent increase. Yet, it wasn't the numbers so much as the diversity that created a new cosmopolitan atmosphere.

Walking along historic Front Street today, you are just as likely to run into a cast member of the "Dawson's Creek" TV show as a tourist sipping coffee in an outdoor cafe or a retiree heading for a day's volunteer work. It seems a comfortable contradiction: The city is both conservative and liberal, traditional yet progressive, a place painstakingly preserved in the face of innovation.

"The beaches were a big draw for us," says Dave Spetrino, a retired Navy captain. "So was the climate and the growing economy. But being a history buff, Wilmington had an extra special attraction for me."

In 1998, Dave, now 64, bought an 1890s-era house in the historic district just five blocks from the river. He had been living in Fairfax, VA, and his future wife, Sandi, lived in Denver. The two got married in the spring of 1999 and moved into the totally renovated house, which had previously been used for law offices.

"It had no kitchen, the chimneys were stuffed, the yard was trashed and all the shutters, save one, had fallen off the house," Dave says. Today the historic house has regained its former Victorian elegance, with a modern kitchen and bathrooms, tiled floors, remodeled bedrooms and a library upstairs where Dave has run out of space for all his books. He still works as an independent consultant on international issues, traveling six months of the year, while Sandi, 42, works as a professional mediator and conflict resolution consultant.

"I'm retired, Wilmington-style," Dave says. "I don't have to go to work, but we both like the excitement of doing something. And this city has something for everyone."

Sandi is the author of a textbook on mediation techniques and teaches classes in conflict management at the University of North Carolina-Wilmington. Since moving here, her calendar has been filling rapidly with a number of community projects, including one that requires her unusual expertise in developing mascots for local sports teams. Dave's interests range from working with local charities and fund-raisers to his Civil War memorabilia collection and Navy projects.

"I walk to the end of my street," he says, "and I see the fantail of a battleship. How much better can it get?"

The reference is to the USS North Carolina, Wilmington's top tourist attraction.

The restored World War II battleship is parked in a small inlet of the Cape Fear River, across from downtown, and it symbolizes the city's long association with maritime history.

Pirates like Stede Bonnet once roamed the area, and the British occupied the city after local rebels showed the first armed resistance in the Colonies to the stamp tax. The port boomed after the Revolution, but the Union blockade in the 1860s, as well as Wilmington's subsequent surrender, brought an end to prosperity.

Ironically, it was poverty that prevented people from tearing down the antebellum houses and saved them for another day. Today's 230-block historic district, revitalized by aggressive preservation beginning in the 1930s, is Wilmington's drawing card for tourists, retirees and the film industry.

With nine major sound stages and 650 film crewmembers in residence, Wilmington has become America's Hollywood East. Hundreds of commercials and feature films have been made in the region over the past two decades. The industry generates $66 million a year in local revenues, and becoming a movie extra has become a popular pastime for interested retirees.

Local theater also is strong. There are more than 15 theater groups with numerous year-round performances, including those at Thalian Hall, a beautifully restored 1855 theater that shares a building with City Hall. An active senior center provides bus transportation for free dress rehearsals, and area residents can take their choice of a dozen other performance venues around town, including Shakespeare, opera, comedy and a senior group called the Rocking Chair Players.

On most days, given Wilmington's year-round mild climate, downtown visitors can also find other forms of entertainment, from street musicians and lunchtime jazz sessions to an eclectic assortment of nightclubs along Front Street.

"Wilmington has some of the best restaurants you can find anywhere," says Nick Rhodes, a newcomer to Wilmington but not to the area. He and his wife, Deloris, both grew up in small towns just 40 miles or so away. Today they live in Landfall, a large, gated subdivision of elegant homes on quiet cul-de-sacs and a Jack Nicklaus-designed golf course, located several miles north of downtown and less than a mile from Wrightsville Beach.

"I like being close to the beach, and I try to frequent it every day," says Deloris, 58, who works as an assistant principal at Cape Fear Elementary School. "Besides that, I wanted to be in a college town, and having the movie industry was interesting, too."

The couple moved here in August 2001 from Fairfax Station, VA, where Nick, a retired lieutenant colonel in the Air Force, had been working for 15 years as a civilian in aircraft systems development. He is an active member of the chamber of commerce and the SCORE program (Service Corps of Retired Executives), and three days a week he also drives his 89-year-old mother to dialysis treatment. Deloris, a former school administrator, also has a 79-year-old mother who lives nearby, and the couple's daughter and three grandchildren live in Charlotte.

Deloris and Nick, who is 59, are experimenting for the first time with country club life, joining the club socially and signing up for golf lessons. "I'm really a novice," says Nick, "but I know that when a shot hooks off No. 3 tee box and heads for our kitchen, it's a bad shot."

Like many couples retiring to Wilmington, the Rhodeses first took up temporary residence in a rented condominium. They chose a place near Landfall.

But downtown Wilmington offers a variety of apartments in the historic district. When Nancy Rankin came here nine years ago to be near her elderly parents, who lived in the retirement community of Plantation Village, she and her husband bought an older house as an investment, renting it out. They have since bought another home, retiring here themselves.

Just a few blocks away, Catherine Ackiss and her husband, Walter, own Catherine's Inn, an 1883 Victorian bed-and-breakfast inn on South Front Street. Both retired from active professional lives in busy Charlotte, but they soon found that owning a historic B&B meant considerable work as well as community involvement. Over the years, so many guests staying in Catherine's five guest rooms have retired here themselves that a 10-member group has formed, complete with monthly get-togethers.

"Most bought or built homes after being in and out of here on many occasions, sometimes over a four-year span," says Catherine, a former store manager and fashion director from Charlotte. The couple bought a B&B when they first moved here in 1989 and purchased the current Catherine's Inn in 1994.

"It's a place that grabs you — the climate, the art, music, lots to do, and more restaurants per capita than any city in the United States," says Catherine of her adopted city. "Retirees here are wonderful. They impact the community in so many ways, giving their time.

"The movie business is also going strong here, and retirees love it," she says. "Many who you would never expect become extras. Even reticent personalities can change when people get the spotlight."

The pay is only $30 to $40 a day, but if

Population: 90,000 permanent residents plus approximately 12,000 University of North Carolina students during the school year. Population in New Hanover County is 160,300.

Location: On the northeast bank of the Cape Fear River, approximately four miles from the Atlantic Ocean in southeastern North Carolina, with low-lying countryside and nearby beach communities including Wrightsville Beach and Carolina Beach.

Climate:

	High	Low
January	55	35
July	89	72

Average relative humidity: 74%

Rain: 54.26 inches.

Cost of living: About average at 99.3, based on national average of 100.

Average housing cost: $225,000 in the historic downtown district, $250,000 in older but affluent suburbs, $350,000 in new suburbs and along the coast.

Sales tax: 6%

Sales tax exemptions: Prescription drugs, eyeglasses, some medical supplies and most services.

State income tax: For married couples filing jointly, the rate is graduated from 6% of taxable income up to $21,250 to 8.25%

on amounts over $200,000. For single filers, it is graduated from 6% of income up to $12,750 to 8.25% on amounts over $120,000.

Income tax exemptions: Social Security benefits are exempt. Up to $2,000 of distributions from private retirement benefits and IRAs (up to the amount reported in federal income taxes), or up to $4,000 of government pensions may be exempt. Total deductions may not exceed $4,000 per person.

Estate tax: None, except the state's "pick-up" portion of the federal tax, applicable to taxable estates above $1 million.

Property tax: The rate is 47 cents per $100 of assessed market value in the city of Wilmington, 69 cents per $100 in the county with varying rates in beach communities. Wilmington residents pay city and county rates. The tax on a $250,000 home in Wilmington would be approximately $2,900.

Homestead exemption: Homeowners age 65 and older, or disabled, living in the home and earning $18,000 or less per year qualify for an exemption of $20,000 or 50% of the value of the home, whichever is greater.

Religion: "The City of Steeples" has more than a dozen traditional churches within the historic district, many built in the 19th century. Denominations of all faiths are represented in the city and surrounding environs.

Education: Approximately 10,000 students attend the University of North Carolina-Wilmington, which offers 69 undergraduate degrees and 25 graduate degrees. Cape Fear Community College is one of the fastest-growing in the state with about 5,500 students and a main campus in downtown Wilmington.

Transportation: Wilmington's WTA provides an extensive bus service, including curb-to-curb transportation for the disabled, throughout the city and suburbs. Adult fares are 75 cents with 10-cent transfers, 35 cents for senior citizens, and 11-ride books for $7.50 for adults, $3.50 for seniors and students. Wilmington International Airport, completed in 1990 and less than 10 minutes from downtown, is served by US Airways and ASA, the Delta Connection, with connections in Atlanta and Charlotte. Interstate 40 connects Wilmington with Raleigh, 110 miles northwest, and to Interstate 95, the major interstate on the Atlantic

you have the time and inclination, Fincannon & Associates puts out regular casting calls. Sandi Spetrino spent a day at the Wilmington airport playing a traveler in a Lou Gossett movie, and another retiree, Jane Freeman, and her daughter were extras in "Everybody Wins" with Nick Nolte and Debra Winger. "Everybody Wins" used Wilmington's federal courthouse as a backdrop.

"It's kind of a cult thing," Jane says. "You get to meet actors if you don't mind getting up at 5 a.m."

She and her husband, George, relocated here in 1991 from Goldsboro, NC, after buying two lots almost 20 years earlier on exclusive Figure Eight Island. The island is off the north tip of Wrightsville Beach, about 13 miles from downtown Wilmington, where George, 72, still works at a law firm.

While the Freemans live here year-round, most of the 385 current homes on the gated private island, accessible only

by drawbridge, are rented or vacant during the winter season. The Freemans' 3,200-square-foot home faces the saltwater marshes to the west rather than the windward beaches to the east, where winter storms and four hurricanes have passed by in the past six years.

"We had to wait until the kids got out of school, but we had planned to retire here from the day we bought the property," George says. They decided to build on the marsh side, away from the sea and facing the Intracoastal Waterway, because it was tranquil and private. No one wanders into their watery back yard other than egrets, Spanish mackerel and an occasional bottle-nosed dolphin. George keeps a 30-foot Grady White at his dock for Atlantic fishing excursions in pursuit of yellowfin tuna and mahi mahi.

Jane, who is 74, comes from a distinguished family in Raleigh and has never let go of her professional career as a librarian. She spent three years raising

$1.3 million for what has become an award-winning, state-of-the-art branch library in an abandoned Wilmington grocery store. The rest of the building is a satellite office for UNC-Wilmington and a 250-seat auditorium for piano concerts and public meetings. Jane is also on the United Way board of directors and works as a volunteer in other civic organizations.

And while she still keeps an eye out for those fun roles as an extra, there is no shortage of celebrities right on Figure Eight Island. Noted politicians, artists, publishers and actors live here or visit while making movies. Paul Newman once had to be rescued from the marsh after his boat went aground, and Andy Griffith, whose series "Matlock" was filmed in Wilmington, still has a home on the island. "You never meet anyone dull around here," says Jane Freeman.

And there's rarely, if ever, a dull moment in Wilmington.●

Wilmington, NC

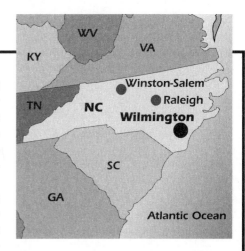

Seaboard.

Health: Wilmington offers a comprehensive, sophisticated array of medical services through the New Hanover Health Network, which includes the New Hanover Regional Medical Center, Cape Fear Hospital, Pender Memorial Hospital and several other entities, making it the ninth-largest health care system in the state with 4,000 employees, 470 physicians and 1,000 volunteers.

Housing options: In Wilmington's historic district, options range from restored or fixer-upper homes dating from the 1890s to new waterfront condos. Beyond Eighth Street, leafy neighborhoods offer a collection of comfortable single-family homes. Country-club developments such as the expansive **Landfall** northeast of the city, (800) 227-8208, have home sites from $75,000 and homes from $300,000. Less expensive is **Magnolia Greens**, (800) 677-7524, with golf villas from $130,000 and townhomes from $146,000. **The Woods of Holly Tree**, (910) 793-1300, is one of many planned retirement communities, and assisted living is available at a variety of locations around Wilmington, including **Champions at Porters Neck**, (910) 686-

6462, and **Spring Arbor of Wilmington**, (910) 799-4999, both of which offer a full range of activities, independent lifestyles or 24-hour nursing care. A number of beach communities are popular, with prices ranging from moderate to extravagant. Wrightsville Beach is mainly a year-round residential area with homes for $350,000 and up. Carolina Beach, a family environment, has condos, vintage cottages and homes starting at $200,000. For more information on housing, call the Greater Wilmington Chamber of Commerce, (910) 762-2611, or visit the Web site at www.wilmingtonchamber.org.

Visitor lodging: An increase of more than 300 rooms a year since 1977 is a reflection of Wilmington's growing popularity with visitors. There are more than 7,000 rooms in the area, with motels, hotels, cottages, condos and B&Bs. Best Western Coast Line Inn, (800) 617-7732, and the Hilton Wilmington Riverside, (910) 763-5900, are both centrally located downtown on the riverfront with rooms starting around $110. Days Inn at (800) 329-7466, Hampton Inn at (800) 426-7866 and Four Points Hotel Sheraton at (800) 325-3535 are located, along with a half-dozen other hotels and

motels, along Market Street closer to I-40 and the airport with rates starting at about $75. Another option is the dozen or so bed-and-breakfast inns, mostly historic houses along Front and Second streets. Catherine's Inn, (800) 476-0723, is a two-story Victorian house at 410 S. Front St. It was built in 1883 and has five guest rooms starting at $100 double, including breakfast.

Information: Greater Wilmington Chamber of Commerce, 1 Estell Lee Place, Wilmington, NC 28401, (910) 762-2611 or www.wilmingtonchamber.org. Cape Fear Coast Convention and Visitors Bureau, 24 N. Third St., Wilmington, NC 28401, (800) 222-4757 or www.cape-fear.nc.us.

Winter Haven, Florida

Florida town has feel of the country, but big-city amenities are easily accessible

By David Wilkening

Robert Price and his wife, Lillie, retired from suburban Chicago to rural Winter Haven, FL, population 24,000. Yet from their new home, they found metropolitan attractions just as easily accessible — and without a traffic hassle.

From this central Florida setting, inviting Atlantic or Gulf Coast beaches are about an hour's drive on normally uncrowded four-lane interstate highways, and cultural amenities are just as close.

The Prices — he's 65, she's 45 — say it's no more difficult to reach the art exhibits of Tampa, Orlando and Sarasota than it was to take in similar downtown Chicago attractions from their former home in Palos Park, IL.

Another couple, Dr. John Petre, 70, and his wife, Catherine, 68, from Erie, PA, live about a half-hour drive from the Prices in an even more rural area — yet they have season tickets to the Orlando Symphony Orchestra's pop concerts.

Why not, they ask? It's only an hour away on an interstate highway.

John and Barbara Riegler, both 61, from Beulah, a small town in northwestern Michigan, crisscrossed Florida for four years looking for the right retirement site. They shunned the state's well-known coastal cities for Winter Haven.

Its attraction? It's near everything and yet secluded, far removed from the "rat race you can get on either coast," as Robert Price puts it.

And it's less expensive, John Riegler adds.

For the Prices and Petres, the environment was a deciding factor in their choice of Winter Haven for retirement.

"We like the quality of life here, the restaurants, lakes, foliage, blue herons, egrets," says Robert Price. "We were surprised at the extent of the lakes and wildlife. Quite a few of the lakes have no population around them

and are probably like they were 10,000 years ago."

Price, who was a vice president of General Mills in Chicago before he retired, now serves as executive vice president of Central Florida Business Solutions in Winter Haven.

The Petres, who both were in the medical field (he as a urologist and she as a nurse), moved into a resort area called Grenelefe, a self-contained golf- and tennis-oriented community outside Winter Haven.

"The environment is similar to what we had in Pennsylvania — tall pine trees, high ridge country, beautiful lakes and oak trees," says John. "You are not allowed to cut a tree under any circumstance."

Winter Haven drew the Rieglers for several reasons. They liked the fact that it had little traffic but was close to such attractions as the beaches, Walt Disney World, Sea World and Universal Studios. And they found the cost of living — particularly recreation and housing — lower in Winter Haven.

"We're golfers, and the cost of golfing had a big impact as to why we went to central Florida as opposed to the coast," John says.

They bought a manufactured home in a community called Swiss Golf and Tennis Club on Lake Henry, where they play golf at least three times a week. The Rieglers spend half the year in Winter Haven and half at their second home on a lake near Traverse City, MI, where they operated supermarkets.

"When we go to Michigan, we get the boat out and get ready for our summer visitors. Down here, we get the golf clubs out and get ready for our winter visitors. It's a year-round vacation," John says.

Despite its quiet nature, Winter Haven sits in the heart of an area where 6.2 million people live within a two-

hour drive and 11.7 million within a four-hour drive. Modern airports at both Tampa and Orlando have won awards for their architecture and, more importantly, their convenience. Tampa — only an hour's drive away — offers its own share of tourist attractions, including Busch Gardens.

"One of the attractions of Winter Haven, I think, is that it's a little more laid-back atmosphere than, say, Orlando, which tends to appeal more to younger people," says Cliff Howell, a 57-year-old attorney who came to the town as a child in the early 1940s.

"The pace is a little less rapid, the costs are a little less, there's available land and the cost of a modest retirement home is less," Howell says.

At press time, the National Association of Homebuilders identified the Lakeland/Winter Haven area as the 17th most affordable place to live in the country. The average single-family home here costs $95,000, according to the local board of realtors.

In addition, an annual price index — released by the Florida governor's office and based on 117 items and services — shows the cost of living in Winter Haven and surrounding Polk County compares favorably with many other Florida counties.

The Prices, Petres and Rieglers — and many other retirees here — have migrated from regions that can be bitterly cold in winter.

"We had seven months of gray days," says Lillie Price of her eight years in the Chicago area. "I used to go to the tanning spa just for the bright light."

Winter Haven, by contrast, has mostly sunny days. It enjoys a balmy climate (average temperature is 73 degrees) with an advantage over coastal areas in that humidity generally is lower than in cities by the sea.

Retirees in Winter Haven find they don't have to go far to keep busy or to find recreation. Many activities revolve around the area's 177 parks and 50 lakes, which provide abundant opportunities for water sports and lakefront living. Citrus groves cover much of the gently rolling terrain. And, Winter Haven is home to Florida's famed Cypress Gardens.

Active retirees can choose among 37 golf courses and numerous tennis courts. For those not inclined toward outdoor activities, the Polk County area has 16 movie theaters, plus bowling alleys and various senior adult centers with organized activities.

Culturally, the Theatre of Winter Haven schedules eight productions a year in the city's 350-seat Chain O'Lakes Convention Center. It's known as one of the best community theaters in the Southeast. Other diversions include a variety of other theater and dance groups and such annual events as arts and crafts festivals and a well-known Bach Festival each March.

Despite its small size, Winter Haven boasts many amenities found in larger cities. There are more than a half-dozen banks and savings and loan offices in the city, for example, as well as a half-dozen stock brokerage firms.

Health care includes Winter Haven Hospital, a major not-for-profit facility with 711 beds. It has a 24-hour emergency room and all-inclusive medical facilities. Educationally, Polk Community College is popular with retirees. Its 130-acre campus offers a varied curriculum. Four-year colleges can be found in Tampa and Orlando.

Clubs and organizations here include dozens of social, fraternal and service groups. Local chapters of the American Association of Retired Persons, Veterans of Foreign Wars Auxiliary and Rotary are active.

Early residents of Winter Haven made

Winter Haven, FL

Population: 24,000 in Winter Haven, 492,751 in Polk County.
Location: At geographic center of state, 50 miles from Tampa on the Gulf Coast and Orlando, tourist capital and gateway to the Walt Disney World complex.
Climate:

	High	Low
January	72	49
July	96	74

Average relative humidity: 55%
Rain: 50 inches.
Climate balmy with mild, sunny winters and hot summers. Humidity high in the morning, lower in the afternoon and normally less than in coastal areas.
Cost of living: Below average (specific index not available).
Average housing cost: $95,000 for a single-family home; $92,600 for a condo or patio home.
Sales tax: 6%
Sales tax exemptions: Most groceries, medical services, prescription drugs.

State income tax: None.
Intangibles tax: Assessed on stocks, bonds and other assets. Tax rate is $1 per $1,000 in assets. The first $20,000 in assets is exempt for individuals. For couples filing jointly, the first $40,000 is exempt. Those who owe less than $60 need not pay.
Estate tax: None, except the state's "pick-up" portion of the federal tax, applicable to taxable estates above $1 million.
Property tax: $24.21 per $1,000 of assessed value with homes assessed at 100% of the appraised value. Yearly tax on an $95,000 home, with the homestead exemption noted below, is $1,695.
Homestead exemption: $25,000 off assessed value for primary, permanent residence.
Religion: More than 80 churches of many denominations, plus one synagogue (reform).
Education: Varied classes at Polk Community College. Also within commuting distance: Florida Southern College, the University of South Florida, the University of Central Florida, the University of Tampa, Warner Southern College and Webber College.
Transportation: Bus, taxi service available, but cars almost a necessity. Amtrak has daily service. Tampa International Airport and Orlando International Airport are both about

one hour away.
Health: Seven general hospitals in the county. Winter Haven Hospital has 711 beds and 24-hour emergency service. There are also 10 medical clinics, two blood banks and about 300 physicians and dentists in area. Full medical services available.
Housing options: A mixture of single-family and condo apartments as well as up to a dozen manufactured-home communities and a half-dozen nursing homes. **Ruby Lake**, a gated lakefront community, has custom homes from the $130,000s, lakefront homes from the low $200,000s. **The Gates of Lake Region**, a new gated development, has lots priced from the $30,000s and homes from the $150,000s. **Cypresswood**, a master-planned golf community, has golf villas from the $70,000s, condos from the $80,000s and patio homes in the low $100,000s.
Visitor lodging: Howard Johnson, $54-$89 depending on season, located downtown, (863) 294-7321 or (800) 654-2000. Lake Roy Beach Inn, $60 -$130 depending on season and room, or $550 and up per week (with kitchenettes), a mile from Cypress Gardens, (863) 324-6320.
Information: Winter Haven Chamber of Commerce, P.O. Box 1420, Winter Haven, FL 33882, (863) 293-2138 or www.winterhavenfl.com.

their living at a canning factory in the late 1800s. By 1911, the city of several hundred people decided it was big enough to build a city hall and pass speed ordinances for the 15 automobiles registered here. Today Winter Haven has a balanced economy based on tourism, commerce and industry, agriculture and phosphate mining.

Not everything is perfect in the Winter Haven area, of course. Summers are hot, though regular rain quenches some of the heat. Howell, who remembers Winter Haven in the early 1940s when it was a fifth of its present size, admits that traffic on main arteries gets congested sometimes —

but nothing like Orlando or Tampa, he adds.

For anyone considering a move to Winter Haven, local retirees offer advice that can smooth the transition to a Florida lifestyle.

"I'd tell people to look at a map to find out where this is. I'd warn them it can be a secluded, rural environment," says John Petre, who adds that he has no desire to live anywhere other than the resort area of Grenelefe.

For retirees who prefer such resort communities away from town, shopping can involve a trip of several miles. But residents say the drive to find needed services is a fair trade for a

less-crowded lifestyle.

Other advice comes from the Rieglers, who say their move to Florida for half of each year is a "dream fulfilled."

"You should rent for a season and make sure you like Florida and the community before buying. Do some intensive research," says John Riegler.

He says he has met people who moved to Florida and discovered they didn't like the casual lifestyle or the year-round warm climate or who simply missed their friends too much. "Some of them just went back home empty-handed," he says.●

The Woodlands, Texas

This lushly forested community north of Houston boasts small-town ambiance near big-city amenities

By Nina J. Stewart

Residents say the trees — abundant towering pines and majestic oaks — are what make The Woodlands such a popular and booming community. Indeed, some call it "the invisible city" because trees cloak busy neighborhoods behind an enchanting veil of shimmering green, making this master-planned, unincorporated community of more than 60,000 people seem much smaller than it really is. And that's just part of the attraction.

"I like trees. My wife, Carole, and I saw the neighborhood and our new potential home on a Tuesday, and we bought on Thursday," Andre Molnar says.

Andre, 72, and his wife, Carole, 57, had previously lived in Houston, as well as in other parts of the country, and had planned to move to Clemson, SC, for their retirement years, but The Woodlands changed their minds.

This hidden community only 27 miles north of Houston offers the best of both worlds. It's near the city, and yet away from the city. With access from Interstate 45 and the Hardy Toll Road, residents are within easy reach of Houston's theater district, Bush Intercontinental Airport and such attractions as the Museum of Natural Science, the Houston Zoological Gardens in Hermann Park and Space Center Houston. Seafarers have only a 90-minute drive to Galveston and the Gulf of Mexico.

"We love the Houston Symphony, and this is its summer home," says Andre. "Also, we had taken up music lessons. When we visited, we found The Woodlands has everything we wanted — next door to Montgomery College where we take courses, great shopping and restaurants, wonderful sports facilities, friendly community, good library, terrific medical facilities, and miles and miles of hiking trails and lakes. We play a lot of tennis. We've even tried kayaking at Woodlands Lake."

For another couple, Pat and Colleen Hosford, it was business that brought them to The Woodlands but pleasure that made them stay. The transplanted Oklahomans got the idea in 1991 to move the offices of their oil company to the community. "We liked the small-town feel, the community attitude, the nature trails. We found it calming and peaceful, a place where there is a great deal of business, but you don't see miles of concrete and urban buildings," Pat says.

"As an oil executive, first with Amoco and then on my own, we averaged a move every two and one-half years," explains Pat, 64. "Our church has been a stabilizing factor for us throughout the years," adds Colleen, 62. "They have some good ones here. It all adds to the sense of community and family." The Woodlands has more than 30 churches of a variety of denominations, with many more in neighboring communities.

And when local Olympic diver Laura Wilkinson beat all the odds to win the gold medal and gave much of the credit to her family, coaches, friends and God, the community fairly burst with pride over the hometown sweetheart, honoring her with a parade. "She trains here, you know," says Colleen. "We have magnificent sporting facilities, whether you like swimming, tennis, golf — you name it."

Pat especially enjoys the year-round golfing opportunities. "I'm not going to tell you my handicap," he laughs, "but there is golf for everyone here." The Woodlands offers five championship golf courses (two public and three private), including the Palmer Golf Course and The Tournament Players Course, home of the annual Shell Houston Open PGA event. The newest course opened last fall and was designed by Jack Nicklaus.

The 30-year-old, 27,000-acre forested community is comprised of seven "villages," with an eighth under development. The Town Center, with its Cynthia Woods Mitchell Pavilion, serves as the community focus, while each village has its own shopping, dining and neighborhood services based on a turn-of-the-century town square concept. For example, each village has its own neighborhood stores where residents can bike or walk to get a gallon of milk, their dry cleaning or a tank of gas, and dine out or copy some documents. Each community center has its own look and personality designed to reflect its unique neighborhood.

Eighty parks grace the community, which also offers more than 100 miles of hiking and biking trails through native woods. The Mitchell Pavilion is a natural, outdoor performing arts center that sets the stage for musicals, plays, festivals, operas and orchestra performances. "The Pavilion provides all of us with world-class musicians — everything from rock to Bach," says Colleen Hosford.

Another contented couple in The Woodlands is Bob and Vivian Kinnear. "When we moved here, everything clicked," says Bob, 57, who retired from Chevron three years ago. "You can get just about anything you want in The Woodlands — a variety of housing choices, good neighbors, beautiful location, great sporting opportunities, culture, shopping, medical facilities. It's all here."

The Kinnears built a custom-designed home in Stellar Point, while the Molnars chose a one-story, 2,100-square-foot tan brick home already completed in the Windsor Hills community, where homeowners must be over 55 years of age to purchase. "We love our quiet, friendly, adult community," says Andre Molnar. "We have nice neighbors, a wonderful new clubhouse and pool where we meet with friends. We are just minutes away from everything we like to do."

The Woodlands offers a range of housing options, from apartments, condominiums and townhouses to patio homes and custom-built dream homes. Prices start at around $11,000 a year to rent condos and $120,000 to buy single-family homes. The median sales price for new home purchases, according to The Woodlands Operating Co., is $200,446.

Lakefront homes are available, as are golf vista homes for those who can't leave the course. Community associations levy deed restrictions on construction, and the approved custom builders must meet Houston's building codes. "The restrictions are good, like the prohibition against cutting trees. Trees make this community," says Colleen Hosford.

"Also, fencing must be uniform. You can't have a chain link fence. But you can experiment with your housing styles. You'll see everything from traditional to futuristic," she says. However, residents note that you won't see purple houses, pigs or goats in back yards, or even RVs parked in the driveways.

Since The Woodlands is unincorporat-

The Woodlands, TX

Population: 55,650 in The Woodlands, 293,770 in south Montgomery County.
Location: In southeast Texas, about 30 miles north of downtown Houston on Interstate 45. Elevation is 130 feet.

Climate:

	High	Low
January	61	41
July	94	73

Average relative humidity: 59%
Rain: 47 inches.
Cost of living: Below average (specific index not available).
Median housing cost: $200,446 is the median sales price, according to The Woodlands Operating Co.
Sales tax: 7.25% in the Town Center, 6.25% outside the Town Center.
Sales tax exemptions: Food and produce, pharmaceuticals and some agricultural services.
State income tax: None.
Intangibles tax: None.
Estate tax: None, except the state's "pick-up" portion of the federal tax, applicable to taxable estates of more than $1 million.
Inheritance tax: None.
Property tax: Varies from village to village. Generally, the average combined tax rate is $3.42 per $100 of assessed valuation and includes utility district taxes, school taxes, county taxes and association fees. Using the average rate, the tax on a $200,000 home is about $6,840 annually without exemptions.
Homestead exemption: All qualified homeowners receive a $15,000 homestead exemption for school district taxes. Other taxing units may offer an exemption of up to 20% of the value of your home but not less than $5,000. Homeowners age 65 and older qualify for an additional $10,000 school district exemption, bringing that total to

$25,000.
Religion: More than 30 congregations of virtually all faiths serve The Woodlands. These groups find common ground in Interfaith, which works with the clergy of each congregation to extend human services beyond individual religious groups. Interfaith also has a full-time seniors advocate who organizes a calendar of social events for retired residents.
Education: College Park in The Woodlands is home to Montgomery College, a two-year community college, as well as The University Center, which delivers course work from six major Texas universities and offers 30 bachelors programs and 23 masters programs.
Transportation: Interstate 45 runs north and south through The Woodlands, and the Hardy Toll Road to Houston is easily accessible. The Woodlands Express offers bus service to residents who work in Houston, utilizing two park-and-ride areas. In addition, there are various van pool services. Bush Intercontinental Airport has 20 major air carriers averaging 500 departures a day to 150 destinations, and is only 20 miles south of The Woodlands.
Health: Memorial Hermann Hospital is a 92-bed, acute-care facility with a 24-hour, fully equipped emergency center. The Sadler Clinic in The Woodlands opened in 1999 with more than 60 physicians. Conroe Regional Medical Center is a 10-minute drive, with 262 beds. The Woodlands Healthcare Center is a 206-bed convalescent and nursing center that also offers rehabilitation. There are a number of other clinics nearby offering rehabilitation services, Alzheimer's assistance and care to uninsured patients, and more are under construction.

Housing options: Options range from apartments, condominiums, patio homes, assisted-living services and single-family homes beginning at around $90,000 and peaking at more than $1 million for luxury estate homes. Neighborhoods are divided into "villages," including Alden Bridge, Cochran's Crossing, Grogan's Mill, Indian Springs, Sterling Ridge, Panther Creek and College Park. Carlton Woods is a new gated golf-course community. Windsor Hills is an active-adult community, in the Village of College Park, requiring at least one homeowner to be 55 years of age or older. Contact The Woodlands Homefinder Center, 2000 Woodlands Parkway, The Woodlands, TX 77380, (888) 504-5050.
Visitor lodging: The Woodlands Town Center has Courtyard by Marriott, (281) 292-3262; Drury Inn, (281) 362-7222; and Marriott's Residence Inn, (281) 292-3252. The four-star Woodlands Resort offers a special rate of $99 per night to house hunters, (800) 433-2624.
Information: South Montgomery County Woodlands Chamber of Commerce, 1400 Woodloch Forest Drive, Suite 500, The Woodlands, TX 77380, (281) 367-5777 or www.smcwcc.org. Also visit www.thewoodlands.com and www.wcscwoodlands.com.

ed, residents pay taxes to municipal utility districts, and the taxes tend to run slightly higher than city rates. Residents pay no state income tax, but the fees they pay neighborhood districts do cover school, county and utility district taxes, community association fees, trash pick-up and, in some cases, club memberships. The 2001 average combined tax rate for communities in The Woodlands was $3.42 per $100 of assessed property value. For example, owners of a $140,000 home in Harper's Landing in The Woodlands would expect to pay $5,278. "Taxes are a little higher than in some places we have lived," admits Andre Molnar, "but we get a lot for our money."

In Windsor Hills, the homeowners association (which levies a monthly fee of $180) mows and maintains front yards, refinishes front doors every two years and repaints homes and repairs fences if needed, according to an established schedule. Community association fees tend to decline as the area develops. There is no city government, but two community associations (both nonprofit corporations) operate as the governing authority along with The Woodlands developers, Crescent Operating Inc. and Morgan Stanley Partnership. Public schools are in the Conroe Independent School District.

More than 400 businesses call The Woodlands home, including 150 stores in The Woodlands Mall. Research Forest has attracted 40 companies that develop ground-breaking technologies in such fields as biomedicine, technology and telecommunications. College Park houses Montgomery College and The University Center, a campus where six major Texas universities offer a range of bachelors and masters degrees.

Woodlands residents and business entrepreneurs are pleased with the construction of a new waterway connecting the mall and business areas with the outdoor Pavilion. The 1.25-mile waterway offers three modes of transportation — water taxi, trolley or walkway — which add to the considerable ambiance already prevalent in the community.

Residents appreciate clean streets, the well-maintained walking and biking paths, the profusion of wildflowers planted along the roadways and, most of all, the wildlife. The forests are home to squirrels, songbirds, raccoons, possums, rabbits, deer and roadrunners. Hawks cruise the air currents by day, and by night, stars blanket the skies, unadulterated by city lights. Winding streets and cul-de-sacs sometimes conjure images of Hansel and Gretl, necessitating the dropping of breadcrumbs to find one's way back, but it is exactly this bewildering but secluded layout that has prompted new friendships after people stop to ask for directions. Other attractions to visitors and residents alike are the outdoor art sculptures sprinkled liberally throughout the villages. Even security wears an appealing face, in the form of red-coated mounties atop gleaming horses that patrol Town Center.

The Woodlands provides quality medical care at Memorial Hermann Hospital, an acute-care facility, and adjoining professional center. The community also has neighborhood health centers located conveniently throughout the area. Specialized nursing and assisted-living facilities are also available. Of course, residents are within easy reach of Houston's world-class medical facilities such as M.D. Anderson, the famous cancer research center.

Crime statistics for The Woodlands compare favorably with Houston. The Montgomery County Sheriff's Department patrols the area, and neighborhood watch programs have won awards for their work. Town Center hires the mounted patrol officers in the business district. The Woodlands has full-time, paid firefighters. "We feel very safe," Colleen Hosford says.

Only the summer heat and humidity bring occasional laments. While winters are mild, the humidity in this coastal area of Texas can be high, which can make summers steamy. Says Pat Hosford, "You learn to stay out of the noontime heat and take advantage of twilight golf."

Visitors likely will find their favorite lodging facility somewhere near the community. In The Woodlands itself, lodging includes Courtyard by Marriott, Drury Inn and Marriott Residence Inn. The four-star Woodlands Resort offers a home-hunter discount package (currently $99 per night) available exclusively to individuals and families searching for a home in the community. The package includes breakfast, access to the health and fitness center, and deluxe room accommodations. Potential buyers also should take advantage of The Woodlands Homefinder Center, where staff is available seven days a week to assist in relocations. New residents also can choose rented homes or extended-stay hotels before making their move final.

Retirees have unlimited choices when it comes to community involvement. Religious organizations, charities and clubs for all interests have been organized in the area. Pat Hosford likes working with The Woodlands Chamber of Commerce. His wife, Colleen, enjoys the Arganauta Organization, where women come together to expand their minds on political, societal, medical and environmental topics.

And if you can't find what you're looking for in The Woodlands, claims Andre Molnar, you just aren't looking.●

Also Available
From Vacation Publications

Retirement Relocation Magazine

Print Cost Here

❑ *Where to Retire*, one-year subscription, $18 _____

Retirement Relocation Books

❑ *America's Best Low-Tax Retirement Towns,* Eve Evans and Richard Fox, $16.95 _____

❑ *Where to Retire in Florida* (Ratings for 99 Cities and Towns), Richard and Betty Fox, $16.95 _____

❑ *Choose the Southwest* (Retirement Discoveries for Every Budget), John Howells, $14.95 _____

❑ *Choose Mexico* (Live Well on $600 a Month), John Howells and Don Merwin, $14.95 _____

❑ *Choose Costa Rica* (A Guide to Retirement and Investment), John Howells, $14.95 _____

❑ *Choose the Northwest* (Includes Washington, Oregon and British Columbia), John Howells, $14.95 _____

Retirement Relocation Special Reports

❑ SR1 How to Plan and Execute a Successful Retirement Relocation, 48 pages, $4.95 _____

❑ SR4 Should You Retire to a Manufactured Home? 32 pages, $4.95 _____

❑ SR5 Retiring Outside the United States, 48 pages, $4.95 _____

❑ SR7 America's 100 Best Master-Planned Communities, *Where to Retire* _____
Special Issue, Summer 2001, $4.95 _____

❑ SR8 America's Most Affordable Retirement Towns, 48 pages, $4.95 _____

❑ MSS How to Get the Most Out of Your Social Security, 32 pages, $4.95 _____

Subtotal _____

Texas residents only add 8.25% sales tax
Add $2.50 postage and handling per book. Add $2.25 total postage and handling
for any number of Special Reports. Postage included in magazine subscription price.

Tax _____

Postage _____

Total Due _____

Name _____

Address _____

City, State, Zip _____

Check the appropriate boxes and fill in the price for each title ordered. Total at the bottom.
Include your payment and return this order form or a copy to: Vacation Publications, 1502
Augusta Drive, Suite 415, Houston, TX 77057. **For faster service call (800) 338-4962 or**
order online with a credit card at www.wheretoretire.com.

Notes

Notes